Sock It To 'Em Tigers

The Incredible Story of the 1968 Detroit Tigers

Sock It To 'Em Tigers

The Incredible Story of the 1968 Detroit Tigers

Edited by

Mark Pattison

&

David Raglin

Produced in association with the
Society for American Baseball Research (SABR)
and the Mayo Smith Society

HANOVER, MASSACHUSETTS

© 2008 SABR. All rights reserved.

No portion of this publication may be reproduced in any way, stored in any type of retrieval device, or transmitted by any method or media, electronic or mechanical, including, but not limited to, photocopy, recording, or scanning, without prior permission in writing from the publisher.

Topps® baseball cards that appear with essays are courtesy of the Topps Company, Inc. Reprinted with permission.

"Denny McLain Game-by-Game in 1968," "Interesting Facts About the 1968 Tigers," "The Greatest Inning in Tigers World Series History," and the lyrics to "Go Get 'Em, Tigers" originally appeared in *Detroit Tigers Lists and More: Runs, Hits, and ERAs*, by Mark Pattison and David Raglin, © 2002 by Wayne State University Press, Detroit. Used with permission.

The opinions expressed in the essays contained in this book are those of the author(s) and not necessarily those of Maple Street Press. Maple Street Press, LLC is in no way affiliated with Major League Baseball, the Detroit Tigers, or their minor league affiliates.

Cover design: Garrett Cullen
Front cover photo: Herb Scharfman/Sports Imagery/Getty Images
Back cover:
Denny McLain 30th win ticket stubs courtesy Evelyn & Norm Young
1968 team photo courtesy Carrie Martin
World Series ticket stubs and 1968 scorebook courtesy Chuck Ailsworth

Mark Pattison & David Raglin, Eds. *Sock It To 'Em Tigers: The Incredible Story of the 1968 Tigers.*
ISBN 978-1-934186-16-9

Library of Congress Control Number: 2008924925

All product names and brand names mentioned in this book are trademarks or service marks of their respective companies. Any omission or misuse (of any kind) of service marks or trademarks should not be regarded as intent to infringe upon the property of others. The publisher respects all marks used by companies, manufacturers, and developers as a means to distinguish their products.

Maple Street Press LLC
1100 Washington Street, Suite 7
Hanover, MA 02339
www.maplestreetpress.com

Printed in Canada
08 7 6 5 4 3 2 First Edition

Contents

Foreword vii
Introduction xi
Acknowledgements xiii

The Players

Gates Brown 3
Les Cain 9
Dave Campbell 15
Norm Cash 21
Bob Christian 27
Wayne Comer 31
Pat Dobson 35
Roy Face 41
Bill Freehan 49
Lenny Green 55
John Hiller 61
Willie Horton 67
Al Kaline 73
Fred Lasher 79
Mickey Lolich 83
Tom Matchick 89
Eddie Mathews 95
Dick McAuliffe 101
Denny McLain 109
Don McMahon 115
Jim Northrup 121
Ray Oyler 127
Daryl Patterson 133
Jim Price 137
Dennis Ribant 141
Jim Rooker 147
Joe Sparma 153

Mickey Stanley 159
Dick Tracewski 165
Jon Warden 169
Don Wert 173
Earl Wilson 179
John Wyatt 183

The Management

Mayo Smith 189
Jim Campbell 197
Tony Cuccinello 203
Wally Moses 207
Hal Naragon 213
Johnny Sain 217

The Broadcasters

Ernie Harwell 225
George Kell 231
Ray Lane 237
Larry Osterman 239

Sock It To 'Em Tigers

Detroit in 1968 245
Detroit Managers 249
The Rise and Fall of the Tigers 251
Interesting Facts About the 1968 Tigers 256
Denny McClain Game-by-Game in 1968 258
Tiger Stadium 259
The Greatest Inning in Tigers Word Series History 264
The Switch 265

Contributors 269

Foreword

by Lynn Henning

Each summer for the past few years, I have been a guest at the Fr. Vincent Welch Memorial Dinner in Troy, Michigan, which celebrates baseball and some of its special people, all before an audience of almost 400 men and women.

Whoever does the seating is to be commended (evidence points to Fr. Don Worthy). I get to sit at a table alongside a handful of men who over the decades have become professional acquaintances and, in a couple of cases, even friends: Mickey Lolich, Gates Brown, Willie Horton, Bill Freehan, Jim Northrup, etc., are the former Detroit Tigers stars who have been on hand in recent years for a big and festive July dinner.

One thing in particular is appreciated about the above names, beyond the fact they're good guys and fun to be around. They were part of the 1968 Detroit Tigers world championship team.

For those old enough to remember the '68 Tigers, no explanation is necessary for why the above names carry such magic 40 years later. Accordingly, anyone would understand why, when it has been a *Detroit News* sportwriter's turn to speak to the crowd, I have twice said something personally important to the audience and to the ex-Tigers seated at that front table.

In essentially these words, the message has been this:

> *I want to thank Mickey Lolich, and Willie Horton, and Bill Freehan, and Gates Brown, and Jim Northrup (and whoever else might have made it) for being here tonight. I want to thank them because I'm not yet sure these men understand that their 1968 team and World Series victory was, for so many of us, the greatest gift of our sports lives.*
>
> *It is difficult to convey what one baseball team, during one year, did for so many people. It is impossible to overstate the emotions, the spiritual fire, the sheer glee, which yet flows from one baseball team that was able to generate such passion and goodwill within the context of a single big-league baseball season.*
>
> *How was it, why was it, that the '68 Tigers remain the crown jewel of a mid-50s man's lifelong absorption with the teams of Detroit and Michigan?*

The reasons are as broad and as diverse as the Tigers' 1968 roster. But we can isolate on a few of that season's phenomena, all of which melded to form an unmatched six months of baseball in Detroit.

Timing

We must remember 1968 in the context of Detroit's recent sports history. Essentially, nobody had won a doggone thing in more than a decade. The Lions had seen their '50s heyday pass into (permanent?) history. The Red Wings had not won a Stanley Cup in 15 years. The Pistons were awful.

And the Tigers—the unquestioned kings of Detroit sports—had not won a pennant since 1945.

To say the town was championship-starved is to say Detroit during the past few years could have benefited from a healthier automobile market.

It was into this distressing vacuum that manager Mayo Smith's 1968 Tigers began to fill minds and hearts and souls with the joy and pride of attachment to an extraordinary baseball team.

Another factor, to be sure, was 1967, and not only because Detroit had experienced during the summer of 1967 the worst urban rioting in American history. The Tigers had come excruciatingly close in '67 to winning the American League pennant (divisional playoffs did not begin until 1969). They missed by one lousy game of tying the Red Sox. The '67 near-miss helps to provide an emotional backdrop for a baseball team that had an underlying mission to erase '67's bitterness and to get it right this time.

Individuals

When you talk about the stars who made the '68 Tigers champions, most discussions turn, initially, to three people: Denny McLain, Mickey Lolich, and Gates Brown. Yes, Gates Brown.

McLain won 31 games during a season of pitching mastery that yet defies explanation. He remains the only big-league pitcher since Dizzy Dean in 1934 to win 30 games in a single season. His grandiose performance, coupled with his one-of-a-kind rock-star persona, made him an eternal, unforgettable Detroit sports figure.

The rubber-armed craftsman, Lolich, won three games during the World Series. He personified a tremendous career, bordering Hall of Fame status, with a pitching virtuoso that, like McLain's 30 victories, was from another realm.

Brown won games with his ability to pop out of the Tigers dugout, needing desperately to get a big hit even if he had not swung a bat in a game the past two or three days, and delivering: a home run into Tiger Stadium's upper deck, a double, a single. It never mattered. The Gator might have been as cold as a morning in winter but he would deliver and the Tigers would steal another comeback victory.

And then there were the others: Al Kaline, coming back from a broken arm to put together the single most dramatic at-bat during the '68 World Series, when he fouled off pitch after pitch against Joe Hoerner and then singled in the go-ahead runs in the pivotal fifth game at Tiger Stadium.

Willie Horton, crushing the ball all season long, and crushing the Cardinals in Game 5 when he threw out Lou Brock at the plate; Jim Northrup hitting grand slams galore, including two in one game against the Indians; Pat Dobson, Jon Warden, and Daryl Patterson, pitching brilliant relief in a bullpen that seemed always to deliver; Earl Wilson, winning games on the mound and bashing long home runs in the pre-designated hitter era; Mickey Stanley, playing silken defense in center field and then, improbably, incredibly, starting at shortstop in the World Series, and performing impeccably; Dick McAuliffe, the tough second baseman and leadoff hitter, showing how much he meant to the club during an August suspension (for charging pitcher Tommy John) when his absence triggered a brief losing streak; Don Wert, holding down third base and singling in the pennant-clinching run; Bill Freehan, blocking the plate against Brock and helping to ring the Cardinals' death knell; Tom Matchick, parking a two-out, two-run home run off Moe Drabowsky into Tiger Stadium's lower-deck seats in right to win a classic, 3–2, against the Orioles on a wild Friday night in July.

Comebacks and Winning Streaks

From the season's second game and first Tigers victory, when Gates Brown's ninth-inning home run beat the Red Sox, the Tigers specialized in late-inning theater. It is one of those special, unique, endearing facets of the '68 team, and it contributed mightily to the way in which an extraordinary ballclub is remembered.

Brown's pinch-hitting wizardry in helping the Tigers sweep an August doubleheader against the Red Sox is a chief reason why so many discussions today about individual players from '68 so often involve The Gator. His exploits on that hot, sultry Sunday all but made him a Mount Rushmore figure in Motown sports lore.

The Tigers won 40 games after the seventh inning, 30 of those games in their last at-bat. McLain won his 30th game of the season, on September 14, thanks to one of those patented ninth-inning rallies.

The Tigers also used winning streaks to take the American League pennant race by the throat. In a span of six weeks from Memorial Day to the Fourth of July, the Tigers rolled up five winning streaks of five games. It was during their torrid transition from spring to summer that the Tigers caught fire and set ablaze a fan base that began to sense something for the ages was beginning to bubble at the corner of Michigan and Trumbull. McLain, of course, was integral here as he pitched with such dominance that the Tigers could just about count on a victory in any particular series.

All of the above made 1968 riveting, exhilarating, and, we now can say with greater perspective, so utterly enchanting with respect to one Tigers baseball season. We remember it, as well, for the sound of Ernie Harwell's voice at a time when televised games were few and fans were more regularly tethered to their radios as their primary Tigers attachment.

We remember J.P. McCarthy and his epic WJR morning program, and the way in which it served as something of an electronic nerve center for the city's, and the state's, collective excitement.

It was on J.P.'s show that the Tigers' pennant-drive theme song ("We're all behind our baseball team—go get 'em, Tigers") became an evergreen melody, as easily recalled today as it was sung four decades ago. It was on J.P.'s show that the magic each morning seemed to be validated and amplified and reviewed, all so blissfully for fans and citizens who were hungry for something to feel good about, and to communally celebrate.

I was blessed to cover the 1984 Tigers, their 35–5 start, and their World Series crescendo. I was on hand every step of the way for the Tigers' 2006 renaissance and for their improbable march into another World Series.

But I was 16 years old in 1968, when the greatest year of my sports-loving life took place. Forty years later, it remains untouchable.

November 30, 2007
Lynn Nenning covers the Detriot Tigers
for the Detriot News

Introduction

by Dale Petroskey

As a lifelong Detroit Tigers fan, it has been exciting to witness the resurgence of the Tigers these past few seasons. I have many fond memories of the 1984 "Bless You Boys" Tigers team that roared off to a 35-5 start on the way to the World Series championship. But no Tigers team is closer to my heart than the 1968 Tigers. My office wall is filled with baseball items—lots of it Tigers-related—but no piece has more meaning for me than my framed 1968 Detroit Tigers World Series champions pennant. It's hard to believe that we are celebrating the 40th anniversary of that team.

Probably my greatest memory of the 1968 Tigers was Game 5 of the World Series. We were a bit discouraged as the Tigers were down three games to one, but never gave up hope, even after the Cardinals took a 3-0 lead off Mickey Lolich in the top of the first.

We were rewarded later in that game with maybe the most-remembered play in Tigers history. The Tigers were down, 3-2, with one out in the fifth when Julian Javier lined a sharp single to left. Lou Brock came around third determined to extend the Cardinals' lead to two runs, but Willie Horton made the throw of his life to the plate. Bill Freehan had the plate well blocked, so Brock decided not to slide. We were holding our breath in the stands as we waited for the umpire's call. Out!

The Cardinals argued the call, and to this day, Hall of Famer Lou Brock insists to me that he was safe, but the umpire ruled otherwise. A rally in the seventh inning gave the Tigers a 5–3 lead they would not relinquish.

The Tigers of that era were a stable—and in many instances, a homegrown—team. Nine of the players on the 1968 club were teammates for 10 seasons: Gates Brown, Bill Freehan, Willie Horton, Mickey Lolich, Al Kaline, Norm Cash, Dick McAuliffe, Jim Northrup, and Mickey Stanley. They lived in Detroit, and were involved in the community. Several were Michigan natives—Freehan, Horton, Northrup, and Stanley—and the others made Michigan home after their careers. There is no finer gentleman in baseball than Al Kaline, and it has been a privilege to get to know him in my time as the president of the National Baseball Hall of Fame and Museum. Some may not remember that another member of the Hall of Fame, Eddie Mathews, was also a member of the 1968 Tigers; he provided a powerful left-handed bat at third base in the last season of his career, and spelled the right-handed-hitting Don Wert.

The 1968 Tigers also provided us with the name for the Tigers fan club my brother, Dennis, my friend, Bill Mackay, and I founded in Washington in 1983 to follow our beloved team. We named the group the Mayo Smith Society, in honor of the 1968 manager, the last manager at the time to lead the Tigers to a world championship. The name was also a bit of a litmus test, as Mayo Smith, despite his 1968 success, was not one of the more well-known managers in Tigers history. We wanted only loyal and knowledgeable Tigers fans in our club. At that time, the Tigers were turning the corner; they would finish in second place that season, six games behind the Orioles, and then win the world championship the following year. Lots of Johnny-come-lately fans were piling onto the Tigers' bandwagon at that time, but we wanted none of them in our club and adopted as our motto, "Tigers Fans Who Always Care."

As word spread, and the Tigers were showing themselves to be one of baseball's premiere teams, attendance at our breakfasts grew. The *Detroit News* and *Detroit Free Press* began paying attention. Even the *Wall Street Journal* profiled the Mayo Smith Society. With that publicity, the Society grew rapidly inside—and outside—Washington. We needed a reason for Tigers fans living outside Washington to be connected to us, so passionate and talented Society members Roger Conner and David Raglin began researching and writing a regular newsletter filled with information you couldn't get anywhere else. We called it *Tigers Stripes*, and it was mailed to members every month.

It's hard to believe a quarter-century has passed since those exciting early days of the Society, and life has moved on. The creativity and workload has shifted to others who are just as talented, dedicated, and excited as we were in those early days. Todd Miller, originally of Ann Arbor who now lives with his family in Pittsburgh, has done a great job of running the Society since 1997. Today's Society is as alive and vibrant as ever. *Tigers Stripes* is still fresh and interesting; David Raglin continues to provide interesting perspectives, as he has since our first days, and Mark Pattison has been a great contributor for several years now. David and Mark bring their talents—and passion for the Tigers—to this interesting book as its editors.

It is so fun to read the biographies of all the 1968 Tigers, and remember them. Our mission here in Cooperstown is "Preserving History, Honoring Excellence, Connecting Generations." That's also a good description of what this book does. It's the result of a collaboration of many members of the Society of American Baseball Research and the Mayo Smith Society, and I am proud that the Society Dennis, Bill, and I helped found is still strong and vibrant, and has been the genesis of this book so many will enjoy.

Enjoy this wonderful trip down memory lane.

Dale Petroskey is president of the National
Baseball Hall of Fame and Museum

Acknowledgements

So many people, so little space. The project editors would like to thank:

- For advice on this project: Mark Armour (who suggested it in the first place), Rod Nelson, and Bill Nowlin.
- For making this work easier: Every single writer, editor, fact-checker, and proofreader associated with *Sock It to 'Em Tigers*.
- For help on the Norm Cash biography: Sonny Eliot and Ernie Harwell.
- For incredible help with photos: Peter Irwin, Deana Carr, Ashley Koebel of the Detroit Public Library, Andrew Newman of the National Baseball Hall of Fame Library, and Rick Thompson of the Detroit Tigers.
- For research facilitation: Mark Patrick of the Ernie Harwell Collection in the Burton Historical Collection at the main branch of the Detroit Public Library.
- For past professional courtesies and, in some cases, ongoing personal courtesies: Danielle De Lucia Burgess, Adela Garcia, Brandon Kelley, Sarah Murphy, Emily Nowak, Alison Reeves, Maya Rhodes, Renee Tambeau, and George Waldman.
- For standing ready: Rebecca Cook and Daymon Hartley.
- For unconditional love and patience: Our wives and families, especially Barb Mantegani, Dave's wife; Judith McCullough, Mark's wife; and Cyntia ("Go Tigers Go!") Pattison, Mark's daughter.

The Players

Gates Brown

by Dave Gagnon

Season	Age	G	AB	R	H	2B	3B	HR	RBI	BB	SO	SB	CS	BA	OBP	SLG
1968 Tigers	29	67	92	15	34	7	2	6	15	12	4	0	0	.370	.442	.685
Career Totals		1051	2262	330	582	78	19	84	322	242	275	30	8	.257	.330	.420

Ask any serious Tigers fan over the age of 50 and they'll tell you that the sound of Tiger Stadium was always a little bit louder than normal when Gates Brown was announced as a pinch-hitter. And why not? After 13 seasons in Detroit, not only did the "Gator" retire as the American League's all-time pinch-hitting king, but so many of his hits were of the clutch variety, either tying the game or putting the team ahead. One would think that in order to have enjoyed that kind of success off the bench, Gates would've had to have been ready to hit at all times. You would think he studied pitchers like a hawk for nine innings—trying to gain any advantage he could for when he took the plate. But, surprisingly, that wasn't always the case for Gates.

Once in 1968, Mayo Smith decided to put in his pinch-hitting specialist far earlier in the game than normal. Gates, who usually didn't come off the bench until a tight spot near the end of the game, was caught off-guard. "I was sitting at the end of the dugout, eating a couple of hot dogs," Gates recalled. "It was only the fifth inning (and) I never expected Mayo to call on me to pinch hit that early." Since he didn't want Smith—who often harped on Gates to lose a few pounds—to see him eating during the game, Gates quickly shoved the dogs down his shirt before heading to the plate. "That's the only time I ever wished I'd strike out," said Gates. But being the clutch hitter he was, Gates didn't get his wish. Instead, he cracked a double and ended up having to slide head-first into second. While Tigers fans roared and cheered, Gates realized he had made quite a mess of himself. "I had mustard and squashed meat all over me," Gates laughed, recalling that all his teammates were bent over laughing.

So despite his success as one of the greatest hitters off the bench in major league history, Gates Brown wasn't a pinch-hitting robot after all. He was simply one of the guys. He played poker with teammates. He snored. He played catch with relievers during games. He was a press-favorite. But most importantly, he always supported his teammates—so much so that his first big league manager, Charlie Dressen, often referred to him as "Governor Brown." But that was Gates Brown in a nutshell—a team player who always said and did the right things to help his team win.

William James "Gates" Brown was born in Crestline, Ohio, May 2, 1939 (the same day that Lou Gehrig's consecutive games streak came to an end). He was nicknamed "Gates" by his mother when he was just a toddler—although, to this day, he has never figured out why his mother chose it. "My mother started calling me Gates when I was small," Gates said. "I still don't know where she got it. But the name stuck."

Crestline, like much of northern Ohio in the 1940s and '50s, wasn't the greatest area to grow up in. Poor, flat, and desolate, most kids from the area got in trouble with the law at some point. A sociologist would say it wasn't their fault the kids turned to a life of crime, but a result of where they grew up.

Brown didn't make it out of Crestline with a clean record. Even though he was a standout football star at Crestline High School, Gates got into more than his fair share of trouble growing up. When he turned 18, he was arrested for breaking and entering and was sent to the Mansfield State Reformatory in nearby Mansfield, Ohio. The same prison used in the film *The Shawshank Redemption*.

Even though he had played some baseball in high school, it was in the Mansfield prison where Brown's true talents as a ballplayer were developed. At 5-foot-11 and 200-plus pounds of pure muscle, a prison guard who coached the pen's baseball team encouraged Brown to try out at catcher. In awe of his raw ability with the bat—and encouraged that baseball might lead Brown out of a life of crime—the coach wrote letters to several major league teams, including the Detroit Tigers.

In fall 1959, Detroit sent scouts to the prison to see Brown. Impressed, one of them called onetime Tiger Pat Mullin, now the team's top scout. Mullin made the trek from Detroit to see for himself. After Brown belted a daunting home run in Mullin's presence, the Tigers decided to help him get paroled a year early. Gates was signed to a $7,000 bonus pact almost immediately upon his release.

Brown mentions that other clubs, including the Cleveland Indians and Chicago White Sox, were interested in springing him. But he stuck with Detroit because "they didn't have any Negroes at that time and I figured they'd have to have some soon." In fact, Ozzie Virgil, a Dominican, had joined the Tigers in 1958—becoming the Motor City's first black ballplayer. But Gates was right in that the Tigers obviously lacked the integration of most other big league clubs in the late 1950s.

Prior to his first professional season in 1960, Mullin advised Brown to give up catching and switch to the outfield. The switch was fine with Gates, who was more concerned about staying out of trouble than he was about a position change.

Brown—on legal probation from Mansfield during his first season—joined the Tigers' organization in Duluth that year. Gates shone almost immediately—especially for someone only a few months out of prison. In 121 games, Gates hit .293 with 10 homers. He also led the Northern League with 13 triples and was second in both stolen bases (30) and runs scored (104). But his real character test wouldn't come until later.

The following year he headed south to Durham of the Carolina League. It was here that Brown found out firsthand that being black and an ex-con was fuel for the fire for Southern crowds. "It was tough just being a Negro down there," Gates said. "They still used the N-word down there, you know?"

Being an ex-con didn't help as Southern newspapers printed stories about his criminal history, leading to more quips and threats from the crowds. "They called me all the names, 'Con,' 'Jailbird,' the whole thing. They were pretty vicious," Brown recalled. But Gates had to learn to ignore the jeers and to use the negativity as motivation to improve. "Some of the guys wanted to go up into the stands after those people, but I told them to just let it lay. It made me do better. It made me try harder. I decided that they could beat me physically, but no way were they going to beat me mentally," he recalled. "And do you know something, I hit the ball hard that season and led the league in hitting," topping the circuit in 1961 with a .324 mark. His outstanding play actually began to win over the same Durham fans who had heckled him earlier in the season. "By the end of the year, they were all on my side," Brown said, laughing.

After showing continued success at the minor league level—including another .300 campaign for Denver in 1962—it was clear that Brown was on the fast track to join the big club. And with the Tigers' lack of early-season success in 1963, Brown was called up from Triple A Syracuse June 17—one day before Dressen was named the team's new manager. It would be Dressen who would call on Gates to take his first major league hacks.

Brown officially debuted for the Tigers against the Boston Red Sox on June 19 at Fenway Park. With Boston up 4–1 in the fifth inning, Brown entered the game as—what else—a pinch-hitter for pitcher Don Mossi.

With Dressen getting his first look at the young outfielder, the situation was much like when Pat Mullin came to see Brown play at Mansfield for the first time. Ironically, Mullin was in attendance that day in Fenway—having been hired by Dressen to serve as the first-base coach. Again, as he had during his Mansfield tryout, Gates would not disappoint his onlookers. He hit a booming 400-foot home run well into the Boston sky, becoming only the third Tiger in history to homer in their first at-bat.

Brown remained with the club for the rest of the season, primarily as a pinch-hitter. Detroit rebounded with him on the team and had a winning record for the rest of the year. Overall, Brown hit .268 with two home runs in his rookie season. He stuck on the parent club for 1964. He was used primarily as the starting left fielder for Dressen. Playing alongside Al Kaline in right field and a troika (Bill Bruton, George Thomas, and Don Demeter) in center, Brown hit .272 with 15 home runs and was second on the team with 11 stolen bases.

Despite his solid 1964 season however, Brown lost his starting job in the outfield in 1965 to a young power hitter named Willie Horton. And even though he was disappointed in returning to his role as a pinch-hitter and reserve outfielder, Gates would never let his personal frustration get in the way of the team. He slugged 10 home runs that season in barely half the at-bats he had in 1964. And despite his stocky 225-pound frame, Brown also managed to steal another six bases and was regarded unofficially as the fastest Tiger on the team. He didn't know it then, but Brown was on his way to becoming the most successful pinch-hitter in American League history.

Despite Brown's clutch contributions, his reserve status—and a budding mix of young outfielders—made it difficult for him to get raises from his bosses in Detroit. In fact, prior to the 1965 season, Brown had to pass up winter ball for the first time. With a wife and one child—plus a second on the way—Brown took a second job as a furniture salesman in the off-season.

Brown pressed on, however, and returned in 1966 and had similar success in the same role—hitting .325 as a pinch-hitter. Overall he hit .266 with seven home runs in only 169 at-bats. Although he remained quietly disappointed with his role, it was clear that Brown was the Tigers' best offensive option off the bench.

Tragedy befell Brown and the Tigers that season, however. Charlie Dressen, the Tigers skipper who arrived less than 24 hours after Gates was called up, died August 10. Dressen had been suffering from heart and kidney problems for most of the season.

Brown struggled with injuries in 1967 before finally being shelved with a dislocated wrist. Even when he played, he never could find his swing under new manager Mayo Smith. As a pinch-hitter, he hit only .154 (4 for 26). However, that Tigers team nearly made the World Series before they were beat out by the "Impossible Dream" Red Sox on the final day of the season. Mayo Smith and the rest of the Tigers vowed to return to the 1968 season with a vengeance. But the greatest turn around of all would come from Gates Brown.

Discouraged by his poor season in 1967, Brown came to spring training on a mission in 1968. He was no longer upset about a lack of playing time, he just wanted to contribute. The Tigers, however, weary of Brown's poor and injury-filled campaign in 1967, decided to bring back Eddie Mathews as the team's primary left-handed pinch-hitter. General Manager Jim Campbell and Smith even said that they thought about trading Brown, but couldn't come close to pulling a trade because Gates had packed on a few pounds while waiting for his wrist to heal, a turnoff for prospective trading partners.

Brown got his chance to prove them wrong, however, on the second day of the season; when Smith, having already used Mathews earlier in the game, called on Brown to pinch-hit in the ninth inning in a tie game. Brown grabbed a bat and hit a game-winning home run off John Wyatt. It was how the 1968 Tigers won their first game of the season. "We took off from there," said Brown.

Brown did everything he could to tarnish the image of what would be known as the Year of the Pitcher. He hammered six hits in his first 10 pinch-hit at-bats on his way to an AL-record 18 pinch hits that season. Tigers fans soon became accustomed to watching the Gator come off the bench and deliver over and over in key situations. But none was more key than during a Sunday doubleheader August 11 against the defending American League champs, the Boston Red Sox.

In the lid-lifter that day, the Tigers were in an extra-inning struggle with the Bosox until Mayo Smith finally found a time for Brown to get in the game in the bottom of the 14th inning. Tiger Stadium erupted when he was announced. But their cheers were nothing compared to when Brown smacked the game-winning home run a minute later.

Then in the second game, Brown strode to the plate in a tie game in the bottom of the ninth. With Mickey Stanley creeping off of third, Gates singled to right to drive in the winning run, giving him an unheard-of two game-ending hits in the same day. Even 16-year vet Kaline admitted he had never heard the Tiger Stadium crowd cheer like they did for Brown that day.

In fact, Brown hit so unbelievably well in 1968 that Smith even started him in 16 games. Not bad for a guy who was trade bait when the season began. In the end, Brown hit an astounding .370 in 1968—more than over 100 points higher than his career average, 135 better than the team average, and 140 better than the American League's collective average. He was the only full-season Tiger to hit above .300 that season. He also averaged an extra-base hit every six at-bats—a remarkable stat when you consider that the mighty Alex Rodriguez only averaged one every 7.2 at-bats in his MVP season of 2007.

Brown was not only clutch with the bat in 1968, he was also clutch as a teammate. One night during the season, he interrupted a melee between Denny McLain and Jim Northrup and made them understand the importance of what the team was trying to accomplish as a whole. During a road trip in the middle of the 1968 season, Brown was playing poker with a bunch of other players, including Northrup and McLain. Halfway through a hand, Northrup caught McLain cheating. Enraged, he flew across the bed and grabbed McLain by the throat. John Hiller, who was seated next to Brown, recalls Northrup screaming, "I'm gonna kill you, you bastard! I'm gonna kill you!" Red-faced and exasperated, Northrup continued to wring McLain's neck in anger. But he was eventually pulled off from behind by Gates. A shocked Hiller remembers Brown looking Northrup dead in the eye and saying, "You're not gonna touch him until after we win the pennant. Then he's all yours."

Brown also remained popular with the Detroit writers that season. When asked about his remarkable success in the clutch, Gates developed a common response to give to reporters: "I'm square as an ice cube, and I'm twice as cool," he always told them. Detroit media couldn't get enough of Gates.

Neither could Tigers fans. When the World Series rolled around and the Tigers lost Game 1 to St. Louis' Bob Gibson—who also struck out 17—Mayo Smith was bombarded by letters to put Brown into the starting line-up. One Tigers fan even wrote Smith asking him to start Brown at shortstop and bat lead-off during the series. "That guy must be nuts," reacted Gates when told of the letter.

In fact, Brown only had one appearance during the World Series: a pinch-hit fly out to left off Gibson in Game 1. But for anyone who remembers how untouchable Gibson was that October day, it's a miracle any man could come off the bench and even touch the ball. But Gates did. In fact, he just missed the sweet spot.

Throughout the rest of his career, Brown enjoyed continued success as a pinch-hitter—including a .346 pinch-hitting campaign in 1971—but nothing quite like the 1968 season. Gates did enjoy more time in the baseball spotlight by becoming Detroit's first-ever designated hitter in 1973, a position tailor-made for the game's Gates Browns.

Moreover, Brown became so beloved that some sportswriters who were adamantly against the DH when it was first implemented later said it didn't bother them as much as they thought it would. One of the reasons: it was great for Tigers fans to see Brown at the plate every day.

The whole country got a chance to see Brown a year later when Joe Garagiola, host of NBC's pregame show, *Baseball World of Joe Garagiola*, did an unusual two-part story on Gates. Garagiola rarely devoted his weekly show to anyone for two separate shows, but did so for Brown. The shows, which aired July 8 and 15, 1974, featured Brown and Garagiola back in Gates's old stomping grounds at the Ohio State Reformatory in Mansfield. The program consisted of an interview in Brown's former prison cell, as well as several rap sessions with current inmates.

Brown said he agreed to the interview inside the prison itself in hopes that it might prevent "even more youngsters" from making the mistake of a lifetime. But he also mentioned that even if you did make the mistake of breaking the law, incarceration didn't mean the end. "It's what you do when you get out that counts," Gates told the inmates. The two-part program received wide acclaim.

After suffering through a 102-loss season in 1975, Brown decided to hang up his cleats at age 36. However, Gates loved the game too much to give it up completely. So he became a scout for the club less than three weeks after the season ended. Almost immediately, Brown went from sitting in a major league dugout to scouting teams in Florida; assisting in the free agent draft; instructing the Tigers' rookie league team; and visiting various colleges nationwide to find new talent.

Brown continued his work as a scout until 1978, when he returned to the Tigers to become the new hitting coach under manager Ralph Houk. The Tigers' team batting average rose from eighth in the American League in 1977 to second overall in Gates's first season. That year the Tigers also enjoyed their first winning season in five years.

When Sparky Anderson arrived in Detroit in 1979, he kept Brown on. Gates helped bring along the hitting talents of Kirk Gibson, Alan Trammell, and Lou Whitaker. Brown remained with the Tigers through their world championship in 1984. Gates wanted to continue coaching the Tigers beyond 1984, but couldn't agree on a contract extension with the front office. He quit November 14, 1984—almost 25 years since he signed his first professional contract fresh out of Mansfield.

Things weren't always rosy for Brown in his years since the 1984 championship. In 1991 he was part of a business group that purchased Ben G Industries, a plastics molding company that was relocated from the Detroit suburb of Mount Clemens, Michigan, to Detroit after its purchase. The company was doomed almost from the start. First it was alleged that the previous owners had stolen $458,000 from Ben G before it was sold to Brown's group. Then the Internal Revenue Service got involved and found that as the company's president, Brown had failed to oversee the payment of taxes during his first two years of ownership. A civil suit was served to Brown by the IRS seeking more than $61,000. However, Gates never faced criminal charges.

Brown also had to settle another IRS allegation a few months before the trial with Ben G began. This time it was at the personal level. Brown and his wife, Norma, were accused of shorting income on their personal taxes and ordered to pay more than $36,000 in back taxes and penalties dating from 1992 to 1997.

Brown was not forgotten from the baseball world, however. He was inducted into the Michigan Sports Hall of Fame in 2002. Beside Gates during his acceptance speech was his former hitting pupil, Lance Parrish, and former big-league pitcher and Zeeland, Michigan, native, Jim Kaat. Many of the voters admitted that Gates's amazing story was a huge reason why they chose him.

Brown has always liked to revisit and reflect upon that magical season of '68. He had reached the pinnacle of his profession. He was a World Series champion. His climb from a prison cell to shaking hands with the likes of Bob Hope and Ed Sullivan is truly a great comeback story. But if you asked Gates, his contribution to the 1968 season was for his parents.

"I can never make up for all the grief I gave them in my life. I can never make up for all the humiliation they suffered, all the torture, when I spent time in [Mansfield]," Brown said. "But I promised them, when I got out of there I would never go back. If I didn't make it in life, it would not be because I didn't try. You know, you can do bad things in a big city and nobody ever knows about them. But do something wrong in small town [Crestline's population was only 6,000] and everybody knows. That's why I was so happy we won it all. I could finally give them something else to talk about."

In his 13 years as a player with Detroit, Brown was a part of nine winning ball clubs. He also was a part of seven more as a coach. Most Tigers fans will tell you that, despite his reserve role, Brown was a huge part of the successful era in Motown. His ability to come through in the clutch has not been matched by any in the annals of AL history. His .370 average in '68 was the eighth-best season ever for a pinch-hitter. He had 107 pinch hits in his career, the most ever in the American League. He also still holds the AL records for pinch-hit at-bats (414) and home runs (16).

But it wasn't just with his bat, but with his attitude, in which Brown became so successful on the diamond. He was everyone's favorite teammate. He was a huge crowd favorite. He was Gates Brown, the underdog who went from prisoner to champion.

References

Publications

Brown's quotes about being hounded by Southern fans while in the minors: Joe Falls article, *The Sporting News*, March 22, 1975, and Rich Koster article, *St. Louis Globe Democrat*, October 19, 1968.

Brown's troubles with the IRS: David Shepardson article, *Detroit News*, date unknown, and Anthony Neely article on the Summa-Harrison scandal, April 1993.

Hot dog story and quotes: Detroit Tigers press release, August 18, 1978.

Joe Garagiola interview info. and quotes: Detroit Tigers press release, July 1, 1974.

Poker story with McLain and Northrup and quotes: *Detroit Tigers Encyclopedia*, p. 99.

Reference to Mayo Smith receiving letters to start Gates at shortstop during the World Series: Rich Koster article, *St. Louis Globe Democrat*, October, 19, 1968.

Rich Shook presents:
Tigers In the News

Monday, April 8
The Tigers held an off-day workout prior to their Wednesday season opener, which was pushed back a day from its scheduled April 9 start to honor the memory of assassinated civil rights leader Rev. Martin Luther King Jr. Manager Mayo Smith announced Mickey Stanley would start the first game at first base, instead of left-handed hitting Norm Cash, because Boston was going with left-hander Dick Ellsworth. "Stanley is the best first baseman we have," he said. "His hitting improved a great deal this spring." That let Smith have an outfield of LF Willie Horton, CF Jim Northrup, and RF Al Kaline. Earl Wilson, a 22-game winner in 1967, was nominated to start the opener.

Tuesday, April 9
Another workout. "Mickey had a good spring (.310 after hitting .210 in a reserve role in 1967) and deserves to play as long as he keeps hitting," Smith said of his new leadoff man. "As long as he continues hitting he will play first base against left-handers." "Yeh, I'm nervous," Stanley admitted. "I'm going to be trying extra hard out there." Smith's batting order: Mickey Stanley, 1B; Dick McAuliffe, 2B; Al Kaline, RF; Willie Horton, LF; Bill Freehan, C; Jim Northrup, CF; Don Wert, 3B; Ray Oyler, SS, Earl Wilson, P. "I'm just as nervous about this opening day as I have been about the others," Kaline said. (Sign of the times I: Mickey Lolich had National Guard duty when the season began, so Wilson, Denny McLain, and Joe Sparma were slated to do the bulk of the early pitching.) (Sign of the times II: 147 days of no newspapers in Detroit, except strike papers, because the *Detroit Free Press* and the *Detroit News* were on strike.)

Wednesday, April 10
"Detroit started 1968 the same way it ended 1967—one game behind Boston," was how UPI's Rich Shook led his first game story of the season. A less-than-capacity 41,429 turnout for the first game, won by Boston, 7-3, behind Ellsworth's nine-hitter. Wilson, who tied Boston's Jim Lonborg for most wins in the AL last season, lost his first game in six decisions against his former team. Carl Yastrzemski slammed home runs in the seventh and ninth innings, the second an inside-the-park job that banged off the fence some 15 feet to the left of the 415-mark in right center. Yaz easily beat McAuliffe's relay of Northrup's throw. Both home runs came with the bases empty. The noticeably nervous Stanley had three hits, one a double, in five at-bats, prompting Smith to say, "As long as he hits, he plays. I don't know if we'll keep him at first base."

Thursday, April 11
Gates Brown, annually the subject of rumors he was available for trade, hit a home run leading off the ninth inning to give Detroit its first victory of the year, 4-3, over Boston. "I needed it," Brown said. "I need all I can get." Jon Warden, 21, who made the jump from 15-game Class A winner to the majors, won in his first appearance with two innings of one-hit relief. Warden made the club in spring training after pitching for Rocky Mount in the Carolina League in 1967. Brown was batting for Warden against John Wyatt (who himself would be a Tiger later in the year). McLain, who gave up 35 home runs the year before, shut out Boston for five innings but surrendered three in the sixth, including a two-run home run to 20-year-old rookie Joe Lahoud, who was filling in for Tony Conigliaro, still recuperating from his 1967 beaning—and barely out of his teens himself. Warden relieved McLain and walked Elston Howard to load the bases before getting PH Joe Foy lined out to Horton in left to end the inning. "I like his coolness out there," Smith said of Warden. "He doesn't get flustered. Sure, he was nervous in his first big league game. But he didn't show it." Starting lineup: McAuliffe, 2B; Wert, 3B; Kaline, RF; Horton, LF; Cash, 1B; Northrup, CF; Freehan, C; Oyler, SS (replaced by Matchick); McLain, P.

Friday, April 12
No game.

Saturday, April 13
Daryl Patterson, in only his second major league game, took over for starter Joe Sparma with one out and two on in the fifth. He got Ken Boyer to hit into an inning-ending double play and pitched until the ninth to record his first victory, a 5-2 win over the visiting Chicago White Sox. Fred Lasher got the final out after singles by Tommy Davis and Boyer. (Curiosity note: Don McMahon, who would pitch later in the year for the Tigers, walked Patterson with the bases loaded to finish a two-run fifth, making it 5-2.)

Les Cain

by Brian Borawski

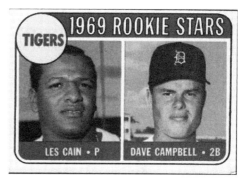

Season	Age	W	L	Pct	G	GS	CG	SV	IP	H	R	ER	BB	SO	ERA
1968 Tigers	20	1	0	1.000	8	4	0	0	24	25	9	8	20	13	3.00
Career Totals		23	19	.548	68	64	8	0	374	331	190	165	225	303	3.97

In 1976, Mark Fidrych made his major league debut at the age of 21 and took the city of Detroit by storm in a spectacular rookie season. He started the All-Star Game for the American League, won the Rookie of the Year Award, and finished second for the Cy Young Award. Of course, Mark Fidrych's career wound up being cut extremely short because of injuries to his pitching shoulder, and an unfortunate ending came to what could have been a fantastic career.

While Les Cain's rookie season, six years earlier, wasn't nearly as prolific, it was nearly as good. The young left-hander had a strong first half that well could have put him on the American League All-Star team, and the media were talking about his chance to win 20 games. Then, in the second half of the season, the shoulder problems began to develop, hence the parallel to Fidrych. Just two years later Cain was out of baseball.

Cain's story is still interesting. He's had some brushes with Hall of Famers, and he's also done something that no other pitcher has yet done. And he took a stand against the baseball establishment, so Cain's story, while short, goes beyond his playing days.

Les Cain was born January 13, 1948, in San Luis Obispo, California, about halfway between Los Angeles and San Francisco. His family moved to El Cerrito, California, a suburb of Oakland. He required skin graft surgery on his right arm when he was 18 months old after hot grease was spilled on his arm.

Cain attended El Cerrito High School and played both basketball and baseball. He was all-league in baseball as a sophomore, but broke his foot between his sophomore and junior years. This didn't seem to affect his performance too much; on April 28, 1965, Cain had a truly spectacular performance on the mound, pitching ten innings of a 12-inning contest and striking out 20.

None of his past exploits compared to what he did in 1966, his senior year, when he put the El Cerrito Gauchos on his back and carried them to the Alameda County Athletic League pennant. In one week in April, Cain threw a two-hit shutout then followed that with a no-hitter. The no-hitter pushed the Gauchos to a league-leading 7–1 record at the time. Then on May 24, he not only held the opposition to a single run in an extra inning, eight-frame game but also scored the winning marker in the Gauchos' final game of the season. The win gave El Cerrito an 11–5 record that was good enough to win the pennant.

For his efforts, Cain was the only player on his team to be named on either the first or second All-Alameda County Team; he was also the only unanimous choice of league coaches. With a 9–5 record on the mound and a .363 batting average at the plate, he was named player of the year.

Just one day after his selection as player of the year, the Tigers made Les Cain their fourth-round pick (74th overall) of the major league player draft. He was signed by former major league player and longtime Tigers scout

Bernie DeViveiros. The Tigers shipped him off to their Florida State League affiliate, the Daytona Beach Islanders. There, Cain's strengths and weaknesses began to show. While he definitely had a live arm and had no problem striking batters out, he also had control problems that led to an inordinately high number of walks. He finished the season with a 4–4 record in eleven starts and five relief appearances, and while he struck out an impressive 85 batters in 92 innings, he also walked 56. Cain's inability to find the strike zone at times would follow him throughout his pro career. Still, hopes were high for Cain, and Tigers general manager Jim Campbell was quoted by correspondent Watson Spoelstra in the December 3, 1966, issue of *The Sporting News* as calling him "a real prospect."

The team felt that Cain pitched well enough to earn a promotion for 1967 to the Double A Southern League, where he played for the Tigers' affiliate, the Montgomery Rebels. Cain got off to a rough start and lost his first four decisions before he finally picked up a win on a six-hit shutout May 12, 1967. He fell to 6–9 in mid-July but on July 22 Cain threw a no-hitter against the Birmingham Athletics. Barry Morgan, who would never play in the majors, made a diving catch of a line drive by future Hall of Fame outfielder Reggie Jackson for the final out of the game.

Cain showed some improvement in the second half of the season, finishing with an 11–13 record. He led the loop with 31 starts (he pitched twice in relief) and 104 walks, and was sixth in the league with a 2.77 ERA. Once again, he struck out his fair share of batters (133 in 185 innings) but also struggled with his control with all of the walks. Over the winter, Cain pitched for the Tigers' Florida Instructional League team at Dunedin, which won the league crown.

At age 20, Cain was the youngest player invited to the Tigers' spring training camp heading into the 1968 season. While he was probably a long shot to make a team that had fallen just one game short of tying for the American League pennant the year before, Cain made an immediate impact by throwing three shutout innings in his first spring game, on March 10. He gave up just one hit and struck out two against a Minnesota Twins first-string lineup. He tossed three more shutout innings against the Washington Senators in a relief appearance on March 26. For his efforts, he joined infielder Tom Matchick and pitchers Daryl Patterson and Jon Warden as one of four rookies to make Detroit's opening day roster. In the April 20, 1968, issue of *The Sporting News,* manager Mayo Smith said, "When we need a fifth starter, Cain would be the one." Even more impressive was the fact that Cain was the youngest player to make a big league opening day roster (Gary Nolan, four months younger than Cain, supplanted him when he made his season debut that May 31, and all other players who were younger than Cain in 1968 all made their debuts during September call-ups).

Cain didn't see action until two weeks into the season when the Tigers played their a doubleheader against the New York Yankees at Tiger Stadium on April 28. After a tough 2–1 Tigers loss in the first game, Cain made his first major league start in the nightcap and did as well as any first-timer could, pitching into the eighth inning and holding the Yanks scoreless through the first seven. The lone run scored against him came on a solo home run by first baseman Andy Kosco to lead off the eighth inning. Cain then left the game in that inning with the score tied 1–1. The Yanks scored another run in the eighth, but the Tigers pulled out the game with two runs in the ninth on solo homers by Bill Freehan (who caught Cain in his debut) and Jim Northrup. Cain also picked up his first career hit with a double in his first at-bat to lead off the third inning.

For the next three weeks, Cain was used as a reliever. In three appearances, he held the opposition to just one unearned run in 5.2 innings. He finally got another start in a doubleheader against the Washington Senators on Sunday, May 19. This time, he didn't waste the opportunity and with Jim Price as his backstop, threw 6.2 shutout innings and picked up his first major league win. He had problems finding the plate at times, walking six batters, but struck out eight. To cap off a busy week, Cain used a West Coast trip the following weekend to marry his high school sweetheart, Vera Nell Washington.

Cain got two more starts in 1968, but neither went well. On May 28, he was pulled with one out in the third inning after giving up a run on three hits and four walks. Four days later, on June 1, he was humbled by the Yankees, who tagged him for four runs and five hits before he was taken out with just one out in the first inning. In both of those two poor starts, the Tigers came back to win the games so Cain escaped a loss.

After another poor relief appearance on June 15, Cain was demoted. Whether it was to get more seasoning or to work on his control, he put together some nice numbers for the Triple A Toledo Mud Hens. Finishing out the season with Toledo, he went 7–5 with a 3.27 ERA with 76 strikeouts and 41 walks in 77 innings. More importantly, Cain got the start in the Mud Hens' final game of the season, on September 8 against the Rochester Red Wings, with the International League pennant at stake. Cain not only held the Red Wings to three hits in a shutout win, but he also starred on offense with a grand slam home run and six RBI in the 17–0 victory.

The winter of 1968 and the 1969 season were setbacks for Cain with one exception. He played winter ball in the Puerto Rican Winter League for the Mayaguez Indians, and after struggling with a 2–6 record to start the season, he pitched a no-hitter on December 3, 1968. It was only the eleventh no-hitter in the league's history.

Cain found himself once again playing for the Mud Hens in 1969, but this time there was no pennant or happy ending to the season. He struggled most of the season, walking almost as many batters (71) as he struck out (79). He finished the season just 4–12 with a disappointing 5.71 ERA. Things worked out better for Cain in 1970, though, and despite finding himself back in Toledo to start the season, he put together three impressive starts in which he gave up just four runs in 25 innings. His performance was good enough to warrant another look by the Tigers, who brought him back after Daryl Patterson was called to serve a few weeks of active Army duty.

Cain's first Detroit start of 1970 didn't go well. Although he struck out nine batters in just five innings, the Chicago White Sox tagged him for six runs in a 13–6 loss on May 1. But he followed with his first major-league complete game and second career win with a solid start on May 6, defeating the Minnesota Twins, 5–2, with a seven-hitter, though he walked six. In his third start, on May 12, he was back in the loss column despite giving up just three runs in seven innings of a 7–2 loss to the Chicago White Sox.

From late May through early July, Cain put together a string of starts that, while not always phenomenal, were good enough to garner the left-hander eight consecutive wins. He gave up his share of walks and two or three runs in each of his starts, but he struck out his share of batters, and as the Tigers headed into the All-Star break, Cain sported an impressive 9–2 record with a 3.62 ERA. His first half was impressive enough to warrant consideration for the All-Star Game, and that year's American League manager, Earl Weaver, was quoted in the August 1 issue of *The Sporting News* as saying, "Cain should have been with us here in Cincinnati," where the All-Star Game was played. He added, "The last time I saw him, he was about the best six-inning pitcher in the league."

The second half of 1970 didn't go nearly as well for Cain and it was later revealed that he was pitching with a shoulder injury that forced him to miss the last two weeks of the season. He did finish the season with 156 strikeouts, a Tigers rookie record that still stands. He did show his propensity to miss the plate with 98 walks, but his 12–7 record and 3.83 ERA were certainly respectable. His 7.77 strikeouts per nine innings were good for third-best in the American League. Only Cleveland's Sam McDowell and Kansas City Royals rookie Bob Johnson had higher marks among starters.

Cain had another setback the next year. The 1971 season paralleled his disappointing 1969 season with the Mud Hens. Cain missed all of April and most of May because of the shoulder injury. But when he came back, he started the season on fire and after his first seven starts had a 5–1 record with a 1.10 ERA. Then when his arm troubles returned in late June and July, he lost seven consecutive decisions, and his ERA ballooned to 4.46. He finally ended his skid August 23 with a 4–2 victory over the Twins in a game in which he struck out a career-high 13 batters. In his next start, on August 28, he won his second straight, 5–4 over the White Sox, and hit his second career homer. (It was the last home run hit by a Tigers pitcher before the institution of the designated hitter—and the last homer hit by a Tigers pitcher until Jason Johnson hit one 24 years later in 2005.)

On September 12, 1971, Cain threw 3.2 unspectacular innings in a start against the Red Sox. One run came on a home run by Red Sox catcher Carlton Fisk, the first hit of what would be 2,356 in his Hall of Fame career.

Cain finished strong in September, winning his last three decisions to put his record at 10–9. He once again showed he could strike batters out with 118 whiffs in 144.2

innings, but he was also handing out lots of free passes, with 91 during the season.

On November 14, 1971, Cain became the first person ever to throw two no-hitters in the Puerto Rican Winter League with a 1–0 victory for the Mayaguez Indians. The three no-hitters as a professional, plus his fourth when he was in high school, had to have been the greatest moments of Cain's baseball life.

Cain's career came to an abrupt end in 1972. After nursing the shoulder injury in his previous two years, he got off to a horrible start, losing his first three starts of the season. Then in his fifth start of the season, on May 28, Cain walked the first batter he faced, the Yankees' Horace Clarke, and then was forced to leave the game because of shoulder pain. He went on the 21-day disabled list, and it turned out to be the end of Cain's major-league baseball career.

Cain almost got one last shot July 8. Tigers reliever John Hiller told the story in the Detroit News in 2005. Hiller was himself coming back from his three heart attacks and intestinal bypass surgery the year before, and Cain was trying to come back from his shoulder injury. As Hiller recalled it, Tigers manager Billy Martin told both Cain and Hiller, "Warm up. I'll keep one of you and release the other." Hiller apparently made more of an impact that day, and went on to be the greatest relief pitcher in Detroit Tigers history. Cain was eventually sold to the San Francisco Giants organization.

With the Phoenix Giants, Cain struggled in two starts and three relief appearances, giving up nine runs in just 11 innings. Those outings with Phoenix were his last in professional baseball. He was invited to spring training by the Giants in 1974, but he failed to make the team.

Les Cain's story doesn't end with his baseball career, though. While players like Curt Flood took on the reserve clause and Andy Messersmith, Dave McNally, and Catfish Hunter paved the way for free agency, Cain took a stand in a different way. With his baseball career over, he filed a disability claim against the Detroit Tigers in 1973 with the Michigan Bureau of Workman's Compensation. He said he was effectively forced to play through the injury. Though Cain was employed when he filed the claim—he was in California working for Bank of America in Oakland—he was unable to play baseball.

In late 1976, Cain received a favorable verdict; the Tigers were forced to retroactively pay him $111 a week for the rest of his life, and The Sporting News said on January 1, 1977, that the decision "could set a precedent for all of professional sports." No longer could a player be abused by his team then dumped without just compensation. Cain said it best in an Associated Press story printed in the February 8, 1977, issue of the Oakland Tribune on February 8, 1977. He said, "I paid into the disability program and felt I should be compensated for the injury. The baseball people look at the verdict as unusual I guess because they'd been saving a lot of money all of those years. They'd never had to pay anybody before."

Les Cain, recently widowed, currently resides in Richmond, California, and he has one son, Brian Earl Cain Sr., and one grandson, Brian Earl Cain Jr. Brian Jr. currently lives with his mother. Although he isn't following in his grandfather's footsteps as a baseball player, he's become one of the top prep soccer goalies in the state of California and an honors student at his high school in Citrus Heights.

References

Articles

"Cain Goes Distance for Tigers In Beating Twins." *Ironwood Daily News*, May 7, 1970.

"Cain Sparks Gauchos." *Oakland Tribune*, May 25, 1966.

"Compensation for Les Cain Landmark Case." *Oakland Tribune*, February 8, 1977.

"El Cerrito Pitcher Fans 20." *Oakland Tribune*, April 28, 1965.

Fox, Bill. "Cain Able; Hens Win Pennant on Final Day." *The Sporting News*, September 21, 1968.

Frau, Miguel. "Cain Reverses Skid—Hurls No-Hit Gem" *The Sporting News*, December 21, 1968.

Frau, Miguel. "Mayaguez' Cain Uncorks Second P.R. No-Hitter." *The Sporting News*, November 27, 1971.

"Gauchos' Cain Fires No-Hitter." *Oakland Tribune*, April 23, 1966.

Paladino, Larry. "Campbell Very 'Scotch' as Detroit Tigers GM." *Benton Harbor-St. Joseph Herald-Palladium*, January 29, 1977.

Spoelstra, Watson. "Horton Hitting Gives Tiger Foes Case of Willies." *The Sporting News*, June 1, 1968.

Spoelstra, Watson. "Pitcher Lolich Fielding Red-Hot Queries In Public Speaking Loop. *The Sporting News*, December 3, 1966.

Spoelstra, Watson. "Tiger Puzzler: Can Lolich Fill Hill-Ace Shoes?" *The Sporting News*, February 27, 1971.

"Two More Eastbay Preps Draft Picks." *Oakland Tribune*, June 9, 1966.

"Two Vikings, One Pirate Named to All-County Nine." *Hayward Daily Review*, June 7, 1966.

Watson, Michael. "Richmond Choice In ACAL." *Hayward Daily Review*, March 16, 1965.

Web Sites

www.baseball-reference.com

www.retrosheet.org

Other Sources

Les Cain file, National Baseball Hall of Fame Library.

1968 TIGERS

Rich Shook presents:
Tigers In the News

Sunday, April 14
Detroit wins its third straight game, 5-4, in 10 innings over Chicago. Freehan's bases-loaded single off Hoyt Wilhelm with nobody out in the bottom of the 10th scored McAuliffe from third. Lasher, who got the save Saturday, earned the win Sunday by retiring Chicago in the top of the 10th thanks to a double-play begun by McAuliffe. He did not allow a hit but did walk two batters. Relievers saved the day in all three wins over the White Sox. Detroit's remade bullpen featured seven relievers not on the roster at this time last season.

Monday, April 15
Detroit at Boston rained out (Red Sox home opener).

Tuesday, April 16
Earl Wilson allowed just four hits, only one over the final seven innings, in a 9-2 victory over Boston. He also contributed two hits of his own. Detroit bumped Ray Culp from the mound in the fourth when 13 Tigers batted and produced eight runs.

Wednesday, April 17
Twice Detroit was one strike from defeat and both times it rallied, defeating visiting Cleveland, 4-3, in 10 innings. Willie Horton drilled a 1-2 Eddie Fisher knuckleball into the lower deck seats in left with Kaline, who had walked with two outs, on first. Jim Price, facing Sam McDowell on a 2-2 count with two out in the ninth, ripped a single to center to score Freehan with the tying run. Freehan had started the ninth with a single and been bunted to second by Don Wert. "That game," Smith said, "was like coming back from the grave." Jon Warden picked up his second win without a loss by retiring the only batter he faced. Freehan threw out Jose Cardenal in his bid for his third stolen base of the game and Warden then got pinch-hitter Jose Vidal to fly out to center. "Feeling great, feeling great," sang Price, who hit for Oyler. "He threw me three curves and I hit the fastball." McLain went the first seven but got no decision. Pat Dobson retired all six batters he faced and Lasher faced just three batters in the 10th before giving way to Warden. Pitcher-turned-outfielder Willie Smith, a former Tiger, led off with a single, Chico Salmon sacrificed, and Cardenal hit an RBI single.

Thursday, April 18
Detroit finally saw first place, defeating Cleveland, 5-0, for its sixth straight win. "Streaks," Smith cautioned," are usually followed by other streaks." Home runs by Horton, Dick McAuliffe, and Kaline sparked the offense while Joe Sparma allowed seven hits and walked just one. He had five shutouts in 1967. He retired the side with the bases loaded in the fourth. "I didn't have the feeling I could throw the ball where I wanted to," Sparma said. Kaline played his 2,000th major-league game.

Friday, April 19
Detroit at Chicago, postponed due to cold weather.

Saturday, April 20
McAuliffe's 10th-inning single gave Detroit its seventh straight win, 4-1, at Chicago. Combined with a loss by Minnesota, it gave the Tigers sole possession of first place. Walt Williams, who had taken over in left for the White Sox at the start of the inning, misjudged a leadoff fly ball by Ray Oyler and it fell for a double. Dick Tracewski pinch-hit and tried to sacrifice but Oyler was tossed out at third. Mickey Stanley followed with a double, however, and McAuliffe's single broke a 1-1 tie. Kaline singled Norm Cash home later in the inning. Chicago's loss was its seventh straight, leaving the White Sox the only team in baseball without a victory. Both teams scored in the ninth. Jon Warden walked pinch-hitter Wayne Causey with the bases loaded to tie the score 1-1, but his rookie luck held when Detroit rallied for three in the 10th to improve his record to 3-0.

Sunday, April 21
Detroit runs its winning streak to nine games with a doubleheader sweep at Chicago, 4-1 and 4-2, dropping the White Sox to 0-9. The Tigers were now in first place by 1.5 games. "This is not a spontaneous group, which is good," Smith said. "You can go up and down too much. They've got a job to do and they do it. It's a better club than last year because we've had a year to get together. The experience of being in contention last year has helped us immensely." Pete Ward has made errors or mistakes that helped Detroit to four of those wins: "Every mistake we make now seems to mean a ball game and unfortunately mistakes have been mine." Ward bobbled a ground ball at third base in each game to jump-start two Detroit rallies. The last time the clubs played, Ward misjudged a fly ball in the outfield that went for a two-run double in one game and saw the game-winning hit carom off his glove in the 10th inning of another. Almost lost in the sweep was the second-game winner, Denny McLain. McLain went nine innings, allowing seven hits and two runs, walking one and fanning eight.

14 LES CAIN

Dave Campbell

by Alex Kupfer

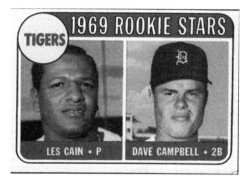

Season	Age	G	AB	R	H	2B	3B	HR	RBI	BB	SO	SB	CS	BA	OBP	SLG
1968 Tigers	26	9	8	1	1	0	0	1	2	1	3	0	0	.125	.222	.500
Career Totals		428	1252	128	267	54	4	20	89	102	254	29	18	.213	.272	.311

Seemingly the only assured thing in Dave Campbell's career as an infielder was the inconsistency. Over an eight-year career with the Detroit Tigers, San Diego Padres, St. Louis Cardinals, and Houston Astros, Campbell was only able to play one season as a full-time regular—with the Padres in 1970. Otherwise, his career was stalled by being buried on depth charts and later by recurring injuries. Yet for a player who moved 42 times as a player, Campbell's post-playing days have been characterized by a relatively stable broadcasting career which has enabled him to become one of the most knowledgeable and respected baseball announcers working today.

David Wilson Campbell was born January 14, 1942, in Manistee, Michigan, a small town with fewer than 9,000 residents located on the eastern shore of Lake Michigan. Along with his younger sister, Nancy, the family moved to Lansing when Dave was a small child. His mother, Frances, worked for the Michigan Highway Department and his father, Robert, was a teacher as well as a baseball and football coach at Sexton High School in Lansing. Robert Campbell had been a two-sport athlete at the University of Michigan, playing baseball and football there from 1935 to 1938. Coming from what he described as a "wonderful, supportive, sports-minded family," Dave, coached by his father, played baseball and football for the Sexton High School Big Reds, graduating in 1959. Despite living in Lansing, the home of Michigan State University, Campbell always knew that he wanted to attend the University of Michigan because of his father.

Switching from shortstop to first base upon joining the Michigan baseball team in 1962, Campbell helped the Wolverines win their second NCAA baseball championship title. Although they finished second in the Big Ten, because of a sweep of Western Michigan—in which Campbell hit the game-winning home run in the final game—the Wolverines garnered an at-large invitation to the District 4 Regional Championships. The team largely rode to the College World Series on the back of pitcher John Kerr, who threw an astounding 320 pitches in 17 innings in a doubleheader victory over Illinois and Western Michigan to make the College World Series.

The Michigan team reached the finals facing the heavily favored Santa Clara Broncos. Not only were the Broncos the nation's top-ranked team, but they also featured a then-record five players who would go on to play in the major leagues. In the longest title game in College World Series history, the Wolverines held tough, scoring two runs in the 15th inning to upset Santa Clara 5–4. Although he went hitless in six at bats in the championship game, Campbell was nonetheless named to the all-tournament team, joking, "It's a good thing they voted on it in the eighth inning, because I didn't do much in the title game." The team went on to win the International Collegiate World Series by defeating Hosei University of Tokyo, the Japanese college champions, in a tournament held in Hawaii. Campbell's talents also quickly attracted the attention of big league scouts and he was offered a contract by the Milwaukee Braves. He turned them down, however, wishing to remain in school. He was also approached by the Boston Red Sox, but declined to sign with them. As he recalled, "I could have signed with the Red Sox two years earlier [than signing with the Tigers] for more money but kids in Michigan dreamed of playing with the Tigers."

The following season, although the starting infielders who turned 60 double plays in 44 games—including Campbell at first—all returned, the program underwent a major change when longtime coach Don Lund left the program to become farm director for the Tigers. Under new coach Moby Benedict, the Wolverines limped to a 7–7 conference record and did not qualify for the postseason. Batting cleanup, Campbell continued to play a key role for the team, knocking in the two winning runs in the ninth inning with the Wolverines trailing 5–4 against second-ranked Western Michigan. He was also the first player in three years to hit a home run out of the University of Arizona's Hi Corbett Field—hitting it over the scoreboard at the 375-foot mark in left field.

The following year, with a number of graduation losses, Campbell was named captain of the squad. The team improved significantly, finishing second in the conference. Campbell switched back to shortstop and played well enough to earn All-Conference honors. Taking after his father yet again, Dave graduated with a bachelor's degree in education, working in the off-season as a substitute teacher. His sister Nancy also became an educator, teaching for many years in the Wacousta, Michigan, school district. His dream of playing with the Tigers came true when Detroit scout Ed Katalinas signed him as a shortstop to a contract for a $10,000 bonus.

Campbell's first assignment in the minor leagues was to the club's Lakeland team in the Florida State League. He jumped off to a fast start with the club, hitting .369, with 13 RBI and a home run in 17 games. Campbell's goal of playing for the Tigers was aided by a considerably larger number of younger players, since, as *The Sporting News* pointed out, "Vietnam and the draft situation, many prime prospects from the higher minors are back in school or involved in a reserve program." As a result, clubs and managers were looking for more rookies and prospects than usual and Campbell was able to move up to Class AA Knoxville.

Over 51 games Campbell's batting average at Class AA dropped to .209, although more than a third of his hits (13 of 33) went for extra bases, including three home runs. The next season, Campbell was still in Double A, now with the Montgomery Rebels, playing alongside former Wolverines teammate Fritz Fisher. Campbell's average had rebounded to .310 by the time he was promoted to Triple A Syracuse of the International League.

He spent slightly over half of the season with the Chiefs, his nine home runs and 27 RBI helping the team to a 74–73 record and a spot in the playoffs. Campbell even received a vote in a poll conducted by *The Sporting News* as "Best Hustler." He began the next season with Syracuse, although was sent back to Montgomery after struggling at the plate. He finished the season strongly there, driving in 28 and hitting six home runs in 53 games.

Campbell reported to the Tigers' spring training in 1967 in Lakeland, trying to make the club as a utility infielder and number-three catcher. Full of exuberance and energy, on March 20 he played in his first exhibition game as a Tiger, hitting a single off Atlanta Braves pitcher Cecil Upshaw in his first at-bat. Unfortunately for Campbell, within the Tigers infield, anchored by Norm Cash, Don Wert, and Dick McAuliffe, there was no space for him at the beginning of the season, and started the season with Class AAA Toledo (Syracuse had switched its affiliation to the New York Yankees that winter).

Establishing himself at second base, 1967 was a breakout season for Campbell. His defense was spectacular, leading International League second basemen with a .977 fielding average while his offense improved dramatically as he hit 20 home runs. Even though Toledo was picked to finished last in the International League, they finished third and earned a playoff berth. After beating Richmond in the semifinals, the Mud Hens faced Columbus for the Governor's Cup. After losing the first game, they won the next four games behind the clutch hitting of Campbell and took the title. Campbell hit a solid .350 in the series while scoring four runs. His three-run home run in the ninth inning of the fourth game proved decisive, giving the Mud Hens a 7–4 victory and a commanding 3–1 series lead. The next night, in a 0–0 tie in the bottom of the ninth, Campbell scored the game-winning run to clinch the title for Toledo.

Only two days after the club's dramatic victory, Campbell finally got his chance in the majors when on September 17 he made his debut in the major leagues for the Detroit Tigers in a game against the Washington Senators at Tiger Stadium when he pinch-hit for shortstop Ray Oyler in the sixth inning. Campbell's only other appearance for the 1967 Tigers came later that week, taking over for Eddie Mathews at first base in the seventh inning. He finished the season with the Tigers as the club nearly won the pennant in one of the closest races in major league history—finishing tied with the Twins one game behind the Red Sox.

That fall, Campbell went to play in the Florida Instructional League. His strong hitting, including a .315 average that placed him third in the league, helped the Tigers' entry in the league win the pennant. Trying to make himself even more versatile, he even worked as catcher for a few games in the Florida Instructional League. Detroit vice-president Rick Ferrell commented on the "Florida experiment": "Dave handles low throws real well and also did some good throwing." In 23 innings behind the plate Campbell did not allow a passed ball.

Once again, Campbell reported to spring training in 1968 trying to find a permanent position with the Tigers. But with McAuliffe still firmly entrenched at second Campbell had to start the season in Toledo. Campbell's offense continued to improve, as he raised his batting average 20 points to .265, and despite playing 40 fewer games than the year before, increased his home run total to 26, establishing a Toledo club record, and raised his RBI total from 36 to 64. His most dramatic home-run hitting that year came in the opener of a doubleheader July 6 against Louisville. He accounted for all of the team's runs beginning in the bottom of the sixth inning when he hit a solo shot with the Mud Hens trailing 2–0. In the bottom of the next frame, Campbell hit a game-ending grand slam. Exactly a week later, Campbell had another two-homer game in a 16–12 slugfest against league-leading Rochester.

Campbell was among four Mud Hens selected to the all-star tilt in Louisville pitting the International League stars against the Cincinnati Reds. Flying from Indianapolis, the four were delayed as a result of a bomb scare when airline officials received two calls warning that a bomb had been planted on the plane. After making the passengers leave the plane, a search was unable to find any explosives. The FBI did pick up a 13-year-old boy from Chicago who admitted making the calls as a joke. The players eventually arrived safely, although three hours late.

After the excitement in Indianapolis, Campbell hit eight home runs in July, including two grand slams in four days, to help lead the Mud Hens to a seven-game winning streak to extend their lead at the top of the standings. While leading Toledo in most offensive categories, Campbell garnered a call-up to the Tigers at the end of July for two weeks when Tom Matchick was on summer military duty. Playing in a substitute role for his first five games, Campbell got his only start with the team August 7 against Cleveland at Tiger Stadium. His first hit was a dramatic one—a home run off Mike Paul in the eighth inning, helping the Tigers beat the Indians 6–1. It would be his only hit during his time with the Tigers in 1967 and 1968. Sent down to Toledo upon Matchick's return in mid-August, everyone assumed that he would be back soon with the club, unfortunately however, his return to the Tigers would have to wait a year as he finished the season in the minors.

The 1968 season came to represent Campbell's frustrations with the Tigers. Although he had been playing great offensively and defensively for Toledo, the local boy who had always dreamed of playing for the team, even turning down better offers from the Braves and Red Sox because he would have to leave the state of Michigan, now was unable to get a chance to play, and could only watch the Tigers' championship 1968 season because he was buried too low on the depth chart. He was stuck behind Dick McAuliffe, the club's All-Star second baseman. Although Campbell had "great admiration for Dick and the way he played the game," and considered McAuliffe to be his favorite player, nonetheless he urged General Manager Jim Campbell (no relation) to trade him to another team.

Dave Campbell was so frustrated at being sent down to Class AAA once again that he considered quitting professional baseball. He was eventually convinced to play in the minors by the Tigers' GM since it would give him exposure for any interested ball club. Dave told *The Sporting News*, "There are 24 major league teams and I feel I'm good enough to play for some of them. And this is the best summer job I could find."

Stricken with mononucleosis, Campbell played only a limited role in Toledo's dramatic pennant race, which like the Tigers' in 1967 went down to the final day of the season. Trailing Columbus by a single percentage point, as the Mud Hens had more losses than the Jets (due to Columbus rainouts which were never made up), Toledo—needing a win combined with a Columbus loss to clinch the pennant—crushed Rochester 17–0 behind a marvelous game by pitcher Les Cain, who pitched a three-hit shutout in addition to belting a grand slam. Columbus lost their first game of a doubleheader, giving Toledo the title. Facing Jacksonville in the Governor's Cup playoffs, the Mud Hens were eliminated in the semifinal round.

Campbell and his wife moved to Lakeland, the Tigers' spring training home, in order to better improve his chances of making Detroit's roster at the start of the season, and spent the winter working as a substitute teacher. Campbell's power numbers with Toledo, particularly his 46 round-trippers 1967–1968, caught the attention of Detroit brass for 1969. *The Sporting News* wrote, "Dave's right-handed power gives him the best chance to make it as one of Mayo Smith's extra infielders. Campbell also qualifies as an emergency catcher." Playing both first and second, Campbell's early hitting in spring training impressed coach Wally Moses and he was rewarded with a spot on the roster to start the season.

Campbell began the year with the Tigers as a utility infielder. Playing in 32 games, he bounced between first, second, and third base and occasionally appearing as a pinch-hitter. While the Tigers as a team suffered through a post-championship malaise throughout the season, Campbell's numbers in particular plummeted. He hit just .103—by far the worst of any the position players, although he only committed two errors all year. During the year, he made two short trips down to Toledo to try and improve his hitting. In 25 games with the Mud Hens, in what would be his final minor-league trip, Campbell hit a remarkable .427, with 15 RBI and three home runs. He seemed to be unable to transition his minor-league hitting to the majors, however.

While playing in the Puerto Rico Winter League, Campbell finally found his chance to be an everyday player when Tigers management traded him. With McAuliffe prepared to return to regular duty at second base, and the other infield positions filled by Don Wert at third, Cesar Gutierrez at shortstop, and Norm Cash (spelled occasionally by Al Kaline) at first, and looking to shore up their starting pitching behind Denny McLain and Mickey Lolich, the Tigers dealt Campbell along with pitcher Pat Dobson and $25,000 to the San Diego Padres for pitcher Joe Niekro in December 1969. Although he would be playing baseball outside of Michigan for the first time in his life, with the Padres he could now expect to be an everyday player.

Joining a San Diego franchise in only its second year of operation, Campbell was penciled in as the starting second baseman. Playing a full season for the only time in his career, Campbell was excited about his new team, telling *The Sporting News*, "Until this season, I'd never played five games in a row in the majors. I wasn't getting any younger and couldn't see much future with the Tigers." San Diego manager Preston Gomez was also excited about his presence, saying, "Campbell's been a big plus for us. He's steadied the right side of the outfield. I like the way he takes charge out there. He has very good baseball instinct." Playing in 154 games, Campbell led the National League second basemen in putouts (359) and assists (455) although tying for the league lead in errors with 22. Shifting to the leadoff and number-two spots in the lineup after getting off to a strong start, Campbell tailed off badly during the season. He led the team in stolen in bases with eighteen, but finished the season with a dismal .219 average; he nonetheless was one of eight Padres in double figures in home runs.

In a somewhat dubious distinction, Campbell got one of only two Padres hits against Mets pitcher Tom Seaver in his record-setting pitching performance on April 22 at Shea Stadium when he struck out 10 batters in a row, breaking the major-league record, and 19 total to tie Steve Carlton's record. Seaver only allowed two hits that day, one a single to Campbell and the other a solo home run to left fielder Al Ferrara. In an omen of things to come for the Padres, they finished their season last in the NL West, 39 games behind the Cincinnati Reds, with a 63–99 record—worst in the league.

In order to give the Padres a sorely needed quality leadoff man, Campbell worked on switch-hitting in the Arizona Instructional League to improve his batting and on-base percentages. Going into the 1971 season Campbell was one of the standouts in the Padres' spring training. The quandary was where to play Campbell. With competition from recently acquired Don Mason at second and starting third baseman Ed Spiezio holding out, Campbell was tried out at third base.

Early-season injuries to Spiezio, Mason, and shortstop Enzo Hernandez created an infield shortage for the Padres, giving Campbell once again the opportunity to play second, third, and shortstop on a daily basis. His utility value was again apparent to Gomez, who commented, "I don't know what we would have done without Dave to fill in at shortstop and third base. He did a good job for us." While continuing to play strong defense, Campbell started his second full season in the majors well, but once again his offense tailed off and his average dropped to .227 by season's end, though his on-base percentage was up 31 points to .299. On September 6, in a game against the Cincinnati Reds, Campbell was injured running out a sacrifice bunt. He underwent Achilles' tendon surgery a few days later, ending his season. Campbell's next two seasons with the club were overshadowed by recurring injuries to his Achilles' tendon. He played in only 55 games total in 1972–1973 as he struggled to stay healthy.

The Padres' 1973 season became dominated by talk of a move to Washington after only four years in San Diego, when the team was sold to interests hailing from the capital. The team's dire financial straits forced them to sell off a number of players for little in return. Campbell was in the midst of one of the worst slumps in baseball history, going 0-for-45 beginning May 16 for three different teams. A week before the June 15 trade deadline, still hitless in the last month, the Padres shipped Campbell to the St. Louis Cardinals for $30,000 and erratic infielder Dwain Anderson.

After only thirteen games with the Redbirds, continuing his slump after going hitless in 21 at-bats, Campbell was traded once again—this time to the Houston Astros for outfielder Tommie Agee. He responded to moving yet again by telling *The Sporting News*, "It's tough to leave a club that is in first place and has a shot at the big money. But due to my past association with Preston Gomez, it could be a break for me. Preston was the manager at San Diego when I was a regular there for four years. So he knows what I can do." Reunited with his former skipper, Campbell broke his slump seven games in his tenure with the Astros, hitting a double September 19 against his old San Diego team. After the 1974 season, in which he played only 35 games and hit .087, Campbell decided to retire after eight years in the majors, finishing his career with a .213 average, 89 RBI, and 20 home runs.

Campbell's broadcasting career had begun in 1972 following his season-ending surgery. Campbell recalled in the *San Diego Union-Tribune*, "After I got hurt I called Buzzie (Bavasi, Padres general manager) and volunteered to do the color commentary. I told him I'd do it for free if he'd pick up my hotel and meal money." Bavasi agreed, and Campbell, to his recollection, "did 10 or 11 games that year." Unfortunately, after retiring from the Astros he was unable to find an announcing job, and worked as a cameraman, reporter, and later sportscaster for a San Diego television station.

In 1977, frustrated that no broadcasting job had been offered, Campbell took a job managing the Padres' Class AA team in Amarillo in the Texas League. The year before, the Gold Sox were one of four Padres affiliates to win minor league championships. Campbell had been offered coaching opportunities before. "Houston offered me a job as manager of its Columbus, Georgia, club in the Class AA Southern League following the 1973 season. At the time, I was just kinda tired of the travel, and perhaps baseball in general." But when Gold Sox manager Bob Miller left to join the Toronto Blue Jays and the Padres called, Campbell decided the time was right. Unfortunately, under Campbell's tutelage the team did not repeat its past success, finishing in last place, and he was fired after only one year, ending his efforts at coaching.

Campbell quickly moved back to the broadcast booth, calling Padres games with former second baseman and legendary broadcaster Jerry Coleman. He added another job to his resume, co-writing from 1984 to 1986 the annual *Scouting Report* alongside Brooks Robinson, Duke Snider, Denny Mathews, and Harmon Killebrew (who replaced Mathews in 1986). He also hosted a postgame and baseball history show in San Diego. However, unexpectedly in October 1988, Campbell's contract was not renewed, ending his association with the club and creating an enormous amount of backlash for the club. A ballot in the sports section of the *San Diego Union-Tribune* asked fans if they agreed or disagreed with Campbell's firing; only 150 of 2,500 took the Padres' side. While it was never fully explained, many speculated his being let go was the result of personality conflicts with team officials due to his often critical comments of Padres' players and management.

Unable to find another baseball broadcasting position for a major league team, Campbell called San Diego State football and baseball games for a time. During his time off, he also had the idea to in his words, "develop a game for anybody who like baseball at all– kids, women, anybody." Campbell created a board game, X-Tra Bases, that combined trivia and baseball strategy.

Campbell found two positions shortly thereafter, first hosting a Christian-oriented talk show, "Talk from the Heart," for KBRT-AM in Costa Mesa, California. A decidedly non-baseball show, it dealt with such issues as abortion, pornography, and a perceived antireligious bias in the media. He was also hired by ESPN in 1990 to work as a baseball analyst on Tuesday and Friday night games. In 17 years with the network he has worked in a number of positions ranging from TV analyst, correspondent on "Baseball Tonight," and calling games on ESPN Radio.

In 1993, while working for ESPN, Campbell was hired as the TV announcer for the Colorado Rockies. He stayed in Colorado until 1997 when Fox Sports Rocky Mountain purchased the TV rights to the games. And since "Fox didn't want an ESPN personality on its telecasts, and ESPN was not about to allow Campbell to work for a competitor," he was let go.

Campbell's career as a broadcaster is in many ways defined by two things: his broad and in-depth knowledge of all components of the game and his willingness to speak his mind. *The Sporting News* perhaps best summed this up when it nominated him as the best television analyst of 1991, calling him the "master of the 'first guess,' [who] wouldn't try to sugar-coat even his mother's efforts if she booted a ground ball." The *Denver Post* similarly noted his devotion to broadcasting, stating, "He estimates, he studies statistical references, scouting reports and historical books from four to eight hours almost daily in the off-season, then spends about four hours a day when the season starts compiling the statistics, anecdotes, and other material that seem to flow so easily and at such appropriate moments on a broadcast." The respect for Campbell's broadcasting is also demonstrated through the sadness expressed upon his departure from the Rockies; lamented his leaving, the *Denver Post* opined the "Colorado Rockies television viewers will be learning the game from a new teacher this year."

From a playing career that was largely defined by inconsistency, Campbell's broadcasting career has been remarkably stable. Working for the Padres, Rockies, and ESPN for 30 years had enabled Campbell, in the words of baseball broadcasting historian Curt Smith, to remain "tall and tan and young and lively," and to become "baseball's bronze warrior," and one of the most respected baseball broadcasters of the past generation.

References

Publications

Adler, Richard. *Baseball at the University of Michigan.* Charleston, S.C.: Arcadia. 2004.

Madden, W.C. and Patrick J. Stewart. *The College World Series: A Baseball History: 1947–2003.* Jefferson, N.C.: McFarland & Co. 2004.

San Diego Union Tribune.

Smith, Curt. *Voices of Summer.* New York: Carroll and Graf Publishers. 2005.

Sullivan, George, and David Cataneo *Detroit Tigers: The Complete Record of Detroit Tigers Baseball.* New York: Collier Books. 1985.

The Sporting News.

Denver Post.

Rich Shook presents:

Tigers In the News

Monday, April 22
Detroit was off but it did sign "The Monster," Dick Radatz, to a contract for its Toledo farm club.

Tuesday, April 23
Detroit was rained out of its scheduled game at Cleveland and it ticked off Mayo Smith. "I'd rather have played it if we could," he said. "I thought we might have played Thursday. Both teams have an off day. But they have the option of rescheduling and they picked June 24th, after a Sunday doubleheader." (You can page ahead to find out what happened June 24.)

Wednesday, April 24
Steve Hargan shut out Detroit, 2-0, on just one hit at Cleveland. Northrup got the only hit leading off the third. Horton collided with Oyler chasing a fly ball in the seventh and suffered a concussion.

Thursday, April 25
No game.

Friday, April 26
Mel Stottlemyre shut out Detroit, making it 20 straight scoreless innings for the Tigers, and Mickey Mantle hit his 521st career home run in a 5-0 Yankees victory. Horton remained hospitalized in Detroit for observation. The crowd yelled for Mantle to take a bow but he remained in the clubhouse, saying, "I don't like to do it. I think it is distracting to the next hitter." Detroit got just three hits off Stottlemyre. The Tigers got good news when it learned Horton had been released from the hospital just prior to the game.

Saturday, April 27
Detroit ended its scoreless innings streak, exploding for a 7-0 victory over New York behind Denny McLain's five-hitter. The Tigers had 14 hits and McLain scattered five singles in five different innings and fanned six in his complete game win to raise his record to 2-0. (Historical aside: Baltimore's Tom Phoebus pitched a no-hitter in 6-0 victory over Boston. The 26-year-old struck out nine, walked three. He was aided by a controversial call and a spectacular catch. Mike Andrews hit a high chopper in the third that the 5-8 Phoebus appeared to tip. Shortstop Mark Belanger sped in to grab the ball but his off-balance throw to first baseman Boog Powell appeared to be too late—until umpire Bill Valentine signaled Andrews out. Andrews was kicked out of the game for objecting to the call. Most press box observers thought Andrews was safe—but this was before instant replays, which nowadays prove most press box observers wrong. Third baseman Brooks Robinson dove to his left to spear a vicious liner by Rico Petrocelli with one out in the eighth.

Norm Cash

by Maxwell Kates

Season	Age	G	AB	R	H	2B	3B	HR	RBI	BB	SO	SB	CS	BA	OBP	SLG
1968 Tigers	33	127	411	50	108	15	1	25	63	39	70	1	1	.263	.329	.487
Career Totals		2089	6705	1046	1820	241	41	377	1103	1043	1091	43	30	.271	.374	.488

Norm Cash would have loved it. The story drew upon metaphors including baseball, the Old West, and camaraderie. Its title, *City Slickers*, was evocative of the relationship between the burly cowboy and the legions of brewers, auto manufacturers, and teamsters who became his fans. Billy Crystal, who played the protagonist Mitch Robbins, later directed and produced a motion picture about the 1961 American League baseball season, using Tiger Stadium to portray Yankee Stadium. In a poignant scene in *City Slickers*, an elderly cattle driver named Curly teaches Mitch the meaning of life. Moments later, "Mitchy the Kid" delivers a calf, which he names Norman. Sadly, Norm Cash never had the opportunity to see *City Slickers*. It was released in theaters in 1991, five years after he drowned in a tragic accident. But just who was Norm Cash? He was a larger-than-life first baseman from Texas who lived, drank, and played hard, sang country-and-western songs in the clubhouse, and could be depended upon in clutch situations. This is his story:

Norman Dalton Cash was born November 10, 1934, in Justiceburg, Texas. A railroad junction southeast of Lubbock, Justiceburg boasted a population of 25, according to the 1925 population census. Fittingly, its most famous citizen wore 25 as his uniform number for most of his professional baseball career. Cash's dominant childhood memories were of helping on the family farm:

"My dad's life was hard work ... he had 250 acres of fertile land, and we grew cotton on 200 acres. I drove a tractor from the time I was 10. Sometimes I drove it 10 to 12 hours." Working with a hoe on the farm also allowed him to develop his wrists. Ironically, those who knew Cash during his youth remember his athletic abilities not on the baseball diamond but on the football gridiron. In 1954, during his senior year at Sul Ross State College in Alpine, he set the school rushing record with 1,255 yards. Following graduation, Cash was drafted in the 13th round as a halfback by the NFL's Chicago Bears. Instead, he chose baseball, signing with the Chicago White Sox as an outfielder on May 21, 1955. Earlier, Cash had married his childhood sweetheart, schoolteacher Myrta Bob Harper, on January 24, 1954.

After two seasons at Waterloo—and all of 1957 in military service—the left-handed hitter and fielder was promoted to Comiskey Park midway through the 1958 season. Cash was soon converted to a first baseman and, after some seasoning at Indianapolis, he was recalled by the White Sox in 1959. Playing backup to Earl Torgeson, Cash batted .240 and fielded .984 in 31 games. The White Sox, led by speedy infielders Luis Aparicio and Nellie Fox, raced to the summit of the American League standings, hitting 46 triples and stealing 113 bases in posting 94 victories. The "Go-Go Sox" outdistanced second-place Cleveland by five games to capture their first pennant in 40 years. However, the Sox were badly overmatched in the World Series by the Los Angeles Dodgers, losing the fall classic in six games. To upgrade the Chisox offense in the off-season, team president Bill Veeck added veterans Roy Sievers, Gene Freese, and Minnie Minoso to a lineup that already included Ted Kluszewski. However, he was forced to mortgage his future prospects, including Earl Battey, Don Mincher, Johnny Callison—and Norm Cash. No match for Kluszewski and Torgeson, Cash was sent to Cleveland with Bubba Phillips and Johnny Romano in the seven-player Minoso deal on December 6, 1959.

Although Cash wore a Cleveland cap on his 1960 Topps baseball card, he never played an inning for the Indians. On April 12, as the Tribe headed north from Tucson at the conclusion of spring training, Cash found himself traded yet again. This time, he was dispatched to Detroit in exchange for third baseman Steve Demeter. Detroit General Manager Rick Ferrell was dumbfounded when Frank Lane, his Cleveland counterpart, offered Cash for Demeter, unsure if he meant "cold cash or Norm Cash." While Demeter's career with the Indians consisted of merely four games, Cash became a fixture at first base in Detroit for 15 years. Lane was not through making controversial trades with the Tigers. Five days later, he sent Rocky Colavito to Detroit for Harvey Kuenn, and later in 1960, the two clubs swapped managers, Joe Gordon going to Detroit for Jimmie Dykes.

Cash's teammates took an immediate liking to him. A comedian both on the field and in the clubhouse, he once tried to call time after being picked off first base. In another instance, Cash was stranded on second base during a thunderstorm. Once play resumed, however, he returned to third base. The umpire was baffled.

"What are you doing over there?"

"I stole third," he answered.

"When did that happen?"

"During the rain."

On several occasions, he gave a muddy infield ball to the pitcher instead of the game ball so the hitters could not see it as well. Al Kaline remembers: "Whenever you mention Norm Cash, I just smile. He was just a fun guy to be around and a great teammate. He always came ready to play. People don't know this, but he often played injured, like the time he had a broken finger."

Sonny Eliot, Detroit's wacky weatherman, describes Cash as "just old-fashioned likable," comparing his physical form to a kewpie doll from a state fair. "Whenever he came to bat, I would yell 'Hey kewpie doll,' and he'd turn around and laugh."

It was another Southerner and recent transplant to Detroit who presented Cash with his nickname:

"I was in Baltimore [for six years] and there was a fellow there named Norman Almony," remembers Ernie Harwell. "Everybody called him Stormin' Norman. When Norman Cash lost his temper once in a while, I gave him the nickname Stormin' Norman. I don't think he liked it at first, but after a while, he started treasuring it."

After a respectable 1960 season in which he batted .286 with 18 home runs, Cash captivated the baseball world in 1961. Although playing in the shadow of Mickey Mantle and Roger Maris, Cash posted some of the most outstanding offensive single-season statistics in American League history. The man Harwell nicknamed "Stormin' Norman" led the junior circuit with 193 hits and a .361 batting average. Cash also established personal marks of 41 home runs, 132 RBI, and eight triples. Even more astounding, he hit .388 on the road. Facing Washington's Joe McClain on June 11, Cash became the first Detroit player to clear the Tiger Stadium roof, hitting a home run that landed on Trumbull Avenue. Another roof-clearing blast that season against Boston's Don Schwall struck a police tow truck. He was equally skilled at first base, fielding a sterling .992 as he caught dozens of foul balls before they could fly into the stands. With Kaline's .324 batting average and Colavito's .290 complementing Cash in the lineup, the Tigers, led on the mound by Frank Lary and his 23 wins, challenged the Yankees for the American League pennant. The Bengals were within a game and a half of the Bronx Bombers on September 1 before retracting to finish eight games behind with 101 victories.

Was Norm Cash destined to become a one-year wonder? Even at the time, he knew his '61 season was "a freak. Everything I hit seemed to drop in, even when I didn't make good contact. I never thought I'd do it again." After Lary injured his leg in the 1962 season opener, and Kaline broke his shoulder during a nationally televised game in May, it became clear that the Tigers would not challenge the Yankees again. The season was equally disappointing for Cash, who batted only .243. The 118 points shaved from his 1961 average remains the record for decline among batting champs. Cash ultimately found his swing, batting .342 in an autumn exhibition trip to Japan, but by that point the regular season was long over. Still, the 1962 season was far from a write-off for the affable Texan. Cash hit 39 home runs, including three more roof shots, as the league runner-up to Harmon Killebrew's 48. His .992 fielding percentage was identical to his 1961 average.

Cash never again cracked the .300 plateau. Years later, when Mickey Lolich asked why, Cash replied that "Jim Campbell pays me to hit home runs." Indeed, Cash's career total of 373 home runs for the Tigers remains second only to Kaline's 399. However, it soon became evident that other factors besides the maturation of expansion pitching compromised Stormin' Norman's batting average. Cheating in baseball was as much an issue in 1961 as it remains today, and Sonny Eliot remembers why Norm Cash called that season "the Year of the Quick Bat."

"We used to sit in the old Lindell A.C.," a popular bar near Tiger Stadium. "We'd just rib the hell out of him. 'Did you put cork in the bat? If not cork, was it lead?' Or whatever it was, we'd just rib him." He struck out frequently, and fans expecting another batting title consistently booed Cash for the balance of his career. Even his wife joined in the chorus on occasion. Stormin' Norman knew that inherently, the jabs were good-natured. After all, when Mayo Smith removed Cash from the lineup during a slump, the manager was also booed. Although he was not bothered by the sounds of tens of thousands of boos, "when one or two guys get on your back, they drive you nuts." For their appreciation of his congeniality and humor, Cash was crowned King Tiger in 1969 by the presidents of individual Tigers fan clubs for his congeniality. George Cantor, a Tigers beat writer at the time, described Cash as "the most popular man on the team," who knew "all the best watering holes" throughout the American League.

Although Cash stifled the cork in 1962 and thereafter, he soon found himself fighting a much larger battle against alcoholism. Denny McLain described his roommate as "a modern medical miracle," who abused his body so mercilessly that he "should [have turned] it over to the Mayo Clinic." Stormin' Norman violated every curfew rule in the book, but he somehow arrived at the ballpark every day, "not only eager to play, but madder than hell if he didn't." Granted, Cash rarely showed up on time; he "could not make 9 a.m. workouts because he threw up until 10 a.m.," according to his roommate. McLain credited hustle and determination as the secrets to Cash's big-league longevity, although the bespectacled right-hander did admit he was often bewildered "how he managed to remain upright" when he took the field. Still, McLain admitted that "I always felt better about everything when I looked over and saw Stormin' Norman at first base." As pitcher Jerry Casale once recounted, "On a team with so many friends, there was no one nicer than Norm Cash."

Cash was nothing if not consistent for the balance of the 1960s. He was the only American League hitter to slug 20 or more home runs each year from 1961 to 1969. In 1964, he set a record among Detroit first basemen by fielding an outstanding .997. On July 9, 1965, Stormin' Norman hit an inside-the-park home run against the A's at Municipal Stadium in Kansas City. The blast must have ignited Cash's non-corked bat, as he decimated American League pitching with 23 home runs and 58 RBI in 78 games after the All-Star break. His second-half exploits earned him Comeback Player of the Year honors, and in 1966, he was invited to the All-Star Game. Cash once again led AL first sackers in fielding with a .997 percentage. Meanwhile, the Cash family was expanding, as Norm and Myrta welcomed son Jay Carl on April 28, 1963, and daughter Julie Lee on December 28, 1964.

Stormin' Norman proved to be the exception on the 1968 Tigers as he was fighting an early-season slump. On July 27, the 6-foot Cash was barely hitting his weight, batting .195 on a team cruising to its first American League pennant in 23 years. In dramatic fashion, he hit a torrid .332 in his last 54 games to finish the season at .262. Included in his 11 home runs and 32 RBI in August and September was a three-run blast against Oakland on September 14. The winning pitcher of the 5–4 decision was Denny McLain—his 30th win of the season. Cash led Detroit's batsmen in the World Series, hitting .385 against St. Louis pitching. After being Bob Gibson's record-setting 16th strikeout victim in Game 1, Cash redeemed himself the following afternoon, homering off Nelson Briles in an 8–1 complete-game win for Mickey Lolich. With the Tigers facing elimination in Game 6, Cash enjoyed another productive day at the plate, scoring two of the 13 Detroit runs, tying the Series at three games. This set the stage for a historic Game 7. The Tigers were unfazed at the prospect of facing a pitcher, Bob Gibson, who specialized in winning Game 7. In the clubhouse after practice, manager Mayo Smith encouraged his players, saying that Gibson "can be beat, he's not Superman!" To this, Cash rejoindered, "Oh yeah? Just a little while ago, I saw him changing in a phone booth!" Tigers hitters proved to be Kryptonite. With two outs and no score in the seventh inning, Cash ignited a Detroit rally with a single off Gibson and later put the Tigers ahead, scoring on Jim Northrup's triple. The final score was 4–1, and the Detroit Tigers were world champions.

After playing in the field for only 114 of his team's 162 games in 1970, Cash enjoyed a renaissance season playing in the Renaissance City in 1971. So torrid was his first half that spectators across major-league ballparks voted him to start the All-Star Game on July 13. Played in Detroit, it drew 53,559 spectators.

When the dust cleared on the 1971 season, the Tigers had won 91 games but finished 12 games behind Earl Weaver and the Orioles. Stormin' Norman clubbed 32 round-trippers—one shy of Bill Melton's league lead—while driving in 91 runs and batting a respectable .283. His offensive record was enough to win his second AL Comeback Player of the Year Award. It would have surprised nobody to hear Cash proclaim, after accepting the honor, "I hope I win this again next year." Cash was, however, named to the All-Star team once again in 1972, his fourth and final year in the midsummer classic. (Cash played in both 1961 tilts for a total of five All-Star Game appearances.) His offensive output may have slackened in 1972, but the Tigers vaulted ahead in the standings to win their first American League East Division title.

A player known for his pranks, Cash saved his most famous stunt for the twilight of his career. It occurred on July 15, 1973, as the Tigers entertained the visiting California Angels. Not one Detroit batsman had hit safely off starting pitcher Nolan Ryan. With two away in the bottom of the ninth, the Ryan Express had fanned 17 as his Angels led 6–0. Potentially the final hitter of the game, Cash strode to the plate substituting a table leg for a bat. Home plate umpire Ron Luciano forbade Cash's creative use of equipment. Cash protested, "But Ron, I've got as much chance with this as I do with a bat." As Jim Northrup remembers from the third-base dugout, Cash reluctantly retrieved a bat—and grounded out against his fellow Texan. The no-hitter was Ryan's second in as many months; as Cash returned to the dugout, he turned to Luciano and said, "See, I told ya."

The 1974 season was a transitional one for the Tigers. For only the second time in franchise history, Detroit finished the season in last place. Stormin' Norman received a fateful telephone call from General Manager Jim Campbell on August 7. Batting only .228 with seven home runs and 12 RBI, Cash was let go. "I thought at least they'd let me finish out the year. Campbell just called and said I didn't have to show up at the park."

Norm Cash was a player who knew his baseball career would not last forever. As a player, his off-season occupations included banking, ranching, and auctioning hogs. In the early 1970s, Cash hosted a local variety show in Detroit called *The Norm Cash Show*. In 1976, he teamed with former October archrival Bob Gibson as broadcasters for ABC's *Monday Night Baseball*. Although Cash continued to display his brand of humor, it was not appreciated by all. On-air remarks such as equating entertainment in Baltimore with going "down to the street and [watching] hubcaps rust" earned Cash his dismissal from the network. In 1978, he made his film debut with a cameo appearance in *One in a Million: The Ron LeFlore Story*. In a scene filmed in Lakeland, Florida, Cash was standing with Kaline, Freehan, and Northrup to watch LeFlore in his first spring training after being released from Southern Michigan Prison in Jackson. When the others marveled at his speed, Cash chimed in with "He can't be too fast, the cops caught him."

Divorced from Myrta, Cash married his second wife, Dorothy, on May 22, 1973. They moved upstate from Detroit, first to Union Lake, where Cash worked as a sales representative for an automobile machinery manufacturer. When asked, Cash remarked that "it's good money…but to tell the truth I'm looking for something else to do." Sadly, the good times did not last long. As Detroit automakers' supremacy took a hit from Japanese imports, Cash's financial windfall proved to be short-term. His health began to deteriorate; he suffered a massive stroke in 1979. As Ernie Harwell remembers, he was "out of commission for quite a while." Fortunately, by 1981 he was healthy enough to broadcast Tigers games for ON-TV, a subscription television service that leased time from a Detroit UHF station to show its programming. He and Hank Aguirre provided color commentary alongside Larry Adderly's play-by-play. By 1983, partial paralysis of his face made him slur his words, and he could no longer continue. In 1986, Cash returned to Tiger Stadium to participate in the Equitable Old Timers Game. Fans were shocked to see the first baseman a shadow of his former self. He could no longer field routine infield balls. A throw from third base hit him in the head before bouncing away. Cash handled the situation with humor, but privately he was embarrassed by the incident. What nobody realized at the time is that the appearance would be his last at the corner of Michigan and Trumbull.

Scott McKinstry remembers Sunday evening of the Columbus Day weekend in 1986 being a gray, misty one. "I was standing at the lighthouse…on Lake Michigan looking out over the water to where boats head out from Charlevoix to Beaver Island." The weather forecast echoed the somber mood that would all too soon be shared by Tigers fans. Earlier in the day, Cash left his condominium to meet Dorothy and a friend for dinner at the Shamrock Bar on Beaver Island. Those present could affirm that Cash had been drinking. After dinner, he returned to the dock to check on his boat. Unable to navigate the slippery pier in his cowboy boots, he fell into the water and could not pull himself out. The next morning, he was found floating in 15 feet of water in St. James Bay. Norman Dalton Cash was pronounced dead on October 12, 1986. He was 51 years old. Tragedy would hit the Cash family a second time in 1987 when Norm's son, Jay, committed suicide.

Like Buddy Holly before him, the Texas legend of Norm Cash lives on. Ernie Harwell recalls receiving an au-

tographed photo from Cash inscribed with his trademark humor: "To the second best broadcaster in the big leagues. The other 25 tied for first place." Gary Peters, who broke in with the White Sox with Cash, remembers his former teammate's diverse collection of hobbies, which included horseback riding, fencing, waterskiing, dancing, and playing the ukulele. Whitey Herzog, Cash's roommate in 1963, once claimed that "there was nothing Norm Cash couldn't do." Describing Cash as his roommate, however, might have been an exaggeration; Herzog recalls the experience as "just like having your own room." On April 23, 2005, the sandlot in Post, Texas, where Stormin' Norman played Little League ball, was rededicated in memory of Garza County's most famous athlete as Norm Cash Field.

Perhaps the most vocal and outward posthumous tribute to Cash came in the final hours of the ballpark whose first base he called home from the Eisenhower administration to two days shy of Gerald Ford taking the oath of office. A sellout crowd of 43,556 jammed Tiger Stadium on September 27, 1999, for the final game against the Kansas City Royals. Several Tigers switched uniform numbers to pay homage to players who starred before them. Rookie Robert Fick switched his number 18 for 25 to honor Cash. But Fick went one step further. The Tigers enjoyed a comfortable 4–2 eighth-inning lead when Fick crushed a Jeff Montgomery fastball for a grand slam. In true Norm Cash fashion, the ball nearly cleared the right-field roof. Fick said that he "looked up in the sky and thought of my dad," who had passed away the year before. "I know that he had something to do with all this."

So did Norm Cash.

References

Publications

Barnes, Tyler. *Detroit Tigers 1999 Information Guide.* Detroit: Tigers Public Relations Department, 1999.

Barnes, Tyler. *The Inaugural Season: Detroit Tigers 2000 Information Guide.* Detroit: Tigers Public Relations Department, 2000.

Britten, Brian. *Detroit Tigers 2006 Information Guide.* Detroit: Tigers Public Relations Department, 2006.

Cantor, George. *The Tigers of '68: Baseball's Last Real Champions.* Dallas: Taylor Trade Publishing, 1997.

Cohen, Irwin. *Tiger Stadium.* Charleston, S.C.: Arcadia Publishing, 2003.

DeWalt, Tim. "Tribute: Norm Cash" in TigersCentral.com (2001–2005): 53 pars. Available from *www.tigerscentral.com/comments.php?id=239_0_1_0_C.* Internet. Accessed April 5, 2007.

Dewey, Donald, and Nicholas Acocella. *Total Ballclubs: The Ultimate Book of Baseball Teams.* Toronto: Sport Classic Books, 2005.

Harrigan, Patrick. *Detroit Tigers Club and Community: 1945–1995.* Toronto: University Press, 1997.

Harwell, Ernie. *Life After Baseball.* Detroit: Detroit Free Press, 2004.

Lyons, Jeffrey, and Douglas B. *Curveballs and Screwballs: Over 1,286 Incredible Baseball Facts, Finds, Flukes, and More!* New York: Random House, 2001.

McLain, Denny, and Dave Diles. *Nobody's Perfect.* New York: The Dial Press, 1975.

McLain, Denny, and Mike Nahrstedt. *Strikeout: The Story of Denny McLain.* St. Louis: The Sporting News, 1988.

McMillan, Robin. *Official Major League Baseball 1995 All-Star Game Program.* New York: Sports Publishing Group Inc., 1995.

Middlesworth, Hal. *Detroit Tigers 1973 Press Radio TV Guide.* Detroit: Tigers Baseball Club, 1973.

Middlesworth, Hal. *Detroit Tigers 1974 Press Radio TV Guide.* Detroit: Tigers Baseball Club, 1974.

Middlesworth, Hal. *Detroit Tigers 1975 Press Radio TV Guide.* Detroit: Tigers Baseball Club, 1975.

Middlesworth, Hal. *Detroit Tigers 1971 Yearbook.* Detroit: Tigers Baseball Club, 1971.

Middlesworth, Hal. *Detroit Tigers 1974 Yearbook.* Detroit: Tigers Baseball Club, 1974.

Paladino, Larry. *Detroit Tigers 1987 Yearbook.* Detroit: Tigers Baseball Club, 1987.

Russell, Cliff. *Detroit Tigers 2004 Information Guide.* Detroit: Tigers Media Relations Department, 2004.

Stanton, Tom. *The Final Season: Fathers, Sons, and One Last Season in a Classic American Ballpark.* New York: St. Martin's Press, 2001.

Smith, Fred T. *Tiger S.T.A.T.S.* Ann Arbor, Mich: Momentum Books Ltd., 1991.

Stern, Chris. *Where Have They Gone? Baseball Stars!* New York: Grosset & Dunlap, 1979.

Thorn, John, Phil Birnbaum, and Bill Deane. *Total Baseball: The Ultimate Encyclopedia,* 8th edition. Toronto: Sport Classic Books, 2004.

Articles

Dow, Bill. "Former Tiger Norm Cash." *Baseball Digest,* September 2001: 27 pars. [Journal Online]. Available from *www.findarticles.com/p/articles/mi_m0FCI/is_9_60?ai_76928886.* Internet. Accessed April 5, 2007.

Hunt, William. "Justiceburg, Texas." *The Handbook of Texas Online* (2001): 2 pars. Available from *www.tsha.utexas.edu/handbook/online/articles/JJ/hnj13.html.* Internet. Accessed April 6, 2007.

"Lobos Fall in Season Finale; Barber Breaks 1,000 Yard Mark." *The Sul Ross Skyline* (November 16, 2006): 18 pars. [Journal

Online]. Available from *www.sulross.edu/pages/3998.asp*. Internet. Accessed April 6, 2007.

"Norm Cash." Brooklyn: Topps Chewing Gum Inc., 1960: 488.

Shaikin, Bill. "California Strikes Gold in Ryan," in *Nolan Ryan: The Authorized Pictorial History*. Fort Worth: The Summit Group, 1991.

Shlain, Bruce. "Stormin' Norman," in *Oddballs: Baseball's Greatest Pranksters, Flakes, Hot Dogs, and Hotheads*. New York: Penguin Books, 1989: 131–146.

"There Are So Many Norm Cash Stories . . .", in "Detroit Tigers History" (2005): 15 pars. Available from *www.detroit-tigers-baseball-history.com/cash.html*. Internet. Accessed April 5, 2007.

Web Sites

www.baseball-almanac.com
www.baseball-reference.com
www.imdb.com

Rich Shook presents:
Tigers In the News

Sunday, April 28
Detroit split two at New York. The Yankees win first, 2–1, on Roy White's single capping a two-run rally in the bottom of the eighth. Tigers retrieved the second, 3–2, on Jim Northrup's two-out home run in the ninth. Some fans in their early teens sitting in the left field seats had been throwing items at Northrup—oranges and apples plus such potentially lethal things as cherry bombs and a rubber ball with steel wires running through it. "One guy hit me with his lunch," Northrup said. "Once, I turned around and told them I'd knock their (bleeping) heads off, and that really set them off. You don't feel too good when you have to run back against that wall and catch something. We used to have fun at games when we were kids, but my dad would have broken my neck if I'd done stuff like that." Detroit entered the ninth trailing, 2–1, but Bill Freehan's one-out home run off Dooley Womack tied the score and one out later Northrup whacked his second home run of the season to give the Tigers the win. Les Cain made his first major league appearance and took a 1–0 lead into the eighth when Andy Kosco tied the score with a booming home run into the left field bleachers, only the 20th homer into that part of Yankee Stadium since it had been built. It was only the sixth hit off Cain, who walked four and struck out two while working out of several jams. He was relieved by Dobson. Frank Fernandez singled in the go-ahead run later in the inning. In the opener, Mantle drove in a run with a ground-rule opposite-field double and scored on White's single, beating Northrup's high throw to the plate. Bill Monbouquette, who pitched for Detroit the previous season, scattered six hits to lower his ERA to 0.87 and improve to 3–1. Sparma pitched hitless ball for six innings for Detroit and had a two-hit shutout entering the eighth.

Monday, April 29
Norm Cash piled into third-string Oakland catcher Rene Lachemann with two out in the ninth inning to give Detroit a 2–1 victory over the A's. Mickey Lolich won his first game of the season with a four-hit complete game, walking three and striking out three. Lolich had lost 10 straight in 1967 with Detroit scoring 16 runs total in them. He missed his scheduled start in New York due to National Guard duty and had pitched seven scoreless no-decision innings against Chicago April 20, a game Detroit eventually won 4–1. Cash was on second with two out when Don Wert, whose home run off Chuck Dobson in the eighth broke a scoreless tie, singled to center. Rick Monday, inserted for defensive purposes by manager Bob Kennedy, fired a perfect strike to the plate but Lachemann, playing because Phil Roof and Jim Pagliaroni were injured, muffed the ball and Cash crashed into him. "I hit him between the eyes with my knee," Cash said. "I'm no gazelle. I couldn't change directions in midair. I missed the plate and had to come back to touch it."

Tuesday, April 30
Ramon Webster hit a three-run home run off Earl Wilson in the first inning and Paul Lindblad's perfect relief pitching gave Oakland a 3–1 victory over Detroit. Detroit stranded nine in the first five innings. The Tigers had a team batting average of .235 and a team ERA of 2.18.

Bob Christian

by John Milner

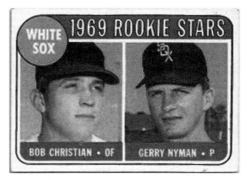

Season	Age	G	AB	R	H	2B	3B	HR	RBI	BB	SO	SB	CS	BA	OBP	SLG
1968 Tigers	22	3	3	0	1	1	0	0	0	0	0	0	0	.333	.333	.667
Career Totals		54	147	14	33	5	0	4	19	11	23	3	0	.224	.278	.340

Robert Charles Christian was born on October 17, 1945, in Chicago to a family of Dutch and Scots-Irish descent. His family would move to Southern California early on in his childhood and would remain in the city of El Cajon throughout his childhood. It was there that he would begin to be involved in sports and eventually would lead him to a career in professional baseball.

Bob attended Magnolia Elementary School for eight years before moving on to El Cajon Valley High School, where he would graduate in 1963. While attending high school, he developed into a three-sport athlete by competing in baseball, basketball, and football. He continued his academic and athletic career by attending Grossmont Junior College in El Cajon for two years. While attending the junior college, he was a member of the baseball and football teams.

His baseball career that began on the Little League, Pony League, and Colt League fields of El Cajon, advanced to the professional level when he was signed as an amateur free agent by the New York Yankees in 1964. Gordon (Deacon) Jones signed him to his first contract as a right-handed-hitting third baseman for the Yankees. Bob weighed 180 pounds and stood 5-foot-10 as he began his climb up the ladder to the major leagues.

The climb began with him playing for Johnson City of the Appalachian League in 1964. He saw action in 58 games and finished with a .319 batting average, which was good enough to finish fourth in the race for the league batting title. He had 76 hits, 6 doubles, 2 triples, 3 home runs, and 28 RBI, in his first professional season. He led the league's third basemen in fielding percentage, coming in at .833. Based on his accomplishments, he was named to the Appalachian League all-star team.

Due to his potential, the Detroit Tigers acquired him by selecting him in the first-year player draft November 30, 1964. The following spring, the Detroit organization sent him to the Daytona Beach club of the Florida State League where he played 139 games during the 1965 season. He finished sixth in batting with an average of .274 with 135 hits, 13 doubles, 5 triples, 1 homerun, and 57 RBI. Defensively, he led the league's third basemen with 293 assists, 472 chances—and 52 errors. Also, for the second consecutive year, he was chosen to be on the league all-star team.

Before beginning the new season, Bob married Vicki Lynn Manahan on January 29, 1966, and had two children. During the 1966 season, Bob spent the majority of his time at Rocky Mount in the Carolina League. He played in 103 games there and batted .276 with 101 hits, 9 doubles, 2 triples, 7 home runs, and 49 RBI. He also hit .269 in 17 games with Montgomery of the Southern League.

Christian stayed with Montgomery for the entire 1967 season. Due to recurring arm problems, Bob became the regular second baseman for Montgomery rather than third base as he had played the three previous seasons. He had been bothered by a sore arm off and on since 1965. He played in 126 games and finished eighth in the league batting race with a .274 average. His batting totals included 116 hits, 17 doubles, 6 triples, 10 home runs, and 53 RBI.

The 1968 season proved to be his best in professional baseball. He began the year with Triple A Toledo of the

International League, which put him one step away from the Detroit Tigers' major league roster. In spring training, he was back playing his original position of third base, but experienced some difficulties due to the arm problems that seemed to be following him. Because of these problems, he was not in manager Jack Tighe's opening day lineup for Toledo. He played third base in the third game and then for a few days after that, but he seemed unsteady and unsure of himself. On May 1, his manager moved him to the outfield and things started improving for him almost immediately. In a *Sporting News* article from June 1968, he said, "I was a little tense and felt the pressure at third base, possibly because of moving up to Triple A. I'm more comfortable and more relaxed in the outfield. I don't worry about my fielding, as I had been doing at third base, and I'm able to concentrate on hitting." Concentrate on his hitting he did, Christian had a 14-game hitting streak (only two away from the club record at the time) that was stopped by Jacksonville's Gary Gentry, who defeated Toledo with a two-hit shutout. Bob began an eight-game hitting streak the next day by getting four hits. By hitting safely in 22 of 23 games, he was leading Toledo with a .365 batting average by the latter part of May. He was able to get three hits in a game on three different occasions during his hitting tear. His key hits also included a two-run homer in the seventh inning that broke up a three-hit shutout by Jacksonville's Tug McGraw. His hitting success did little to change his humble attitude, though. He credited his high school coach from El Cajon Valley, Harry Elliot, with helping him develop his style of swinging down on the ball in order to hit more line drives rather than pop-ups. Christian also spoke highly of veteran teammate Lenny Green, whose left-field job he had taken: "Lenny has been very good with the younger guys on our club. In my case, he suggested I shorten my swing by bringing the bat down and in closer to my body. The big thing is that I have better control of the bat and I'm getting into the pitch more quickly." Christian played 123 games for Toledo and finished second in the league with a .319 batting average and 151 hits. He also had 16 doubles, 7 triples, 5 home runs, and 57 RBI. He was an IL all-star team member and as the season wore on, the parent club took notice of his hitting exploits, eventually calling him up in September. Christian made his major league debut September 2 with Detroit against the Oakland Athletics and had one at-bat without getting a hit. In his three at-bats with Detroit that month, he collected one hit, a double. He played in just one game defensively, splitting time between first base and the outfield.

On September 30, 1968, Christian was purchased from Detroit by the Chicago White Sox as part of the midseason trade for Don McMahon. The early portion of the 1969 season was affected by Bob's six-month stint with the Army Reserve. He returned from duty in late May and was sent to play with Tucson in the Pacific Coast League. Christian played 49 games combined there during two stints and batted .240 with 37 hits, 3 doubles, 2 triples, 1 home run, and 17 RBI. He returned to the big leagues with the White Sox when Buddy Bradford was put on the military list and went into the National Guard in late June. By August, Christian was in a position to finish out the season with the White Sox, playing in 39 games and batting .217 with 28 hits, 4 doubles, 3 home runs, and 16 RBI overall. Despite his six years of experience, Christian had the appearance of a "baby-faced" youngster and was known for his shy demeanor. White Sox manager Don Gutteridge attested to that saying, "He's kind of quiet, he doesn't say much, but he's been making noise with the bat lately." The noise that he was referring to included a ten-game hitting streak in September. He also was making noise with his glove, including two instances where he had to dive into the stands in order to catch the ball and retire the batter. Gutteridge conceded at that point that Christian could wind up as one of the regular outfielders and that he probably would have had a good chance going into the 1969 season if his military service had not caused him to have a late start. Christian played with the White Sox entry in the Florida Instructional League following the regular season, batting .280 in 26 games.

Bob was able to start the 1970 season with the White Sox and played in 12 games before being sent back to Tucson. In those twelve games, he batted 15 times with an average of .267, with 1 home run and 3 RBI. His appearance May 24, 1970, was the last of his major league career. He went to Tucson and played in 62 games and batted .333. He had 73 hits, 16 doubles, 4 triples, and 40 RBI.

He was placed on Tucson's winter roster for the following season, but on March 27, 1971, he was given his outright release from the Tucson ball club. He had an opportunity to play in Japan that season. He signed on with the Tori Flyers and ended his professional baseball career playing in Japan.

As his baseball career was coming to a close, his life was also approaching an unforeseen ending. Bob Christian became ill with leukemia and on Wednesday, February 20, 1974, in San Diego, he succumbed to the disease. He was 28 years old and left behind his wife, Vicki, and two children.

His major league totals include parts of three seasons with the Tigers and White Sox. He played in 54 games, had 147 at-bats, scored 14 runs, had 33 hits, 5 doubles, 4 home runs, 19 RBI, 3 stolen bases, 11 walks, 23 strikeouts, an average of .224, an on-base percentage of .278, and a slugging percentage of .340. Defensively, he notched 43 games in the outfield and one at first base, had 71 putouts, 3 assists, and 3 errors for a fielding percentage of .961.

Although he only had a brief stay with the 1968 Detroit Tigers, who went on to win the World Series that year, he said that he had no regrets. "I was there when Mantle hit his 536th homer, the one off [Denny] McLain, " he said. "It was a great thrill seeing Mantle hit one."

References

Publications
The Sporting News, June 1968 and October 1969.

Articles
Bob Christian clip file, National Baseball Hall of Fame and Museum Library.

Web Sites
www.baseball-reference.com

Rich Shook presents:
Tigers In the News

Wednesday, May 1
Here was the story of the season ahead of Denny McLain. First-place Detroit was entertaining second-place Minnesota and McLain was nursing a 3-2 lead through the ninth. McLain got the first two outs but Harmon Killebrew pulled a single to left and Rich Reese crushed a single off the wall in right to put pinch-runner Jim Holt on third. Out strolled Mayo Smith. "Don't take me out. I'm all right," the newly red-haired McLain said. "I'm not here to take you out," the manager responded. "That made me feel about this tall," McLain said later, spacing about an inch between his thumb and forefinger. "Just throw your best stuff. If you get beat, get beat with your best stuff." Ted Uhlaender popped a McLain fastball into foul territory near the Tigers' dugout and Don Wert lost his cap making the catch for the final out. McLain struck out nine, walked none, scattered six hits—including two homers—in going 3-0. The game took 2:02. Jim Northrup hit only the second Detroit home run of the season off a left-hander. It was his third of the week, and the season. Detroit got only five hits off lefty Jim Merritt, who fanned seven, but they came at the right time for the Tigers. Northrup's home run came following a leadoff single by Wert in the fifth. In the eighth, Dick McAuliffe tripled to left center with one out, Al Kaline walked, and Willie Horton then lofted a long fly to left that brought McAuliffe in with the winning run. Killebrew and Reese both pulled home runs off McLain.

Thursday, May 2
Detroit lost to Minnesota, 3-2, in 10 innings. Bill Freehan and Dick Tracewski both fanned with the bases loaded in the 10th. Rod Carew doubled and Tony Oliva broke out of a slump with a single off Dennis Ribant in the top of the 10th. Detroit had scored 19 runs in the last nine games, including seven in one game. Ribant was the first Detroit reliever to lose. Northrup got his fourth home run of the week. It came with one out in the bottom of the ninth to force the extra inning.

Friday, May 3
Those devilish Angels picked up where they left off against Detroit last year—knocking the Tigers out of first place. You may recall that California, under manager Bill Rigney, split back-to-back doubleheaders in Detroit on the last two days of the 1967 season, allowing Boston to win the AL pennant. California's 6-5 victory shoved Detroit a half-game behind Baltimore. Mickey Lolich was tagged for five runs, four earned. Willie Horton drove in three runs with a pair of homers.

Saturday, May 4
The Angels slugged the Tigers, 7-2, behind a pair of three-run home runs by Roger Repoz. Jim McGlothlin pitched a six-hitter. Repoz led the league with 8 homers and 19 RBI. The Angels won the sixth of their last seven.

Sunday, May 5
Denny McLain snapped a three-game Detroit losing streak with a seven-hitter (five of them bloops) in a 5-2 win over California, making him 4-0. Bill Freehan had a leadoff home run in the fourth and Mickey Stanley hit his first home run of the year with Dick Tracewski on base in the fifth inning to put the Tigers up to stay, 3-2. After the game McLain ripped into Detroit's fans. "Norm Cash and I were going bad last year and they got on us real bad. How do they think a guy's wife feels after he goes 0-for-8 or 0-for-16 and the fans cut loose while she's in the stands? If they think we're stupid for playing this game, how stupid are they for watching us?" Asked if he thought the fans' attitude had an effect on the 1967 race, McLain responded, "I think it did. There were certain guys on this club who didn't want to go out and play last year because of fan abuse." McLain cited the booing of All-Star and future Hall of Famer Al Kaline as an example. Kaline was hitting .241 with just two RBI. "Now the fans are on Kaline. He's produced for 15 years and he'll produce again this year. They don't realize how good a ballplayer he is. I don't care if I get booed here the rest of my life. Detroit is a great town. I like it. I've bought a home here and have roots. But the fans in this town are the worst in the league."

Monday, May 6
The UPI lead on the game in Baltimore: "The next pitcher who has ideas about throwing a no-hitter against the Detroit Tigers had better walk Jim Northrup every time he comes to bat." For the second time of the young season, Northrup collected the Tigers' only hit in a game. His two-out single in the seventh inning was the only hit Detroit managed off Dave Leonhard and Baltimore took a 4-0 start in their battle for first place. The Orioles' win was their eighth in a row, and 13th of 15, to go 2.5 up on the Tigers. Detroit tied a major-league record in the game by only collecting 23 at-bats in a nine-inning game. Leonhard, 2-0, struck out six and walked seven in pitching the first shutout of his career. Converted outfielder Curt Blefary threw out three of four Detroit runners who tried to steal.

Wayne Comer

by Brian Borawski

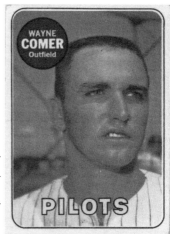

Season	Age	G	AB	R	H	2B	3B	HR	RBI	BB	SO	SB	CS	BA	OBP	SLG
1968 Tigers	24	48	48	8	6	0	1	1	3	2	7	0	0	.125	.160	.229
Career Totals		316	687	119	157	22	2	16	67	106	106	22	9	.229	.331	.336

Harry Wayne Comer was born February 3, 1944, to Harry and Pearl Comer in Shenandoah, Virginia, about 100 miles southwest of Washington, D.C. He grew up there and attended Page County High School, where he was a multi-sport star. He lettered in all four years in baseball, football, and basketball, eventually earning all-district honors in all three sports. He was an all-state honorable mention in football in his senior season in 1961.

After being scouted by the Pittsburgh Pirates, Kansas City Athletics, and Washington Senators in high school, Comer was signed in 1962 by Senators scout George McQuinn, a former major leaguer himself. Comer played his first season in 1962 for the Raleigh Capitals, the Senators' affiliate in the Class B Carolina League, where he struggled as an 18-year-old. Comer himself admitted that he was probably in over his head, and he hit just .228 against some stiff competition that included future Yankees All-Star pitcher Mel Stottlemyre. Of Comer's 61 hits, only 17 were for extra bases. He also had yet to establish the patience at the plate that helped him later in his career and struck out 46 times with just 26 walks. In only one other season in his professional career did Comer have that many more strikeouts than walks.

On January 11, 1963, he married Joyce Nauman. Two months later, he was traded by the Senators to the Detroit Tigers for infielder Bobo Osborne, who had played parts of five seasons for the Tigers. In the spring, Comer reported to the Tigers' Class A affiliate in the Florida State League, the Lakeland Tigers. He put together a solid season there, and while his power had yet to develop (just two home runs in 417 at-bats), he had an impressive 62-to-67 strikeout-to-walk ratio while he hit .264.

In 1964, Comer played for another of the Tigers' Single A affiliates, the Duluth-Superior Dukes of the Northern League. There, he continued to progress as a hitter and refined his effectiveness on the basepaths. He hit .279 with 26 extra-base hits (the most of any season up to that point), and he stole 20 bases in 99 games. He continued to show a good eye at the plate and walked 75 times with just 54 strikeouts.

Comer's performance earned him a promotion in 1965 to the Tigers Double A affiliate, the Montgomery Rebels of the Southern League in 1965, where he had his best season yet. He stole a league-high 31 bases (and was caught stealing a league-high 14 times) and hit .285 with nine home runs. It was good enough to warrant him a spot on the Southern League All-Star Team. Just as important as his quality season, Comer and his wife had their first child, Timothy Wayne Comer, on June 22, 1965. For his performance at Montgomery, he was rewarded with a promotion to the Tigers' Triple A affiliate in the International League, the Syracuse Chiefs, just a step away from the majors, for the 1966 season.

But after playing 35 games for the Chiefs, Comer was traded to the New York Yankees' Triple A affiliate, the Toledo Mud Hens, for Art Lopez. Toledo needed a right-handed bat while Syracuse was looking for a lefty to round out its lineup. Comer was the right-handed hitter sent to Toledo. Between Toledo and Syracuse, Comer finally broke into double digits with 11 home runs but took some adjusting to the better competition, as his batting average dipped to .266. The trade turned out to be temporary, though; after the season ended, he was sent back to the Tigers.

In 1967, though again Tigers' property, Comer remained in Toledo. The Tigers and Yankees swapped minor league affiliates. His second season in Toledo was arguably his best as a pro. He hit .290, and led the International League with 86 runs and 229 total bases. As an outfielder, he led the league with 306 putouts, 14 assists—and nine errors. He was one of the leaders of a team that, for the first time in franchise history, won a Triple A title: the Governor's Cup, the championship of the International League; Toledo had never won an American Association title when it was part of that circuit. In a cross-state, best-of-seven series with the Columbus Jets, the Mud Hens prevailed four games to one. Comer's biggest contribution during the International League playoffs came in the deciding game of the Mud Hens' first-round series against the Richmond Braves. In that game, he had three hits and drove in one of the Hens' runs in the 5–1 win.

His all-star performance in 1967 earned Comer a look by the big-league club after the playoffs. In his first big-league at-bat September 17, 1967, Comer belted a pinch-single off Frank Bertaina in a 5–0 loss to the Washington Senators. Three days later he made his first big-league start, in center field in the middle of a heated pennant race. He went 0 for 2 in his last two at-bats of the season. He got into two more games, but both times they'd be as a pinch-runner.

In 1968, behind five Detroit outfield stalwarts on the depth chart, Comer once again found himself in the minors playing for Toledo. He got his break in May, at the expense of a future Hall of Famer. On the 25th, Kaline was hit by a Lew Krausse pitch that broke his forearm. Comer was called up to help out in the outfield as a reserve but also served as the team's third catcher. He was used often as a pinch-hitter—21 times in 48 games played—but batted just .125. He picked up only 48 at-bats in 48 games, but he did hit his first major league homer in a pinch-hitting role August 11. On September 18, 1968, the day after the Tigers clinched the American League pennant, Comer's second son, Paul Allan, was born.

Comer made the Tigers' World Series roster. In his only at bat, as a pinch-hitter for pitcher Daryl Patterson in Game 3, he laced a single to center field. (Another important role was catching Mickey Lolich's pregame warm-up pitches.)

In 1969, Comer would get his first chance at a regular job, but it wasn't going to be the defending World Series champion Tigers. With both the American League and National League expanding by two teams in 1969, Comer was selected by the Seattle Pilots in the expansion draft, and he took advantage of his chance to start by having a solid season. On a team that was immortalized in Jim Bouton's book *Ball Four*, Comer belted 15 home runs, hit .245, and walked 82 times. He was probably the team's most productive hitter after first baseman Don Mincher—who came over in the expansion draft from the California Angels—second to Mincher on the team in home runs and fourth in RBI. The best game of Comer's career also came in 1969, when he belted two homers and drove in four on May 16 in a 10–9 win at Fenway Park over the Boston Red Sox.

His solid play didn't carry into 1970, and while Comer went with the Pilots to Milwaukee, his time with the Brewers was short. Comer lost his starting center-field job when he started the season 0-for-15. He finally picked up his first hit May 10, a game-winning RBI single in the bottom of the ninth inning against the Washington Senators. That same day, he was traded to Washington for infielders Hank Allen and Ron Theobald. Comer said he was warned of the trade by Nats catcher Paul Casanova during the game and that Casanova told him not to get a hit because he was a Senator. Not sure whether to believe it and still doing his job, Comer got the game-winning hit anyway. The deal was announced the following day, and Comer played for Washington that night. But in Washington, Comer was once again relegated to a reserve role for the team that had originally signed him in 1962. He floundered, finishing the season hitting .233 for Washington—and .212 between the two teams—with no homers.

On December 5, 1970, the Tigers purchased Comer from the Senators and from then on, he was a career minor-league player. He spent three years, 1971 through 1973, with Toledo, with a two-plus-month stay in Detroit, from late May to early August of 1972, during which he had just nine at-bats in 27 games. His pinch-single on July 19 was his 157th and last major league hit. After a year in Double A Reading in 1974, Comer called it quits on his 13-year professional baseball career.

Comer had a few different jobs during the off-season while he played ball. He worked in a grocery store and he purchased a men's haberdashery. Once he left baseball, he got into sporting goods sales. Comer and his wife also had a third son, Shaun Christopher, in 1980, after leaving baseball. Comer eventually became a teacher and a baseball coach. He continues to live in his hometown of Shenandoah, Virginia. He got to see all three of his sons play college baseball and is the proud grandfather of six granddaughters and three grandsons.

References

Articles
Albuquerque Journal, April 3, 1970.
Andrews, Jack. "Toledo Drugs Chiefs Twice." *Syracuse Post-Standard*, July 23, 1966.
Benton Harbor News-Palladium. Articles of September 21 and October 8, 1967, and December 5, 1970.
Coshocton Tribune, Coshocton, Ohio, October 25, 1970.
European Stars and Stripes. Articles of September 12 and 17, 1967.
Manitowoc Herald-Times, Manitowoc, Wisconsin, May 11, 1970.
Pacific Stars and Stripes, September 2, 1968.
Petersburg Progress Index, Petersburg, Virginia, September 11, 1967.
Reddy, Bill. "Chiefs Get Lopez From Hens in Trade for Comer," *Syracuse Post-Standard*, June 10, 1966.
Syracuse Herald-Journal. Articles of April 3, 6, and 21, 1966.
Syracuse Post-Standard. Articles of March 13, 1966; April 29, 1966; June 4 and 7, 1966; and July 23 and 27, 1966.

Web Sites
www.baseball-reference.com
www.retrosheet.org

Other Sources
Wayne Comer file, National Baseball Hall of Fame Library.

Rich Shook presents:
Tigers In the News

Tuesday, May 7
Rookie Tom Matchick's pinch-hit two-run double with two out in the ninth gave Detroit a 2-1 victory over Baltimore. Matchick credited a tip from hitting coach Wally Moses with producing the game-deciding swing, which broke up a scoreless duel between Mickey Lolich and Tom Phoebus. The left-hander, who gained his ninth consecutive victory over the Orioles, checked Baltimore without a hit until the sixth. "He told me I was swinging too hard if I hit the ball to the fence," said Matchick. "Wally likes me to hit line drives." His winning blow hit at the base of the fence after Curt Blefary, returning to right field after catching, had some difficulty getting back from a shallow position. "I went about 14-for-104 with Toledo at the start of last season," said Matchick, 24, "and I was about to quit the game. Then the Tigers sent Moses down to work with me and I credit him with straightening me out." Matchick wound up hitting .289 in 1967 and was the International League's all-star shortstop.

Wednesday, May 8
Jim Northrup kept saving the Tigers, this time with his glove, as he made a sensational diving catch at Baltimore with the bases loaded and two out in the eighth inning of a 3-1 victory that pulled Detroit within a game of the first-place Orioles. He also slammed his fifth home run to get Detroit off to a 1-0 start against Dave McNally in the first inning. A sacrifice fly by starting second sacker Dick Tracewski in the second inning, plus an Al Kaline double and a Willie Horton single in the sixth frame, produced Detroit's other runs. Earl Wilson raised his record to 3-4, allowing seven hits with a walk and four strikeouts. Jon Warden relieved and closed down the game after Boog Powell and Dave Johnson led off the ninth with singles, although the Orioles did score their only run. Warden retired pinch-hitter Frank Robinson—making his first appearance since April 20—and Belanger on routine flies, but Don Wert fumbled Andy Etchebarren's grounder for an error that let Powell score. Paul Blair struck out to end the game. (Historical aside: Catfish Hunter pitched a perfect game and drove in three runs with a pair of singles to lead Oakland to a 4-0 victory over Minnesota. It was the first regular-season perfect game in the AL in 46 years—since the White Sox' Charley Robertson tossed a perfecto against Detroit in 1922.)

Thursday, May 9
Detroit had a day off halfway through a six-game road trip. At the start it was batting .229. The Tigers had gone 7-8 after a nine-game winning streak. One hit has won nine games for the Tigers—three in the 10th, four in the 9th, one in the eighth and one in the fifth—by eight different players (Horton twice).

Friday, May 10
Denny McLain allowed seven hits and fanned seven without walking anyone in a 12-1 win over Washington. Detroit retook first place from Baltimore by a half-game, and never gave up the lead for the rest of the year. Al Kaline, 33 and in his 16th season, entered the game hitting .228 with just one homer and two RBI, and broke out of a slump by going 3-for-4 and driving in six runs. The classy veteran hit a two-run double in the four-run first, singled home a run in the four-run second, and slammed his 306th career home run, a three-run shot in the fourth that tied Hank Greenberg's all-time Tigers mark. McLain was now 5-0 with five straight complete games.

Saturday, May 11
Bill Freehan and Willie Horton hit home runs and drove in three runs each. Don Wert also homered, in the ninth, as the Tigers thumped the Senators, 12-4. Joe Sparma earned the win.

Sunday, May 12
Daryl Patterson relieved Mickey Lolich with one out in the sixth and gave up three straight singles, a sacrifice by Joe Coleman (who later pitched for the Tigers), and another single before retiring the side. Frank Howard added a typically monstrous home run in the seventh as Washington beat Detroit, 6-3. Still, Detroit increased its AL lead because Baltimore dropped a doubleheader to Cleveland. The Indians and Orioles were both two games behind the Tigers. Kaline had three more hits and drove in another run.

Monday, May 13
A day off to reflect. A year ago this day Detroit was 17-7 and in first place by a half-game. After 28 contests in 1967, though, the Tigers were 18-10 but 1.5 games out.

Tuesday, May 14
Earl Wilson, 4-4, pitched only the ninth shutout of his nine-year major league career with Detroit taking Baltimore, 4-0. "I don't pitch too many shutouts," said Wilson, 18-5 lifetime against the Orioles. "I make too many mistakes." Willie Horton hit a pair of home runs good for three runs while Ray Oyler added his second in two years. Baltimore had now lost seven straight after gaining first place. Cleveland, winner of 11 of its last 12, is second by two games.

Pat Dobson

by Bill Bishop

Season	Age	W	L	Pct	G	GS	CG	SV	IP	H	R	ER	BB	SO	ERA
1968 Tigers	26	5	8	.385	47	10	2	7	125	89	39	37	48	93	2.66
Career Totals		122	129	.486	414	279	74	19	2119	2043	939	833	665	1301	3.54

Patrick Edward Dobson Jr. was born February 12, 1942, in Depew, New York, a small village ten miles east of Buffalo. In his youth, Pat often took the bus there to watch his heroes Joe Caffie and Luke Easter, stars of the Buffalo Bisons of the International League. Pat attended Lancaster Central High School, where he was the star pitcher, amassing an impressive 19–1 record. His high school buddies gave him the nickname "The Cobra." A lanky, hard-throwing right-hander, Pat stood 6-foot-3. Scouts from Boston, Detroit, and San Francisco pursued him, and he eventually was signed by Tigers scout Cy Williams. At the age of 17 he received an impressive $25,000 signing bonus. Pat would later say, "I blew my money on cars and good living, but I enjoyed it and I'd do it again."

In 1960, Pat made his professional debut with the Durham Bulls, at that time a Class A Detroit affiliate. He compiled a 7–9 record, striking out 137 batters in 157 innings, but he also walked 98. The following year was split between Knoxville and Durham. His 4–10 record was reflected by his elevated WHIP (walks plus hits per innings pitched) of 2.01 over 119 innings. In 1962, Pat pitched for Montgomery, going 8–7. He significantly lowered his WHIP to 1.39 and struck out better than a batter per inning. He finished the year with Duluth-Superior in the Northern League, appearing in four games and being treated rather roughly by opposing teams.

The 1963 season found Pat still toiling in the lower minors, starting with Jamestown in the New York-Penn League and finishing in Knoxville of the Double A South Atlantic League. He showed some promise by year's end, winning five and losing one at Knoxville with an impressive 1.33 ERA. Dobson began 1964 in Knoxville, reclassified a Double A club, and in midseason was promoted to the Tigers' Triple A farm team in Syracuse. He struggled a bit with the top minor league talent and was demoted to Double A Montgomery in 1965. There he appeared in only 17 games, going 4–1. He finished the year back in Syracuse, pitching four times in relief. Pat spent the winter playing ball in Puerto Rico. He said later that his success there was instrumental in rebuilding his confidence.

Dobson was at a crossroads in 1966. He didn't believe he was getting a real chance in the Detroit organization. He found himself on loan to Cleveland's Portland team in the Triple A Pacific Coast League. Dobson started slowly, not getting into the starting rotation until the third week of the season. Despite missing a week to bursitis, he ended up becoming one of the top pitchers in the league. Pat finished with a record of 12–9 and an 3.45 ERA. His manager, John Lipon, remarked, "Pat's got a good fast ball and slider, and at times a good curve. In fact, when he gets his big curve working effectively, he reminds me of Tommy Bridges." Pat played winter ball that year in the Dominican League and was one of the most impressive American pitchers, jumping out to a 3–0 record.

Dobson started 1967 with the Triple A Toledo Mud Hens, by then the Tigers' top farm team. After an impressive 4–1 start, he was called up to the parent club. He made his major league debut May 31, 1967, against Cleveland. He came into the game in the sixth inning with a runner on second and promptly surrendered a run-scoring single. He settled down and got the next two batters. In the seventh inning he surrendered a two-run home run to Leon

Wagner. In his inning and two-thirds, Pat gave up two runs on four hits, but did not walk a batter and recorded three strikeouts. He was in the major leagues to stay.

Dobson appeared in 28 games in his rookie season. Initially, he was used only in Detroit blowout losses. But on August 2 Pat came in and pitched three strong innings against the Orioles to preserve a 1–0 lead. Manager Mayo Smith showed great confidence in the rookie by leaving Dobson in to start the ninth inning. But disaster struck when Pat walked Frank Robinson and then gave up a game-ending home run to Brooks Robinson. Still, his strong showing earned him his only start of the 1967 season on August 6 in the nightcap of a doubleheader against Cleveland. He surrendered four runs in the first inning, three of them coming on a Duke Sims homer. He left for a pinch-hitter in the top of the third, trailing 4–0. Dobson ended up with the loss as the Tigers fell 6–3. Then, from August 16 through September 15, Pat strung together eight appearances with 18.1 innings of shutout relief. Mayo Smith called him "the most improved pitcher on the staff." Dobson earned his first major league victory September 9 against the Chicago White Sox when the Tigers overcame a 3–0 deficit by scoring seven runs in the ninth inning. His scoreless string ended abruptly September 17 against Washington as he surrendered a three-run home run to the Senators' Hank Allen that turned a close game into a rout. Smith didn't use Dobson again until the final game of the season when he faced two California Angels, walking the first and giving up a sacrifice before being pulled in favor of Mickey Lolich in a Detroit defeat. The Tigers saw the 1967 pennant go to the Boston Red Sox.

Pat spent the winter playing ball in Puerto Rico. He impressed a lot of baseball men when he rewrote the record books December 10, 1967, by striking out 21 batters, eclipsing Juan Pizzaro's old league mark of 19.

Dobson entered 1968 full of confidence. He developed a strong working relationship with pitching coach Johnny Sain. Pat said Sain told him that he gripped the ball too tight and was teaching him to relax. As Dobson explained, "This gives my pitches better movement, better everything." Sain also taught him a different grip for his slider; it became his best pitch. Dobson commented, "I can throw it anytime I want to for a strike. I used to have a slider that was flat. It broke away from a right-handed hitter. The one Sain gave me is better because it dips."

Dobson worked a couple of innings in relief of Earl Wilson during the April 10 opening day loss to Boston. He contributed two scoreless innings in each of two Tigers come-from-behind victories in April. He then had a bad outing against the Yankees, allowing three batters to reach base without recording an out; he also threw two wild pitches. But the Tigers once again rallied for the victory. Pat got little work from manager Smith the first two months. He appeared in only 10 games, working 12 innings. On June 1, he was called upon to relieve Les Cain, who had been knocked around by the Yankees for four runs in the first inning. Pat shut the Yankees down for 5.2 innings, and the Tigers came back to win the game.

Following an injury to Earl Wilson, Dobson and John Hiller undertook several starts in his place. Pat hurled a complete-game shutout at Boston June 4. Coach Wally Moses called it the Tigers' most important victory of the season. A week later he earned a victory against the Minnesota Twins, allowing just one run in 7.2 innings, while striking out 10 batters. He had a string of 25 scoreless innings snapped by a Tony Oliva home run. Three days later he pitched five scoreless innings in relief as the Tigers went on to beat the White Sox in 14 innings. Pat saved the second game of a doubleheader against Chicago June 16. Over the next eight days he racked up three more saves. On June 21, Dobson came on to start the tenth inning and shut the Indians down through the twelfth. When the Tigers took the lead in the top of the thirteenth, Pat was in line for another victory. But he surrendered a single to Duke Sims and a home run to Tony Horton. Pat bounced back to save three more games before the All-Star break. In a string of 13 games won by the Tigers, Dobson won one and saved five.

Dobson's contributions weren't limited to the ball field. He had a flair for having fun with his teammates. He coined nicknames for many of them, including "Pizza" for Tom Matchick in honor of his red hair. He also hung the name "Ratso" on his roommate John Hiller, naming him after the Dustin Hoffman character in the movie *Midnight Cowboy*. He said, "When I fool around in the bullpen, I do it for a purpose. I stay relaxed and so do the guys around me." Pat was known simply as "Dobber," a nickname he carried the rest of his life. Bill Freehan emphasized Pat's competitiveness. "He goes after the hitters now and really challenges them. The pressure is on them, not him."

The Tigers appeared sluggish after the All-Star break. They dropped five out of eight games heading into a big four-game series with the Baltimore Orioles. In the first game, the Tigers trailed 4–2 in the ninth inning as Dobson came in to retire the side. When Matchick hit a dramatic two-run homer with two out and a 3–2 count on him, Dobson ended up with his third win of the season. Two days later Mayo needed a starter for the second game of a doubleheader against the O's. Dobson only lasted 2.1 innings, giving up two runs on four hits and a walk to suffer his second loss of the season. He started once again in Washington on August 1 and was handed another defeat as he gave up a grand slam to light-hitting Ron Hansen. Pat got five more starts in August, losing two and getting no decisions in the other three games. He pitched well in the games he lost, falling 5–3 and 1–0. Twice the bullpen cost him victories. Eventually, however, Joe Sparma was returned to the starting rotation, and Pat was sent back to the bullpen.

Dobson started September off with a bang, winning back-to-back games against the Oakland A's in relief, then saving the third game of the series. He was given another starting assignment against the Twins. Dobson pitched brilliantly except for two pitches to rookie Graig Nettles that were lined into the seats. The second one proved to be the winner in a 2–1 loss for the Tigers. Pat appeared in only four of the last 19 games, for a total of six innings. He got a save and took two losses in those four games. His final numbers for the pennant-winning Detroit Tigers were 5–8, a 2.66 ERA, and seven saves. He pitched in 125 innings and had an impressive WHIP of 1.10. He led the staff with 47 appearances.

Dobson appeared in the three games the Tigers lost in the 1968 World Series. He mopped up for Denny McLain in Game 1, allowing a home run to Lou Brock. In the third game, he came on for an injured Earl Wilson with the Tigers up 2–1 and two runners on. He got Orlando Cepeda out, but gave up a three-run home run to Tim McCarver as the Cardinals went on to win the game 7–3. His final appearance was in Game 4, in which he shut down the Cards for two innings on one hit.

In 1969 Pat appeared in 49 games, winning five games, losing ten, and saving nine. As in 1968, he worked as both a starter and reliever. He had one complete-game victory on July 1 against the Red Sox. He appeared in his last game as a Tiger on September 16, pitching two scoreless innings against the Yankees. His season ended prematurely when Wayne Redmond jumped on the little toe of his left foot after being startled by a mouse in the dugout.

Dobson once again went to Puerto Rico for winter ball. While down there he railed against Detroit management for firing pitching coach Johnny Sain and not making any moves during the season. He criticized the Tigers' aging infield and declared that General Manager Jim Campbell had "no guts to make the trades we need to make." On December 4, 1969, Campbell promptly made a trade, sending Pat Dobson and Dave Campbell to the San Diego Padres for Joe Niekro.

Despite going from a perennial contender to a second-year expansion team, Dobson was excited to finally get a chance to be a full-time starter. He beat the Atlanta Braves 8–3 on opening day in San Diego. He struck out six batters, including Hank Aaron. For the season, Dobson compiled a 14–15 record for the worst team in the National League. He was a workhorse for the Padres, starting 34 games and even picking up a save in seven relief appearances. Despite pitching on a bad knee all year, Pat was not about to give up his spot in the rotation now that he was a starting pitcher. "I waited three years to become a regular starter. They can have the bullpen" Dobson said. He said being in the rotation allowed him to work on his control. "It was excellent discipline. And I learned that control pitchers get the corners from the umpires," he said. Dobson established single season records for wins and strikeouts for the young franchise.

Dobson's stay in San Diego was limited to one season. On December 1, 1970, he was traded to the Orioles along with Tom Dukes for Tom Phoebus, Al Severinsen, Fred Beene, and Enzo Hernandez. Earl Weaver, the Orioles manager, was elated. He had been a fan of Dobson "ever since the night I saw him strike out 21 guys in a game in Puerto Rico." His first start of the season was against his old team, the Tigers. He gave up three runs in the first inning, then shut Detroit out for the next seven. He was pulled for a pinch-hitter, and the Tigers went on to win in extra innings. Pat won his next start against the Yankees, only allowing one run in the complete-game victory. But he won one of his next nine starts. Before his June 17 start, his record stood at 3–4 with an ERA of 3.70. Starting with a victory over the Yankees that day, Pat would win 12 starts in a row. Eleven of the twelve victories were complete games. Then, starting with a loss to the Yankees, Pat slumped, winning only two of nine starts. He finished strong, however, winning his last three starts to reach the coveted twenty-win level. Dobson and teammates Mike Cuellar, Dave McNally, and Jim Palmer all won 20 or more games, and the 1971 Orioles were only the second team in major league history to boast four twenty-game winners.

Baltimore swept the Oakland A's in the American League playoffs, and went into the 1971 World Series as the favorite over the Pittsburgh Pirates. Pat at first was the odd man out as Weaver decided to go with a three-man rotation for the postseason. Pat did not appear in the AL Championship Series but finally got a chance to start Game 4 of the World Series. The O's staked him to a 3–0 lead in the first, but Pittsburgh came back with two runs in the bottom of the inning. They tied it up in the third, and Pat was pulled in the sixth inning with the score 3–3. The Pirates went on to win, 4–3. Pat made another Series appearance in Game 6, coming on to start the 10th inning. He retired the first batter, but then gave up a single to Dave Cash, who stole second on a strike-three pitch to Richie Hebner. Dobson intentionally walked Roberto Clemente and then was replaced by lefty Dave McNally to face the left-handed batting Willie Stargell. McNally ended up with the win when the Orioles scored in the bottom of the tenth. In Game 7, Dobson came on to start the ninth inning with the Orioles down 2–1. He retired the first two batters, striking out Clemente. But he gave up back-to-back singles, and McNally was once again summoned to face Stargell, whom he retired for the final out. The Orioles went down meekly in the ninth, and the Pirates were world champions.

After the Series, the Orioles and Dobson were scheduled for an exhibition tour of Japan. On November 2, 1971, in Toyama, Japan, Pat hurled a no-hit, no-run game against the Tokyo Yomiuri Giants, winning 2–0.

The Oriole dynasty slipped in 1972, finishing five games behind the Tigers. Dobson's record fell to 16–18 despite his posting a lower ERA and WHIP than he had in his 20-win season. He made the All-Star team, although he did not appear in the game. Pat stirred up a little controversy in Detroit when he suggested that Billy Martin was misusing Tom Timmerman, saying he made a better relief pitcher than a starter. When Baltimore came into Detroit for a four-game set, they were trailing the Tigers by two games. Dobson was scheduled to pitch the opener for the O's. Martin suggested Dobson would tremble and flee under the Tiger Stadium long ball hex. Instead, Pat threw a complete-game four-hitter, winning 3–2.

Dobson loved it in Baltimore and was shocked when the Orioles traded him to Atlanta on November 30, 1972. Along with Dobson, Atlanta got Davey Johnson, Roric Harrison, and Johnny Oates while sending Earl Williams and Taylor Duncan to Baltimore. Dobson's debut for Atlanta was inauspicious as he was bombed by the Astros 10–3. He beat San Diego in his next start, then went 1–6 in his next nine starts. After beating the Cubs to raise his record to 3–7, he was traded to the Yankees on June 7, 1973. He had hated it in Atlanta. He complained, "I went from the best defensive team to the worst. I throw ground balls. I need defense. Their whole game is tailored to offense—the park, the wind, and the grass." He was happy to be in New York and compiled a 9–8 record for the Yankees. He enjoyed playing for Ralph Houk, and the Yankees were in contention up until late August.

Dobson was a little concerned when manager Ralph Houk was replaced by Bill Virdon. He felt Houk had been forced out by management. Pat won his first game in 1974, but lost eight of his next ten decisions. At that point, he started butting heads with Virdon over the pitching rotation. Virdon was experimenting with a five-man rotation, while Dobson insisted he needed to work every fourth day. The manager relented and went back to the four-man rotation. Dobson suddenly got hot and went on a 16–7 run the rest of the way. The Yankees were in first place on September 23, but wound up two games behind Baltimore as the Orioles won their last eight games while New York was winning five and losing three. Pat ended up 19–15 with a 3.07 ERA.

The Yankees believed that 1975 would be the year they returned to their former glory. Dobson started slowly, but he won six games in a row to raise his record to 8–5. He complained to the press after being pulled with two out in the seventh inning in a game against the Twins. At the time the Yankees were trailing 1–0, and there were two outs. Sparky Lyle came in and gave up a two-run single to Lyman Bostock. Virdon held a clubhouse meeting the next day and said, "One guy is causing dissension on the club." When the manager reinstituted the five-man rotation, Dobson went into a tailspin, winning only three more games all year. Virdon was fired in August and replaced by Billy Martin. But Martin and Dobson didn't get along well, either. Pat said Billy "had a habit of second-guessing what you threw, too."

In November, Dobson found himself traded once more, this to Cleveland in exchange for Oscar Gamble. Dobson's outspokenness didn't always sit well with management. But he said, "I have never regretted one word I've said. 'Course, there have been repercussions, but if you're right you have to take the consequences."

His manager with the Indians was Frank Robinson, his old Orioles teammate. Dobson respected Robinson, calling him the finest player he'd ever teamed with. Pat was considered the "elder statesman" of a young Indians staff that also included a rookie named Dennis Eckersley. Dobson had a fine season with the Indians, posting a 16–12 record with a 3.48 ERA. Cleveland finished above .500 for the first time since 1968. But in 1977, his record plummeted to 3–12, and his ERA soared to 6.14. He didn't get his first victory until June, after losing his first five decisions. His last victory came early in July against the Kansas City Royals. Shortly after that he lost his spot in the rotation and was relegated to the bullpen. What would be his final major league appearance came on September 19, 1977—fittingly, at Tiger Stadium. Dobson came on in relief in the seventh inning, getting the final two outs. He gave up a leadoff single in the eighth and was pulled from the game. The runner eventually scored, and Pat ended up taking the loss. He was released by the Indians on April 14, 1978, without making an appearance that year.

Pat Dobson won 122 games while losing 129 in the major leagues and saved an additional 19 games. His ERA for his career was a solid 3.54, and his WHIP was 1.28. In 17 seasons of professional ball, he played for 19 different teams.

Dobson developed a second career as a pitching coach. He summed up the logic behind the move: "Who knows more about pitching than me? Just take a look at the crap I'm getting away with out there [on the mound]. I rest my case." He was working for Triple A Nashville in 1982 when he was summoned to the parent club, the Milwaukee Brewers. Their pitching coach, Cal McLish, had become ill, and Pat was asked to fill in. This was the year of Harvey's Wallbangers, and the Brewers advanced to the World Series, losing to the St. Louis Cardinals in seven games. Pat's son Chris fondly remembers the days in Milwaukee. His dad would work his charts, chug coffee, chain smoke his menthol cigarettes, and complete the crossword puzzle in the *New York Times*. "I never saw a crossword puzzle my father couldn't finish," Chris said. After the Brewers fell to last place in 1984, Dobson and all the coaches were let go. He returned to coaching in the minor leagues before returning to the majors with San Diego from 1988 to 1990.

Dobson managed of the Fort Myers Sun Sox in the Senior League in 1989 and 1990. The Senior League was a new winter ball league set in Florida for players 35 and older. There were eight teams in two divisions. Pat's team finished second and was eliminated in the first round of the playoffs. The league folded halfway through its second season.

In 1991, Dobson became the Royals' pitching coach. He was considered a key man on the team, trying to restore the confidence of reliever Mark Davis. He had handled the star pitcher before at San Diego. Another project was Mark Gubicza, coming back from shoulder surgery. Pat was considered as a possible replacement for manager John Wathan, who was fired in May 1991. The job went instead to Hal McRae. Dobson's relationship with the new manager was rocky, and Pat resigned on September 9 when he could not get assurance that he would be asked to return the next year. Later that year, Pat attended the final-day ceremonies at Memorial Stadium in Baltimore and reunited with his fellow 20-game winners, Jim Palmer, Dave McNally, and Mike Cuellar.

Dobson joined the Colorado Rockies expansion team as an advance scout in December 1992, serving in that capacity until 1995. He left the Rockies to take the Baltimore pitching coach job in 1996, working with his close friend, manager Davey Johnson.

Despite the Orioles finishing a close second to the New York Yankees, Dobson was fired at the end of 1996 by owner Peter Angelos. Pat and the Orioles' young ace, Mike Mussina, did not see eye to eye and after a shouting match at the mound during a crucial September game, the writing was on the wall. Over the objections of General Manager Pat Gillick and manager Johnson, Ray Miller was hired as the new pitching coach.

Dobson next took a position as an advance scout with the San Francisco Giants in 1997, eventually becoming a special assistant to General Manager Brian Sabean. He was one of Sabean's top talent evaluators and scouted many of the players the Giants acquired, particularly pitchers. In 1998, Dobson was elected to the Greater Buffalo Sports Hall of Fame. His induction notice credited him with enlivening every clubhouse he entered. One writer even suggested that Pat may have been the funniest man who ever wore a baseball uniform.

Dobson played a key role in persuading Bruce Bochy to take the manager's position with the Giants in 2006, even jetting to San Francisco with Bochy when he went for an interview. Shortly afterward, Pat began to feel ill. After two weeks, he went to a hospital for tests and was diagnosed with leukemia. One night after checking in to the hospital, Pat Dobson died on November, 22, 2006, in San Diego. He was survived by his wife Kathe, and six children, Pat III, Nancy, Stacy, Chris, Shannon, and Stephanie.

References

Articles

Baggerly, Andrew. "Dobson played role in Bochy's decision." Oakland Tribune, December 6, 2006. Accessed at http://findarticles.com/p/articles/mi_qn4176/is_20061206?pnum=2&opg=n16893475

Cour, Paul. "Bulldog Dobson—Padre Workhouse and Battler." *The Sporting News*, September 19, 1970, p. 20.

Flaherty, Tom. "McLish Loses Out In Coaching Change." *The Sporting News*, November 29, 1982, p. 60.

Frau, Miguel. "Dobson Eclipses Pizarro's Strikeout Record, Fans 21." *The Sporting News*, December 23, 1967, p. 47.

Hatter, Lou. "Dobson Turns Detroit Into Bengal Snakepit." *The Sporting News*, July 22, 1972, p. 9.

Jackman, Phil. "Pat Dobson Acquired to Fill No. 4 Spot on Oriole Staff." *The Sporting News*, December 19,1970, p. 38.

Jackman, Phil. "O's Thank Their Lucky Stars for New Ace Dobson." *The Sporting News*, August 14, 1971, p. 10.

Jackman, Phil. "O's Boast Four 20-Win Aces, Equal Feat of '20 Chisox Stars." *The Sporting News*, October 9, 1971, p. 11.

Kaegel, Dick. "Kansas City Royals." *The Sporting News*, September 23, 1991, p. 26.

Kubatko, Roch. "O's 'gamer' won 20 in '71." *Baltimore Sun*, November 24, 2006, p. D11.

McKean, Dale. "'All I Needed Was a Chance'—Beaver Ace Dobson Proving It." *The Sporting News*, July 29, 1966, p. 38.

Nightengale, Bob. "Orioles Functioning Like a Dysfunctional Family." *The Sporting News*, October 28, 1996, p. 15.

Nightengale, Dave. "1991: Hello to Odd Ball." *The Sporting News*, April 1, 1991, p. S12.

Pepe, Phil. "Sleight of Hand Provides Dobson Toehold on Wins." *The Sporting News*, September 14, 1974, p. 29.

Powers, Roger. "Sports of All Sorts." *Grit*, (Williamsport, Pa.), November 14, 1971, p. 43.

Reidenbaugh, Lowell. "Cardinals Flash Muscle, Speed in a 7–3 Triumph." *The Sporting News*, October 19, 1968, p. 9.

Spoelstra, Watson. "Winter Loop Whiff Feats Mark Dobson as '58 Bengalani to Watch." *The Sporting News*, January 6, 1968, p. 50.

Spoelstra, Watson. "Unheralded Dobson and Hiller Win Tiger Headlines." *The Sporting News*, June 29, 1968, p. 11.

Spoelstra, Watson. "Tiger Jokester Dobson Wipes Grin Off Batters' Faces." *The Sporting News*, June 21, 1969, p. 12.

Spoelstra, Watson. "Kilkenny Is Tough Pitcher In a Paradise for Swingers." *The Sporting News*, October 11, 1969, p. 17.

Sudyk, Bob. "The Travels and Travails of Pat Dobson." *Baseball Digest*, Vol. 36, No.1 1977, pp. 74–78.

Vicioso, Fernando. "Dobson Helps Tigers Bare Sharp Teeth." *The Sporting News*, November 26, 1966, p. 43.

Web Sites
www.buffalosportshallfame.com
www.espn.com
www.sfgate.com
www.thebaseballcube.com
www.thebaseballpage.com

Rich Shook presents:
Tigers In the News

Wednesday, May 15
Denny McLain lost for the first time in 1968, 10–8, to Baltimore. He gave up four runs on four hits. Boog Powell hammered a three-run home run in the first and Elrod Hendricks opened the second with a home run. McLain was lifted for a pinch-hitter.

Thursday, May 16
Detroit played its then-annual exhibition game at Toledo. Al Kaline hit a long home run off Mud Hens reliever Dick Radatz. Dick McAuliffe relieved Al Kaline in right field for six innings and outfielder Gates Brown switched positions with catcher Bill Freehan the last two innings.

Friday, May 17
Frank Howard powered his eighth home run in five successive games to break one of Babe Ruth's records (Jim Bottomley of St. Louis Cards and Vic Wertz of Tigers had seven in five). It came with one on and one out in the ninth and gave the Senators a 3–2 lead in a game Detroit came back to win, 7–3. Jim Northrup upstaged Howard by touching rookie lefty Steve Jones for a grand slam in the bottom of the ninth after Jim Price pinch-hit an RBI single to tie the score. It was the fourth grand salami of Northrup's career and his second in two years on May 17. Sparma had a no-hitter for 6.1 innings before Ken McMullen hit a home run.

Saturday, May 18
Howard belted a pair of home runs as visiting Washington drubbed Detroit, 8–4, giving him 10 in six games and another major league slugging mark. The old record of seven was held by Roger Maris of the Yankees, plus George Kelley, Walker Cooper, and Willie Mays, all of the Giants. Hondo's second was a mammoth drive over Tiger Stadium's left field roof off Mickey Lolich—only the second time to that date a ball had cleared Tiger Stadium's left field roof since it was remodeled in 1933. Harmon Killebrew had hit the other six years earlier.

Sunday, May 19
Detroit took a doubleheader from Washington, 5–4 and 7–0. Earl Wilson was breezing along with a 4–0 lead in the opener's eighth inning when Howard doubled with one out and Ken McMullen singled him in, bringing on Jon Warden, who gave up an RBI single to Cap Peterson and a base hit to Ron Hansen, followed by a two-run home run to tie the score. Fred Lasher (2–0) got out of the inning and John Hiller finished up. Right fielder Ed Stroud fell down on the wet grass and Norm Cash's hit fell in front of him for a double. A walk and a pinch-RBI single by Gates Brown won it in the ninth. Rookie Les Cain fanned eight to overcome a six-walk, six-hit outing over 6.2 innings and gain his first major league victory in the second game. Lasher finished up. Eddie Mathews hit his 510th career home run.

Roy Face

by Gary Gillette

Season	Age	W	L	Pct	G	GS	CG	SV	IP	H	R	ER	BB	SO	ERA
1968 Tigers	40	0	0	.000	2	0	0	0	1	2	0	0	1	1	0.00
Career Totals		104	95	0.523	848	27	6	193	1375	1347	591	531	362	877	3.48

Baseball is a game in which one or two numbers can become burned into collective memory, ultimately defining a player's career. In the case of Babe Ruth, the numbers are 60 and 714. In the case of Ty Cobb, they are 4,191 and .367 (even though those numbers were shown to be inaccurate more than 25 years ago). "Joltin' Joe" DiMaggio's career has been forever entwined with 56, while "The Splendid Splinter" Ted Williams has been permanently branded with .406. In the case of Cy Young, the number everyone knows is 511. Bob Gibson's immortal number is 1.12; Orel Hershiser is bonded to 59.

Like many great players, Elroy Leon Face's career in the major leagues was defined by a pair of numbers: 18 and 1. Face's 1959 season, when he won 18 games against a single loss in relief for the Pirates, is certainly a remarkable achievement. At .947, it was the highest single-season winning percentage ever for a pitcher: only three other pitchers have posted a .900 winning percentage in a season since 1901 (minimum, 15 wins). A stalwart member of the Pirates from the mid-1950s through the late 1960s, the slight right-handed relief ace became one of the best-known "faces" of the postwar Pittsburgh franchise.

Standing only 5-feet-8 and listed at between 155 and 160 pounds, Roy Face would seem an unlikely candidate to play a key role in revolutionizing the way the game was played. Since the end of World War II, only seven other pitchers shorter than 5-feet-9 have made their big-league debuts and either started in 50 games or appeared in 100—none since 1976. Only three of those were shorter than Face, who was far from the prototype of the intimidating closer later made famous by practitioners like Goose Gossage, Rollie Fingers, and Bruce Sutter.

Durability is one of the hallmarks of the greatest relief pitchers, and Elroy Face clearly met that test. The right-hander pitched for 16 years, all but two of them exclusively or almost exclusively in relief. In 1956, Face tied the major league record by appearing in nine consecutive games September 3–13, including five games in four days September 7–10. Even though he shouldered a heavy workload, Face was on the disabled list only once in his career, after knee surgery in 1965.

Consistency is another quality of great relief pitchers. Again, Face made the grade by posting double-digit save totals in all but two seasons from 1957 to 1968. (In that period, the average NL-leading save figure was less than 23.) He led the league in saves three times and in appearances twice and was a member of the NL All-Star team in 1959, 1960, and 1961.

In the 1950s, the national pastime witnessed many profound changes. Among them was a new philosophy of pitching that coalesced after many teams experimented with true relief pitchers in the 1940s (as opposed to starters coming on in relief in key games between starts). Relievers, heretofore mostly considered to be failed starters, were gaining prominence as many pennant-winning clubs featured a bullpen ace. Nevertheless, most top relievers lacked one or both of the key qualities of consistency and durability.

Joe Black, a Negro League veteran, won the 1952 NL Rookie of the Year Award while going 15–4 with 15 saves for Brooklyn. He never had another season anything like that. Reliever Joe Page of the postwar Yankees had only two really good years. The Phillies' Jim Konstanty was more durable than most, but his MVP-winning 1950 was his only outstanding campaign. Ellis Kinder had several good seasons out of the bullpen for the Red Sox in the 1950s, but he lasted only four years as a full-time reliever. The Dodgers' Clem Labine probably was the most durable and consistent reliever prior to Face, though Labine never achieved Face's level of excellence.

The only relief pitcher of the pre-expansion era whose career was comparable to Face was Hoyt Wilhelm, the ageless knuckleballer who made a brilliant debut at age 29 with the New York Giants in 1952. Wilhelm went 15–3 with 11 saves, leading the NL with 71 appearances, all in relief. However, after two more good seasons, Wilhelm's career stalled. Bouncing from the Giants to the Cardinals to the Indians to the Orioles, he was converted to starting before finally settling in as a relief ace for good in 1961. Wilhelm's career eventually eclipsed Face's, but it was Face who was the pioneer in defining the role of the ace reliever in the 1950s.

Star relievers of the 1960s like Lindy McDaniel (who learned his forkball from Face in the early 1960s), Ron Perranoski, and Stu Miller were, thus, following in Face's footsteps. None of them ever garnered serious support for the Hall of Fame, never climbing above 2 percent of the vote. Face peaked at 19 percent in Hall balloting in 1987, showing that he was regarded much more highly than any reliever of his time aside from Wilhelm, inducted into Cooperstown in 1985.

Retroactive save statistics first compiled in 1969 show that Face held the all-time saves lead from 1962 through 1963, being passed by Wilhelm in 1964. Face was the career leader in games finished from 1961 to 1964, again until passed by Wilhelm. From 1956, when he was permanently moved to the bullpen, through 1968, Face led all major league pitchers in relief games with 717 (87 more than Wilhelm) and in saves with 183 (20 more than Wilhelm).

Considering that he didn't attend college, Face got a late start on his professional career for someone of his level of accomplishment. Born on February 20, 1928, in Stephentown, New York, just over the state line from Pittsfield, Massachusetts, he played baseball at Averill Park High School, a dozen miles east of Albany, before serving in the U.S. Army from February 1946 to July 1947.

Signed by the Phillies at age 20 and assigned to Class D, Face spent two years with Bradford in the Pennsylvania-Ontario-New York (PONY) League. Even though the right-hander pitched well for the PONY League champion Blue Wings in his professional debut (14–2 with a league-leading .875 winning percentage), he was not promoted. The following year, Face was even better, leading the PONY with a 2.58 ERA and compiling an 18–5 record for a fourth-place club. Yet Philadelphia left him exposed to the annual winter draft, allowing Branch Rickey of Brooklyn to snatch Face in December 1950.

Two years later, after successful campaigns with Pueblo in the Class A Western League (three levels above Class D, confirming that the Phillies made a mistake in not promoting him) and Fort Worth in the Double A Texas League, Rickey (now with Pittsburgh) again drafted Face at the 1952 Winter Meetings. The following spring, Face made his major league debut on April 16. He spent the whole season with the Pirates, making 41 appearances, including 13 starts, but posting a 6.58 ERA.

At that time, the diminutive right-hander was what scouts used to call a "blow-and-go guy": a moundsman who threw as hard as he could for as long as he could, but who was not an experienced pitcher. Despite his small stature, Face threw as hard as, or harder than, Bob Friend and the other Pirates pitchers, according to catcher Hank Foiles, who was with Pittsburgh from late 1956 through 1959. As a rookie, Face's repertoire consisted of a fastball and a curveball. While the young right-hander's success in the minors argued that he might get by with just two arrows in his quiver, big-league hitters argued—successfully—to the contrary in 1953.

As a result of his first-year struggles, Face was sent in 1954 to Pittsburgh's highest-level farm club, New Orleans of the Double A Southern Association. His assignment was to learn an off-speed pitch—a career-changing move that would catapult him to stardom. Contrary to accounts that say Face learned his forkball from veteran relief pitcher Joe Page, Face says he simply got the idea for developing a fork from watching Page as the erstwhile Yankees reliever was trying to make comeback in Pittsburgh's spring camp in 1954. After practicing the new pitch on his own on the sidelines for half the season, Face started using it in ballgames with the Pelicans.

Danny Murtaugh, the Pelicans' skipper who would later manage the Pirates to world championships in 1960 and 1971, converted Face to a full-time reliever. Murtaugh scratched his new charge from his second scheduled start after he took over in the Crescent City, never asking him to start another game. Years later, Murtaugh reaped the benefits of that conversion when he was the man in the Forbes Field dugout during Face's peak years from 1958 to 1962.

After completing his assignment by mastering his new pitch, Face went north with Pittsburgh in the spring of 1955.

> "I don't, but neither does the batter."
> —Face, as quoted in *The Cultural Encyclopedia of Baseball*, about whether he knew which way his forkball would break

A forkball is a pitch that is hard to define, hard to throw, hard to control, and very hard to hit. Essentially, it is a change-of-pace offering that gets its sudden drop because the pitcher jams the baseball between his index and middle fingers, allowing the ball to depart his hand with minimal spin. Properly delivered, it should "tumble" toward home plate, dropping out of the strike zone as befuddled batters futilely swing over it. If thrown slowly enough, á la Elroy, the pitch can also break unpredictably to either side, á la the knuckleball.

The forkball that Roy Face ultimately mastered and which, in turn, allowed him to master NL hitters, is a little-used pitch with a long history. Assuming one accepts that forkballs and split-finger fastballs are different pitches—notwithstanding that many think it a distinction without real meaning—the forkball was invented in 1908 by Bert Hall, a pitcher with Tacoma in the Northwestern League who made his only major league start for the Phillies in 1911. The next pitcher known to employ the fork was "Bullet Joe" Bush in the 1920s; the only other really prominent pitchers to use it regularly before Face were Ernest "Tiny" Bonham (an All-Star starter for the Yankees during World War II whose career was ended by his premature death while with the Pirates in the late 1940s), and Mort Cooper (who starred for the Cardinals in the 1940s).

Baseball analyst Rob Neyer rated Face as throwing the best forkball of all time (if one separates the fork from the splitter), though Neyer lumped the two pitches together in his top-10 list after devoting several pages to distinguishing them.

Though now identified most closely with his devastating forkball, Face has always maintained that he wasn't dependent on that pitch. When the fork was working, he might throw it 70 percent of the time; when it wasn't working, he might use it only 20 percent of the time. Though he later added a slider, he kept his curve, ultimately providing four pitches in his arsenal to choose from.

Even in his superb 1959 and 1960 seasons, Face mixed his pitch selection according to what was most effective that day.

The epigraph to Chapter III of Christy Mathewson's classic *Pitching in a Pinch* reads: "Many pitchers Are Effective in a Big League Ball Game until that Heart-Breaking Moment Arrives Known as the 'Pinch'—It Is then that the Man in the Box is Put to the Severest Test...Victory or Defeat Hangs on his Work in that Inning."

Armed with his new pitch, Face took off on his excellent career. He split his time between starting and relieving in '55, then led the NL in appearances the next year with 68 (including three starts). In '57, Face registered his first year with double-digit saves; in '58, he led the NL in saves for the first time. His sensational 1959 season marked his first All-Star honors and is now, of course, the stuff of baseball legend.

"When he had that great year in 1959 you had to wonder how he did it, but he did, had that great forkball and I don't think he weighed more than 145 pounds," said Sam Narron, Branch Rickey's first bullpen catcher (as quoted in *Pen Men*).

Face's sole loss in '59 snapped a relief record 17-game winning streak that year as well as a 22-game winning streak over two seasons. Perhaps more remarkable in an era where ace relievers often were called upon with the score tied, it was also his first loss in 99 appearances, dating back to early 1958.

Sally O'Leary, who worked in the Pittsburgh PR department for 32 years and now edits the Pirates alumni newsletter *The Black and Gold*, recalls how Face's record-setting season—which included a healthy dose of good luck, as virtually all great seasons do—has been remembered by retired Bucs pitchers. "[T]he Pirate starters love to tell stories of how they would start a game, pitch really well, and somehow the game would get tied—Elroy would come in—and get the win! This always provides good copy!"

A key actor in Pittsburgh's 1960 pageantry, Face again topped the NL in appearances while saving 24 and compiling a 2.90 ERA in 114.2 innings. Though bordering on heroic, Face's efforts in the 1960 World Series have been largely forgotten by fans—including many who remember Bill Mazeroski's famous homer. Coming in from the pen to save Games 1, 4, and 5, Face narrowly missed becoming the winning pitcher in Game 7 when the Yankees came from behind to knot the score in the top of the ninth. (Face had been removed for a pinch-hitter in the bottom of the eighth at the start of a five-run Pittsburgh rally.)

Face logged 10.1 innings in that Series, more than any other Bucs pitcher—including starters—except Vern Law. Only one year earlier, the Dodgers' Larry Sherry had become the first pitcher ever to save or win every game for a World Series winner.

After an off-year in 1961 (6–12 record, though he again led the league in saves), Face enjoyed his best year in "The Show" in '62. Although Roy's 1962 season isn't as well known as his 1959 or 1960 campaigns, at age 34, Face won his only *Sporting News* Fireman of the Year Award. (*TSN*'s award was first given out in 1960.) The unflappable veteran posted a league-leading, career-high 28 saves to go with a 1.88 ERA (2.09 adjusted for park factor and league offensive level) as well as an NL relief-high 20 Adjusted Pitching Runs (runs allowed compared to the average pitcher).

The durable righty was never as good thereafter, struggling through a mediocre 1963, a rocky 1964, and an injury-shortened 1965. Afterward, with lighter usage, the seasoned stopper rebounded to post three consecutive solid seasons before his Pittsburgh career came to an end.

When he was sold to Detroit, Face held the NL records for games pitched (802), games in relief (775), games finished (547), and relief wins (92). In all of those categories, Face was second to future Hall of Famer Hoyt Wilhelm for the major league lead. Wilhelm, the first relief pitcher enshrined in Cooperstown, had an advantage in that he had spent most of his career to that point with first-division teams.

According to longtime Pittsburgh sportswriter Lester Biederman in the September 14, 1968, issue of *The Sporting News*, "There was a little dash of cloak and dagger mystery to Roy Face's final turn with the Pirates August 31 before he was sold to the Tigers for a reported $100,000." The deal with Detroit had already been agreed upon, but it hadn't been announced since the Tigers wouldn't have a roster slot open till September 1. (*TSN* also asserted that Face had saved 233 games for the Pirates, apparently using a different definition for the unofficial stat that would finally be codified for the following season.)

Pittsburgh sold Face to Detroit despite his leading the Bucs with 13 saves in only 43 games and posting a 2.60 ERA (Adjusted ERA 13 percent better than the NL norm). His last appearance for the Bucs tied Walter Johnson's record for most appearances with a single team (802); it was arranged as somewhat of a going-away present by Pittsburgh management. Face was invited to start this last game, but declined. Instead, Face relieved Steve Blass after the Pirates' starter had retired the leadoff hitter in the first inning. Blass went to left field temporarily as Face threw a single pitch and recorded a groundout before walking off the mound. While the Pirates had not yet announced Face's sale to Detroit, it seemed that everyone with the club knew what was happening and wanted to bid Roy adieu.

When he pitched his last game in the majors less than a year later, Face stood second with 193 on the all-time saves list to Wilhelm's 210; he was six saves behind Wilhelm when he left Pittsburgh in 1968. That was no mean feat considering that, in Face's 14 years in the Steel City, the Bucs won only one pennant and finished in the first division only three other times. Face remains today atop the Pirates' all-time list in games with 802 and saves with 188.

According to O'Leary, the Pirates' alumni newsletter editor, Face remains extremely popular today, almost four decades after he last pulled off his Pirates uniform. "He is always ready to help the alumni in one way or another—appearances, signing autographs, giving little talks (question and answer things)—and the public enjoys having him at their events," she says.

In one of those fascinating twists of fate, the world champion 1968 Tigers turned to one of the all-time great firemen—the predominant term of that day for what would today be called closers—late in their season to give them extra insurance for the final month. After only two brief appearances and two more unexpected twists of fate, Face was all but forgotten in Detroit.

In hindsight, the '68 Tigers now seem to have been invulnerable. Yet, after ascending to first place on May 10 and holding leads between 5.5 and eight games for the next three months, they didn't appear to have the American League pennant in the bag in late August. Upon sweeping a doubleheader from the Athletics on August 27, rookie manager Earl Weaver's hard-charging Orioles had blazed to a 35–17 record after Weaver had replaced Hank Bauer at the helm. Worse, the second-place Birds had narrowed the gap to four games when the Tigers dropped a 2–1 decision to the White Sox on the same day. The No. 1 and No. 2 teams were set to clash in a big three-game weekend series starting on August 30 in Motown, then potentially fight it out for the pennant in the last week of the season in Crabtown.

Detroit was only six games ahead of Baltimore at the end of August when Face was purchased from Pittsburgh on August 31. No one knew at that time that Detroit would finish with a flourish, winning 21 of their last 30 games as Baltimore stumbled to the finish line, losing 17 while winning 13 and finishing a distant 12 games back.

Still reeling from the devastation—both physical and psychological—of the 1967 riots, the city of Detroit was going gaga over its Tigers in the summer of 1968. As the long season ground on, however, Detroit's bullpen looked like a potential problem. Such is the luxury of having a great team: worrying about potential problems rather than having to deal with pressing problems. General Manager Jim Campbell, therefore, tried to bolster the club's relief corps by the time-honored tradition of adding several experienced arms.

In that glorious summer of '68, Detroit's bullpen was an amalgam of untested youngsters (rookie righty Daryl Patterson was 24, while rookie lefty Jon Warden was a tender 21) and sophomores with about a year or so of big-league experience (lefty John Hiller, 25, and righties Pat Dobson and Fred Lasher, both 26). Hiller and Dobson filled the swingman roles, making 12 and 10 starts, respectively. The only Detroit pitcher over 27 years old for the first half of the season was veteran starter Earl Wilson (33).

Despite the doubts, the Detroit bullpen as a group was spectacular that year, holding opponents to a .200 batting average (remember, however, that the league batted only .230 in the watershed "Year of the Pitcher") and compiling a 2.26 ERA with a 29–13 record and 29 saves. Their unofficial saves total was tied for sixth in the league. No Detroit pitcher posted more than seven saves, with three relievers each earning at least 17 percent of the team total (Dobson and Patterson with seven each; Lasher with five).

As the season wore on, Campbell strengthened his callow pitching staff by acquiring a handful of old-timers. Don McMahon, who became the Tigers' closer, was 38, though he would soldier on for another six seasons and 244 games, mostly with the Giants. The Tigers also auditioned two other veteran closers, acquiring John Wyatt (only 33 but at the end of his career) from the Yankees in mid-June and Roy Face, age 40. Unlike McMahon, neither veteran thrived in Detroit. Both would finish their careers in 1969, with Wyatt appearing in his final four games for Oakland and Face spending most of the year in Montreal.

On September 2, the day after he reported to Detroit, Face made his AL debut. He was called on in the eighth inning of the second game of a doubleheader, allowing a run-scoring hit and blowing the lead while pitching 0.2 inning. Face also appeared the next day, again being nicked for an RBI single and blowing the lead. He never saw game action for Detroit afterward. His stat line for the 1968 Tigers reads: one inning pitched, five batters faced, two hits allowed, one (intentional) walk, and one strikeout.

The Detroit rotation soon made Campbell's insurance policy superfluous by logging complete games in half of its 26 September starts on the way to leading the AL with a total of 59—including a remarkable 12 consecutive complete games from September 6 through September 19.

By the time that streak was over, the gap between the Tigers and the Orioles was an insurmountable 12.5 games, and Face sat unused for the rest of the season. The veteran closer returned home as Detroit battled St. Louis in what would become one of the greatest fall classics ever.

Face's career came to a close in 1969, the year when the save was officially endorsed as a statistic. The great reliever was released by Detroit late in spring training and was picked up three weeks later by the expansion Expos, for whom he appeared in 44 games before being released in mid-August. Face pitched briefly for Triple A Hawaii in 1970 before hanging up his spikes permanently.

In a November 2, 1968, column by Watson Spoelstra in *The Sporting News*, Tigers pitching coach Johnny Sain was optimistic about the Detroit pitching staff's prospects for the next season. One reason mentioned by Sain was that he thought the club would be helped by the presence of four veteran closers: McMahon, Face, Wyatt, and Dick Radatz (who pitched in the Tigers' organization in Toledo in 1968 after being released by the Cubs).

Sain's prognostication for his veteran quartet would remain mostly unfulfilled, with only Radatz and McMahon pitching for Detroit in 1969. "Four pretty good country relief pitchers" was the way Radatz remembered that group years later in *Pen Men*.

That seems like a fair way to sum up Roy Face's career: A pretty good country relief pitcher who became a pioneer.

References

Publications
Abramovich, Joe, and Paul A. Rickart. *Baseball Register*. St. Louis: The Sporting News. 1964.
Cairns, Bob. *Pen Men*. New York: St. Martin's Press. 1993.
Dickson, Paul. *Dickson Baseball Dictionary*. New York: Facts on File. 1989.
Dickson, Paul. *Dickson Baseball Dictionary*. 2nd ed. New York: Avon Books. 1991.
Duxbury, John, and Cliff Kachline. *Baseball Register*. St. Louis: The Sporting News. 1966.
Duxbury, John, and Cliff Kachline. *Baseball Register*. St. Louis: The Sporting News. 1967.
Duxbury, John. *Baseball Register*. St. Louis: The Sporting News. 1968.
Duxbury, John. *Baseball Register*. St. Louis: The Sporting News. 1969.
Enders, Eric. *100 Years of the World Series: 1903–2003*. New York: Barnes & Noble Publishing. 2004.
Felber, Bill. *The Book on the Book*. New York: St. Martin's Press. 2005.

Gietschier, Steve. *The Complete Baseball Record and Fact Book*, 2006 ed. St. Louis: Sporting News Books. 2006.

Gillette, Gary, and Pete Palmer. *The ESPN Baseball Encyclopedia*, 4th ed. New York: Sterling Publishing Co., Inc. 2007.

James, Bill. *The Bill James Historical Baseball Abstract*. New York: Villard Books. 1986.

James, Bill, and Rob Neyer. *The Neyer/James Guide to Pitchers*. New York: Fireside Books. 2004.

Johnson, Lloyd. *Baseball's Dream Teams*. New York: Crescent Books. 1990.

Kachline, Cliff, and Chris Roewe. *Official Baseball Guide for 1966*. St. Louis: The Sporting News. 1966.

Kachline, Cliff, and Chris Roewe. *Official Baseball Guide for 1967*. St. Louis: The Sporting News. 1967.

Light, Jonathan Fraser. *The Cultural Encyclopedia of Baseball*. Jefferson, North Carolina: McFarland & Company, Inc. 1997.

MacFarlane, Paul, Chris Roewe, and Larry Wigge. *Official Baseball Guide for 1970*. St. Louis: The Sporting News. 1970.

MacFarlane, Paul, Chris Roewe, Larry Wigge, and Larry Vickrey. *Official Baseball Guide for 1971*. St. Louis: The Sporting News. 1971.

MacFarlane, Paul, Chris Roewe, Larry Wigge, and Larry Vickrey. *Official Baseball Guide for 1972*. St. Louis: The Sporting News. 1972.

Mathewson, Christopher. *Pitching In a Pinch*. Mattituck: N.Y.: Amereon House reprint of 1912 Knickerbocker Press edition.

Morris, Peter. *A Game of Inches: The Game Behind the Scenes*. Chicago: Ivan R. Dee. 2006.

Morris, Peter. *A Game of Inches: The Game On the Field*. Chicago: Ivan R. Dee. 2006.

Neft, David. S, Lee Allen, and Robert Markel. *The Baseball Encyclopedia*, 1st ed., updated. New York: The Macmillan Company. 1969.

Peary, Danny. *We Played the Game*. New York: Hyperion Books. 1994.

Pickard, Charles, Cliff Kachline, and Paul A. Rickart. *Baseball Register*. St. Louis: The Sporting News. 1965.

Pietrusza, David, Matthew Silverman, and Michael Gershman. *Baseball: The Biographical Encyclopedia*. Kingston, New York: Total/Sports Illustrated. 2000.

Quigley, Martin. *The Crooked Pitch*. Chapel Hill, N.C.: Algonquin Books. 1984.

Reichler, Joseph L. *The Baseball Trade Register*. New York: Collier Books. 1984.

Rocwe, Chris, and Oscar Kahan. *Official Baseball Guide for 1968*. St. Louis: The Sporting News. 1968.

Roewe, Chris, and Paul MacFarlane. *Official Baseball Guide for 1969*. St. Louis: The Sporting News. 1969.

Spatz, Lyle. The SABR *Baseball List & Record Book*. New York: Scribner. 2007.

Spink, J.G. Taylor, Paul A. Rickart, and Joe Abramovich. *Baseball Register*. St. Louis: The Sporting News. 1955.

Spink, J.G. Taylor, Paul A. Rickart, and Joe Abramovich. *Baseball Register*. St. Louis: The Sporting News. 1956.

Spink, J.G. Taylor, Paul A. Rickart, and Joe Abramovich. *Baseball Register*. St. Louis: The Sporting News. 1957.

Spink, J.G. Taylor, Paul A. Rickart, and Joe Abramovich. *Baseball Register*. St. Louis: The Sporting News. 1958.

Spink, J.G. Taylor, Paul A. Rickart, and Joe Abramovich. *Baseball Register*. St. Louis: The Sporting News. 1959.

Spink, J.G. Taylor, Paul A. Rickart, and Joe Abramovich. *Baseball Register*. St. Louis: The Sporting News. 1960.

Spink, J.G. Taylor, Paul A. Rickart, and Joe Abramovich. *Baseball Register*. St. Louis: The Sporting News. 1961.

Spink, J.G. Taylor, Paul A. Rickart, and Joe Abramovich. *Baseball Register*. St. Louis: The Sporting News. 1962.

Spink, J.G. Taylor, Paul A. Rickart, and Joe Abramovich. *Baseball Register*. St. Louis: The Sporting News. 1963.

Spink, J.G. Taylor, Paul A. Rickart, and Clifford Kachline. *The Sporting News Baseball Guide and Record Book*. St. Louis: The Sporting News. 1961.

Spink, J.G. Taylor, Paul A. Rickart, and Clifford Kachline. *The Sporting News Baseball Guide and Record Book*. St. Louis: The Sporting News. 1962.

Spink, C.C. Johnson, Paul A. Rickart, and Clifford Kachline. *Official Baseball Guide for 1963*. St. Louis: The Sporting News. 1963.

Spink, C.C. Johnson, Paul A. Rickart, and Clifford Kachline. *Official Baseball Guide for 1964*. St. Louis: The Sporting News. 1964.

Spink, C.C. Johnson, Paul A. Rickart, and Clifford Kachline. *Official Baseball Guide for 1965*. St. Louis: The Sporting News. 1965.

Sumner, Benjamin Barrett. *Minor League Baseball Standings*. Jefferson, N.C.: McFarland & Company, Inc. 2000.

Thorn, John, and John Holway. *The Pitcher*. New York: Prentice-Hall. 1988.

Trdinich, Jim, and Dan Hart. *Pittsburgh Pirates 2007 Media Guide*. Pittsburgh: Pittsburgh Pirates Baseball Club. 2007.

Trdinich, Jim, Dan Hart, and Patrick O'Connell. *Pittsburgh Pirates 2004 Media Guide*. Pittsburgh: Pittsburgh Pirates Baseball Club. 2004.

Articles

Biederman, Les. "Buc Scribe Gives Bengals An Intimate Look at Face." *The Sporting News*, September 21, 1968. Available from *www.PaperOfRecord.com*.

Biederman, Les. "Face Leaves Bucs In a Blaze of Glory." *The Sporting News*, September 14, 1968. Available from *www.PaperOfRecord.com*.

Felber, Bill. "The Changing Game," in John Thorn and Pete Palmer's *Total Baseball*, 1st ed. New York: Warner Books. 1989.

Felber, Bill, and Gary Gillette. "The Changing Game," in John Thorn and Pete Palmer's *Total Baseball*, seventh edition. Kingston, New York: Total Sports Publishing. 2001.

"National Nuggets," in *The Sporting News*, p. 54, October 5, 1968. Available from *www.PaperOfRecord.com*.

Spoelstra, Watson. "It Looks Like Northrup Can Buy Cowboy Boots," in *The Sporting News*, September 21, 1968. Available from *www.PaperOfRecord.com*.

Spoelstra, Watson. "Sain, Naragon Give Tigers Early Line on '69," in *The Sporting News*, November 2, 1968. Available from *www.PaperOfRecord.com*.

Web Sites

www.baseballindex.org

www.baseball-reference.com

http://members.SABR.org [SABR encyclopedia, including Home Run Log and Scouting Database]

http://pittsburgh.pirates.mlb.com/

www.retrosheet.org [including Transactions Log]

Other Sources

Gillette, Gary. Interview with Jim Price.

Gillette, Gary. Telephone interview with Elroy Face.

Gillette, Gary. Telephone interview with Pete Palmer.

Gillette, Gary. Telephone interview with Lenny Yochim.

Nelson, Rod. E-mail messages to author.

O'Leary, Sally. E-mail message to author.

Palmer, Pete. E-mail messages to author.

Notes

Ages quoted are seasonal ages (i.e., age as of June 30 of each season)

Adjusted ERA stats per Pete Palmer's calculations in *The ESPN Baseball Encyclopedia*. They may differ slightly from similar statistics on baseball-reference.com or those previously published in *Total Baseball*.

1968   Tigers

Rich Shook presents:
Tigers In the News

Monday, May 20
Denny McLain went 10 innings and improved to 6-1 with a seven-hitter in a game Detroit won, 4-3, over Minnesota. The Twins might have won the game, 3-1, but for four errors they made that let in three runs, including one that let in the winning run. It was the 11th game the Tigers had won in their last at-bat.

Tuesday, May 21
Joe Sparma scattered eight hits over eight innings with three walks and seven strikeouts but Dean Chance pitched a four-hitter and Minnesota topped the Tigers, 3-1. Rich Rollins lined a two-run single to left in the eighth to break a 1-1 tie. Twice during the winning rally the Twins successfully challenged left fielder Willie Horton's arm.

Wednesday, May 22
Detroit's bid to win its 12th game in its last at-bat ended when Norm Cash flied out with two on to end Minnesota's 4-3 victory. Jim Perry held the Tigers to two hits over the first seven innings and whacked a three-run home run in the second, his second of the season. Don Wert slammed a home run in the fifth and belted another in the eighth. One out later Gates Brown, pinch-hitting for Mickey Lolich, tripled to chase Perry; Ron Perranoski relieved. Al Kaline, who didn't start because of a sore back, batted for Tom Matchick and singled Brown home with the tying run. But Tony Oliva opened the bottom of the eighth with a double to right off Fred Lasher. Killebrew drove home Oliva with a single to right.

Thursday, May 23
No game. News of the day: Manager Smith has used 20 different lineup combinations in 37 games.

Friday, May 24
Detroit and Oakland played a 2-2 tie in a rare game halted by rain on the West Coast. The game was stopped after a 54-minute wait. Bill Freehan and Willie Horton hit back-to-back home runs in the second. Earl Wilson balked in Oakland's first run in the fourth and another balk in the fifth let Jim Pagliaroni move to third, from where he scored on Reggie Jackson's single.

Saturday, May 25
Denny McLain pitched a six-hitter with eight strikeouts to move to 7-1 as Detroit nipped Oakland, 2-1. Denny McLain showed his skill at bunting by beating one out for a single to open the eighth off Lew Krausse. Dick McAuliffe sacrificed, Jim Northrup walked, and Mickey Stanley drove the pitcher in with a single. The Tigers and A's each scored unearned runs in the ninth. Stanley entered the game in the sixth as the replacement for Al Kaline after Krausse hit him with a pitch. It was costly as Detroit learned the next day Krausse's pitch put a hairline fracture in Kaline's right forearm and he would be out of action two to three weeks.

Sunday, May 26
Bad blood between Oakland and Detroit contributed to a nearly 15-minute brawl in the sixth inning of a game the A's won, 7-6, in 10 innings. The score was deadlocked at 6-6 when reliever Jack Aker hit Northrup in the back of his batting helmet with a pitch. The "Gray Fox" got up from the dirt and charged Aker. Mathews belted Aker below the right eye and the reliever had to leave the game due to injuries suffered in the melee. The right side of his uniform was in shreds and he had cuts and bruises all over his body. "I was trying to brush him back but the pitch didn't sail," Aker said. "It sank and Northrup ducked right into it." Umpires Ed Runge and Cal Drummond booted Northrup "because he used some badly chosen words" and tossed John "Blue Moon" Odom "because he kicked McAuliffe in the ribs." Pinch-hitter Rene Lachemann's single in the tenth won it, scoring pinch-runner Jim Hunter. Smith kept the clubhouse closed for 30 minutes after the game. When told Aker had called Northrup to apologize, Smith said, "Then ask Aker what happened. He seems to have all the answers." During the brawl, some of the 14,587 fans threw debris on the field and a Tiger unidentified at the time—it was later determined to be Dennis Ribant—threw a ball into the stands and hit Mary Alamieda, 52, of San Leandro, California, above the right eye, causing a three-inch gash.

Monday, May 27
Detroit's trip continued to California, where the Angels edged the Tigers, 7-6, in 12 innings. Mathews slammed the last two home runs of his major league career, leaving him at 512, one more than Mel Ott for sixth place (at the time) on the all-time list. Detroit's fourth loss in five games shrank its lead to a half-game over Baltimore and a full game over Cleveland. Daryl Patterson gave up a leadoff single to Rick Reichardt in the 12th. He advanced to second on a balk and scored on Tom Satriano's double over Willie Horton's head in left. Detroit made a roster move before the game, placing Kaline on the 21-day disabled list and recalling outfielder Wayne Comer from Toledo.

Bill Freehan

by Trey Strecker

Season	Age	G	AB	R	H	2B	3B	HR	RBI	BB	SO	SB	CS	BA	OBP	SLG
1968 Tigers	26	155	540	73	142	24	2	25	84	65	64	0	1	.263	.366	.454
Career Totals		1774	6073	706	1591	241	35	200	758	626	753	24	21	.262	.340	.412

Widely regarded as one of the game's best defensive catchers and the best catcher in the American League during his prime, Bill Freehan was a fierce competitor and a committed leader on the diamond. Described by sportswriter Arnold Hano as "a thinking man's catcher" and "an elemental ballplayer," the 6-foot-2, 205-pound Freehan displayed "an unusual blend of brawn and brains." Freehan is in select company with Charlie Bennett, Mickey Cochrane, Lance Parrish, and Ivan Rodriguez as one of the most popular and talented backstops in Detroit baseball history.

The eldest son of Ashley Freehan, a sales representative for a seat insulation company, William Ashley Freehan was born on November 29, 1941, in Detroit. Growing up in suburban Royal Oak with his three siblings, the young Freehan began catching on the Detroit sandlots one day when his Little League team's catcher didn't show up and he moved from shortstop to behind the plate. During one Little League all-star game, Freehan was bowled over in a collision at home plate by future teammate Willie Horton. When Bill was 14, his father bought a mobile-home development, and his family moved to St. Petersburg, Florida, where Freehan attended Bishop Barry High School, playing baseball, basketball, and football. During the summers, Freehan returned to Detroit to play sandlot baseball, where, only 15, he captured the eye of Tigers scout Louis D'Annunzio, who called Freehan "the best sandlot catcher he'd seen."

After graduating from high school in 1959, Freehan hoped to attend the University of Notre Dame, but the school required that he choose football or baseball, so he accepted an athletic scholarship to the University of Michigan, catching on the baseball team and playing end and linebacker on the football squad. At Michigan, Freehan once caught all three games of a tripleheader between Michigan and Michigan State, then, according to his mother, "he went out dancing until one in the morning." Always strong defensively, the sophomore catcher pounded Big Ten pitching, batting .585 in 1961 and drawing the attention of major league scouts. Although he entertained offers from several teams, the 19-year-old Freehan signed with his hometown Tigers for a $125,000 bonus in 1961. But, even as he was breaking into the big leagues, the Tigers' bonus baby continued attending school part-time over the off-season, completing his bachelor's degree in history with a 3.1 grade point average from Michigan in 1966. Freehan explained, "My deal with my dad was, I didn't see a dime of my bonus until I got my degree."

For the 1961 season, the Tigers farmed him out to Duluth-Superior in the Class C Northern League, where Freehan hit .343 with seven home runs and 26 RBI in 30 games for manager Bill Swift before he was promptly promoted to Knoxville in the Sally League. There, he batted .289 in 47 games before a late-September call-up to Detroit, where Freehan managed four singles in 10 at-bats. In 1962, Freehan played the entire season for Denver's American Association entry, playing stellar defense behind the plate and batting .283 with nine home runs and 58 RBI. Called up to Detroit after the season, he saw no action. On February 23, 1963, Freehan married Patricia O'Brien, his high school sweetheart from St. Petersburg and the sister of St. Louis Cardinals pitcher Dan O'Brien (1978–1979).

Brought up to the Tigers again in 1963, Freehan got on base nine straight times, managing three home runs, one triple, three doubles, two singles, and three walks in 15 plate appearances. Over the remainder of his rookie season, the 21-year-old receiver committed only two errors in 73 games behind the plate, although he hit only .243. "I wanted to hit well," Freehan said. "I just never put that ahead of my primary responsibility. The catcher has to be the captain of the field. I felt if I did my job behind the plate, I was contributing to the team in the best way I could." Always a perfectionist, one Tigers front-office man said, "Bill's biggest trouble is that he thinks he never should have a bad day."

The next year marked Freehan's arrival as the dominant catcher in the American League. A right-handed hitter who crowded the plate, Freehan became the first Detroit catcher to hit .300 since Mickey Cochrane batted .319 in 1935. At the time of his first all-star selection in 1964, Freehan had caught fewer than 200 major league games, but over the course of the season, the Detroit backstop demonstrated that he deserved to be an all-star. Freehan committed only seven errors in 141 games—catching the final 56 games of the season and logging a stretch of 517 consecutive innings behind the plate—with a .993 fielding percentage, and he belted 18 home runs with 80 RBI. More importantly, during the 1964 campaign, Freehan became the team's "spiritual leader," according to writer Jim Sargent. Manager Charlie Dressen noted that even a veteran pitcher like Dave Wickersham was willing to let the young catcher call the game. "He suddenly grew up," Dressen remarked, "and his pitchers have confidence in him now. So do the other players. Quick-like, the Tigers had a leader." Arnold Hano noted that Freehan "leads the way sergeants lead, not second lieutenants. He leads by example." General Manager Jim Campbell said, "We put the full load on Freehan's shoulders and he didn't stumble."

Although Freehan caught 129 games in 1965, he was frequently dinged up by injuries. In spring training, Freehan suffered a severe muscle spasm in his lower back while rounding second base, the injury putting him on the bench for three weeks. On May 29, a foul tip off the bat of Cleveland's Max Alvis injured his throwing hand and, on June 25, a pitch deflected off Minnesota rookie Sandy Valdespino struck Freehan's bare hand in the exact spot as the foul tip. While he avoided the disabled list, Freehan only hit a meager .234 in both 1965 and 1966. Still primarily known for his defensive prowess and his game-calling skills, Freehan won the first of five consecutive Gold Gloves in 1965 and, on June 15, 1965, he set a record by making 19 putouts in a single game—thanks in large part to Denny McLain's 15 strikeouts in 6.2 innings of relief work.

At the beginning of the 1967 season, Freehan experimented with moving closer to the plate on the advice of new manager Mayo Smith and batting coach Wally Moses, and his hitting improved. Although he was hit by pitches 20 times that year, he hit .282 with 20 home runs and 74 RBI. It was an exceptional season, as Freehan caught 138 games with only six passed balls and eight errors, and he played in 155 games; no other catcher in the majors led his team in games played. Moreover, much to the consternation of Smith and the Tigers, Freehan caught all 15 innings of the 1967 All-Star Game in Anaheim. On September 10, Freehan was hit by a pitch in the third inning of the first game of a doubleheader, spoiling Joel Horlen's otherwise-perfect game. At the end of the season, on September 26, Freehan was ejected from a game for the first time in his career, slamming his mask into the dirt after the Yankees' Horace Clarke stole second base. "I wasn't arguing about the stolen base," Freehan explained later. "The pitch was a strike.... [Umpire Hank] Soar called it a ball. I couldn't believe it." His next ejection would occur nearly eight years later, on August 12, 1975, when he argued over a ball-four call to the Texas Rangers' Mike Hargrove. Although Detroit finished one game behind Boston's "Impossible Dream" team for the AL flag, Freehan had an outstanding season, and he was voted the 1967 Tiger of the Year by the local chapter of the Baseball Writers Association of America.

During the Tigers' 1968 championship season, Freehan caught 155 regular-season games and all seven World Series games. In the regular season, he set career-high marks with 25 home runs, 73 runs scored, and 84 RBI, and he was hit by pitches 24 times. Bothered that he was hitless in the first five games of the World Series, Freehan shrugged, "You've got to understand that you're facing Bob Gibson in three of those games. That's not a joy for anybody." In the first five games of the World Series, the Cardinals tested Freehan's arm, stealing 11 bases in 16 attempts, but he managed to corral the running game in Games 6 and 7.

Freehan's role in one of the most controversial plays in World Series history is familiar to most Tigers fans. The Cardinals led 3–2 when speedster Lou Brock tried to score from second on Julian Javier's single to left field. Freehan caught Willie Horton's perfect one-hop throw and blocked the plate, and Brock, who decided not to slide, was tagged out. "I've got to thank [University of Michigan football coach] Bump Elliott if I block the plate well," Freehan said. Writing about the play, the *Los Angeles Herald*'s Milton Richman said, "What makes [Freehan] so extraordinary is that he plants his two big feet firmly in the ground, doesn't bother giving the base runner barreling down on him from third base so much as a sidelong glance and plain refuses to budge even when said base runner hits him at midship like a torpedo. For that he has the respect of ballplayers everywhere. They know they don't make catchers like Freehan anymore." White Sox manager Eddie Stanky added, "On any close play at the plate, it's like running into a freight train."

Freehan also caught Tim McCarver's foul popup near the first-base dugout to secure the final out in Game 7. The sight of Mickey Lolich leaping into Freehan's arms will always be an iconic image in Detroit baseball lore. "When Lolich jumps on you, well, he's not a small man," Freehan said. "But it was a great feeling!" Finishing the World Series 2-for-24 with a double, Freehan observed, "I know I wasn't very successful in hitting, but I've got the same World Series ring as everybody else." Remarkably, Freehan was the only AL player to finish among the top three in MVP voting in both 1967 and 1968.

In 1969, the Tigers finished in second place, a distant 19 games behind Baltimore, and Freehan batted a respectable .262 with 16 home runs in 143 games. Throughout the 1969 season, the catcher kept a ballplayer's clubhouse diary, which would be published the next year as *Behind the Mask: An Inside Baseball Diary*. Published a decade after Jim Brosnan's *The Long Season* and the same year as Jim Bouton's *Ball Four*, Freehan's *Behind the Mask* did not display the literary insights of Brosnan's book or the scandalous revelations of Bouton's. For the most part, the book was, as Freehan explained, "a story about a ballclub. A catcher, a manager, and the pitcher." Unfortunately, as the 1970 season opened, pitcher Denny McLain was in the headlines again, serving a suspension related to a gambling investigation, so when *Sports Illustrated* published excerpts from Freehan's diary, it was no surprise to anyone that the McLain passages were featured in the magazine. At the center of the controversy was Freehan's accusation that McLain was often allowed to break club rules and that the coaching staff was powerless to stop him. McLain is "the best pitcher in the American League," Freehan wrote, "but it's an individual thing vs. a team thing." Ironically, after these excerpts were published, the same Tigers who resented McLain's special treatment felt Freehan had violated the sanctity of the clubhouse. "My book is about what it's like to be a catcher and go through a season," Freehan explained, "but what appeared in the magazine was not an accurate representation." Sportswriter Joe Falls speculated that some of the vitriol surrounding Freehan's book was due to poor timing: "If they had won the pennant last year, what Freehan had to say about McLain might have come out as being rather humorous: Look at that Denny, will you? Isn't he a rascal?"

Thus, 1970 was a rough year for Freehan. While his defense behind the plate was still impeccable, his batting average dropped to .241, and the team fell to fourth place. Still bothered by the 1965 spring training base-running injury, Freehan consented to spinal surgery to prolong his career as an everyday catcher. "Some days were good and some days were bad," Freehan recalled. "It got so my legs would be numb on certain days when I stepped out of my car at the ball park." On September 2, 1970, Freehan had bone graft surgery on the fifth vertebra of his lower back. As always, the durable catcher recovered quickly, and three months later, he was hiking on a deer-hunting weekend with Al Kaline, Mickey Stanley, and other players.

Although fans booed Freehan after the publication of *Behind the Mask*, all was forgotten when the catcher made a strong comeback from the surgery in 1971. Under Billy Martin, the Tigers bounced back into second place, and Freehan topped AL catchers with a .277 batting average, 21 home runs, and 71 RBI, while he caught 144 games, more than anyone else in the league. Freehan had the opportunity to start the All-Star Game at Tiger Stadium in place of the injured Ray Fosse, and had a three-homer game in a 12–11 loss to Boston that August 9.

With a healthy back and the acquisition of new backup catcher Tom Haller, Freehan anticipated another good season behind the plate in 1972. Freehan caught 105 games that season, batting .262, hitting 10 home runs and driving in 56 RBI, but he fractured his right thumb late in the season when tagging out Boston's Carl Yastrzemski on a play at the plate. The Tigers finished first in American

League East, but they were defeated by Oakland in the American League Championship Series. Freehan hit better in this postseason than he did in 1968, securing a .250 average and a home run in Detroit's Game 3 victory, but the Athletics stole seven bases thanks in part to Freehan's bum thumb.

"Defense…isn't just talent," Freehan believed, "that's concentration and work. I always called my games. Sure, I always had eye contact with my manager, but I was the one calling the pitches." The next year, when Billy Martin platooned him at catcher and questioned his game-calling skills, the proud Freehan resented his manager. Feeling that he was not given sufficient opportunity to prove himself, Freehan struggled with a lowly .234 average and 29 RBI, playing in only 110 games (his lowest total in 10 years). "I was never platooned before, not even part-time. I wouldn't have minded if the figures showed I couldn't hit right-handers. But they don't. I wouldn't mind losing my job if I was doing a lousy job." What bothered Freehan more than his poor performance at the plate was that Martin also second-guessed the pitches Freehan called, even publicly questioning some pitches that were ordered from the bench.

Freehan returned in 1974 prepared to prove himself, splitting time at catcher and first base under new manager Ralph Houk. With his poor showing the previous season and with the rise of Thurman Munson and Carlton Fisk as the league's premier catchers, Freehan felt he had to reestablish himself, but only two months into the season, the American League's all-star catcher for the past 10 years was shifted to first base. In the Tigers' biggest offensive bonanza of the year, Freehan belted a grand slam and drove in seven runs against the Yankees on September 8, 1974. Although his offensive production improved from the previous year—he hit .297 with 18 home runs and 60 RBI in 1974—Freehan was the cornerstone of a December deal that would have sent him with Mickey Stanley—"remains of a bygone era," according to Detroit sportswriter Jim Hawkins—to the Philadelphia Phillies for catcher Bob Boone. As Freehan was preparing his family for the move to Philadelphia, the deal was nixed by the Phillies at the last minute.

Nevertheless, after the trade failed, Freehan could see the writing on the wall. Going into spring training in 1975, Houk tabbed Freehan as the Tigers' starting catcher, unless "one of these other guys proves he's better than Bill is." At age 34, Freehan caught 113 games, hitting .246 with 14 home runs and 47 RBI, and he returned to the All-Star Game for the eleventh time. But over the winter, the Tigers traded for Milt May, putting Freehan in a reserve role for the first time in his career. May caught only six games before being sidelined for the season with a broken ankle. Freehan, as part of a backstop triumvirate, caught 61 games in 1976 as did Bruce Kimm (John Wockenfuss was behind the plate in 59 contests), and on December 12, 1976, the Tigers gave Freehan his unconditional release. Although he still believed he could contribute on the diamond, he realized how fortunate he was to have played on his hometown team for his entire 15-year major league career. Still, when the Tigers offered Freehan a job managing Montgomery in the Class AA Southern League, he declined, explaining that "I can't feed my family on a minor league manager's salary."

In retirement, Freehan still felt the pull of the game, particularly when he saw the opportunity to teach. "You can't take the baseball out of the boy," he said. After he retired from major league baseball, Freehan served as the president of Freehan-Bocci & Company, an automobile manufacturer's representative agency he founded in suburban Detroit in 1974, where he worked with former teammate Jim Northrup. In 1989, disturbed by an NCAA investigation that revealed illegal payments to players, Freehan called University of Michigan athletic director Bo Schembechler to ask about the once-successful baseball program. Two weeks later, he put his business career on hold and took over as the Wolverines' head baseball coach. Weathering two years' probation, Freehan coached Michigan baseball until 1995, reestablishing the integrity of the program and finishing with a 166–167–1 record. He left coaching to devote more attention to his business interests, although he was lured back to serve as Detroit's organizational catching instructor from 2002 to 2005. Today, Freehan lives in the Detroit suburb of Bloomfield Hills with his wife, Pat. The Freehans have three daughters: Corey Sue, Kelley, and Cathy.

A driven leader and the best catcher in the American League for almost a decade, Freehan was an intelligent and durable backstop who caught more than 100 games for nine consecutive seasons. He won five Gold Gloves, was selected for 11 All-Star teams and played in eight All-Star games, retiring with a .262 lifetime batting average, 758 RBI, and 200 home runs (100 at home and 100 on the road). When he retired, Freehan held the major league career records for most chances (10,714) and putouts

(9,941), and highest fielding average for a catcher (.993). Bill James ranks Freehan as the twelfth-best catcher of all time. Freehan was inducted into the Michigan Sports Hall of Fame in 1982, and Tigers fans voted him as catcher in 1999 for the All-Time Tiger Team.

References

Publications

Cantor, George. *The Tigers of '68: Baseball's Last Real Champions.* Dallas: Taylor. 1997.

Freehan, Bill (Steve Gelman and Dick Schaap, eds.). *Behind the Mask: An Inside Baseball Diary.* New York: World. 1970.

Hawkins, Jim, and Dan Ewald. *The Detroit Tigers Encyclopedia.* Champaign, Ill.: Sports Publishing. 2003.

James, Bill. *The New Bill James Historical Baseball Abstract.* New York: Free Press. 2001.

Articles

Hano, Arnold. "Bill Freehan: Tough Leader of the Tigers." *Sport,* August 1968, pp. 57–62.

Sargent, Jim. "Bill Freehan: A Key Member of the 1968 Champion Tigers." *Baseball Digest,* June 2000, pp. 58–65.

Web Sites

"Bill Freehan." *www.baseball-reference.com.*

Other Sources

Bill Freehan clipping file, National Baseball Hall of Fame Library.

1968   Tigers

Rich Shook presents:
Tigers In the News

Tuesday, May 28
John Hiller relieved Les Cain in the third inning and shut out the Angels the rest of the way for a slump-stopping 4–1 victory. George Brunet, a native of Houghton, Michigan, allowed four in the first with Bill Freehan hitting a two-run double and scoring on Horton's home run.

Wednesday, May 29
Denny McLain became the AL's first eight-game winner with a 13-strikeout effort. (In the NL, Juan Marichal of the Giants also had eight wins.) McLain pitched a four-hit shutout with one walk. Horton hit a two-run home run, giving him five home runs and eight RBI in six games of batting against California pitching.

Thursday, May 30
The Tigers made believers out of Angels manager Bill Rigney with a 7–3 win over California. "From what I saw the last four days, I'd have to say the Tigers are the team to beat in our league," said Rigney, whose Angels knocked Detroit out of a chance to win the 1967 race. "They have good pitching, good hitting and a strong defense. What more can you ask?" Joe Sparma won his sixth straight decision from the Angels dating back to August 19, 1964.

Friday, May 31
Detroit 1, New York 0. Willie Horton hit a seventh-inning home run, his 12th in May and third in four games, and Mickey Lolich spun a four-hitter for his first victory since May 7. He left following his first shutout of the season for another weekend of National Guard duty. Lolich gave up singles to Ellie Rodriguez and pinch-hitter Charlie Smith in the eighth, fanned Horace Clarke, then got Roy White on a deep fly ball to Northrup in right. Pinch-runner Gene Michael tagged up and advanced to second, which gave manager Smith the opportunity to intentionally walk Mantle, which he did. Andy Kosco flied out to end the inning. "We would have pitched to Mantle if Michael stayed on first," Smith said, but we wouldn't have given him anything to hit."

Saturday, June 1
Six of the first seven New York batters singled as the Yankees jumped out to a 4–0 lead. Pat Dobson relieved shaky starter Les Cain and gave up a pop-fly RBI single to a young third baseman by the name of Bobby Cox, who went on to much greater fame as a manager. He pitched to 18 more batters with only one of them reaching base, on a walk. Bill Monbouquette, who once pitched for the Bengals, had Detroit baffled for two innings but Bill Freehan hit a two-run single in the third and solo home runs by Willie Horton and Norm Cash opening the sixth tied the score. Jim Northrup singled to open the seventh against Dooley Womack, stole second and continued to third when second baseman Horace Clarke cut in front of shortstop Tom Tresh, allowing catcher Jake Gibbs's throw to go into center. With the infield drawn in, Freehan grounded a single through the left side for a 5–4 lead. Lasher worked the final three innings to gain the 5–4 win.

Sunday, June 2
Denny McLain took a rare no-decision in the opener, which New York won, 4–3, but Detroit came back to win the second game easily, 8–1. John Hiller made his first start of the season in the second game and carried a three-hit shutout into the ninth that was spoiled by three New York singles. "It's not as hard to go from relief to starting as it is to go from starting to relief," said Hiller, 3–1 on the season. "When you start, you can give up a hit and it won't hurt too much. But in relief you go in and bear down right away." Mickey Stanley hit his first career grand slam off Steve Barber in the six-run fifth. Manager Mayo Smith was ejected in the ninth inning of the opener—his first thumbing ever in the majors—when the Yankees scored the winning run; Tresh had slid in under Jim Price's tag. Jon Warden took the loss. Ray Oyler went 0-for-7 in the doubleheader and his batting average dipped to .154. "Detroit may be the first team in history to win the pennant with a shortstop hitting .120," one wag said. "What makes you think he'll be hitting that high?" Cash cracked.

Monday, June 3
Boston scored four runs in the fifth off Joe Sparma while Jim Lonborg, making his second relief appearance of the season after off-season left knee surgery following a ski injury, held off Detroit in a 4–3 Red Sox victory. The Tigers had scored twice in the seventh and had the tying run on third when Lonborg was summoned by manager Dick Williams. Lonborg hit Bill Freehan with a pitch (he was hit 44 times in 1967–68 and 114 times in his career) to load the bases but Willie Horton hit into a threat-ending fielder's choice.

Lenny Green

by Bill Nowlin

Season	Age	G	AB	R	H	2B	3B	HR	RBI	BB	SO	SB	CS	BA	OBP	SLG
1968 Tigers	35	6	4	0	1	0	0	0	0	1	0	0	0	.250	.400	.250
Career Totals		1136	2956	461	788	138	27	47	253	368	260	78	41	.267	.351	.379

Scout Joe Krich of the St. Louis Browns followed ballplayer Lenny Green during his days at Detroit's Pershing High School and soon after Green graduated, Krich signed him on the very last day of 1952 to a contract with York (Pennsylvania) of the Class B Inter-State League. Green never played for York, though, nor for the Browns. His next games were for the Army.

Leonard Charles Green (born January 6, 1933, in Detroit) was the middle of three sons born to Eugene and Anna Green. Gene Green worked at the Ford Motor Company stamping plant in suburban Dearborn. Anna ran a flower shop. Lenny's older brother Willie and younger brother Donald both became teachers. Neither really pursued baseball; Willie ran track in college, and Donald played baseball in high school but didn't take it any further. Lenny's father first inspired him to play ball. It came naturally, he explained in an August 2007 interview. "I've always liked baseball. My dad liked it. Dad worked for the Ford Motor Company and he played for the plant team. Only in the plants. He mostly played in the outfield. We had good sandlot programs here in Detroit and I got involved in them early." Lenny himself primarily played outfield.

He played for his high school team and played in the Detroit Baseball Federation at Northwestern Field. Jerry Griffin, a member of the Mayo Smith Society and a contemporary of Green's, recalls seeing Lenny on the Detroit sandlots: "Lenny was a very graceful athlete, who could run like a deer and was a strong line drive hitter," Griffin remembers. Green was "the ultimate team player who always had a big smile for everyone he met." Lenny was drafted into the Army not long after he finished high school and spent two years in the infantry, stationed at Camp Atterbury, Indiana, and Fort Carson, Colorado. He kept up his baseball skills, though: "I played a lot of ball. Billy Martin and Zach Monroe, a lot of guys played. Martin was on my team. We played in the Army tournament in San Antonio, Texas. Willie Mays was there, too. Don Newcombe and them. We all met at the tournament. I played against them. And then the next year, I went down there and played baseball."

Green was referring to his first assignment in pro ball, coincidentally with San Antonio in the Texas League in 1955, after his discharge from the Army as a corporal. He was still in the same system in organized ball, but since the Browns franchise had relocated from St. Louis after the 1953 season, Lenny was now playing in the Baltimore Orioles chain. With San Antonio he hit .216 as he got his feet wet with 116 at-bats. He downplays his stint in San Antonio: "I never even hardly got on the field. I'd sit there a while and then I went to Wichita. I don't remember 59 games (laughs). I was there about a month or so. They didn't give me much opportunity to play. I played a lot when I got to Wichita." And he took full advantage of the opportunity, batting .302 in 78 Western League games.

In 1956, Green spent the full season with Columbus in the Class A South Atlantic League, which the left-hander led both in batting average (.318) and runs scored (92). After hitting just one home run the year before, he showed some power, hitting 13 for Columbus and driving in what would be a career-high 83 runs. In 1957, Lenny played outfield for the Triple A Vancouver Mounties. Over the course of 505 at-bats, he averaged .311 at the plate (five homers, 57 RBI) and was center fielder on the Pacific Coast League all-star team. On August 25, he was called up to the Orioles and hopped right into action, appearing in both halves of a doubleheader against the White Sox in Chicago. He was 0-for-3 in his first game, and a second-inning error in center allowed Chicago to score the third run of a 6–2 White Sox win. Lenny's first major league hit came in his fifth game, at Cleveland on August 29. He entered the game in the third inning, replacing Bob Nieman in the lineup, and found himself batting with the bases loaded in the top of the fifth with nobody out. Mike Garcia was pitching for the Indians, and Green tripled to right field, then scored two batters later on Tito Francona's sacrifice fly. Those were the only four runs in a 13–4 loss. He hit his first major league home run during a September 18 night game at Baltimore's Memorial Stadium, off Chicago's Jim Wilson, a solo blast, also in a losing effort. In 1957, Green appeared in 19 games, and hit .182 in 22 at-bats, driving in five runs.

In the winter of 1957–1958, Chico Carrasquel arranged for Green to play ball in the Venezuelan League. Green believes the extra work helped: "I hadn't had a chance to play regularly in the big leagues, and if you don't play every day it's tough … I got my playing in and got a chance to see a lot of pretty fair ballplayers down in South America." Green broke spring training with Baltimore and appeared in 69 games, playing at all three outfield positions. It wasn't a productive season offensively, his first RBI not coming until the last day of May. He scored only five runs over the first couple of months, too, batting with an average that declined as the season progressed to the point that he was hitting an even .200 on Memorial Day. He played through July 26, raising his average to .231 but with only four RBI and increasingly as a late-inning defensive replacement who saw only one at-bat in his last 13 games. After the game on the 26th, he was optioned to Baltimore's International League farm club in Rochester. There, Green completed the season, hitting .261 over his next 180 at-bats.

Green had kept busy, though, and had his own daily sports program—when the team was at home—on Washington radio station WUST beginning in the summer of 1958.

In 1959, he made the big-league club again, and was again used late in games for his first half-dozen appearances. His first start came on April 19 against the Senators, and he had hits in both halves of the day's doubleheader. Green hit .292 with the Orioles, but not that productively. His only two RBI came on April 26 at Yankee Stadium when he hit a sixth-inning home run off Duke Maas. He scored only three runs, one on his homer. The Washington Senators were looking to replace Albie Pearson, who had been the American League Rookie of the Year in 1958 but was slumping badly in his sophomore season. They wanted Green and dealt Pearson for him May 26. Lenny played for Washington against the O's in Baltimore the very next day as a sixth-inning defensive replacement. He flied out in his only at-bat. At the time of the trade, the *Washington Post* called Green "a great fielder with tremendous speed and a better-than-average arm" and revealed that Baltimore had been thinking of releasing him as far back as 1955 but that Orioles manager Paul Richards was so impressed with his defense that he "issued orders to keep Green in the Baltimore organization."

Green, however, did not enjoy playing under Richards. He was straightforward about it: "I didn't enjoy playing for him. I didn't like his managing." Allowing that "he was a good one, manager and all that, but just…. If you knew him, you either liked him or you didn't." Happy to be with Washington, playing for Cookie Lavagetto, Green found a much better situation. With more playing time (he had 190 at-bats the remainder of the season, batting .242 with two homers and 15 RBI), he contributed but was still most highly regarded for his defense. He was lucky to escape serious injury in mid-September when his car struck an ambulance returning from a hospital with such force that Green's car slammed the ambulance into three parked cars. There were no injuries, and the worst Green suffered was a speeding ticket. The *Washington Post*'s Shirley Povich reported that Lavagetto considered him sure-handed in the field and the best baserunner on the club.

In the winter of 1959, Green signed to play ball in the Venezuelan League. It was in 1960 that he first broke through offensively, with a very strong .294 season and a .383 on-base percentage. He drove in 33 runs and scored 62 times. Then he found himself in another franchise shift as the Senators resettled in Minnesota as the Twins, while an expansion team began its first year in Washington. Lenny much enjoyed three-plus seasons with the Twins. "I loved it," he recalls. In 1961, he hit .285 in an even 600 at-bats as the team's regular center fielder, playing between Jim Lemon in left and Bob Allison in right. He led the club in base hits with 171, hit nine home runs, and drove in 50 runs. Green enjoyed a 24-game hitting streak May 1–28, 1961, which remained the Twins record until Ken Landreaux surpassed it in 1980. Sam Mele took over as manager in mid-June.

In 1962, the Twins made a run for it. Vic Power came in to play first base, and Harmon Killebrew moved to left field. The Twins finished in second place, just five games behind the Yankees in the 10-team league. Green's .271 was a higher average than those of Killebrew or Allison, but the two flanking outfielders combined for 77 homers and 228 RBI (The Killer led the league in both categories). Lenny hit a career-high 14 home runs and had his best year driving in runs in the major leagues with 63 RBI. Green had a good sense of humor. One Twins fan, accepting the Minnesota Historical Society's invitation to reminisce about the club, fondly remembered, "One early summer night, the fog was so thick the game was delayed. The crowd roared when Lenny Green ran to center field with a miner's hat with the light on atop the helmet. The game did eventually resume."

As did the Twins, Green had an off-year in 1963, batting .239 as rookie Jimmie Hall earned more at-bats. Hall homered a then-rookie record 33 times for the Twins that year. "I knew I was in trouble," Green later told Boston sportswriter Larry Claflin. "Mele had to keep Hall in there the way he was hitting." Green still appeared in 145 games, but had only 280 at-bats. His best day came on May 29 in Cleveland, when his two-out, two-run homer in the top of the ninth beat the Indians, 7–6.

In the off-seasons, Green was often invited to team functions and promotional events. In early 1964, he ranked tops among the players in a bowling tournament. He was also one of four Twins players named to an in-house committee to study the problem of planning for racially integrated housing arrangements at their Orlando spring training locale. In 1964, he led the Twins in hitting during the exhibition season but became a well-traveled ballplayer, playing for four teams: the Twins, the Angels, the Hawaii Islanders, and, again, the Orioles. With Jimmie Hall taking over in center, and with Killebrew and Tony Oliva in the outfield, Green was marginalized and spent what must have been a very discouraging first two months with the Twins. He only had 15 at-bats and never once hit safely, though he walked four times and scored three runs. On June 11, he was packaged in a three-team, five-player trade, traveling to the Angels with Vic Power. With only occasional work, he was hitting .184 through July 10 but, as he explained, "I never got a chance to play. They sent me to Honolulu to get in shape." In 16 late-July games in the Pacific Coast League, Lenny hit .333 with six home runs for Hawaii and was brought back up. Six multi-hit games helped him bring his .184 average up to a more respectable .250, and the Orioles reacquired him for a sum reported as slightly more than the $20,000 waiver price. For the second time, he played his next game against the team that had just traded him. Sold to the Orioles on September 5, he played against the Angels that day, coming on in the eighth to replace Charlie Lau defensively in left. With Baltimore, Lenny hit .190 with just one run batted in during 21 at-bats; and went hitless as a pinch-hitter.

Green was a nonroster invitee to spring training with the Boston Red Sox in 1965, the property of Baltimore's Rochester ballclub but with Boston on a "look-see" basis. Green had telephoned Orioles GM Lee MacPhail and asked if he could be placed with another team during the exhibition season to see if he could catch on. MacPhail found interest from both Boston and Houston, and Green chose Boston. If he made the team, the Orioles would sell him at a predetermined price, believed to be $25,000. He excelled, leading the Red Sox in spring training with a .385 mark. On March 30 Boston announced his purchase from Rochester. "I had no intention of starting the season with Green in center field," acknowledged Red Sox manager Billy Herman. "But Lenny hit so well he forced his way in there. He's a real hustler." Green kicked off the year for the Red Sox with two home runs on Opening Day in Washington. It was the fourth time Green had hit a home run on an opening day. In 1961 and 1962, he hit homers in the home opener for the Twins, and in 1963 he hit one in the season opener.

Green was the primary center fielder for 1965, between Carl Yastrzemski in left field and Tony Conigliaro in right. His .276 average was a little higher than Tony C's, but Conig hit a league-leading 32 homers. Green drove in just 24 runs, though two of those came on another day he hit two home runs—June 19 in Chicago. Pitcher Bill Monbouquette appreciated Green's work; the two round-trippers accounted for the only two runs in a 2–1 win over the White Sox.

This was a season in which the Red Sox drew few customers, and 1966 wasn't much better—though the team played very well indeed in the second half. They nonetheless finished just a half-game out of last place, and few could have foreseen that they would win the pennant in 1967. "I enjoyed Boston," Green reflects. "They treated us real nice. I had a real nice time." On the team, he says, "It wasn't that we were that bad. We didn't win like we should have won."

That there were racial undertones in Boston is undeniable. The Red Sox were the last major-league team to integrate, in 1959, and there were strong suspicions that there was an unspoken racial quota in place. Larry Moffi and Jonathan Kronstadt report a story from Earl Wilson: "When the Red Sox acquired two black players, pitcher John Wyatt and outfielder José Tartabull, on June 6, Wilson told his black roommate, Lenny Green, that there were now too many black players [seven] on the ball club. Although the remark was made half in jest … to no one's surprise, the phone rang the next morning." Wilson and Joe Christopher had been shipped to Detroit for Don Demeter and a player to be named later. A week later, Julio Navarro was named as that player. Now Green became a big help to one of the other black players, rookie George Scott. The two become roommates after Wilson left. Scott says, "He was definitely a tremendous help to me … trying to get me to recognize the curve ball and all of that. Lenny was not only good for me, Lenny was good for the Red Sox. He was one of them guys who knew where he was in baseball, and knew what he could do in baseball. And he'd just stretch out and help as many guys as he possibly could. And it wasn't only the black guys." Scott thought Green would have become a coach or manager had he played in a slightly later era.

With Yaz fixed in left and Conigliaro in right, Green shared playing time with Demeter, Tartabull, and a number of other outfielders. Limited to 133 at-bats, he hit .241, and with center-fielder heir apparent Reggie Smith waiting in the wings, there wasn't room for Lenny Green under incoming manager Dick Williams. To no one's surprise, he was released by the Red Sox on October 21, 1966. "I wasn't surprised at being released," he later told the *Chicago Daily Defender*. "They had to make room for this kid Reggie Smith. He's a real good one." Lenny figured he wasn't quite finished yet. The team he signed with was a surprise, though. It hardly seemed as if the Tigers needed him in their outfield. They had Gates Brown, Willie Horton, Al Kaline, Jim Northrup, and Mickey Stanley—but farm director Don Lund still succeeded in talking Lenny Green into signing a minor league contract with the Toledo Mud Hens, just in case.

Green hadn't experienced being a free agent before, though. Neither had he won a pennant. Part of Lund's pitch was that Green could commute back and forth between Toledo and his home in Detroit. The chance that he might get called up and have the chance at last to play for the team he'd dreamed of playing for as a kid was appealing as well. There were the road trips, though, and there were times it seemed a struggle as he told the *Washington Post*'s Bill Gildea, "Down there, we had to ride a bus almost everywhere. You would think we would have a good bus, but we didn't."

With Kaline hurt with a broken finger, once Gates Brown hurt his wrist crashing into the outfield fence, the Tigers put Brown on the disabled list and called up Green on June 30. He'd been hitting .329 for Toledo at the time and kicked off July with the Tigers hitting .429 through the first game of a July 9 doubleheader, with four multi-hit games in his first seven games. "I knew I wasn't done after Boston," he told UPI on July 11. "I was gonna keep playing, waiting for a break like this." He roomed with Earl Wilson, now a star pitcher for the Tigers. Wilson tied for the American League lead with 22 wins in 1967.

Naturally, that initial pace of Lenny's was bound to slacken, but, asked in mid-July if manager Mayo Smith would have a place for Green in his lineup once Brown and Kaline came back, Smith replied, "Yeah, he will, even if I have to give him mine." Green was a steady contributor, played for the rest of the season, and hit a very good .278 with 13 RBI. In the season's last week, Green's leadoff double in the sixth set him up to score the only run in a 1–0 win September 26 over the Yankees in New York and put the Tigers in a position to tie for the pennant on the final day. Rainouts helped give Detroit a three-day layoff before a pair of weekend doubleheaders at home against the Angels. As the Red Sox listened to the radio to learn whether there would be a playoff against Detroit, the Tigers fell just short in the ninth inning of the last game.

At spring training in 1968, Green was a nonroster invitee at the Tigers' camp in Lakeland, Florida. He was two weeks short of playing 10 full seasons in the major leagues. Those two weeks of service time could make a major difference in pension plans, but there's no indication that the invitation was merely an act of generosity. Green had performed very well in 1967 and hoped to contribute again in 1968. He admitted he'd been ready to hang it up after 1966, but was looking forward to the chance to help the Tigers go all the way. "Mayo asked me to come to spring training this year," he told the Associated Press. "I guess I'll wind up at Toledo. But I'm in good shape. And next year there will be expansion and some new ball teams."

It proved to be Green's last year. He was assigned to the Mud Hens as he expected. He played in 95 games that year, batting .257 with five homers and 28 RBI. And he had one last stint in the big leagues, appearing in six games between June 19 and June 30, four times as a pinch-hitter and twice defensively in left field. He was 1-for-4, and was walked once. Once back in Toledo, he continued to share pointers with some of the up-and-coming Tigers prospects but found he was being used less and less frequently. He had come to the end of the road in baseball.

In 1965, the year after he'd been traded from Minnesota, the Twins won the pennant. In 1966, the Orioles made it—and swept the World Series. In 1967, the year after he'd been released by Boston, the Red Sox won the pennant. Now, in 1968, a little more than three months after he'd last played for Detroit, his hometown Tigers won the pennant and the World Series. Lenny attended a couple of the games, but was no longer part of the team. The Series shares came to a little over $10,000; Lenny and five other bit players were given $200 apiece. Money completely aside, though, did he feel disappointed in some way, left out of the glory? "No, no. I had a good career and I enjoyed it. No, I don't ever feel left out. I feel blessed to ever have been able to play."

Green got a job with Ford, like his father before him, after his baseball career was complete and worked as a security supervisor for 27 years. He was not involved in baseball in any way; he told interviewer Ron Anderson that he was never tempted to seek out a managerial or coaching position. It simply wasn't his priority. He had his fill and wanted to move on. Family came first. He and his wife have one child, a daughter born late in the 1962 season. He had been fully enjoying his retirement from Ford until back miseries necessitated surgery in 2007.

References

Publications
Moffi, Larry, and Jonathan Kronstadt. *Crossing the Line: Black Major Leaguers 1947–1959*. Iowa City: University of Iowa Press. 1994.

Articles
Chicago Daily Defender, August 7, 1967.
The Sporting News, April 24 and May 1, 1965.
The Washington Post, September 19, 1959, and July 12, 1967.

Web Sites
www.mnhs.org/exhibits/baseball/memories.html

Other Sources
Anderson, Ron. Interview of George Scott, August 6, 2007.
Nowlin, Bill. Interview of Lenny Green, August 1, 2007.

1968 TIGERS

Rich Shook presents:
Tigers In the News

Tuesday, June 4
Boston and Detroit traded 2–0 wins in a doubleheader, the Tigers taking the second game. Mickey Lolich lost the first game as Gary Bell allowed three hits over 8.2 innings and Sparky Lyle retired Jim Price (batting for Gates Brown) to end the game. Lolich had a no-hitter until George Scott boomed a two-run double off the Green Monster with two out in the sixth. Pat Dobson took a two-hitter into the eighth in the second game and gave up a pair of two-out singles, bringing up Carl Yastrzemski. "I didn't seriously consider taking him out," Mayo Smith said. "He had good stuff and he was getting them out." Dobson got Yaz on a fly to center and got his first complete game in the majors. Don Wert hit a home run in the seventh, Price singled, and three straight walks forced in the second run.

Wednesday, June 5
Denny McLain started on two days' rest due to injuries and doubleheaders, giving up three runs in the first. He was taken out for pinch-hitter Eddie Mathews in the seventh. Mathews singled and Lolich ran for him. With runners on first and second and one out, Stanley grounded to short but Rico Petrocelli threw the ball into right field trying for a force at second to let the tying and winning runs score in Detroit's 5–4 win. "I had to have somebody pitch the game," Smith said of the decision to work McLain.

Thursday, June 6
Joe Sparma started on two days of rest, too, and beat Boston for the first time in nearly three years, 5–3. Detroit had a 2–0 lead after its first at-bats and scored three more in the third. Jim Northrup had a two-run home run in the opening inning and Norm Cash slugged a three-run shot in the third. Sparma gave up two singles plus a home run to Yastrzemski to bring Smith to the mound. "I told him he was throwing some lousy pitches and he wouldn't be around very long if he kept it up," Smith said.

Friday, June 7
A two-out triple in the ninth by Mickey Stanley gave Detroit its latest last-at-bat victory, 5–4 over Cleveland. Rookie left-hander Mike Paul had fanned six in 2.2 innings before Stanley's looping drive to right fell in front of Jose Cardenal and caromed off his knee toward the foul line, allowing Bill Freehan and Dick McAuliffe to score. "I wasn't going to right field," Stanley said. "I was just trying to keep from making an out." Paul had walked and scored on a single by Tony Horton in the top of the inning to give Cleveland a 4–3 lead in the battle between the first- and second-place AL teams. Paul slid in under Freehan's tag on a throw from right fielder Northrup, bringing Smith out for his second ejection of the week. "He (Jim Honochick) said Freehan juggled the ball," Smith said. "Bill had the ball in his bare hand. There's no way he can juggle it unless he drops the ball." Norm Cash and Willie Horton had hit consecutive homers to chase Steve Hargan in the seventh and Cash added another blast off Paul in the eighth to tie the score. The win boosted Detroit's margin over Cleveland to 3.5 games. (An in-game curiosity: Paul had retired the first two in the ninth when Dark switched him to first base in place of Tony Horton and brought in veteran right-hander Stan Williams to face Freehan. Freehan singled and Dark pulled Williams, returning Paul to the mound and bringing in outfielder Lee Maye to play first—a move that promptly backfired when Maye fumbled McAuliffe's ground ball for an error. Then came Stanley's hit.)

Saturday, June 8
The game's starting time had been pushed back to 8 p.m. two days earlier per Commissioner William D. Eckert's request no games be played during the funeral of assassinated presidential hopeful Robert Kennedy. Mickey Lolich pitched a seven-hitter with 10 strikeouts and no walks to pace Detroit to its fifth straight victory, 3–1, over Cleveland, expanding the club's lead to 4.5 games. McAuliffe tripled off left-handed fireballer Sam McDowell in the first after Lolich had given up a home run to Tony Horton in the top of the inning. Dick Tracewski struck out but Northrup grounded to short and McAuliffe beat a relay from Larry Brown to third sacker Max Alvis to catcher Jose Azcue. Freehan walked and Horton scored Northrup with a single. In the seventh, Stanley beat out a two-out infield single and Jim Price doubled him home.

Sunday, June 9
Luis Tiant bested Denny McLain, who lost for just the second time in 11 decisions, with a four-hit, 2–0 Cleveland win. McLain gave up just three hits but Duke Sims doubled and scored a run and also hit a home run. Gates Brown doubled for McLain in the eighth, making him 8-for-12 as a pinch-hitter.

John Hiller

by Larry Hilliard and Rob Hilliard

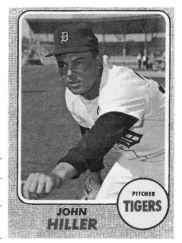

Season	Age	W	L	Pct	G	GS	CG	SV	IP	H	R	ER	BB	SO	ERA
1968 Tigers	25	9	6	.600	39	12	4	2	128	92	37	34	51	78	2.39
Career Totals		87	76	.534	545	43	13	125	1242	1040	438	391	535	1036	2.83

When John Hiller retired in 1980 after 15 seasons, all with Detroit, he was the last member of the 1968 world champion Tigers still playing in the majors. Best known, perhaps, for his work out of the bullpen, Hiller in fact started 43 games for the Tigers, 12 of them in the star-struck 1968 season. During his career, he pitched 13 complete games and racked up six shutouts. Of his 1,242 major league innings pitched, 962.2 were in relief. Hiller compiled these figures despite suffering a three heart attacks one off-season; he missed the entire 1971 season, and was perhaps the only major league player to resume his career after a heart attack.

Hiller's most remarkable season may have been 1974, when, pitching for a team that finished last in the American League East Division with a 72–90 record, Hiller won 17 games and lost 14, all in relief (he had no starts that season). His 17 relief victories were one less than the record of 18 set by Roy Face (his teammate on the 1968 world champions) in 1959 when Face was with the Pittsburgh Pirates. And his 14 defeats were two less than the record for relief losses later set by Gene Garber of Atlanta. All this by a native of Canada who grew up as a hockey fan.

Born on April 8, 1943, in Toronto, Ontario, the son of an auto body repairman and a homemaker, Hiller grew up in Scarborough, outside Toronto, playing hockey as a goaltender and hanging around Maple Leaf Gardens. He once jokingly said he would have given up a year of baseball just to spend a game between the pipes in the National Hockey League. But the die was cast when, to have something to do between hockey seasons, he took up baseball in the summer with the Kiwanis Club. He told an interviewer in 2006 that at a tryout camp in Toronto when he was 16 or 17, Charlie Dressen told him, "Son, I hope you haven't thrown out your hockey skates."

But the baseball bug persisted. "I just loved playing and got better and better," he recalled. "One time, I struck out 22 guys in seven innings— I think one guy got [on base] on a wild pitch—and that got some more attention. A great old scout named Cy Williams, out of Buffalo, took a look at me for the Tigers. ... Williams offered me $400 a month to play baseball. This was a time when I was finishing up eleventh grade, making $10 a week bagging groceries. Wasn't an especially hard decision. My bonus was a pair of shoes he had stashed in his car trunk."

Hiller played in Jamestown, New York, in the New York-Penn League in 1963, going 14–9 with 172 strikeouts in 181 innings and earning a promotion to the Class A Duluth-Superior Dukes of the Northern League in 1964. There he went 10–13, although he lowered his ERA from 4.03 with Jamestown to 3.45. He finished 1964 with a promotion to Double A Knoxville of the Southern League, making three starts for the Smokies. In 1965, he became a reliever for the Tigers' new Southern League affiliate, the Montgomery Rebels, and got a summons to Detroit in September. The first big-league hitter the 22-year-old Hiller faced that September 6 was Boston Red Sox shortstop Rico Petrocelli. Hiller said he was "totally intimidated" by the major leagues, but he wound up pitching five games in relief, allowing no runs in six innings and getting one save. (That month he also married Janis Patricia Baldwin.) Hiller started the 1966 season with the Tigers but pitched in only one game before catching pneumonia and being sent down to Syracuse, the Tigers' Triple A team, where he spent the rest of the year, except for one game with the Tigers. He started the 1967 season with the Tigers' new Triple A club in Toledo before being called up to the Detroit, with Pat Dobson, Fred Lasher, Daryl Patterson, and Mike Marshall, other untested players. The young pitchers bonded with one another on the way up, as they would with Tigers backup catcher, Jim Price. Hiller said, "Collectively, the younger guys called themselves the scrubbinis, we were just happy to be there." In relief, Hiller won the second game of a home doubleheader on July 23, 1967, against New York. (By the third inning of that game, smoke from rioting in Detroit was visible inside Tiger Stadium.) In late August Hiller was given a chance to start and he shined. He threw back-to-back shutouts against the Indians and Athletics, followed by a win over the contending California Angels in which he carried a shutout into the ninth inning. He had three more starts, but did not go more than six innings in any of them, and finished the season in the bullpen. Hiller was hit hard in the season's final game, giving up three runs after relieving Denny McLain in the third inning and being charged with the loss that eliminated the Tigers from the 1967 pennant chase. Despite that last game, it was a successful rookie season for Hiller. He pitched in 23 games, going 4–3 with a 2.63 ERA and an outstanding 49/9 strikeout/walk ratio.

In 1968 Hiller stayed with the Tigers all year as they won the pennant and World Series. He spent most of the first four months in the bullpen, but made three starts in June. He got a chance to move into the rotation in August when Mickey Lolich was moved to the bullpen (Lolich relieved in seven games that season) and the doubleheaders started piling up. In the first of those starts, on August 6, Hiller struck out the first six Indians, tying a major league record (the record has since been broken).

Hiller made nine starts the rest of the way, including a shutout of the White Sox in the first game of an August 20 doubleheader. Three days later against New York, he came in with nobody out in the eighth inning and wound up pitching a "complete game"—throwing nine shutout innings in a game that was called with the scored tied, 3–3, after 16 innings. He had two complete-game wins in September, including the game that clinched a tie for the American League pennant on September 16 against the Yankees. (Had the Baltimore Orioles lost that night, Hiller—not Joe Sparma—would be remembered as the man who won the pennant-clinching game.) He finished the year with 39 appearances, 12 of them starts, and went 9–6 with a 2.39 ERA. He led a quartet of relievers—Don McMahon (5–2), Fred Lasher (5–1), and Pat Dobson (5–8) were the other three—who were credited with two dozen wins for a 103–59 club.

Hiller pitched in World Series Games 3 and 4, in both cases doing mop-up duty in games in which the Tigers were well behind. He gave up four runs, three earned, in his second appearance, and ended the Series with a 13.50 ERA.

With a newly developed slider taught to him by pitching coach Johnny Sain, Hiller pitched in 40 games in 1969, eight of them starts. He shut out the Yankees on June 17, the third time he had kept New York scoreless over nine innings (counting the 16-inning tie) in a year. He went 4–4 but his ERA jumped by almost two runs, to 3.99. The next season was similar, with Hiller spending most of his time in the bullpen. He ended the year in the rotation, making four starts. On the last day of the 1970 season, Mayo Smith's last game as Detroit's manager, Hiller threw possibly the best start of his career, shutting out Cleveland 1–0, allowing only two hits and walking two while striking out 11—including seven in a row—to tie an American League record. It was his last major league game for 20 months. On January 11, 1971, Hiller suffered three heart attacks.

Hiller's recovery was one of the greatest sports comeback stories of all time. He underwent an experimental procedure called intestinal bypass surgery, intended to help him lose weight. The surgery was successful and by November 1971, Hiller was working out for three hours a day and losing weight (between 1968 and his heart attack, it had gone up from 185 pounds to 220 pounds). With renewed confidence he began to plan his comeback.

Hiller worked out at the YMCA in Duluth, Minnesota, until spring training of 1972. The Tigers offered him a $7,500 contract to be a minor league instructor, starting in spring training. "It was a comedown from $20,000 a year to play ball, but I hadn't had a paycheck for a year, so I took it," Hiller said. In dealing with young pitchers, he applied some of Sain's lessons about psychology. Meanwhile, while instructing young pitchers, he learned a changeup from John Grodzicki, a minor league pitching coach. It gave him a third pitch and made the fastball and slider more effective.

Hiller refined the changeup against the minor-leaguers he was instructing, getting feedback from Grodzicki. To go with his 90–91-mph fastball the changeup became the difference-maker in Hiller's baseball career. Still, the Tigers were nervous about playing him, so they took him north as a batting-practice pitcher. Before that, Hiller exercised a bit of bravado to keep himself in the Tigers' sights. When General Manager Jim Campbell came to Lakeland, Florida, Detroit's spring training headquarters, Hiller spotted him and took the offensive. "The second I saw him, I knew, I just knew—he was there to cut me loose," Hiller recalled. "Supposedly, he was there to check on the minor-leaguers, but I just knew it. So I got up from the bleachers, walked straight up to him, and said, 'Jim, if you're here to release me, go home. I'm not letting you release me.' And I walked away."

In July Hiller finally got a chance to pitch because Tigers hurlers Les Cain and Fred Scherman were having arm troubles, and he made the best of it. He hadn't faced any game action since the 1970 season. By now the Tigers had given him a contract for $17,000, a cut of $3,000 from what he was making before the heart attack. He faced Dick Allen, the American League MVP, in his first game back, and Allen clubbed a home run off him. The outing wasn't spectacular—in three innings pitched, Hiller gave up four hits, two runs, and one walk with two strikeouts—but he was back.

Hiller ended 1972 having pitched in 24 games with a 2.05 ERA. His strikeout/walk ratio was 26/13, and manager Billy Martin was holding him up as an example to the other pitchers. (Hiller says Martin liked veteran players, and "strategy-wise he was probably one of the best, he and Earl Weaver.") Still, his favorite manager was Ralph Houk. He says Houk didn't get enough credit for the 1984 team that won the World Series, many of whose star players got their start under Houk's 1974–1978 tenure in Detroit.

Hiller won Game 4 of the 1972 American League Championship Series in relief over Oakland, shutting off the Oakland A's after they had scored two runs in the top of the 10th and taking the win when the Tigers got three in the bottom of the inning. If not for a controversial call at first base, he might have saved the decisive Game 5 and returned the Tigers to the World Series. It was not to be, as Oakland won, 2–1.

In 1973, Hiller saved a league-leading (and at that time a major league record) 38 games, added 10 wins to his ledger, and was in at game's end 60 times in 65 appearances, finishing the season with a 1.44 ERA and striking out 124 batters in 125.1 innings. His record-tying 37th save occurred when he came into a 10–0 game in the ninth inning and allowed a run. That game, among others, helped prompt changes to the save rule. Hiller won both Comeback Player of the Year and Fireman of the Year honors. He finished fourth in the Cy Young Award voting and tied for fourth in the MVP voting.

Hiller and fellow fireman Rollie Fingers of Oakland contributed to the evolving thinking of the value of relief aces. Hiller was a pioneer in making the save a popular statistic. But he was used very differently than today's closers are. His 125.1 innings pitched in 65 games in 1973 were an average of almost two innings per game. He pitched more than one inning in 40 games. He came into the game in the sixth inning or earlier 13 times, in the seventh 11 times, and in the eighth 15 times. In 22 of his games, the Tigers were losing or tied when he came in. He pitched five or more innings three times, including a game on July 22 that he entered in the second inning and pitched 8.1 innings, striking out 10 before losing the game in the 10th on the only run he allowed.

Hiller followed up that performance by winning 17 games, losing 14, and saving 13 in 1974, throwing 150 innings. His playing weight, as listed in the 1974 Tigers yearbook, was 165 pounds. By now, he was the old hand in the bullpen. In 1975, he was having another fine season until a pulled muscle suffered during a game on July 25 put him out for the year. Mickey Stanley also suffered an injury in that game that would end his season, and without the two 1968 veterans, the Tigers went 13–51, including a team-record 19-game losing streak.

Hiller returned healthy in 1976 and resumed his role as the Tigers' main reliever. After pitching 55 games out of the bullpen, he started the final game of the season and shut out Milwaukee on four hits to gain his 12th win. In 1977, he returned to a starting role for a while, with seven starts between May 18 and June 26, going 2–5 in those games. His ERA ballooned to 3.56, his highest since 1969, and he went 8–14 with only seven saves. Again, he ended the season on a high note, beating the Yankees, 5–2, while throwing a complete game.

In 1978, Hiller's 92.1 innings were his fewest in a full season since 1967, even though he pitched in 55 games. He threw more than four innings in a game four times. He won nine games and had 15 saves and 7 blown saves (for his career, Hiller had 125 saves and 60 blown saves). It was clear in 1979 that Hiller's career was coming to an end. His 5.22 ERA was his career worst and his season ended prematurely in late August with a shoulder injury. Early in the 1980 season, Hiller pitched in 11 games, including four of four or more innings. He retired on May 30. His last game was on May 27, against the Yankees, but this time, they got the best of him, getting four runs and 10 hits off him in four innings.

Hiller retired with a then-franchise record of 125 saves. He had become the Tigers' all-time leader in games pitched with 545. Hiller reaped post-retirement rewards recognizing his inspiring comeback story, and his incredible record as a relief pitcher. "I was happy, my family was happy with my career," said Hiller. "I was 38 years old, the oldest guy on the team and the last link to our '68 championship. We had a young club, with Sparky Anderson in as the new manager, and he wanted to clean house from the old establishment. I told Jim Campbell that it was time for me to go and the comment was, 'I respect your decision.'" Hiller was the last of the 1968 Tigers to leave the playing ranks.

After retiring, Hiller tried to return to the Tigers as a roving pitching coach, but a circulatory blockage behind one knee ended that. In Lakeland, Florida, a surgeon told Hiller his leg would have to be amputated. In response, John headed home to Iron Mountain in Michigan's Upper Peninsula, where he lives year-round with his second wife, Linette. "I just enjoy the small-town flair.... You better just be like you're everybody else, and they'll accept you in a heartbeat."

Of his early days as a relief pitcher, Hiller says, "In those days, there was no one stopper. Pitchers who had a bad go ended up in the bullpen. You had to pitch your way out of the bullpen to get back in the lineup by doing spot starting and long relief. Then you might get a chance, say, in a doubleheader."

The Hutch Award in 1973 for fighting spirit and competitive desire—named for former Tigers manager Fred Hutchison, who died of cancer—and the American Heart Award are Hiller's "most honored moments."

John and Linette Hiller have been married since 1985. Linette has a son from a prior marriage and John has two children who reside in Orlando, Florida, and a third in North Carolina from his first marriage. He has a brother, Jim, who lives in the Toronto area.

Said Hiller in "Baseball Men—The Comeback": "Well, some people have told me I've been an inspiration, You don't know what it's meant to me. What can I say? I was just a ballplayer who wanted to make a living; I didn't set out to be a spokesman for anything, but I was happy for the opportunities to help when they came up. Every time I visited quite a few kids in the hospital or in cancer units, and every time I went there to help them, they helped me by showing their inner strength."

References

Publications

Cantor, George. *The Tigers of '68: Baseball's Last Real Champions*. Dallas: Taylor Trade Publishing. 1997.

Middlesworth, Hal. *Detroit Tigers 1974 Yearbook*. Detroit: Tigers Baseball Club. 1974.

Articles

Harwell, Ernie. "Hiller survives another scare" *Detroit Free Press*, September 19, 2005.

Handrinos, Peter. "Baseball Men—The Comeback" Available online at http://angels.scout.com/2/586736.html (accessed November 4, 2006)

Markusen, Bruce. "Comeback Kids—Remembering the Tigers of '68." *Cooperstown Confidential*, August 22, 2003. Available online at http://www.baseballguru.com/archives/entries/00000498.htm

Leggett, William. "Those Big Tiger Muscles" *Sports Illustrated*, June 5, 1967, p. 24, 27.

Sargent, Jim. "Jim Northrup Recalls His Playing Days with Tigers. (Turn Back the Clock)(Detroit Tigers)." *Baseball Digest*, February 1, 2004. Available online at http://www.encyclopedia.com/doc/1G1 112167130.html

Schechter, Gabriel. "John Hiller's Amazing Comeback" Originally posted at http://www.baseballhalloffame.org/li.../gs_050625.htm and available online at http://www.motownsports.com/forums/showthread.php?p=652441

Web Sites

www.baseballlibrary.com/ballplayers/player.php?name=John_Hiller_1943&page=chronology—"BaseballLibrary.com, The Home of Baseball History: John Hiller—chronology"

www.members.cox.net/hholtsb/HillerJ.jpg

www.usfamily.net/web/trombleyd/Northern%20L%20History.htm#Duluth—"Northern League Organization and Team Histories"

www.usfamily.net/web/trombleyd/Northern%20PlayersGL.htm—"Baseball The Biographical Encyclopedia," cited in "Northern League Players Who Made the Majors"

Other Sources

Hilliard, Larry, and Rob Hilliard. Interview with John Hiller, August 12, 2007.

Acknowledgments

Thanks to the Mayo Smith Society, to my co-author and brother Rob Hilliard, and of course to John Hiller for granting us the interview.

1968 TIGERS

Rich Shook presents:
Tigers In the News

Monday, June 10
No game. The Tigers announced the signing of University of Michigan sophomore outfielder Elliott Maddox, 20, who had led the Big Ten with a .467 average.

Tuesday, June 11
Detroit increased its lead over Baltimore and Cleveland to 4.5 games with 3-1 and 3-2 victories over Minnesota. Only two of the runs were earned. Jim Price drove in a pair of unearned runs in the first game while second baseman Cesar Tovar made two errors in the second. Tovar's wild relay on a double play try with one out and runners on first and second in the ninth let Tom Matchick score the winning run from second. Pat Dobson (2-0) struck out 10 and allowed five hits in 7.2 innings of the opener. Daryl Patterson finished up. Price's single gave Detroit two in the second. He doubled and scored on a Dobson single in the fifth. A single by Mickey Stanley plus an outfield error put him on second in the eighth inning. A Norm Cash single tied the score in the eighth inning. Tovar's first error let Stanley in with first Detroit run in the third. Joe Sparma pitched four-hit ball over seven innings with John Hiller (4-1) getting the win for two perfect innings of relief.

Wednesday, June 12
The Tigers topped the Twins, 2-1, for their eighth win in nine games. Dick McAuliffe's eighth-inning home run snapped 1-1 tie and gave Mickey Lolich (5-3) the win. Lolich gave up five hits but none after the fifth inning. He walked two and struck out nine. Eddie Mathews, 37, was placed on the disabled list with a herniated disk in his back. He was hitting .194 with three home runs and six RBI in 22 games with the Tigers. (Historical aside: One of the players mentioned as a possibility to replace Mathews was left-handed hitting first baseman Don Pepper, better known in later years as the father of golfer and golf commentator Dottie Pepper.)

Thursday, June 13
Denny McLain got back on the winning track, improving to 10-2 with a six-hit, 3-1 victory over Minnesota. He had six strikeouts and walked one against a Twins team that was without benched Harmon Killebrew (who pinch-hit later) and Bob Allison.

Friday, June 14
Earl Wilson made his first start since May 24 (sore heel) and pitched seven innings, allowing Chicago four runs over the first two innings. The Tigers came back to tie and Don Wert hit a home run in the 14th inning to give Detroit a 6-5 win over the White Sox. Ray Oyler had an RBI and Wilson smacked his second home run of the season and 28th of his career in the fifth with two teammates on base. Dobson entered in the eighth and pitched five scoreless innings. Mickey Stanley, Jim Northrup, and Bill Freehan had singles off Bob Priddy that gave Detroit a 5-4 lead in the top of the 13th. Pinch-hitter Gates Brown suffered a left thigh injury pulling back from an inside pitch in the inning. The White Sox tied the score when shortstop Luis Aparicio singled, went to third on a sacrifice, and scored when Norm Cash couldn't make a play at the plate on Pete Ward's grounder. Wert smacked Priddy's first pitch to give the Tigers their 15th win in their last turn at bat. John Hiller (5-1) went two scoreless innings to win.

Saturday, June 15
The White Sox stopped the Tigers' five-game winning streak with a 7-4 victory. Ken Berry hit a grand slam off Joe Sparma in the fourth inning to make it 5-1. Detroit purchased the contract of right-hander John Wyatt from the New York Yankees (who also sold Jim Bouton to minor league Seattle). Wyatt, 33, had been with New York just 30 days, having been bought from Boston. Wyatt was 1-4 with a 3.32 ERA over 19 innings covering 15 games. (Historical notes: Gene Mauch, manager during Philadelphia's 1964 collapse, was fired as Phillies manager, replaced by Bob Skinner. And Tigers Hall of Famer Sam "Wahoo" Crawford died at age 88 in Hollywood, California.)

Willie Horton

by Dan Holmes

Season	Age	G	AB	R	H	2B	3B	HR	RBI	BB	SO	SB	CS	BA	OBP	SLG
1968 Tigers	25	143	512	68	146	20	2	36	85	49	110	0	3	.285	.352	.543
Career Totals		2028	7298	873	1993	284	40	325	1163	620	1313	20	38	.273	.332	.457

A standout on the sandlots of Detroit, Willie Horton became the first black superstar for his hometown Tigers and spent parts of 15 seasons with the team. A tremendously powerful right-handed slugger, Horton was one of the strongest men in the game and launched 325 homers in his career. Extremely popular in Detroit, Horton worked in the Tigers front office after his playing career, where he helped bridge relations between the club and the African American community.

Born in Arno, Virginia, on October 18, 1942, William Wattison Horton was the youngest of 14 children—eight of them boys—of Clinton and Lillian Horton. His father moved the family to Detroit when Willie was five years old. Raised in the shadows of Briggs Stadium in the Jefferson Projects in downtown Detroit, Horton was a talented athlete despite his short, stocky frame that carried extra baby fat. Horton was a left-handed batter until age 10, when his father changed him to right-handed in Little League.

As a 17-year-old in 1960, he played outfield for the Detroit Lundquist team that won the national sandlot championship in a tournament in Altoona, Pennsylvania. Horton batted third on that team, directly in front of Bill Freehan, who would later be a teammate of Willie's on the Tigers. As a star slugger at Northwestern High School in Detroit, Horton hit a home run at Tiger Stadium in the city championship game, and earned the nickname "Willie the Wonder." After his senior year, the Tigers signed Horton to a $50,000 bonus.

At Duluth-Superior in the Northern league in 1962, Horton enjoyed a fine rookie season in pro ball, batting .295 with 15 home runs and earning comparisons to a young Roy Campanella because of his physical appearance and power from the right side of the plate. The performance earned him a promotion to Triple A Syracuse in 1963, but he was overmatched and quickly sent down to Knoxville of the Sally League, where he flourished with a .333 mark and 14 home runs. At Knoxville he earned a reputation for hitting the ball well to all fields. Called up by the Tigers at the tail end of the '63 season, Horton came through in his first two pinch-hit at-bats and finished the season with a 6-for-10 stretch against the Orioles.

Willie made a name for himself during spring training in 1964 when he led the team in home runs and drove in 18 runners. On Easter Sunday, he clubbed a ninth-inning, pinch-hit homer more than 420 feet to deep center field to win the first game of a doubleheader, and hit another game-winning homer in the second game. His play—and his weight—caught the attention of manager Charlie Dressen. The Tigers skipper stripped more than 20 pounds from Horton's frame during the spring, after the youngster reported weighing 222 pounds.

"He looks like a natural hitter to me," Dressen said. "Willie throws good, and he can run."

His spring heroics earned Willie a spot on the Tigers' roster, and he began the season platooning with veteran Bill Bruton in left field. But Horton struggled, especially against off-speed pitches, and slumped to an 8-for-59 start (.136 with no home runs). In mid-May, the Tigers shipped Horton to Triple A Syracuse, where Willie felt more comfortable playing every day, slugging 28 homers and batting

.288 with 99 RBI for the Chiefs. His efforts earned him another late-season call-up to Detroit. In his final game of the season, Horton clubbed a home run against Milt Pappas in Baltimore.

While playing winter ball in Puerto Rico in early 1965, Horton received tragic news. Both of his parents were killed in a New Year's Day car accident in Albion, Michigan. Horton quickly flew home to attend the services. The youngest child, Horton had been particularly close to his father, who had been in the stands at Tiger Stadium when his son hit his first major league home run, victimizing Robin Roberts.

Overcoming the death of his parents, Horton lost his usual off-season weight during the spring and made the big league club. "Whatever I do this year, I'm doing for my dad and mother," Willie said. He began the 1965 season as Detroit's fourth outfielder. But his hot-hitting quickly won him the left field job from Jim Northrup and earned him a spot on the American League All-Star team. In 143 games, the 22-year-old batted .273 with 29 homers and 104 RBI, finishing eighth in Most Valuable Player Award voting. During an East Coast road trip to Washington and Boston in May, Horton socked six homers in four games, each of the blasts traveling more than 400 feet. "Willie the Wonder" had arrived on the big-league scene.

Having established that he could hit right-handed pitching well enough to be in the lineup on a daily basis, Horton was entrenched in the starting lineup for Detroit in 1966. Once again he put up big offensive numbers, driving in 100 runs on the strength of 27 home runs. An ankle problem hampered him in 1967, but Willie still managed 19 homers and 67 RBI in 122 games. With the Tigers battling into the final weekend in a four-team race for the pennant, Horton hit homers in the first inning of the first games of doubleheaders on the last two days of the season to help defeat the Angels. However, Detroit lost the flag by one game.

That season, Horton thrust himself into the Detroit riots, fleeing Tiger Stadium in uniform to address the irate crowds in the streets of fire. Showing tremendous courage, Horton pled with Detroiters to calm the violence, but his efforts were in vain, and the city burned for nearly a week.

Horton was the most consistent bat in the Tigers' lineup in the magical 1968 season. In a season dominated by brilliant pitching performances, Horton's .285 average was fourth in the league, and his 36 homers were second to Frank Howard's 44. In the World Series against the Cardinals however, it was Willie's right arm that won him eternal fame with Detroit rooters. In the fifth inning of Game 5, with Detroit trailing 3–2 and St. Louis threatening to extend its lead, Lou Brock tried to score standing up on Julian Javier's single to left field. Horton fielded the ball and fired a one-hopper to home plate. Freehan caught the ball and tagged Brock to swing the momentum in Detroit's favor. The Tigers came back to win the game, 5–3, and captured the final two games to win the title. Horton batted .304 with six runs scored and three extra-base hits in the Series victory.

In contrast with the previous season, 1969 was filled with disappointment for Horton. Mired in a 4-for-35 slump on May 15, Willie left the team midgame and disappeared for four days due to "personal pressures." When he came back, he had lost more than $1,300 in pay and was admonished by Detroit General Manager Jim Campbell. On June 28 in Baltimore, Horton pulled up at second base on a double and tore thigh muscle in his right leg. The injury forced him to miss 10 games and relegated him to the bench for seven more. He played the final weeks of the season with a sore right hand. Nonetheless, Horton still managed 91 RBI and 28 home runs.

Horton tried something different during the off-season, doing road work in Detroit in the ice and snow to keep his weight down. He arrived for spring training in Lakeland in 1970 in the best shape of his career. But an injured ankle ended one of his best seasons on July 24 with his batting average at .305 with 17 home runs and 69 RBI. He enjoyed a career-high 15-game hitting streak and had one of the best days of his career on June 9, when he slugged three homers, including a grand slam, and knocked in seven runs in Tiger Stadium against Milwaukee.

More adversity came Horton's way in 1971, when on August 27, he was struck in the left eye with a pitch from Rich Hinton of the Chicago White Sox. The injury kept him out of the lineup for a month, but Willie still managed 22 homers, 72 RBI, and a .289 average in 119 games. On team picture day, sulking over a perceived slight by the front office, Willie refused to pose for the team photo. In the final game of the season at Cleveland, Horton butted heads with manager Billy Martin. After grounding out, Horton failed to run down the baseline, and Martin pulled Willie from the game, embarrassing the slugger. "I'm through playing in Detroit," the sensitive Horton snapped. But, Martin and Horton, who later became very good friends, mended their differences.

Detroit returned to the postseason in 1972 while Willie suffered one of his most frustrating seasons, hitting .231 with 11 homers in 108 games. He reported to spring training overweight and fought hard to shed the pounds, but never got on track, and suffered foot and shoulder ailments that hampered his effectiveness.

Following that disappointment, Horton arrived at spring training in 1973 in good shape and focused on a return to form. He did just that, hitting .316 in 111 games, spending much of the season among the batting leaders in the league. Now 30 years old, Horton continued to have troubles with his legs, especially after the All-Star break, which limited his playing time. "By the fourth inning my legs are so stiff the way it is that I can hardly move," Willie said. Horton also injured his wrist when he ran into a wall chasing a fly ball, but he credited his new roommate, veteran slugger Frank Howard, with helping him have one of his better seasons. He was also helped by a new daily exercise regimen that involved a broom handle Willie called "the wand."

Yet despite the broom handle, his nagging legs bothered Horton again in 1974, and in early July, after nearly a month without hitting a homer, he was shut down and underwent knee surgery. Even though he had been unable to run very well all season, Horton had managed to hit .298 with 47 RBI in 72 games. In April he was involved in a bizarre incident at Fenway Park when he lofted a high foul fly directly over home plate that struck a pigeon. The bird landed at the feet of Red Sox catcher Bob Montgomery. On the next pitch, Willie singled.

With the retirement of Al Kaline following the 1974 campaign, Horton was now an elder on the club. Having always been sensitive to his status in the clubhouse, Horton aimed to have a big 1975 and boost his salary into the $100,000 mark that Kaline had received. Spurred by that possibility, Horton stayed healthy all season for the first time in six years. Manager Ralph Houk helped the situation by using Horton exclusively as a designated hitter. Horton played in 159 games and set career marks at that time for hits and at-bats. His 92 RBI were 32 more than any other Tiger, and his 25 homers were nearly double that of any of his teammates. He was named DH on *The Sporting News'* AL All-Star team. Though he was not sure at first if he would like being a DH, Horton warmed to the role as the season wore on.

"The only reason I thought I might not like it was because I thought it might feel like I wasn't doing enough for the club," Horton said. "It's not that way though. Now I have to keep up with what's going on all the time."

But in November, Willie expressed his desire to put a glove on again, either in left field, or at first base. "I just turned 32 [he was really 33] and I don't want to think I can't do nothing but sit around and hit the rest of my life," Horton said.

With a fresh new $105,000 contract when the 1976 season opened, Horton was in the DH spot again as a veteran bat on a team rapidly getting younger with outfielders Ron LeFlore, Danny Meyer, and Ben Oglivie, first baseman Jason Thompson, and pitching phenom Mark Fidrych. "These kids are just coming along, just getting started, and I want to help them," Horton said. "I want them to learn to live on and off the field. I want them to learn to live together."

Horton got off to a strong start, leading the league in homers in April and earning Player of the Month honors. But Houk sat Willie against certain pitchers, shuttling Rusty Staub into the DH spot once or twice a week. Sulking, at one point Horton refused to take batting practice or shag flies. Then, in early June he hurt his knee and missed more than a month. When he returned, he was less than 100 percent and his average dropped from .299 to a season-ending mark of .262 with spotty power. With Staub, a defensive liability in the outfield, having an All-Star season, it was apparent Horton's DH slot was in jeopardy. Willie still begged to play left field again, but the emergence of Steve Kemp made that unlikely. Years of injuries had caught up with Willie, who at 33 was breaking down more often every season.

"If I had been the type of guy who could go out there and not play hard, I probably would have never gotten hurt," Horton lamented. "But when you play hard, you're going to get hurt—I don't care who you are. I'm the type of guy who, if there's a fly ball hit to me, and I've got a chance to catch it, I'm going to try to catch it—even if we're 12 runs behind. That's one of the reasons I get hurt so much, running into walls and falling and stuff like that."

Horton's tenure with his hometown team came to an end early in the 1977 season. After going 1-for-4 in left field on opening day against the Kansas City Royals, he sat on the bench until he was traded to the Rangers five days later. With a backlog of outfielders and Staub at DH, the Tigers shipped their disgruntled slugger to Texas for reliever Steve Foucault. Willie packed his bats and his helmet (he wore the same helmet throughout his career, having it painted when he changed teams) and joined his new club. It began an odyssey for Horton that took him to six different teams in three seasons.

Horton never was accepted in Texas, where the team owner, Brad Corbett, had made the deal for him without consulting his baseball people, least of all manager Frank Lucchesi. The Rangers had several DH candidates on their roster and their own outfield logjam. Yet with his thundering bat, Willie found playing time, appearing in 139 games, blasting 15 homers, and finishing second on the club with 75 RBI. But in the off-season, he was dealt to Cleveland with former pitching phenom David Clyde for reliever Tom Buskey and outfielder John Lowenstein. The Indians were the first of three teams that Horton played for in 1978, finding himself released in July, signed by Oakland, and then swapped to the Toronto Blue Jays a month later with Phil Huffman for Rico Carty. Through it all, Willie still proved to be a run producer—driving in 60 runs in 115 games.

In the off-season, Horton tested the free agent market for the first time and received his long-sought-after two-year deal—with the Mariners. In Seattle, as a veteran on an expansion club, Willie found a comfortable environment and enjoyed playing for manager Darrell Johnson, who inserted Horton's name in the lineup every day. Willie rewarded Johnson's confidence, slugging 29 homers with 106 RBI, a career best, and earning American League Comeback Player of the Year honors. Seattle fans fell in love with 36-year-old Horton, dubbing him the "Ancient Mariner."

Facing his former Tigers team June 5, 1979, Horton belted a ball at the Kingdome in Seattle that disappeared in the roof in left-center field. Initially ruled a home run—the 300th of his career—it was changed to a single when it was determined that it had struck a speaker. The next game, Horton hit his for-real 300th homer off Detroit's Jack Morris.

With a two-year extension in his pocket, Horton got off to a dreadful start in 1980, and without a home run to his credit and his average languishing below .200, he sat for two three-game stretches during May. Later he spent two stints on the disabled list with a hand injury. He finished his 18th season with a .221 average and just eight home runs. He entered the off-season knowing he would have to fight for a job on the Mariners, but that didn't matter on December 12, when he was dealt to the Rangers as part of an 11-player trade. After spring training in 1981, Horton was released by Texas. His career seemed over, but a month later the Pittsburgh Pirates signed him to a minor league deal and assigned him to Portland in the Pacific Coast League. Willie showed flashes of his power for the Beavers, stringing together a 10-game hitting streak at one point. Just seven hits away from 2,000 for his career, Willie was determined to get back to the major leagues, but it never materialized. He spent one more season in the minors and played briefly in the Mexican League in 1983, but returned home frustrated.

"I know I can still help a club," Horton said. "Even if I never touch a bat again, I know one thing: I can still help somebody."

Horton finally found that opportunity with an old ally—Billy Martin. The Yankees skipper brought Horton to New York in 1985 as his "harmony coach." Essentially, Willie was responsible for making sure that Martin's players didn't divide into warring factions in the clubhouse. Much of Horton's time was spent spying on the players and reporting to Martin. He served in a similar capacity for the Chicago White Sox in 1986. In 2000, he was brought back into the Tigers organization by owner Mike Ilitch as a special adviser, and he still serves the team's front office today. A bronze statue of Horton taking a mighty swing is located at Comerica Park beyond the left-field stands, and Willie is the only non-Hall of Famer to receive that recognition. His uniform number 23 was also retired by the club.

In 2004, Horton was dealt a setback when he was hit by a car, and in 2006 he was diagnosed with prostate cancer. Horton and his wife, Gloria, with whom he shares seven children and 19 grandchildren, reside in Bloomfield Hills, Michigan. Throughout his post-playing years, Horton busied himself with charity work for many organizations, including the Foundation for Fighting Blindness, the Boys and Girls Club of America, Meals on Wheels, the Red Cross, and the United Way. He also established the Horton Foundation to provide scholarships for needy students in inner-city Detroit. In 2004, Michigan Governor Jennifer Granholm declared Willie's birthday, October 18, as "Willie Horton Day" in Michigan.

"Willie Horton is one of those rare baseball players who doesn't need a diamond to truly sparkle and shine—he's a star on and off the field," Granholm said. "This fitting recognition will continue to inform future generations of his accomplishments."

On September 27, 1999, the final game was played at Tiger Stadium in Detroit. As part of the postgame festivities, former Tigers ran onto the field in uniform and took their positions. When Horton ran into left field, he was greeted with a tremendous ovation from fans who appreciated his 15 seasons and 262 home runs wearing the Detroit uniform. Willie Horton, the slugger who starred for the 1968 World Champions, the little kid from the streets of Detroit, the teenager who belted a homer nearly out of the ballpark, the strong man who shattered bats with brute strength, broke down and cried like a baby.

References

Publications
Detroit Tigers Yearbooks, 1963–1976.

Eldridge, Grant, and Karen Elizabeth Bush. *Willie Horton: Detroit's Own Willie the Wonder.* Detroit: Wayne State University Press. 2001.

Ewald, Dan. *John Fetzer: On a Handshake—The Times and Triumphs of a Tiger Owner.* Detroit: Wayne State University Press. 2000.

Harrigan, Patrick. *The Detroit Tigers: Club and Community, 1945–1995.* Toronto: University of Toronto Press. 1997.

Articles
The Sporting News: April 4, 1964, p. 23; April 11, 1964, p. 8; July 4, 1964, p. 31; January 1, 1965, p. 10; March 20, 1965, p. 8; May 29, 1965, p. 13; June 19, 1965, p. 18; July 24, 1965, pp. 3–4; January 22, 1966, p. 6; January 22, 1966, p. 12; February 26, 1966, p. 29; August 6, 1966, p. 13; March 25, 1967, p. 11; October 28, 1967, p. 19; December 23, 1967, p. 29; June 1, 1968, p. 7; July 20, 1968, p. 3; September 28, 1968, p. 7; February 1, 1969, p. 29; August 16, 1969, p. 15; February 21, 1970, p. 34; June 6, 1970, p. 19; July 4, 1970, p. 9; May 8, 1971, p. 19; January 15, 1972, p. 51; February 10, 1973, p. 41; April 14, 1973, p. 26; May 5, 1973, p. 11; September 8, 1973, p. 13; March 30, 1974, p. 30; June 15, 1974, p. 7; February 22, 1975, p. 42; June 28, 1975, p. 21; November 1, 1975, p. 15; May 22, 1976, p. 3; March 26, 1977, p. 8; April 30, 1977, p. 6; April 30, 1977, p. 16; May 28, 1977, p. 29; June 3, 1978, p. 29; August 19, 1978, p. 13; December 9, 1978, p. 42; May 26, 1979, p. 11; January 19, 1980, p. 35; May 17, 1980, p. 11; November 8, 1980, p. 49; January 17, 1981, p. 38; June 13, 1981, p. 48; November 7, 1981, p. 61; August 1, 1983, p. 24.

Willie Horton player file; National Baseball Library (various clippings)

Web Sites
www.retrosheet.org

Rich Shook presents:
Tigers In the News

Sunday, June 16
Manager Eddie Stanky of the White Sox had some caustic comments after Chicago split a doubleheader with Detroit. The White Sox won the first, 3-2, while the Tigers took the second, 6-1. "I said last year they should have won it by 10 games," the opinionated Stanky said. "If they don't do it big, they won't do it. Why do I think so? I'll tell you when they win it or lose it. They know why. They're running scared and it's only June. Guys like Willie Horton, Bill Freehan and Norm Cash bunting for base hits? If that isn't an indication of what I mean then I can't tell you any more." Detroit trailed 1-0 in the second game when Tom Matchick singled, Don Wert was hit by a pitch, and Chisox right-hander Cisco Carlos messed up Wayne Comer's double-play grounder in the eighth to load the bases. Willie Horton batted for Denny McLain against knuckleballing righty Hoyt Wilhelm and dribbled a checked-swing ball to the left of the mound on which Wilhelm fell down trying to field. Not that anybody was covering first anyway. The score now tied, Dick McAuliffe walked to force in the winning run and Jim Northrup rammed a double past first for two runs. Cash then dribbled a single past the mound for another. "Funny thing," manager Mayo Smith said, "even if we had lost two, we weren't in trouble. Cleveland had lost and Baltimore had lost the first game of a doubleheader." Mickey Lolich lost the first game to drop to 5-4 but McLain, now 11-2, was the beneficiary of the late second-game rally.

Monday, June 17
No game. Detroit optioned seldom-used lefty Les Cain to Toledo and recalled outfielder Lenny Green. Cain had appeared in eight games for the Tigers with a 1-0 record and 3.00 ERA over 24 innings. Green, 35, who hit .278 in 58 games for Detroit in 1967, was to appear in just six games—his last in the majors.

Tuesday, June 18
Earl Wilson (5-4) took a four-hit shutout into the ninth but walked Carl Yastrzemski and threw a wild pitch. Pat Dobson came on and gave up an RBI single to Ken Harrelson and a hit to Reggie Smith that put runners at the corners. Rico Petrocelli tapped one back to Dobson, who turned to second but then whirled and threw to the plate where Bill Freehan got Harrelson in a rundown for the first out. Dobson then fanned pinch-hitters Dalton Jones and Jerry Adair to close the Tigers' 2-1 win.

Wednesday, June 19
Boston's 8-5 victory, achieved on Harrelson's three-run home run in the seventh, was marred when Tigers fans threw debris at the Red Sox outfielder in the ninth inning. Included was a firecracker that struck him in the back and exploded behind him. "What if it landed in front of my face? I'm blind," he said. "A few fans like that give a city like Detroit a bad name all the time. Detroit is the only town in the league where this happens. You don't get that stuff in the rest of the league." General Manager Jim Campbell, disturbed over the incident, ordered an announcement with two out and two strikes on Don Wert in the bottom of the ninth that the game would be forfeited if fans didn't stop. Boston made five errors in the game but Joe Sparma (5-7) took the loss. "This race is far from over," manager Dick Williams of defending champion Boston said. "We've got a long way to go. I'm sure Detroit manager Mayo Smith is as well aware of that as anybody. He's reminding his players of it, too."

Thursday, June 20
Denny McLain (12-2) didn't allow a hit until George "Boomer" Scott singled over Ray Oyler's glove with two out in the seventh as the Tigers trumped the Red Sox, 5-1. Mickey Stanley drove in four runs with a double and a three-run home run as Detroit upped its lead to 8.5 games going to second-place Cleveland.

Friday, June 21
Detroit took a taste of its own late-inning medicine as Tony Horton hit a two-run home run off Pat Dobson (2-1) in the 13th inning to give Cleveland a 4-3 win. Jim Northrup's hit-and-run double had provided the Tigers with a 3-2 lead in the top of the inning.

Saturday, June 22
Steve Hargan and three relievers shut Detroit down on five hits in a 2-0 Cleveland win. Max Alvis hit a two-run home run off Earl Wilson in the fourth.

Al Kaline

by Nick Waddell

Season	Age	G	AB	R	H	2B	3B	HR	RBI	BB	SO	SB	CS	BA	OBP	SLG
1968 Tigers	33	102	327	49	94	14	1	10	53	55	39	6	4	.287	.392	.428
Career Totals		2834	10116	1622	3007	498	75	399	1583	1277	1020	137	65	.297	.376	.480

Albert William Kaline was born December 19, 1934, to Nicholas and Naomi Kaline in Baltimore. His father, a broom maker by trade, was a semipro baseball player, and began working with young Al to develop a pitcher's arm. Nicholas would squat down, while his son threw a variety of pitches. By the time he was nine, Al had learned a fastball, curveball, and changeup, and the work paid off. Kaline, while pitching for Westport Grammar School, won 10 straight games. The legendary arm strength and accuracy that would make Kaline one of the most complete ballplayers of his time was evident early on. During a picnic festival, Kaline threw a ball 173.5 feet. The disbelieving judges ordered him to throw again, believing that the measurement was off. Kaline threw again, this time 175 feet. While developing his arm, Kaline also learned to overcome osteomyelitis, a chronic bone disease that forced the removal of diseased bone from his left foot. To combat the physical impairment left behind, Al taught himself to run on the side of his foot. The determination to overcome injury became a trademark of Kaline's career.

A freshman at Southern High School in Baltimore 1949–1950, he tried out for the football and basketball teams. He quit football midway through the season when he broke his cheekbone, but in basketball, he led all scorers as a freshman. When spring came, Al tried out for baseball. Coach Bill Anderson immediately noticed Al's pitching, but because there was no place for Kaline as a pitcher, Anderson began teaching him to play center field, with the idea that Kaline would play one year of junior varsity ball and move up to varsity as a sophomore. That idea was short-lived, however, as Anderson placed Kaline on the varsity after watching his defensive prowess and offensive skills during a practice game. Position changes would follow Kaline to the majors as well.

Scouts from every major league team followed Kaline's every move. They watched as he hit .333 as a freshman and .418 as a sophomore, improving his defense as the year went on. After his sophomore year, Kaline was chosen in 1951 to play in an annual game sponsored by the Hearst newspapers, played at the Polo Grounds in New York. This game became a proving ground for Kaline, who hit two singles and a home run, and was named most valuable player. The next day, Kaline traveled to Yankee Stadium to watch his first-ever major league game, as the Yankees took on the St. Louis Browns.

Despite two great seasons in high school ball, the best for young Kaline was yet to come. He hit .469 as a junior and .488 as a senior to go along with his stellar defense. The combination earned Kaline more attention from the major leagues, specifically the Brooklyn Dodgers, St. Louis Cardinals, Philadelphia Phillies, and Detroit Tigers.

Tigers scout Ed Katalinas had followed Kaline's high school career, and was determined to make him the next Tigers great. When asked about Kaline's ability, Katalinas said, "To me he was the prospect that a scout creates in his mind and then prays that someone will come along to fit the pattern." Katalinas watched as Kaline played in seemingly every recreational ball league Baltimore had to offer during the summer, even hitting .609 one year in American Legion ball. The Tigers had finished the previous season last for the first time in franchise history, and were determined not to repeat that performance. Katalinas tried desperately to persuade Tigers president John McHale Sr. to sign Kaline, but McHale was more interested in pitcher

Tom Qualters. After Philadelphia signed Qualters, the door was open for the Tigers to sign Kaline. Katalinas wrote McHale asking that he fly to Baltimore to watch Kaline play in person. McHale did, and was so impressed by Kaline's abilities that he immediately flew back to Detroit to get permission from Tigers president Spike Briggs to sign Kaline to a bonus contract. Briggs agreed, and Katalinas was given the task of signing Kaline.

Players could not be contacted by major league clubs until after high school graduation. The day after Kaline's graduation, Katalinas descended upon the Kaline residence with a contract in his pocket. Katalinas was greeted by Nicholas and Al, but was quickly left alone with the young player. Katalinas offered $15,000 in bonus money and $20,000 in salary over three years. Kaline discussed the offer with his parents, and agreed to the contract. He later said the bonus money helped pay off his parents' mortgage and his mother's eye surgery. Al signed the contract and turned it over to his father, who was also required to sign. Before Nicholas could sign, Al said he had promised to play in an Amateur Day game in a few days, and asked if he could still play. Katalinas realized then that he had a special talent in the young Kaline—not only with baseball, but with life. He knew Kaline would never break a promise, and agreed to let Al play. Nicholas then signed the contract, and Al Kaline became a Detroit Tiger. Since the bonus was more than $6,000, Kaline was assured he would be with the big-league club for at least two years.

On June 25, 1953, Katalinas drove 18-year-old Kaline to his first game at Shibe Park in Philadelphia, where the new team was playing against the A's. The idea was to have Kaline play sparingly for two years with the major league club, and then be farmed out to a minor league team for two or three years for seasoning. Kaline quickly saw action that day, though. Wearing number 25, Kaline was told to play right field in the bottom of the eighth. Kaline had never played right field, but ran out with his glove and took the position. No ball was hit anywhere close to him, and he jogged back to the dugout with relief, until he realized he would lead off the top of the ninth. Kaline stepped in against Harry Byrd for his first big league at bat. Kaline dug in and drove a belt-high fastball to center field for an out. Kaline got his first hit, a single, July 8, 1953, off the Chicago White Sox' Luis Aloma. He scored his first run July 21 when he pinch-ran for Walt Dropo and came home from first on a double by Don Lund against the Washington Senators. That run from first to home earned Kaline the nickname "Baltimore Greyhound."

Kaline's first brush with greatness occurred later in 1953 when manager Fred Hutchinson introduced the budding star to Ted Williams. Williams spent ten minutes with Kaline, giving him tips on how to hit low balls, and on off-season workouts like swinging a heavier bat and squeezing a baseball. Williams's advice became a trademark of Kaline's game, especially his off season. The hitting advice Williams gave Kaline was on display September 16 when Kaline started his first game, this time in center field. He rapped out three singles and drove in his first run in an 8–3 Tigers victory over the Boston Red Sox. Kaline continued to show flashes of brilliance, even getting a hit off the great Satchel Paige in a game against the St Louis Browns. Kaline's first home run came during a ninth-inning pinch-hitting appearance at Cleveland. Although Kaline played in only 30 games, he had done enough to impress Hutchinson. According to a 1953 *Sporting News* article, the Tigers worked with Kaline at second base and shortstop, but eventually kept him in the outfield.

After the 1953 season, Kaline returned to Baltimore to work during the off-season in a sporting goods store, allowing him to take Williams's advice and squeeze a baseball during the day. While on breaks, Kaline would take a bat in the backroom and swing until his arms got tired. He also continued dating his high school sweetheart, Madge Louise Hamilton. Al was attracted to her not only because of her beauty, but also because she could talk baseball. Just before Kaline left for spring training, he proposed to Louise, who accepted. They were married after the 1954 season.

While playing winter ball in Cuba, everyday outfielder Steve Souchock broke his wrist, allowing Kaline to get valuable spring training time in right field. It was assumed that Souchock would be the starter in right when his wrist healed and Kaline would return to the bench. But Souchock's wrist didn't heal, and the 19-year-old Kaline became the starting right fielder in 1954. Kaline impressed everyone that season with his defense, and his offense soon became adequate; he hit around .250 for most of the season before the All-Star break. After the break, Kaline went on a tear and increased his average to .283 by the end of August. About a month later, in a home game, Kaline suffered his first major injury. A fly ball hit toward right at Briggs Stadium had Kaline racing toward some box seats that poked out into foul territory. Kaline ran into the wall protecting the seats, and was knocked out. He also twisted his knee and was hospitalized for five days. After the incident, Tiger president Spike Briggs ordered the seats removed lest Kaline be injured again. Kaline finished up his first full season with a .276 average. His lack of power, though, was a concern. Kaline had only 25 extra-base hits, including four home runs, and only 43 runs batted in.

Kaline went into the off-season knowing he had to improve his prowess at the plate. He didn't disappoint the fans or new manager Bucky Harris that year, even earning comparisons to Joe DiMaggio. On April 17, he blasted three home runs, including two in the sixth inning. By the end of April, Kaline had a 14-game hitting streak to go with a .453 batting average. He was voted by the fans as the American League's starting right fielder for the All-Star Game. After the break, Kaline continued to hit. By the end of July, Kaline was leading the league in batting average, runs, runs batted in, hits, and home runs. The hot hitting continued until the beginning of September, when Kaline fell into a slump. To help himself out of it, Kaline focused on the fact that he was only a few hits away from 200 for the season, and that if he achieved that plateau, he would be the first Tigers outfielder in 12 years to have 200 hits. Kaline broke out of the slump, and ended the season with exactly 200 hits. He won the American League batting championship with a .340 average. Kaline, at the age of 20, was one day younger than Ty Cobb when Cobb won the batting title in 1907, making Kaline the youngest batting champion ever, a mark that has endured for more than a half-century. The comparisons to DiMaggio that had followed Kaline all season were summed up in the October 5 issue of *The Sporting News*, which outlined how Kaline was more similar to DiMaggio than Cobb.

Before the 1956 season, Kaline bulked up—perhaps due to being on the "banquet circuit." In an effort to become more comfortable with reports and the public, Kaline made as many appearances as possible. Early in the season, Kaline seemed to be uncomfortable at the plate because, according to manager Bucky Harris, he was reaching too much for pitches and being too impatient. Kaline had put extra pressure on himself to follow up his amazing 1955 season. Despite his slow start, Kaline was voted to start the All-Star Game for the second straight year. During the festivities, Kaline sought out Ted Williams, who reaffirmed what Harris had already told him: He was pressing, and needed to be more disciplined at the plate. After that, Kaline went on a tear, and raised his average from .276 to finish at .314. During the off-season, the estate of Spike Briggs' father sold the Tigers to an 11-man syndicate headed by radio station owners Fred Knorr and John Fetzer. Briggs stayed on as general manager.

Before the 1957 season, Al Kaline met businessman Frank Carlin, who offered Kaline and Detroit Red Wings forward Gordie Howe positions in a new business venture. Howe and Kaline were to be salesman gaining subcontracts for automotive parts design. Kaline was reluctant, but Louise was certain it was a good venture, which is all Al needed to hear. Kaline, Howe, and Carlin formed Michigan Automotive Products Corporation (Mapco). Kaline was vice president, and found the business easier than he had originally believed. The business was so successful, the trio also formed Howe-Kaline-Carlin Corporation.

The off-season was not without controversy, though. Kaline believed he deserved a raise, as did Briggs, but Briggs did not offer a figure near what Al wanted. Briggs sent Kaline a contract, which was reportedly sent back unsigned, without a note. Briggs was insulted, and declared in a speech that Kaline thought he was as good as Mickey Mantle, and wanted to be paid as such. Briggs said he was offended by the returned unsigned contract, which he said included a $3,000 bonus, and Kaline returned it without an explanation, and without a holiday greeting. Kaline eventually got his contract, but the price he had to pay was larger. Many fans viewed Kaline as an ego-driven player, and many reporters implied as such with pointed, sometimes hostile questions. Kaline became so upset that he began to ignore the press, becoming more introverted than he already was.

The 1957 season was successful for Kaline. As in 1956, he started slowly, but was still chosen to start in the All-Star Game. Again, as in 1956, after the All-Star break, Kaline began to hit, and raised his batting average to .300 near the end of August. His success was coupled with the birth of his first son, Mark Albert, on August 21. Kaline's strong hitting and stellar defense helped the Tigers finish fourth, and gave Kaline his first of 10 Gold Gloves. Kaline repeated his strong hitting and stellar defense in 1958, as he hit .313 and earned a second straight Gold Glove as the Tigers still finished fifth.

The 1959 season was one of change and of improvement for Kaline. He was shifted to center field after regular Harvey Kuenn was hit on the arm. Kaline preferred right field, but played well in center. When Kuenn returned from his injury, new manager Jimmy Dykes kept Kaline in center and moved Kuenn to right. Kaline thrived in the new position, and began to show signs of being a gritty and tough leader. After being hit in the cheek by an errant throw, Kaline sat out five games. He began to get restless on the bench, demanding that Dykes play him. When Dykes expressed concern because the cheek was still swollen, Kaline replied

"I don't bat or throw with my cheek." Kaline was selected to start in the All-Star Game, this time over fellow center fielder Mickey Mantle. Kaline also got his 1,000th career hit off Billy Pierce of the White Sox. The Tigers finished in fourth place, while Kaline finished second in the batting race with .327 to Kuenn's .353. Kaline also picked up his third Gold Glove.

Before the 1960 season Bill DeWitt was hired as president and general manager of the Tigers. DeWitt immediately shook up the team by trading for Norm Cash, then sending batting champion Kuenn to Cleveland for home run leader Rocky Colavito. By May, the Tigers and Kaline had both had their ups and downs. Kaline was hitting only .250, which many people figured was due to off-field distractions. In an effort to reduce taxes, Frank Carlin, Kaline's partner with Howe, persuaded Kaline and Howe to purchase racehorses because the expenses were tax-deductible for three years. Horse racing was considered taboo for ballplayers, and the story became a focal point. Kaline quickly sold his interest in the HKC stable, distancing himself from racing and betting. The season grew to be more frustrating for the Tigers and for Kaline. Normally mild-mannered, Kaline was ejected for arguing a strike call with an umpire, but true to his form, Kaline approached the umpire after the game and apologized. He admitted he knew he was wrong as he walked back to the dugout. The prolonged slump cost Kaline a chance at starting another All-Star Game, although he was chosen as a reserve, making his sixth straight appearance. After DeWitt made history by trading a hitting champion for a home run leader, he made history again by trading manager Dykes for Cleveland manager Joe Gordon. The turmoil of the season took its toll on Kaline, as he finished with a .278 average, his lowest since 1954. (Gordon resigned after the season.)

In 1961, the Tigers hired Bob Scheffing as their new manager. Scheffing immediately turned to Kaline to become more of a leader, and the star responded. Kaline was not vocal but led by example, stepping up when needed. Kaline flourished all season, and was chosen to for seventh All-Star Game. He ended the year second in the batting race with a .324 average, and was voted AL Comeback Player of the Year.

In 1962, Kaline began the season by expressing the desire not only to play in the World Series, but to have a 20-year career. He also decided to be more aggressive at the plate, citing his low number of strikeouts from the previous season as the reason. Kaline shot out to .358 by May 21, but that good fortune ended five days later in Yankee Stadium. In the bottom of the ninth with two out and the Tigers leading 2–1, Elston Howard hit a fly to shallow right. Second baseman Jake Wood and first baseman Norm Cash could not reach it. The only hope was for Kaline to make the grab. He dove for the sinking ball, landing on his right shoulder. Kaline made the catch but broke his collarbone. It was predicted that he would miss at least two months. Before the game, Scheffing told reporters, "We're where we are because of Kaline. Where we go from here depends on him." Scheffing did not realize how right he was. During the 57 days that Kaline missed, the Tigers lost 7.5 games in the race for the pennant, falling to 10.5 games back. The layoff was not all bad for Kaline, though, as Louise gave birth to their second son, Michael Keith. Kaline was also chosen to start the first of the two All-Star Games that season—his eighth straight start—but could not play because of the injury. By the time the season was over, Kaline hit .304 and 29 home runs, two more than his previous best, all while missing 54 games. The Tigers finished 10.5 games behind the first-place Yankees, but Kaline earned his fifth Gold Glove, and finished sixth in the AL MVP voting.

As the 1963 season began, Kaline again changed his approach, deciding to get on base more, and let the slugging duo of Cash and Colavito drive in the runs. The team started slowly, but Kaline's approach kept him hitting well enough to be chosen for another All-Star Game. Kaline battled a knee injury all season, which eventually cost him a batting title to Carl Yastrzemski when he was forced to miss a few games. He finished second with a .312 average to Yaz's .321, hit 27 home runs, drove in 101 runs, placed second in MVP voting, and earned his sixth Gold Glove.

Kaline experienced more injuries in 1964. He injured his left foot, the same foot on which he had had surgery as a child, while running in a spring training game. Kaline hid the injury from manager Charlie Dressen at first, believing he could overcome it. By the end of April, however, the injury became too painful, and Kaline was forced to sit out a few games. Still, he was chosen to the All-Star Game for the tenth straight year, but withdrew due to injury, saying the rest would do his foot some good. The Tigers finished in fourth place that season, and Kaline finished with a respectable .293 average and his seventh Gold Glove.

Kaline's average dropped to .281 in 1965 while he was wearing a special shoe to protect his foot. He did earn his eighth Gold Glove splitting his time between center field and right field. During the off-season, Kaline had surgery on the foot. It helped him hit better in 1966, which became a tough year for the Tigers on and off the field. Dressen, who missed time the previous season after a heart attack, fell ill again on May 16. He was replaced by coach Bob Swift, who himself was diagnosed with cancer that season. Dressen and Swift both died later in the year. Frank Skaff finished the season as manager. Despite the distractions, Kaline was chosen for his 12th straight All-Star Game, and helped the Tigers finish third, while hitting .288 with 29 home runs. He also earned his ninth Gold Glove.

The Tigers had high hopes for 1967 under new manager Mayo Smith. Smith moved Kaline back to right field. Kaline was chosen to the AL All-Star team for the 13th year in a row, but a freak injury kept him out for 26 games. After a strikeout in a frustrating loss to Cleveland, Kaline slammed his bat into the bat rack and broke his hand. Unlike 1962, the Tigers stayed in contention without Kaline, going 15–11. The Tigers battled all year, but finished tied for second behind the Red Sox. Kaline hit .308 with 25 home runs (including his 300th) and 78 runs batted in, despite missing 31 games. Kaline won his 10th and final Gold Glove. The Red Sox lost to the St Louis Cardinals in the 1967 World Series. It would be that same Cardinals team against which Kaline would live out his dream.

Nineteen sixty-eight was a season of new endeavors. During the off-season, Kaline, now 33, withdrew from Mapco to focus on baseball. He played in his 2,000th game April 18 in a 5–0 victory over the Indians. Kaline hit his 307th home run on May 19, passing Hank Greenberg as the Tigers' career homer leader. The success was short-lived; Kaline's arm was broken by a Lew Krausse pitch just six days later, and he did not return until July 1. In Kaline's absence, Jim Northrup took over right field and played well. When Kaline returned, he was used mostly as a pinch-hitter, and filled in at first base. Despite the reduced role, Kaline figured prominently in the pennant run. He scored the tying run in Denny McLain's 30th victory on September 14. On September 17, Kaline pinch-hit for Norm Cash, and ended up scoring the run that won the Tigers the pennant. After the game, Kaline told Smith he did not deserve to play in the World Series because other players had stepped up in his absence. Smith, knowing what Kaline meant to the Detroit organization, had other ideas. To get his star in, Smith put center fielder Mickey Stanley at shortstop, Jim Northrup in center, and Al Kaline in right. The move proved successful as the Tigers rebounded from a three-games-to-one deficit to win three straight games, including Game 7 over Bob Gibson. The Tigers had won the World Series behind Kaline's .379 batting average and two home runs.

Kaline had reached one of his goals, to play in the World Series. Now it was time to fulfill his goal of a twenty-year career. As Kaline marched toward that mark, he continued to hit, and gain accolades. In 1969, he was voted to the Greatest Tiger Team of All Time. August 2, 1970, was Al Kaline Day, upon which the city renamed Cherry Street behind the stadium Kaline Drive. In 1971, Kaline was selected to play in his 17th All-Star Game, held that year in Detroit. He went 1-for-2 and scored on a Harmon Killebrew home run in the bottom of the sixth. On July 1, 1972, Kaline hit his 369th home run, tying Ralph Kiner for 18th place all-time. He also helped the Tigers to the playoffs, in which they lost to the eventual champion Oakland Athletics. It was also Kaline's 20th season in the big leagues. The 1974 season was Kaline's last, and his first as a full-time designated hitter. He was named to his 15th and final All-Star team. He rapped his 3,000th hit September 24, a double off Dave McNally, in his home town of Baltimore.

Kaline finished his career with 3,007 hits, 498 doubles, 75 triples, 399 home runs, 1,622 runs scored, and 1,583 run batted in, while batting .297. What makes his numbers even more impressive is the fact that he missed 594 games in his career, the vast majority due to injury—the equivalent of two and a half seasons. With a career .987 fielding percentage, he was also one of the best fielders of his time, with 10 Gold Gloves to prove it. In a 2001 *Sporting News* article, both Ernie Harwell and Yogi Berra declared that Kaline had the best arm in the outfield ever.

In 1976, Kaline began a second career as a color commentator on Tigers television broadcasts. In 1980, Al Kaline was elected to the Baseball Hall of Fame alongside Duke Snider, Chuck Klein, and Tom Yawkey. Kaline thanked his family for their support, then said:

"If there is one accomplishment of which I am particularly proud, it is that I have always served baseball to the best of my ability, never have I deliberately done anything to discredit the game, the Tigers, or my family. By far, being inducted into the Hall of Fame is the proudest moment of my life."

Kaline spent more time as a broadcaster—25 years—than as a Tigers player. He also participated as a spring training instructor, even teaching a young Kirk Gibson about playing the outfield. In 2001, Kaline left the broadcast booth to become a special adviser to Tigers owner Mike Ilitch. In 2003, new General Manager David Dombrowski named Kaline and his former teammate Willie Horton as special assistants to the general manager. Because of the broadcasting and special assignments, Al Kaline has been associated with the Tigers for more than 50 years. For that, some people know him as Mr. Tiger. Others still refer to him simply as Number Six.

References

Publications
Butler, Hal. *Al Kaline and the Detroit Tigers*. Chicago: Henry Regnery Co. 1973.

Cantor, George. *The Tigers of '68: Baseball's Last Real Champions*. Dallas: Taylor. 1997.

Harrigan, Patrick J. *The Detroit Tigers: Club and Community 1945–1995*. Toronto: University of Toronto Press. 1997.

Hirshberg, Albert. *The Al Kaline Story*. New York: Julian Messner. 1964.

Whitt, Alan. *They Earned Their Stripes: The Detroit Tigers All-Time Team*. Champaign, Ill.: Sports Publishing, Inc. 2000.

Articles
Berra, Yogi and Ernie Harwell. "The Best I Ever Saw." *The Sporting News*, July 9, 2001.

Falls, Joe. "Summer Without Baseball: Kaline Making Adjustments." *The Sporting News*, February 1, 1975.

Salsinger, H.G. "Kaline More Like DiMaggio Than Cobb." *The Sporting News*, October 5, 1955.

Web Sites
www.baseball-almanac.com
www.baseballhalloffame.org
www.baseball-reference.com
www.detroittigers.com
www.retrosheet.org

Rich Shook presents:

Tigers In the News

Sunday, June 23
The Indians took their third straight from the Tigers, 3-0, on Luis Tiant's (11-5) three-hitter in the first game, but Dick Tracewski hit a three-run home run off Sam McDowell in the fifth inning of the nightcap, which Detroit won, 4-1. "Now I have nothing to look forward to for the rest of the year," said Tracewski, who entered the game batting .170 and equaled his home run output for 1967. "Trixie" later added three more home runs to double his career output—to eight. Joe Sparma (6-7) won the second game, allowing six hits in seven innings, with Pat Dobson allowing just one walk in the final two frames. John Hiller (5-2) started the opener and lasted just one-third of an inning.

Monday, June 24
Jim Northrup tied a major league record with two grand slams to lead Detroit's 14-3 thumping of Cleveland and help Denny McLain raise his record to 13-2. "That's a heckuva way to come out of a slump, isn't it?" Northrup said. He bushwhacked an Eddie Fisher knuckleball in the fifth and creamed a Bill Rohr delivery his next time up, in the sixth. "The second time I was thinking more of myself. I said to myself, 'Here's your chance to tie the record.'" Jim Price hit his first career home run. Don Wert was hit in the head by a pitch in the sixth and hospitalized overnight. McLain fanned eight, gave up nine hits and, typically, did not walk a batter.

Tuesday, June 25
A six-run seventh inning helped Detroit take a wet 8-5 victory from host New York in a game that endured three rain delays totaling 99 minutes and didn't end until one tick before 1 a.m. EDT. Dennis Ribant earned his first AL win. Dick Tracewski doubled off the glove of third baseman Bobby Cox to drive in the first run of the seventh and cut the Yankees' lead to 5-2. All-Star voting results were released and Bill Freehan was the leading vote-getter with 248 of a possible 251. Carl Yastrzemski had 246 of 252. Voting in those days was done by players, managers, and coaches. Horton was also voted to the AL's starting team. (Historical footnote: A 22-year-old rookie became the first modern-era player to hit a grand slam in his major league debut: outfielder Bobby Bonds of the San Francisco Giants.)

Wednesday, June 26
The rain that bedeviled Tuesday night's game washed out this night's tilt. It was rescheduled as part of a twi-nighter for August 23. (Historical footnote: Right-hander Bob Gibson of St. Louis hurled his fifth straight shutout, one short of the record set earlier in the month by the Dodgers' Don Drysdale.)

Thursday, June 27
No game scheduled. Denny McLain was named to the AL's mound staff for the All-Star Game by manager Dick Williams of Boston; McLain had started the 1966 game. Don Wert, still suffering the effects of his beaning three days earlier, was expected to miss the weekend series with Chicago. He was hitting .224 with seven home runs and 17 RBI at the time he was hit in the head.

Fred Lasher

by Don Petersen and Mike Lassman

Season	Age	W	L	Pct	G	GS	CG	SV	IP	H	R	ER	BB	SO	ERA
1968 Tigers	26	5	1	.833	34	0	0	5	49	37	19	18	22	32	3.31
Career Totals		11	13	.458	151	1	0	22	201.2	179	103	87	110	148	3.88

Many young boys will ponder the important matters of the day, and some young boys will just daydream as they skip rocks across the surface of a lake. In the case of Fred Lasher, the enjoyment of skipping rocks across a tranquil lake helped transform Fred into a nasty submarine pitcher that minor and major league batters did not want to face.

Frederick Walter Lasher was born in Poughkeepsie, New York, on August 19, 1941. At least 11 professional baseball players were born and raised in this Queen City along the Hudson River, including Mickey McDermott, who had success in the major leagues and pitched a short time for the Tigers in 1958.

As a youngster, Fred played various positions and was a fine hitter. He batted and threw right-handed. But while at Poughkeepsie High School, Fred began to concentrate on pitching. Ultimately, he became a star pitcher for the Poughkeepsie High School baseball team.

Major League Baseball had not yet conducted its inaugural free agent draft of amateur baseball players. As a result, Fred was free to sign with any professional team after graduation from high school. At 6-foot-4 and a hard thrower, he attracted the interest of more than one team. Eventually, in 1960 he signed with the Washington Senators as an amateur free agent. Lasher pitched for Wytheville, a Class D Appalachian League aggregation. It was not the most auspicious of pro beginnings, as he had a 7.31 ERA and a 2–2 record in 32 innings over seven games.

At the conclusion of the 1960 season, the Senators moved to Minnesota and became the Twins. Lasher moved on as well, pitching for the Class D Fort Walton Beach Jets in the Alabama-Florida League during the 1961 season.

The highlight for Lasher was a game against the Montgomery Rebels in which he allowed five hits and struck out 18 batters. The Jets and Lasher still lost in 10 innings, 5–4, due to two Jets errors. The Jets compiled a 61–55 record under manager Vern Morgan and finished in third place. Fred's performance earned him an appearance on Minnesota's Florida Instructional League team along with future Twins star Tony Oliva.

Lasher left the warmth of Florida for the cooler temperatures of North Dakota when the Twins assigned him to the Bismarck-Mandan Pards in the Class C Northern League for 1962. Morgan served once again as Fred's manager after leaving Fort Walton Beach for the minor league advancement. Fred dominated hitters, and on June 10, 1962, his record was 3–0 with a spectacular 0.26 ERA. He had struck out 45 batters in 35 innings. The Northern League Sportswriters Association named Lasher to the all-star team. Also appearing on the all-star squad were future teammates Mickey Stanley and Jim Price. After the all-star game, Lasher was named the Northern League Player of the Month by the league's sportswriters and broadcasters. He immediately established himself as a major league prospect by winning eight games for Bismarck-Mandan while losing only five. Moreover, he sported a dazzling 2.03 ERA and struck out 132 batters in 115 innings. At the end of the season, Bismarck-Mandan was 60–62. Fred's performance earned him a return trip to the Florida Instructional League team that was coached by a young Jim Kaat.

Lasher's progress through the minor league ranks impressed the Twins, as the parent club invited him to spring training. In a little more than two seasons, Lasher had given up only 205 hits in 274 innings to go along with

309 strikeouts. Fred's teammates gave him the nickname "Whip" due to his sidearm pitching that would last through his career. In order to provide some variety, pitching coach Gordon Maltzberger helped Lasher learn a new arm angle by showing him a three-quarter overhand delivery. Lasher had made four consecutive scoreless relief performances in exhibition games due to an effective fastball and a devastating curve. This caused Twins manager Sam Mele to make a late-hour recommendation for Fred to make the big leap from Class C to the major leagues. Lasher was given uniform number 29, which was worn later by Hall of Famer Rod Carew and retired by the Twins.

Lasher made his major league debut at age 21 at Memorial Stadium in Kansas City on April 12, 1963. The Twins lost the game, but Lasher contributed by pitching a scoreless inning. Lasher pitched 9.1 innings for the Twins, but his 10 walks presumably brought about his demotion to the Charlotte Hornets in the South Atlantic League. Lasher pitched both ends of a doubleheader in his first appearance and went on to pitch 57 innings with a 2.84 ERA. Fred was called back to Minnesota when the rosters were expanded in September. He pitched two innings and gave up one earned run after his call-up. Lasher finished with no wins or losses and 4.76 ERA during his two stints in the American League. The Twins invited Fred to some more Instructional League training in October, and Lasher rewarded them with 64 innings and a 2.39 ERA.

The Twins invited Lasher to spring training in 1964, but he did not make the team as he had in 1963. The Twins sent Fred to play for the Atlanta Crackers in the International League. Future major league manager Jack McKeon managed the Crackers. Lasher did not stay in Atlanta very long, for the Twins sent him back to Charlotte.

Lasher continued to pitch in the Twins' system through 1966. On November 29, though, the Tigers paid $4,000 and rescued Fred from the Twins' organization via baseball's annual minor league draft. The Tigers assigned Lasher to the Montgomery Rebels of the Southern League. Through July, Lasher was putting up numbers similar to those he posted early in his professional career. At one point, Fred's record was 8–1 with a 0.68 ERA. He pitched 53 innings and struck out 50 batters. The Tigers wisely promoted Lasher to Triple A Toledo.

As a Toledo Mud Hen, Fred pitched in nine games before another promotion. He struck out 17 batters in 17 innings and posted a minuscule 0.53 ERA. Tigers pitcher Johnny Podres went on the disabled list with tendinitis in his left elbow. While reliever Fred Gladding had pitched well earlier in the season, he was apparently worn out. This enabled Lasher to return to the majors after being away for four years. Manager Mayo Smith called Lasher to the mound in his first game with the Tigers on August 13 in a clutch situation. Light-hitting Ray Oyler had hit a three-run homer early in the game to give the Tigers the lead. Starter Earl Wilson gave up a home run in the seventh inning, and the Tigers were narrowly leading the Orioles, 3–2. Lasher entered the game in the eighth inning and pitched two scoreless innings. Lasher retired three future Hall of Famers—Luis Aparacio, Brooks Robinson, and Frank Robinson—to help the Tigers secure a key pennant-race win. The win gave Wilson his 16th victory and provided Lasher his first major league save.

Lasher got a taste of his first pennant drive after missing some quality opportunities when the Twins won the 1965 American League pennant. Fred had an unsuccessful second appearance, but got two huge outs for Denny McLain one week later for his second save. Another highlight for Lasher included a three-inning appearance on August 22 in front of 40,291 at Tiger Stadium against the Twins. Lasher earned his first major league victory against his former team. Fred struck out four and gave up only one hit. Then, on, September 3, the Tigers played at Metropolitan Stadium against the Twins and their 43,444 faithful fans. Earl Wilson pitched 5.1 innings and was on his way to a shutout. Smith lifted Wilson, and Lasher entered the game. Fred pitched a rare 3.2-inning save to preserve a key victory for the Tigers. Lasher added six strikeouts.

Fred had a successful run late in the season and was one of the young Tigers hot hands Mayo Smith used, including future National League Cy Young Award winner Mike Marshall. Lasher responded with nine saves and two victories. His ERA was 1.35 at one point in September, and his fortunes were going well. Unfortunately, the Tigers lost a close game on September 18 in Tiger Stadium against the eventual pennant-winning Boston Red Sox. Lasher gave up a homer to Triple Crown winner and MVP Carl Yastrzemski with one out in the ninth inning, and the Red Sox tied the game at five runs. In the 10th inning, Boston's Dalton Jones hit a solo homer off reliever Marshall, and the Red Sox won the game, tying the Tigers for first place with identical 85–66 records. Lasher had a couple of rough outings after that game, but rebounded on October 1 with a solid two-inning performance in the first game of the final-day doubleheader against the California Angels. The Tigers fell short in the pennant drive, but Lasher gained some key experience in crucial games that helped him and the Tigers in 1968. Lasher finished the 1967 season with 30 innings pitched and a 3.90 ERA to go along with a 2–1 record and nine saves, his career high for a single season.

The Tigers gave one of their bullpen jobs to Lasher during spring training in 1968. In the first week of the season against the Chicago White Sox, Fred earned a victory and a save. These events caused Tigers radio broadcaster Ernie Harwell to proclaim, "Sound the siren, flash the flasher; here's our fireman, big Fred Lasher!"

During the Tigers' magical season, Lasher roomed with Tom Matchick, who pinch-hit for Lasher on occasion. A strange statistical event occurred during the season with regard to Fred's wins. Lasher won five games during the season, and each victory was a 5–4 Tiger win. Fred gave up only two homers during the season, to renowned long-ball hitters Boog Powell and Frank Howard in May. Also, on May 19, Fred pitched 2.1 innings and combined with rookie Les Cain on a shutout to enable the Tigers to win 7–0 against the Senators in the nightcap of a twin bill in front of 45,491 Tigers fans.

Lasher finished the season with a 5–1 record and five saves. He maintained a 3.33 ERA while pitching 48.2 innings. Fred had the opportunity to pitch in Game 4 of the World Series. The Tigers lost the game, 10–1, but Lasher pitched two scoreless innings. In the seventh game of the World Series, Lasher and Earl Wilson warmed up in the bullpen when Mickey Lolich gave up some hits in the middle of the game. Lasher would not be needed in this game as Lolich threw a complete game—his third of the Series—against Bob Gibson and the Cardinals, and sent the team and city into ecstasy.

Lasher made the Tigers' opening day roster for the second straight season in 1969. Fred had a frustrating start to the season as he believed manager Smith did not have confidence in him. He pitched only 7.1 innings through May 13 and did not give up a run. From a statistical standpoint, Lasher pitched well with a career-best 3.07 ERA in 44 innings and a 2–1 record. But Fred was only given one save opportunity and did not convert the chance on June 1 in Seattle against the expansion Pilots.

In 1970, Lasher and Tom Timmerman came into the season as the top relief men for the Tigers. Fred picked up his first win on April 17 against the Red Sox and pitched three scoreless innings. He earned his first save since 1968 on April 21 against the Indians with a scoreless inning of relief. Lasher pitched well, but gave up some runs against the Yankees and Red Sox in mid-May. The Tigers traded Lasher—the only trade of his career—to the Cleveland Indians on May 22 for baseman-outfielder Russ Nagelson and pitcher Billy Rohr. Nagelson made limited appearances for the Tigers as an outfielder, and Rohr never played for the parent club.

Apparently, the Indians were anxious to use Lasher as he pitched two scoreless innings the next day against the Yankees in Cleveland. The day after, Indians and Yankees had a doubleheader, and Lasher pitched in both games. The Yanks' Lindy McDaniel won both games of the doubleheader while Lasher lost both games. In the opener, John Ellis hit a tie-breaking homer for the Yankees, while Horace Clarke drove in the winning run with a single in the 11th inning of the nightcap. Fred earned his first victory in an Indians uniform by pitching three scoreless innings on June 18 against the Senators. Former American League Cy Young winner Dean Chance got the save.

Lasher took part in history in three remarkably different games. On June 21 against the Tigers, Fred gave up one of Cesar Gutierrez's seven hits when Gutierrez made baseball history by going 7-for-7 in an 11-inning game. On June 24, Lasher was part of Yankees history as he surrendered Bobby Murcer's fourth homer of the day in the second game of a doubleheader. Then, Roy White proceeded to hit a game-winning single in the bottom of the eighth inning, tagging Lasher with the loss. Finally, Lasher started his first and only major league game against the Red Sox on July 24, 1970. In the first inning, Fred hit understandably sensitive Tony Conigliaro in the arm. In 1967, Conigliaro had been hit in the face with a pitch, nearly losing his sight and ruining his career. Conigliaro reacted angrily to Lasher's pitch, and a bloody brawl ensued. In the second inning, Lasher gave up consecutive homers to Conigliaro's brother Billy and Tom Satriano, causing Fred's exit. This was the second straight game that Lasher hit a batter. On July 9, Lasher hit the Senators' Ed Stroud and broke his jaw.

Lasher's season came to a dramatic close on September 26. In the 11th inning of a 7–4 loss to the Orioles, Lasher walked Boog Powell and made a wild throw on a Mark Belanger bunt, allowing Powell's pinch-runner, a rookie named Don Baylor, to score the tie-breaking run. After Fred threw two balls to Paul Blair, Tribe manager Alvin Dark pulled Lasher for pitcher Steve Mingori. Lasher did not like the manager's decision and threw down the ball in disgust, then proceeded to toss his glove into the stands. The Indians fined and suspended Fred for the remainder of the season. Lasher finished the season with a total of two wins and 10 losses and a 4.19 ERA with

eight saves in a career-high 55 games. He also pitched in a career-high 66.2 innings. At the conclusion of the season, Dark vowed that Lasher would not be back in a Cleveland uniform.

At the conclusion of the 1970 season, Lasher pitched for Ponce in the Puerto Rican Winter League, and the Indians demoted Lasher to Wichita. Then, on November 30, the California Angels drafted Lasher from the Cleveland during the Rule 5 draft based on Angels coach Fred Koenig's recommendation; Koenig had managed Ponce, for which Lasher had pitched 78 innings and had a 2.85 ERA.

Fred pitched for the Salt Lake City Angels in the Pacific Coast League to start the 1971 season. Lasher struggled with some arm problems, but was able to save six games in 11 days to earn another shot at the majors. Lasher pitched a scoreless inning on June 23 for California. On July 1, though, he struggled and gave up four runs in one-third of an inning. This was Fred's last appearance in the major leagues. Lasher was not being used and asked to be returned to Salt Lake City in order to pitch more often. Lasher was a key reliever for Salt Lake City as he picked up two victories and five saves down the stretch and did not lose a game. Lasher finished the season with Salt Lake City and pitched 62 innings, notching a 3.92 ERA. Salt Lake City won the PCL's Southern Division flag and defeated Northern Division champion Tacoma to win the title. One of Lasher's Salt Lake City teammates was fellow 1968 Tiger Ray Oyler.

After retiring from baseball, Fred operated a drywall company and served as a recreation therapist for youth with drug and alcohol problems in Merrillan, Wisconsin, where he still lives.

References

Publications
Green, Jerry. *Year of the Tiger*. New York: Coward-McCann. 1969.

O'Brien, John, and Jerry DeBruin with John Husman. *Mud Hen Memories*. Perrysburg, Ohio: BWD Publishing. 2001.

Web Sites
www.alabama-florida-league.com/
www.baseball-almanac.com
www.baseball-reference.com
www.minnesotatwins.com
www.minorleaguebaseball.com
www.pkny.info/city.php
www.retrosheet.org

Other Sources
Lassman, Mike. Interview with Tom Matchick, August 18 and 19, 2007.

Rich Shook presents:
Tigers In the News

Friday, June 28
Mickey Stanley hit a two-run home run in the seventh to give Detroit a 5-4 win over visiting Chicago in the first game of a scheduled doubleheader. The second game was postponed due to rain. The first game was delayed for 79 minutes by rain, making the field nearly unplayable. Stanley had singled in a run in the fourth after Dick McAuliffe legged a hit in front of right fielder Leon Wagner into a double. Norm Cash hit a home run off the top of the third deck in the second with Willie Horton, who had been hit by a pitch, on first. Earl Wilson lined a triple off the center field fence in the second. Fred Lasher won it with three perfect relief innings. He was 5-1 with all the wins coming at home by 5-4 scores.

Saturday, June 29
Jim Northrup's third grand slam of the week gave Denny McLain his 14th victory. It was an opposite-field smash off the facing of the second deck in left with nobody out in the third off Chicago's Cisco Carlos. (I started dictating my lead: "Jim Northrup set a major league record with his third grand slam of the week," only to get halted by my New York dictation-taker, 'How do you know it's a record?' "Well, because I just dictated he tied the record on Monday.") Of the 11 home runs to date by the "Gray Fox," four had come with the bases loaded. He came up with the bases loaded in the fifth but struck out against Jack Fisher in a bid to tie the major league mark for slams in a season in one week. McLain allowed eight hits in the 5-2 win, walking two and striking out five. (Historical footnotes: Don Canham began his reign as University of Michigan athletic director on Sunday, succeeding H.O. "Fritz" Crisler. "We've got to fill those places," he said of 101,001-seat Michigan Stadium for football and the 15,000-seat Events Building for basketball. Also: A two-mile D-shaped oval was being bulldozed and paved out in the Irish Hills near Brooklyn, Michigan. Michigan International Speedway was scheduled to host its first race October 12, a 250-mile USAC race.)

Mickey Lolich

by Dan Holmes

Season	Age	W	L	Pct	G	GS	CG	SV	IP	H	R	ER	BB	SO	ERA
1968 Tigers	27	17	9	.654	39	32	8	1	220	178	84	78	65	197	3.19
Career Totals		217	191	.532	586	496	195	11	3640	3366	1537	1390	1099	2832	3.44

Mickey Lolich described himself as "the beer-drinker's idol." With his portly physique and likable disposition, the pitcher was popular with Tiger fans during his 13 seasons in their uniform. His talented left arm didn't hurt his cause either.

Of Yugoslav descent, Lolich was born in Portland, Oregon, September 12, 1940, the same day that Schoolboy Rowe defeated the Yankees to keep the Tigers a half-game ahead of the Indians in the American League pennant race. Lolich's father was a parks director, which kept him outside, and his kids near the parks and play equipment. Consequently, Mickey (born Michael Stephen Lolich) developed into an outdoorsman and an athlete. Lolich said that as a kid he threw rocks at "birds, squirrels, and anything else that moved."

As a result, he built a strong arm. But Lolich was initially right-handed. As a toddler, he was favoring his right arm, until one day he tipped over a motorcycle onto himself. The bike landed on his left side, damaging his left arm and shoulder. That summer he wore a cast on the arm and performed exercises to strengthen the torn muscles. When the cast came off, Lolich was a southpaw.

As a youth in Oregon, Lolich played lots of baseball, though there wasn't a major league team to follow. "The only games we would get were national broadcasts of the Yankees," Mickey said, "so I grew up idolizing Mickey Mantle and Whitey Ford in the 1950s." Later, Lolich and Ford would pitch against each other in the big leagues.

Young Mickey served as visiting batboy for the Portland Beavers of the Pacific Coast League, where he met several baseball legends, including Lefty O'Doul. Lolich also met an umpire named Emmett Ashford, who later became the first African American umpire in the major leagues.

As a teenager, Lolich pitched brilliantly for local Babe Ruth and American Legion teams, setting Oregon records for strikeouts that still stand. Lolich's 1955 Babe Ruth team played in the Babe Ruth League World Series in Austin, Texas, in 1955 and his American Legion team was in the American Legion World Series in Billings, Montana, in 1957. One pitcher who Lolich battled in amateur tournaments was Al Downing, also a left-hander, who was signed by the Yankees at the same time Mickey was being scouted. "My uncle told me Al had signed with the Yanks," Mickey said, "and I knew I'd be battling him to get to the majors, so I signed with the other team that was really interested in me, the Detroit Tigers."

Lolich posted a 19–5 record at Lincoln High School in Portland and signed on the dotted line June 30, 1958, for $30,000 with Tigers scout Bernie deViveiros.

In his first season in the minor leagues, playing under Johnny Pesky with Knoxville in the Sally League, Mickey weighed 160 pounds, and as he said, "was nothing but skin and bones." Displaying an independent attitude that was his trademark, one year Lolich reported late to spring training because he took the civil service exam in Portland. With his eye on a job as a letter carrier should his arm ever fail him, Mickey was making sure he had a backup plan in place. During a stop in Triple A Denver he was struck by a line drive below his right eye. Lolich was gun-shy afterward, and his pitching suffered badly.

Lolich's refusal to take a demotion inadvertently led to him learning a pitching style that in turn led to his later success in the big leagues. After three seasons of bouncing on both sides of the Double A divide, Tigers General Manager Jim Campbell asked Lolich to report to the A-ball Knoxville Smokies again in 1962. Lolich, who didn't like Smokies manager Frank Carswell, balked and instead flew home to Portland, telling the Tigers he was done. Shortly after, he toed the rubber for a semi-pro team, fanning 16 batters in relief and catching the attention of the Portland Beavers. Campbell arranged a deal to loan Lolich to Portland for the season. Pitching at home, the 21-year-old Lolich won 10 games and received pivotal advice from pitching coach Jerry Staley. A former big-league hurler, Staley advised Lolich to stop trying to fire the ball hard all the time, and to focus on throwing strikes.

Lolich pitched brilliantly in spring training in 1963 but failed to make the Tigers' roster. After a brief spell with Triple A Syracuse, Lolich was called up to Detroit in May, initially working out of the bullpen. Ironically, it may not have been his considerable fastball that enabled him to beat out other more highly touted lefties for the open spot on the roster. "That young Lolich is all business out there," Detroit vice president Rick Ferrell observed. "I like his breaking stuff." Staley's advice had paid off. Lolich was evolving from a thrower into a pitcher.

Lolich's big-league debut came May 12, 1963, in a 9–3 Detroit loss to the Cleveland Indians. He struck out the first two batters he faced, Max Alvis and Sam McDowell. Later inserted into the rotation by manager Bob Scheffing, Mickey earned his first win May 28 in Los Angeles against the Angels, going the distance. Complete games became a Lolich trademark. Later in 1963, he pitched a one-hitter for eight innings against the Baltimore Orioles only to surrender a two-run homer in the ninth, losing to veteran Robin Roberts. "I guess you can't beat an old pro," Mickey said philosophically.

In his first full season in the Detroit rotation in 1964, helped by a tip from new Tigers skipper Charlie Dressen, Lolich won 18 games with a 3.26 ERA and 192 strikeouts in 44 games, 33 of them starts. As a scout with the Dodgers the previous season, Dressen had noticed that Lolich was tipping his pitches and helped the left-hander fix the flaw. In his windup, Lolich had been raising his arms higher when he threw his fastball and lower for breaking pitches. Mickey adopted a new windup and continued to show that he was more than just a fastball pitcher.

"Lolich's fastball is so good that he can get away with a mistake once in a while," Dressen said. "But the big difference is that he comes in with the curve when he's behind the hitter."

On April 24, 1964, Lolich fired a 5–0 shutout against the Twins in Minnesota, which was not only his first shutout in the big leagues, but his first as a professional at any level. On September 9, he fulfilled a dream when he shut out the Yankees and his idol Whitey Ford, 4–0, at Tiger Stadium. American League batters began to take notice of the 23-year-old. "Lolich throws so easy," Yankees slugger Mickey Mantle observed. "He keeps the ball down," said Leon Wagner of the Cleveland Indians, "that's why he's so good." Over a stretch in September, Mickey pitched 30.2 consecutive scoreless innings.

During the season, Lolich met Joyce Feenor, an airline stewardess from Hollywood, Florida, and the two were married on November 21. Mickey credited Joyce with his breakout season. "I called her each night before I pitched, and I called her after every game."

The following year, Lolich's 15 wins were surpassed by only three other AL lefties—Jim Kaat, McDowell, and Ford. His 226 whiffs ranked second in the league—the fist of four times he would be runner-up in that category (he led the league once). "I know I have some good years ahead in Detroit," Lolich said after the 1965 campaign. "I don't want to be an average pitcher. I want to be among the best." On May 29, Lolich twirled a 10-inning complete game two-hitter to defeat the Indians 1–0 at Tiger Stadium.

In 1966, Lolich struggled to get into a groove, battling inconsistency all season as he posted a 14–14 mark and saw his ERA inflate to 4.77. However, he did become the first Tigers pitcher since Hal Newhouser to win opening day starts in back-to-back seasons.

By the end of the 1967 season, which saw Detroit battle for the pennant until the final day of the campaign, Lolich was establishing himself as one of the finer hurlers in the league. He finished the season with 28.2 scoreless innings. "That's the best left-hander I've seen all year," Boston slugger George Scott said after Mickey fanned 13 Red Sox batters late in the season at Tiger Stadium. Even curmudgeon Eddie Stanky, the White Sox manager who once tagged Lolich as a "second-line pitcher," compared the southpaw to Hall of Famer Lefty Grove.

A member of the Michigan Air National Guard, Lolich missed 15 days due to military service in 1967, seeing action during the riots in Detroit that served to fuel racial tensions in the city. After suffering a 10-game losing skid in the middle of the season—his 5.09 ERA during this stretch was one cause, but his teammates scored just 16 runs—Lolich roared through his last 11 starts, going 9–1 in the process. He threw 87.2 innings in those 11 starts, allowing only 50 hits and 18 walks while striking out 81 and posting a 1.33 ERA. Lolich credited pitching coach Johnny Sain, who became a good friend of his, with helping him become a complete major league pitcher. Sain's laid-back approach and his reluctance to run his pitchers appealed to Mickey.

Gradually filling out his frame, Lolich accumulated a noticeable belly, which some observers called flabby, but which he insisted, half-serious, was "all muscle." Tigers manager Mayo Smith called him "my sway-backed left-hander."

"I do have a big tummy, I'll admit," Lolich once said. "There's nothing I can do about it. It's my posture. When I'm going good, nobody says anything about it. If I lose a few games they start saying I'm out of shape."

In 1968, the Tigers had the best team in the American League, coming from behind to win several games on the way to the pennant. Teammate Denny McLain won 31 games that year, overshadowing another fine season by Mickey (17–9, 3.19 ERA, 197 Ks), who actually had been pulled from the rotation in early August for poor performance. He had six appearances out of the pen before returning to the rotation. But after going 0–2 to close the season, Lolich took center stage in the World Series.

The Tigers squared off against the St. Louis Cardinals, the defending world champions. After McLain lost Game 1 to Cardinal ace Bob Gibson, Lolich righted the ship by winning Game 2, 8–1 on a six-hitter. In that game, Lolich hit a home run off Nelson Briles in his first at-bat—amazing considering he was a career .110 hitter. "I wish I could pitch against hitters like me all the time," Lolich once quipped about his lack of offensive prowess.

In Game 5, with Detroit trailing three games to one in the Series, Lolich outdueled Briles again, winning 5–3 in his second complete game. Cardinals speedster Lou Brock admitted that Lolich was tough, saying it was hard to pick up the delivery until the ball was almost on top of the plate.

Detroit won the next game in a rout to set up a seventh game match between Gibson and Lolich, both of whom had two wins in the fall classic. Detroit erupted for three runs in the seventh inning and Mickey went the distance to win, 4–1, on just two days' rest. In the game, Lolich picked off two runners—Brock and Curt Flood—in the bottom of the sixth inning as he stymied the favored Redbirds. The southpaw had become the 12th pitcher to win three games in a World Series, and the last to win three complete-game Series contests in one year.

"I didn't know how long I could go," Lolich recalled. "After the fifth inning, Mayo looked at me every inning and I would tell him I was okay. Then, when [they] got me some runs in the seventh, I told Mayo I would finish it."

As MVP of the World Series, Lolich earned a new sports car. "I hope it has a stick shift," said Lolich, a car and motorcycle lover known for his fondness for going fast. In fact, during most of his career in Detroit, Lolich traveled the 33 miles from his suburban home to Tiger Stadium on his motorbike on the days he pitched. Another perk for the Series hero: Vice President Hubert Humphrey invited Mickey and Joyce Lolich to watch the liftoff of Apollo 8, the first mission to the moon. Lolich was already a space buff; he arranged annual tours of the space center at Cape Kennedy for Tigers players and their wives during spring training.

His performance in the 1968 Series seemed to buoy Lolich. In 1969 he won 19 games and earned his first All-Star selection. His 271 strikeouts were the third-highest total in Detroit history, trailing only Denny McLain's 280 in 1968 and Hal Newhouser's 275 in 1946. Twice in '69, Lolich fanned 16 batters in a game, his career high.

Two years later Lolich shattered that team mark for Ks as he racked up 25 victories and finished second in Cy Young Award voting to Vida Blue. In 1971, his 308 strikeouts paced the league, he started 45 games and completed 29, and he logged an incredible 376 innings pitched. "I don't like to hold back," Lolich said of his stamina. "I have a God-given good arm."

Lolich credited part of his success in 1971 to the addition of the cut fastball, a pitch that Sain had been trying to teach him for years. Warming up one day in spring training, Lolich noticed his fastball dipping and moving in unusual ways and realized he had finally gotten what Sain had been preaching. Armed with his new pitch (which some batters mistakenly assumed was a slider because it moved down and away so much), from 1971 through 1974, Lolich reached the 300-inning mark every season. The lefty used an unusual method to keep his arm fresh in order to rack up all those innings.

"I never used ice. I would stand in the shower after a game and soak my pitching arm under hot water for 30 minutes," Mickey explained. "The water was scalding hot. After 30 minutes [my arm] would be red, but it would feel fine and I'd be throwing on the sidelines in two days. I never had a sore arm."

Lolich was nearly as effective in 1972, winning 22 games as he helped lead the Tigers back to the postseason. In his final start of the regular season, the lefty dominated the Red Sox at Tiger Stadium, fanning 15 batters to vault Detroit ahead of Boston by a half-game. As usual, Mickey was a workhorse, pitching 41 games, completing 23, and hurling more than 300 innings. He finished third in Cy Young voting behind Gaylord Perry and Wilbur Wood. In the playoffs against the A's, Mickey pitched brilliantly, posting a 1.42 ERA in two starts, but he lost one game and got a no-decision in the other as the Tigers took Oakland to the limit before losing the decisive Game 5.

Through most of his career, Lolich was a two-pitch pitcher. He threw his fastball in the low to mid-90s and relied on a curveball to set it up. In 1971, he added the cut fastball which he could throw in a few different ways to have it dip or move in or out. Regardless of what pitches he used, Mickey's philosophy was simple: stay ahead of the hitters and let them get themselves out.

"I tried to throw two of my first three pitches to a batter for strikes," Lolich said. "I was like, 'Here, hit it.'"

But his fastball was hard to hit, and Lolich went on to fan more batters (2,679) than any other lefty in American League history, a record that still stood in 2007, more than three decades after he tossed his last pitch in the league.

"I can't throw as hard as [Sam] McDowell and a lot of guys," Lolich said early in 1966. "Dave Wickersham showed me something two years ago. He doesn't throw hard at all. [He's] got control and he makes the hitter go after his pitch. That's what I have to do."

Lolich captured 16 victories in both 1973 and 1974, and on May 25, 1975, he defeated the White Sox, 4–1, in a rain-shortened seven-inning game at Comiskey Park for his 200th career victory. But the season was one of frustration for the veteran left-hander.

Mickey suffered one of the worst stretches of offensive support in baseball history in the second-half of 1975. While the Tigers were on their way to their most dismal season in more than two decades, Lolich pitched effectively but had little help. Over the course of 14 starts from July 11 through September 13, Mickey received a total of 14 runs from his offense! Not surprisingly, Lolich's record was 1–13 during the stretch, which included a 19-game losing streak by the Tigers. When Mickey toed the rubber on July 11, he was 10–5 with a 3.31 ERA. When he lost the last of the 13 games during the 14-game stretch, his ERA was just 3.88, but his record had sagged to 11–18. He won his next start September 20—his teammates scored five runs for him—but it was his final game in a Detroit uniform.

After the season, Lolich was dealt to the New York Mets for Rusty Staub in a trade that was unpopular with Tigers fans. Mickey never took to the Big Apple and never moved his family there. During his one season as a Met, he battled with the trainer and pitching coach, who wanted him to run and treat his arm with ice. Lolich balked at the advice. He managed a decent 3.22 ERA for the Mets, posting an 8–13 record in 1976. His biggest highlight in a Mets uniform came July 18, 1976, when he fired a two-hit shutout over the Braves at Shea Stadium in which he fanned four and did not walk a batter.

At the end of the 1976 season, fed up with New York, Lolich retired in order to get out of the last year of his two-year contract. After sitting out a year, Mickey signed with the San Diego Padres, who pursued him and gave him a two-year deal. While playing with the Mets, Lolich had enjoyed visiting San Diego and felt it would be a wonderful place to finish his career. With a young Padres club he performed well in 1978 out of the bullpen, going 2–1 with a 1.56 ERA in 20 games. The following season, Lolich introduced a new weapon to his pitching arsenal: the knuckleball. After an inconsistent 1979 season, Lolich retired and returned to his home in Michigan.

For several years, Lolich ran a doughnut shop in the Detroit suburbs of Rochester and Lake Orion before selling the business and retiring to his homes in Oregon and Michigan with his wife, Joyce. In retirement, Lolich remained active in charitable work and served as a coach at the Tiger Fantasy Camp in Lakeland, Florida, nearly every year. His hobbies included biking, shooting, archery, and ham radios, and briefly during his playing career he took pilot lessons, played the banjo, and sang on stage in Las Vegas.

In 2003, Lolich was one of 26 players selected to the final ballot by the Hall of Fame's Veterans Committee. He received 13 votes, placing him far below the 75 percent required for election. Again in 2005 and 2007, Lolich was one of the few players to appear on the Hall's Veterans ballot, but he fell far shy of enshrinement.

Lolich won 217 games in his 16-year career, fanning 2,832 batters in 3,638.1 innings. He was named to the All-Star team three times, and earned the 1968 World Series Most Valuable Player Award for his historic performance and three victories over the Cardinals. He completed nearly 40 percent of his starts, and hurled 41 shutouts.

References

Publications
Detroit Tigers Yearbooks, 1961–1975.
Harrigan, Patrick. *The Detroit Tigers: Club and Community, 1945–1995.* Toronto: University of Toronto Press. 1997.

Articles
The Sporting News: September 5, 1956, p. 17; September 18, 1957, pp. 18–19, 22; June 24, 1959, p. 36; December 20, 1961, p. 41; May 16, 1962, pp. 27, 36; August 11, 1962, p. 40; April 25, 1964, p. 41; September 19, 1964, p. 11; November 14, 1964, p. 5; May 8, 1965, p. 15; January 15, 1966, p. 12; January 22, 1966, p. 12; October 7, 1967, p. 22; December 30, 1967, p. 31; May 18, 1968, p. 3; October 19, 1968, p. 7; October 26, 1968, pp. 8, 12; June 7, 1969, p. 13; May 2, 1970, p. 13; April 3, 1971, p. 27; June 12, 1971, p. 21; May 22, 1971, p. 9; November 13, 1971, p. 40; November 18, 1972, p. 51; June 23, 1973, p. 11; February 23, 1974, p. 32; February 15, 1975, p. 38; May 3, 1975, p. 13; August 2, 1975, p. 15; September 27, 1975, p. 16; October 25, 1975, p. 26; December 27, 1975, p. 53; January 17, 1976, p. 36; March 6, 1976, p. 50; May 22, 1976, p. 3; August 19, 1978, p. 13; April 14, 1979, p. 48; May 17, 1980, p. 19; July 26, 1980, pp. 9, 20; October 31, 1981, p. 19; December 31, 1984, p. 11

Mickey Lolich player file; National Baseball Library (various clippings)

Other Sources
Holmes, Dan. Interview with Mickey Lolich; January 2004, Lakeland, Florida.
Holmes, Dan. Telephone interviews with Mickey Lolich; September 2006 and May 2007.

Web Sites
www.retrosheet.org

1968   Tigers

Rich Shook presents:
Tigers In the News

Sunday, June 30
The White Sox halted another five-game Tigers winning streak, blanking Detroit, 12–0. Bill Voss, hitting .157 at the time, hit a grand slam—his second home run in two days and only the third of his career, all of which were in Tiger Stadium. Jim Price pulled his right hamstring, forcing him out of action in the third.

Monday, July 1
Al Kaline finally returned to the Tigers' lineup—as their first baseman. "He's the kind of guy that if you handed him a catcher's glove and told him to go to work would do a great job behind the plate for you without any previous experience," said California Angels manager Bill Rigney. Kaline had appeared in—can you believe it?—1,968 games as an outfielder (right and center) before manager Mayo Smith had him debut at first base in Detroit's 5–1 victory over the Angels. "He played well out there and I was well satisfied," Smith said. "I have no intention of playing him every day there but he showed he can do the job." Kaline worked out at first in the spring and recalled playing third for part of one game against Washington in September 1961. "I was nervous until the game started," Kaline said, "for I had never played first base, either in high school or pro ball, and I was not sure of all the moves." The first hitter of the game, Vic Davalillo, hit a grounder right at Kaline, who made the play with little hesitation. He was charged with an error later but also delivered the single that broke a 1–1 tie in the sixth. "I was lucky there were no real tough plays out there," he said. "The play on which I got an error came when I pulled my foot off the bag. But happily it did not hurt us. My arm still hurts when I swing, especially if I try to hold up on it." Mickey Stanley tripled in the sixth before Kaline lined a 2-2 pitch to left. Mickey Lolich improved to 6-4 with a 14-strikeout performance. Bill Freehan hit two home runs and Dick Tracewski also hit one, his third. (Historical footnote: Bob Gibson's streak of shutouts ended at six when he wild-pitched home a run in the first inning of a 5–1 victory over Los Angeles. He ended with 47 straight scoreless innings.)

Tuesday, July 2
Earl Wilson fanned six in the first three innings en route to nine-strikeout seven-hitter. Willie Horton hit a two-run single with two out in the first to stake him to a 2–0 lead as the Tigers beat the Angels, 3–1. (Historical footnote: Juan Marichal improved to 15–3 with a five-hit shutout of Atlanta.)

Wednesday, July 3
Denny McLain ran his record to 15–2 with a four-hit complete game in which he gave up one earned run. McLain struck out 10 and walked two in Detroit's 5–2 victory over California. Norm Cash's two-run home run in the sixth broke a 1–1 tie. His error in the top of the inning had allowed the Angels to tie the score. Dick Tracewski, still subbing for Don Wert at third, and Horton also hit home runs. It was slugger Tracewski's second in three games.

Thursday, July 4
The Tigers tied their club record with six home runs in a 13–10 win over the Angels. First-place Detroit noted with some degree of optimism the team in first place on July 4 had gone on to win the pennant 45 times since the AL began in 1901. "I said way back last spring the race this year wouldn't be as close as it was last year," said Jim Northrup, who had two home runs and a triple good for five RBI. The Tigers sent 14 batters to the plate while scoring nine runs in the second inning to wipe out four runs the club had generously provided the Angels in the top of the inning. Bill Freehan, Norm Cash, and Horton hit home runs in the inning. Cash hit another later in the game. Joe Sparma could retire just one batter in the second so Dennis Ribant (2–1) came on to get the win. John Wyatt (one inning), Fred Lasher (four), and John Hiller (one) finished up.

Tom Matchick

by Mike Lassman

Season	Age	G	AB	R	H	2B	3B	HR	RBI	BB	SO	SB	CS	BA	OBP	SLG
1968 Tigers	24	80	227	18	46	6	2	3	14	10	46	0	2	.203	.248	.286
Career Totals		292	826	63	178	21	6	4	64	39	148	6	6	.215	.254	.270

Before the term "walk-off" homer became a cliché, a Huck Finn–like figure from Pennsylvania coal country, Tom Matchick, hit a dramatic two-run homer off Moe Drabowsky in the ninth inning with two out to beat the Baltimore Orioles, 5–4 on July 19, 1968. Many longtime Detroit Tigers fans have claimed they were at that game, or at least heard the game on radio while at home or in their automobiles. There were 53,208 fans in attendance on that glorious Friday night, which was the Tigers' largest crowd in seven years. An estimated 5,000 fans were turned away.

Earlier in the game, Baltimore starting pitcher Wally Bunker held the Tigers hitless until the sixth inning, when Dick McAuliffe hit a two-run homer to cut the Orioles' lead to 4–2. In the bottom of the ninth, the Tigers staged another of their trademark rallies of 1968. Detroit was able to get runners, prompting new Baltimore manager Earl Weaver to call his crafty bullpen veteran, Drabowsky, into the game to face Bill Freehan. Freehan reached base on a fielder's choice, scoring one Tigers run. This set the table for the left-handed-hitting, freckle-faced Matchick, who had played for Weaver when Matchick was loaned to Elmira during its Eastern League pennant run of 1964. Drabowsky had given up only one home run during the season and squared off against the rookie infielder.

"I usually did not get concerned with who was pitching," Matchick said. "I was just looking to make contact and I hit a 3–2 slider." Matchick's disciplined contact approach caused the ball to arc high into the upper-deck overhang of Tiger Stadium's right-field porch. Tom hit three home runs in 1968; this was obviously the biggest of his career. This was a key victory as it pushed the charging O's to 8.5 games behind Detroit. Al Kaline jokingly referred to the victory as routine. But, this game was one of many the Tigers won in their last at-bat, and this day's hero was Matchick. It was yet another example of a Tigers player who contributed to the team's success during the fabulous summer of 1968.

John Thomas Matchick was born September 7, 1943, in Hazleton, Pennsylvania, to John Wesley and Anna Matchick. He was sandwiched between older sister Mary Ann and younger sister Anna Mae. He obtained his love of baseball from his father, who was a good catcher during his youth. His father admired Yogi Berra and the New York Yankees. Of course, Tom followed in his father's footsteps and admired the Yankees as well. Tom's favorite player as a boy was Yankees shortstop Tony Kubek.

Matchick enjoyed playing baseball, and his father did his part by helping his son practice. "My dad was a crane operator at Bethlehem Steel and would drive 60 miles each way to work," Matchick said. "He would come home at 6:30 p.m. and would practice different baseball drills with me." As a young boy, Tom would play baseball with other boys in the neighborhood. They would place electrical tape around the balls and put nails in the bats in order to keep them in use. The boys would play games of three-against-three and would make up their own rules.

Matchick played organized ball as well by playing Little League, Babe Ruth, and American Legion baseball, and usually played shortstop. His Babe Ruth team went to the World Series in Stockton, California, and, was the national runner-up. During the summer of 1960, Tom's father managed the Jeddo Stars, the premier amateur baseball team in the area. Tom attended Hazleton-Freeland High School and in addition to playing baseball, he was the star guard on the school basketball team. A 24-point and 12-assist average caused Stetson University to offer Matchick a basketball scholarship. But Matchick had other aspirations; baseball was his true love.

Prior to the 1962 season, St. Louis Cardinals scout Ollie Vanek signed Matchick to his first professional baseball contract, which included a $17,000 bonus. This began a 15-year journey in professional baseball. Matchick started his first pro season playing for Brunswick and hit .311 while playing in 71 games and smacked three homers in 264 at-bats. He remarked that the bus trips in Georgia and Florida were awfully long and hot. But the heat would not be a concern later in the season as the Cardinals moved Matchick to the cold weather in Winnipeg and he hit .227 in 176 at-bats.

At the conclusion of the 1962 season, major league baseball revised its first-year player rule and permitted the drafting of all rookies in the minor leagues. On November 26, 1962, major league teams raided the rosters of other teams for prices of $8,000 and $12,000. The Tigers drafted Matchick from the Cardinals for $12,000, which is ironic, as he would later appear for the Tigers in the 1968 World Series against his former organization.

Tom made his Tigers organizational debut for the Class A Lakeland team in the Florida State League in 1963. Later in the season, the Tigers promoted Matchick to Class AA Knoxville and Tom got the opportunity to play with future Tigers Willie Horton and Jim Northrup. After playing in the Florida Instructional League in the late fall of 1963, the Tigers thought about moving Matchick to their Triple A club in Syracuse, but eventually the Tigers decided that future shortstop Ray Oyler should play there.

Matchick played for Knoxville in early 1964 before the Tigers loaned him in July to the Elmira Pioneers, who played in the Eastern League. Weaver managed Elmira during the season and Matchick contributed to the Pioneers winning the league championship. Late in the 1964 season, Oyler had his Triple A all-star season come to a halt due to an ulcer, and Matchick was summoned to Syracuse to play for the Chiefs. Matchick nearly obtained a second title with Syracuse, but the Chiefs fell short in the quest for the Governor's Cup and lost the International League championship to the Rochester Red Wings.

Matchick spent the 1965 and 1966 seasons playing for Syracuse. During the 1965 campaign, he played with future Tigers center fielder Mickey Stanley and participated in a triple play. The Tigers invited Matchick to spring training in Lakeland along with future managers Jim Leyland and Gene Lamont in 1966. During the 1966 season in Syracuse, Matchick played in 145 games and hit .250 to go along with 12 homers and 54 RBI. After the conclusion of the 1966 season, the Tigers regarded Matchick as the best young infielder in the system and sent him to the Florida Instructional league to try him at second base.

The Tigers summoned Matchick to spring training in 1967 and hitting coach Wally Moses convinced Matchick to choke up on the bat and use a heavier 34-inch, 34-ounce bat instead of his typical 33-inch, 31-ounce bat. "I do not think that the Tigers wanted me to think about pulling the ball to the short right field at Tiger Stadium," Matchick said. According to Matchick, manager Mayo Smith told him that Tom would get a lot of playing time, but after a spectacular spring training that had Matchick going 15-for-31 and hitting .467, the Tigers sent Matchick to Triple A and kept Oyler on the roster. Smith thought his best position would be second base, and was open to the idea of moving Dick McAuliffe back to shortstop if Matchick performed well in Toledo.

The Tigers and Yankees switched Triple A affiliates prior to the 1967 season, the Yankees taking Syracuse and the Tigers claiming Toledo. Although Matchick did not want to go to Toledo, he did receive a blessing as he met his future bride that April. When he told Linda that he played for the Mud Hens, she asked Matchick what a Mud Hen was. This employment inquiry was understandable as Toledo had no minor league team from 1956 through 1964. Despite Linda not knowing much about the Mud Hens at first, the two got married after the season ended.

From a baseball standpoint, Matchick had a bad start to the 1967 season. The Tigers sent hitting coach Wally Moses to Toledo in order to help Matchick regain his hitting stroke. Tom eventually regained his stroke and raised his average to .290. Mud Hens skipper Jack Tighe proclaimed that Matchick was the best lefty hitter in the league against left-handed pitching. Tom became an all-star on the Toledo team and hit .289 with 11 homers along with 55 RBI. Matchick led the league in putouts, assists, and double plays, which helped earn him a Silver Glove—sporting goods manufacturer Rawlings' minor league equivalent to the Gold Glove—for his fielding. Toledo won the Governor's Cup championship, but Matchick did not play in the playoffs because the Tigers promoted Tom to the majors as part of the September roster expansion.

Matchick made his Tigers debut September 2 against the Minnesota Twins in front of 29,155 fans at Metropolitan Stadium in Bloomington, pinch-hitting for Ray Oyler in the eighth inning against Dave Boswell. "I went up to the plate and I was weak in the knees," Matchick exclaimed. "I probably took a swing at the first pitch that was near my shoulders." Tom popped out to Cesar Tovar at third base. Matchick came into the game at shortstop and made a putout in the bottom of the eighth inning.

On September 6, Matchick pinch-hit for Fred Gladding in the seventh inning and stroked a single off future Hall of Fame pitcher Catfish Hunter of the Kansas City Athletics at Tiger Stadium for his first major league hit. The Tigers eventually scored four runs in the inning and beat the A's, which kept the Tigers in a first-place tie with Boston, with Chicago and Minnesota breathing down their necks. Eventually, the Tigers fell short by one game to Boston. Matchick pinch-hit for Hank Aguirre in the fifth inning of the nightcap of a doubleheader against the California Angels in the last game of the season and struck out. Tom was 1-for-6 during his September call-up. Matchick was able to experience a successful pennant race after the season ended, however, as he helped lead Dunedin to the Florida Instructional League Championship and led the team with 29 RBI.

"I could tell that the 1967 team had a taste of winning the pennant and really was focused on winning the championship," recalled Matchick. Even though Tom did not have a spectacular 1968 spring training with a .191 batting average, he won a job and obtained uniform No. 2. Some of Tom's biggest games during 1968 were against the Orioles. In addition to his July 19 heroics, Matchick participated in a rare triple play September 1 against the Orioles in Detroit. Eventual 31-game winner Denny McLain caught a line drive and threw the ball to Matchick, who tagged second and threw to first base to complete the trifecta. Matchick pinch-hit for Mickey Lolich in the top of the ninth inning on May 7 in Baltimore and hit a clutch two-run double to help break the Orioles' eight-game winning streak.

"I thought that Mickey Lolich was a much underrated pitcher. He had an excellent sinking fastball and slider and did not get much run support," said Matchick. "He really challenged the hitters. If I was not playing and Lolich was pitching, both Gates Brown and Dick Tracewski would disappear when Bill Freehan was putting on his catching gear. I would often get stuck warming up Lolich and it was a tough job," joked Matchick. The Brown-Tracewski disappearing act notwithstanding, "we had a 25-man team and we played for the purpose of winning," Matchick said. "Everyone got along on that team and you couldn't find nicer people.

Tom's first career homer came on July 2 against Larry Sherry and the California Angels at Tiger Stadium. In addition to Matchick's iconic July 19 homer, Matchick's third and final homer of the season came against the Orioles on July 21 against Jim Hardin. Tom started every game but one July 16–25 and played well. Then, Matchick served in the Army National Guard and missed about 20 games. During the regular season, Tom hit .203 in 227 at-bats— weak, but better than his shortstop counterparts Tracewski (.156) and Oyler (.135).

Matchick has great memories of the 1968 season and remembers the sweet smell of Tiger Stadium. "Norm Cash was the leader off the field and kept us loose with his practical jokes. On one occasion he invited us for a boat trip in Chicago, but no boat arrived," said Matchick. Tom also remembers laughing September 19 when McLain was on his way to his 31st victory and grooved a fastball to Mickey Mantle, then knocked Joe Pepitone to the dirt when Pepitone requested a similar pitch. "But, when we needed a spark, Dick McAuliffe set the tempo on the field and would get the team going on the field and he never avoided a confrontation like when Tommy John hit him with a pitch," explained Matchick.

Matchick cherishes the 1968 World Series championship and had the opportunity to pinch-hit in three different games, but went 0 for 3. Matchick and Gates Brown are the only batters who did not strike out against Bob Gibson during his 17-strikeout performance in Game 1. When the Tigers were down three games to one, Matchick indicated that the clubhouse seemed like they were up three games to one instead. He said, "Placing Mickey Stanley at shortstop was a great move by Mayo. Stanley could play anywhere and we needed to get Kaline in the lineup."

Matchick returned to the Tigers in 1969 and it looked like he would compete for the shortstop job. But Mickey Stanley played mostly shortstop for the Tigers early in the season after his successful World Series play until the Tigers traded for Tom Tresh from the Yankees. Matchick proceeded to lead the American League in pinch-hitting, going 8-for-16. When Matchick started, he played mostly at second and third base during the season, and started at second base while McAuliffe recovered from knee surgery. He hit .242 for the season and had 298 at-bats. At the end of the 1969 season, Matchick had a meeting to negotiate a contract with Jim Campbell for the 1970 season and Matchick thought he would continue with the Tigers.

The Tigers traded Matchick to the Boston Red Sox, however, in return for Dalton Jones. The Red Sox doubled his salary and looked for Matchick to contribute with the glove and back up infielders Rico Petrocelli and Mike Andrews. Also, Tom had a better batting average than long-time Bosox utility player Jones in 1969—although Jones had better power numbers. But Matchick did not get much playing time and only had one hit in 14 at-bats. On May 28, 1970, the Red Sox traded Matchick to the Kansas City Royals for Mike Fiore. Unfortunately, in a pre-game drill on May 29 he was struck by a liner and cracked his right thumb and could not make his first appearance until June 21. No injury is timely, but this time, more than the thumb hurt. The Royals acquired veteran second basemen Cookie Rojas from the Phillies on June 13, which greatly diminished Matchick's future playing time. Tom did get 158 at-bats for Kansas City and finished with a .196 average.

Matchick started the 1971 season with the Royals' farm club in Omaha, with Jack McKeon the skipper. The Royals traded Tom to Milwaukee May 11, 1971, for Ted Savage. Matchick played for Evansville and became an American Association all-star as a utility man. Matchick hit .304 for the Triplets and won a promotion to Milwaukee, playing his first game in a Brewers uniform July 30. Tom was hitting .300 on September 7, but faded during the month and finished with .219 in 114 at-bats for the Brewers. At the end of the 1971 campaign, on October 22, the Brewers traded Matchick to the Orioles.

Tom played for Rochester during the 1972 campaign and made the International League all-star team. Matchick led the league in putouts, assists, and double plays, which helped earn him another Silver Glove. He had 11 homers and 58 RBI to go along with his .252 average and earned a call-up to the Orioles in September. Ultimately, Tom played in the last three games of his major league career and went 2 for 9. Matchick looked forward to playing for the Orioles in 1973 and was due to back up Bobby Grich at second. Matchick was told that he made the Orioles team in 1973 by Weaver, but Tom was traded on April 5 to the New York Yankees for Frank Baker.

Refusing to retire, Matchick spent the next four seasons playing in the minor leagues. He played for the Syracuse Chiefs in 1973 and hit .271, but he missed seven weeks due to a hernia operation. His 1974 season was spent playing for the Charleston Charlies and he hit .228 while playing alongside future manager Tony La Russa. In 1975, Matchick played again for the Toledo Mud Hens, by this time a Phillies affiliate, during spring training. The Phils allowed Matchick to sign a contract with the Rochester Red Wings. Matchick played for Joe Altobelli and helped mentor the Orioles' infield prospects. Dennis Martinez served as Matchick's roommate; other teammates included pitchers Mike Flanagan and Scott McGregor. Tom hit .274 for the Red Wings. Matchick was 50 days away from his four-year major league baseball pension and tried to get back to the Orioles, but fell short of a promotion.

Matchick started the 1976 season with the Red Wings, but Rochester released him July 7 in order to make room for Rich Dauer and Bob Bailor. The Yankees' Triple A farm team, the Syracuse Chiefs, signed Matchick, and Bobby Cox was the manager. He batted .299 for the Chiefs in 1976 in addition to pitching a scoreless inning. After the 1976 season, Matchick was told that he was sent an offer to be a player-coach. However, he never received the letter. "I was a student of the game and I thought I had good instincts and could judge baseball talent," Matchick said. "It would have been interesting to see what would have happened."

During Matchick's career, he played all four infield positions. "I have the utmost respect for utility players because it is tough to adjust and play many positions," said Matchick. "They are underappreciated." Tom would have liked the opportunity to get 400 at-bats during a major league season to see how he might have performed as a full-time player. Matchick, however, was a successful professional player for 15 seasons and he was named the top all-star in the International League on four occasions.

Over the course of Matchick's career, he had the fortune of playing for managers like Mayo Smith, Bobby Cox, Earl Weaver, Jack McKeon, and Joe Altobelli. He also played with Tony La Russa, Jim Leyland, and Gene Lamont. "Mayo was one of the mellowest managers that I played for during my career and he made the players feel comfortable," Matchick said. Also, Tom really enjoyed playing under Weaver and Cox.

After Matchick's playing days ended, he went into the sporting goods business as a manager. Subsequently, Matchick became involved in the photography business. In 2007, 40 years after his big-league debut, he was a vice-president of Great Lakes Aerocam, which does aerial photography. In his spare time, Tom likes to hunt for deer and turkey and play golf. Tom and his wife, Linda, have three children, Brian, Heather, and Amanda, and four grandchildren. Matchick is a member of the Hazeltine, Pennsylvania, Hall of Fame.

It has been 40 years since that magical midsummer night of July 19, 1968, but that memory will never be forgotten by Tom Matchick and the Detroit Tigers fans who witnessed it. And Matchick will never forget a very long and distinguished career as a professional baseball player.

References

Publications

Green, Jerry. *Year of the Tiger*. New York: Coward-McCann. 1969.

O'Brien, John, and Jerry DeBruin with John Husman. *Mud Hen Memories*. Perrysburg, Ohio: BWD Publishing. 2001.

Web Sites

www.baseball-almanac.com
www.baseball-reference.com
www.minorleaguebaseball.com
www.retrosheet.org

Other Sources

Lassman, Mike. Telephone interviews with Tom Matchick, July 16 and August 9, 2007.

Lassman, Mike. Interviews with Tom Matchick, August 18 and 19, 2007.

Rich Shook presents:
Tigers In the News

Friday, July 5
Freehan stroked a pair of three-run home runs to continue his power streak in Detroit's 8-5 victory over Oakland. The round-trippers gave him 14 for the season, five in the Tigers' current five-game winning streak. The Tigers' All-Star catcher was irritated at being struck in the left shoulder by a pitch in the fourth inning, the 12th time he had been hit by a pitch to that point in the season. Freehan was hit by 20 pitches in 1967. "I'm not trying to start a fuss," he said, "but I think it's about time something was done to protect the hitters. I'm not saying Catfish (Hunter) threw at me deliberately. I talked with (umpire Cal) Drummond about it later in the game and he said the A's were trying to pitch me high and inside and that the pitch got away and bounced off my shoulder. I don't know why I have been hit so often but I do think it is strange to see a fellow hit one or two home runs and then get hit. I think there ought to be an immediate fine. Not $50 or so, but $500 imposed right on the spot on a pitcher who throws at a batter. My view is that if the umpires do not fine these pitchers, the players are going to take things into their own hands. Some day a batter who has been hit will get real irritated and go out and hit a pitcher with a bat. I don't agree that deliberately throwing at batters is a way of baseball life." It bothers hitters, he agreed, "but if you get shy you will never get a hit and you might as well go out and buy yourself a shovel and get a job as a ditch digger or something." Freehan's home runs came in Detroit's four-run first and again in the fifth. Wert returned to the lineup and went 1-for-3 with an RBI. Mickey Lolich (7-4) worked 5.1 innings, allowing six hits and four runs. Pat Dobson completed the game.

Saturday, July 6
Earl Wilson (6-6) literally got knocked out of the game in the fifth as Oakland took a 4-1 decision. Rick Monday lined a shot off Wilson's neck, jaw, and thumb but the Detroit pitcher was able to jump up and back up at third, where the play was made after Don Wert fielded the carom and threw wildly to first for an error on what was ruled a single. One out later Reggie Jackson smashed a grounder off Wilson's throwing hand for an RBI single. He was taken for X-rays but there were no fractures. (Historical footnote: Billie Jean King won Wimbledon for the third straight year, defeating Judy Tegart, 9-7, 7-5, then teamed with Rosemary Casals to take the doubles crown.)

Sunday, July 7
The Tigers swept a doubleheader from the A's, 5-4 and 7-6, to take a 9.5-game lead on Cleveland heading into the All-Star break. "Nobody has asked for any (World Series) tickets yet," manager Mayo Smith said, "but I get the feeling some of them are building up to it. I'm getting a lot of those `Hi Buddy,' calls." Detroit entered the break 55-28 (.663). Leading the NL was St. Louis at 53-30 (.639) with a 10-game margin over Cincinnati and Atlanta. "Never in my fondest dreams did I imagine we would go into the All-Star recess with a lead like that," Smith said. "I think the Tigers really have a shot at the American League title now," Oakland manager Bob Kennedy said. "About the only way they could blow it would be if they played .400 ball the second half and some other club played at an .800 clip." In the opener, Denny McLain and Lew Krausse were tied at four runs and five hits through 8.5 innings. Krausse retired his 12th batter in a row, Norm Cash, to start the ninth but Kennedy brought in Ed Sprague to pitch to Willie Horton. Sprague made two pitches—the second turning into Horton's 21st home run. McLain entered the break as the majors' winningest pitcher at 16-2. Joe Sparma shrugged off the boos that greeted him when he took the mound as the second-game starter and raised his record to 7-8, walking four and giving up four hits in five innings. He left after facing two batters in the sixth with a 5-2 lead. Sal Bando's third home run of the day brought Oakland up to 7-3 in the eighth and the A's rallied for three in the ninth before Mickey Lolich, in his first relief appearance of the season, slipped a third strike past Reggie Jackson to end the game. Phil Roof singled and Dave Duncan walked off reliever John Hiller. John Donaldson stroked a one-out double to score Roof, and Hiller knocked down Rick Monday's smash and threw him out for the second out. Fred Lasher relieved and Bando ripped a two-run single to make it 7-6 before Lolich was brought in. (Historical footnote: Rookie pro Mike Hill missed a five-foot par putt on the 18th green and lost the $125,000 Buick Open at Warwick Hills in Grand Blanc to Tom Weiskopf. "It was just a terrible putt," said Hill, tied with Weiskopf at 8 under par until the $10,000 miss [$25,000 first, $15,000 second]. "The minute I hit it I knew I missed it.")

Eddie Mathews

by David L. Fleitz

Season	Age	G	AB	R	H	2B	3B	HR	RBI	BB	SO	SB	CS	BA	OBP	SLG
1968 Tigers	36	31	52	4	11	0	0	3	8	5	12	0	0	.212	.281	.385
Career Totals		2391	8537	1509	2315	354	72	512	1453	1444	1487	68	39	.271	.376	.509

Eddie Mathews played in only 31 games for the Tigers in 1968, batting .212 with three home runs, but his contribution to that championship season far outweighed his statistics. Mathews, who arrived in Detroit in 1967 after a long and illustrious career in the National League, had led the Milwaukee Braves to two pennants and the 1957 World Series title. This respected veteran provided a much-needed dose of leadership to the Tigers, only a handful of whom had ever played in a Series. When Mathews retired as a player after the 1968 World Series, he stood in sixth place on baseball's career home run list with 512 and held the all-time record for games played by a third baseman. Ten years later, he became the first member of the 1968 championship team to gain election to the Baseball Hall of Fame.

Edwin Lee Mathews Jr. was born in Texarkana, Texas, on October 13, 1931. His parents moved the family to Santa Barbara, California, four years later. Eddie inherited a passion for baseball from his father, a Western Union telegraph operator and former semipro athlete, though his mother participated as well. "My mother used to pitch to me, and my father would shag balls," he recalled many years later. "If I hit one up the middle close to my mother, I'd have some extra chores to do. My mother was instrumental in making me a pull hitter."

He excelled in football and baseball at Santa Barbara High and received college scholarship offers in football, but his prowess as a third baseman and a left-handed hitter stamped him as one of the most sought-after baseball prospects in the nation. Eddie and his parents weighed offers from several major league teams during his senior year. Mathews' autobiography explains how the rules then stated a player could not be signed until he graduated from high school. To be safe, Eddie and Boston Braves scout Johnny Moore waited until midnight on the night of his graduation in June 1949 and signed the contract a few minutes after midnight. Mathews got a $6,000 bonus. Several other teams had offered more money, but Eddie and his father had studied major league rosters and determined that the Braves, with aging third baseman Bob Elliott, would likely have an opening at that position a few years down the road.

The Braves sent Mathews to High Point-Thomasville of the North Carolina State League, where he hit .363 and belted 17 homers during the last half of the 1949 campaign. Promoted to Atlanta in 1950, the 18-year-old Mathews led the Crackers to the pennant with 32 homers, 106 RBI, and a .272 average. He was considered the best hitting prospect in baseball, and even Hall of Famer Ty Cobb marveled at the youngster's ability. "I've only known three or four perfect swings in my time," said Cobb. "This lad has one of them."

Eddie's career was interrupted by the Korean War, but after a few months in the Navy he received a hardship discharge due to his father's illness and his status as sole support of his family in Santa Barbara. He returned to the Braves organization and played for three teams during the 1951 season, ending the year with the Braves' top farm club, the Milwaukee Brewers. Invited to spring training with the parent team in 1952, Eddie won the third base job, beating out Bob Elliott, just as he and his father had foreseen.

Still only 20 years old, Mathews belted 25 homers as a rookie for the Boston Braves that year. Though he struck out 115 times, batted .242, and drove in only 58 runs, Eddie impressed onlookers with his potential and finished tied for third in the Rookie of the Year balloting. He capped the season on a high note with a three-homer game against the Brooklyn Dodgers on September 27, showing promise for the future. However, his future would not unfold in Boston. After years of declining attendance, the team's owners moved the team to Milwaukee for the 1953 season.

The Milwaukee fans were excited about the arrival of major league baseball, and in Eddie Mathews they found their first hero. Eddie grew into his own as a hitter in 1953, walloping 47 homers and driving in 135 runs while boosting his average to .302. He continued his hard hitting with 40 homers in 1954 and 41 in 1955, raising expectations that he could someday pass Babe Ruth's career record of 714 round-trippers. On August 16, 1954, the premiere issue of *Sports Illustrated*, with Eddie Mathews on the cover, appeared on the nation's newsstands.

Mathews was a hard-working, determined ballplayer who took pride in his fielding as well as his hitting. "Eddie was a below-average fielder when he came up, but he made himself into a good third baseman," longtime teammate Johnny Logan said. "Connie Ryan, one of our coaches, would hit 50 to 100 groundballs to Eddie every day in spring training. He'd knock them down with his chest and pick them up. He broke his nose three times fielding balls." By 1954, Mathews had established himself as a perennial All-Star and the top third baseman in the league, a distinction he held for the next decade.

He was one of the toughest men in the National League and drew almost as much attention for his fighting prowess as for his hitting. On August 1, 1954, after Brooklyn pitcher Clem Labine hit Milwaukee's Joe Adcock in the head with a fastball, the Braves' Gene Conley retaliated by knocking down Jackie Robinson. Later that inning, Robinson slid into third with his spikes high and found himself in a fistfight with Mathews. In August of 1960, Frank Robinson of the Cincinnati Reds slammed into Eddie at third and received the same response. "Eddie hit him with three punches that not even Muhammad Ali could have stopped," recalled teammate Warren Spahn years later. "Eddie was a tough competitor and a tough guy. He didn't back down from anybody." Another beanball war against the Dodgers in 1956 ended with Eddie pummeling rookie pitcher Don Drysdale.

"With Eddie, you never worried about anything," said former Braves teammate Lew Burdette. "If somebody charged the mound when you were pitching, you knew he was going to be there. Eddie used to tell me, 'Let the son of a gun charge you and get the hell out of the way.'" Mathews' tenacity, as well as his willingness to protect his teammates at all times, made him one of the most respected players in the National League during the 1950s.

Aside from his fights, however, Eddie rarely showed emotion on the field. "I'm not the type to make a big production out of everything I do," he said. "I think it's a joke when a guy strikes out and throws his bat. If I have to do that to show the fans I'm mad, to heck with it. I shouldn't have to fling bats or kick water coolers. Hustling to me means taking the extra base, beating out the slow roller, breaking up a double play, knocking the ball out of the catcher's glove, backing up throws and keeping my mind on the game at all times."

The steadily improving Braves finished in third place in 1954 and climbed to second in 1955, largely due to the hitting of another powerful slugger who joined Mathews in the Milwaukee lineup. Hank Aaron, a 20-year-old outfielder from Mobile, Alabama, made his debut with the Braves in 1954 and quickly adapted to major league pitching. By 1956 Aaron was the National League batting champion and formed a potent left-right hitting combination with Mathews, who hit 37 homers and drove in 95 runs that season. The Braves led the league by 3.5 games on Labor Day but faded in the stretch, losing the National League pennant by one game to Brooklyn.

The Dodgers, with their aging roster, had won their last pennant in Brooklyn, and the Braves were ready to take charge. In 1957 Aaron, the Milwaukee cleanup hitter, announced his arrival as a power threat with 44 home runs, while Mathews, batting in the third spot, chipped in with 32 homers of his own. Mathews and Aaron were now the best one-two power punch in baseball, and the hard-hitting Milwaukee club, buoyed by the pitching of Warren Spahn, Lew Burdette, and Bob Buhl, won its first pennant, taking the flag by eight games over the second-place Cardinals. The Braves entered the World Series as underdogs against the perennial American League champions, the New York Yankees.

All the Braves, except for Aaron, had been hitting poorly during the Series, but the team refused to collapse. The Yankees won two of the first three games and had a 5–4 lead in the 10th inning of Game 4 at Milwaukee. In the bottom of the 10th, Milwaukee's Nippy Jones was hit in the foot with a pitch, which he proved to the umpire by showing a mark made on the ball by the polish on his shoe.

Red Schoendienst sacrificed pinch-runner Felix Mantilla to second, and then Johnny Logan doubled to score Mantilla and tie the game. This brought Eddie Mathews, batting .091 during the Series up until then, to the plate.

First base was open, but the Yankees elected to pitch to Mathews rather than walk him and face Hank Aaron, who was waiting in the on-deck circle. With Milwaukee fans roaring, Mathews belted a Bob Grim pitch over the right-field fence for a game-ending homer and a 7–5 victory. "He didn't get many hits in that Series," recalled Aaron, "but that was the big one. That set up the whole Series for us."

This unexpected victory energized the Braves, who won a 1–0 squeaker the next day as Eddie scored the only run of the game. After a Yankees win in Game 6 tied the Series at three games apiece, Lew Burdette pitched the Braves to the title with a 5–0 shutout in the seventh game. Mathews, who doubled in the first two runs of the contest in the third inning, was the hitting hero once again as the Braves won their first, and only, championship in Milwaukee. "Without (Mathews) in that Milwaukee lineup," moaned losing manager Casey Stengel, "it would have been a different Series."

The Braves won the pennant again in 1958, but the Yankees enjoyed revenge in the Series. Mathews, who had slumped during the regular season with a .251 average and 31 home runs, managed only four hits and struck out 11 times as the Yankees regained the title. Eddie rebounded in 1959 with one of his greatest seasons, leading the league with 46 homers and finishing second in the Most Valuable Player balloting, but the Braves finished the campaign in a tie for the pennant with the Los Angeles Dodgers. After his team dropped the first game of a best-of-three playoff, Eddie walloped a homer off Don Drysdale in the second contest, extending the Braves' the lead in the fifth inning. However, the Dodgers tied the game in the ninth and won it in the 12th to clinch the pennant.

Mathews and Aaron supplied the power for the Braves over the next several seasons, though the team faded from contention after 1959. In 1962, Eddie tore the ligaments in his right shoulder while swinging at a high pitch thrown by Houston's Dick Farrell. He was never as dangerous a hitter after the injury, and his total of 29 homers in 1962 ended a nine-year streak in which he hit 30 or more. His first home run of the 1963 season was the 400th of his career, but his output began to diminish due to back and shoulder problems. He rebounded in 1965 with 32 homers and 95 runs batted in for the Braves. Home run No. 28, smacked August 20 in Pittsburgh, totaled 773 for the Mathews-Aaron tandem, passing the Babe Ruth-Lou Gehrig mark of 772. Aaron and Mathews combined for 863 home runs between 1954, when Aaron joined the club, and 1966, the team's first season in Atlanta.

Eddie, the only man to play for the Braves in Boston, Milwaukee, and Atlanta, lasted only one season in the Deep South. In November 1966, the Braves obtained Clete Boyer from the Yankees to play third base, then traded the fading Mathews to the Houston Astros. Eddie's career was winding down, though his short tenure with the Astros provided one bright moment. On July 14, 1967, he belted a Juan Marichal pitch into the right-field stands at San Francisco's Candlestick Park to become the seventh member of baseball's 500-homer club. However, Eddie played mostly as a first baseman and occasional pinch-hitter for Houston. He was expendable, and in August, when several American League teams inquired about his availability, the Astros cleared Mathews through waivers. The Detroit Tigers, in need of a third baseman after an injury to Don Wert, acquired Eddie on August 17, 1967, in exchange for a player to be named later. That November, the Tigers sent reliever Fred Gladding to Houston to complete the deal.

Eddie displayed his leadership mettle on his first day as a member of the Tigers when he discovered that not all of his new teammates were content with manager Mayo Smith. When he walked into the Detroit clubhouse for the first time, Mathews spotted a chalkboard on which an anonymous Tigers player had written, "We'll win it despite Mayo." Eddie erased the offending message and gave his teammates a lecture on the importance of supporting their manager. "That little episode made me a friend of the whole team because some idiot had written that down there," recalled Mathews. "Starting from that moment, I was accepted right away."

"You don't appoint guys to be leaders like that," Detroit General Manager Jim Campbell said several years later. "They either have it in them to take over, or they don't. And Eddie had it. We knew that when we traded for him. We got him as a player, but we got him to be a leader, too. Even Kaline looked up to him. He took a lot of pressure off Al."

Mathews played third for the Tigers until Wert's return in early September, then shared first base with the slumping Norm Cash for the remainder of the season. He batted .231 in 36 games for Detroit, adding six home runs to raise his career total to 509. On the final weekend of the season, when the Tigers needed to win three out of four from the California Angels to clinch a tie for the pennant, Eddie started all four games at first base. He drove in four runs, but the Tigers won only two of the contests and lost the pennant to the Red Sox by one game. In the final game, as Detroit's hopes for victory faded, Eddie nearly tripped over a news photographer while chasing a foul ball. The frustrated Mathews caught the ball and threw it at the unlucky man's feet, earning a chorus of boos from the crowd.

In the spring of 1968, Mayo Smith decided that Eddie's days as a regular third baseman were over. Don Wert reclaimed the third base job, while Mathews and Norm Cash competed at first base. Smith even suggested that he might platoon Mathews and Cash, though both were left-handed batters. Cash had struggled against lefties, while Mathews had enjoyed more success against them. Cash, however, established himself as the regular at first with Eddie on the bench. Mathews finally hit his first homer of the 1968 season on May 19 against the Washington Senators. Eight days later, Eddie hit the 511th and 512th homers of his career against the Angels, passing Mel Ott for sixth place on the all-time list. The two blows lifted his batting average above the .200 mark for the first time in 1968.

The veteran also gave his team a lift against the Athletics on May 26, after Oakland's Lew Krausse broke Al Kaline's forearm with a pitch the day before. When Jack Aker hit Detroit's Jim Northrup in the helmet, both benches emptied for what umpire Ed Runge called "the best fight I have ever seen on a baseball field." The charge from the Tigers dugout was led by Mathews, who raced to the mound and clocked Aker in the cheekbone. The skirmish, which raged for more than 10 minutes, energized the Tigers, who won 16 of their next 21 games and opened up a lead in the pennant race that they maintained to the end of the season.

Unfortunately, Eddie's back problems flared up again, and in early June the Tigers put him on the disabled list with a ruptured disk. Neither rest nor traction helped ease the pain, and on July 5 doctors at Henry Ford Hospital in Detroit operated to remove the offending disk.

Most observers figured that Eddie's season, and his storied career, were over, but the veteran soon returned to the Tigers and worked hard to get into shape. By early September he was back on the active roster, making a few starts at third and appearing as a pinch-hitter. He lifted his average to .212 by season's end, but the two homers he hit against the Angels in May proved to be his last in the major leagues. Mathews was surprised and pleased that the Tigers decided to put him on the roster for the World Series against the St. Louis Cardinals, though he had already decided that 1968 would be his last season. His third World Series appearance, coming a decade after his performances in the fall classic for Milwaukee in 1957 and 1958, would mark the end of his playing career.

Mathews played in only two of the seven games against the Cardinals. In Game 1, he pinch-hit for Don Wert in the eighth inning and struck out against Bob Gibson, who set a Series record by setting 17 Tigers down on strikes in that game. In the fourth game, Mayo Smith gave Eddie the starting assignment at third, with Gibson once again on the mound for St. Louis. Eddie walked once and hit a single, one of only five hits managed by the Tigers in a losing effort. Mathews rode the bench for the rest of the Series as the Tigers won the final three games and claimed their first world title since 1945. Though Eddie modestly described himself as a "cheerleader" for the club—"all I needed was the pompons and the little skirt," he said—he was thrilled to retire as a World Series champion. "We finished on top in Class D in my first year in organized baseball, and we finished on top my last year," said Eddie. "What more can a ballplayer ask?" The title eventually made Mathews only the third Hall of Famer, after Joe DiMaggio and Johnny Mize, to retire a World Series winner.

Jim Campbell offered Eddie a job as a scout, but Mathews decided instead to go into business. This effort was a failure; as Eddie later put it, "I didn't like being a salesman. I wasn't a closer. I'd go in and talk baseball for half an hour and walk out without mentioning my product." In 1971 he returned to baseball as a coach with his old team, the Atlanta Braves, and in August 1972 he replaced Luman Harris as manager of the club.

The biggest controversy of Eddie's managerial tenure occurred as his old teammate Hank Aaron, still a fixture in the Atlanta lineup, stood on the verge of breaking Babe Ruth's career mark of 714 home runs. Aaron entered the 1974 season with 713 round-trippers, and hit the record-tying blow on opening day in Cincinnati. Eddie then announced that Aaron would sit out the next two games in Cincinnati, the better to break the record at home in Atlanta the following week. Commissioner Bowie Kuhn angrily ordered the Braves to play Aaron against the Reds, threatening to fine or suspend Mathews if Aaron was not in the lineup. After a heated exchange of opinions between Kuhn and Mathews, Aaron sat out the second game of the season, then went hitless in the third and left Cincinnati still tied with Ruth. In the Braves' home opener, on April 8,

1974, Aaron hit his 715th homer, breaking the record that many had once expected Mathews to shatter.

The Braves floundered in mid-1974, and in July of that year the owners fired Eddie as manager. He spent the next several years coaching and scouting for the Texas Rangers, the Milwaukee Brewers, and the Oakland A's. In 1978, he was elected to the Baseball Hall of Fame in his fifth year of eligibility. Though Eddie had publicly questioned why Ernie Banks, who compiled statistics similar to his, entered the Hall on his first try while he waited five years for induction, he was a happy man at the ceremony in Cooperstown that summer. "I'm just a beat-up old third baseman," Eddie told the crowd. "I'm just a small part of a wonderful game that is a tremendous part of America today."

Eddie's later years were filled with difficulty. Married four times, the hard-drinking Mathews admitted in his 1994 autobiography that his alcohol intake caused him to lose several baseball jobs, including his position as Braves manager. In 1982, he developed a serious case of pneumonia and was hospitalized for months. Fourteen years later, he slipped while boarding a boat; fell into the water and was crushed between the vessel and the pier, smashing his pelvis. The old ballplayer never regained his health after that devastating injury, and on February 18, 2001, he died of pneumonia and respiratory failure at the age of 69.

"I think he was one of the greatest third basemen of all time," Johnny Logan said. "He had one of the sweetest swings I ever saw. There was only one Eddie Mathews."

References

Publications

Allen, Bob, with Bill Gilbert. *The 500 Home Run Club: Baseball's 16 Greatest Home Run Hitters from Babe Ruth to Mark McGwire.* Champaign, Ill.: Sports Publications. 2000.

Mathews, Eddie, and Bob Buege. *Eddie Mathews and the National Pastime.* Milwaukee: Douglas American Sports Publications. 1994.

Articles

Associated Press, February 19, 2001.

Haudricourt, Tom. "Eddie Mathews Overlooked As One of the Game's Greats." *Baseball Digest,* June 2001.

Milwaukee Journal-Sentinel, February 19, 2001.

New York Times, January 20, 1978; August 8, 1978.

The Sporting News, January 15, 1958, p. 4; August 26, 1978, p. 12.

Web Sites

The Eddie Mathews page at *www.baseball-almanac.com*

1968 TIGERS

Rich Shook presents:
Tigers In the News

Monday, July 8
First day of All-Star break.

Tuesday, July 9
Americans held to three hits in a 1-0 game that was the Nationals' sixth straight win. The three hits were a record low for a nine-inning game, as was the total of eight by both teams. Twenty AL hitters in a row were retired at one point. The game, played at Houston's Astrodome, was the first indoor All-Star contest and, as Bill Freehan noted, "it ruins your depth perception." "I don't like it," Willie Horton said. "It's nothing I can put my finger on. It is just odd. It is kind of awesome. [Juan] Marichal threw me a slider and I saw it so good I said to myself, 'I'm going to murder this,' and I swung and that ball hasn't got to me yet." Horton flew out to right fielder Hank Aaron in the second and was thrown out on a fine play by second baseman Tommy Helms of the Cincinnati Reds on his slow roller in the fifth. Freehan bounced out to third in the second and struck out against Marichal in the fifth. Third baseman Don Wert collected one of the AL's three hits, a double into the right-field corner against Tom Seaver in the eighth. The lone run of the game was set up when Freehan called for a curve and Luis Tiant threw him a fastball in the first. Mays started the game with a single off Tiant, who threw badly to first (although Harmon Killebrew was charged with an error on the play) on a pickoff attempt to let the Giants' center fielder move to second. Tiant's wild pitch was above Freehan's head, permitting Mays to move to third, from where he scored on a double play. (Mays was starting only because Pete Rose was hurt.) Denny McLain pitched the fifth and sixth innings, allowing a hit and two walks and fanning two. The Tigers' chances in the pennant race were helped by an unfortunate injury to Killebrew. He pulled his left hamstring catching a wide throw (by California shortstop Jim Fregosi) and had to be carried from the field on a stretcher. He was expected to miss about a month of action, but was sidelined into September. (Historical footnote: Spencer Haywood, who with Ralph Simpson led Detroit Pershing High School to the Michigan prep Class A basketball title in 1967, signed a letter of intent with the University of Detroit. The 6-foot-8, 225-pound center was a member of the 1968 U.S. Olympic basketball team and spent his freshman year at Trinidad Junior College in Colorado.)

Wednesday, July 10
The National League voted to break into two divisions beginning with the 1969 season. The two leagues voted at their annual All-Star meetings to go to a best-of-five format for their divisional playoffs, to be followed by the best-of-seven World Series. Originally the NL was going to have Montreal and San Diego join and keep their league at 12 teams with no divisions. Commissioner William D. Eckert urged the NL to reconsider and adopt a format similar to what the AL had approved earlier. They agreed, provided the AL agree to a 162-game schedule. The moves needed the players' approval. Hank Bauer was fired as manager of the Baltimore Orioles and replaced by a relatively unknown career minor league player and manager named Earl Weaver. Bauer was manager of the year twice in his four seasons at the helm of the Orioles, including the championship season of 1966 when Baltimore swept Los Angeles in four straight in the World Series. Weaver, 37, was one of three new coaches added after Baltimore finished sixth in 1967.

Thursday, July 11
Rod Carew hurt Detroit with a two-run single in the seventh to tie the score and another in the ninth to give Minnesota a 5-4 victory. Mickey Lolich started but John Hiller was charged with the loss. Baltimore won in Weaver's first game as manager, tying Cleveland for second, 9.5 games behind.

Dick McAuliffe

by John Cizik

Season	Age	G	AB	R	H	2B	3B	HR	RBI	BB	SO	SB	CS	BA	OBP	SLG
1968 Tigers	28	151	570	95	142	24	10	16	56	82	99	8	7	.249	.344	.411
Career Totals		1763	6185	888	1530	231	71	197	697	882	974	63	59	.247	.343	.403

Richard John McAuliffe was born in Hartford, Connecticut, November 29, 1939. He grew up in the tiny town of Unionville, a burg "not exactly a breeding spot for major league athletes," according to *Los Angeles Times* columnist Jim Murray, another Connecticut native. "Chickens are more along its line.... Unionville has about nine months of winter," Murray recalled. "And summer is apt to be three months of thunder showers." McAuliffe played baseball at Farmington High School under legendary coach Leo Pinsky, whose teams won 411 games and three state championships. "He was an excellent baseball coach," McAuliffe recalls. "A very tough individual. When you didn't show up for practice, when you didn't run hard, when you didn't hustle, he'd take you right out of the ballgame and sit you right down. I thought those were good rules he had, and I think that gave me a lot of desire and hustle." At 5-foot-10 and 140 pounds, Dick was also the fullback on Farmington's football team, and a star basketball player.

Dick caught the attention of Red Sox scout Joe Dugan during a tryout camp at Bristol's Muzzy Field during his junior year in high school. McAuliffe was 16 years old. Dugan told him to come back around the next year when he turned 17. Unfortunately, the McAuliffe family was a victim of a 1955 flood that damaged many houses in Collinsville and the Farmington River valley, and Dick spent the year helping restore housing instead of returning to Farmington High. He did finish school a year later, leading the Indians baseball team to the state tournament at Muzzy Field as a pitcher and third baseman. "I was pitching a game in the state championships.... I always had a good arm in high school," Dick says. "My first eleven pitches I threw were all balls. And we had two guys on and a 3–0 count on the next hitter, so Leo Pinsky took me out. [H]e put me at third base ... and I made a couple of good plays ... and got a couple of hits." Detroit Tigers scout Lew Cassell was in the stands during that tournament, and McAuliffe recalls their conversation after that game. "You're not a pitcher, by the way, are you?" Dick remembers Cassell asking. "I think he already knew that, but he was pulling my leg. Then he gave me an application to fill out ... and about two weeks later he was in the area, and he called my parents on a Sunday afternoon and he asked if I wanted to sign professionally ... and I said, 'Yes, I do.'" McAuliffe signed shortly after the class of 1957 graduated, guaranteeing a $500 bonus and an opportunity to play professional ball immediately.

The June 22, 1957, *New York Times* reported the signing of the "infielder-outfielder from Hartford, Conn." He would report to the Class D New York-Penn League Erie (Pennsylvania) Sailors, one of nine Detroit farm teams in 1957. "I flew from Bradley Field in Hartford to Erie," McAuliffe remembers. "I go to the ballpark ... and the team had just left to go on the road to Jamestown, which was a couple-hour bus ride, but they would return that evening." The cab driver took him downtown to the general manager's office. The GM told Dick to go across the street and check into the team hotel, and come back for dinner. "I had my only suit and tie on, thinking he's going to take me out to a fancy restaurant," Dick says. "I get there, and he takes me to the corner drugstore and buys me a 69-cent macaroni and cheese dinner! And then we drive over to Jamestown.... We watched the ballgame and the first thing that came to my mind after I watched ... was yes, I can handle this." The 18-year-old played 60 games, mostly at shortstop, had 175 at-bats, 36 hits, 9 doubles, 16 RBI, and a .206 batting average. "Don't they throw curves in Unionville, sonny?" he was asked. Charles Kress was the Erie manager, and the team led the league in attendance with a total of 54,923. The Sailors won the Eastern League championship, beating the Batavia Indians three games to one.

"My first year in pro ball, the velocity that the pitchers threw compared to high school was a lot more," the lefty-hitting McAuliffe remembers. "I was hitting everything to left field. I wasn't getting around on pitches." Tigers hitting instructor Wayne Blackburn had a fix. "They were flooding me to the left side, and it was difficult, there weren't any holes out there to get hits," Dick says. "So [Wayne] got me to open up, get my hip out of the way, and pretty much develop the stance that I had, and I was pretty successful with it. I stayed with it that whole spring training and after six or seven weeks of spring training I got familiar with it, and I was hitting the ball to right field, left field, and up the middle.... By the time I left spring training I was very comfortable with it." Many compared the new McAuliffe "foot in the bucket" stance to that of Mel Ott, the former New York Giants star. Bill James, who ranked McAuliffe 22nd all-time among second basemen in his *Historical Baseball Abstract*, described it this way:

"[H]e tucked his right wrist under his chin and held his bat over his head, so it looked as if he were dodging the sword of Damocles in mid-descent. He pointed his left knee at the catcher and his right knee at the pitcher and spread the two as far apart as humanly possible, his right foot balanced on the toes, so that to have lowered his heel two inches would have pulled his knee inward by a foot. He whipped the bat in a sort of violent pinwheel which produced line drives, strikeouts, and fly balls, few ground balls, and not a lot of pop outs."

It was back to Class D and the Valdosta franchise in the Georgia-Florida League in 1958. McAuliffe, now 5-foot-11, made the all-star team as a shortstop, hitting .286 with 17 doubles, 5 triples, 8 home runs, and 62 RBI. "I just started progressing," Dick once recalled. "Started hitting for average, hitting with power. Making less mental mistakes and physical mistakes." His fielding left much to be desired, as he tallied 45 errors in 93 games. Valdosta, under manager Stubby Overmire, won the league title over Albany in the playoffs. McAuliffe wasn't around for the postseason, however, having been sent to the Class A Augusta Tigers in the South Atlantic League for the end of the 1958 season. The 18-year-old played 41 games with Augusta, hitting .241 with no home runs and 13 RBI. The Tigers finished the season in first place, but lost in the first round of the Sally League playoffs to the eventual champion Macon Dodgers.

The 1959 season began for McAuliffe with the Durham Bulls of the Class B Carolina League. He was again an all-star shortstop, despite 35 errors in 94 games at Durham. (The all-star second baseman and league MVP from the pennant-winning Raleigh Capitals was Carl Yastrzemski—who would become McAuliffe's teammate 15 years later.) Dick hit .267 for the Bulls, driving in 43 runs on 84 hits, 20 doubles, 4 triples, and 4 home runs. He finished up the '59 season back in the Sally League with the Class A Knoxville Smokies, managed by former Red Sox great Johnny Pesky. "I liked Johnny, his brand of baseball," McAuliffe said. "He was a tough man to play for. You know, a real red-ass." He played only 11 games for Pesky that year, getting four hits in 26 at-bats for a .154 average.

Back to Knoxville in 1960, this time under manager Frank Skaff. Dick was again an all-star, making the club as a "utility infielder." McAuliffe's 109 runs scored led the league. He batted .301, hit 27 doubles, a career-best 21 triples, and 7 homers, and drove in 54 runs. It was a season that earned him a promotion to the big club at the end of the year. On September 15, 1960, the Tigers purchased the contract of the 20-year-old shortstop from the Smokies.

The 1960 Detroit Tigers were on their way to a 71–83 record, good for a sixth-place finish in the American League, 26 games behind the pennant-winning Yankees. Rocky Colavito slugged 35 home runs for Detroit. Al Kaline was fourth in the league in stolen bases with 19. Jim Bunning led the league in strikeouts with 201 and had a 2.79 ERA. Frank Lary topped the junior circuit in complete games with 15. McAuliffe remembered his first major league appearance, on September 17, 1960:

"[It] was in Detroit, in a game that I pinch-hit for the pitcher [Paul Foytack], and we were way behind [8–4 to the White Sox]. [Mike Garcia] walked me on four straight pitches, and there was one out at the time, and we were behind by a lot of runs, and [had] no chance of winning the ballgame. So I get on first base, and there's one out, and all I want to do is don't make any mistakes out on the base paths. So Coot Veal got up, and hits a real soft line drive to shortstop, and I don't know what made me do it—I guess the excitement that I was in the big leagues and all the people there and everything combined—and I just broke for second base ... and I got doubled off first base. So it wasn't a very good impression."

His first official at-bats came against the Indians. "Jim Perry was pitching for Cleveland, in Cleveland," McAuliffe remembers, and he smacked a single in the first inning, another single in the second, and then the triple in the fifth. "And then [Dick Stigman] came in, and [he] was just throwing balloons up there, and he threw one down the middle of the plate and I popped it up. And that was my first big-league out." (McAuliffe would even the score with Stigman in 1961, hitting his first major league home run off the Indians hurler that June 23 at Cleveland Stadium.) McAuliffe's defense was still a work in progress in 1960; in seven games at shortstop, Dick committed five errors.

At the end of the season, manager Joe Gordon wanted his young shortstop to come to California. "[He] wanted to take me to Sacramento, where he lived," says McAuliffe. "He wanted to tutor me while I was out there, and he would get me a job at one of the big factories…they have great baseball, semipro baseball out there. He wanted me to hook up with one of the teams and play, get in shape…while I was out there. And at the end of the season they fired Joe Gordon, so I never did get to go." Bob Scheffing would be brought in for the 1961 season. "The best manager I played for was…Joe Gordon." Dick recalls. "He was tough, he was fair. He treated the player…like a man."

McAuliffe started 1961 in the rarefied air of Colorado, playing for manager Charlie Metro and the Triple A Denver Bears. After 64 games with Denver, the 21-year-old shortstop was hitting .353, with 95 hits, 14 doubles, 14 triples, 5 home runs, and 31 RBI. He made 24 errors, but his hitting earned him a call to the Motor City. Joining the team for a game against the Washington Senators June 22, 1961, shortstop Dick McAuliffe was a Tiger to stay. In July, there was some concern that President John F. Kennedy would expand the military draft, leaving McAuliffe vulnerable. It didn't come to pass. (He finished a six-month stint in the Air Force prior to spring training in 1962.) The 1961 Tigers had an excellent campaign, posting a 101–61 record. Norm Cash led the league in hitting, and Al Kaline led in doubles. Frank Lary's 22 complete games topped the AL as he went 23–9 for the year. But this was 1961, and the New York Yankees were a dominant 109–53. McAuliffe played 55 games at short and 22 at third in '61, spelling regulars Chico Fernandez and Steve Boros.

Dick added a wife and second base to his repertoire in 1962. He married JoAnne Lee Cromack on March 3. Dick played 71 games at second, 49 at third, and 16 at short. He committed 30 errors, but more than made up for them with his bat—hitting 20 doubles, 12 home runs, 63 RBI, and compiling a .263 average hitting predominantly sixth and seventh in the order. He had his first career four-hit game against the Red Sox at Tiger Stadium on May 11. His first child, Mary Elizabeth, was born in the off-season, on January 2, 1963.

The Tigers' regular shortstop in the early 1960s was journeyman Chico Fernandez, a native of Havana, Cuba. They had no other shortstops in their system capable of replacing him. With his average hovering at .143 in early May 1963, it was time for the Tigers to make a change. Fernandez was traded to the Milwaukee Braves for Lou Johnson (who would never play for Detroit) and cash. McAuliffe took over as the regular shortstop, starting 133 games there and committing 22 errors. The '63 Tigers tied with Cleveland for fifth in the American League at 79–83, 25.5 games behind the Yankees.

The next year, 1964, was a breakout season for McAuliffe. He played in 162 games, 160 of them at shortstop, and started 159 of those. His career-high 32 errors were tied for third most in baseball. But his offensive output—for a 1960s shortstop—was remarkable. The 24-year-old led the Tigers and set a team record for shortstops with 24 home runs. His 77 walks were good for ninth in the American League. He drove in 66 runs batting mostly in the bottom third of the order. The '64 Tigers had a decent season, finishing 85–77 (with one tie), good for fourth in the AL, 14 games behind the pennant-winning Yankees.

In 1965, Dick became an All-Star. Chosen the American League starter at short, he led off the bottom of the first against NL starter Juan Marichal at Metropolitan Stadium in Bloomington, Minnesota. He popped out to shortstop Maury Wills in foul territory. Jim Maloney came in for the Nationals in the fourth, and McAuliffe singled and later scored on a Rocky Colavito hit. Cincinnati Red Jim Maloney was still in the game in the fifth, and Dick faced him again. "He threw me a high fastball, and in fact it was a funny thing, because Bill Freehan, our catcher, was out in the bullpen," McAuliffe remembered. "And Bill was talking to one of the catchers in the NL, and he was saying, 'How the hell does a guy like McAuliffe hit with that type of stance?' And no sooner was it out of his mouth than I hit the ball over his head…[a]nd Freehan just turned to him and said, 'Just like that!'" The National League went on to win the game, 6–5. "I played in three All-Star games," says Dick. "And…we lost by one run each and every time."

McAuliffe's numbers fell off a bit in '65, due in part to a broken hand that limited him to 113 games. Still, he hit .260, slugged 15 home runs, and drove in 54 runs. He began a transition into the leadoff spot that year, batting first in 48 games. "I was the type of guy who had a pretty good eye at the plate and got a fair amount of walks," McAuliffe says of his leadoff hitting. "My on-base percentage was always good, so therefore if I'm on base quite often it gives a chance for the number two, three, and four hitters to drive me in." He hit quite a few leadoff home runs in his time as well. "I think it's great for a ball club," Dick said. "Because if you have the power to hit the ball out of the ballpark before the other team comes up … that's a plus. Not that I'd do it that often … but it is a big plus and it gives an incentive to the rest of the [team], especially the starting pitcher that day. … It gives him a little incentive that before he goes to the mound he's going to be ahead one to nothing at least." Nineteen times in his career Dick gave his pitcher a leadoff home run.

Dick and JoAnne's second child, Michael John, was born February 1, 1966. That season, illness and injury again affected Dick. He was limited to 124 games, but made only 17 errors at short. He spent some time at third base, and was again voted the starting shortstop in the All-Star Game. He went hitless, and struck out against Juan Marichal. His season was outstanding, as he connected for 23 home runs, drove in 56 runs, and brought his average up to a career-best .274.

By 1966, it was clear to the Tigers that second baseman Jerry Lumpe was near the end of the line. The starter at the keystone since 1964, the Missouri native's offensive production had been trending downward since 1963, and his career-high in home runs (10) had come in 1962. To solve the problem, for the 1967 season Detroit moved its All-Star shortstop to second, and installed defensive whiz Ray Oyler at short. "The Tigers had no illusions about Oyler's lack of ability with the bat," says Brad Smith in his article "A History of Detroit Tigers Shortstops." "[T]hanks to McAuliffe's injuries, he had batted 400 times [actually, 404] over the course of the 1965–66 seasons, hitting .178."

In 1967, the All-Star starters were chosen by the players, and Rod Carew was tapped to start at second. Dick came in as a defensive replacement in the seventh. He flied to right in the eighth, again in the 11th, and once more in the 14th inning—his final career All-Star at-bat. And yes, the AL lost by one run, 2–1, on a Tony Perez dinger in the top of the 14th.

Dick had another fine offensive year in '67, hitting in the top third of the order. Twenty-three home runs, a career-high 105 walks, and 65 RBI helped the Tigers to a 91–71 record (with one tie) and an epic battle down to the final out of the season with the "Impossible Dream" Boston Red Sox. In fact, it was McAuliffe's 4–6–3 double-play grounder in Detroit, against the California Angels in the season's finale, that kicked off a pennant celebration in Boston. It was only the second GIDP for McAuliffe that year, both in the season's last five games. He would set a major league record the next season when he didn't ground into a double play all year. "I wasn't quick … I wasn't fast," Dick told interviewer Peter Zanardi in the early 1990s. "I could get down to first base, being left-handed and had a quick start at home plate. But one thing that helped me … was leading off so many times with nobody on base."

The 1968 Detroit Tigers ran away with the American League, finishing 103–59 (with two ties), 12 games ahead of runner-up Baltimore. "[We were] absolutely phenomenal for that particular year," McAuliffe remembers. "I mean, when you think a guy like Denny McLain won 31 ballgames. … But it was more than that. We averaged five plus runs for Denny throughout that year. Mickey Lolich was a great pitcher for our team, won [17] ballgames, but the key factor I think is that everybody contributed at the right time. I'd have to say that 1968 was the highlight of my life."

Al Kaline was in the outfield. "The best right fielder you'd ever want to see," Dick says. "Never [made] a mistake in the outfield, never drop a ball, always throw to the right base. Quick release, not only a strong arm, but very accurate." Norm Cash was "the comic of our ball club," says McAuliffe, and "Stormin' Norman" slugged 25 home runs. Big Willie Horton led the team with 36, and outfielder Jim Northrup drove in 90 runs. Bill Freehan was "a good catcher, excellent with knowing how to pitch teams," recalls McAuliffe. "[A] good, solid man behind the plate. Knew how to call a ballgame, knew the pitchers that he had[.]"

When asked about manager Mayo Smith, Dick says, "I don't call him a great manager, but … I think the biggest plus that he asserted to the club was that … he would have everybody moving on the bases. No matter who was on base. If a guy was on first and second and the count was 3–1 or 3–2, you'd be running. We were so successful with it that it was unbelievable. We'd stay out of double plays, we'd put the bat on the ball, we got base hits, and it really created a spark."

Some sparks flew at Tiger Stadium with the Chicago White Sox in town on the night of August 22, 1968. "I was sort of the sparkplug of the Tigers … scoring a lot of runs and playing good defense." Mickey Lolich was on the mound for Motown, Tommy John started for the Sox. McAuliffe played second, and led off the bottom of the first with a single. He scored on a Willie Horton single.

The Tigers still led 1–0 when McAuliffe came up with one out in the bottom of the third. He remembers what happened next this way:

"[T]he first pitch at me was right at my head, and I mean right at my head. The catcher never laid any leather on it, and it hit the backstop. And I didn't think too much of it. … Tommy John has got some of the best control you'll ever see, and he's a low-ball, sinker-slider type of pitcher with great control [and] not a great deal of velocity, but he was throwing the ball hard at me that day. So he threw… the next pitch, he spun me down, threw it behind me. And I turned around to the umpire, Al Salerno, and I said, 'Boy, if that thing hit me it would really put me away.' Al didn't say anything… and I've got a glare in my eye then but I didn't say anything. The count worked to 3–2, so I dug in, and there's no way that John is going to throw at me again. The next pitch… it hit the backstop again. And now I'm mad. But not mad enough to go out and charge him. So I take about two steps, and I'm glaring out at the mound at him … and he starts popping off at me [saying] 'What the hell are you looking at you. . .' or something like that. And all I saw were stars after that, and I just rushed out at him, and both benches emptied."

Tommy John remembers the incident differently. "I was 10–5 with a 1.98 ERA and pitching against the Tigers in August. A 3–2 pitch slipped out of my hand and sailed over Dick McAuliffe's head. I didn't throw at him, but McAuliffe was yelling at me as he went to first, and he charged the mound. McAuliffe drove his knee into my left shoulder and separated it." John was out for the year; McAuliffe was suspended for five games and fined $250 by league president Joe Cronin. "John hit us four times in Chicago in June," said manager Smith. "They hit eight of our guys in the series there and we didn't hit any of theirs." Tigers General Manager Jim Campbell said, "Cronin used bad judgment."

John indeed had hit four Tigers in a game that June 15, though he pitched against them again on June 30 and pitched a five-hit shutout with no hit batters. There was only one HBP in that four-game August series and it was when the Tigers' Pat Dobson hit Pete Ward. The John game was the series finale.

McAuliffe had another sterling season in 1968. Most significantly, he reduced his error total from 28 in 1967 to nine in 1968. (He was shocked that he didn't win the Gold Glove that year—Bobby Knoop, who made 15 errors, did.) McAuliffe hit 24 doubles, 10 triples, and 16 home runs, drove in 56 runs, and hit .249. His 95 runs scored led the American League. Dick would play in his only World Series, against the St. Louis Cardinals. His offensive stats weren't impressive, but he didn't commit an error in the Tigers' seven-game Series win. And he added a home run in a losing effort in Game 3 against the Cards' Ray Washburn. "It was a high fastball," Dick remembers.

A knee injury and subsequent surgery derailed the 1969 season, limiting the 29-year-old McAuliffe to 74 games. He still managed 11 homers and 33 RBI. He matched 1968's error total with nine. He would play four more years with Detroit, never quite reaching the heights of the 1960s, although still productive in a more limited role. By 1973, he was a platoon player, sharing time at second with Cuban journeyman Tony Taylor. On July 15, 1973, the Tigers hosted Nolan Ryan and the California Angels. "Ryan was tough," McAuliffe says. "You couldn't dig in against him back then as you could [later in his career]. That [day] was the best stuff I've seen from a pitcher in my whole career." So good that Ryan fanned Dick three times in three at-bats. Not that the rest of the Tigers fared better—Ryan threw his second no-hitter of the season that day.

Dick made one more postseason appearance, back at short for four games and second for one in the 1972 AL Championship Series against Oakland. He hit only .200 for the series, but hit a big home run off Catfish Hunter in Detroit's Game 4 win. The A's would go on to win the series in the decisive Game 5.

Dick had a decent season for the Tigers in 1973, playing in 106 games, hitting .274, and hitting 12 homers. But at age 33, he knew the end was near. "I wanted to move back East, I told them I wasn't coming back," McAuliffe says. "I wasn't pressuring [the Tigers] into trading me to Boston, but I knew my career was near the end, and I wanted to maybe make a connection and get into business of some sort, and Detroit obliged me."

On October 23, 1973, the Red Sox announced they had acquired the veteran infielder for young outfielder Ben Oglivie. According to an article about Oglivie in the December 13, 1975, *Sporting News*, Oglivie was the "only body Boston was willing to give up to get [McAuliffe.]" Manager Darrell Johnson expected Dick to challenge Doug Griffin for the second base job at best, and at worst, back up Rico Petrocelli at third. McAuliffe would wear number 3 for

Boston, a number worn by another Connecticut-born player—Moosup's Walt Dropo—from 1949 to 1952. Dick was excited about playing at Fenway. "[It's] a great stadium to play in because the fans are close to you. Just has that aroma in the air." As for the Boston fans, "[they] are very, very critical, very tough," McAuliffe said. "But they know the game. They really do."

Things didn't work out exactly as manager Johnson had planned. McAuliffe served in a utility role in 1974, playing 53 games at second, 40 at third, three at short, and three as the Bosox' designated hitter. He batted only 272 times, and hit .210 with five home runs. It was clear that at age 34, the end had come. Dick retired at the end of the season, and accepted the Red Sox' offer to manage in their minor league system.

Muzzy Field in Bristol, Connecticut, was a 20-minute commute from McAuliffe's home in Simsbury, and home to the Double A Eastern League Bristol Red Sox. With Dick as their manager in 1975, Dick would manage the B-Sox. Bristol went 81–57 on the year, behind young hitting star Butch Hobson. They swept the Reading Phillies in a best-of-five series to capture the Eastern League championship. McAuliffe wasn't around to taste the champagne, however.

In August, Red Sox third baseman Rico Petrocelli was suffering from headaches, inner ear trouble, and vertigo, possibly the result of a 1974 beaning. The 32-year-old Petrocelli left the Sox in Chicago on August 17, at the time hitting .254, with four home runs and 44 RBI. Some wondered if his career, much less the 1975 season, was over. "I just don't see certain pitches well at all," Petrocelli told *The Sporting News*. Rico was placed on the disabled list, Bob Heise was installed as the regular third baseman, and Dick McAuliffe was pulled from his managerial job in Bristol. "I'm in good shape," McAuliffe told Peter Gammons of *The Sporting News*. "I'm seven pounds lighter than I was. I've been throwing in batting practice every day so my arm's strong, my legs are in good condition, and I've been hitting off and on."

When Petrocelli went down, the Sox inquired about the readiness of Butch Hobson. "Butch had a pretty good bat for me all year long," McAuliffe said. "But in the field he'd make an awful lot of mistakes. Especially throwing mistakes. And I didn't think he was ready right then. [A]nd they asked, 'Would you be interested in coming up?'" There were about six weeks left in the season, and the Sox had a big lead in the AL East. "I really didn't think about it, and I said, 'Well, yeah, I would be.' Six weeks or so, you know, it's not long." But the veteran hadn't been completely honest with the parent club or the press. "[T]he only bad thing about it was I wasn't in shape," Dick said some 15 years later. "I hadn't picked up a bat all year. I threw batting practice—that was the only thing that was in shape was my arm."

McAuliffe played in seven games, all at third base, making his first appearance as a defensive replacement on August 23. He batted 15 times, with only two singles, for a .133 batting average. His career ended on a sour note on September 1. The Red Sox were hosting the rival Yankees, and the 35-year-old McAuliffe started the game at third, batting eighth. With one out in the second, Yankees DH Walt Williams hit a popup between third and home. McAuliffe dropped the ball for an error. With one run in, Yanks shortstop Fred Stanley tapped a ball to third, and McAuliffe's throw pulled first baseman Carl Yastrzemski off the bag. It was scored a single, and another run came in. Dick drove in his only run of the season in the contest, but the Sox lost the game, 4–2, and Dick McAuliffe's major league career was over. "I never, ever remember being booed in the big leagues," Dick remembers. "But that one game everything stood out, and the fans in Boston were tough. And I really felt bad after that and that was the only time after making an error that I felt really bad about losing a ballgame. And I said, 'Well, I guess I am over the hill.'" The Red Sox obviously agreed—McAuliffe was left off the postseason roster. In the classic 1975 World Series, Rico Petrocelli was back at third base.

The Sox wanted McAuliffe to manage in their system in 1976, but Dick had had enough. "You know, the salary wasn't very… big," he says. "I enjoyed doing what I did, but it was tough being on the road once again after 20 years of playing [baseball]. Leaving your family… and I said that's enough." Would he have changed anything in his career? "I think the only mistake I made was I should have stayed back in Detroit, where I felt more comfortable, and finished up there," Dick said. [T]hey would have given me a job in the minor leagues either as a hitting instructor—or in the big leagues—or managing in the minor leagues, which would have been fine. And gave me a decent salary."

McAuliffe went into business, running a couple of baseball schools and teaching kids how to play the game. "If you've got the desire, you don't need to have superstar skills," Dick told author Chris Stern in 1979. Shortly after retiring, he bought a business that repaired and installed coin-operated washers and driers. "I did quite well with it," said McAuliffe. "I was in the laundry business over 10 years… and then got tired of doing it." He sold the business and went into semi-retirement, playing golf, appearing occasionally at minor league games, and at autograph tables at county fairs and card shows.

"The game was very important to me," McAuliffe says. "I took it to heart. I played as hard as I could. I always thought I gave 100 percent, and was proud of the feats I'd done. I thought overall … I should have done better. That's just my personal feeling. I think I've been successful."

References

Publications

Detroit Tigers 1969 Press Guide.

Detroit Tigers 1972 Yearbook.

James, Bill. *The New Bill James Historical Baseball Abstract*. New York: Free Press. 2001, p. 497–8.

Johnson, Lloyd, and Miles Wolff, eds. *The Encyclopedia of Minor League Baseball*, 2nd ed. Durham, N.C.: Baseball America, 1997.

McConnell, Bob, and David Vincent, eds. *SABR Presents the Home Run Encyclopedia*. New York: Macmillan. 1996.

Stern, Chris, *Where Have They Gone?* New York: Tempo Books. 1979, p. 118.

Articles

Chass, Murray. "Yanks Use Munson at 3d and Win." *The New York Times*, September 2, 1975, p. 39.

Doyle, Al. "Tommy John: The Game I'll Never Forget." *Baseball Digest*, May 2004.

Gammons, Peter. "McAuliffe Back as Bosox Lose Rico." *The Sporting News*, September 6, 1975.

Green, Jerry. "Time Hasn't Taken Fight out of Tigers Franchise." *The Detroit News*, August 20, 2001.

Hawkins, Jim. "Tigers Tabbing Oglivie as a Regular." *The Sporting News*, December 13, 1975, p. 50.

"Majors Fear Loss of Players From a Possible Military Draft." *New York Times*, July 23, 1961, p. S2.

Murray, Jim. "Sticks to Riches." *Los Angeles Times*, June 9, 1965, p. B1.

O'Gara, Roger. "Eastern's Openers Hit Fouls in Bad Weather." *The Sporting News*, 1975.

"Ryan Hurls His 2nd No-Hitter of Year." *New York Times*, July 16, 1973, p. 37.

Smith, Brad. "A History of Detroit Tigers Shortstops." Available at *www.people.virginia.edu/~pw7e/tigershistory/shortstops.html*, (accessed January 27, 1999).

Spoelstra, Watson. "Kaline Marks 27th Birthday." *The Sporting News*, January 3, 1962.

"Tigers Buy McAuliffe." *New York Times*, September 16, 1960, p. C2.

"Tigers Sign Two Schoolboys." *New York Times*, June 22, 1957.

Zanardi, Peter. "An Interview With Dick McAuliffe." *Oldtyme Baseball News*, Vol. 5, No. 2, 1993.

Web Sites

www.baseball-almanac.com

www.hphshall.com/PINSKYHOF.htm

www.retrosheet.org

Other Sources

Zanardi, Peter, Oral History Interview with Dick McAuliffe, circa 1990–1991.

Acknowledgments

Dick declined to be interviewed for this project, and this biography would have been far less illuminating without the wonderful interview Connecticut sports journalist Peter Zanardi did with him in the early 1990s. Thanks to the SABR oral history committee for making it available. Thanks also to fellow SABR members David Paulson, Ed Washuta, David Vincent, and Bill Dunstone.

Notes

An earlier version of this biography appeared in *'75: The Red Sox Team That Saved Baseball*, published by Rounder Books.

Rich Shook presents:
Tigers In the News

Friday, July 12
All the talk centered on Denny McLain's chances to win 30 games after he ran his record to 17-2 with a three-hit, four-walk, five-strikeout performance in a 5-1 Detroit win. The only run off him was unearned, the result of a Don Wert error in the seventh. "I've got a chance for 18 now," McLain said. "I'd like to win just enough to win a pennant, that's all. Anybody who wins 25 has got to pitch well." No pitcher had won 30 in 34 years, since Dizzy Dean went 30-7 for St. Louis in 1934. "I'm pitching better this year than I was last year," he said, "there's no one or two ways about that. I've won every year I've been up here, but this just seems to be a real good year, that's all." "I think he's pitching better this year," pitching coach Johnny Sain said. "He's improved himself. He's pitching differently. He's got a better assortment of pitches and he's got them organized. He's an organized pitcher out there now. He hasn't pitched a bad ball game all year." "Nothing's routine, believe me," McLain said. "But once I get up four or five runs, I consider myself as having won." Wert's two-run home run, his eighth of the season, in the sixth provided McLain with enough runs to win. (Historical footnote: Eddie Stanky said he quit as manager of the skidding White Sox—probably just beating the ax. He was replaced by veteran Al Lopez. Chicago agreed to pay Stanky through 1971, the duration of his contract. GM Ed Short said it was "about half and half" whether Stanky quit or was fired. Owner Arthur Allyn was probably about to fire him. Lopez previously managed Chicago until 1965, guiding the club to the 1959 pennant. He managed the Cleveland Indians before joining the White Sox for a nine-year run. Stanky's reign marked an extension of Chicago's "Hitless Wonders" reputation as he searched to scratch out enough runs to win with tough pitching and good defense. The White Sox were 34-45, 18.5 games out, at the time the change was made. Stanky was famous for his double-switches and overbearing manner.)

Saturday, July 13
John Wyatt walked pitcher Jim Roland with the bases loaded in the 14th inning, handing Minnesota a 7-6 victory over Detroit. The Tigers had taken a 6-5 lead in the top of the 14th when Jim Northrup doubled leading off, made it to third, then came in when shortstop Rick Renick threw wildly to first on Al Kaline's grounder. Willie Horton and Bill Freehan both fanned with the bases loaded in the top of the ninth. Tony Oliva scored on an infield groundout to tie the score, 6-6, in the bottom of the 14th. Dennis Ribant was the losing pitcher.

Sunday, July 14
Earl Wilson started and complained of a sore wrist after getting cuffed by California for seven hits and six runs (three earned) in three innings of California's 7-3 win over Detroit. He had been hit on the wrist July 6 by Oakland. Wilson, Joe Sparma, and Mickey Lolich stood at a combined 20-19, including Lolich's 7-4 mark. (Historical footnote: Agreement on a $3 million pension plan ended a labor disagreement between National Football League players and owners that had kept the veterans out of training camps.)

Monday, July 15
Houghton, Michigan, native George Brunet handcuffed Detroit on five hits in California's 4-0 victory. It marked just the third time the Tigers had lost three in a row but Detroit was now 1-4 since the All-Star break. Jim Fregosi and rookie third baseman Aurelio Rodriguez hit two-run home runs off Lolich, who gave up two earned runs. Three of the hits off Brunet, who had a six-game losing streak to the Tigers, were singles by Al Kaline.

Tuesday, July 16
Denny McLain became the first 18-game winner with an eight-hitter for a 4-0 victory at Oakland that stopped Detroit's three-game slide. McLain did not walk a batter in his ninth straight win. Smith elected to play Kaline, a right-handed hitter, at first base against a right-handed pitcher rather than the lefty-swinging Norm Cash. Kaline made Smith the hunch-player look good by leading off the fourth inning with his fifth home run of the season.

Wednesday, July 17
Oakland beat Detroit, 3-2, with Reggie Jackson throwing out Dick McAuliffe at the plate in the seventh inning to preserve the A's one-run lead. Joe Sparma (7-9) failed to retire a batter in the second, allowing all three runs. Jon Warden and Pat Dobson combined to pitch two-hit shutout ball the rest of the way. McAuliffe stood on second in the seventh when Mickey Stanley lined a single to right. Jackson threw a strike to Dave Duncan at the plate. Duncan became better known as Tony La Russa's pitching coach when his playing days ended. Willie Horton hit his 23rd home run for Detroit.

Denny McLain

by Mark Armour

Season	Age	W	L	Pct	G	GS	CG	SV	IP	H	R	ER	BB	SO	ERA
1968 Tigers	24	31	6	.838	41	41	28	0	336	241	86	73	63	280	1.96
Career Totals		131	91	.590	280	264	105	2	1885	1646	778	711	548	1282	3.39

On September 19, 1968, at Tiger Stadium, Detroit right-hander Denny McLain was cruising along in the top of the eighth with a 6–1 lead over the New York Yankees. He had won his 30th game five days earlier, and the Tigers had already clinched the American League pennant. When Yankees first baseman Mickey Mantle came to bat with one out and nobody on, McLain let Mantle know that he would give him whatever pitch Mickey wanted. After a few batting practice fastballs were skeptically ignored or fouled off, Mantle signaled for a fastball letter high, McLain delivered it, and the Mick deposited it into the right-field seats. It was Mantle's 535th career home run, passing Jimmie Foxx for third place all-time. McLain was coy in the locker room, and later received a stern rebuke from Commissioner William Eckert, but has freely admitted the circumstances of the event over the subsequent years.

It was classic McLain: charming, cocky, arrogant, reckless. Just 24 years old, and arguably the biggest star in his sport at that moment, McLain had played by his own rules his whole life, and as baseball's first 30-game winner in 34 years, he was not going to be changing any time soon. He had a prickly relationship with his teammates, managers, the fans, and the city of Detroit, all of which he was apt to criticize at the slightest provocation. Bill Freehan, his catcher, once wrote, "The rules for Denny just don't seem to be the same as for the rest of us."

A virtual gunfighter on the mound, McLain pulled his hat brim down so low that he had to tilt his head backward to see the signs from his catcher. He worked fast and without deception, throwing pitch after pitch in the strike zone, even ahead in the count. Although he had a change and overhand curve, he used fastballs and hard sliders for the most part, challenging the hitter with every pitch, often throwing one letter-high fastball after another. If a batter hit the ball hard, the next time up McLain would just give him the same pitch in the same location. "Here you go," he seemed to say, "let's see you hit it again."

Off the field, McLain's life was equally carefree and, it would turn out, even more reckless. His idol was Frank Sinatra, not just for the legendary singing voice but because Sinatra exuded wealth and power. "Sinatra doesn't give a damn about anything, and neither do I," said Denny. Likely due mainly to his pitching prowess, Denny had a successful side career as organist; he played on *The Ed Sullivan Show*, headlined performances in Las Vegas, and cut a pair of LPs. Not content with traveling like the rest of us, he bought his own airplane, and learned to fly it himself. *Time* magazine put McLain on its cover in 1968, comparing him to a "high-school wise guy."

For his 31 victories and 1.96 ERA, McLain won the American League's Cy Young and Most Valuable Player awards in 1968, and his team won its first World Series in 23 years. He won the Cy Young again in 1969 (tying with Baltimore's Mike Cuellar) when he won 24 games. He made nearly $100,000 from the Tigers, and much more than that off the field. He was living the dream life. Until he wasn't.

Dennis Dale McLain was born March 12, 1944, in Markham, Illinois, to Tom and Betty McLain, both Irish Catholics. Tom had been a star high school shortstop in Chicago, but married Betty at age 18 in 1941, and adhered to her demand that he not travel around chasing a baseball career. When Dennis was born, Tom was in the Army in Europe; he later held jobs as a truck driver and insurance advisor, and made extra money giving electric-organ lessons.

Denny remembers Tom as a hard worker who chain-smoked and guzzled beer. Denny and his brother Tom lived in fear of their father's angry outbursts, which often resulted in beatings. Tom also got in frequent fistfights, on at least one occasion responding to the heckler at one of his son's Little League games. Denny did not try very hard to avoid his father's wrath, though—once, at age 12, taking the family car for a joyride. This behavior became more and more typical. Denny's memories of his mother are no better; he remained bitter over her failures to intervene on her children's behalf, and he has depicted Betty as a cold and heartless woman.

Tom encouraged Denny's baseball career, organizing the first youth baseball league in their hometown of Markham when Denny was seven, and a few years later driving his son to a neighboring town to play in a Babe Ruth baseball league. Denny dominated these leagues as a pitcher, just rearing back and throwing one fastball after another. Tom died suddenly of a heart attack at age 36 when Denny was a 15-year-old high school freshman. Betty quickly remarried, and Denny began doing whatever he pleased.

McLain attended Catholic schools, first at Ascension Grade School, then receiving a baseball scholarship to attend Chicago's Mt. Carmel High School. An indifferent student (one teacher later recalled, "He had a lot of trouble keeping his mouth shut"), Denny led his team to three city championships, amassing a 38–7 record on the mound. Upon his graduation in June 1962, McLain signed with the White Sox, receiving a $10,000 bonus, and another $7,000 if he made it to the major leagues. Days later he reported to Harlan, Kentucky, to play for the Smokies in the Class D Appalachian League.

McLain had a spectacular professional debut on June 28 against the Salem Rebels, tossing a no-hitter and striking out 16. He lost his second start, but allowed no earned runs and struck out 16 more batters. Though he was in Harlan only a couple of weeks, that was sufficient time for McLain to exhibit the reckless behavior that would become his trademark, defying team rules by making a 30-hour round trip to visit his girlfriend in Chicago on an off-day. He figured, correctly, it would turn out, that throwing a no-hitter would entitle him to more leeway than other players. This notion had been applied growing up in Chicago, and would stay with him all the way to the major leagues. After just two games, with a 0.00 ERA and 32 strikeouts, McLain was deemed to have mastered the Appalachian League, and was promoted to the Clinton, Iowa, C-Sox in the Single A Midwest League.

The Midwest hitters weren't as overmatched by a pitcher who threw almost all fastballs, and Denny had to settle for a 4–7 record, but with 93 strikeouts in 91 innings. In Clinton he went AWOL on the team several times, costing himself several hundred dollars. On the mound, his promise was still apparent.

That off-season McLain began dating Sharon Boudreau, daughter of former star shortstop Lou Boudreau, then an announcer for the Chicago Cubs. The two had met in high school, but their relationship escalated enough that they were engaged by January 1963, and married the following off-season.

Because McLain had received a bonus larger than $4,000, the White Sox were required to place him on the team's major league roster in 1963, or put him on waivers. Faced with a similar dilemma with pitcher Bruce Howard, the White Sox ultimately chose to waive McLain, the local boy, and keep Howard. The Detroit Tigers claimed McLain.

McLain did not take long to soar through the Detroit system. He began the 1963 season in the Single A Northern League with Duluth-Superior, but after 18 starts he was 13–2 with a 2.55 ERA, with 157 strikeouts in 141 innings. He then moved on to Double A Knoxville in the Sally League, and finished 5–4 in 11 starts. In September he was in the major leagues.

His major league debut was almost as spectacular as his pro debut in Harlan. Taking the hill against the White Sox in Tiger Stadium on September 21, he came away with a 4–3 complete-game seven-hitter, starting the Tigers' scoring by belting a home run off Fritz Ackley in the fifth inning. This would be the only home run of his major league career.

McLain began the 1964 season with Syracuse in the Triple A International League, but he did not stay long. After fashioning a 3–1 record and a 1.55 ERA in eight starts, he was promoted to the Tigers in early June. Just 20 years old, Denny joined the rotation for the rest of the season, winning four of nine decisions for the fourth-place Tigers.

McLain later claimed he turned the corner as a pitcher in the winter of 1964–1965 when he pitched for Mayaguez in the Puerto Rican Winter League, finishing 13–2 to help his team to the championship. Back in the States, Denny's first full season resulted in a 16–6 record and a 2.62 ERA. McLain relied essentially on one pitch—a letter-high fastball with movement, a pitch that was a strike in the 1960s but would not be a generation later. Tigers manager Charlie Dressen advised McLain to just throw strikes, and said he'd get a lot of hitters out with his stuff. He struck out 192 in 220 innings, including a league record seven in a row in a relief appearance on June 15.

His success continued in 1966. Starting the season 13–4, he was selected to start the All-Star Game in St. Louis and responded by retiring all nine National League hitters he faced. He did not pitch well after the break, but finished 20–14 with a 3.92 ERA, with 192 strikeouts. Dressen, whom McLain has always credited for his breakthrough ("God gave me an arm, but Charlie made me a pitcher"), had to leave the team after suffering an early season heart attack, and died soon thereafter. Denny would never find another manager to his liking.

McLain's outsized personality, combined with his pitching success, began to earn him a lot of money off the field. He played the organ, either by himself or with a group, in clubs around the Midwest, and earned a $25,000 endorsement deal with Hammond organs. McLain's biggest personal vice was his huge appetite for Pepsi-Cola, on the order of 24 bottles every day. When the company heard of his obsession, they signed him as a sponsor, paying him $15,000 a year, plus 10 cases (240 bottles) delivered to his house every week. By the age of 22, McLain was earning more money off the field than he was from the Tigers.

Detroit lost a heartbreaking four-team pennant race in 1967, due in large part to an off-year from McLain. McLain finished 17–16 with a 3.79 ERA, and was winless after August 29. After several poorly pitched games—no wins, two losses, 13 runs in 13.2 innings in four starts—on September 18 McLain reported that he had severely injured two toes on his left foot. His foot had fallen asleep while he was watching television, he said, and he stubbed it getting up when he heard some raccoons that were getting into his garbage cans. In the heat of the pennant race, McLain did not pitch again for thirteen days, until the very last game of the season. If Detroit had won, the club would have forced a one-game playoff with the Red Sox for the American League pennant. Unfortunately, McLain was again ineffective, and the Tigers lost to the Angels to fall one game short. His teammates were not happy about McLain's efforts that season, and doubted his injury story. "A lot of guys think he did it kicking a water cooler when he was knocked out of the game the day before," said one teammate. "He can still be damn irresponsible." It would get worse.

Entering the 1968 season, the Tigers were considered a talented group of individuals who could not play together. They proceeded to debunk that theory by leading the league nearly wire to wire on the way to a 103-win season and an impressive 12-game margin over the second-place Orioles. The star of the team, and of all of baseball, was Dennis Dale McLain, who captured the attention of the sports world with his 31–6 record. No pitcher had won 30 games since Dizzy Dean in 1934, and by midsummer McLain's pursuit drew attention across the country. The 30th win came September 14 on national television against the Athletics, a 4–3 victory. His 31st came five days later, the game in which he grooved the pitch to Mantle. In the Tigers' World Series triumph over the St. Louis Cardinals, McLain lost twice to Bob Gibson to help put the Tigers in a 3–1 hole, but won Game 6 as the team pulled out the series. Mickey Lolich won three times to lead the Tigers.

After the season, McLain won the American League Cy Young and Most Valuable Player awards, among many other honors. He spent the off-season flying around the country playing the organ, making money, and running his mouth. When asked during a performance in Las Vegas about teammate Mickey Lolich, who had saved the Tigers' season with his performance in the World Series, McLain responded: "I wouldn't trade (one) Bob Gibson for 12 Mickey Loliches."

McLain had another big year in 1969, winning 24 games and capturing a second consecutive Cy Young Award (tying with Baltimore's Mike Cuellar). The best pitcher in the game, the 25-year-old McLain was also raking in money on endorsements, appearing on national talk shows, and performing as a headliner in Las Vegas. As the 1960s ended, Denny McLain had reached a level of fame that very few baseball players have ever reached. When considering his outside income along with his baseball salary, he made more money than anyone in the game, and he spent it as fast as it came in.

The good times ended very suddenly.

In February 1970, *Sports Illustrated* featured McLain on its cover next to the headline "Denny McLain and the Mob, Baseball's Big Scandal." The mob? According to the magazine, in early 1967 McLain invested in a bookmaking operation based in a restaurant in Flint, Michigan; several of his partners were part of the Syrian mob. When a gambler named Edward Voshen won $46,000 on a horse race, his bookie couldn't pay it off, suggesting instead that Voshen find the bookie's partners. One of his partners was McLain. Voshen spent several months trying to get his money, finally enlisting the aid of mobster Tony Giacalone. According to the magazine's sources, Giacalone met with McLain in early September and, while threatening much worse, brought his heel down on McLain's toes and dislocated them. This would have coincided with time of McLain's ankle-toes injury in September 1967. The magazine also reported that Giacalone had bet heavily on the Red Sox and Twins to win the pennant, and had made a large bet on the Angels in McLain's final start.

McLain denied most of the story. He admitted to investing in the bookmaking business to the tune of $15,000, but claimed that his partners reneged on him, causing McLain to withdraw his support. He told Bowie Kuhn, baseball's commissioner, that he was completely uninvolved in the ring at the time of the Vashon bet, but oddly admitted that he had loaned $10,000 to one of the partners to help pay off the debt. Furthermore, he had never met Giacalone, and McLain retold the story of his toe injury. (In subsequent years, McLain recalled that it was an ankle sprain, not injured toes.) Just prior to spring training, Kuhn suspended McLain indefinitely while he conducted an investigation.

The problem with all of these accusations was that many of the people making them were criminals and low-lifes, as *Sports Illustrated* acknowledged. Although he has continued to deny the allegations regarding his injury, his denials have been in themselves damning. In his 2007 memoir *I Told You I Wasn't Perfect*, he writes that he was heavily distracted in September 1967. "I was spooked about Ed Voshen and worried about being exposed," he writes. "I kept expecting someone to tap me on the shoulder and say, 'Hey, where's my money?' or that my car was going to blow up." This fear is precisely why baseball has a paranoia about gambling.

If these problems were not enough, McLain was also suddenly broke. Though his annual income was close to $200,000, McLain had entrusted it all with a lawyer, who either mishandled it or stole it before fleeing to Japan. Without his baseball income, McLain's financial problems caused him to file for bankruptcy. Claiming that all of his problems were due to "poor business decisions," his petition listed debts of $446,069 and assets of only $413.

On April 1, 1970, Kuhn announced his decision. He continued McLain's suspension until July 1, roughly half of the season. Kuhn's report, among other things, said: "While McLain believed he had become a partner in this operation and has so admitted to me...it would appear that he was the victim of a confidence scheme. I would thus conclude that McLain was never a partner and had no proprietary interest in the bookmaking operation." Kuhn also absolved McLain from any charges that his actions had any effect on baseball games or the 1967 pennant race. (On the contrary, McLain's later recollection that he feared for his life in September 1967 suggests that the pennant race was quite affected.)

After Kuhn read his statement, a reporter asked him to explain the difference between McLain attempting to become a bookmaker, and actually becoming one. "I think you have to consider the difference is the same as between murder and attempted murder," responded the wise commissioner. Reporters all over the country, and especially in Detroit, thought the decision was a whitewash. Denny's teammates seemed surprised as well. Dick McAuliffe spoke for many when he said: "If Denny's innocent, it should be nothing. If he's guilty, then this is not enough." Jim Price, the Tigers' player representative, said that most Tigers thought McLain would get one or two years, or else nothing at all. Nonetheless, three months it was.

McLain returned on July 1 to a packed house, but struggled that night and for the next several weeks. On August 28, in what he claimed was a harmless prank, he doused two Detroit writers with buckets of ice water, earning a seven-day suspension from the Tigers. Before the week was up, Kuhn discovered that McLain had carried a gun on a team flight in August, so Denny was declared through for the season. His 1970 record was 3–5 with a 4.63 ERA.

McLain had lived the past several years by his own rules, and his stunning success on the pitcher's mound allowed him tremendous leeway. He showed up late, flew his plane to music gigs after games, and popped off about teammates, management, the fans, the ballpark, or the city. When you win 31 games, all of this is forgivable. When you finish 3–5, you are a pain in the neck.

A few days after the 1970 season, McLain was traded to the Washington Senators in an eight-player deal. Although he was just 26 years old—and was just six months removed from being considered one of the best players in the game—the Tigers considered themselves fortunate to acquire pitchers Joe Coleman and Jim Hannan and infielders Aurelio Rodriguez and Eddie Brinkman. They were fortunate indeed.

In his one year in Washington, McLain carried on a yearlong battle with manager Ted Williams, and finished 10–22. He spent 1972 with the Oakland A's, the Birmingham Barons, and the Atlanta Braves, getting hammered at all three stops, before finally drawing his release by the Braves the next spring. He spent a few weeks with Des Moines in 1973, but the magic was long gone.

His baseball career was over, at age 29, four years removed from winning 55 games over a two-year period. How could this have happened? McLain claims to have suddenly lost his fastball in 1970, but one couldn't help but notice that he was putting on ten pounds of fat a year. At the time of his release, he was 29 and looked 45. Denny McLain had a remarkable right arm, but he did not seem willing to do the work necessary to stay in the game. He had time to fly around the country playing the organ, but he didn't have the time to stay in shape. The case of Pepsi he still drank every day likely did not help his waistline.

Without his baseball career to get in the way, McLain could now devote all his energies to his "successful" business ventures. Always looking for the fast buck, he invested in a big-screen television business, ran a bar, wrote a book, opened a line of walk-in medical clinics. In the mid-1970s he was the general manager of the minor league Memphis Blues, who soon went belly up. McLain filed for bankruptcy again in 1977. His wife, Sharon, left him several times, but he always managed to get her back.

Denny made a living for a while hustling on the golf course. While involved with a financial services company in Tampa, he turned to loan sharking and bookmaking. With losses piling up, he and his colleagues got more adventurous. He once made $160,000 smuggling a fugitive out of the country in his airplane.

Eventually, the U.S. Justice Department began to sniff around Denny's associates, several of whom were willing to talk. In March 1984, McLain was indicted on charges of racketeering, extortion, and cocaine trafficking. McLain was tried, convicted, and sentenced to 23 years in prison. Thirty months later, an appeals court threw out the verdict on procedural grounds, setting McLain free, and the government ultimately decided to not retry the case.

McLain spent the next several years putting his life back together. He wrote another book, appeared at card shows, worked for a minor league hockey team, and got his own radio show. He was doing what he could have done all along—making a living being Denny McLain. It was a good living, reportedly making him $400,000 a year.

It wasn't enough. In 1993 he and a friend bought Peet Packing, a struggling 100-year-old meatpacking firm in Chesaning, Michigan. Within a month after the sale, $3 million was taken from the company's pension fund, and by 1995 the company was bankrupt. McLain and his partner were eventually convicted on charges of embezzlement, money laundering, mail fraud, and conspiracy. McLain spent seven more years in prison.

Released in 2003, McLain is giving life another shot. His wife, Sharon, divorced him when he returned to prison, but they remarried when he got out. They had four children: Kristen, Denny Jr., Tim, and Michelle. Kristen McLain was killed in an automobile accident in 1992 at age 26, a tragedy that McLain says caused his downward spiral that led to the debacle with Peet Packing. The remaining children have uneasy relationships with their father, understandably scarred by his repeatedly onerous behavior.

McLain was a great pitcher for a few years before his shocking downfall. He lived by his own rules, and hurt countless people along the way, including teammates, friends, and his own family. He has owned up to many of the mistakes he has made, but it is not clear that he really understands how much the world gave him and how little he has given back. It's an open question as to whether McLain will realize this before he dies. In March 2008 he turned 64 years old, and time is running out.

References

Publications
Freehan, Bill, with Steve Gelman and Dick Schaap. *Behind the Mask*. New York: World. 1970.
McLain, Denny, and Dave Diles. *Nobody's Perfect*. New York: The Dial Press. 1975.
McLain, Denny, and Mike Nahrstedt. *Strikeout*. St. Louis: Sporting News Press. 1988.
McLain, Denny, with Eli Zaret. *I Told You I Wasn't Perfect*. Chicago: Triumph. 2007.

Articles
Frady, Marshall. "You can be in Vegas before the game's half over." *Saturday Evening Post*, September 7, 1968.
"Tiger Untamed." *Time*, September 13, 1968.
Sharnik, Morton. "Downfall of a Hero." *Sports Illustrated*, February 23, 1970.
Stevens, David. "Denny's Vegas Debut Called 'Less Than Smashing.'" *Detroit News*, reprinted in *The Sporting News*, November 2, 1968.
Wolf, David. "Tiger on the Keys and the Mound." *Life*, September 13, 1968.
Wright, Alfred. "Golden 30 for Show Biz Denny." *Sports Illustrated*, September 23, 1968.

Web Sites
www.baseballreference.com
www.retrosheet.org

1968 TIGERS

Rich Shook presents:
Tigers In the News

Thursday, July 18
Earl Wilson (7-7) returned to form with a six-hitter in Detroit's 3-1 win at Oakland. Bill Freehan had a sacrifice fly in the fourth. Mickey Stanley's infield single plus a sacrifice fly by Jim Northrup brought in two more in the fifth.

Friday, July 19
Tom Matchick's two-out, two-run home run in the bottom of the ninth inning, his second of the season, capped a three-run ninth that gave Detroit a 5-4 comeback win over visiting Baltimore in front of 53,208, the largest Tiger Stadium crowd since 1961. Matchick had beaten Baltimore 2-1 earlier in the season with a two-run double in the ninth. Willie Horton strained some left-side abdominal muscles attempting a shoestring catch in the sixth and had to leave the game. It was not a serious injury. The Orioles had a 4-0 lead after the top of the sixth but Dick McAuliffe's two-run home run shaved the deficit in half in the bottom of the inning. Pat Dobson (3-1) pitched the ninth to earn the win. Detroit scored on a force play at second with runners at the corners to make it 4-3 before Matchick hit his home run on a 3-2 pitch.

Saturday, July 20
Dave McNally made his first hit in 42 at-bats, a two-run home run, in a 5-3 victory over Detroit and Denny McLain. McNally's first major league home run and a two-run shot by Frank Robinson chased McLain (18-3) in the fifth. It was the first time in 24 starts he had been knocked out of the box. Detroit had just one hit until Mickey Stanley doubled with one out in the seventh and scored on an Al Kaline single. Mickey Stanley added a two-run single in the eighth. "Funny," McLain said, "I've lost three games and all of them have been here [Tiger Stadium]. Funny, I've won every game I've started on the road. I hate to pitch in this bleeping place. It's not the fans, no, it's the fences. I wish we could take our own fans to Washington or some place."

Sunday, July 21
At the All-Star break Detroit held a 9.5-game lead. It was down to 5.5 games following 5-2 and 4-1 losses to second-place Baltimore, which shared the runner-up spot with Cleveland. Cleveland and Baltimore opened a three-game series on Monday. Earl Wilson started on just two days' rest in the opener and made it through six innings before getting knocked out in the seventh. Detroit stranded seven men in the opener and nine in the second in their first double-header loss of the season. Pat Dobson replaced Joe Sparma as the second-game starter. Al Kaline played left field in the second game. "I've been on eight pennant winners," said masterful pitching coach Johnny Sain, credited with developing Detroit's young pitching staff, "and so far this club has had less trouble than any of them."

Monday, July 22
Detroit played Pittsburgh in the Hall of Fame exhibition game at Cooperstown, New York. Don Wert hit a three-run home run in a 10-1 win. The Indians grabbed second place by defeating the Orioles.

Tuesday, July 23
Denny McLain also started on two days' rest, pitching Detroit to a 6-4 victory at Washington. A three-run sixth gave Washington a 4-3 lead but Al Kaline walked to open the eighth, Willie Horton laid down an unordered sacrifice bunt, and Bill Freehan walked. Jim Price pinch-hit and singled to tie the score and one out later Gates Brown pinch-hit an RBI single for a 5-4 lead. Jim Northrup doubled and scored on a single by Kaline in the ninth. It was the third time in the month a Detroit starter had worked on short rest. This was not as serious a move in those days of four-man rotations as it would be once teams moved to use five starters in turn.

Wednesday, July 24
The Senators slapped the Tigers, 6-3, handing them their fourth loss in five games. "We're in one of those ruts we have to battle out of, both in hitting and pitching," Mayo Smith said. "Everybody expects you to win, win, win. You just don't do that. There isn't a club in baseball that hasn't had this kind of rut happen to them this year." Detroit has a return match at Baltimore this weekend but Smith said, "You can't call it critical. We've got too much left to play." Detroit has just six games against the top three challengers the last six weeks of the season but has seven games coming up against Cleveland and nine versus Baltimore in the next month. "If we can split those 16 games, we're in good shape," Smith said. Mickey Lolich (6-7) lasted less than four innings in the loss. Gates Brown singled in the ninth and stood 11-for-18 as a pinch-hitter.

Thursday, July 25
Joe Sparma rallied Detroit with a rain-shortened one-hitter in Detroit's 4-1 victory over Washington. Rain stopped the game in the top of the seventh with Sparma striking out five and walking six in the game's 1:59 playing time. The only hit he allowed was a single by Paul Casanova in the fourth. Jim Northrup had a pair of home runs in Sparma's eighth win. He drove in three runs with his round-trippers. (Roster move: Detroit called up infielder Dave Campbell, an International League all-star, from Toledo as Tom Matchick reported for two weeks of National Guard duty. Campbell, 26, had 53 RBI. He starred for the University of Michigan.)

Don McMahon

by John Vorperian

Season	Age	W	L	Pct	G	GS	CG	SV	IP	H	R	ER	BB	SO	ERA
1968 Tigers	38	3	1	.750	20	0	0	1	35.2	22	8	8	10	33	2.02
Career Totals		90	68	.570	874	2	0	153	1312	1054	482	431	579	1003	2.96

History has not been kind to Don McMahon. Now largely forgotten, McMahon had a very long—often excellent—career, pitched in the postseason four times, helped win two world championships, and was clearly one of baseball's best relief pitchers in a number of seasons.

Playing in the days before the closer became such a highly prized position, Donald John McMahon worked for seven teams in 18 major league seasons. Upon his retirement at age 44, records show that only three pitchers (Hoyt Wilhelm, Lindy McDaniel, and Cy Young) had appeared in more games. The two-pitch (fastball and overhand curve) right-handed McMahon pitched in 874 games, racking up 1,310.2 innings and 1,003 strikeouts. He notched 153 saves and posted a 90–68 (.570) win-loss record with a career 2.96 ERA. Born on January 4, 1930, in Brooklyn, New York, McMahon grew up there as well. The youngster of Irish American descent went to St. Jerome Elementary School and Brooklyn Prep. In 1948, he graduated from Erasmus Hall High School. McMahon played baseball for the local Flatbush Robins in 1949. He was signed by Boston Braves scout John "Honey" Russell before the 1950 season.

Although mainly a third baseman in high school, McMahon was converted by the Braves into a pitcher. In 1950 at Owensboro (Kentucky) in the Kitty League, the 20-year-old won 20 games, with 143 strikeouts and a 2.72 ERA. He led the league in all three categories. The next year, he was sent to Denver in the Western League but appeared in only four games—in relief—before entering the Army, where he served from May 22, 1951, to May 14, 1953. After completing his service time, McMahon remained in the Braves' organization, though the club had relocated to Milwaukee just before the 1953 season.

McMahon was assigned to Evansville in the Three I League and pitched 114 innings in 1953 for a 6–5 won-lost record with 91 strikeouts and a 4.50 ERA. In 1954, he was assigned to the Atlanta Crackers in the Southern Association, where he improved his game and got his ERA down to 3.56.

On the personal front, 1955 was a big success; he married Dolores Darlene Sater on February 5. But it was a dismal baseball year. Now with Toledo of the American Association, McMahon finished 2–13 with an ERA that ballooned to 5.01. He returned to Atlanta the following year. Incoming Braves pitching coach Charlie Root acknowledged the 2–13 record, but said, "I don't see how anybody ever hits him. He throws so hard that catchers have a hard time hanging onto his pitches." McMahon always credited the Atlanta Crackers' field manager, former Brooklyn Dodgers hurler Whitlow Wyatt, for moving him from the rotation to the bullpen in 1956. It was a switch that proved very successful. That year, McMahon posted a 4–2 mark in 36 innings, struck out 34, and recorded a low 2.00 ERA and earned a midseason move to Wichita in the American Association. He took a while to adapt to the new league, but led off 1957 with a 2.92 ERA in his first 71 innings of relief and got himself a call-up to the big leagues in June. Clyde King also was credited with helping

McMahon develop. By this time, McMahon was pitching exclusively in relief.

On June 30, 1957, McMahon made his major league debut against the Pittsburgh Pirates in a Sunday doubleheader nightcap game before 36,283 in Milwaukee's County Stadium. Called upon to start the ninth inning to replace southpaw Taylor Phillips, he entered a game the Pirates were leading, 4–2. McMahon set down the three batters he faced. In the bottom of the ninth, the hometown Braves knotted the score on a Felix Mantilla home run with Frank Torre on board. In the Braves' 10th, McMahon popped out to first base in his first major league at-bat. Taken out in the 12th for a pinch-hitter, McMahon ended his part of the game with four innings pitched, giving up just two hits and striking out seven. Milwaukee won the match in the 13th by a come-from-behind score of 6–5 when Eddie Mathews hit a two-run home run. In his first eight appearances, he threw 14 scoreless innings. Milwaukee captured the 1957 National League pennant with a 95–59 record (plus one tie). McMahon ended a great first season with nine saves and a 1.54 ERA. He made three appearances in the 1957 fall classic against the Yankees, which the Braves won four games to three. McMahon threw five innings in relief without allowing a run. After the season, he played winter ball for San Juan in Puerto Rico. In December, though, he was traded to Estrellas Orientales in the Dominican League. The idea was to place McMahon with a team that didn't need as much relief help, so he wouldn't get overworked. McMahon pitched very well to open the 1958 season and was named to the 1958 All-Star team. He won seven games and lost two, with an ERA of 3.68. It wasn't until June 6 that he gave up his first home run in major league ball, to Don Zimmer, after 47 appearances without one. McMahon might have first become the answer to a trivia question sometime in 1958 at Milwaukee's County Stadium when he was the first pitcher driven from the bullpen to the mound; he arrived in a motor scooter with sidecar. McMahon saved the pennant-clincher for Warren Spahn on September 21 and the Braves repeated as NL champs. McMahon again made three appearances in the World Series but this time Milwaukee fell in seven games to the Yankees.

In 1959, relief specialist McMahon led the National League with 15 saves, complementing a 2.57 ERA. He claimed to have counted 132 times he was up and throwing in the bullpen; accurate or not, he was used in 60 games. He helped keep the Braves in the race, but the hitting wasn't sufficient and Milwaukee finished the year tied for the league lead with the Los Angeles Dodgers. The Dodgers took the first two games in the best-of-three playoff. McMahon got a good pay raise but had a disappointing year in 1960, with a 5.94 ERA and a 3–6 mark. The Braves still contended, finishing second, seven games behind the Pittsburgh Pirates. Bob Wolf wrote in *The Sporting News* that "the Braves' relief pitching was far short of championship caliber. The failure of Don McMahon to regain his form of the last three years was becoming more costly as the season wore on."

Bouncing back from what Wolf called a "season-long slump" in 1961, McMahon brought his ERA back under 3.00 and finished a decent season with a 6–4 mark and a 2.84 ERA. He'd started 1961 very well indeed, but tailed off significantly in August and September, and the team was not convinced that he'd entirely returned to form. They chose not to protect him in the expansion draft as the New York Mets and Houston Colt .45s both joined the league for 1962. Neither team picked him up, and Bob Wolf wrote in February that he "doesn't seem to have the old hop on his fastball, but he does have a good slider and a pretty fair curve."

On May 9, 1962, though, Houston was ready to make a move. Though McMahon had not worked much and not pitched well, the 32-year-old right hander was purchased by the Colt .45s for a relatively modest $30,000. When the Braves came to Houston for the first time, he unleashed a barrage at his old manager Birdie Tebbetts, bitter over the fact that he'd hardly been used by Milwaukee (three innings of work in the first month) and that Tebbetts had told him not to use his fastball except as a waste pitch. He blazed several fastballs past Braves batters and got credit for beating his old team June 7. A *Sporting News* account in the June 23 issue makes it clear there was no love lost between Tebbetts and McMahon. Don later admitted he got a letter from his mother admonishing him. "She told me to quit saying things against Mr. Tebbetts," he reported. He'd also had a flare-up over salary with Braves General Manager John McHale, so a change of scenery was probably in order.

Looking back on the year, McMahon was able to tell reporter Clark Nealon that 1962 was "the most gratifying year I've had since I came up to the Braves in 1957, helped them win the pennant and pitched in the World Series" (*The Sporting News*, March 16, 1963). He'd found his fastball again, liked the hot weather, and felt Houston treated its players better (and had a better philosophy of sharing relief work). He appeared in 51 games for Houston and contributed a stellar 1.53 ERA.

In 1963, McMahon put in a full year for Houston, but it wasn't nearly as strong as '62. His ERA ballooned to 4.05. He did witness teammate Don Nottebart's no-hitter. It was the eighth no-hitter McMahon had seen. McMahon had been the one to recommend signing Nottebart to Houston GM Paul Richards. Right at the end of the 1963 season, McMahon was bought by the Cleveland Indians, reuniting him with Birdie Tebbetts, now the Tribe's manager. It was Tebbetts who recommended getting McMahon, though it was a cheap enough acquisition at the $20,000 waiver price. The Indians weren't desperate for bullpen help, but Birdie spotted something in Hoot Evers' scouting report on McMahon and thought he saw a bargain.

McMahon lamented leaving Houston, saying that a bad shoulder had hampered him during a large part of the 1963 season. After the winter off, he established himself as Cleveland's bullpen ace right out of the gate. Coming to a new league gave him a bit of an advantage at first. He still relied mainly on his fastball. "My control isn't so sharp that I can pitch to the inside corner on one guy and the outside on another. All I want to know is whether I should pitch him high or low" (Regis McAuley, *The Sporting News*, June 6, 1964). By midyear, he had a 1.71 ERA. By year's end, he'd made 70 appearances in relief, breaking the previous club record of 63 appearances. He was 6–4 with 16 saves. In November, he was named Man of the Year for the Indians.

He was a holdout in the spring, and it took a while before Cleveland GM Gabe Paul and his pitcher came to terms—while seated at the February writers' dinner. He contributed a solid and respectable 1965 season (3.28 ERA), though not nearly as spectacular as in 1964. He wasn't being used quite as much in early 1966, throwing 12.1 innings in 12 games through the end of May. His ERA was good, though, at 2.92. In early June, the Indians traded McMahon and fellow pitcher Lee Stange to the Red Sox for Dick Radatz. In *Lost Summer: The '67 Red Sox and the Impossible Dream*, author Bill Reynolds described Radatz as the "…most dominant relief pitcher in the game, a large hulking man nicknamed 'the Monster'…" Radatz had a really disappointing year in 1965, losing 11 games, and wasn't off to such a hot start in '66, losing his first two decisions. First baseman Dick Stuart called him "that former fastball pitcher" and unforgiving Fenway crowds weren't making his life easy. The Red Sox were on a bit of a swapping spree; the trade was the seventh the team had made since September 1965, as GM Dick O'Connell moved to remake the team.

Despite Radatz's struggles, the trade was condemned by many in Boston. Stange was acquired for long relief and spot starts; McMahon was seen as the short relief specialist—though his first appearance was a four-inning stint June 4 against the Yankees, and he faced the minimum 12 batters in the seventh through the 10th innings in a game the Sox won on a three-run homer by Jim Gosger in the bottom of the 16th. He put out a fire the following night, also against the Yankees. On July 6, he earned wins in both halves of a doubleheader at Yankee Stadium and began to win hearts and minds in Boston. The last pitcher to win both ends of a doubleheader from the Bombers was Dave Davenport of the St. Louis Browns a half-century earlier, in 1916.

McMahon took over the fireman role, leading the 1966 pen with nine saves and a 2.65 ERA. Stange won seven games, but lost nine. Radatz had had his day; he disappointed Cleveland with an 0–3 record and a far higher ERA than either Stange or McMahon. In the end, Larry Claflin wrote that the Sox felt they "jobbed" the Indians and may have cost Birdie Tebbetts his job managing the Tribe. But Boston still wound up just a half-game out of last place. The Boston baseball writers noted McMahon's contribution nonetheless, and voted him the club's most valuable pitcher for 1966.

At the start of 1967, Don, his wife Darlene, their six kids, and two dogs all drove cross-country from his home near Anaheim, California, for Red Sox spring training in Florida. He and John Wyatt were seen as the core of the Boston bullpen. McMahon didn't pitch as well, though, as his ERA was up a run in April and May over his 1966 numbers.

Exactly one year from the day he was acquired by the Red Sox, they sent him to Chicago. It was June 2, 1967, as Red Sox management sought to bolster their infield by trading for veteran utility man Jerry Adair. McMahon was not getting a lot of work, having thrown just 17 innings. The White Sox had lost their primary reliever, Dennis Higgins, who suffered a detached retina, and were anxious to make a trade, anxious enough to give up a player like Adair. O'Connell found it a very attractive deal, and he pounced on it, throwing in highly touted minor league pitching prospect Bob Snow (who went 20–2 for Winston-Salem the year before).

Boston's 1967 skipper, Dick Williams, told SABR interviewer Jeff Angus that it was "a trade that helped both clubs." He added, "McMahon was disgruntled to leave, but he was just bouncing the ball off the plate with us. When he went over to Chicago, [he] pitched very well for them … [while] Adair played short for us for three weeks when Rico [Petrocelli] was hurt, and contributed." The shift agreed with McMahon; he finished the year with a 1.67 ERA for the White Sox and a 5–0 record, making a key contribution to Chicago's pennant drive. Adair contributed in a number of ways, and a number of writers felt his acquisition one of the key moves the Sox made in 1967.

McMahon didn't last much more than a year in the Windy City. The White Sox really needed another starter, and in a straight-up swap on July 26, 1968, they sent McMahon to the Detroit Tigers for right-hander Dennis Ribant. Chicago was worried about Gary Peters' health and wanted a pitcher with starting capabilities. McMahon again posted a final 1.98 ERA (consistent throughout the year, he was 1.96 for Chicago and 2.02 for Detroit). He'd missed being in the 1967 World Series with the Red Sox, but he found himself with another pennant-winning team as Detroit captured the AL flag in 1968. McMahon collected his second world championship ring, as the Tigers beat the St. Louis Cardinals in the fall classic—McMahon himself appearing twice, though briefly and not effectively.

McMahon returned to the National League later the following year, joining his seventh major league team, when the San Francisco Giants purchased him August 8 from the Tigers. Playing with Cooperstown-bound Willie Mays, Juan Marichal, Willie McCovey, and Gaylord Perry must have agreed with him. He was 39 at the time of the transaction, and he still kept getting batters out. He posted a 3.04 ERA for the remainder of 1969 and a 2.96 ERA in 61 appearances in 1970. In 1971, he was still relying on his fastball but admitted he hadn't used his slider for a couple of years. He was getting his breaking ball over the plate better than ever, and so featured that more.

In 1972, when the Giants signed him, they did so in two capacities. He was to be a pitcher, of course, but he also served as pitching coach, taking over from Larry Jansen. He still got into 44 games, throwing 63 innings and tallying a 3.71 ERA.

Over four seasons, McMahon posted an overall 25–15 won-loss record with 30 saves. After the 1972 season ended, the Giants released him as a player. He continued with his duties as pitching coach. When San Francisco's bullpen began to falter in mid-1973, McMahon was reactivated on June 25. He'd been throwing batting practice all year, so was in excellent shape, and hopped into a game against Atlanta on July 2. The score was 6–5 Giants, there was a runner at first and no one out, with Hank Aaron due up. McMahon closed the game, setting down six straight batters. He notched a 4–0 mark with six saves and an excellent 1.48 ERA. The following year, the same situation presented itself. He was the team's pitching coach, returned to the active roster on May 21, and the following day shut down the Braves in two full innings of work. He threw only 11.2 innings, though, appearing in nine games with no decisions and a 3.09 ERA. Six weeks later, San Francisco called up Phoenix (Pacific Coast League) farmhand right-hander Ed Halicki and placed McMahon on waivers. Once he cleared waivers, McMahon returned as the pitching coach. His last appearance as a pitcher had been on June 29, 1974, in a home game against the Dodgers. He threw two innings in relief.

McMahon coached for San Francisco through 1975. In 1976 and 1977 he was a coach with the Minnesota Twins. For a couple of years, Don worked in sales for the Rawlings Sporting Goods Company and turned up at Anaheim Stadium to present Rick Miller with a Gold Glove.

He returned to the major league ranks to reprise his role as pitching coach with the Giants for three more seasons, 1980–1982. Within a few weeks of his release, he was hired by the Cleveland Indians in the same capacity, 1983–1985. In November 1985, he was hired by the Los Angeles Dodgers "to position players from the press box" as the team's "eye in the sky." He even worked some in the off-season as a football scout for several years, helping out the Oakland Raiders even while still an active player. Al Davis and he had both gone to school at Erasmus Hall High in Brooklyn.

On July 22, 1987, at Dodger Stadium, while pitching batting practice, the 57-year-old McMahon suffered a heart attack and died a few hours later in a local hospital. He had been working for Los Angeles as an instructional coach and scout and threw batting practice almost every Dodgers home game.

Hall of Fame outfielder Duke Snider said of Mac: "I played against him. He never gave in to a hitter. He was a great competitor." The *New York Times* ran a heartfelt appreciation of Don McMahon by Ira Berkow, headlined "He

Died With Spikes On." The Dodgers wore an arm band reading "MAC" in his memory. Survived by his wife and six children, Don McMahon was buried at Good Shepherd Cemetery in Huntington Beach, California, with a baseball in his hand.

References

Publications

Looney, Jack. *Now Batting Number….* New York: Black Dog & Leventhal Publishers. 2006.

Pietrusza, David, Matthew Silverman, and Michael Gershman, eds. *Baseball: The Biographical Encyclopedia.* Kingston, N.Y.: Total Sports/Sports Illustrated. 2000.

Other Sources

Angus, Jeff. Interview with Dick Williams, February 24, 2006.

Notes

An earlier version of this biography appeared in *The 1967 Impossible Dream Red Sox: Pandemonium on the Field*, published by Rounder Books.

1968　TIGERS

Rich Shook presents:
Tigers In the News

Friday, July 26
This game was later seen as one of the season's possible turning points. Daryl Patterson was called to the mound in the sixth inning with the bases loaded, nobody out, and his team holding a 2-0 lead. Earl Wilson had strained his left knee during the inning. He struck out Fred Valentine, Brooks Robinson, and Dave Johnson on just 13 pitches to preserve the margin and Detroit went on to win, 4-2, over new manager Earl Weaver's hard-charging second-place Baltimore Orioles. It restored the Tigers' lead to 6.5 games over the Orioles. RBI singles by Bill Freehan and Dick McAuliffe in the fifth had given Detroit a 2-0 lead before starter Wilson and reliever Jon Warden loaded the bases with two singles and a walk. Patterson worked four innings and the only hit he allowed was a solo home run by Boog Powell in the eighth. (Roster move: Dennis Ribant was traded by Detroit to the Chicago White Sox for Don McMahon in a straight waiver deal. The 38-year-old McMahon was 2-1 with Chicago.)

Saturday, July 27
Denny McLain posted his 20th victory with a three-hit shutout in a 9-0 win over the Orioles. Willie Horton had a pair of home runs while McAuliffe, Don Wert, and Al Kaline added one each. McLain did not allow a runner past second base, moving 11 days ahead of the pace set by Dizzy Dean when he won 30 games for St. Louis in 1934. It was the first time a pitcher had won his 20th game in July since Robert Moses "Lefty" Grove for Philadelphia in 1931. Kaline played right field for just the second time since he broke his arm.

Sunday, July 28
Dave McNally three-hit Detroit in a 5-1 Baltimore victory. Mickey Lolich gave up seven hits in 1.1 innings in his first loss to the Orioles since May 24, 1964. Horton ruined the shutout with his 26th home run with two out in the ninth. Ray Oyler jammed his left ankle and had to leave the game in the first inning. Detroit was left with just Dick Tracewski as a shortstop with Matchick away on National Guard duty. "I'm going to take Lolich out of the rotation for a while," Smith said after the game. "He has not been good in his last three starts."

Monday, July 29
The Yankees beat the Tigers, 7-2, but the Orioles lost twice to fall back into a second-place tie with the Indians at seven games back. Joe Sparma was roughed up for five runs and nine hits in less than six innings.

Tuesday, July 30
Earl Wilson (9-8) allowed three hits despite a left knee that was heavily bound in a leather and metal harness. He developed the sore knee during his July 26 start in Baltimore. Wilson came out after walking Mickey Mantle in the ninth. Daryl Patterson came on to complete the 5-0 shutout. Wilson hit his third home run of the season into the right field seats to open the third inning and Dick McAuliffe then lifted one into the upper deck in right for his 13th. Al Kaline had a two-run double in the fourth. (Historical footnote: Shortstop Ron Hansen of Washington executed the first unassisted triple play in 41 years—since Detroit first baseman Johnny Neun pulled it off in the ninth inning of a 1-0 Tigers victory over Cleveland in 1927.)

Wednesday, July 31
Dick McAuliffe adjusted his batting stance and went 4-for-4 with four runs scored to back Denny McLain's 21st victory. McLain pitched a four-hitter for his second straight shutout, 4-0 over visiting Washington. McAuliffe used a very open stance with his front foot pointed almost toward first base. He said he shortened his stride and moved his bat handle a little closer to his body because "it makes me follow the ball better." He hit his 14th home run, two doubles and a single, scoring on two of Al Kaline's three hits (a double and two singles).

Thursday, August 1
Ron Hansen hit a grand slam to lead last-place Washington to a 9-3 victory over Detroit. Norm Cash hit his 15th home run for the Tigers. Jim Northrup tripled in Dick McAuliffe, who had singled, in the third. (Historical footnote: Hansen was traded later in the day to Chicago's White Sox, leading several writers to note he was the only major league player to make an unassisted triple play, hit a grand slam, and then get traded all in the same week.)

Friday, August 2
Veteran Don McMahon plus kids John Hiller and Daryl Patterson preserved a one-run lead to help Detroit take a 6-5 win from host Minnesota. Bill Freehan drove in three runs including the game-winner as Detroit blew a four-run lead. McMahon worked four shutout innings after Joe Sparma and Mickey Lolich squandered the lead to earn his first Detroit victory. Sparma allowed two runs and Lolich three before McMahon was brought on. McMahon allowed three hits before a leadoff single in the ninth prompted Mayo Smith to call on Hiller for two outs and Patterson for the last. Freehan doubled home two runs in the first and Don Wert staked Sparma to a 4-0 lead with an RBI single. Freehan drove in his other run to cap a two-run fifth.

Jim Northrup

by Jim Sargent

Season	Age	G	AB	R	H	2B	3B	HR	RBI	BB	SO	SB	CS	BA	OBP	SLG
1968 Tigers	28	154	580	76	153	29	7	21	90	50	87	4	5	.264	.324	.447
Career Totals		1392	4692	603	1254	218	42	153	610	449	635	39	38	.267	.333	.429

James Thomas "Jim" Northrup, who was born and raised in a small town in Michigan, starred in several sports, including baseball and football, at Alma College in the Michigan city of the same name. Later, he made it to the major leagues and enjoyed a fine career as an outfielder with the Detroit Tigers. Highlighting his fourth full season with Detroit, Jim was one of several Tigers heroes when the Motor City ball club won the 1968 World Series over the St. Louis Cardinals.

In 12 big-league seasons, 11 of them in Detroit, the left-handed-hitting fly chaser averaged .267, connected for 153 home runs, scored 603 runs, drove in 610 runs, and played in 1,392 games, mostly in the outfield. However, the downside of Northrup's career is that he played in an outfield that often featured a future Hall of Famer in right fielder Al Kaline; an excellent athlete and four-time Gold Glove center fielder in Mickey Stanley; and a solid left fielder with great power in Willie Horton.

A clutch hitter and a good run producer, Northrup belted 21 home runs—including four grand slams—during the 1968 regular season. The lefty hit two slams in consecutive at-bats against the Cleveland Indians Monday, June 24, and three in the same week—blasting his third against the Chicago White Sox at Detroit's Tiger Stadium the following Saturday, June 29. The Tigers right fielder had five opportunities for slams in that week. But in addition to his three four-baggers, he struck out swinging with the bases loaded once each against the Indians and the Chisox.

Also, Northrup is remembered by Tigers fans for his World Series heroics in 1968. His two biggest hits were a grand slam in Game 6, which the Tigers won 13–1, and a two-run triple in the seventh inning of climatic Game 7, which Detroit won, 4–1.

Born November 24, 1939, Northrup grew up in Breckenridge, in the heart of the Great Lake State. His father taught Jim and younger brothers Jerry and Mickey to love team sports as well as hunting and fishing. After developing into an excellent athlete at St. Louis High, Jim became a five-sport star at nearby Alma College.

Northrup was a standout in every sport young men could play at Alma. As a junior he started at quarterback in football (he made small college All-American) and forward in basketball. In baseball he was a righthanded pitcher (he once hurled a no-hitter) who often played center field or first base. Jim also ran track and golfed, a sport he still plays. Further, he was a good student, although his graduation was delayed 40 years because he signed with the Tigers in 1961.

The personable Northrup has a disarming sense of humor. On the field, however, he was an intense competitor who worked hard to focus his talent and his emotions and to make the most of his first-rate athletic skills. Jim had offers from the New York Titans of the American Football League, and from the Chicago Bears of the National Football League. But the Tigers offered guaranteed money, so he decided on baseball.

In spring 1961 Northrup began his pro career with Duluth-Superior of the Class C Northern League. Calling the circuit "over my head," he hit only .222 with one homer and eight runs batted in. Detroit sent him to sixth-place Decatur of the Class D Midwest League. In Iowa, the former Alma star finished the 1961 season hitting .291 with 13 home runs and 73 RBI. He also married his college sweetheart, Jean, and later the couple had three children: James Thomas II (born in 1961), Paige Leigh (born 1963), and Maria Kate (born 1969).

Northrup steadily improved in three more seasons of minor league ball. In 1962 the Tigers sent him to Knoxville of the Class A South Atlantic League, but he batted .244 and again found himself "over my head." He finished the season at Class C Duluth-Superior, where he averaged .324 and produced 11 homers and 61 RBI. The .324 mark tied the Michigan standout for the league's batting title with Donald Wallace of Aberdeen.

In 1963, the year the major leagues began player development contracts with minor league affiliates and the minors were reorganized into different levels of Class A ball, Jim spent the season with Knoxville of the Double A Sally League. Hitting .309 with 10 homers and 66 RBI, he won the circuit's Rookie of the Year award.

Playing for second-place Syracuse of the Triple A International League in 1964, Northrup again won Rookie of the Year honors with a .312 season that included 18 homers and a career-best 92 RBI. The former Breckenridge star had produced three straight .300-plus seasons, and the Tigers called him up near the end of the year.

Making his major league debut September 30, 1964, the 6-foot-3, 190-pound Northrup had an inauspicious beginning, going 1-for-12 and making two outfield starts in five games.

In 1965 Northrup started in left field, until Willie Horton got hot and took over the job. Thereafter, Jim was platooned in the outfield. "Willie pretty much played every day, and I filled in where I could in 1965," Northrup said in 2003. Reflecting his lack of regular playing time in 1965, Jim got into 80 games, 54 in the outfield, and he averaged .205 with two homers and 16 RBI.

But the Tigers were building a fine young team. In 1966 Detroit, although lacking in depth, finished third in the American League with an 88–74 record. But the club suffered emotional turmoil due to playing for three managers under tragic circumstances. Chuck Dressen suffered a heart attack early in the season and died after the All-Star break. Coach Bob Swift succeeded him, but he had to leave the team after cancer was diagnosed. As a result, Frank Skaff, the third base coach, worked on holding the Tigers together.

Northrup said he got more playing time in 1966 because he had played for Swift in winter ball and at Duluth and for Skaff in Knoxville. Beginning in 1966, Northrup played at least 130 games a year for Detroit until the 1973 season, when, due partly to differences with manager Billy Martin, Jim played 119 games—even though he batted a career-best .307.

Finishing at 91–71 under new pilot Mayo Smith in 1967, the Tigers missed the pennant by one game on the last day of the season. In 1967 Northrup gave Detroit another good season, going .271 with 10 homers and 61 RBI. A supremely confident but streaky clutch hitter who used an inside-out swing to hit explosively to all fields, Jim didn't often go for the fences. But his career totals of 218 doubles, 42 triples, and 153 home runs show he could hit with power. Northrup said all the breaks went against the Tigers: "If you believe in destiny, we were not destined to win in 1967. Everything that could go wrong, did. But it was a great, great pennant race, and we learned from it. We knew when we went to spring training in 1968 there was nobody who could stop us. And they didn't."

Commenting on the club's best pitchers in 1968, Northrup said, "We had Denny McLain, Mickey Lolich, Earl Wilson, and Joe Sparma. Then we had 'bullpen by committee.' We picked up Elroy Face and John Wyatt and Don McMahon. We had Fred Lasher, Daryl Patterson, John Hiller, and Pat Dobson. So we handled relief pitching and spot starting by 'committee.' In those days, there was no one 'stopper.' Pitchers who had a bad go ended up in the bullpen. You had to pitch your way out of the bullpen to get back in the lineup by doing spot starting and long relief. Then you might get a chance, say, in a doubleheader."

In 1968 the pennant-tested Tigers got off to a good start and kept on winning. The Baltimore Orioles finished a distant second, 12 games behind Detroit. Even when Al Kaline suffered a forearm injury in late May and sat out two months, it made little difference. Detroit led the league in homers with 185 and in runs scored with 671.

Northrup, dubbed the "Gray Fox" by his teammates due to the flecks of premature gray in his hair, made a major contribution to Detroit's excellent team effort in 1968. Hitting .264 with 21 homers, Jim led the Bengals with 153 hits and 90 RBI. Close behind came Horton with 85 RBI and Freehan with 84 RBI, and Willie led the club with 36 four-baggers.

But Northrup bunched 16 of his 90 RBI in four at-bats! On Friday, May 17, Sparma, working on a one-hitter against the Washington Senators, yielded a ninth-inning homer to slugger Frank Howard—his record-breaking eighth four-bagger in five games—and gave the Senators a 3–2 lead. In the bottom of the inning, Northrup connected for his first grand slam of the year to cap a five-run rally and give the Tigers a 7–3 victory.

Five weeks later, on Monday, June 24, against Cleveland, Northrup hit two grand slams in consecutive at-bats, and the Tigers beat the Indians, 14–3. Jim shares the distinction for two slams in consecutive innings with three others: Tony Lazzeri of the Yankees in 1936, Jim Tabor of the Red Sox in 1939, and Jim Gentile of the Orioles in 1961.

Five days later, on June 29, against Chicago, Northrup hit another bases-loaded homer to beat the White Sox, 5–2, and help McLain notch win number 14. Northrup's heroics tied the major league record for three grand slams in a month set by Detroit's Rudy York in May 1938. But Jim set a new major league mark for slams in a week with three.

Regarding the two grand slams against Cleveland, Northrup recalled, "In the first inning I struck out with the bases loaded on a pitch right down the middle. The next time I came up, the bases were loaded in the fifth inning. Eddie Fisher threw me a nothing knuckleball, and I hit it about four miles! The third time I came up, Billy Rohr threw me a fastball and I hit that one out of the ballpark. So I got two out of three with the bases were loaded. Five days later I hit one in the upper deck in left field off Cisco Carlos of the White Sox. And I came up two innings later with the bases loaded and nobody out, swung at two in the dirt, and took one right down the middle! So I had an opportunity to hit five grand slams in a week, and I didn't do too well on a couple of 'em."

Detroit won the American League pennant—the last season before Major League Baseball began divisional play and playoffs—and faced the St. Louis Cardinals in the World Series. Mayo Smith made a seemingly bold move by putting Al Kaline back into right field. By September the longtime star had recovered fully from a fractured forearm suffered in early May. (Northrup took over in right at the time.) When Kaline was able to return to the lineup on July 1, Smith used him at first base (the first time in Al's career), where he played 22 games. The regular, Norm Cash—who hit .263 with 25 homers and 63 RBI in 1968—was a notorious streak hitter who was then more than 20 points below his final season average. For the Series, Northrup moved to center field and Mickey Stanley took over at shortstop to displace the fine-fielding but .135-hitting Ray Oyler.

The Redbirds, led by right-hander Bob Gibson's excellent 22–9 mark and his major league–leading 1.12 ERA, opened the Series in St. Louis against McLain. Gibson hurled a five-hit shutout and won, 4–0. After yielding a leadoff single to Stanley in the ninth, the Cardinals ace set a World Series record with 17 strikeouts by fanning Kaline, Cash, and Horton to end the game.

"Bob Gibson was the toughest pitcher I ever faced for one game," Northrup observed in 2003. "He was throwing hard, and the ball moved all over. I don't know how we got any hits. He struck out 17 of us, and we were fastball hitters. But he blew the ball right by us. And he had a nasty slider that was jumping all over the place."

Detroit won Game 2, 8–1, when the weak-hitting Lolich spaced six singles and hit a two-run homer, the only home run of his professional career. Horton and Cash added solo homers. The Cardinals pitched 19-game winner Nelson Briles, followed by three relievers. "When Mickey hit that home run," Northrup quipped, "it was the only extra base hit he got in his life. When he got to first, he had to ask Wally Moses, our first base coach, where to go. Mickey was in uncharted waters! He was a bloop hitter to right field, but he got around on a high fast ball, and it jumped out of the ballpark. None of us in the dugout could believe it!"

St. Louis won Game 3, 7–3, behind Ray Washburn and Joe Hoerner. Earl Wilson started and lost, as Kaline's two-run home run and McAuliffe's solo blast couldn't overcome a three-run homer by Tim McCarver and a two-run shot by Orlando Cepeda.

In Game 4, Gibson fired a five-hitter and won, 10–1, giving St. Louis the Series lead, three games to one. While Gibson hurled a complete game, McLain gave up six hits and four runs in 2.2 innings. Sparma, Patterson, Lasher, Hiller, and Dobson all pitched in relief. "Denny was tired," Northrup remembered. "He'd pitched over 330 innings in 1968. Denny's arm was sore and tired, and he didn't have any heat left, no speed. He started 41 games, and he completed 28 of those. Denny struggled, but he won the sixth game when we got 13 runs for him."

Facing elimination in Detroit, the Tigers responded with a 5–3 win, keyed by Al Kaline's bases-loaded two-run single in the seventh inning. In the top of the fifth, Willie Horton threw out fleet Lou Brock (who doubled) at home on Julian Javier's single to left. Freehan's foot blocked the plate, and Brock chose to try to score standing up. "If Willie doesn't throw him out," Northrup said, "and if Brock slides, we probably lose that ball game. But Brock didn't slide, and Freehan had the plate covered. They gave us a chance to come back, and we did. We came back about 37 times in 1968, where we were behind in the seventh inning or later but won the game. We always figured that if we were within two runs with an inning or two to go, we'd catch 'em. And we did—all year long."

Through the first five games, Northrup had produced three singles in 19 trips to the plate (he hit .250 for the seven games). But rising to the occasion in Game 6, Jim belted a grand slam in Detroit's 10-run third inning—matching the single inning scoring mark set by the Philadelphia Athletics in Game 4 of the 1929 World Series against the Chicago Cubs. McLain scattered nine hits and Detroit won easily, 13–1.

In the decisive seventh game, Lolich, pitching on two days' rest, and Gibson both hurled shutout ball into the seventh inning. With two outs in the top of the frame, Cash and Horton singled. Northrup then smashed a terrific shot to center, and the ball carried over the head of Curt Flood—who first took a step in, then pivoted and ran back—for a two-run triple. Freehan doubled home Northrup, Lolich gave up only a ninth inning two-out solo homer to Mike Shannon, and the Tigers won the world championship. Commented Northrup, "We saw the film afterwards, and Curt Flood did slip on that ball I hit to center field, because it was wet out there. But that ball went 20 or 30 feet over his head. He wasn't going to catch it, no matter what.

"You can call that a misplay if you want. I call it a triple that won the World Series. I don't fault Flood, but he was playing me too much to pull. I wasn't a pull hitter, especially with Gibson on the mound. Flood probably didn't see the ball at first. It was a low stadium with a lot of white shirts behind home plate. I played out there, and you had to break where you thought the ball was going, because you could not see the ball for the first second or two. Flood broke the right way, and he slipped. But we got the opportunity to win the World Series, and we won it."

Detroit's club had good camaraderie and enjoyed a good run for eight seasons, including 1967's second-place finish and 1968's world championship. Continuing in 1969, the year each major league was divided into an East and West Division and played a League Championship Series preceding the World Series, the Tigers performed well. Northrup consistently made good contributions to his team, hitting .295 with 25 homers and 66 RBI as Detroit finished second in the AL East with a 92–70 record in 1969. In 1970, he averaged .262 with 24 homers and 80 RBI as Detroit ranked fourth in the division with a 79–83 mark. Jim hit .270 with 16 homers and 71 RBI as the Tigers placed second under new manager Billy Martin with a 91–71 mark in 1971. And he batted .261 but produced only eight homers and 42 RBI in 1972, when Detroit won the AL East with an 86–70 finish. Still, while his offensive production fell during the regular season, the Alma star rose to the occasion and batted .357 in the 1972 playoffs against Oakland.

Martin, a sparkplug pilot who often soured a team's management with his caustic and aggressive style as well as his off-field problems, helped turn the Tigers around. The club rose to second in the East in 1971. In 1972 Detroit won the division, finishing a half-game ahead of the Boston Red Sox. Northrup did not respect Martin: "We got sick and tired of reading Martin say in the papers, 'I manage good, and they play bad.' 'I'd like to bunt, but my players can't do it.' 'I'd like to hit and run, but my players can't do it.' It was all, 'I, I, I,' and 'me, me, me.' I did not respect him in any way, but I had to play. So I ignored what he said and played ball."

To win the competitive East Division, the Tigers had to beat out the Orioles, the Yankees, and the Red Sox. By September newspaper reports were calling Detroit the "over the hill gang," led by "granddaddy" Kaline, now 37 (as was Cash). For example, Lolich, one of the most underrated left-handers in baseball history, and Woodie Fryman, both 32, led the moundsmen. Lolich won 22 games for the Tigers, and Fryman won 10 times after arriving in August.

A key player in Detroit's late-season surge was catcher-first baseman-outfielder Duke Sims, a versatile athlete who came up through the Cleveland system, spent eleven years in the majors, and hit .239 lifetime. Purchased from the Los Angeles Dodgers on August 4, 1972, Duke averaged .316 in 38 games as a Tiger.

In the League Championship Series, the Tigers lost to the Oakland Athletics in five games. Oakland won the first two contests by scores of 3–2 and 5–0, but Detroit won the third and fourth games, 3–0 and 4–3. Northrup singled to score the winning run in the 10th inning of Game 4.

Jim believed Detroit had a chance to make the World Series again: "I thought we should have won the playoffs in 1972, but we got some bad breaks. In Game 3, Billy Martin put Freehan behind the plate with a broken thumb. He put our backup catcher, Duke Sims, who hit .316 after he came over from the Dodgers, in left field. Both positions cost us a run. The A's scored on a double steal, which should have been an out at home. In the last game the first-base umpire called [George] Hendrick safe who was out by two steps at first base. That ended up being the winning run. Duke Sims got a ground ball where he could have thrown the guy out at home, but he didn't. He shouldn't have been out there, but Billy played him. It's not the player's fault. It's the manager's fault. Should have, would have, could have, whatever. But if we had Duke behind the plate where he belonged and Willie out in left field, I believe we'd have won Game 5, 1–0."

Down 2–1 in the ninth inning of Game 5, Cash singled with one out. Martin used Stanley to pinch-hit for Northrup, and Stanley forced Cash at second. Tony Taylor lined to deep center to end the game and the last hurrah of the Tigers who had played together since the mid-1960s.

Northrup said, "In the fifth game I had one hit already off Vida Blue, a left-hander. But Martin pinch-hit for me in the ninth. Who knows why Martin did what he did? I will say this: Billy Martin put most of us in a frame of mind where he took the fun out of the game. And when there's no fun, it's not worth playing. That's what I didn't like."

Northrup produced another good season in 1973, hitting .307 with 12 homers and 44 RBI while playing 116 games. Jim's final Detroit season came in 1974. On August 7, when it was clear the Tigers would finish last, Detroit sold him to the Montreal Expos. On September 16, after the Expos lost any shot at the playoffs, the club sold him to Baltimore: "The Tigers dumped me because if I had finished the season, I would have had 10 years in the majors, and I could have negated a trade. The club didn't want that," Northrup says.

Northrup enjoyed playing the 1975 season for Baltimore's Earl Weaver. Jim hit .273 with five homers and 29 RBI, but he decided to call it quits after the season. "I'd had enough. I'd been away from home too much, and I wasn't with my kids enough. So that was the end of it. You have to quit sometime, and I did. I was making $76,000 with Detroit in 1973. But I was mainly going to pinch-hit in 1974, so they dropped me to $67,000. Baltimore paid me the same, $67,000. In 1975, the major league average was $35,000. I made $418,000 altogether in baseball, counting my bonus and winter ball. But we were owned and controlled by the team. That was a different era—before free agents."

Later, in the mid-1980s, Northrup became a broadcaster for the Tigers, serving for nine years. He worked as an analyst with play-by-play man Larry Osterman, on the Detroit area's regional sports cable channel PASS (Pro-Am Sports System). Today he is in the insurance business. Jim was inducted into the Michigan Sports Hall of Fame in 2000.

"I enjoyed the challenge of hitting," Northrup explained. "I wanted to see what the Hall of Famers were like. Who knows? If I got a hit or two off them, maybe I was as good as they were. I never accepted failure. You have to believe you can hit anyone, and I did. I can hit anybody out there at certain times, if you give me enough shots. And that's the way you have to believe. Guys like McLain and Lolich and Gibson feel the same about hitters: 'I can get anyone out.' They have the same positive attitude. It's a challenge. That's what makes the game so much fun. I enjoyed the challenge every day. I felt like I was born to play the game, and I did."

References

Publications
Baseball Encyclopedia, 1993 edition. New York: Macmillan. 1993.

Articles
Chass, Murray, "Tigers Living It Up in Old Folks Home." *New York Times*, Oct. 5, 1972.
Forman, Ross, "Northup's Collection is Now Just a Memory," *Sports Collectors Digest*, Jan. 21, 2000.
Jim Northrup clipping file, National Baseball Hall of Fame Library, Cooperstown, New York.
New York Times and *Washington Post* stories from ProQuest database about 1968 World Series and 1972 ALCS.
Spoelstra, Watson, "Bengals' Northrup Knows He Can Hit." *The Sporting News*, April 15, 1967.

Other Sources
Pat Doyle's Professional Baseball Player Database, version 6.0.
Northrup, Jim. Letter to author, November 2006.
Sargent, Jim. Interview with Jim Northrup, February 2003.
Sims, Duke. Letter to author, February 2003.

Note
This article is a revised version of the author's profile of Jim Northrup that appeared in the February 2004 issue of *Baseball Digest*.

1968 TIGERS

Rich Shook presents:
Tigers In the News

Saturday, August 3
A four-hit shutout by the Twins' Dean Chance slowed Detroit, 4–0. Earl Wilson (9–9) allowed six hits and three runs in 2.2 innings.

Sunday, August 4
Denny McLain beat Minnesota, 2–1, to win his 22nd game and excitement began to build over the prospect of the right-hander becoming the first 30-game winner since 1934. He would need eight more wins in the 13 or 14 more starts he figures to have left to join Dizzy Dean as the most recent 30-game winners. McLain walked four and struck out four. Mickey Stanley tripled and Bill Freehan's single in the fourth scored Detroit's first run and the Tigers made it 2–0 in the eighth inning on a leadoff triple by Dick McAuliffe and a sacrifice fly by Al Kaline.

Monday, August 5
No game.

Tuesday, August 6
Detroit beat Cleveland, 2–1, in 17 innings in the first game of a twi-night doubleheader. The second game was suspended due to a 1 a.m. curfew, with Detroit needing just three outs to complete a 5–2 victory. John Hiller opened the first game by fanning the first six Indians he faced to establish what at the time was a modern major league record for strikeouts at the beginning of a game. The Indians broke the string and scored their only run in the third but Wert reached Luis Tiant for a solo home run in the eighth to force extra innings. Prior to the home run, Don Wert was in a 14-for-102 slump since being hit in the head. Willie Horton singled to start the 17th and Bill Freehan was hit by a pitch for the 16th time this season before Wert bunted into a force at third. Dick Tracewski lashed a game-winning single to right-center on Polish American Night. John Wyatt (2–4) worked one inning for the win. Norm Cash hit his 16th home run in the second inning of the second game but Joe Sparma was typically wild and Cleveland took a 2–1 lead in the fourth. After the game Mayo Smith announced Sparma was going to the bullpen. Brown's double started a four-run sixth, with singles by Norm Cash and Wert providing the first run. Jim Price was removed for pinch-hitter Freehan with a 1–0 count and the All-Star catcher drew a walk. Al Kaline pinch-hit a two-run double and a wild Eddie Fisher knuckleball brought in the last run.

Wednesday, August 7
Dave Campbell got his first major league hit, a two-run home run, in the eighth inning of a 6–1 victory over visiting Cleveland. John Wyatt got three outs prior to the regularly scheduled game, completing Tuesday night's 5–2 Detroit victory. Campbell got the start in the regularly scheduled game because Smith felt Dick McAuliffe needed a rest in the wake of playing 25 innings the night before. Campbell played despite a fever of 102. His parents, who lived in Lansing, were unaware their son was starting and listened to the game at home on the radio. "I'm really sorry my parents missed it," he said. "They sat through the 17-inning game hoping I would get a chance to play." Indians manager Alvin Dark removed Sam McDowell after just two batters, a walk and a single. "Dark came out and asked me if that was all the harder I could throw. I said, 'yes.'" Kaline greeted Eddie Fisher with an RBI single and Freehan followed with a two-run double. Horton added his 27th home run, in the eighth, and Campbell followed with his two-run blow in the same inning. Earl Wilson (10–9) left after giving up a single in the seventh.

Thursday, August 8
Denny McLain improved to 23–3 with a 13–1 win over Cleveland in Tiger Stadium. Freehan backed his pitcher with a pair of home runs, bringing his total for the season to 16. The game was delayed at its start for 90 minutes by rain. McLain gave up four hits in the first three innings but only two in the final six. He also hit a double. Freehan's three-run home run highlighted a six-run third. He hit a solo home run in the eighth. McLain moved three games ahead of the pace of Lefty Grove when he won 31 games for Philadelphia in 1931. (Historical footnote: It was announced Detroit's nine-month newspaper strike was over. "When we have player meetings," Mayo Smith cracked, "we sit around and interview one another. That's so when the writers come back we won't be out of practice.")

Friday, August 9
Boston beat Detroit, 5–3, on an eighth-inning grand slam by Joe Foy, prompting Red Sox manager Dick Williams to observe, "I've been telling you guys this race is far from over." Boston's fifth win in a row snapped a five-game Detroit winning streak. Foy's grand slam came off the erratic John Wyatt, who had been ordered to intentionally walk the previous batter to load the bases. Gates Brown pinch-hit his second home run of the year in the eighth. Mickey Stanley (ninth home run) and Dick Tracewski (fourth) hit solo homers for Detroit. Pat Dobson started for the Tigers with Daryl Patterson scheduled for his first major league start Saturday.

Ray Oyler

by Richard Newhouse

Season	Age	G	AB	R	H	2B	3B	HR	RBI	BB	SO	SB	CS	BA	OBP	SLG
1968 Tigers	29	111	215	13	29	6	1	1	12	20	59	0	2	.135	.213	.186
Career Totals		542	1265	110	221	39	6	15	86	135	359	2	6	.175	.258	.251

Perhaps the greatest example of the old baseball cliché "good field, no hit," Raymond Francis Oyler was the regular shortstop for two late-1960s Detroit Tigers teams, including the world champion 1968 squad, as well as the original Seattle Pilots the following season. Ray compiled a sub-"Mendoza line" .175 career batting average—the lowest of any player to bat more than 1,000 times since the deadball era. The right-hand-throwing and -hitting Oyler, who stood 5-foot-11 with a playing weight of 165 to 170 pounds, was solid, however, defending his shortstop position. Johnny Sain said Oyler was "one of the best fielders" he saw in a half-century in the game.

Significant about Ray's career, other than the lack of hitting—but a direct result of having not much of a bat to offer—was his involvement in one of the most risky managerial moves in baseball history. Mayo Smith, manager of the 1968 Tigers, inserted Gold Glove center fielder Mickey Stanley to play Oyler's shortstop position for each of the seven games of that season's World Series. Smith then could play all four of his outfielders, with the fourth, Stanley, playing shortstop. The four—Stanley, Al Kaline, Willie Horton, and Jim Northrup—were significantly better hitters than Oyler, who hit a scant .135 that season.

Ray honed his skills—as a defensive whiz in his favorite game—as well as his polite and humble demeanor while growing up in Indiana. He was born August 4, 1938, in Indianapolis, to Raymond H. "Bus" Oyler and Frances M. Harrington Oyler.

Ray's father Bus, otherwise known as "Big Bus" and Ray as "Little Bus," encouraged Ray's development in baseball by working with him for hours, especially in fielding ground balls. "The only ball that gets by you is the one that goes through you," Ray's father said.

Oyler got a taste of professional baseball at age 12 when he became the official batboy of the Indianapolis Indians after winning an essay contest. This whetted his appetite to continue pursuing that common childhood fantasy of being a professional athlete, with baseball now ahead of other sports for Ray, who went on to be the captain of the Indianapolis Cathedral High baseball squad his junior and senior years. Ray also developed talent on the gridiron, leading Cathedral High to a city championship as quarterback, while also filling out his prep schedule on the basketball team.

Immediately upon graduating, Ray joined the Marines and played service ball during his years there, 1956–1959. It was during these years that he met his future teammate with Detroit, Earl Wilson, who pitched and hit cleanup.

His military stint, as well as his Midwestern manners, engendered the already soft-spoken Oyler to refer to others politely as "sir." Ray also had a humorous side that was often self-effacing.

Early in 1960, Oyler was signed to a professional contract with the Detroit Tigers by longtime Tigers scout Wayne Blackburn, who patrolled ball diamonds for talent in the Great Lakes region, following Ray's discharge from the military.

He was immediately assigned to the Tigers' Duluth-Superior club in the Class C Northern League, where he was installed as the Dukes' regular shortstop, appearing in all 121 games played. Ray scored 90 runs that season, by far his highest single-season total, fostered by a career-high .396 on-base percentage.

Oyler returned to the Dukes to play shortstop in 1961. While batting .261 to match his 1960 average, with a .388 on-base percentage through 84 games, the Tigers promoted

Ray to play shortstop in Knoxville of the Class A South Atlantic League. The promotion slowed Oyler's offense to a .171 crawl in 22 games for the Smokies. Shortly following his promotion to Knoxville, Ray's second daughter was born. Kathleen Marie joined the Oyler team—Ray, wife Joanne, and five-year-old sister Cynthia Kae.

1962 saw Oyler adjust to Sally League pitching, increasing his average to .236 and his home runs, from a previous high of six in 1960, to 11 for the Smokies. Ray patrolled shortstop while appearing in all 140 Knoxville games in 1962, smacking a career-high six triples to go with the 11 homers. Oyler's defense shined as he led Northern League shortstops in putouts and fielding percentage. The Smokies finished 86–54 and made it to the league finals, where they came out on the losing end.

The Detroit organization saw enough in Oyler's 1962 performance that they again promoted him, this time to play with its Triple A International League affiliate in Syracuse. As it did two seasons earlier, Ray's offense swooned as he saw his average dip to .213, with a career-high 130 strikeouts in 146 games for the Chiefs. However, again he flashed the leather, leading IL shortstops in assists.

The following spring, Oyler, now 25, found himself opening the season in the minor leagues for a fifth season. Assigned to repeat with the Syracuse Chiefs for 1964, Ray responded as he did two summers prior in the South Atlantic League, by showing more comfort at the plate, hitting IL pitching at a .251 clip with surprising authority—slugging 19 homers and driving home 61.

With his slick fielding and maturing bat, Oyler's talents were now catching the eye of the Tigers' front office and yet another promotion was just around the corner. Ray didn't see any action with the 1964 Tigers, but he had seen the last of the minor leagues for a while.

Oyler stayed with the big club as they gathered in Lakeland, Florida, in spring 1965. Watson Spoelstra, Tigers beat writer for the *Detroit News* and *The Sporting News*, noted that Oyler's 1964 season at Syracuse made him a candidate to unseat the Tigers' incumbent at short, Dick McAuliffe. Tigers skipper Charlie Dressen announced that Ray would play "at least half the games down here," noting that "several scouts have told me he is the best fielding shortstop they've seen. Not our own, but Pittsburgh and New York scouts." Dressen went on to suggest that with Oyler at short, McAuliffe may get a look at third base, sharing time with Don Wert.

Oyler showed enough that spring to prompt Dressen to take him north.

On Sunday, April 18, 1965, Oyler debuted in the majors by starting at shortstop, batting eighth, in place of McAuliffe, as the Tigers played the Angels at Dodger Stadium in Los Angeles. Oyler stepped to the plate in the top of the second against left-hander Rudy May, also, incidentally, making his major league debut. May struck him out—one of ten he recorded that afternoon. Ray went 0-for-2 and participated in five plays at short, with four assists and a putout.

Oyler appeared in several more games, mostly—believe it or not—as a pinch-hitter, batting a total of nine times before collecting his first hit. In a game against Baltimore at Detroit on Sunday, May 23, Oyler singled to center off of lefty Dave McNally in the bottom of the fifth while pinch-hitting for pitcher Phil Regan. Ray's first multi-hit game occurred a week-and-a-half later at Cleveland June 4. His initial extra-base hit took place off of Yankee Pedro Ramos at Detroit on Thursday, July 8, when he doubled to right in the bottom of the eighth, driving in a run and helping to extend the Tigers lead in a 6–1 victory.

Two weeks later, with Cleveland in town, Oyler stepped in against veteran lefty Jack Kralick, leading off the bottom of the second and slashed his first of fifteen major league home runs, igniting a four-run rally that helped propel the Tigers to a 10–5 win.

Oyler collected three hits, including another home run, his third, a solo shot off of the Angels' George Brunet in a 9–5 victory at Detroit Sunday, August 15. Brunet and McNally were each victimized twice by Ray for home runs.

During the course of his rookie season, Oyler's playing time gradually increased due to McAuliffe's being sidelined with a broken wrist. Ray appeared in 27 games in September as the regular shortstop as the Tigers proceeded toward an 89-win season, 13 games behind the pennant-winning Twins. He finished 1965 with a .186 average and five homers, his most in four seasons with Detroit.

Oyler returned to his backup role the following spring. Starting the 1966 season well—batting .297 on the first of June—acting manager Bob Swift started platooning Ray at short in June, July, and early August with McAuliffe against left-handed pitching. His failure to continue his early production (just a single homer in his first game, off Buster Narum of Washington, in April and only nine RBI in more than 200 at-bats) relegated him to fewer appearances—just four games after September 1. The Tigers, 44–27 through June, again finished in the first division, this time with 88 wins, 10 games behind the Orioles.

A highlight for Oyler in 1966 occurred July 17 when he had a pair of hits in each game of a doubleheader against the Indians. He went 4-for-8, as the Tigers were swept in the twin bill, raising his average above .200 for the final time that season. Ray's averaged slipped to .171 by year's end, though.

Oyler's deftness afield impressed the Tigers' new manager, Mayo Smith, enough to move stalwart Dick McAuliffe—who himself noted that Oyler was "the best shortstop I ever played with"—to second base.

Skipper Smith noted, "You've got to see Oyler day in and day out to appreciate him. He's done the job for us. He plays the slow-hit ball as well as I've ever seen it done." Even Tigers' owner John Fetzer weighed in by stating during the 1967 season that "putting Oyler at shortstop was the best move [Smith] made."

Despite the intentions of manager Smith, as the 1967 season wore on, Oyler was forced to split time at short with veteran Dick Tracewski due to continuous nagging leg ailments.

In an effort to pick up his offense, Oyler had arrived in Lakeland early that spring after returning from winter ball in Puerto Rico, where he experimented with switch-hitting. Ray worked on his stroke with a few local amateurs and then spent a great deal of time with hitting coach Wally Moses. "I got so bad I was listening to tips from everybody. I was using a different stance and holding my hands a new way every time I went up to the plate. Now I'm just listening to Moses, using a little, light bat, and going up there with the confidence I'll be able to meet the ball." Ray was able to contribute offensively in his own way, leading the 1967 Tigers with 15 sacrifice bunts.

An example of Oyler's defensive wizardry was what was known as a "daylight" pickoff play at second base. Reporter Watson Spoelstra described this play, which Ray performed with old military pal, pitcher Earl Wilson, and how they were able to catch Mickey Mantle, among others. Spoelstra notes how the play was often triggered by a sign from the catcher, Oyler sneaking in behind the runner at second base with Wilson firing back only if he sees "daylight" between the runner and Oyler.

During the heat of the 1967 pennant race, Oyler showed a rare display of anger when he got involved in a shoving match with Yankees outfielder Bill Robinson. After tagging Robinson out in a rundown, Oyler got an elbow to the ribs, an apparent attempt by Robinson to jar the ball loose. Ray made a running charge at Robinson only to be intercepted by other players on the field. Later, Ray said, "I lost control of myself. I'm sorry I did." Nevertheless, five years later, the two scuffled again after a similar play while both were toiling in the Pacific Coast League.

Oyler's stake at the shortstop position gave way to the desire for more punch with the bat for the last month of the 1967 pennant race when Mayo Smith restored McAuliffe to short, putting Jerry Lumpe in the lineup at second base. Tigers General Manager Jim Campbell brusquely noted the need for "a shortstop who can hit," following the Tigers' near-miss at the 1967 pennant. They praised him for his glove but loathed the lack of hitting. Ray did lift his average to .207, with 29 RBI, both high marks for his big-league career.

Following the conclusion of the 1967 season, several teams inquired about Oyler, due to his defensive prowess. At a postseason banquet, pitcher Dave Wickersham, traded from the Tigers that winter, noted how "Oyler [as the starting shortstop] had a lot to do with" the Tigers allowing 111 fewer runs in 1967 than in 1966.

After an attempted deal with Baltimore for Luis Aparicio fell apart during the 1967–1968 off-season, the Tigers found themselves with the Oyler-Tracewski combo they featured in 1967.

Following a winter as a sporting goods salesman in Detroit, Oyler arrived at camp in Lakeland in February 1968, determined once again to add some more wood to his cache of leather: "I know I can do better than (hit .207) if I play every day. … I've put on a few pounds to 178 and I feel good. You're more relaxed at the plate when you play every day. … I hope to hit .250. I think I've that much in myself."

During spring training, Oyler took to wearing glasses to help him see the ball better while hitting, causing teammate Norm Cash to compare Ray with a World War II German tank soldier. Ray also was one of the first players to have a protective side flap on his batting helmet due to having been hit in the head more often than he cared for.

Tigers fans were also impatient with the "woodless wonder," as Oyler was greeted with boos when introduced as the starting shortstop on opening day. He was cheered derisively when connecting for foul balls and ended the day with a pair of strikeouts and a groundout. "I hated to see them making fun of Ray," said manager Mayo Smith.

As early as April, with fourth outfielder Mickey Stanley off to a hot start with the bat, and Mayo suggesting that "If Mickey keeps hitting, he'll play somewhere," the idea of Stanley taking over at shortstop was brought up. To this Mayo replied, "You're not going to start changing it all in one day," without denying that a shortstop switch could happen.

Low-key Oyler's roommate was Tigers ace pitcher Denny McLain, the antithesis of low-key. On the road, Ray took to answering the phone: "Mr. McLain's office." As many others noted, McLain remarked how Ray was the "finest defensive shortstop I've ever seen." McLain also reflected how Ray "couldn't hit his way out of a room full of toilet paper with a crowbar.... But the way he could field, I'd keep him on my club if he couldn't hit his weight."

As the season progressed, Oyler's anemic hitting became virtually nonexistent—after singling off of Minnesota's Bob Miller in the eighth inning July 13, Ray failed to collect even one hit in his last 37 trips to the plate, walking just once—and his role was reduced to that of a defensive replacement at short for Tom Matchick and Dick Tracewski.

Oyler gained notoriety for his weak bat with Mayo Smith's move of center fielder Mickey Stanley to start in Oyler's place as Detroit shortstop during the 1968 World Series. In preparation for this World Series position change, the manager had inserted Stanley into the shortstop position in seven September contests and decided to proceed with this daring arrangement for the Series.

Ray was not left shelved on the bench, however, as he supplanted Stanley at shortstop as a late-inning defensive replacement in each of the Tigers' victories, while also contributing a successful sacrifice in his only plate appearance.

As Stanley noted in George Cantor's book *The Tigers of '68: Baseball's Last Real Champions*: "He never carried a grudge about my replacing him during the series," said Stanley. "He was simply a great guy. To get into the Series and then to have some guy moved entirely out of position to take your place. He'd take me out there during workouts and tried to give me a crash course in shortstop. He was such a great competitor. He played hurt, he played hungover. He never complained. We all loved that guy."

During the series, Mayo Smith assured that Stanley would play short in Oyler's place "only for now." What neither manager Smith nor Oyler knew at the time was that Game 7 at Busch Stadium in St. Louis would be Ray's last appearance as a Tiger.

On October 10, 1968, Oyler celebrated with his Tigers teammates and their fans everywhere as Detroit came back from a 3-games-to-1 deficit to defeat the St. Louis Cardinals for the Tigers' first championship in 23 years. Five days later, Ray was no longer a Tiger. Unprotected for the American League's expansion draft, he was nabbed as the third player chosen by the new league entry in Seattle.

Oyler was to be that rare defensive gem so often absent on new teams. Manager Joe Schultz responded at spring training when asked whether Oyler's hitting would be a liability: "Ah, hell. Ray Oyler will bat .300 for us with his glove." In Jim Bouton's diary of the Pilots, *Ball Four*, Ray became known as "Oil Can Harry," after the old cartoon character.

Oyler homered in the Pilots' second home game at Sick's Stadium. He went on to hit a career-high seven blasts, due in part to the coziness of Sick's Stadium Oyler was quickly endeared to his new fan base when Seattle disc jockey Bob Hardwick organized a "Let's Help Ray Oyler Hit .300" drive, prompting thousands to join the Ray Oyler "Sock-It-To-Me" fan club. Ray started strong, hitting .350 through the first two weeks, but tailed off, predictably, to a final mark of .165, ten points below his career average In August, Ray reinjured his knee that had hampered him at the start of the 1967 season, while playing in Washington for Seattle, on turf damaged by football players in a recent Redskins game.

The one-year run for Seattle's initial major league franchise ended with 98 losses and a one-way trip to Milwaukee to become the Brewers in 1970. Oyler was traded to Oakland, which then sold him to California in the spring of 1970.

In the aftermath of delivering his first hit as an Angel to ignite a winning rally, Oyler happily exclaimed: "I finally feel like I'm part of the team. I finally did something to help out." Ray replaced Jim Fregosi in the fifth inning in an August 5 tilt against the Twins. He had been just 0-for-9 prior to the hit and he followed the single with a squeeze bunt adding another run for the Angels in the ninth inning. Oyler smiled and said, "I used Fregosi's bat. Heck, I've never had a model of my own." Ray's only other hit was his last in the majors, connecting in the ninth inning of a September 9 Angels loss to the White Sox off of Jerry Janeski.

The 1970 season marked Oyler's final round at the major league level, lasting just 24 games, primarily because of his .083 batting average. Ray's last big-league appearance took place in the Angels' final game October 1. Ray stepped in as a pinch-hitter for pitcher Greg Garrett in the bottom of the seventh and took a called third strike from White Sox rookie hurler Don Eddy. Incidentally, Angels manager Lefty Phillips used Ray as a pinch-hitter nine unsuccessful times, or six more times than during the previous four seasons combined. Ray had collected three pinch hits in eleven such opportunities as a rookie in 1965.

Oyler's played shortstop in 502 games with a fielding percentage of .966—which, as a mark of fielding ability is only part of the picture—and, at .966, is above average but certainly not outstanding; Omar Vizquel's career mark is .984 and Ray's contemporaries, Dal Maxvill at .973 and Luis

The official shot of the 1968 American League Champions—wait, make that World Champions!

Mickey Lolich had more pop-ups in his bat than pop in his bat, but he slugged an unlikely homer in 1968 World Series Game 2 to pace Detroit to victory.

John Hiller was best known as the Tigers' bullpen ace in the 1970s, but he made a career-high 12 starts for the 1968 Tigers.

Mayo Smith managing his penultimate game as Tigers skipper in 1970. After he got sacked, he criticized Detroit baseball fans, saying, "They couldn't tell a baseball player from a Japanese aviator."

Bill Freehan was the top catcher of his era in the American League. He finished second in the MVP voting in 1968 and third in 1967.

Dick McAuliffe attempts to complete a double play over a sliding Tom Tresh. McAuliffe was arguably the heart of the 1968 team; their only big slump came while Mac was suspended for charging Tommy John on the mound.

Willie Horton finished fourth in the MVP voting in 1968. Four Tigers claimed the first seven spots in the final tally (McLain, Freehan, Horton, and McAuliffe). Notice the uniform number on the sleeve, a feature of Tiger road uniforms of that time.

Two lifetime Tigers: A young Gates Brown, a player 1963-75 and a coach 1978-84, and Pat Mullin, who played 1940-41 and 1946-53 and coached 1963-66.

The veteran Al Kaline getting ready to swing at a pitch. Notice the uniform; the Tigers switched to the blue-and-orange road uniform in 1972.

Mickey Stanley was one of the best center fielders in the American League, but Mayo Smith eyed him to move to shortstop. The first St. Louis batter, Lou Brock, hit the ball to Stanley, who fielded the ball flawlessly and threw out the speedy Redbirds left fielder.

Al Kaline chases a ball in Yankee Stadium that is perched on the top of the right-field scoreboard.

Someone forgot to tell Mickey Lolich (left) and John Hiller not to make a racket! Here, they practice their badminton moves at spring training in Lakeland, Fla., with Joker Marchant Stadium in the background.

Gates Brown was one of the best pinch hitters of all time. As a pinch hitter in 1968, Brown hit .450 with a .542 on-base percentage, with three home runs in 45 at-bats.

A young Al Kaline poses for a picture. Kaline played for the Tigers from 1953 to 1974.

Norm Cash finishes his home-run trot in a 1960 home game with congrats from third-base coach and onetime Tiger Jo-Jo White, who came over from Cleveland with manager Joe Gordon in the infamous "managers' trade" involving Jimmy Dykes.

Earl Wilson had the best home-run-per-at-bat rate on the 1968 Tigers, a team that had 52 more home runs than any other team in the American League. Wilson had seven round trippers in 88 at-bats.

Denny McLain delivers a pitch against the Athletics at Tiger Stadium. McLain beat the A's on September 14 for his 30th victory of the season, the only pitcher in the past 73 seasons to reach that mark.

Jim Northrup was known in 1968 for his grand slams. Fans remember his two in one game, three in one week, and his World Series blast, but he hit one other grand slam in 1968, and it was a game-ender, on May 17 versus the Senators.

Mickey Stanley speaks his mind during a 1969 game at Tiger Stadium. He is pictured on the infield dirt, but the outfielder's glove on his hand suggests he was playing center field that day.

Mayo Smith had a lot to smile about in 1968. Not only did his Tigers win the World Series, but his move of centerfielder Mickey Stanley to shortstop in the Series paid off. Smith had considered playing Stanley at short since the manager's first spring with Detroit in 1967.

Jon Warden poses for a photo before a game. The 1968 season was Warden's only season in the majors; he was taken by the Royals in the 1969 expansion draft but injuries derailed a promising career.

Mickey Lolich delivers the ball to the plate. Lolich won three games in the 1968 World Series. The next season, he won a then-career high 19 games and later won 20 games twice.

Aparicio at .972, are higher with many more chances. Another part of the fielding measurement is chances per game (TCG), which characterizes range. Oyler's TCG of 3.8 shows, again, above-average capabilities, but is behind Maxvill (4.1), and way behind the great Aparicio (5.0). Keep in mind, though, they started games more regularly while Oyler was quite often a defensive replacement. Regardless, he was steady, showing excellent instincts, and great afield in 1968, with a .977 fielding average.

Interviewed for an article in *The Sporting News* in 1970, Oyler's double play partner back in Detroit, Dick McAuliffe, lamented the Tigers' inability to replace Ray's glove, declaring, "Oyler made my job easy because he would show you the ball all the time on ground balls to shortstop. The big thing on double plays is getting the throws at second base at the same speed, Oyler was tops at this too."

After seeing minor league action briefly in the Pacific Coast League in 1970, going 2-for-7 while with the Hawaii Islanders, Oyler joined the Salt Lake City Angels for 1971 as a player-coach, hitting .192 with six homers in 58 games. Salt Lake City won the PCL South Division title and defeated Tacoma, the North Division titlist, in the playoffs.

Oyler returned to play with Hawaii in 1972. Islanders pitcher and former big leaguer Dave Baldwin reminisced: "Ray was my teammate in Hawai'i [in the PCL] in 1972. The Islanders acquired him as the team was beefing up to get a major league franchise. We also had players like Clete Boyer, Mike McCormick, Leon Wagner, and Jimmie Hall. Ray was to be our shortstop and John Donaldson was at second—an outstanding double play combination."

In May 1972, Ray was injured three different times the same week. He left a game against Eugene with a swollen hand after a bad bounce from a grounder hit by Joe Lis smacked him on the right wrist. He missed a game and returned only to be struck in the nose by a pickoff throw from pitcher John Purdin in a game against Salt Lake City. Again, he had to leave the game. The next evening, in game two of a twin bill, Oyler collided with outfielder Jim Hicks on a fly off the bat of the Salt Lake City Angels' Rudy Meoli. He had to be taken off the field on a stretcher to a hospital. The bruised ribs from the collision landed Ray on the disabled list.

Oyler came back a player-coach for Hawaii of the PCL in 1973, his final year in professional baseball. He did not appear as a player that season, however.

While with the Pilots, Oyler fell in love with the Seattle area and retired there following his baseball career, managing a bowling alley in Bellevue and working for Boeing. He also was employed by Safeway Stores as a salesperson.

Oyler resurfaced briefly as the Tigers' batting practice pitcher when they visited Seattle to play the Mariners during the 1977 and 1978 seasons.

He suffered a fatal heart attack January 26, 1981, at age 42, at his home in Redmond, Washington. He was buried at Sunset Hills Memorial Park in Bellevue.

For students of baseball, Ray Oyler will forever be noted for his being able to play regularly while never being able to experience any prolonged offensive success, to a historic extent. Al Pepper notes in *Mendoza's Heroes: Fifty Batters Below .200*, his book about weak hitters, as their version of the "Mendoza Line" the Tigers had the "Ray Oyler Divide."

Rich Shook, who covered the Tigers for UPI during Oyler's tenure in Detroit, describes Ray's weakness this way: "Almost as soon as a game began, Oyler would come unglued. Perhaps somewhere along the line he'd hit a home run that entranced him. Because Oyler was forever trying to put a power swing on a 5-foot-11, 165-pound body, fastballs defeated him. His head would fly off the ball and he'd end up one-handing an upper cut swing that would miss any pitch with the slightest wrinkle in it."

In Oyler's home town of Indianapolis, they commemorate a favorite son with the Ray Oyler Scholarship, established to recognize students who are overcoming significant obstacles to earn a diploma.

References

Publications

Bak, Richard. *A Place for Summer*. Detroit: Wayne State University Press. 1998.

Cantor, George. *The Tigers of '68: Baseball's Last Real Champions*. Dallas: Taylor Trade Publishing. 1997.

McLain, Denny, and Diles, Dave. *Nobody's Perfect*. New York: The Dial Press. 1975.

Middlesworth, Hal. *1968 Detroit Tigers Official Yearbook*. Detroit: Detroit Tigers. 1968.

Pattison, Mark, and David Raglin. *Detroit Tigers Lists and More: Runs, Hits, and Eras*. Detroit: Wayne State University Press. 2002.

Pepper, Al. *Mendoza's Heroes: Fifty Batters Below .200*. Clifton, Va.: Pocol Press. 2002.

Rousso, Nick. *Rain Check: Baseball in the Pacific Northwest*. Cleveland: The Society for American Baseball Research. 2006.

Society for American Baseball Research. *The SABR Baseball List & Record Book*. New York: Scribner. 2007.

The Baseball Encyclopedia, 10th ed. New York: MacMillan, 1996.

Articles

Herbat, Ray. "Rice Shuffle Salt Lake Deck, Came Up With Winning Hand." *The Sporting News*, September 25, 1971.

Newhan, Ross. "Queen of Angels Finds Relief in Bullpen." *The Sporting News*, August 22, 1970.

"Coach Me a Little Bit." *Newsweek*, April 10, 1967, p. 88.

Sargent, Jim. "Jim Northrup." Society for American Baseball Research BioProject. Accessed at http://bioproj.sabr.org/bioproj.cfm?a=v&v=l&bid=1583&pid=10478

Seattle Times. January 29, 1981 (obituary, courtesy of Eric Sallee at www.thedeadballera.com).

Spoelstra, Watson. "Dressen Taking Hard Look at Glove Smoothie Oyler." *The Sporting News*, March 13, 1965.

Spoelstra, Watson. "Slick Fielder Oyler Works to Lubricate Batting Stroke." *The Sporting News*, March 4, 1967.

Spoelstra, Watson. "Sparma Regains Old Yankee-Killer Rep—Bengals Lick Chops." *The Sporting News*, June 17, 1967.

Spoelstra, Watson. "Oyler Bat Lacks Something, But His Glove Is Super-Sweet." *The Sporting News*, September 2, 1967.

Spoelstra, Watson. "Mayo Recommends Shortstop Who Can Hit as Cure for Tigers." *The Sporting News*, October 21, 1967.

Spoelstra, Watson. "Gladding's Departure Saddens Lolich." *The Sporting News*, December 9, 1967.

Spoelstra, Watson. "Five Clubs Seek Oyler, But There'll Be No Deal." *The Sporting News*, December 30, 1967.

Spoelstra, Watson. "Anemic Bats Put Oyler On Tiger Spot." *The Sporting News*, February 17, 1968.

Spoelstra, Watson. "Strike-Bound Writer Couldn't Resist Camp." *The Sporting News*, March 9, 1968.

Spoelstra, Watson. "Oyler Receives a Barrage of Boos on Opening Day." *The Sporting News*, April 27, 1968.

Spoelstra, Watson. "'Only for Now,' Says Mayo of Stanley's Tenure at SS." *The Sporting News*, October 12, 1968.

Spoelstra, Watson. "McAuliffe No. 1 Tiger When It Comes to Praising Cesar." *The Sporting News*, April 11, 1970.

"Tiger Untamed." *Time*, September 13, 1968. Accessed at http://www.time.com/time/magazine/article/0,9171,838702-1,00.html

Whittlesey, Merrell. "Gridders Rip Soft Turf; Senators Fighting Mad." *The Sporting News*, August 23, 1969.

Web Sites

www.baseballanalysts.com
www.BaseballLibrary.com
www.en.wikipedia.org
www.retrosheet.org
http://sunnyside.ltschools.org/news_events/press_release.detail.php?id=1065.
www.thedeadballera.com

Acknowledgements

Dave Baldwin
Jim Bouton
Pete Cava
Peter Morris
National Baseball Hall of Fame & Museum/A. Bartlett Giamatti Research Library
Rod Nelson
Jeff Samoray
Rich Shook
Trey Stecker
www.PaperOfRecord.com

Rich Shook presents:

Tigers In the News

Saturday, August 10
Norm Cash atoned for an eighth-inning error with a home run in the bottom of the inning to give Detroit a 4–3 victory over visiting Boston. Cash's 17th home run of the season came off lefty Bill Landis, too, and it gave Detroit its 20th win of the season in its last turn at bat. Cash also made an error, one of six he'd made this season, on July 3 against the Angels and also ripped a home run in that game. Mickey Lolich picked up his second straight victory in his four relief appearances to improve to 9–7. He struck out four of the six batters he faced in closing out the game. Patterson started, worked 4.1 innings and left trailing, 3–1.

Sunday, August 11
The one drawback to starting Gates Brown was that it took baseball's best pinch-hitter off the bench. Detroit beat Boston twice—taking the first game 5–4 in 14 innings and winning the second by a 6–5 count. Brown, whom Detroit reportedly tried in vain to trade in the spring, pinch-hit his second straight home run in the opener to reward 13.1 innings of shutout relief by five Tigers pitchers. He is now 16-for-27 pinch-hitting. He started in left field in the second game, went 2-for-4 and drove in the winning run with a one-out squib single to first in the ninth that capped a four-run rally. "I have never in my life had anything happen to me to compare to this," Brown said after helping Detroit restore its first-place margin to seven games. He has beaten the Red Sox with hits four times and all three of his home runs are off Boston pitching. In the first game, Wilson was battered for four runs in just 0.2 of an inning. Joe Sparma, Jon Warden, Don McMahon, Fred Lasher, and Mickey Lolich shut the door. Lolich worked five two-hit innings to improve to 10–7. Warden relieved in the second game and became 4–1 due to the rally. Jim Northrup hit a sacrifice fly in the third, Bill Freehan added his 17th home run in the sixth, Wayne Comer pinch-hit his first major league home run in the seventh and Don Wert hit an RBI triple in the eighth after Willie Horton was safe on an error to tie the score.

Daryl Patterson

by Parker J. Bena

Season	Age	W	L	Pct	G	GS	CG	SV	IP	H	R	ER	BB	SO	ERA
1968 Tigers	24	2	3	.400	38	1	0	7	68	53	19	16	27	49	2.12
Career Totals		11	9	.550	142	3	0	11	231	223	119	105	119	142	4.09

Daryl Alan Patterson was born on November 21, 1943, in Coalinga, California. He graduated from Coalinga High School in 1962 and entered the College of the Sequoias in Visalia, California, that fall. At 6-foot-4, he entered college intending to play basketball as a point guard, but switched to baseball after pitching for an amateur team in Melville, Saskatchewan. Since it was an amateur team, it did nothing to hurt his collegiate eligibility. After attending the College of the Sequoias, he was signed to a free-agent contract with the Los Angeles Dodgers by scout Dwight "Red" Adams. During Patterson's years at Sequoias, the team finished with an overall record of 30–29–1 and a conference record of 20–20 under coach Roy Taylor. Aside from Patterson, Sequoias sent several other players to the major leagues, including pitchers Jack Aker and Bob Ojeda, outfielder Jim Wohlford, and former Montreal Expo Brad Mills, bench coach for the 2007 world champion Boston Red Sox. Patterson was put on the roster of the Dodgers' Triple A farm team, the Spokane Indians, but never got the chance to pitch in the L.A. system.

Patterson would not make his major league debut until he joined the roster of the Detroit Tigers in 1968 ("just in time to get a ring," he'd say), having been selected from the Dodgers by the Tigers in the first-year minor league draft in November 1964. Before making his debut with Detroit, Patterson was part of the Toledo Mud Hens team that won the 1967 Governor's Cup as champions of the International League, winning the best-of-seven series in five games over the Columbus Jets (affiliates of the Pittsburgh Pirates). During the regular season, the Hens finished with a record of 73–66, which was good for third place, seven games out of first. Outfielder Wayne Comer and relief pitcher John Hiller were among the Hens who joined Patterson in Detroit the next year.

His debut major league game came April 10, 1968, at home against the defending American League champion Red Sox. It was a two-inning mop-up relief appearance in a 7–3 Tigers loss, pitching the eighth and ninth innings. After hurling a perfect eighth, he ran into a little trouble in the ninth. He got Mike Andrews to strike out looking and Dalton Jones to ground out, but Carl Yastrzemski belted an inside-the-park home run to center field. Patterson then struck out Reggie Smith. He went 4.1 innings but did not figure in the decision in a 4–3 Tigers win. On June 5, Patterson pitched a scoreless three-inning save in relief of eventual 31-game winner Denny McLain in a 5–4 Detroit win over the Red Sox at Fenway Park. Daryl also made one start in his rookie season. In the start, which came at home August 10 against the Red Sox, he allowed all three Bosox runs on four hits, walked two, and struck out three and gave way to future star reliever John Hiller in the fifth inning. However, in a case of role reversal, it was eventual World Series hero Mickey Lolich who pitched the final 1.2 innings and picked up the victory.

Patterson did have a couple of highlights against the once-mighty New York Yankees in 1968. His first came at home July 30 when he came into the game in relief of Earl Wilson, who had gone eight strong innings. Patterson pitched a perfect ninth after Wilson walked Mickey Mantle; he got Joe Pepitone to fly out to left, Rocky Colavito to line out to right, and then struck out Tom Tresh to earn his fourth save of the year as he and Wilson combined on a 5–0 whitewashing of the Bronx Bombers. His second highlight came at Yankee Stadium August 23. Patterson came into the game in the seventh inning in relief of John Wyatt, who had relieved starter Wilson—who himself had given up two runs in 5.2 innings. He was perfect in his two innings of work, even striking out Mantle to end the eighth inning. Patterson got Mantle on a 3–2 breaking ball that he called "one of the best breaking balls I ever threw in my life." Patterson added, "Even in his final years, watching Mickey swing was like watching a stick of exploding dynamite." However, the Tigers could not score in their half of the ninth to make a winner out of him, and Wilson was saddled with a 2–1 loss. All in all, Patterson appeared in 38 games in 1968 with one start, 22 games finished, 68 innings pitched, 27 walks, 49 strikeouts, a 2–3 record, seven saves, and an impressive 2.12 ERA.

Patterson was on the roster for the 1968 World Series against the defending world champion St. Louis Cardinals. He pitched a perfect seventh inning in Game 3 at Tiger Stadium, getting Tim McCarver to pop out to third, Mike Shannon to ground out third to first, and Julian Javier to fly out to center. He was then lifted for pinch-hitter Wayne Comer. Patterson's two-inning relief appearance in Game 4 at Tiger Stadium, however, was a bit more eventful. He came into the game in the fourth inning to replace Joe Sparma after Cardinals pitcher Bob Gibson had homered and Lou Brock had tripled. With Daryl on the hill, Curt Flood flied to right. Brock (the runner Patterson inherited) scored on a ground out by former New York Yankees slugger Roger Maris. Future Hall of Famer Orlando "Baby Bull" Cepeda then drew a walk. However, he ended the inning by being caught trying to steal second base by Tigers catcher Bill Freehan. Patterson opened the fifth inning by getting Tim McCarver to fly out to center and Mike Shannon to fly out to left. Julian Javier singled, but was erased trying to steal second when Patterson caught him leaning the wrong way and fired a dead-on pickoff throw to end the inning. Patterson was lifted for pinch-hitter Jim Price. Game 4 ended in a 10–1 Cardinals victory; but that was their last 1968 Series win as the Tigers swept the last three contest to take the Series in seven games. In his three innings of World Series work, Patterson allowed only two base runners, and both were erased trying to steal.

In 1969, the year after the Tigers' World Series triumph, Patterson saw action in only 18 games. He finished with a 0–2 record and with 19 walks and 12 strikeouts, and an ERA of 2.82. His longest outing of the year was a 2.1-inning stint July 11 against Cleveland at Tiger Stadium. He came into that game in the third inning and was greeted by a Ken Harrelson grand slam, but he settled down and pitched a scoreless fourth and fifth in an 8–1 Tigers loss. He also threw two innings against Baltimore on September 5 at Tiger Stadium. He pitched a scoreless eighth and ninth, allowing only a single to Paul Blair, in an 8–4 loss to the eventual American League champions. The winning pitcher that day was co-1969 Cy Young Award winner Mike Cuellar, who posted his 20th victory of the 1969 campaign.

The year 1970 proved to be an important one for Patterson. After being roughed up in a May 23 home game against the Washington Senators and saddled with the loss in a two-inning relief stint in which he failed to hold a 5–4 lead, he reeled off seven straight wins, all in relief. Patterson finished 1970 with a 7–1 record, 43 appearances, two saves, 55 strikeouts, and a 4.85 ERA. One of his highlights came in a September 4 game against the Senators at RFK Stadium. Patterson entered the game in relief of Lolich in the eighth inning. Bernie Allen, batting for Tim Cullen, opened the inning by singling to left. Darold Knowles struck out on a bunt attempt. Eddie Brinkman then flied out to center. Ed Stroud came up, batting for Patterson's former teammate Wayne Comer, and drew a walk, sending Allen to second. Frank "The Capital Punisher" Howard singled to right, scoring Allen and sending Stroud to third. The inning ended when Stroud was caught trying to steal home. Patterson was lifted for pinch-hitter Ike Brown during a four-run Tigers rally in the top of the ninth to take a 6–3 lead. Tom Timmerman then pitched the ninth and picked up his 24th save, ensuring Patterson's seventh win of the 1970 campaign.

Patterson started off the 1971 season on the Tigers' roster. He got into 12 games and posted a 0–1 record with a 4.82 ERA. He was traded May 22 to the Oakland Athletics in exchange for infielder John Donaldson. Patterson got into only four games with the eventual AL West champs, posting no record and a 7.94 ERA before being sold June 25 to the St. Louis Cardinals. Patterson made two starts with the Cardinals in 1971. In his second start, he achieved a somewhat dubious honor. Bob Gibson had been taken out of the rotation once the Cardinals fell out of the 1971 National League East race. This meant that Patterson would be the starter (and loser—in his only Redbirds decision of the year) in a September 30 game against the Mets at Shea Stadium. The winning pitcher in that game was Tom Seaver; with the win, Seaver posted the second of his five career 20-win seasons en route to 311 career wins. Patterson went 5.1 innings with five runs, four hits, four walks and one strikeout. Among the hits were two home runs to

Ken Singleton. Incredibly enough, Patterson had retired the first 14 batters he faced before the Mets' bats came alive. It wasn't the first Patterson-vs.-Seaver confrontation; they had pitched against each other when they played junior college ball in California. Seaver pitched for Fresno City College before transferring to the University of Southern California. Patterson recalled his time in St. Louis as being "very enjoyable" and the fans as being "very knowledgeable." His locker was right next to Gibson's. He had very fond memories of Gibson: "He was very tough to get along with, but he liked me," Patterson said. On October 21, though, Patterson was returned to the Athletics.

Patterson played winter ball for Ponce in Puerto Rico in the 1971–1972 off-season and pitched a shutout against Mexico February 7, 1972, to win the Caribbean World Series. That spring, he reported to the Oakland A's minor league club in Tulsa, Oklahoma.

In 1973, Patterson was sold by the A's to the Pittsburgh Pirates. He spent the season pitching for the Pirates' top farm club, the Charleston Charlies, in Charleston, West Virginia. The Charlies were managed by Joe Morgan, who managed the Boston Red Sox in the late 1980s and early 1990s. Among his teammates were: Frank Tavares and Omar Moreno, who played key roles on the Pirates' 1979 world championship team, and future big-league player and manager Art Howe. The Charlies finished the 1973 International League regular season in first place. However, they lost the Governor's Cup finals to the Pawtucket Red Sox.

Patterson returned to the majors in 1974 and pitched in his first game with the Pirates on June 15 at Three Rivers Stadium against the San Francisco Giants. Coming in with two out in the eighth inning, he got Bobby Bonds to ground out short to first, Chris Speier to strike out, and Gary Maddox to ground out second to first. He then gave up a single before the rains came, giving the Bucs—and Patterson—the victory. For the year, Patterson finished his final major league season with a 2–1 record, 14 appearances, one save, eight strikeouts, but a 7.29 ERA.

The Pirates' manager that year was Danny Murtaugh, in one of his four stints as Pittsburgh's skipper. According to Patterson, "nobody could handle pitchers like Danny Murtaugh." Though the Pirates won the NL East with an 88–74 record, Patterson was left off the postseason roster for the National League Championship Series against the Los Angeles Dodgers, which they lost 3 games to 1. His final major league appearance came on September 14 in a somewhat bizarre game—a 17–2 shellacking at the hands of the Montreal Expos at Parc Jarry in Montreal. He came into the game in the sixth inning and pitched 2.2 mop-up innings. Patterson was roughed up—allowing eight runs on nine hits with two walks and two strikeouts and a home run by first baseman Mike Jorgenson. Patterson recalled succinctly his final appearance in the majors: "I didn't have anything that day."

After retiring from baseball after the 1974 season, Patterson went to work for Pacific Gas & Electric. In twenty years with the company, he rose from helper to chief inspector. One of his major projects was a $7 billion hydroelectric job. In 2007, Patterson was reunited with some of his 1967 Toledo Mud Hens teammates when the Mud Hens hosted a reunion of the 1967 Governor's Cup championship team. Today, he makes his home in Clovis, California.

References

Publications

Gillette, Gary, and Pete Palmer, eds. *The ESPN Baseball Encyclopedia*, 2007 edition. New York. Barnes and Noble Books. 2006.

Web Sites

www.cos.edu
www.retrosheet.org

Other Sources

Bena, Parker. Interview with Daryl Patterson. September 21, 2007.

Rich Shook presents:
Tigers In the News

Monday, August 12
McLain became a 24-game winner with a 6-3 victory over host Cleveland. "I've been thinking about 30 since [win number] 15," he said. "I think it's natural to think about winning 30 games. But I'm not losing any sleep over it." Tony Horton's two home runs accounted for the three Indians runs. Norm Cash broke a 1-1 tie with his 18th home run in the sixth. Mickey Stanley had sacrifice flies in the fifth and seventh innings.

Tuesday, August 13
Sonny Siebert's three-hit shutout cooled off Detroit, 1-0. Pat Dobson (3-5) worked the first seven innings and three of the four hits he allowed came in the second inning.

Wednesday, August 14
Mickey Lolich relieved Joe Sparma in the fourth inning and pitched Detroit to a 3-0 victory over host Cleveland. "I don't like it," the lefty said of relieving. "I don't think my arm is adjusted to relief. I think I'll be back in the starting rotation next week." Lolich (11-7) has given up three runs and 10 hits in six games covering 16.2 innings since Smith yanked him from the rotation. He has won four games with 12.2 shutout innings since August 6. Bill Freehan's 18th home run gave Joe Sparma a 1-0 lead in the second and the Tigers added two more in the sixth on Al Kaline's double, a single by Gates Brown, and Norm Cash's triple. Sparma walked three in 3.1 innings and left with two on.

Thursday, August 15
Detroit was not scheduled to play but Sparma ripped Smith for what he felt was humiliating treatment the night before. (Denny McLain was going for his 25th win and 16th road victory of the season the next day at Boston.) Sparma was irked at Smith having Lolich warming up as early as the first inning Wednesday before finally bringing him in with Detroit leading, 1-0, and two runners on with one out in the fourth. "He even had him up in the first inning, as soon as I walked the second batter I faced," Sparma said. "If that's all the confidence he had in me, why did he start me in the first place? I don't know if I can pitch for that man any more. I was completely embarrassed when Mayo came out to get me. I felt humiliated." At the time, Sparma was 8-10 with a 3.98 ERA. For his part, Smith felt Sparma has a better chance for success as a starter than he would in relief, due mainly to his excessive walk total. Part of the reason Smith wanted Lolich pitching was because he'd miss the weekend with National Guard duty. "All he had to do was talk to me, tell me what was going on," Sparma said. "But I go out there and all I can see is Mickey down there throwing in the bullpen. I've always had pride in my work but you can't keep that pride when your manager doesn't treat you like a man. Woody Hayes never even treated me that way." Sparma was Hayes' quarterback at Ohio State before Detroit signed him as a pitcher.

Friday, August 16
McLain says his arm is tired. Well, gee, could it be all those innings in all those wins? "I've pitched more than 250 innings already," McLain said after making host Boston his 25th victim of the season with a 4-0 shutout. "I think it's understandable that my arm is more tired. It has to be. It's beginning to tell on me, especially in the eighth and ninth innings." McLain said it was taking him a few innings to get really loose now. Detroit held a 2-0 lead when Boston put runners at second and third with nobody out in the sixth. No problem. McLain whiffed Dalton Jones, Carl Yastrzemski, and Ken Harrelson in order to help nail down his sixth shutout, 22nd complete game, seventh win in a row, 16th in his last 17 decisions, and up his record away from Tiger Stadium to 16-0. Dick McAuliffe doubled and Al Kaline hit a home run in the third to give the Tigers their 2-0 lead. They added two in the eighth on McAuliffe's triple, a wild pitch, a walk plus singles by Mickey Stanley and Norm Cash. Bill Freehan was hit by pitches three times in the game, tying a major league record.

Saturday, August 17
Freehan belted a home run in the 11th inning to provide the Tigers with a 10-9 victory over the Red Sox. His 19th home run went into the left-field screen atop the Green Monster off lefty Lee Stange with two out in the 11th to give Detroit its 12th win in its last 14 games. Harrelson had hit his 32nd home run in the ninth to tie the score at 9-9. Harrelson reached 100 RBI in the game. Cash had five RBI, the last on an eighth-inning single for a 9-8 Detroit lead. Boston had erupted for seven in the sixth to tie it. Cash hit a two-run home run, as did McAuliffe as Pat Dobson carried a three-hitter into the sixth. Don McMahon (4-1) pitched four innings of two-hit, one-run ball for the win with Jon Warden getting two outs in the 11th despite giving up two hits and Wyatt getting the last out.

Jim Price

by Gary Gillette

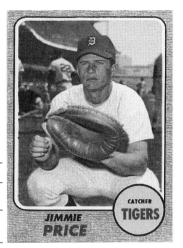

Season	Age	G	AB	R	H	2B	3B	HR	RBI	BB	SO	SB	CS	BA	OBP	SLG
1968 Tigers	26	64	132	12	23	4	0	3	13	13	14	0	0	.174	.253	.273
Career Totals		261	602	58	129	22	0	18	71	62	70	0	0	.214	.287	.341

"One of the most ignorant things ever said about baseball was the labeling of catcher's gear as "the tools of ignorance." The origins of that regrettably memorable phrase date back at least to the 1930s, though the etymology is disputed. Suffice it to say, however, that anyone who repeats that ignorant utterance must never have met Jim Price.

For more than two decades after Price last donned what he calls the "tools of intelligence," Price's fame rested on his membership in the exclusive 1968 Tigers club—whose members are veritable demigods in Michigan. Now, however, after 15 years in the Detroit broadcast booth, Price's reputation rests on the smooth way he has been able to meld his analysis with play-by-play partners Dan Dickerson, Ernie Harwell, and others.

One of the fascinating aspects to Price as a broadcaster is that he combines the knowledge of an old-school ballplayer without the undercurrent of bitterness or condescension that some old-timers display when commenting on the modern game. In an interview, Price related—in the same, matter-of-fact way—an anecdote about playing on a broken ankle in winter ball early in his career. "They taped it up and gave me pain pills. That's just the way it was in those days." The ankle never healed properly, and Price to this day displays a swollen ankle and a slight limp as a reminder of the physical toll of catching.

Born in Harrisburg, Pennsylvania, on October 13, 1941, Price was a standout athlete in three sports at nearby Hershey High School and is now a member of that school's hall of fame. According to Price, "It was a good place for an athlete to grow up, because it was football, football, football—and basketball. Baseball was very minor." On the gridiron, Price earned "Big 33" honors, the equivalent of all-state selection.

Price's boyhood idols were Smoky Burgess, plus Mickey Mantle and Yogi Berra. This was partly due to the fact that his Little League coach was a big Yankees fan, Price remembers, to the point of "having grass from Yankee Stadium in his wallet."

Like most high school football heroes, the youthful Price wanted to play college football and was heavily recruited. The Tigers' Ed Katalinas scouted Price, but Price told him he intended to play football, even though Price's father wanted him to play baseball. Ultimately, the son decided that he wanted to get married, so he signed a professional baseball contract in 1960 with Pittsburgh that included a small signing bonus. He signed as a shortstop and pitcher, as so many outstanding high school ballplayers start out.

Then known by his given name of Jimmie, Price began his career with Kingsport in the Appalachian League in 1960, playing third base and first base. He started catching in '61 with Grand Forks of the old Northern League, where he spent two years and started developing some power. In 1963, Price began catching full-time, earning Carolina League Player of the Year honors at Kinston while hitting .311 with 19 home runs and a league-leading 109 RBI.

At that point, however, the catching prospect's career stalled. Sent by Pittsburgh to Triple A, he spent three years with Columbus of the International League while awaiting his chance to break into the Pirates' lineup. After losing out to Jerry May in 1967 in the battle for the third catcher's slot at the end of spring training, Price told the Pirates that he wouldn't go back to Columbus again. Since the Tigers had been asking about Price for a couple of years, the Pirates promptly sold him to Detroit for a reported $50,000 on April 7. May quickly moved up to become the Pirates' regular catcher that season.

Price went north with his new club as the reserve catcher. "It was a double-edged sword," he recalls. "Great to be in the big leagues, but behind an All-Star." All-Star Bill Freehan's backup would be the sole role Price would fill for the next five years. During that time, the rugged Freehan spent only one month on the disabled list and started only 54 games at other positions (mostly first base). Thus, Price's big-league career was limited to only 261 games and 602 big-league at-bats, despite never being sent back to the minors and despite spending only 21 days on the disabled list in those five seasons. Part of his conditioning regimen was weightlifting, which was unusual among baseball players of his era.

Freehan, a three-time All-Star by age 24, was already the best catcher in the AL when Price came to Detroit. He was still the best in the league when Price retired. Though the Tigers' stalwart would never again reach the heights he achieved in 1967 and 1968 (when he was third and second, respectively, in AL MVP voting), Freehan remained an All-Star every year through 1972 and was the AL's starting catcher for seven straight midsummer classics from 1966 to 1972.

Because the Tigers carried only two catchers, manager Mayo Smith was reluctant to use Price, even as a pinch-hitter. (Price averaged less than 20 pinch-hit at-bats per season in Detroit.) During Price's tenure, all other Tigers catchers (besides Freehan and Price) appeared in fewer than eight games per season on average. "Mayo was the type of guy that just let us play.... He didn't mess things up; didn't overmanage," recalls Price. Despite the natural rivalry at the position, Price says that he has "great memories" of his playing days. He also became "best friends with Freehan" and had "great respect for him."

The new Tigers' catcher made his major league debut on April 11, 1967, as a pinch-hitter. His first game behind the mask was in the nightcap of a doubleheader at Kansas City on April 16, where he went 3-for-4 with a double and two RBI. Even with a career hitting line of .214 (batting average)/.287 (on-base percentage)/.341 (slugging percentage) in spot usage, Price experienced several individual highlights—aside from participating in the barn-burner AL pennant race in 1967 and in winning a world championship in 1968. Price hit a dramatic solo homer at Tiger Stadium in the bottom of the 10th inning on August 21, 1968, off knuckleballing White Sox reliever Wilbur Wood. However, in the '68 fall classic, Price saw only two at-bats as a pinch-hitter, even though Freehan was catching every inning while going only 2-for-24 (.083) in the Series.

Price posted an adjusted OPS of 95 in 1969, more than respectable for a little-used backstop. Offensively, Price's best power numbers were posted that year when he slammed nine home runs and eight doubles in only 192 at-bats. Despite a .234 batting average, One of those was a game-ending round-tripper on June 23, 1969, off the Yankees' Steve Hamilton at Tiger Stadium. Price hit the only grand slam of his career off Sonny Siebert on September 1, 1970, in Boston.

While not exactly a highlight, Price was behind the plate September 19, 1968, when Denny McLain grooved a batting practice–caliber fastball to Mickey Mantle, allowing the Yankees' legend to blast his 535th career homer to surpass Jimmie Foxx and become (then) the third-most prolific home run hitter in baseball history. Many accounts of that day—including, curiously, those in McLain's first two autobiographies—erroneously say that Freehan was the catcher.

Unlike many ballplayers who leave only when they are no longer wanted, Price retired voluntarily after 1971. "I was fed up making no money.... When you don't play every day, you lose your skills." Also unlike so many ballplayers, Price had a plan for his life after baseball. He had already started working at a small television station in Lebanon, Pennsylvania, in the off-season while still playing, doing interviews to hone his skills and increase his future employment prospects.

After retiring, Price remained in the Detroit area, taking a manufacturer's representative job like many other ex-Tigers. For two decades, the ex-catcher paid his dues and slowly climbed the ladder in sports television. He was one of the earliest ESPN analysts, covering College World Series games, softball, and other events for the fledgling network. As honorary chairman of Special Olympics, Price ended up on the other side of the microphone, being interviewed frequently. Eventually, he would also work for several TV stations in Detroit.

The big break in Price's broadcasting career came in 1992 when Mike Ilitch purchased the Tigers. Hired first to work in the club's community relations department, Price was asked the following year to do Tigers games on cable on Pro-Am Sports System (aka PASS Sports), paired with his old teammate Jim Northrup in the booth. The following year, legendary announcer Ernie Harwell was added to the PASS team. In 1996, Price worked over-the-air games with George Kell and Al Kaline on Detroit TV station WKBD while continuing with PASS. In '97, PASS' last year on the air, Harwell replaced the retired Kell and worked with Price on both the WKBD and cable telecasts.

The Tigers signed a 10-year deal with Fox Sports Network Detroit in 1998, leaving Price momentarily out in the cold. However, he was back in the booth in June when Lary Sorensen left as the analyst on WJR's radio broadcasts. It was Price's first venture into radio after decades of working for TV. In 1999, Harwell switched back to radio, teaming with Price. In 2000, the two veterans were joined by Dan Dickerson for WJR's final season as the Tigers' rights holder after 36 consecutive years as their flagship radio station. (WJR had also shared the Tigers' radio contract off and on prior to 1965.) The trio switched to WXYT in 2001, enjoying a yearlong outpouring of affection for Harwell after he announced he would retire at the end of the 2002 season.

Because Price's forte is breaking down the inside game, radio was a perfect fit as the medium allows broadcasters to speak at greater length. Catchers frequently make great analysts because they can speak about pitching like a pitcher but can also speak knowledgeably about hitting, whereas pitchers-turned-analysts sometimes can't turn things around when they get into the booth. Needling his former batterymates, Price jokingly says, "Pitchers aren't the brightest guys."

Dan Dickerson praises his partner, "Jim recognizes if a pitcher doesn't have his best stuff early in the game, and he'll say so. Or, if the pitcher makes an adjustment during the game, Jim recognizes it."

Since 2003, Dickerson and Price's reputations have grown along with the club's prowess on the field. Their first season without Harwell was a nightmare, as they endured calling 119 Detroit losses and more than a month of speculation at the end of the season about whether the toothless Tigers would tie or set the modern record for losses in a single season (120). Unexpectedly, Detroit finished with a flourish, winning five of its last six games.

With his long-term experience as a ballplayer and TV analyst, Price's tenure in the radio booth was important, as the franchise was reeling in the early years of the first decade of the new century. After Harwell and Kaline retired, the ex-catcher with the smooth, reassuring manner was the only direct link still on the air to the glory year of 1968. Jack Ebling, a Lansing sportswriter, talk radio host, and author of *Tales from the Detroit Tigers Dugout*, said that it took a long time for Detroit fans to get past the loss of Kell, Kaline, and Harwell. Ebling thinks Price "might have been a balm in some way, especially with the youth of their other three broadcasters."

Stuart Shea, vice chair of SABR's Business of Baseball Committee and a historian of baseball broadcasters, also compliments Price. "Not many former players are as good at analyzing the game as he is. He could probably even do play-by-play, because he's quite smooth. I'd compare him to [Tim] McCarver in that he has good behind-the-plate insight." McCarver, of course, is another ex-catcher.

References

Publications

Britten, Brian, ed. 2007 *Detroit Tigers Information Guide*. Detroit: Detroit Tigers. 2007.

Duxbury, John. *Baseball Register*. St. Louis: The Sporting News. 1968.

Duxbury, John. *Baseball Register*. St. Louis: The Sporting News. 1969.

Ebling, Jack. *Tales from the Detroit Tigers Dugout*. Champaign, Ill.: Sports Publishing. 2007.

Enders, Eric. *100 Years of the World Series: 1903–2003*. New York: Barnes & Noble Publishing. 2004.

Gillette, Gary, and Pete Palmer. *The ESPN Baseball Encyclopedia*, 4th ed. New York: Sterling. 2007.

Kachline, Cliff. *Baseball Dope Book*. St. Louis: The Sporting News. 1966.

Kachline, Cliff, and Chris Roewe. *Official Baseball Guide for 1966*. St. Louis: The Sporting News. 1966.

Kachline, Cliff, and Chris Roewe. *Official Baseball Guide for 1967*. St. Louis: The Sporting News. 1967.

MacFarlane, Paul, Chris Roewe, and Larry Wigge. *Official Baseball Guide for 1970*. St. Louis: The Sporting News. 1970.

MacFarlane, Paul, Chris Roewe, Larry Wigge, and Larry Vickrey. *Official Baseball Guide for 1971*. St. Louis: The Sporting News. 1971.

MacFarlane, Paul, Chris Roewe, Larry Wigge, and Larry Vickrey. *Official Baseball Guide for 1972*. St. Louis: The Sporting News. 1972.

Marcin, Joe. *Baseball Register*. St. Louis: The Sporting News. 1970.

Marcin, Joe. *Baseball Register*. St. Louis: The Sporting News. 1971.

Roewe, Chris, and Oscar Kahan. *Official Baseball Guide for 1968*. St. Louis: The Sporting News. 1968.

Roewe, Chris, and Paul MacFarlane. *Official Baseball Guide for 1969*. St. Louis: The Sporting News. 1969.

Spink, J.G. Taylor, Paul A. Rickart, and Clifford Kachline. *The Sporting News Baseball Guide and Record Book*. St. Louis: The Sporting News. 1961.

Spink, J.G. Taylor, Paul A. Rickart, and Clifford Kachline. *The Sporting News Baseball Guide and Record Book*. St. Louis: The Sporting News. 1962.

Spink, C.C. Johnson, Paul A. Rickart, and Clifford Kachline. *Official Baseball Guide for 1963*. St. Louis: The Sporting News. 1963.

Spink, C.C. Johnson, Paul A. Rickart, and Clifford Kachline. *Official Baseball Guide for 1964*. St. Louis: The Sporting News. 1964.

Spink, C.C. Johnson, Paul A. Rickart, and Clifford Kachline. *Official Baseball Guide for 1965*. St. Louis: The Sporting News. 1965.

Sumner, Benjamin Barrett. *Minor League Baseball Standings*. Jefferson, N.C.: McFarland & Co. 2000.

Articles

Biederman, Les. "Bucco Regulars Make It Rough for Newcomers." *The Sporting News*. April 9, 1966. Available from www.PaperOfRecord.com.

Fisher, Eddie. "Pitching, Power Helped Jest Cop Int Flag in 'Upset of The Year." *The Sporting News*. September 11, 1965. Available from www.PaperOfRecord.com.

Gillette, Gary. "The Voice of Summer Evenings in the Motor City." *Tigers Corner 2007*. Hingham, Mass.: Maple Street Press. 2007.

Spoelstra, Watson. "Freehan Feeling Rosy Over Black And Blue Marks," *The Sporting News*. June 3, 1967. Available from www.PaperOfRecord.com.

Spoelstra, Watson. "Siege in Sick Bed Leaves Northrup's Batting Eye Sharp," *The Sporting News*. July 1, 1967. Available from www.PaperOfRecord.com.

Web Sites

http://DennyMcLain.US/
http://Detroit.Tigers.MLB.com/
http://members.SABR.org [SABR encyclopedia, including Home Run Log and Scouting Database]
www.baseball-reference.com
www.retrosheet.org [including Transactions Log]
www.themick.com/mickeyquotes7.htm
www.tigersweekly.com

Other Sources

Ebling, Jack. E-mail message to author.
Gillette, Gary. Telephone interviews with Dan Dickerson and David W. Smith.
Gillette, Gary. Interview with Jim Price.
Lahman, Sean. E-mail messages to author.
McLain, Denny. Remarks at Mayo Smith Society meeting. August 3, 2007.
Shea, Stuart. E-mail message to author.

Notes

Adjusted OPS stats per Pete Palmer's calculations in the *ESPN Baseball Encyclopedia*, 4th ed. They may differ slightly from similar statistics on *baseball-reference.com* or those previously published in *Total Baseball*.

Rich Shook presents:

Tigers In the News

Sunday, August 18

A suicide squeeze killed Detroit. Pitcher Juan Pizzaro laid down a perfect squeeze bunt while Joe Foy steamed in from third with the tie-breaking run during a 4-1 victory by Boston. Pizzaro bunted a 3-2 pitch to the right of the mound in the seventh inning of a 1-1 game. "We were looking for the squeeze," Earl Wilson (10-10) said after starting with two high fastballs to foil the strategy. "The first pitch was a pitchout and I wasn't trying to get the second one over the plate either. But you can't look for it on a 3-2 count with the pitcher batting and a hot hitter like Mike Andrews coming up next." Willie Horton belted his 28th home run, in the fifth, for the Tigers' lone run.

Monday, August 19

Detroit did not play but organ player McLain hit a couple of sour notes. McLain told UPI's Milton Richman, while in New York to plug Hammond organs, that he had a torn shoulder muscle. "My arm hasn't been giving me much trouble until lately," he told the Hall of Fame columnist, "but I've got a torn muscle in back of my shoulder and that's giving me a lotta pain. The pain is there all the time. That goes whether I'm playing the organ, playing cards or doing anything which requires moving my shoulder. When I go out to warm up, I have to throw sidearm at first because it pains me so much. Then I gradually begin throwing overhand. I get this kind of trouble at the beginning of every year but this was the first year I didn't have it until five weeks ago. It was cold one night and all of a sudden I felt the strain." The other bad news for the Tigers' 25-game winner was a tidbit that surfaced about financial trouble McLain was getting into, although nobody recognized it at the time it was a sneak preview of McLain's future. A suit was filed saying he owed a credit card company $743 in unpaid bills and a department store alleged he failed to pay $377 he had been court-ordered to.

Dennis Ribant

by David MacGregor

Season	Age	W	L	Pct	G	GS	CG	SV	IP	H	R	ER	BB	SO	ERA
1968 Tigers	26	2	2	.500	14	0	0	1	24.1	20	7	6	10	7	2.22
Career Totals		24	29	.453	149	56	13	9	518.1	536	245	223	126	241	3.87

Somewhere, back in the swirling mists of time, there existed a magical and wondrous age when aspiring athletes did not commit their lives to the fanatical and single-minded pursuit of one sport by the time they were five years old. Take, for instance, the 1968 Detroit Tigers, who were notable for having a number of extremely versatile sportsmen on their team. Joe Sparma and Jim Northrup were both college football quarterbacks (at Ohio State and Alma College, respectively), Mickey Stanley was a multi-sport high school star, and Willie Horton won a Golden Gloves boxing tournament at age 17, to name just a few. But perhaps the most remarkable of all these athletes was an unheralded journeyman reliever who was traded from the Tigers to the Chicago White Sox midway through the 1968 season—Dennis Joseph Ribant.

Born on September 20, 1941, Ribant, catcher Bill Freehan, and outfielder Lenny Green were the only three members of the 1968 Tigers actually born in Detroit. His mother and father, Helen and Arthur Ribant, raised Dennis and his brother and sister in the East Forest-Chene area of Detroit's near east side. Long before the era of personal trainers, video analysis, and sports gear as a fashion statement, Ribant honed his baseball skills at a nearby school the old-fashioned way. He and a few of his buddies would outline a strike zone on the wall and then use rubber balls to pitch and hit for hours, with younger kids from the neighborhood assigned the task of chasing down balls hit into the field. In addition to this, Ribant's father would come home from his job as a foreman for the Farmcrest Baking Company and spend time teaching Dennis how to throw a curveball.

The lessons paid off, because as a teenager Ribant became known as the best pitcher in the city. He never bothered playing baseball for St. Joseph High School because the season was too short and the quality of the play was too low. Instead, he lived on the sandlots, playing with and against players like Horton, Freehan, Alex Johnson, and Carmen Fanzone. He played in the Pony League in Hamtramck, the Colt League, and the Firemen's League, finally ending up on an extremely good team sponsored by Herbert Smith Roofing in 1960. They were ultimately beaten in the city championship by Lundquist Insurance, which entitled Lundquist to travel to Altoona, Pennsylvania, to compete in the Class D National Baseball Federation Tournament for kids 19 years old and under. However, Lundquist (which already had Freehan on its team) was allowed to cherry-pick three extra players from other teams to take with them, and with an unerring eye for talent they chose Horton, Johnson (who would win the American League batting title in 1970), and Ribant. This team, loaded with future major leaguers, went on to win the championship in Altoona against a team from Cincinnati featuring future Tiger Eddie Brinkman and future NBA star John Havlicek.

But as gifted as Ribant was as a pitcher, it wasn't the only sport in which he excelled. In the winters he played hockey, often skating out on Belle Isle. As he says, "I had a good shot and I was a good skater, and not popping off or bragging, but I certainly held my own." As a 17-year-old, he found himself playing for the Teamsters' hockey team, with none other than James Hoffa Jr.—son of the legendary Teamsters leader and a future Teamsters president himself—playing goalie. By the time the 1960–1961 hockey season rolled around, Ribant was playing left wing and center for the Hamilton Red Wings (a farm team of the Detroit Red Wings) in the Ontario Hockey Association. Playing on the same line as future National Hockey League star Pit Martin, the team also featured future 1972 "Summit Series" hero Paul Henderson and future NHL coaches Pat Quinn and Nick Polano. Up against the St. Michael's Majors in a semifinal playoff game at Maple Leaf Gardens, Ribant was checked into the boards and dislocated his left elbow. This in itself was bad enough, but even worse, Ribant was scheduled to report to spring training with the Milwaukee Braves and showed up with his left arm in a sling.

Just how did a teenage phenom from Detroit wind up with the Milwaukee Braves? That was the work of Ray Garland, a Milwaukee scout who had seen Ribant pitch on the Detroit sandlots and arranged for him to try out for Milwaukee during the 1961 season. As Ribant relates:

"[Tigers General Manager] Jim Campbell told me before I went to Milwaukee, 'Dennis, before you sign, we'd like to talk to you. We're really interested in having you join the Tigers.' But I'm 19 years old, I'm happy as can be. The Milwaukee Braves fly me out there and I'm in County Stadium with my dad, throwing batting practice to Eddie Mathews and Joe Adcock. I see Warren Spahn walking by and they say, 'Dennis, we want you to sign, otherwise we don't know if we'll make any offer.'"

The Braves' stratagem worked beautifully and they had Ribant's signature on a contract before he left town. In 1961, Ribant joined the Class D Quad Cities Braves in Davenport, Iowa, and proceeded to overpower the entire league. He went 17–2, with a league-leading 1.86 ERA, five shutouts, and 17 complete games. His most memorable outing was the first nine-inning perfect game ever pitched in the Midwest League, shutting down the Clinton C-Sox 1–0 on July 2, 1961. As Ribant recalls, "The thing I remember was that ten thousand people were in the stands and the last batter, with two outs in the ninth inning, tried to bunt to get on base. I wouldn't say it was unethical, but it was a little weak. Anyway, I picked up the bunt and threw him out."

Voted Midwest League Rookie of the Year, the Braves moved Ribant all the way up to their Double A team in Austin, Texas, for the remainder of the 1961 season, where Ribant went 4–2. This was the year that determined Ribant's athletic future: "After my first year in baseball, when I was 21–4, the Braves said, 'Dennis, you'd be foolish to continue playing hockey. Look what happened to your left arm. You have a good chance to be a big league ballplayer.' So that was the last year I played hockey."

In 1962, Ribant began the year at the Braves' Triple A affiliate, the Louisville Colonels, but a tired arm and a 0–3 record (along with a 13.05 ERA) got him sent back to the Austin Senators in the Texas League. By the time 1963 rolled around, the Braves decided to send Ribant to another one of their Class AAA teams, the Toronto Maple Leafs, where he was used in relief. This worked for the manager of the Maple Leafs, but it didn't work for the Braves' front office, who were grooming Ribant to be a starting pitcher. He was told to pack his bags once again to join yet another AAA affiliate of the Braves, the Denver Bears in the American Association, where Ribant went 14–9. When the 1963 season was over, Ribant headed down to Puerto Rico to play winter ball, pitching for Lobos de Arecibo (the Arecibo Wolves), but also developing some arm problems in the form of calcium deposits in his right elbow. Still, Ribant was back in Denver in 1964 and crafted an 8–2 record to go along with a respectable 3.53 ERA. This drew the attention of the New York Mets, who traded Frank Lary to the Braves for Ribant on August 8, 1964. The very next day, Ribant made his major league debut, pitching two-thirds of an inning in relief against the Philadelphia Phillies.

In 1965, Ribant spent the majority of the year with the Triple A Buffalo Bisons, going 3–12 for a farm team every bit as woeful as their parent club. But gradually, Ribant made his way into the Mets' starting rotation, where he soon became the best starting pitcher the Mets had ever had during their short history. In 1966, Ribant achieved folk hero status among Mets fans when he became the first full-time starting pitcher in Mets history to actually record a winning season, going 11–9. Even more remarkably, this was the first season that the Mets didn't wind up in last place. While Ribant would later declare, "I loved playing in New York," his glory days as a Mets pitcher were short-lived. At the end of the 1966 season the Mets brought up a young fireballer named Nolan Ryan, and in 1967 Tom Seaver appeared on the scene, followed by Jerry Koosman in 1968. But Ribant wouldn't be there to see any of these pitchers blossom, because he was traded to the Pittsburgh Pirates along with Gary Kolb for Don Bosch and Don Cardwell after the 1966 season.

As Ribant recalls it: "I remember Bing Devine [de facto GM of the Mets] called me up and said, 'Dennis, sit down.' I mean, I wasn't crying, but God, I couldn't believe it. I really had a good year, but then I thought, well, get over it.

You're going to a good ballclub with Roberto Clemente and Willie Stargell."

In Pittsburgh for the duration of the 1967 season, Ribant had a decent but unspectacular year. Used both as a starter and a reliever, he went 9–8, but his ERA ballooned to 4.08 in a year when the ERA for the entire National League was 3.38. Still, he had the distinction of taking the mound for what could be considered a historic major league game. On June 17—aside from Ribant—every other member of the Pirates starting nine was either black or Hispanic, a fact that wasn't lost on anyone. To this day, Ribant can rattle off his teammates in that particular game, and as Bruce Markusen relates in his book, *Roberto Clemente: The Great One*, Pirates pitcher Dock Ellis observed what was going on and joked, "We got to find a way to get Ribant out of there early and get Alvin O'Neal McBean in there so we have nine brothers playing." Another ephemeral bit of baseball trivia that season that had to do with Ribant: On July 19, Ribant and Mike McCormick of the San Francisco Giants combined to issue a total of seven intentional walks during the game—one for Ribant and six for McCormick. It was an 11-inning contest; no game before or since of that length or less has had more intentional passes. A 17-inning Giants-Cubs tilt May 2, 1956, featured 11 such free passes, but only a Mets-Pirates games June 27, 1979, and a 16-inning Phillies-Orioles marathon July 3, 2004, matched the Ribant-McCormick number of seven.

But as was becoming a pattern in his career, Ribant didn't stay too long in Pittsburgh. After one year with the Pirates, Ribant was traded to Detroit, with Dave Wickersham going to Pittsburgh to complete the deal. Tigers GM Jim Campbell, who had once coveted the teenaged Ribant, now brought in the versatile right-hander as insurance for the economical salary of only $24,500 for the year. For Ribant, the adjustment of moving from the National League to the American League was eased by the fact that he already knew several Detroit players, having played with or against Horton, Freehan, Stanley, and Jim Northrup. He wound up rooming with Mickey Lolich and appreciated being in a clubhouse with the likes of Al Kaline ("number one, one of the best ever to play the game"), Freehan ("a class guy, a good person") and Denny McLain ("pretty good golfer, a hustler, a fun guy…he was cocky, but he stood behind what he did.").

In the 1968 *Detroit Tigers Yearbook,* a short article entitled "Welcome Home, Dennis Ribant" declared, "He is expected to add stability to the Tiger bullpen and double as a spot starter when needed." But those starts never came.

While other relief pitchers like John Hiller and Pat Dobson started 12 and 10 games, respectively, days and days would go by as Ribant sat in the bullpen cooling his heels. He was used sporadically in relief, winning two games and losing two, but despite his glowing 2.22 ERA, Mayo Smith apparently had little use for the hometown boy. As it turned out, the number 14 on Ribant's back was a portentous sign, as he pitched in only 14 games for the Tigers. Looking back on 1968, Ribant remembers, "I was happy to be coming back to Detroit, but I didn't get much of a chance to pitch. Only 24 innings in three-and-a-half months." While respecting Mayo Smith's knowledge of the game and the players, Ribant concluded, "I wasn't crazy about him, because I didn't pitch much for him."

Ribant's final appearance as a Detroit Tiger would take place in the Hall of Fame game, played July 22 at Doubleday Field in Cooperstown. Ribant collected the win in this exhibition game over his former Pirate teammates, with future Hall of Famer Jim Bunning taking the loss as the Tigers romped to an easy 10–1 victory. Four days later Ribant was gone, traded to the Chicago White Sox for veteran reliever Don McMahon. Why had the Tigers made the trade? In *The Tigers of '68: Baseball's Last Real Champions*, author George Cantor claims it went back to a May 26 brawl the Tigers had in Oakland. A day after Al Kaline had his arm broken by a pitch, Jim Northrup got beaned by Oakland's Jack Aker and both teams rushed onto the field for what umpire Ed Runge described in Jerry Green's *Year of the Tiger* as "the best fight I have ever seen on a baseball field." As the Oakland A's fans pelted the Tigers with garbage and verbal abuse, one of the Tigers hurled a ball into the stands, striking a middle-aged woman who subsequently sued the Tigers. In Cantor's account, he writes: "No one would say who had thrown the ball. But pitcher Dennis Ribant was discreetly traded and the Tigers settled the case. Some of the players privately said that it was the hardest pitch Ribant had thrown all year."

Ribant denies the charge, pointing out that a full two months elapsed before he was traded and offering the more mundane explanation that the transaction took place because "they were in a fight for a pennant and they wanted an experienced relief pitcher in Don McMahon, which he was."

Being moved from the Tigers to the White Sox in the middle of the season hit Ribant hard. Not only was he leaving his hometown, but the Tigers were in first place by 6.5 games when he was traded. Reflecting on his brief and unhappy tenure with Chicago, Ribant says, "My head really wasn't into it. I was really depressed to go from a team that's going to the World Series to Chicago. It knocked the stuffing out of me." When the season was over, the Tigers reacquired Ribant, but then sold him to the expansion Kansas City Royals. Ribant spent the winter in Puerto Rico, playing winter ball for Leones de Ponce (Ponce Lions) and compiling an 8–1 record. Hopeful of moving into the Royals' starting rotation in 1969, he was instead told that they were sending him to the minor leagues to begin the season. Having spent $175,000 for each of their players in the expansion draft, the Royals wanted to see what their drafted players could do before using a pitcher they had acquired for a paltry $25,000.

After five years in the majors and being bounced from team to team, Ribant had had enough, telling the Royals, "If I can't be on this ballclub now with the way I pitched in spring training, trade me." The Royals duly sold him to the St. Louis Cardinals, who promptly sent Ribant to their Triple A farm club, the Tulsa Oilers. They brought him up to their major league roster where he pitched just once—and pinch-ran for Joe Torre once—before trading him to the Cincinnati Reds for Aurelio Monteagudo. The Reds sent Ribant to their Triple A farm team, the Indianapolis Indians, before finally calling him up late in the season. Ribant subsequently appeared in seven games in relief and proved his worth by posting a sterling 1.08 ERA. As he walked off the field on September 27, 1969, Ribant could have been excused for looking forward to what the next year might bring. He had just turned 28 years old, he had finished the season strong, and maybe 1970 would be the year he would be able to put his vagabond baseball days behind him and stick with one club. He had no way of knowing that he would never again appear in a major league uniform.

After the season, the Reds traded Ribant to the Pirates for Bo Belinsky. And in a pattern that had become dismayingly familiar to Ribant, the Pirates immediately sent him to the Columbus Jets, their Triple A team in the International League. After laboring in the minors for the entire season, Ribant once again pitched winter ball in Puerto Rico for Lobos de Arecibo, hoping to recapture the form that would allow him to return to the majors. As Ribant noted of his three seasons playing winter ball, "It was fun to play in Puerto Rico. Good baseball. At least as good as AAA and maybe a little bit better, because they had all the major leaguers like Orlando Cepeda, Jose Pagan, Juan Pizarro, Roberto Clemente, they would all play."

Despite his best efforts, Ribant failed to make a major league roster in 1971 and joined the Hawaii Islanders, the Triple A minor league affiliate of the San Diego Padres who made their home at Aloha Stadium in Honolulu and played in the Pacific Coast League. Even with a geographical location that required alternating three-week road trips and home stands, Ribant philosophically observed that "if you had to be in the minor leagues, Hawaii was awesome." Unfortunately for Ribant, his contract was owned by the Islanders, not the Padres, and they were disinclined to sell him unless the price was right. Ribant continued to pitch for the Islanders in 1972, but his dream of returning to the majors was drifting further and further over the horizon. At the conclusion of the season, Ribant stepped back and assessed his situation.

"I was 31 at the time and I figured if I'm not going back to the big leagues after the way I've been pitching the last three years in AAA, then I'm not going back. Especially when I found out that I had a chance to go to the Chicago Cubs for $25,000, but the deal never materialized because Hawaii wanted $50,000 for me."

He would give professional ball one more shot, appearing in ten games for the Triple A Eugene Emeralds in the Pacific Coast League in 1973, going 0–0 with a 7.36 ERA, before packing it in for good. All told, he had appeared in 149 major league games as a pitcher and another 16 games as a pinch-hitter or pinch runner. He had started 56 games and come on in relief on 93 occasions. This was one of the aspects of his career that Ribant found most exasperating, because in his view, "I've always been a better starting pitcher than in relief. I put everything into every pitch and after pitching a few innings or so, I need three or four days to be strong again."

Looking back on his career, Ribant can point to several highlights: his perfect game in the minor leagues, getting called up to the big leagues from Denver, and his first win in the majors, a 5–0 shutout of the Pittsburgh Pirates on August 19, 1964, where he struck out 10 men. He felt he had good success against Pete Rose and Ernie Banks, and lists Willie Stargell, Willie McCovey, Frank Robinson, Lou Brock, and Hank Aaron as among the toughest hitters he faced. His biggest regret in baseball is refusing to report to the minor leagues for the Kansas City Royals in 1969: "I should have shut up and gone to AAA because they were bringing up pitchers left and right and I'm sure I would have been called up by them during the course of the summer."

Just what sort of pitcher was Ribant? After his career year with the Mets in 1966, Ribant described his pitching approach in the January 1967 issue of *Baseball Digest*: "I got away with my curve in Class D, but I use a slider now instead of a curve. I'd throw maybe three good curves, then one wouldn't break and would really get tagged. I've always had control. Now I have a sinker, a fastball and a change-up taught to me by Warren Spahn when he was a Met in 1964 [actually, 1965] and polished up by Harvey Haddix, who is Met pitching coach now. Control does it up here. I'm not overpoweringly fast. My slider's good when I'm able to keep it down…I go for the corners, using my slider to break low for the 'out pitch.'"

What Ribant doesn't mention is the dark rumors that he had another very special pitch in his arsenal as well. On four separate occasions in 1967 and 1968, *The Sporting News* published articles on pitchers suspected of throwing spitballs, and Ribant's name appeared in all of them. As if to confirm the rumors for American League hitters, in Ribant's very first appearance as a Detroit Tiger in a spring training game in Lakeland (against the Minnesota Twins on March 9), Ribant faced only two hitters before being ejected for throwing a spitball. Subsequently, when Newsweek ran an article entitled "The Soggy Art" in its April 1, 1968, issue, it was Ribant's name that once again floated to the surface. Despite the passage of forty years, Ribant is reluctant to go into the details of this aspect of his career, saying, "I don't know if I really want to talk about the spitball. Let's just say I experimented with it."

What happened to Dennis Ribant following his peripatetic baseball career? After bouncing from Toronto to Puerto Rico to Hawaii and seemingly every town and state in between, it should come as no surprise to learn that once he had the chance to put down some roots, Ribant was both eager and grateful for the opportunity to stay in one place. He had met Bette Neelands in Ontario while attending business college and playing hockey for the Hamilton Red Wings and they got married in 1962. In 1970 they decided to settle in Newport Beach, California, where they live to this day. They have two children, Tracy and Deron (named after former major leaguer Deron Johnson) and Ribant took up a career in the insurance business. This isn't to suggest that he gave up sports completely. He began playing tennis with the same passion he had once devoted to hockey and baseball, and in 1983 the father-daughter team of Dennis and Tracy Ribant won the Equitable Family Tennis Championship held at the National Tennis Center in Flushing Meadows, New York. Even at age 65, Ribant still hit the tennis courts three times a week, and played in the occasional celebrity golf tournament as well.

With the various tantalizing peaks and demoralizing valleys of his baseball career long behind him, there is a bittersweet quality to his reminiscences. There is regret that he was never able to fully reach the potential he felt he had, mingled with relief that it's all over. As Ribant himself says, "It was frustrating, because after 1969 I did have good years in the minor leagues, and not getting called up was a little bit maddening. But in the business that I'm in now, the life insurance business, no one can trade me. I like it here."

All told, Ribant contributed only two wins to the 103–59 season of the 1968 Detroit Tigers. And just as he was one of the best all-around athletes on that team, he is one of its most forgotten members as well. But the hometown boy was here. From swatting rubber balls on the playground, to the sandlots, to taking the mound in Tiger Stadium for the most legendary team in Detroit sports history—Dennis Ribant was here. And that's a slice of Detroit sporting history that most definitely should be remembered.

References

Publications
Cantor, George. *The Tigers of '68: Baseball's Last Real Champions.* Dallas: Taylor Trade Publishing. 1997.
Green, Jerry. *Year of the Tiger.* New York: Coward-McCann, Inc. 1969.
Markusen, Bruce. *Roberto Clemente: The Great One.* Champaign, Ill.: Sagamore Publishing.1998.
Middlesworth, Hal, ed. *Detroit Tigers 1968 Official Yearbook.* Detroit: Detroit Tigers. 1968.
Palmer, Pete, and Gary Gillette, eds. *The Baseball Encyclopedia.* New York: Barnes & Noble Books. 2004.

Web Sites
www.robneyer.com/book_04_extras3.html (accessed June 10, 2007)

Other Sources
Interview with Dennis Ribant, June 17, 2007.
Ray Nemec for minor league stats, basebalray@aol.com

1968 TIGERS

Rich Shook presents:
Tigers In the News

Tuesday, August 20
McLain getting bombed was about as likely as John Hiller pitching a one-hitter, yet both occurred as Detroit split a home doubleheader with the Chicago White Sox. Hiller (6-3) hurled his one-hitter in the opening game, a 7-0 win. He walked two and struck out seven. Ron Hansen's leadoff single in the fifth inning was the only hit he gave up. Gates Brown made a rare start and slammed his fourth home run of the season on the first pitch he saw in the game. He also had an RBI single in the fourth. Mickey Stanley had a two-run single in the seventh while Hiller got his second single of the season and second RBI in the same inning. McLain was shellacked in the White Sox' 10-2 second-game win a day after saying he had a "torn muscle" in his shoulder. Tigers' team physician Dr. Russell Wright said his examination of the "torn muscle" McLain said he had was just a minor irritation of the trapezius muscle that has been present for several years. Detroit made four errors behind McLain, who gave up nine hits and nine runs in 5.2 innings. Only two of the runs were earned. Pete Ward reached him for a grand slam. Two of the errors were by Al Kaline, who heard boos for one of the few times in his career.

Wednesday, August 21
The Price was right. Jim Price was called on to pinch-hit in the 10th inning of a 2-2 game and lined a two-strike knuckleball from Wilbur Wood into the left field seats for a game-ending 3-2 Detroit victory over visiting Chicago. His reward? A rare scheduled start as Bill Freehan was ticketed to play first base against lefty Tommy John of the White Sox. Price was hitting just .180 before slamming his second home run of the season. Freehan's single drove in Detroit's first run and Stanley hit a two-out home run in the eighth for a 2-2 tie. Daryl Patterson (2-2) pitched two scoreless innings of relief for the win. Pat Dobson allowed four hits and two runs in the first eight innings.

Thursday, August 22
Hit batters were not proving to be a hit with Detroit. Dick McAuliffe took exception to a high inside 3-2 pitch from Chicago's Tommy John in the third inning and charged the mound halfway to first base. The two were seen exchanging words and McAuliffe veered from his stroll to first to charge John. The White Sox' southpaw suffered a left shoulder injury when tackled by the Tigers' gritty second baseman and both were ejected following the bench-clearing brawl.

Back-to-back home runs by Al Kaline and Willie Horton in the sixth cemented Detroit's 4-2 win. John was found to have torn ligaments in his shoulder, putting him out 10 days to three weeks. "If they're all wound up as tight as that guy McAuliffe, they're in trouble," said acting Chicago manager Les Moss, who had replaced Al Lopez and who in 1979 would manage the Tigers for all of 53 games before being dumped so Detroit could hire Sparky Anderson. Chicago said it was ridiculous to think a pitcher would throw at a leadoff hitter on a 3-2 count. McAuliffe countered it was the third pitch John had thrown near his head in the at-bat and added "the White Sox have been throwing at us for two years." Mickey Lolich ended an exile to the bullpen to pick up his 12th win of the season, allowing four hits and two runs in seven innings. He struck out eight and didn't walk a batter. Don McMahon pitched the final two frames.

Friday, August 23
Detroit suffered two losses: McAuliffe for five days and a 2-1 decision to the Yankees in New York. McAuliffe received word he was suspended, and fined $250, for his part in the melee with Chicago lefty Tommy John the previous night. Detroit got just six hits in dropping the first game of what was supposed to be a twi-night doubleheader. Their only run was Earl Wilson's home run. The second game was halted after 19 innings by the 1 a.m. curfew with the score tied 3-3. It was to be replayed in its entirety prior to Sunday's regularly scheduled game. Noteworthy in the second game was Mickey Stanley's first appearance at shortstop. He played the beginning and end in center but worked eight innings at short in between. Stanley was pressed into shortstop duty because of the suspension of McAuliffe and military service of Tom Matchick. He had been regularly taking grounders at short during infield practice for several seasons. Joe Sparma ended his bullpen exile with the second-game start. John Hiller pitched nine innings of shutout relief and McMahon added three.

Saturday, August 24
Denny McLain allowed five hits in seven innings but one of them was Roy White's two-run home run and the right-hander lost on the road for the first time this season, 2-1 to New York. Matchick returned from military duty and played second base in place of McAuliffe, with Dick Tracewski playing short.

1968 TIGERS

Jim Rooker

by Rich Shook

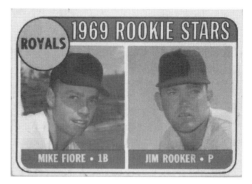

Season	Age	W	L	Pct	G	GS	CG	SV	IP	H	R	ER	BB	SO	ERA
1968 Tigers	25	0	0	.000	2	0	0	0	4.2	4	2	2	1	4	3.86
Career Totals		103	109	0.486	319	255	66	7	1810.1	1694	814	696	703	976	3.46

Jim Rooker's pro baseball career didn't come right out of left field. Center field is more like it. Rooker, who pitched his first two major league games for Detroit's 1968 championship team and then never pitched for them again, was not signed as a pitcher out of high school. The Tigers signed him and prep teammate Lindy Kurt out of the same high school in Decatur, Illinios, on June 21, 1960, soon after they graduated. They were scouted and signed by Jack Fournier. Detroit offered $6,000, decent signing money in those pre-draft days, and Rooker bought "the first real nice car I ever owned—a 1959 Chevy Impala Supersport."

Kurt and Rooker began their pro careers—Kurt as a pitcher and Rooker as the center fielder—later that summer. Rooker, who was born on September 23, 1942, in Lakeview, Oregon, switched full-time to pitching in 1966 and two years later was in the big leagues playing a much smaller role as a newcomer than he felt he should have. But at least Rooker found out right off the bat how a championship team conducts itself, an experience that would help him later with the World Series–winning Pittsburgh Pirates.

"It was fantastic being around those guys," Rooker said of his pro baptism with the 1968 Tigers. "Al Kaline, a Hall of Famer; Norm Cash, one of the funniest guys you'd ever meet; Pat Dobson, Mickey Stanley, Jim Northrup…you did feel comfortable being around them. You felt like you were one of them. They made you feel relaxed. I think it's tougher for some younger players. They weren't as helpful. It was more of holding on to your job and to heck with the other guy."

"Kaline was always nice to me. During spring training it came up there was a possibility he was going to be traded to the [Los Angeles] Dodgers. He asked me what I thought about L.A. and the Dodgers. I was from that area. I pretty much gave him a glowing report. There was [announcer] Vin Scully. How could you not like him? I thought it was real nice of him to come up and ask me those questions. All those guys treated me real nice. Naturally, in any clubhouse there's always going be a jerk or two. But you find on winning clubs that they all get along and everything goes well."

Rooker didn't pitch his first game in the majors until age 25 and then it was just two relief appearances, making in debut June 30, 1968. Over the two games, he pitched 4.2 innings and allowed two runs on four hits with a walk and four strikeouts. But his time with Detroit ended before it barely began at the major league level. He was sent to the New York Yankees as the player to be named later in a late-season deal the Tigers struck to get late-inning relief help in the form of John Wyatt. The veteran was at the end of his career, though, and not helpful enough to be included on the postseason roster. Rooker, meantime, didn't even get to wear pinstripes. He was left unprotected in the expansion draft and taken by Kansas City, where he pitched from 1969 until being fortuitously traded to the Pirates following the 1972 season.

"I guess I was surprised," Rooker said. "I was not sure what was going on at that point. To be drafted by an expansion team, it was a lucky thing for me. I got more of an opportunity to still feel my way along and get my feet wet

SOCK IT TO 'EM TIGERS   147

in the big leagues. Which took a while for me to do. I was still learning at the big-league level in K.C. with an inexperienced ball club." He was traded to Pittsburgh for pitcher Gene Garber.

"It was like walking down the street and finding money," Rooker said of his adjustment to the trade. "From the first day I was around more professional people. You could see it just by the way they went about their work. I was feeling like, 'Where has this been?' I hadn't been around that atmosphere for a long time. I was a little more established. But it was a whole new world. Being there for eight years, taking a big part of winning a World Series, that was the greatest thing that ever happened to me."

Rooker became a successful broadcaster for the Pirates after his career ended with an arm injury during the 1980 season. He worked the team's games from 1981 until retiring from that phase of his life in 1993.

From 1960 through 1964 Rooker played the outfield and tried to figure out hitting, clearly without enough success.

Gail Henley was the Lakeland manager in 1963 and his pitching coach was Stubby Overmire. Rooker credits Overmire with his conversion to pitching. Like hitting your first curveball, it was an accident, of course. "I had pitched in a couple of blowouts," he said. "They saw me in batting practice. I was throwing and they asked me to throw harder, throw harder, throw harder. So I said, 'If I throw any harder, you're not going to be able to hit it.' I cut a few loose and he couldn't get the bat on the ball. So Stubby made the comment to me that if things don't work out as an outfielder, I should consider pitching. He was pretty impressed with the velocity I was throwing with."

Trading the known for the unknown can be like deciding whether to run full speed into a brick wall or only half speed. You know it's going to hurt, the question is how much. "I worked my way up to Double A as an outfielder. I just wasn't very consistent as a hitter. After the change they sent me back down to Class A ball. But there was a period in there of about two, three years of them not knowing what they wanted me to do.... In 1966 is when they let me do nothing but pitch. Things were much more consistent after that. I got called up at the end of the year. Things turned around pretty quickly after that."

Coming up through the Detroit organization in the 1960s placed Rooker on the same fields as some of the Tigers' best players. "Pat Dobson was one. I played with him in Instructional League. I also played with Mickey Stanley, Jim Northrup, Jon Warden, Willie Horton, Denny McLain—Denny and I were roommates in Duluth [Minn.] in Class C ball one year [1963]. I also played with Daryl Patterson, Fred Scherman, Tommy Matchick, and Dave Campbell. The year I roomed with Denny, I was an outfielder and he was a pitcher. With the team we had, we tore up the league that year.

"I remember McLain, he was afraid of the dark. At night I always used to say I heard these noises. I didn't realize he was terrified of the dark. But at the time it was pretty funny. He used to put pots and pans by the door so they'd make noise if anybody came in. I used to say, 'Did you hear that?' Tried to scare him. I didn't realize at the time how afraid of the dark he was. As great a player as McLain was—and he's a friend of mine—he was a jerk. He's still a friend, but you have to know him and what kind of person he is. But on that '68 team, most of the guys got along real well. Some would rub you the wrong way, but in general they were good guys."

Aside from the comparatively poor playing conditions, terribly long bus rides and low wages, life in the minors is probably like walking barefoot through a room full of bear traps in the dark. The journey takes all of your attention.

Rooker didn't have a breakthrough moment, a time when he went from just trying to get by to the point where he absolutely knew for certain he was destined for the major leagues. "You weren't making any money," Rooker recalled. "You were just trying to survive. Other than Duluth, I can't remember any winning teams I played on. You were trying to survive. Lots of guys have hopes, but I can't say I was loaded with confidence. I wasn't sure what direction I was going in.

"In 1966, my first full year pitching, I was 12–6 for a team in North Carolina, Rocky Mount. That's when I got called up at the end of the year. I kind of saw what was going on. I know the times I would warm up in the bullpen, I would look at the reaction of the guys watching. You kind of had the feeling you had the ability. But mentally for me it took a little time to get my confidence, because I didn't start out as a pitcher. Then I went from Class A to Double A to Triple A and basically dominated there. There were things you'd hear from other players, coaches and managers, so in the back of your mind you start thinking, 'It's going to happen, I just don't know when.' In 1967–1968 is when I developed some of the confidence. I knew I had the ability. But it was harder to get to the big leagues then than it is now. And in Detroit they had some good players."

While not making the club out of the starting gate in 1968 was tough for Rooker to deal with, it also fueled his fire a bit. And he got pushed by his Toledo manager, former Tigers manager Jack Tighe. "He kept telling me, 'You're going to be there.' I'd go up and down, up and down. I kept getting called up every time somebody got injured or had to do [two weeks of] military service, that sort of stuff. I might have been in the category where I didn't get the opportunity."

If that sounds like Rooker didn't care a whole lot for Mayo Smith as a manager, he didn't. "He can't defend himself now but I think the ability of the team overshadowed his inability as a manager. I've heard stories since. He was not a great manager, he was not the worst manager. But the one thing he did, the best thing he ever did as a manager, was when he moved Mickey [Stanley] to shortstop for the World Series. He doesn't get enough credit for that. It surprised me there wasn't more made out of it. It was probably one of the gutsiest things ever done—and of all people, him! If you ask anybody about that World Series, probably the first thing they say is, 'Lou Brock.' But I don't think he was any special strategist or anything. Let's make it clear, I didn't like the guy and I don't think I got a shot [from him]. Career-wise, it was proved out by who he kept and who he didn't keep. There are some managers who want to be liked, some want to be respected, and some who want it both ways. I'm not sure guys liked him or respected him. He was in the category of managers who just put the lineup out and stay out of their way."

There was one illustrative incident that stuck in Rooker's mind. There was a game where the pitcher of the moment was struggling, so Smith went out to the mound, probably with the intent of taking the hurler out. "This pitcher [Rooker didn't name him] told Mayo that if he didn't get off the mound, there were going to be some serious repercussions. So finally Mayo just left him in and let the guy get out of his own trouble. Pitchers told him things you really shouldn't say to a manager. But I think the players knew what was going on. Their attitude, I think, was, 'We know what we're doing, just let us do our job.'"

Rooker wasn't on the postseason roster but he still retained a vested rooting interest in the team. But something had happened late in the season that would change his life. "They made a trade late in the season. They got John Wyatt from the Yankees for a player to be named later. He was a veteran relief pitcher at the end of his career. I was the player to be named later. So I went to the Yankees on paper that winter and was drafted in the expansion draft by Kansas City." There he joined former teammate Warden, who had beaten him out for a roster spot the previous spring. Another twist of fate: Warden came down with a sore arm and was never the same. Rooker went on to play many more years. Pitching for the Royals was a mixed blessing, however. On the one hand you're a regular starter in the major leagues, the envy of every kid who likes baseball and everybody pitching in the minors. On the other hand, you're playing solitaire with a 50-card deck.

"When you play for a club like that," Rooker said, "you're more playing for yourself than trying to win a ball game for the organization. Because you know you're not going anywhere. I remember a player who refused to pinch-hit. He wanted to protect his average because he was hitting .300. I'm thinking, 'You gotta be kidding me.' We didn't know how to win, how to play winning baseball. We didn't have the type of leadership you need to teach younger players." Again, Rooker didn't name the player, but the best guess is 1969 AL Rookie of the Year Lou Piniella, who hit .282 that season and was once spotted during one game early in his career taking imaginary swings for nearly a full inning while playing left field.

The '69 Royals were managed by Joe Gordon and actually beat out the Chicago White Sox for fourth place in the AL West by one game and fellow expansionist Seattle by five. The first baseman was Mike Fiore, second baseman was Jerry Adair, and one of the two catchers was Buck Martinez. The pitching staff featured Wally Bunker and Dick Drago plus relievers Moe Drabowsky and Dave Wickersham. Rooker went 4–16 with a 3.75 ERA while logging 158.1 innings in 28 games (22 of them starts), fifth on the team. His hitting background showed up in a July 7 loss to Jim Kaat and Minnesota. Rooker became the first Royal to hit two home runs in a game (both off Kaat).

In 1970 Rooker improved to 10–15 with a 3.55 ERA in 38 games, 29 of them starts. His innings rose to 203.2, third on the staff. One of Rooker's losses came in a 12-inning game June 4 in which Horace Clarke of the Yankees broke up his bid for a no-hitter with a base hit leading off the ninth. "I won 10," Rooker said, "so I started to think, 'I'm getting the hang of things.' It was hard on everybody." But he went 7–13 over the next two seasons, splitting his time between relief and starting, and was traded to Pittsburgh for the 1973 season.

Those Pirates featured Willie Stargell, Manny Sanguillen in his prime, Al Oliver, Richie Hebner, and Richie

Zisk. Pitchers included Nelson Briles, Bob Moose, Dock Ellis, with a bullpen of Dave Giusti, Bob Johnson, and Ramon Hernandez. Rooker responded to his new environment by going 10–6 in 1973 and 15–11 with a 2.78 ERA in 1974, his best season, as Pittsburgh won the AL East. Rooker started the second game of the NL Championship Series, giving up two runs in seven innings without a decision.

The Pirates repeated in 1975 as Rooker contributed a 13–11 record and 2.97 ERA. He pitched the second game of the NL Championship Series, giving up four runs in four innings as the Cincinnati Reds won the series. Rooker was 15–8 and 14–9 the next two years as Philadelphia edged out Pittsburgh for the division title. In 1978 he dipped to 9–11 with a 4.24 ERA and in 1979 Rooker appeared in just 19 games—17 of them starts—going 4–7.

That Pittsburgh team made the World Series and Rooker was a surprise Game 5 starter in a series Baltimore led, 3–1. "I wasn't scheduled to start," Rooker said, "Bruce Kison was. But he had nerve damage to his arm from the first game. It was not a good year for me during the season. But there was one thing: I was very rested for the World Series. I thought I had somewhat of an advantage. I was all charged up and ready to go. Not only was I going to have what I hoped was fun. What a challenge! We were down 3–1. If we stink up the joint, we were going home."

Rooker pitched the first five innings and left trailing 1–0. The Pirates rallied for seven runs over the sixth, seventh, and eighth innings to hand the win to Bert Blyleven, who worked four scoreless relief innings. "I honestly thought we had the better team," Rooker said. "The first four games our hitting was limited. But [Baltimore manager] Earl Weaver made a couple of mistakes. He decided to pitch to Bill Madlock. And then we started swinging the bats. Our pitching was pretty consistent. And from that point we took off. All of us still knew we had the ability to beat 'em because we felt we had the better team. I can't remember if it was the sixth or seventh inning [it was the sixth] but Madlock came up with a runner in scoring position and got a base hit to knock in a run or two. Once he did, the hits just kept coming, coming, coming. Once we won that, it was back to Baltimore for the sixth and seventh games. Our bats came alive from that point on." Before Madlock stepped to the plate, Stargell had scored Tim Foli on a sacrifice fly, sending Dave Parker to third base. Then Madlock got his single, scoring Parker.

That marked Rooker's career highlight because the next year, 1980, he hurt his arm throwing a slider in May to Atlanta's Dale Murphy. "At the time I didn't know how serious it was. I waited for it to heal. It never did. Doctors could not find the injury. But I knew I was not going to be able to pitch again. That winter I went on the [press] caravan. As we went to different places, I kind of became a spokesperson for the club. Some of people thought I spoke so well I ought to do more of this."

So his career ended with a 103–109 record and a 3.46 ERA for 1,810.1 innings and 976 strikeouts. Which brought the left-hander to another career turning point. What to do next? What could be better than playing baseball? Well, for Rooker and many other players, it's extending their association with the game.

"They had fired one of the guys who was going to be one of the broadcasters and I auditioned for the job. I didn't have all the ability in the world, but I think they felt I would get better. And I was terrible—until I started listening to my own tapes. I realized the things I left out. I didn't prepare myself. But I also think I could have had a little more help along the way. But it's a lot like anything else, if you want to work on it, you'll get better. I asked our radio guys to tape the innings and I'd listen to them in my car on the way home. Things got better faster after that.

"I didn't plan ahead to do that. It's different today. You have players listening to broadcasters and they'll tape them for auditions. I thought my job [as a player] was on the field. And I find players don't want to know the truth. When they screw up they don't want to hear it. Had I thought about it, I probably would have gone another route. But what listeners want to know is, 'What's the score and how many outs.' You have to be very descriptive. And that's something you have to work at, especially in radio."

Rooker became a Pittsburgh icon with his ability to combine professional skill as a broadcaster with his propensity to speak his mind and be critical in a nonthreatening manner. No doubt many young Pirates fans don't even know Rooker used to work on the mound instead of the broadcast booth, a professional compliment. His defining moment as a broadcaster came June 8, 1989, after Pittsburgh scored 10 runs in the top of the first at Philadelphia, capped by a three-run Barry Bonds home run. "If we lose this game," Rooker said, "I'll walk home."

Naturally, something happened. Von Hayes answered with two-run home runs in the first and third innings. Steve Jeltz hit home runs in the fourth and sixth and the Phillies found by the bottom of the sixth they only trailed 11–10. The tying run scored in the eighth on a wild pitch, Darren Daulton hit a two-run single, and Philadelphia walked off the field with a 15–11 victory. "I always try to forget that," Rooker said. "We didn't have a good team. Whoever loses 10–0 leads? As long as I've been in baseball, that's never happened. Word spread real quick. The next morning I got a phone call from our radio station. This guy asked if I would go on at noon with him. I thought, 'What's the big deal?' But people were saying, 'Is he going to do it? Is he going to walk from Philadelphia to Pittsburgh? I said I won't do it just for the sake of doing it. Let's get some charities involved, a sponsor. Let's have some reason to do it."

It was billed as "Jim Rooker's Unintentional Walk." It took place that October after the season ended, and the proceeds were to go to Children's Hospital in both Pittsburgh and Philadelphia. "We got people together," he said. With the help of the Pirates and the Phillies, it took me 13 days. And it was hell. You don't realize what it can do to your feet. Day after day. We didn't realize how bad it was going to be. I walked with Carl Dozzi, he was one of those really over-energetic guys. After five days your feet get so bad (blisters). Once you get going for about a half an hour you kind of loosen up. Every five days we went to a half-size bigger shoe, extra socks, and another five days it was another half-size bigger. But we raised $81,000 for Children's Hospital. At least it was something you had to look forward to, a light at the end of the tunnel. There was no way in the world I was going to do it for nothing, no way in the world."

Rooker retired from the broadcast booth in 1993 to spend time at home and helping out with his restaurant, Just Rook's, located in a suburb about 20 minutes from Pittsburgh. "Last July [2006], my wife and I moved down to Jacksonville [Fla.]. My partner and I rotate being at the restaurant. Other than that, I just fish and golf."

1968 TIGERS

Rich Shook presents:
Tigers In the News

Sunday, August 25
Host New York tripped Detroit twice, 6-5 and 5-4, to trim the Tigers' lead over Baltimore to five games. The Tigers played 55 innings with the Yankees over three days and lost four games. Kaline suffered a groin injury in the first game and aggravated it pinch-hitting in the second. Meanwhile, Detroit suffered the indignity of losing to an outfielder in the opener. Former Tiger Rocky Colavito came out of right field and one-hit Detroit over 2.2 innings for the win. Colavito, known for his rocket arm out of right, had pitched in a game 10 years earlier (three hitless innings for Cleveland against Detroit). Daryl Patterson (2-3) lost the first game in relief of Pat Dobson as Detroit squandered a 5-0 lead. Mickey Lolich (12-8) walked seven batters in the first three-plus innings—he walked the two batters he faced in the fourth—and lost the second as New York scored in each of the first four innings, totaling five runs. Bill Freehan walked to the chalkboard in the visitor's clubhouse in Yankee Stadium and wrote a short message: "Anybody who thinks the world ended today doesn't belong here."

Monday, August 26
Earl Wilson rescued the strapped Detroit mound staff by working on two days of rest, pitching a six-hit shutout and driving in two runs to lead the Tigers to a 3-0 victory over Chicago in a game played in Milwaukee. The White Sox honored Eddie Mathews, the Tigers' disabled infielder who played much of his career in Milwaukee with the Braves, in a pregame ceremony. Detroit planned to put Mathews back on the active roster September 1. Wilson was hit on the batting helmet by a pitch with the bases loaded in the second and he singled in a run in the seventh. Norm Cash singled in Detroit's third run in the eighth.

Tuesday, August 27
The Tigers' lead shrank to four games with a 2-1 loss to the White Sox in Chicago, Detroit's fifth defeat in six games without the suspended Dick McAuliffe. His replacement at second base, Tom Matchick, made a wild throw in the ninth that allowed the winning run to score. "We had our shot to bust it open in the top of the ninth and couldn't do it," manager Mayo Smith said. "Bases loaded and nobody out. You can't ask for more than that." Willie Horton hit into a 1-2-3 double play and Norm Cash grounded out to short to squelch the threat. Starter John Hiller committed the sin of walking the leadoff batter in the bottom of the ninth, he was bunted to second and scored from there when Matchick threw away the ball on a grounder to second. Cash's 20th home run of the season accounted for the lone Detroit run. Bill Freehan was hit by a pitch for the 21st time of the season.

Wednesday, August 28
McAuliffe returned to Detroit's lineup, and so did Denny McLain's winning ways. The Tigers had been one run shy in five of their last six decisions (not counting the tie) prior to McAuliffe coming back to the field following a five-day suspension for his part in an on-field altercation with Chicago's Tommy John. McLain (26-5) stopped his season-long losing streak at two games (two games!) by hurling Detroit to a six-hit, 6-1 victory over visiting California. He struck out 11 to extend his club record for strikeouts in a season to 222. He had walked only 50 batters in 277 innings. Freehan, playing first base, socked his 20th home run in the second inning after a Horton single. Jim Northrup doubled and Jim Price looped a single to right for an RBI. Freehan was hit by a pitch again; that's 22 times, three shy of the league record, set by onetime Tiger Kid Elberfeld, then with the Washington Senators, in 1911. Horton had singled earlier and Northrup followed Freehan by hitting his 16th home run.

Thursday, August 29
Mickey Lolich turned in a three-hitter to blank California, 2-0. Lolich (13-8) struck out 12 and improved his August record to 6-1. He allowed his three hits in the first two innings and retired the last 20 batters in a row. Horton blasted his 31st home run in the fourth and added an RBI single in the eighth. His 400-foot home run landed in the upper-right center-field stands, about the same area where he tagged a home run as a 16-year-old high school kid in the Detroit Public School League championship game. Dick Tracewski played third to give slumping Don Wert a rest.

Friday, August 30
Earl Wilson grabbed the spotlight with his arm and bat. Wilson pitched a four-hit, 9-1 win that pushed second-place Baltimore further back and also drove in four runs with a home run and a single. It was Detroit's third straight win since the return of Dick McAuliffe and fourth victory in five games. The Tigers moved back to seven games in front of the Orioles. Wilson (12-11) blasted his 31st career home run and fifth of the season with two teammates on in the second. He capped a five-run third with his RBI single. The game drew 53,575 to Tiger Stadium, the new high for the season and biggest crowd since 1961.

Joe Sparma

by Jeff Samoray

Season	Age	W	L	Pct	G	GS	CG	SV	IP	H	R	ER	BB	SO	ERA
1968 Tigers	26	10	10	.500	34	31	7	0	182	169	81	75	77	110	3.71
Career Totals		52	52	.500	183	142	31	0	865	774	423	379	436	586	3.94

Once a promising right-hander blessed with a blazing fastball and hard overhand curve, Joe Sparma seemed destined to become a mainstay of the Detroit Tigers' starting rotation when he joined the team in 1964. Though he showed flashes of brilliance over his seven-year career, a frustrating lack of control and a perceived inability to remain focused kept him from achieving greater success.

A few too many uninspired starts led to a bitter conflict with Tigers manager Mayo Smith during the 1968 season. Yet Sparma seized a timely opportunity for a brilliant outing—and the most important of his career—when he pitched an exciting complete-game victory over the New York Yankees to clinch the Tigers' first pennant in 23 years. Sparma's continued inability to throw strikes and struggles with Smith in 1969 led to a postseason trade to the Montreal Expos. By June, Montreal sent Sparma to the minor leagues. By 1971, he was out of baseball.

Joseph Blase Sparma was born in Massillon, Ohio, February 4, 1942. As a youngster, he played sandlot ball in Canton and Massillon in the Ohio Amateur Baseball Congress. He gained the attention of Tigers scouts as a pitcher at Massillon High School, where he was also an All-State quarterback. Instead of entertaining baseball contract offers, Sparma opted to be a two-sport athlete at Ohio State University.

Legendary OSU football coach Woody Hayes platooned Sparma and two other players at quarterback in 1961 and 1962. Though he didn't have the chance to fully bloom under Hayes, who favored the running game, Sparma led the Buckeyes in passing both years. He also threw for 200 yards and tossed two touchdowns in OSU's 50–20 win over archrival Michigan in 1961. It was persistently rumored that Hayes recruited Sparma to keep him from playing for a rival Big Ten team.

Sparma was more successful as a starting pitcher for the Buckeyes in 1962 and 1963, compiling a cumulative 11–8 record and 3.16 ERA. He had 102 strikeouts in 1962 and turned down a bonus offer from the Milwaukee Braves so he could return to OSU for his junior year. Sparma struck out 93 batters in 1963 and threw a no-hitter against Michigan on May 18. He ended his collegiate career as OSU's all-time strikeout leader with 195.

Disappointed by a lack of playing time under Hayes, Sparma left OSU and signed as an amateur free agent with the Tigers in 1963, earning a $20,000 bonus. He was assigned to Class AA Knoxville in the South Atlantic League, where he pitched 17 innings over six games before being assigned to Class A Duluth-Superior in the Northern League. Sparma went 2–4 in eight games, striking out 58 in 43 innings. He also threw a five-hit shutout over Bismarck-Mandan to help the Dukes win the 1963 Northern League championship.

While assessing prospects during the winter 1963 Florida Instructional League, Tigers manager Charlie Dressen was especially impressed with Sparma's fastball and overhand curve.

Sparma began the 1964 season with Knoxville, compiling a 2–4 record in seven games before the Tigers called him up in May. He made his major league debut in Washington on May 20, allowing an unearned run in two-thirds of an inning of relief in a 10–3 loss to the Senators. Consecutive wins over New York, Washington, and Boston—the middle outing a 10-strikeout, one-walk, 3–0 complete-game win July 5 over Washington in Detroit—prompted Dressen to marvel at Sparma's rapid success.

"There's nothing freaky about his delivery," Dressen said. "Sparma has speed and gets it over. He has all the pitches to win."

The quick success did not last. Sparma struggled with his command and didn't get another win until mid-August. In 21 mound appearances, 11 of them starts, he went 5–6 with a 3.00 ERA, striking out 71 and walking 45 in 84 innings.

After honing his skills that winter pitching for Mayaguez in the Puerto Rican League, Sparma developed into one of the Tigers' top hurlers in 1965, losing consecutive games only once while compiling a 13–8 record and 3.18 ERA in 30 games (28 starts). He also exhibited improved control, striking out 127 and walking 75 in 167 innings. In the tradition of former Tigers pitcher Frank Lary, the media dubbed Sparma a "Yankee Killer" as he won five of his first six career decisions against New York.

Sparma got off to a bad start during spring training in 1966 when he injured the index finger on his pitching hand while closing a car door. That season he failed to complete a single game, finishing 2–7 with a 5.30 ERA in 29 appearances, only 13 of them starts. Sparma's recurrent control problems prompted interim Tigers manager Bob Swift to remark, "The son of a bitch looks like he never threw a baseball in his life."

Sparma pitched effectively in the winter 1966 Puerto Rican League and entered 1967 with renewed hope and a new pitching coach in Johnny Sain. During a visit to Puerto Rico, Sain suggested that Sparma add a slider to his repertoire. He continued developing the pitch in early 1967 while working out at a Detroit-area high school gym with Tigers catcher Bill Freehan. The Tigers also suggested that Sparma abandon his elaborate windup and decrease the amount of time between pitches (Sparma was known as one the league's dawdlers). He also arrived for spring training weighing 192 pounds, 10 pounds less than in 1966. Sparma, listed at 6 feet, had difficulty controlling his weight and was a chain smoker throughout his career, which some believed had a detrimental effect on his pitching performance.

Sparma's best season turned out to be 1967. The Tigers won his first seven starts, in which he collected four wins—two of them shutouts. Freehan remarked that Sparma was suddenly "thinking like a pitcher, not like a guy throwing through a brick wall." Sparma pitched confidently under Sain's tutelage during the season's first half, stating, "You know you're going to come back in the regular rotation. You don't get tense [for fear of] losing your job."

Tigers vice president and former catcher Rick Ferrell also remarked on Sparma's early-season dominance. "I don't believe anybody is faster in our league," Ferrell said. "[Cleveland Indians pitcher] Sam McDowell is as fast when he's right, but Joe can stay with anybody." By July, Tigers manager Mayo Smith moved Sparma from fifth to first in the starting rotation. A small amount of controversy ensued when Baltimore Orioles manager Hank Bauer did not select Sparma (then 9–1) for the All-Star team. "We knew in spring training that Joe would pitch better," Smith said. "When he has his control, he's as tough as they come."

Sparma didn't have as strong a second half and the Tigers fell a game short of winning the 1967 American League pennant. But he still finished 16–9 with a 3.76 ERA and tied for second in the league with five shutouts (all at home). He struck out 153 and walked 85 in 217.2 innings.

Sparma chose to forgo winter ball in 1967 to work as a manufacturer's representative selling machine parts, plastic, and rubber to automotive accounts. The Tigers expected Sparma to be a frontline starter in 1968. But he performed poorly in the season's first half, going 7–8 with a 4.01 ERA in 20 starts.

"Skipping winter ball seemed to retard Sparma's progress as a pitcher," said George Cantor, Tigers beat writer for the *Detroit Free Press* from 1966 to 1969. "He was like a kid who forgot all the math he learned over summer vacation. The Tigers loved his arm. He threw hard and was hard to hit. But he was always fighting to control his pitches. The coaches were frustrated with Joe, but I'm sure he was frustrated with himself, too."

After allowing five hits and three runs in an inning-plus against Oakland on July 17, Smith took Sparma out of the game. But "take him out" went only so far. "I can't start him, and he's too wild to pitch relief," Smith said after one exasperating outing. "What am I supposed to do—take him out and shoot him?" Sparma brooded endlessly when placed in a long relief role. The lack of communication with Smith made their relationship tense.

Things quickly unraveled during a start on August 14 in Cleveland. Sparma struggled against the Indians, allowing two singles and two walks in the first three innings. Although the Tigers had a 1–0 lead in the third, Smith had left-hander Mickey Lolich throwing in the bullpen. As Lolich warmed up, Sparma seemed to lose his concentration while preparing for the worst. After allowing a single and walk in the fourth, Smith yanked Sparma from the game. Visibly angered, Sparma threw his glove in the dugout and headed straight for the clubhouse. Lolich allowed just three singles the rest of the game and the Tigers won 3–0.

On the flight to Boston following the game, Sparma remained furious. He sat next to *Detroit Free Press* columnist Joe Falls and openly criticized Smith. Sparma said he felt "humiliated" and that he wasn't being treated like a man or a member of the team. "I don't know if I can play for that man anymore," Sparma said. "Even Woody Hayes didn't treat me like that." Smith was unapologetic. "I have to think of the other 24 players, too. I can't be thinking of one man," he said.

In two more starts—each with eight days' rest—Sparma failed to make it past the sixth inning and was in the depths of Smith's doghouse. He wandered aimlessly about the clubhouse and went 15 days without pitching. Trade rumors circulated. But on September 17, Sparma got a surprise start just five minutes before game time.

The Tigers' magic number was one, and right-hander Earl Wilson was scheduled to start against the Yankees at Tiger Stadium. A win would give the Tigers their first pennant since 1945. But Wilson hurt his shoulder warming up, forcing Smith to call on Sparma to pitch. With little time to spare, Sparma quickly took to the mound, much to the dismay of the 46,512 fans who booed as his name was announced.

Sparma allowed two singles in the first but the Tigers erased the threat with a double play. Afterward, Sparma was practically untouchable. He set down 19 of the next 21 batters; the only two who reached base were thrown out trying to steal second. Sparma was consistently ahead in the count and pitching with conviction. The fans got behind him and cheered thunderously when he singled to center to give the Tigers a 1–0 lead in the fifth. He received a standing ovation when he came to bat in the eighth.

Anticipation rose to a fever pitch when Sparma attempted to shut down the Yankees in the ninth. New York scored the tying run with two out, but Mickey Mantle struck out to end the inning. In one of its customary last-licks rallies that season, Detroit won the game 2–1 in the bottom on the ninth on a two-out single by Don Wert. The pennant-clinching win touched off a wild celebration that hadn't been seen in Detroit for more than two decades.

Sparma was highly emotional in the jubilant Tigers clubhouse, giving thanks to his wife, Connie, for her support that season. "I didn't have time to get nervous" about making the start, Sparma said. "All I could think of was all the trouble I've been in this year and how much pain it has caused my wife and my family. [The game] was beautiful, not for me, but for Connie. She's put up with an awful lot from me."

In 34 games (31 starts), Sparma went 10–10 with a 3.70 ERA, striking out 110 and walking 77 in 182.1 innings. His only World Series appearance came in relief of starter Denny McLain in Game 4 against St. Louis. In one-third of an inning, Sparma allowed two runs and two hits in a 10–1 loss.

The hard feelings between Smith and Sparma carried over into the 1969 season, as did Sparma's wildness. In 23 appearances (16 starts), Sparma went 6–8 with a 4.76 ERA. His control seemed to disappear altogether as he struck out 41 and walked 77 in 92.2 innings.

A rare bright spot for Sparma that season came against Seattle in a nationally televised game on May 31. In his first start in more than a month, Sparma missed the plate on eight consecutive pitches before getting a strike across in the first inning. But the Tigers retired the Seattle Pilots on an attempted steal and a double-play groundout. Sparma was erratic through eight innings, walking seven and striking out eight, but he had not allowed a hit. Only four pitches had been hit out of the infield.

"Joe [was] struggling," catcher Bill Freehan recalled. "I was constantly getting on him, chewing him out, trying to get him mad so he'd keep his concentration.… He was in trouble all the time, but he kept getting guys out." After retiring the first batter in the ninth, Don Mincher hit a 2–0 pitch to deep right-center for a double, ending Sparma's only serious bid for a no-hitter. The Pilots had just one hit in the 3–2 loss.

In early August, the Tigers fired pitching coach Johnny Sain, leaving Sparma with little support among the Tigers coaches. During the 1969 World Series, the Tigers attempted to trade Sparma to Pittsburgh for reserve outfielder Carl Taylor, but the deal fell through. On December 3, 1969, the Tigers dealt Sparma to the Montreal Expos for pitcher Jerry Robertson. The Expos sought to acquire Sparma after receiving an enthusiastic report from a scout who watched him pitch a game that winter in Puerto Rico.

After the trade was announced, Sparma did not hesitate to criticize Smith. "Mayo has no idea how to put a pitching staff together," Sparma said. "We might have blown two or three pennants in a row."

Impressed with Sparma's spring training performance, Expos manager Gene Mauch named him the 1970 opening day starter. Mauch hoped a fresh start with a new team might restore Sparma's confidence. "Joe Sparma will never master the strike zone," Mauch said in early April. "But he's a threat to shut you out every time."

Sparma showed good control in his first two starts, but his wildness crept back. He also had problems making accurate throws to first on pickoff attempts. On April 29 against San Diego, he tried to walk a Padre intentionally but his pitch sailed over the catcher's head, scoring a run. The next inning, Sparma's errant pitch broke the jaw of Padres catcher Bob Barton. Later, after losing four of his first five starts, Mauch put Sparma in the bullpen. "It would be different if I had established pitchers, but I've got to go with guys who are winning," Mauch said.

Sparma's most humiliating performance came in what was to be his final major league game. Appearing in relief May 12 against the New York Mets, Sparma threw just five strikes in 28 pitches. Most were over catcher John Bateman's head or in the dirt. The inning ended only when a wild pitch bounced off the backstop and returned to Bateman for a play at the plate. Shortly thereafter, Montreal optioned Sparma to Class AAA Buffalo. He ended the major league season 0–4 with a 7.06 ERA in nine games (six starts). He struck out 23 and walked 25 in 29.1 innings.

On June 11, the Buffalo franchise was transferred to Winnipeg. But the team's home ballpark was not yet ready for play, so the Winnipeg Whips played 23 consecutive road games while wearing Buffalo Bisons uniforms. Sparma's weight dropped to 180, but it didn't help his pitching. He ended the International League season 3–13 with an 8.22 ERA in 24 games (23 starts). He struck out 76 and walked 92 in 116 innings, and was tied for the league lead with 19 wild pitches. "We were a Triple A expansion club," Sparma said of his Winnipeg experience. "It's like one of the guys said—'We're a team of fringe ball players that nobody else wants.'"

Sparma returned to the Detroit area that September to manage a suburban health club. At age 28, he considered retirement. The Expos tried to trade him that winter, but there were no takers. In February 1971, Montreal sold Sparma to Class AAA Toledo, the Tigers' top farm club. The Mud Hens gave Sparma an opportunity to reestablish himself, but he never regained his control. In an April 17 start against Richmond, Sparma walked the first five batters he faced in the second inning. Over one stretch, he missed the plate with 15 straight pitches.

Sparma's baseball career ended when Toledo released him that August. He was 2–5 with a 5.88 ERA. Despite having a sound arm and pitching a one-hitter, he walked 70 batters in 57 innings. "I really feel sorry for [Sparma]," said Mud Hens General Manager Charlie Senger. "He worked his head off, but just couldn't help us."

Looking back, some of Sparma's teammates also wondered about his lack of control. "You couldn't even play catch with the guy," recalled former teammate John Hiller. "He never knew where the ball was going to wind up. It was all mental with him. When he was on, he had better stuff than Nolan Ryan. He just never figured out how to harness it."

After leaving the game, Sparma returned to Ohio and entered a management training program. By the 1980s, he became vice president of sales and marketing at Buckeye Steel in Worthington.

In May 1986, Sparma suffered a heart attack and was treated at a Columbus hospital. Always a clubhouse favorite, Sparma received a call from former Tigers pitcher Earl Wilson, which lifted his spirits immensely. But Sparma died at age 44 May 14, 1986, from complications following triple-bypass surgery. He was buried at Resurrection Cemetery in Worthington.

Following in his father's footsteps, Blase Sparma pitched for Ohio State 1989–1991 and was a member of the Buckeyes' 1991 Big Ten championship team. The Atlanta Braves selected Blase in the third-round (77th pick overall) in the 1991 draft, but he never advanced to the majors.

Joe Sparma ended his major league career with a 52–52 record and 3.94 ERA. Although he left baseball without having reached his full potential, he will remain a fixture in Detroit sports history for winning the game that clinched the 1968 American League pennant.

References

Publications
Cantor, George. *The Tigers of '68: Baseball's Last Real Champions.* Dallas: Taylor, 1997, pp. 95–97, 150–153, 214.

Detroit Tigers 1968 Press Guide.

Freehan, Bill, *Behind the Mask: An Inside Baseball Diary.* Cleveland: World Publishing Company, 1970, p. 86–89, 190.

Official Baseball Guide for 1971. St. Louis: The Sporting News, 1971, pp. 409 and 418.

Articles
"AABC Picks Joe Sparma as its Graduate of Year." *The Sporting News,* March 23, 1968.

Blackman, Ted. "Expos' McGinn Gaining Poise." *The Sporting News,* May 30, 1970.

Blackman, Ted. "Red Hair, Strong Arm—Morton Ticket to Montreal," *The Sporting News,* May 23, 1970.

Blackman, Ted. "Rusty Sees Expos Soaring Over .500." *The Sporting News*, December 5, 1970.

Blackman, Ted. "Sagging Expos Find Raymond a Great Relief." *The Sporting News*, May 16, 1970.

Blackman, Ted. "Stoney, Sparma Revive Sinking Expos." *The Sporting News*, April 25, 1970.

Blackman, Ted. "Wow! Expos' Scout Elated over Sparma." *The Sporting News*, December 20, 1969.

"Class A Highlights." *The Sporting News*, September 7, 1963.

Doerschuk, Steve. "Old Friends Who Don't Meet Anymore." *The Sporting News*, April 29, 1985.

Falls, Joe. "How Important Are Sports?" *The Sporting News*, September 7, 1968.

Falls, Joe. "Trim Sparma Set to Retire?" *Detroit Free Press*, September 16, 1970.

Feeney, Charley. "Pirates Thank Tigers for Reluctance to Deal." *The Sporting News*, October 10, 1970.

"International League." *The Sporting News*, July 4, 1970.

"International League." *The Sporting News*, May 8, 1971.

"International League." *The Sporting News*, August 7, 1971.

Marks, Cliff. "Cripples Team Falls to OSU Power, 50–20." *The Michigan Daily*, November 25, 1961.

Middlemas, Larry. "Time for Laughs—Look at False Forecasts." *The Sporting News*, January 9, 1971.

Mintline, Doug. ".198 Hitter (Wert), Lost Soul (Sparma) Ignite Celebration." *The Flint Journal*, September 18, 1968.

"Obituaries." *The Sporting News*, May 26, 1986.

Otte, Dick. "Brawny Blockers Boost Bucks' Title Bid." *The Sporting News*, October 6, 1962.

Smith, Corinne. "Pressure and Tension of Pennant Tough on Tigers' Wives." *The Detroit News*, September 30, 1968.

Spoelstra, Watson. "Aguirre and Sparma Wake Dozing Tigers." *The Sporting News*, July 8, 1964.

Spoelstra, Watson. "Bengals Beam, Rivals Frown Over Gladding's UFO Pitches." *The Sporting News*, May 27, 1967.

Spoelstra, Watson. "Cash, Finding Norm at Plate, Now Seeks Gold Glove Crown." *The Sporting News*, March 19, 1966.

Spoelstra, Watson. "Don't-Spare-the-Horses Style Improves Sparma's Hurling." *The Sporting News*, March 25, 1967.

Spoelstra, Watson. "Hefty Sparma Diets to Win His Battle of the Bulge." *The Sporting News*, December 16, 1967.

Spoelstra, Watson. "Joe Niekro, Robertson, Buttress Tigers on Hill." *The Sporting News*, December 20, 1969.

Spoelstra, Watson. "Joe Sparma." *The Sporting News*, July 15, 1967.

Spoelstra, Watson. "McAuliffe Horsepower Revives Motor City Model." *The Sporting News*, July 25, 1964.

Spoelstra, Watson. "Pilot Dressen Gets Eyeful in Peek at Bengal Comers." *The Sporting News*, November 16, 1963.

Spoelstra, Watson. "Sparma Beefs to Writer—Raps Mayo's Strategy." *The Sporting News*, August 31, 1968.

Spoelstra, Watson. "Sparma Charm for Tigers: When Joe Starts, They Win." *The Sporting News*, May 27, 1967.

Spoelstra, Watson. "Sparma Regains Old Yankee-Killer Rep—Bengals Lick Chops." *The Sporting News*, June 17, 1967.

Spoelstra, Watson. "Sparma Shutout Star in Batters' Paradise." *The Sporting News*, September 23, 1967.

Spoelstra, Watson. "Sparma to Bolster His Comeback Try with a New Slider." *The Sporting News*, February 18, 1967.

Waldmeir, Pete. "In the Midst of a Hullabaloo, Sparma is an Island of Emotion." *Detroit News*, September 18, 1968.

Web Sites

www.baseball-reference.com
www.ohiostatebuckeyes.com
www.retrosheet.org

Other Sources

Samoray, Jeff. Interview with George Cantor, July 8, 2007.

Shook, Rich. "Joe Sparma," unpublished essay.

WJR-AM. Taped radio broadcast of New York Yankees at Detroit Tigers, September 17, 1968.

1968 TIGERS

Rich Shook presents:
Tigers In the News

Saturday, August 31
Detroit dropped a 5-1 decision to Baltimore. McAuliffe tripled in the sixth and Al Kaline, making his first appearance since pulling a groin muscle August 25, drove an RBI single to left as a pinch-hitter. John Hiller (6-5) started and lost. (Roster note: Detroit purchased all-time great reliever Roy Face, 40, from Pittsburgh for bullpen help down the stretch. The club also activated Eddie Mathews from the disabled list. Both moves came after the deadline for added players to be eligible for the World Series. Face was 2-4 with a 2.60 ERA in 43 games with the Pirates and pitched to one batter earlier in the day so he could tie the NL record for appearances by a pitcher with one team.)

Sunday, September 1
September wasn't very kind to Denny McLain in 1967. This year was going to be different. McLain, who hurt his foot in a mysterious "my foot fell asleep" incident that prevented him from winning a game in the final month of the 1967 season, won his first September start of 1968 thanks to a triple play he started himself. With the Detroit lead trimmed to 4-3 and O's runners on first and second base with nobody out, hulking Baltimore first baseman Boog Powell came to the plate. He smacked a vicious liner right at McLain that the pitcher snared in self-preservation. "If I hadn't caught it, it would have hit me in the head," McLain said of his 1-6-3 triple play with the bases loaded in third, which kept the Tigers' lead and helped them on their way to a 7-3 victory over the Orioles that was also the pitcher's 27th victory. McLain whirled and threw to shortstop Tom Matchick covering second and he relayed to Norm Cash at first base to complete the triple play. He gave up just two more hits in his final six innings. He struck out nine and walked two and survived a 43-minute rain delay at the start of the second inning plus a 31-minute rain delay in the bottom of the inning. Jim Northrup drove in three runs, two coming on his 17th home run in the opening inning. McLain's first September victory since 1966 helped Detroit take a giant step toward clinching the pennant a year after his inability to pitch or win a game in the season's final month cost the Tigers the 1967 flag.

Monday, September 2
Bill Freehan caught 18 innings and ended the second game with a two-out home run in the 10th inning to give Detroit a 4-3 victory and a split of a doubleheader at Oakland. The A's took the first game, 4-0, on a four-hitter by Jim Nash. Mickey Lolich (13-9) got clipped in the first game and Joe Sparma started the second, lasting five innings and giving up two runs on a walk and five hits. Sparma singled in the third and reached second when right fielder Reggie Jackson booted the ball for an error. A double by Dick McAuliffe and a Northrup single produced two runs. Pat Dobson (4-5) worked two scoreless innings of relief to gain the victory. And it became time for Magic Number thoughts. The split meant any combination of Detroit wins and Baltimore losses totaling 17 would clinch the pennant for the Tigers.

Tuesday, September 3
The Tigers won their 27th game of the season in their last turn at bat by scoring four runs in the ninth to grab a 6-3 victory from the Athletics. Northrup, who made an error earlier in the game, drilled a two-run single with the bases loaded and Detroit trailing, 3-2, to put his team ahead to stay. He kicked a ball in the bottom of the eighth that let in two runs and gave Oakland its 3-2 lead. "You usually don't get the opportunity to make up for it when you kick one like that," Northrup said. "I was happy to get the opportunity. I was even surprised the manager let me hit against the lefty [Warren Bogle]."

Wednesday, September 4
Willie Horton's scratch single with the bases loaded in the eighth broke a 2-2 tie and triggered Detroit's 4-2 victory at Oakland. Horton bounced a single off the pitcher's leg to break the tie and Bill Freehan walked to force in the last run. Northrup had an RBI single in the first and Norm Cash hit a sacrifice fly in the sixth.

Thursday, September 5
No game.

Friday, September 6
Denny McLain survived a rough start to post his 28th victory, 8-3, at Tiger Stadium against Minnesota. He struck out 12 and allowed nine hits. Mayo Smith came to the mound to lecture him about bearing down when the Twins had runners on second and third with one out and had already scored twice in the fifth to shave the Tigers' lead to 6-3. McLain induced two infield grounders to snuff out the rally. Detroit rushed out to a 4-0 lead in the first. Dick McAuliffe, Mickey Stanley, and first baseman Al Kaline each had singles. Horton followed with a three-run home run, his 32nd, for a 4-0 lead. Don Wert had an RBI single in the fourth and Horton had a two-run double in the seventh.

Mickey Stanley

by Jerry Nechal

Season	Age	G	AB	R	H	2B	3B	HR	RBI	BB	SO	SB	CS	BA	OBP	SLG
1968 Tigers	25	153	583	88	151	16	6	11	60	42	57	4	3	.259	.311	.364
Career Totals		1516	5022	641	1243	201	48	117	500	371	564	44	23	.248	.298	.377

Everyone has their proverbial fifteen minutes of fame. For Mickey Stanley they came during two weeks in the fall of 1968 when he was cast under the intense spotlight of the baseball world. The shift of a career outfielder to the unfamiliar position of shortstop during the 1968 World Series has been called one of the boldest managerial moves in the history of the game. Most observers were skeptical of the move. In his memoir *Tuned to Baseball*, Ernie Harwell declared, "At the time I thought it was a bad move. I checked about 25 so-called experts on the eve of the Series and they agreed with me.... But it worked."

Beyond the 1968 World Series, the details of Stanley's career appear at first glance to be less noteworthy. However, on closer examination both his career and several of his accomplishments are quite remarkable. His 15 seasons with the Detroit Tigers put him in a category of only 63 others in length of tenure with one team. Stanley won four Gold Gloves, and, through the 2006 season, was 12th all-time in fielding percentage for outfielders. He also was a key contributor to the 1972 AL East Division Championship team.

Throughout the course of Stanley's career, three attributes stand out. First, he was a self-admitted below-average hitter with a career batting average of .248. In 1999 Mickey jokingly told the *Grand Rapids Press*, "My grandkids know I played for the Tigers. I don't tell them I was a bad hitter. They'll find out for themselves soon enough." Stanley is one of only 54 players with a minimum of 5,000 plate appearances with an average below .250.

The compensating factor for Stanley's hitting was his athleticism, versatility, and fielding. He commonly was acknowledged as one of the best center fielders of his era. George Cantor in *The Tigers of '68: Baseball's Last Real Champions*, commented about Mickey's ability to get a jump on the ball: "Whereas other center fielders excelled at sheer speed, Stanley seemed to be operating on clairvoyance, getting to many balls simply on anticipation." On occasion he would run to the spot of an impending home run, scale the fence, and make the catch. Before he injured his arm, runners feared his throwing abilities. Stanley's natural athletic abilities also were widely recognized. In the latter stages of his career, his ability to play seven different positions made him a valuable commodity.

Finally, equally important were Stanley's character and his approach to the game. As Joe Falls observed in a 1975 column in *The Sporting News*, "He really is a throwback to the old-timer who played the game for the sheer joy of it." Stanley simply signed his contract and never complained about playing time. He accepted his manager's decision about where to play and was loyal to his team. Falls wrote, "He is just there, day after day, doing his job and having fun." In 1976 Stanley told *Accent/Grand Rapids* magazine, "I can't wait to play.... I'm the first at the park on a game day and the last to leave."

Mitchell Jack Stanley was born to James and Betty Stanley in Grand Rapids on July 20, 1942. He was the middle of five children whose father supported them as a night truck driver for Oven Fresh Bakery. In the 1976 *Accent/Grand Rapids* interview, Stanley recalled, "No matter how tired he was when he came home, he'd always find time to hit or throw a few to me."

The Grand Rapids area has an established tradition of producing major leaguers, among them first baseman Wally Pipp and former Tigers Dave Rozema and Phil

Regan. Growing up a Tigers fan, Stanley's boyhood baseball idol was Detroit's All-Star shortstop, Harvey Kuenn.

Stanley was a three-sport star in high school, playing basketball, baseball, and football. His athletic versatility contributed to the success of his teams. A 1969 *Pinellas County (Fla.) Evening Independent* story told of a crucial switch in positions by Stanley in an Ottawa Hills High School football game. Playing against rival Grand Rapids South, Mickey played halfback in the first half and his team trailed, 6–0. He was switched to end after halftime. "He caught two 60-yard passes and out-ran his defenders for touchdowns" and his team won, 20–6. On the baseball team, Stanley pitched and played second base wining the 1959 Grand Rapids City League batting title with a .523 average. In his senior year, he was voted the top athlete in the City League.

After graduating from high school, Stanley was signed in July 1960 by local Tigers scout Bob Sullivan for a $10,000 bonus. Sullivan coached several major league prospects, including Kirk Gibson and Jim Kaat. After graduation Stanley played outfield on Sullivan's National Baseball Congress team that won the national championship in Wichita, Kansas; in a 2007 interview, he remembered this as "pretty thrilling for a kid my age."

In 1961 Stanley began climbing up the ladder to the major leagues, which included five seasons in the minors and five years of winter ball. He told *Accent/Grand Rapids*, "I look back at the minors, the 12 hours of doubleheaders; riding the buses all day and I remember then I told myself if I wasn't playing in the majors in three years, that I probably would never make it."

He started in Duluth of the Class C Northern League. Stanley told *Accent/Grand Rapids*, "The first game I played was in Grand Forks and it was snowing. I had a typical day, 0 for 4." Mickey started slowly in Duluth and after 44 games, batting only .223, he was sent down a level to Decatur of the Class D Midwest League. He finished the season there with a respectable .279 batting average. After the 1961 season he married his high school sweetheart, Ellen Ann Terrell.

In 1961 the three members of what was to become a famous outfield tandem met for the first time. In 1968 Stanley told *TSN*, "I first met [Jim] Northrup in 1961 at Tigertown.... The following October, I met [Willie] Horton." Northrup and Stanley later were roommates in the majors, vying with each other for playing time. In a 2007 interview Mickey remembered, "Jim was not a good outfielder early in the minor leagues, but he made himself into a real good outfielder." Horton and Stanley were teammates for 14 years. They became close friends and Mickey was noted for his calming influence on the sometimes volatile Horton. In 2007, Stanley cited a time in Puerto Rico where he intervened in a confrontation between Horton and another player. "I got in front of him ... and Willie grabbed my uniform in two places by my waist, lifted me off the ground and walked me completely off the ball diamond. He was a strong, strong man ... not a mean guy ... not a mean bone in his body."

Returning to Duluth for a full season in 1962, Stanley was joined there by Horton and Northrup. Mickey's hitting had improved. He finished with a batting average of .285 and was selected to the Northern League all-star team.

In 1963 Stanley moved up to the Double A Sally League with Knoxville, again with Horton and Northrup. Despite opening the season strong and hitting .343 on May 7, he finished with an average of .252. Six days after the end of the season, Stanley's first child, Steven Scott, was born September 14. But there was not a lot of time to enjoy fatherhood. It was on to the Florida Instructional League, which opened its season October 8. Managed by Phil Cavaretta and Bob Swift, the team was a precursor of things to come. With seven future members of the 1968 Tigers on the roster, they took the league championship, with Stanley batting .305.

The 1964 season was a year of highs and lows for Stanley. He moved up to Triple A Syracuse of the International League, but he was pushing up against his personal timetable for making it to the majors. After only 19 games, Mickey found himself going backward not forward. Hitting a meager .160, he was demoted to Knoxville. This proved to be a personal day of reckoning for Stanley. He vividly recalled in 2007, "I had the station wagon packed leaving for Knoxville and I made up my mind I was going to the big leagues. I can't go backward any more." Three months later he was a September call-up in the majors. Returning to Knoxville in May he started slowly, going 1-for-8, but then went on a tear, hitting home runs in three consecutive games. Stanley finished the season with a .304 batting average and was named to the Southern League all-star team. And in September, he was a call-up to the majors.

Stanley made his major league debut on September 13, 1964, at Tiger Stadium against the Washington Senators. He singled off Claude Osteen in his first at-bat. In 2007, he laughingly remembered it as a "chopper down the third base line, about sixteen feet, a swinging bunt." Stanley appeared in four games, batting .273.

The Tigers were faced with a crowded pool of outfield talent in the spring of 1965. This included Don Demeter in center as well as Gates Brown, George Thomas, Kaline, Horton, and Northrup. Stanley became the odd man out. Northrup and Horton both stuck with the team. An off-season rules change allowed teams to option out players with less than five years' experience four times, instead of the previous three, and Stanley was moved to Syracuse to start the season. This time he was able to handle Triple A pitching and in 144 games he batted .281 with personal minor league highs of 10 home runs, 152 hits, and 73 RBI. Selected to the International League all-star team he led outfielders with a .992 fielding percentage and won a Rawlings Gold Glove Award.

In late August, Stanley again joined the Tigers as a center-field fill-in for the injured Demeter. He took advantage of the opportunity by hitting .311 in his first 18 games. On September 3 in Detroit against Washington, his first major league home run was a 400-foot line drive off left-hander Marshall Bridges. Stanley's impressive play caused AL president Joe Cronin to rave to *TSN*, "Boy, I like that young outfielder. He looks like an athlete in every respect." However, by season's end, Mickey's average had slipped to .239.

In the spring of 1966 Stanley was poised for his first full big-league season at age 23. He would compete with Demeter for a starting spot in the lineup. Manager Charlie Dressen's plans were for Mickey to play on a regular basis as long as he hit .270. He was the starter at the beginning of the season, but again struggled early with his hitting. He was batting an anemic .182 when he broke his finger in mid May. While on the disabled list, Mickey's former minor league manager, Bob Swift, took over from Dressen, who had suffered a heart attack. Before Stanley returned to the active roster on June 18, Demeter was traded to the Red Sox for pitcher Earl Wilson. With more frequent playing time, Stanley's hitting improved. Inserted into the lineup when Kaline hurt his hip, Stanley went on a rampage, hitting .382 during one stretch July 16–24. In midseason third-base coach Frank Skaff became the manager after Swift was diagnosed with cancer. For the year Stanley appeared in 92 games and batted .289. He was impressive defensively with a perfect fielding average handling 163 chances with no errors. Shortly after the season, Stanley's second child, Karen Michele, was born that October 14.

Mayo Smith became the Tigers' new manager in 1967. With a pool of rising young talent mixed with veterans like Norm Cash and Kaline, the Tigers contended all season for the pennant. They finished second at 91–71, losing out by one game on the last day in a heartbreaking loss in the nightcap of a doubleheader. Stanley's playing time increased to 145 games, but hitting again was a problem. He struggled all season, finishing at a career low of .210. After hitting a two-run homer July 2 in a 3–0 victory over first place Chicago, Mickey told the *Detroit Free Press*, "All I wanted was to do something that would win a ball game for the team." In looking back at that season in 2007 he commented, "All I had to do was have a couple of big hits … I felt pretty bad about that year."

Expectations were high for 1968. The Tigers started strong. After moving into first place on May 10, they never looked back, finishing with 103 wins, 12 games ahead of Baltimore. Stanley recalled in 2007, "The chemistry was so doggone good. Everybody had good years, not great years. Even the guys who didn't play much had big days where they contributed. … A bunch of good guys. There were no bad apples." The one player with an exceptional season was pitcher Denny McLain with 31 victories. Stanley recalled, "I liked playing behind Denny. He worked fast and he threw strikes. He challenged hitters."

To many, 1968 was Stanley's best season. In a year of lower overall batting averages, he finished at .259 with career highs in hits (151) and runs scored (88). In the outfield he had a perfect 1.000 fielding percentage and won his first Gold Glove. Mickey's versatility was an important factor in the team's success. He spelled Cash at first base when a right-handed hitter was needed. When Kaline's arm was broken in May, he returned full time to center field. On June 15 against Chicago he made what was described in Jerry Green's *Year of the Tiger* as "the finest catch Mayo Smith ever saw. Stanley raced 60 yards diagonally across right center and made a diving catch of Tom McCraw's drive. He tumbled onto the gravel track, arose and doubled Luis Aparicio at first base. He was limping but waved off Mayo and trainer Bill Behm." In August, when Dick McAuliffe was suspended, Stanley played second and short in a series against the Yankees.

In late September, Stanley moved to center stage. After the pennant was won, Mayo Smith searched for a way to keep Kaline in the lineup and to deal with the weak hitting at the shortstop position. Stanley had regularly taken infield practice before games.

In 2007 Stanley provided the details. "I would get to the ballpark early and I loved taking ground balls. I was always the first one on the field. … I just loved catching ground balls. Norm Cash said 'You are not too bad over there.' I'm almost positive Norm Cash put a bug in Mayo Smith's ear.... It was a shock when Mayo Smith called me up to the hotel room, I had no idea.... He came right out and said it, 'You are going to be my shortstop in the World Series.' He didn't ask me if I wanted to. You talk about a surprise.... I said I have no problem with it, but what about the other guys, if I screw things up? He said 'You can do it. It's up to me.... You are going to be playing tonight.'"

That night against Baltimore, Mickey was baptized as a middle infielder in the first inning. He made an error when Don Buford "knocked me on my ass.... My first experience was getting flipped over on a double play because I didn't know how to get out of the way."

Obviously a quick learner, Stanley went on to amaze the baseball world in the Series. In the first inning of Game 1 he was tested by a leadoff ground ball off the bat of the speedy Lou Brock. Brock was out on a close play and Mickey's fielding at shortstop became a nonfactor. He successfully handled 30 of 32 chances, making two inconsequential errors.

In the World Series the Cardinals jumped out to a three-games-to-one lead. In pivotal Game 5, the Tigers fell behind 3–0 in the first inning. Stanley told the *Grand Rapids Press* in 1968, "It was a little glum.... but some of the guys, mainly Norm Cash and Al Kaline, started whooping it up. Kaline kept yelling, 'All we need is a few base hits.'" Stanley led off the fourth inning with a triple to start a two-run rally. Kaline's clutch single in the seventh knocked in two runs and the Tigers won 5–3. After a 13–1 win in Game 6, Detroit took the final game 4–1, the victory keyed by a two-run triple by Jim Northrup off Bob Gibson in the seventh to break a scoreless tie. Stanley batted .214, but his replacement in the outfield, Kaline, hit .379 with eight RBI and two home runs.

Mickey looked back in 2007: "It wasn't fun. I was just waiting to screw up. It helped getting the first ball of the Series hit to me, though. I wished I could have played center field because of the pressure.... It wasn't fun because I played out of position."

Stanley's fortunes turned quickly the following spring. The newspapers were filled with speculation about a permanent move to shortstop. On the first day of spring training Mickey injured his throwing arm. In 2007 he remembered that day, "The first ground ball.... Dick Tracewski hit one in the hole; being the young showoff, I picked it up and threw it off the wrong foot.... It hurt my arm and that was it for the rest of my career. I played with a bad arm.... It definitely took the fun out of baseball for me, because that was my biggest asset." Despite the injury, Stanley led the team with 149 games played, 59 of them at shortstop. He returned to the outfield as a regular after Tom Tresh was acquired from the Yankees in June to play short. Stanley won his second Gold Glove and set a Tigers record by playing in 220 consecutive errorless games as an outfielder. His batting average slipped to .235, but he had a career-high 70 RBI as the Tigers finished 19 games behind Baltimore.

In March 1970, Stanley's third child, Pamela Ann, was born. That year, Mayo Smith's last as manger, was a productive one for Mickey. He led the team in runs, hits, stolen bases, and triples while batting .252. He led AL outfielders in fielding percentage at 1.000, winning his third Gold Glove. However, for the first time in his career, the Tigers finished below .500.

In the next three years under Billy Martin, the Tigers again were a winning team. Stanley was a mainstay in the Detroit outfield. Among the Tigers' outfielders, he played the most games. In 1971, he had a career-high batting average of .292. In 1972, he told *TSN*, "Each year starts out pretty much the same way. I don't think I'm playing enough and I wind up with more at-bats than I figured I would." That year the aging Tigers contended all season, clinching the East Division crown on the next-to-last day of the season. Stanley provided many key hits. Despite a .234 average, he led the team with 18 go-ahead RBI. Detroit lost the AL Championship Series to Oakland in a hard-fought five-game series in which Stanley appeared in four contests, batting .333. In 1973, he won his fourth and last Gold Glove and led the Tigers in runs, at-bats, and hits while hitting .244. On July 13 he tied an AL record by making 11 putouts in center field.

Stanley's eight-year reign in center field for the Tigers ended suddenly in 1974. On July 30 he was hit by a pitch and suffered a broken hand. Ron LeFlore was called up from the minors and Stanley again had a permanent playing position. Mickey finished the 1974 season on the DL and hit just .221. In December he was almost traded to Philadelphia along with Bill Freehan, but the Phils pulled out of the deal.

Over the next four years Stanley became a role player. His versatility allowed him to finish his career with the Tigers while many of his original teammates were either released or traded. Stanley played whenever or wherever he was needed. Ralph Houk, who became Detroit's manager in 1974, became a strong supporter of his value to the team. In 1975, Houk commented to *TSN*, "He's done everything we could want him to do. He's just been great. No moaning or groaning. He's worked as hard as anybody. He's a great guy to have on the club." In 1975 Mickey split his playing time between four positions and the designated hitter role. He was hitting .256 when his season again derailed July 25; he injured his thumb sliding into second in a game in which he went 4-for-4. After his departure to the disabled list, the Tigers went on a club record 19-game losing streak.

It 1976 the antics of Mark "The Bird" Fidrych captured the imagination of Detroit fans. Stanley recalled in 2007, "You certainly wanted to play as well as you could behind him. It was phenomenal playing in front of packed crowds." On June 16 Stanley contributed to one of Fidrych's 19 victories by singling in the winning run in the ninth inning. For Mickey personally, it was a pivotal year. In August he became a ten-year man and could not be traded without his consent. There was also speculation that he would be left unprotected in the upcoming expansion draft. His versatility was his saving grace. That year, he played six different positions as well as DH. After passing the ten-year milestone Stanley played regularly over the last 32 games after injuries to LeFlore and third baseman Aurelio Rodriguez. He finished with a .257 average and in November he commented to *TSN*, "I'd rather stay in Detroit even for a lot less money." In December he survived the expansion draft and signed a two-year contract with the Tigers.

In his final two seasons, Stanley was a link between the 1968 champs and the nucleus of what would become the 1984 championship team; playing with Alan Trammell, Lou Whitaker, Jack Morris, and Lance Parrish. In 2007, he remembered, "It made me feel a little more like a leader. It felt pretty good to be the old man of the ball club. Lance Parrish says 'Hi Mr. Stanley. I was in eighth grade when you were in the World Series.'" In August 1977 Mickey preserved Morris's first major league victory with an over-the-fence ninth-inning catch. For the season he hit .230.

In 1978 Stanley played sparingly, appearing in only 53 games and batting .278. He was released in December 1978. General Manager Jim Campbell told the *Detroit News*, "Mickey is one of the finest all-around athletes ever to wear a Tiger uniform. But more important he has been an exemplary individual." The same article quoted Stanley as saying, "I feel very fortunate I was able to stay in the same organization so long. I was never a superstar. I went through some slumps and never heard many boos." Jerry Green of the *News* commented: "Mickey Stanley: Never a superstar, but always The Professional."

After his playing days, Stanley worked as a manufacturer's representative and later with his son developing subdivisions. An avid golfer, he played in numerous charity events. Nearly 30 years after his departure from baseball, he had eight grandchildren and resided in Brighton, Michigan.

References

Publications

Cantor, George. *The Tigers of '68: Baseball's Last Real Champions*. Dallas: Taylor. 1997.

Detroit Tigers 1974 Yearbook. Detroit: Detroit Tigers. 1974.

Green, Jerry. *Year of the Tiger*. New York: Coward-McCann, Inc. 1969.

Harwell, Ernie. *Tuned to Baseball*. South Bend: Diamond Communications. 1985.

Palmer, Pete, and John Thorn. *Total Baseball, 3rd ed.* New York: HarperPerennial. 1993.

Pattison, Mark, and Dave Raglin. *Detroit Tigers Lists and More: Runs, Hits, and Eras*. Detroit: Wayne State University Press. 2002.

Spatz, Lyle, ed. *The SABR Baseball List & Record Book*. New York: Scribner. 2007.

Articles

Cantor, George. "Bubble Has Burst On Mickey Stanley." *Detroit Free Press*, July 28, 1966.

Cantor, George. "Stanley Is Steaming After 1st Key Homer." *Detroit Free Press*, July 4, 1967.

Conklin, Joe. "Definitely Detroit." *Grand Rapids Press*, April, 11, 1999.

"Class AA Kings Cop Star Team Laurels." *The Sporting News*, October 3, 1964, p. 33.

Falls, Joe. "An Unforgettable Player, Even If His Feats Fade." *The Sporting News*, March 15, 1975, p. 35.

"Fielding Flashes." *The Sporting News*, July 16, 1966, p. 45.

"Florida Phenoms." *The Sporting News*, October 5, 1963, p. 40.

"Friday 13th Proves Jinx For Stanley." *The Sporting News*, May 28, 1968, p. 16.

Green, Jerry. "Stanley A Professional." *Detroit News*, December 14, 1978, p. 1C.

Hawkins, Jim. "Expansion May Break Up Tigers' Old Gang." *The Sporting News*, November 6, 1976, p. 16.

Hawkins, Jim. "Mickey Quickie Tailor for Tiger Tears." *The Sporting News*, July 12, 1975, p. 8.

Korreck, G.F. "Climbing The Walls With GR's Mickey Stanley." *Accent/Grand Rapids*, April, 1976, pp. 8–13.

"Minor League Highlights Class C." *The Sporting News*, July 21, 1962, p. 41.

"Minor League Highlights Class C." *The Sporting News*, September 15, 1962, p. 46.

"Sally Averages." *The Sporting News*, May 18, 1963, p. 35.

"Shepard Int's No. 1 Pilot: Suns Head All-Star Picks." *The Sporting News*, October 2, 1965, p. 36.

Spoelstra, Watson. "Campbell Facing Pay Assault by Tiger Players." *The Sporting News,* January 13, 1973, p. 45.

Spoelstra, Watson. "Dressen Hands Garden Post to Stanley Until—." *The Sporting News,* March, 26, 1966, p. 11.

Spoelstra, Watson. "Hitters Learn Hard Way—Lolich Can Throw Strikes." *The Sporting News,* October 6, 1965, p. 6.

Spoelstra, Watson. "Stanley Wins Tiger 'Oscar' for Good-Thief Role." *The Sporting News,* June 3, 1972, p. 5.

Spoelstra, Watson. "Tigers Doff Caps to Stanley, Stickout in CF." *The Sporting News,* August 31, 1968, p. 11.

Stanley, Mickey. "Mickey Stanley on The Series." *Grand Rapids Press,* October 8, 1968, p. 39.

"Stanley In Slugging Spree." *The Sporting News,* June 13, 1964, p. 45.

"Tigers Hoist Pennant With Classy Pitching." *The Sporting News,* December 14, 1963, p. 30.

Zainea, Leo. "Once He Failed In A Different Experiment." *Pinellas County (Fla.) Evening Independent,* March 4, 1969, p. 1C.

Web Sites
www.baseball-almanac.com
www.baseball-reference.com
www.retrosheet.org

Other Sources
Nechal, Jerry, Interview with Mickey Stanley, June 22, 2007.

Rich Shook presents:

Tigers In the News

Saturday, September 7
Detroit's drive to reduce its magic number stalled out under a pair of solo home runs by rookie Graig Nettles as Minnesota downed the Tigers, 2-1. Nettles hit them in the sixth and ninth innings off Pat Dobson (5-6) to offset a solo home run by Wert in the fifth. Detroit still needed 12 wins of its own or in combination with losses by second-place Baltimore to clinch its first pennant since 1945.

Sunday, September 8
Minnesota Nettled Detroit again. Rookie Graig Nettles hit his fourth home run in three games to lift the Twins over the Tigers, 3-1. Earl Wilson had nine strikeouts, no walks, and allowed just five hits but Wilson dropped to 12-12 in coming off his 22-win season of a year ago. Gates Brown, starting in left, hit his fifth home run to give Detroit a 1-0 lead in the fifth. Nettles hit his three-run shot in the sixth.

Monday, September 9
Mickey Lolich (14-9) hurled a two-hit shutout at California in Detroit's 6-0 win over the Angels. Lolich struck out seven and issued just one walk as Detroit reduced its magic number to 10. That gave him a 20-inning scoreless streak over the Angels this season. Mickey Stanley opened a three-run first with a double and later added a single plus his 11th home run. Al Kaline, playing first base, had an RBI single in the first and his ninth home run of the season in the third.

Tuesday, September 10
Denny McLain notched his 29th victory and contributed two singles plus a triple to Detroit's 7-2 victory at California. "I haven't been under as much pressure as I thought I'd be because I've been so busy with all these outside activities," said McLain, who had been recording an album as an organ player while lining up an appearance on Ed Sullivan's popular Sunday TV variety show as well as a tour of one-night musical stands in Michigan. "I know Mayo (Smith) and Jim (GM Campbell) don't like all these things I've been doing on the outside," he said, "but it's kept my mind off baseball and kept the pressure from building up." McLain allowed nine hits but only walked one and fanned 12. Bill Freehan and Willie Horton had RBI singles, Jim Northrup contributed an RBI double, and Dick McAuliffe had two RBI as the Tigers scored six runs in the first four innings to make it easy for their ace.

Wednesday, September 11
A pair of Horton home runs contributed to Detroit's 8-2 victory and completed a three-game sweep at California. They also helped reduce Detroit's magic number for clinching the pennant to eight. Horton raised his home run count to 35 while Bill Freehan hit his 22nd. "If they keep going the way they have been," Angels manager Bill Rigney said, "I think they'll beat St. Louis in the World Series. They're a little stronger than the Boston team the Cardinals beat last year." John Hiller (8-5) scattered 10 hits and struck out six in the Tigers' sixth straight complete game.

Thursday, September 12
No game.

Friday, September 13
Earl Wilson got lucky on Friday the 13th. Wilson (13-12) pitched a 10-hit shutout in Detroit's 3-0 victory over visiting Oakland. He also chipped in his seventh home run of the season, which came in the eighth as Detroit's magic number with Baltimore dropped to five. Wilson said he went out for breakfast and got ticketed for making an improper left turn. But his luck improved once he got on the hill. Dick McAuliffe hit his 16th home run of the season to open the fourth and Freehan had a bloop RBI double in the seventh.

Dick Tracewski

by Peter M. Levine

Season	Age	G	AB	R	H	2B	3B	HR	RBI	BB	SO	SB	CS	BA	OBP	SLG
1968 Tigers	33	90	212	30	33	3	1	4	15	24	51	3	0	.156	.239	.236
Career Totals		614	1231	148	262	31	9	8	91	134	253	15	14	.213	.289	.272

Richard Joseph "Trixie" Tracewski was an average-hitting, good-fielding shortstop whose career in baseball spanned both the National and American Leagues, four World Series rings, and a Detroit Tigers record span as both a base and bench coach. Also known as "Dick Tracy" by many fans in Los Angeles during his four years with the Dodgers (1962–1965), he played shortstop, second base, and third base in his eight years as a player, retiring with a fielding percentage of .961. In a career distinguished by professionalism and respect from virtually everyone he encountered from umpires to managers, Tracewski was a witness to and participant in baseball history.

Tracewski was not only multitalented as a player, but after being promoted from the minors to his first coaching position with the Tigers in 1972, took on a range of coaching roles under multiple managers and general managers. Beloved and remembered by fans in Detroit for his ever-steady presence at both the first- and third-base coaching boxes, he found his career extended and expanded under Hall of Fame manager Sparky Anderson, who invited him to remain with the team in 1980 and gave him additional responsibilities. This included mentoring a new generation of ballplayers such as Alan Trammell and Lou Whitaker, as well as two brief stints as Detroit manager in 1979 and 1989, the latter occurring when Anderson took a leave of absence.

A member of two Dodgers championship teams, 1963 (his rookie year) and 1965, as well as part of the Tigers' 1968 World Series winner, Tracewski played or worked for three of baseball's leading minds in Walter Alston, Billy Martin, and Anderson. Although perhaps better known for his coaching career, as a rookie he scored the eventual winning run in the opener of the Dodgers-Yankees World Series. Tigers manager Mayo Smith also credited him for helping to turn around the 1968 season with a game winning three-run home run against Cleveland June 23 that spurred a winning streak.

Tracewski was born February 3, 1935, in Eynon, Pennsylvania, a small town in the northeastern part of the state, as the youngest of four children. He was always an excellent athlete and baseball player, in some ways following in the footsteps of his older brother, a minor leaguer in the Philadelphia Athletics system who also played professional football. Tracewski's parents were Polish immigrants who instilled in him a work ethic that was reflected in his baseball career—his father having arrived in the United States at age 16 and then returning to Europe at 18 to fight for his newly adopted country in World War I.

Tracewski established himself a rising star during his teen years and in high school, playing for Archibald High and leading teams in the highly popular and competitive sandlot games that took place on Sundays, as well as with American Legion teams. He attracted the attention of major league scouts, including Ray Welsh of the Pittsburgh Pirates, who advised Tracewski, then a high school sophomore, to focus on shortstop. As he approached age 17 and awaited signing offers from the many scouts he had come to know, Tracewski was surprised to find that no offers were forthcoming. This was particularly true of the Cleveland Indians, who had previously indicated a serious interest in the young infielder.

As Tracewski related in a 2007 interview, this was when fortune smiled upon him. Brooklyn Dodgers scout Phil Weinnert got lost on the way back from Binghamton,

New York, to his Philadelphia home. He came across a local baseball game in Jessup, Pennsylvania, which featured the Peckville VFW team and wound up watching the entire game. As was frequently the case, Tracewski stood out, and after the game Weinnert approached him to ask when he might see another game. After several failed efforts, Weinnert returned personally and invited Tracewski to come (with his father) to Brooklyn for a workout. He thus found himself, at 17, at Ebbets Field, spending four days hitting and fielding with Jackie Robinson, Pee Wee Reese, Duke Snider, and Gil Hodges.

Shortly thereafter, the Dodgers signed him as an amateur free agent in 1953 and he launched what was to be a long career, along with a signing bonus of several hundred dollars. He was quickly sent to Dodgertown in Vero Beach, Florida, where he began a six-year career in the minors which saw him crisscross the country, playing at every level in the team's farm system. Tracewski also performed two years' military service during this period, posted with other baseball players at Fort McPherson, Georgia, outside Atlanta. It was during this period where he had his greatest regret as a pro ballplayer. Given the option to develop skills as a switch-hitter, he chose not to. When he finally arrived in the major leagues he realized what a mistake this was as "I had to face pitchers like Bob Gibson and Juan Marichal who were so nasty against right-handers."

Tracewski was called up to the Dodgers from their AAA Omaha farm team in 1962, beginning his 42-year big-league career with a debut as a pinch-runner in the final game of the first-ever series at the new Dodger Stadium. Although he was never to experience a losing season as a player, Tracewski still remembers that first year painfully, as the Dodgers lost a two-game lead at the end of the season courtesy of three straight defeats to St. Louis. This was followed by a playoff loss to the San Francisco Giants in only the fourth-ever such series in major league history. That Dodgers team grew stronger from the experience, however, and behind the pitching of Tracewski's friend, Sandy Koufax, would win the first of two World Series with Trixie as a utility infielder.

It was in the 1963 World Series that Tracewski would experience what he considers his greatest moment as a professional baseball player. In his first-ever postseason at bat, Tracewski singled off future Hall of Famer Whitey Ford and scored what proved to be the winning run on a John Roseboro home run. With Koufax pitching a 2–1 victory, the Dodgers proceeded to sweep the Yankees. Although many still remember him for a key diving stop in Game 4 of the Series, Tracewski still remembers that first World Series hit with fondness and emotion. He was also on the field during the notorious moment in the August 22, 1965, game when Roseboro was struck in the head with a bat swung by Juan Marichal, a strong memory for him even today. It was as a Dodger that Tracewski was nicknamed Trixie, a sobriquet that sticks to this day. During summer pool parties hosted by reliever Ron Perranoski, Tracewski could frequently be found performing back flips, front flips and other tricks and was thus dubbed Trixie by his teammates.

Tracewski played in three of Koufax's four no-hitters (going 3 for 7 at the plate) and also was part of the 1965 world champion team before being traded to the Tigers for pitcher Phil Regan on December 15, 1965. This proved to be the start of a new phase of his career—one which initially frustrated him, as his playing time was already dwindling and he could see the end approaching. Tracewski even went so far as to approach Tigers General Manager Jim Campbell shortly after arriving in Detroit with a request to be traded. He argued that since he'd arrived it was clear his playing time would be limited and asked that Campbell move him where he'd have a chance to extend his career. After considering the request briefly, Campbell refused, asking Tracewski to be patient. Although he indeed became more of a spot player for the team, Tracewski quickly established himself as an important part of the Tigers with his fielding skills, ability to cover multiple positions, work ethic, and knack for clutch hitting. During 1968 he played in 90 games for the Tigers, hitting four home runs, including the three-run shot against Cleveland in the nightcap of a June 23 doubleheader, the opening salvo in a 4–1 Detroit win that Mayo Smith credited with spurring on the team in its pennant run.

It was shortly after the 1969 season that Campbell offered Tracewski a coaching position with the Tigers, which Trixie enthusiastically accepted as a golden opportunity to extend his professional career. He quickly established himself as an excellent coach and mentor to young athletes, leading second-year Tigers manager Billy Martin to promote him from the minors and make him first-base coach. Success followed Tracewski to his new coaching position, as the 1972 team won the American League East. Martin, however, would only last another season, canned after famously ordering his pitchers to throw spitballs. It was during Martin's tenure that Tracewski, generally known as among the nicest men in the game, experienced his only ejection, an incident Martin found highly amusing. The ejection aside, Tracewski established a strong rapport with umpires throughout the major leagues, a relationship of mutual respect and even friendship. This was perhaps strengthened by the fact that Hall of Fame umpire Nestor Chylak was a longtime neighbor of his in Peckville, Pennsylvania.

Tracewski's baseball knowledge and teaching abilities would play a significant role in the Tigers' restructuring efforts, which began with the hiring of Ralph Houk for the 1974 season. Although the next few years saw many losses, they also witnessed the signing of a new generation of Detroit heroes, a group that began to pay dividends in 1978 when the team finished 86–76. In one year alone, the team added Alan Trammell, Lou Whitaker, Jack Morris, and Dan Petry—all instrumental parts of the Tigers' future success. Tracewski remains particularly proud of his work with Trammell, the shortstop he worked with closely as a young ballplayer and watched grow into one of the game's best. Even more than a decade after Trammell's retirement as a player, Tracewski believed strongly that Trammell should be in the Hall of Fame. Tracewski expressed his frustration at the lack of recognition for his student, stating, "There is no justice in baseball" when Ozzie Smith—a great player in his own right whose career paralleled Trammell's—receives more than 300 votes for the Hall while Trammell collected barely 70.

He was named manager for two games in 1979—winning both—pending the arrival of Sparky Anderson, the man Tracewski worked with for virtually the rest of his career. He continued as base coach and mentor for the Tigers, a perennial AL power for much of the 1980s. He also served as bench coach and right-hand man to Anderson, whom he considers among the greatest managers of all time. Tracewski credits Anderson for reinforcing the importance of always giving 100 percent—from spring training to the final out—and also cites his ability to understand and communicate with modern-day players. Working closely, Anderson established plans for every aspect of the game and every player, communicating on a daily basis with those like David Wells, who thrived under such a method—and never with others who were best left alone. Although Anderson was known by some as Captain Hook, Tracewski points out that he only lived up to that moniker when he had a strong bullpen.

Tracewski managed the Tigers again for three weeks during 1989 while Anderson recovered from exhaustion. This was a bittersweet time as he watched his close friend approach the end of his managing career—and the Tigers go from league power to a team that lost more than 100 games. He retired after the 1995 season. He returned to northeastern Pennsylvania, having moved his family there after being traded to the Tigers from the Dodgers three decades earlier.

During a career spanning several decades of baseball history, Tracewski played in virtually every major league ballpark and watched the game change in myriad ways. When Tracewski entered the majors he received a base salary of $7,200, an amount he quickly doubled through a then-record payout of $14,500 to members of the world champion Dodgers. As he recalls it, the manager's authority was unquestioned during that period and players used spring training to get fit for the regular season. Players during his coaching years were more independent and generally arrived fit for spring games. They also enjoyed considerably more job security and were able to focus almost entirely on baseball. Like most of his counterparts, Tracewski always worked during the off-season; the added job security, he asserted, became one of the biggest changes he witnessed in the game. A close second would be the fact that players are now bigger, stronger, and faster. As Tracewski posited, those who reminisce about the good old days perhaps do not realize how much the game has changed. Among other things, Tracewski also believes modern equipment has degraded, noting in particular the low quality of wood used in bats which now shatter with a frequency unheard of during his playing days.

Indicative of the strong friendships and relationships he had in the game, as well as his unique perspective, Tracewski cited the top five players he saw:

1. Sandy Koufax—Tracewski's friend to this day and roommate with the Dodgers who performed "feats which will never be duplicated."
2. Maury Wills—a man who changed the game, bringing back the days of Ty Cobb with his 100 steals a season.
3. Al Kaline—the best all-around field player he'd ever seen and a precursor to today's five-tool player.
4. Dick McAuliffe—his Tigers teammate and a three-time All-Star at second base during the 1960s.
5. Alan Trammell and Lou Whitaker—the shortstop-second base combination that epitomized Tigers teams of the 1980s.

Tracewski considers himself lucky in many ways to have played or worked for some of the greatest baseball minds around. This includes the late Walter Alston who managed him with the Dodgers and was a close second to Sparky Anderson, as the manager Tracewski respected most. He fondly remembers breaking in as a coach under Billy Martin, whose innovations and fire led the younger

Tracewski to believe Martin had invented the game. Tracewski also feels blessed to have worked with Ralph Houk on the successful rebuilding project that GM Jim Campbell oversaw with the mid-1970s Tigers.

In retirement, Tracewski has participated regularly in Tigers fantasy camps, gone to spring training, and maintained contact with current and former Tigers like Alan Trammell. Since retiring from baseball in 1995, Tracewski has continued to be active, playing golf with his friend Sandy Koufax, and at least one trip a year to Detroit. He recently had the opportunity to tour old Tiger Stadium, marveling at the shape of the grass field as his grandson ran the bases on what he considers one of the great ballparks in which to play or watch a game. Tracewski also had one last trip to Vero Beach planned, as the Dodgers prepare to close down Dodgertown and move to Arizona after the 2008 exhibition season, as Tracewski longed for another chance to walk the fields and basepaths where his remarkable four-decade pro career began.

References

Articles

"No. 43—Dick Tracewski—Eynon." *The Times-Tribune* (Scranton, Pa.), November 15, 2004.

McAuliffe, Josh, "Son of immigrant coal miner finds himself on the field with Jackie Robinson," March 11, 2007.

McAuliffe, Josh, "Lion in Winter: A League of His Own, Richard 'Dick' Tracewski" March 11, 2007.

Web Sites

www.baseball-reference.com (Dick Tracewski entry)
www.wikipedia.com (Dick Tracewski entry)

Other Sources

Levine, Peter M. Richard Tracewski telephone interview, June 1, 2007.

Rich Shook presents:

Tigers In the News

Saturday, September 14

"Right now, I'm numb." Denny McLain received his 30th victory in a milestone season when Willie Horton's RBI single capped a two-run ninth that gave Detroit a 5–4 win over Oakland. "We knew something was going to happen," said Al Kaline, who walked as a pinch-hitter for McLain in the ninth. "It was a typical game. We've been winning them that way all year." On hand to see what could be the last 30-win season in major league history was the last previous 30-game winner, Dizzy Dean, who won 30 for St. Louis in 1934. Kaline walked to open the ninth and one out later moved to third on a Mickey Stanley single up the middle. Jim Northrup hit a medium-speed ground ball to first but Danny Cater threw to the third base side of the plate while on the run and Kaline sprawled over the catcher to tag home plate and tie the score at 4–4. Stanley wound up at third on the error and Horton lined a 2–2 pitch over the left fielder's head to send Detroit's dugout into a spontaneous celebration for McLain, who struck out 10 and walked one in a six-hitter. Reggie Jackson hit two home runs off McLain, the second snapping a 3–3 tie in the sixth.

Sunday, September 15

Mickey Lolich turned in a three-hitter as Detroit starters turned in their ninth straight complete game. Lolich (15–9) struck out a dozen and walked two as Detroit pounded out 15 hits in a 13–0 win over Oakland. The southpaw also doubled and scored a run in the fourth and contributed an RBI single in the sixth. Bill Freehan (24) hit a pair of home runs to drive in four runs while Northrup (19) hit a pair to drive in three runs. Willie Horton added his 36th. "We'll get 'em tuned up," Mayo Smith said of his inactive relievers. "They've been pitching a lot of batting practice." Detroit's magic number dropped to two.

Monday, September 16

"We clinched a tie for the pennant and you don't see everyone jumping around and raising hell," Norm Cash said after Detroit drubbed New York, 9–1. "We've been ahead all year so it's not that exciting." Detroit got its 10th straight complete game, an eight-hit, seven-strikeout effort by John Hiller (9–5). The Tigers have won seven straight. Detroit decided the outcome early with nine runs in the first two innings. Northrup had an RBI single in the first, Cash a two-run single, and Freehan closed the first-inning scoring with an RBI single. Cash unloaded a three-run home run in the second, his 22nd.

Jon Warden

by Dan Holmes

Season	Age	W	L	Pct	G	GS	CG	SV	IP	H	R	ER	BB	SO	ERA
1968 Tigers	21	4	1	.800	28	0	0	3	37	30	15	15	15	25	3.65
Career Totals		4	1	.800	28	0	0	3	37	30	15	15	15	25	3.65

Less than two weeks into the 1968 season, Jon Warden had three victories to lead the American League in that category. That fact was quite unexpected considering the rookie left-hander was pitching out of the bullpen. National Guard service interrupted his 1968 season, but the tall hurler still performed well, especially on the road, and helped contribute to the pennant with four wins and three saves in 28 games in relief.

Jon Edgar Warden was born October 1, 1946, in Columbus, Ohio. He starred in baseball, basketball, and football at Pleasant View High School in Grove City, just outside Columbus. Though the Cubs and Giants sent scouts to look at him, he was undrafted out of high school, and Warden accepted a baseball-basketball scholarship to the University of Georgia. There, he pitched well against inferior competition, tossing a no-hitter and several other shutouts. He caught the attention of a Tiger scout who recommended him. Detroit selected Warden in the fourth round of the amateur draft in January 1966. A 6-foot, 205-pound hurler, Warden had an excellent fastball and good command.

Warden reported to Lakeland for spring training and was assigned to Daytona Beach of the Florida State League for his first professional season. A farm boy, Warden took advantage of the many attractions in Daytona Beach. At midseason, his manager asked him to try to "get a few hours of sleep" each night, recognizing that the rookie was having a good time in his first stretch away from home. In the second half, the lefty pitched much better. For the year, he went 9–12 with a 3.24 ERA in 30 games, 29 of them starts.

The 20-year-old spent 1967 at Rocky Mount in the Carolina League, considered the top Class A circuit in baseball. As a member of the starting rotation, he posted a 15–11 record with a 2.88 ERA in 219 innings, and made the all-star team. At Rocky Mount, his manager, Al Federoff, was one of his biggest supporters.

The Tigers sent Warden to Dunedin in the Florida Instructional League that winter. In Dunedin, he pitched on the same staff as fellow lefty John Hiller. The team won 15 of their last 16 to take the league title. Warden started and earned the win in the final game. Also on that team with Warden were future major leaguers Dave Campbell and Tom Matchick.

Fresh off his success in the instructional league, Warden was given a chance to make the big-league club in spring 1968. It was there that he earned the nickname "Warbler," though only one person ever really called him that. The Tigers' base-running instructor, Bernie Di-Viveiros, was notorious at butchering the names of players, and he called Warden "Warbler." When the folks from Major League Baseball came around and asked if he had a nickname, teammates shouted "Warbler" and the nickname was entered into the official record.

Warden's effectiveness in the spring, and that of fellow rookie hurlers Les Cain and Daryl Patterson, prompted the trade of veteran reliever Hank Aguirre at the tail end of camp. The deal cleared the way for Warden, who emerged with Hiller as two of Mayo Smith's primary southpaws out of the pen.

"Warden's lack of wildness is what impressed me in spring training," said Tigers catcher Bill Freehan. Praise from veterans like Freehan helped Smith show confidence in his young rookie hurlers. "You never can be sure how it will turn out," Smith said. "They might not be ready, or they might show all the poise in the world."

After dropping their season opener to the Red Sox, the Tigers used a solid performance from Warden to capture their first victory of the 1968 season. "I didn't think I could stand up I was so nervous. I think my knees were knocking just getting loose in the bullpen," Warden said of his major league debut, which came in relief of Denny McLain in a 3–3 tie. "Then I was on the mound in the eighth inning. The first thing I knew, the bases were loaded. I got out of the inning without a run and the score stayed tied. In the ninth I remember striking out Carl Yastrzemski. That was my first major league strikeout. I'll remember that all my life. I won the game when Gates Brown homered in the ninth."

Six days later, Warden won in relief once again, and three nights later he became the first pitcher in the AL to win three games. In a trip to Baltimore in May, Warden earned his first save and gained another save the next night.

The young Detroit bullpen, which also included sophomore hurlers Hiller and Pat Dobson, played a key role in the Tigers' season. At 21, Warden was the junior member of the roster. His poise and command was appreciated by pitching coach Johnny Sain, who called Warden "a power pitcher who can get away with a few mistakes."

Warden served in the Army Reserve during the 1968 season, fulfilling his duties on the weekends. He played the clarinet in his unit's band. On one Sunday in May, Warden took a plane to Ohio to play with the band but rain canceled the performance. He hopped back on a plane and was back in Detroit in time for the game that day. In July, Warden was replaced on the roster when he had to serve in the reserve for a two-week stint of clarinet playing.

After returning, Warden lowered his ERA from 4.96 to a final figure of 3.62. His longest appearance of the season came on July 17 in Oakland, when he pitched five innings of one-hit relief in a Tiger loss. He also tossed three shutout innings at Yankee Stadium on August 25. After that outing, Warden was used just once more that season. The fact that Detroit starters tossed 12 complete games in a row was one factor. Tigers General Manager Jim Campbell, faced with the off-season expansion draft, chose to keep Warden on the shelf so other teams would think he was hurt.

When the Tigers squared off against the St. Louis Cardinals in the fall classic, Warden was the only player on either roster who did not get into the World Series, though he warmed up a few times in the bullpen. Still, he earned a World Series share of $10,936.66 and a ring in his first season in the big leagues. In the off-season, he reported to Fort Dix, New Jersey, for 18 weeks of reserve duty.

But the euphoria of the world championship was interrupted on October 15, when Warden was drafted by the Kansas City Royals as the 12th pick in the expansion draft. The Royals and Seattle Pilots were joining the circuit for the 1969 season. Each big-league team could protect 30 players on their 40-man rosters. After an unforgettable season in Detroit, Warden was on his way to a new team. "I hated to see Warden go because we had him with us all year," Sain said. "He had the potential."

Unfortunately, a shoulder injury in spring training in 1969 shelved Warden. In a game against the Twins, Kansas City pitching coach Mel Harder asked Warden to pump up the velocity on his fastball. When he did, something popped and the lefty was taken from the game. He was diagnosed with a rotator cuff tear, but the Royals, as was common practice at that time, treated it with cortisone shots and drugs that simply masked the pain. In less than two weeks they had Warden back on the mound. When he returned, the Royals assigned him to High-Point-Thomasville, hoping the warmer climate would help heal his shoulder. Later he reported to Omaha in the American Association where he played under manager Jack McKeon and pitched in the starting rotation with Paul Splittorff, helping the team to the AA title. For the season, Warden was 6-6 in 21 games (121 IP) with a 5.28 ERA and 80 Ks. At one point, free from pain, Warden was 4–1, and thought he may be promoted to the big-league club, but he was passed over for Kansas City hometown product Don O'Riley and veteran Galen Cisco. The Royals did call him up when rosters expanded on September 1, but when he underwent a routine examination by the team doctor, the team shut him down, citing a tired arm. Warden remained on the roster but did not pitch.

With Omaha in 1969, Warden began to hone his skills as an entertainer and baseball personality. Blessed with a great sense of humor, Warden was popular with his teammates and fans. "It makes me feel good to see people laugh and have a good time," Warden said. "I'm hardly ever in a bad mood and when I am, the guys get on me and soon everything's okay." With Omaha, manager Steve Boros helped Warden pull off a stunt at Oklahoma City in which Warden shot a blank pistol after an opposing batter hit a homer, mocking the Oklahoma City practice of shooting off a cannon after their homers. The fans were delighted.

Entering spring training in 1970, Warden was anxious to return to the big leagues. "I'll be the left-handed relief pitcher, all I need is a chance," Warden predicted in January.

The Royals were not so sure. "Let's see if he can be the guy he was supposed to be when we drafted him from Detroit. We need a lefty in the bullpen. He and [Steve] Jones have the inside track," Royals vice-president Cedric Tallis said.

Manager Charlie Metro, a staunch disciplinarian—one Royal called Metro's spring training "Stalag 17"—had Warden on a conditioning program in the spring of 1970. At one point, Metro gave Warden three days to drop his weight from 216 to 207. The southpaw came in at 205 before the three days were over, but still failed to make the big-league club. He was assigned to San Jose, where he spent the balance of the 1970 season. Shoulder problems hampered him again in 1970 and into the off-season. "I would be strong in the spring and then pitch well in the first few months of the season, but by mid-July I would be [less effective] and as the season wore on, my arm was dead," Warden said.

In 1971 he was on injured reserve with Elmira of the Eastern League when the Royals activated him to have him pitch against the big-league club on June 2. The intention was for team brass to have a good look at the former major leaguer. Warden defeated the Royals, 3–0, allowing just two hits in seven innings. In spite of his performance, Warden was not called up to Kansas City, and while he was with Evansville, for whom he had no record, he was released in August. Shortly thereafter he signed with the St. Louis Cardinals and was assigned to Arkansas of the Dixie League.

But Warden never again reached the majors, and the following summer, after being released by the St. Louis organization, he was driving from his home in Columbus to Cleveland to serve as batting practice pitcher for the Cleveland Indians.

In 1974 the Chicago White Sox invited Warden to spring training on the recommendation of Johnny Sain. Warden threw the ball well, but when the team broke camp, the White Sox asked if he would be willing to pitch in Mexico. Still "bitten by the bug," Warden agreed. But after several weeks traveling by bus on long road trips and living in dreadful conditions, he phoned home and told his wife he was through and was coming back to Ohio.

After his playing career, Warden worked in sporting goods briefly, finished his college degree, and got a job teaching and coaching at the high school level, something he did for several years. He became a regular at the Tigers' fantasy camp, where he donned the robe and performed duties as judge in kangaroo court. In that role, his one season in the majors was of little importance to fantasy campers, who quickly grew to love Warden's humor and affable manner. Many campers cited Warden as the reason they returned to camp year after year. In 2005, Warden reprised his role as kangaroo court judge for the Hall of Fame Fantasy Camp in Cooperstown, reaching the heights of fantasy camp status. Warden also stayed busy with speaking engagements through the Major League Baseball Alumni Association. He felt blessed to have had his one season in the big leagues.

"Those guys on that team share a common bond," Warden said of his 1968 teammates. "We made it to the top of our profession together, and we see each other a few times each year and are very close."

Rich Shook presents:
Tigers In the News

Tuesday, September 17
The champagne finally flowed freely. Don Wert's RBI single in the bottom of the ninth scored Al Kaline with the run that gave Detroit a 2-1 victory over New York and its first American League championship since 1945. "The only thing I didn't want to do was to go up there and strike out," said Wert. "I just wanted to hit the ball." The Tigers scored their winning run in their last turn at bat for the 29th time this season. Joe Sparma, who had not pitched in 15 days, notched his first complete game since July 25 and Detroit's 11th in a row as a substitute starter. Earl Wilson was scheduled to pitch but noticed unusual soreness in his shoulder while warming up. Mayo Smith turned first to Dobson, who said, "As long as you want me in the bullpen in the World Series I'd just as soon stay there and be ready if you need me in relief." Smith then asked Sparma, who had thrown a short bullpen session earlier, if he would take the ball. He would. "It's great to be part of this," Sparma said. A double play got him out of a first-inning jam and he then retired 14 in a row before walking a batter in the sixth. Detroit had actually clinched the pennant when Baltimore lost to Boston earlier in the evening but GM Jim Campbell ordered the final result kept off the scoreboard because he feared fans would swarm the field in celebration and cause a forfeit. Kaline drew a walk as a two-out pinch-hitter and Bill Freehan singled to left. After two moves and counter-moves, Gates Brown pinch-hit and walked to load the bases. Wert then lined his single to right and Kaline touched off a celebration when he touched the plate with the pennant-clinching run. "I've had great thrills but this has got to top them all," said Kaline, who played 15 seasons without experiencing the ecstasy of a championship.

Wednesday, September 18
The clinching of its first pennant since 1945 enabled Mayo Smith to start planning for the post-season. And it helped that Detroit's hung-over players got an extra day of merciful rest when its game against New York was rained out. Smith confirmed what came to light two days ago: Kaline would get a trial at third base in an effort to get his bat in the lineup and yet keep the outfield trio of Horton, Stanley, and Northrup intact. As part of the plan, Wert would slide over to see if he's capable of handling shortstop for the World Series. That would solve a problem of light hitting the Tigers have endured at the position all season. "It goes against everything I believe in baseball," Smith said of his experiment, "but I'm willing to give up defense to get his bat in the lineup. We need as many hitters as we can get against the Cardinals." "I'm ready to play anywhere Mayo wants me," the proud Kaline said. Kaline started at third once in 1961, played six innings of a 14-inning game there in 1965 and had played some first base for Detroit this season. Kaline went to Smith before Detroit clinched the pennant the night before and told him to start Stanley in center and Northrup in right because they had played there the most this season. "It's killing me but I know what Mayo is up against," Kaline said. "I've waited all my life to get in a World Series but he's got to go with the kids. They deserve the chance to play; they're the ones who have been winning the pennant." Smith said Detroit's string of 11 complete games by its starters would end because he wants to tune up his bullpen and that only McLain, Wilson, and Lolich would start in the World Series.

Thursday, September 19
Just another day at the office for Denny McLain: a win and some headline-making news. McLain grooved a fastball for Mickey Mantle so the New York Yankees' great could hit the 535th home run of his career, break a tie with Jimmie Foxx, and become third on the all-time home run list. McLain sheepishly denied it but catcher Jim Price more or less confirmed it. The outcome was not in doubt and Detroit defeated New York, 6-2, with McLain posting the staff's 12th complete game in a row. Price tipped off Mantle a fastball was on its way but the slugger, playing first base as his career wound down, didn't believe it. Mantle let another grooved fastball go by and then made a quick motion with his hand around the letters of his jersey. McLain obliged and Mantle creamed the fat 0-2 letter-high fastball into the upper deck in right as the crowd roared its approval. "I got a feeling he wanted me to hit it," Mantle grinned. McLain (31-5) became baseball's first 31-game winner since Lefty Grove for Philadelphia in 1931 with his 28th complete game. Norm Cash put Detroit ahead with a fourth-inning home run, then added his 24th home run of the season in the sixth after Stanley walked to break a 1-1 tie. Eddie Mathews had an RBI single in the sixth also. Wayne Comer entered the game as a late-inning sub and had a two-run single in the seventh. Stanley played shortstop as Smith had Kaline hitting third and playing right field. Northrup patrolled center.

fFriday, September 20
Kaline, playing right field, went 4-for-4 including his 10th home run while Northrup, playing center, cracked a pair of home runs good for four RBI in Detroit's 6-3 victory at Washington. Horton stayed home with a sinus infection while Bill Freehan sat out the game. Mickey Lolich (16-9) was pulled for pinch-hitter Gates Brown after seven innings but survived a seven-walk outing by striking out nine and only giving up three hits. That broke a streak of 12 straight complete games by Tigers starters. Northrup now had 21 home runs and Detroit had a 10-game winning streak.

Don Wert

by John Milner

Season	Age	G	AB	R	H	2B	3B	HR	RBI	BB	SO	SB	CS	BA	OBP	SLG
1968 Tigers	29	150	536	44	107	15	1	12	37	37	79	0	3	.200	.258	.299
Career Totals		1110	3840	417	929	129	15	77	366	389	529	22	24	.242	.314	.343

The Detroit Tigers' magic number for clinching the American League pennant had been whittled to one as they entered play on September 17, 1968. A Tigers win or a Baltimore Orioles loss would give Detroit a pennant the city had been waiting 23 years to enjoy. Heading into the ninth inning, the Tigers led the Yankees 1–0 behind Joe Sparma's brilliant pitching performance. However, the Yankees tied it with a run in the top of the ninth and that left it up to the Tigers to stage a rally in their half of the inning in order to secure the World Series berth. The first two hitters were retired, but then Al Kaline drew a walk. Bill Freehan contributed a single to left field, which caused the Yankees to change pitchers. Lindy McDaniel was brought in to face Gates Brown, who drew a base on balls from the Yankees reliever. As Don Wert walked to the plate, 46,000 fans were on their feet in Tiger Stadium waiting for what they hoped would be the celebration that they had been anticipating. Don Wert, the Tigers' steady third baseman, swung and sent the ball safely into right field for a single that scored Kaline and started pandemonium with the fans rushing the field. Don Wert was the hero of the day for the pennant-winning Tigers.

Donald Ralph Wert was born in Strasburg, Pennsylvania, on July 29, 1938, to a family of German descent. Don attended Harmony Elementary School through the eighth grade, then attended Southern Lancaster County (Solanco) Joint High School. He excelled in athletics and academics in high school. Don was a three-sport star, participating in football, basketball, and baseball. He especially excelled in football, where as a 145-pound junior quarterback he led the team to the conference championship and was named the all-league quarterback and the player of the year. Upon graduation from high school in 1957, Don was offered an athletic scholarship to Franklin and Marshall College in Lancaster to play all three sports and work toward a career as a teacher and coach. It was thought he was primarily needed for his skills as a quarterback As it turned out, he played only football in college. He played for the freshman football team in 1957, but because of finances he could not attend the school after the first semester. His academic record was good, but Franklin and Marshall's expenses were substantial, even with his scholarship. Looking back, Wert said, "I think I made a bad choice. I should have gone to Millersville State College (a teachers' college also in Lancaster County with lower tuition). I think that I could have met my fees easier even without the scholarship and could have acquired my teaching credits more directly. However, I thought a liberal arts college would afford me better grounding. But I have no regrets now." In February 1958, Wert took a job with the Farm Bureau in Quarryville, Pennsylvania, as a loading and delivery man. The job involved him having to load and deliver 100-pound sacks of feed and grain, and this enabled him to keep his arms and legs in shape.

Wert had not worked there too long before his life took a drastic turn. Ralph DeFranco, a Lancaster native, was the Detroit Tigers' scout for eastern Pennsylvania. He had followed Wert's baseball career since his prep days and had continued to follow it as he played American Legion ball and in the Lancaster City and County leagues. DeFranco, along with chief Tigers scout Ed Katalinas, signed the right-handed-hitting Wert to a contract in early 1958 for $5,000. Wert started out working with Idaho Falls of the Pioneer League and then reported to Lakeland, Florida, for spring training in the Tigers camp. An uneventful camp left him being sent to Valdosta in the Class D Georgia-Florida League to play the 1958 season, in which he hit .284.

During spring training at Lakeland's Tigertown complex in 1959, the Detroit brass attempted to move Wert to shortstop, but he resisted the move and remained at third base. This resistance may have slowed his trek to the big leagues. He was assigned to Durham of the Class B Carolina League for 1959 and finished with a .220 average. At season's end, Don married his high school sweetheart, Marlene Fay Rineer, on October 3, 1959. (They had three children, Scott, Barbara Ann, and Kimberly.) In 1960 he returned Durham, where his batting average rose to .276 and he led the Carolina League with 259 assists.

In 1961, because of his solid 1960 season at Durham, Wert was promoted to Triple A Denver of the American Association. Going from B ball to AAA was quite a jump, and the Denver club was apprehensive when the Tigers asked that Wert be its regular third baseman. As the season progressed, Denver was more than happy to have him on its roster. In Denver, Wert was able to work with manager Wayne Blackburn, who was also Detroit's minor league hitting instructor. "Wayne changed my hitting almost completely, " Don said. "I was throwing my weight forward on my left foot on the swing too fast and too far. He taught me how to keep my weight distributed and in reserve on my right foot, swiveling my weight, as it were. I worked hard at it this and Wayne kept at it with me." The hard work paid off as Wert won the American Association batting title by hitting .328. His glove work was also making people take notice. "He's in the class with guys like George Kell, Kenny Boyer, and Brooks Robinson as a fielder at third base," commented Indianapolis manager Cot Deal after watching Wert come up with nine assists—at least five of them sensational—in a game against Indy in August. It was the second time that season that Wert had accumulated nine assists in a game, one below the league record. After this breakthrough season, Wert began to feel that the major leagues could be within his grasp. Since high school, he had always been known for his fielding, but this was the first time he had experienced this much success at the plate. He attributed his fielding success and his fundamental knowledge of the game to his high school coach, Harold Suder, who mentored him as a pitcher, outfielder, and—Don's favorite position—third base.

And 1962 was another solid year. Wert's batting average fell to .267, but his walks doubled, from 44 to 96. He now had confidence in himself and his abilities, and contributed many clutch hits along with his steady glove work.

In 1963, the Tigers brought in John "Bubba" Phillips from the Cleveland Indians to be their regular third baseman. After Wert couldn't dislodge Phillips in spring training, he went back to the minors, with Syracuse of the International League (the American Association had folded). Wert continued his clutch hitting and steady, if not spectacular, work with the leather at third base; and in May, the Tigers called him up. Don Wert, at 24 years of age, made his major league debut before a crowd of 5,540 on Saturday, May 11, at Tiger Stadium in a game against the Cleveland Indians. The Tigers lost, 6–5 in ten innings to the Indians. Wert got into the game as a pinch-runner and scored in a four-run rally in the bottom of the ninth that tied the score. In the tenth inning, after Cleveland scored twice in the top half, Wert hit an RBI double off Jerry Walker in his first major league at-bat to bring the score to 6–5, as close as the Tigers got that day. He went on to play in 78 games for the Tigers that year. He had 251 at-bats, 31 runs, 65 hits, 6 doubles, 2 triples, 7 home runs, 25 RBI, and a .250 batting average. He played 47 games at third base, but also played second base (21 games) and shortstop (8 games). That year, the Tigers got off to a slow start that eventually cost manager Bob Scheffing his job. He was replaced by former Brooklyn manager Charlie Dressen. The Tigers tied with Cleveland for fifth place at 79–83, 25.5 games behind the Yankees.

The tables turned during spring training in 1964; Wert won the regular third base position, and Phillips was relegated to the backup role. It was Dressen's first full season as manager and he felt Wert's potential for improvement would be better served by his being in the lineup on a regular basis. It was during this spring training that Wert acquired his nickname of "Coyote." Manager Dressen reportedly requested Wert to become more vocal at third base and Don responded with high-pitched chatter that sounded like the yip-yip-yipping of a coyote. Don Demeter is reported to have saddled him with the moniker. Wert played in 148 games for the Tigers in '64, with 525 at-bats, 63 runs, 135 hits, 18 doubles, 5 triples, 9 home runs, 55 RBI, and a .257 batting average. He finished third in the American League with seven sacrifice flies. The team again started the year slowly, but did better toward the end, and had a 20–10 record in August. They finished at 85–77, in fourth place, 14 games behind the pennant-winning Yankees. Wert's solid everyday play put him in the mix for Dressen's plans for 1965 and beyond. Dressen was primarily given credit for giving Wert a chance where others had not. The Tigers' surge during the latter part of the season coincided with Wert's bat warming up. He crushed a three-run homer on September 9 off the Yankees' Whitey Ford into the upper deck at Tiger Stadium, then two nights later he went 4-for-4 with a triple and scored the winning run in the ninth to defeat the Senators. In a span of 19 games, Wert mashed the baseball at a .370 pace and raised his batting average 17 points. Wayne Blackburn, Wert's former manager in the minors and in 1964 a Tigers coach, commented, "I said last year that Wert could make the plays over there like a Brooks Robinson or a Clete Boyer and everybody laughed at me, but they're not laughing anymore."

With Phillips released by the Tigers in February 1965, Wert knew that third base was all his. Dressen spoke highly of his 5-foot-10, 160-pound third sacker by saying, "There isn't a better fielding third baseman in the American League. The little guy makes all the plays that Brooks Robinson and Clete Boyer make." The respect for Wert's defensive prowess was beginning to expand outside the Tigers' organization as well. After the Minnesota Twins watched him make a bevy of remarkable stops and throws in a series at Tiger Stadium, Twins manager Sam Mele said, "I'd like to take him with us." It was believed that Wert's solidifying the third base position led to the overall defensive improvement of the Tigers. He finished 1965 with just 12 errors, strides ahead of the 39 that had been committed by Tiger third basemen in 1962. And although he did make spectacular plays, it was his steadiness on a daily basis that led observers to realize just how valuable he was. Wert became a great friend of the developing Tigers' pitching staff, especially left-handers like Mickey Lolich and Hank Aguirre. Typically the third baseman gets a lot of action at the "hot corner" with lefties on the mound and Wert did not disappoint because he could handle anything hit his direction. Statistically, Wert had the best season of his blossoming career in 1965. He played in all 162 games for the Tigers and had 609 at-bats. He scored 81 runs, had 159 hits, 22 doubles, 2 triples, 12 home runs, 54 RBI, and 73 walks, and batted .261. Defensively, he contributed 163 putouts and 331 assists, and was involved in 33 double plays. Also, his name began to appear in the American League Top Ten for certain categories. He was first in games played, third in at-bats, fourth in times on base, sixth in walks and singles, and ninth in runs and hits. He finished tenth in the AL Most Valuable Player voting for 1965. As a team, the Tigers improved to 89–73 and finished in fourth place, 13 games behind the Twins. They accomplished this despite having to deal with Charlie Dressen's having a heart attack during the season and being temporarily replaced by coach Bob Swift. Dressen had been the one to show confidence in Wert, especially at the start of 1965, and Don had commented: "When Dressen stayed with me, I felt, finally, that I had it made. This is what I needed and I think it made a major leaguer out of me once and for all."

During the off-season, Don went back home to New Providence, Pennsylvania, to work in the sports department of the local Sears-Roebuck store. It was his second off-season working there so that he could establish himself for a possible post-career position with the company. While at home, he received news of being selected Tiger of the Year by the Detroit chapter of the Baseball Writers Association of America. Watson Spoelstra of the *Detroit News* described Wert by using a quote from Branch Rickey: "Don't ever put it down that the quiet fellow is not smart or resourceful. Vocalization is not the test of courage." Spoelstra said this described Wert perfectly. "He is smart and resourceful without talking about it." Spoelstra wrote. Fans had also taken notice when they proclaimed Don as King Tiger through the fan club voting process for that season. Along with these awards, Wert also was honored by his hometown Lancaster sportswriters and broadcasters. At the time, he was the first position player from Lancaster to make it to the major leagues since the early 1900s.

In January 1966, Wert accepted the Tiger of the Year Award from Detroit baseball writers and spoke with promise for the coming season. He declared, "We can go all the way this year, I really think so." In what turned out to be an ironic counterpoint, Dressen agreed: "We've added enough to a young club to make us a contender. We'll be all right if the Good Lord keeps them all healthy." But the 1966 season was one of adversity for the Tigers. They had three managers during the campaign with two of them eventually dying. In May, Dressen suffered his second heart attack in two years and died in August. After Dressen was hospitalized, coach Bob Swift took over on an interim basis. He led the Tigers on a 19–5 surge in June to close within 1.5 games of first place. But by mid-July, manager Swift was hospitalized with lung cancer and eventually died in October. That left the reins to coach Frank Skaff, and under him, the team finished 88–74 in third place, ten games behind the winning Orioles. Skaff had been the third-base coach before taking over the team and had a good relationship with Wert, having coached him in the minors at Durham and Denver. Of Wert, Skaff said, "He has all the equipment to be one of the top third baseman in baseball. The esteem of his mates and his election as Tiger of the Year ought to provide the spark to stardom." Wert played in 150 games in 1966 and had 559 at-bats. He scored 56 runs and had 150 hits, 20 doubles, 2 triples, 11 home runs, 70 RBI, and a .268 average, the latter two numbers career high. In the field, he had 128 putouts and 253 assists and committed only 11 errors for a fielding average of .972.

In 1967, the Tigers came oh-so-close to reaching the World Series. Under new manager Mayo Smith, they finished 91–71, tied for second with the Twins, one game behind the Boston Red Sox. Wert started the season slowly, hitting only .200 after the first 35 games. Along with batting coach Wally Moses, he determined that he was restricting his swing by leaning too much at the plate. With a changed stance, Wert hit nearly .300 over the next 35 games, even though many of his well-struck balls were finding their way into opposing fielders' mitts. "You can't feel too bad about it when you hit the ball hard," Wert said. "You tell yourself, 'Things even up and maybe I'll get my share of bloops.'" The new manager thought highly of Wert's capabilities as a hitter by using him in the leadoff, second, and third spots on occasion. Wert had his share of key hits during the season. They included a double on May 21 that was the last hit off the Yankees' Whitey Ford—as Ford left the game with arm trouble and never returned to competition—and a fourth-inning, game-winning double on June 6 against Kansas City Athletics pitcher Blue Moon Odom after Bill Freehan had been intentionally walked. Wert ended up playing in 142 games with 534 at-bats. He scored 60 runs and had 137 hits, 23 doubles, 2 triples, 6 home runs, 40 RBI, and a batting average of .257. He had 112 putouts, 280 assists, only 9 errors while at third base for a fielding average of .978. Wert had some unforeseen competition when Eddie Mathews was picked up from Houston for an added boost during the pennant drive. Mathews ended up playing 21 games at third base for the Tigers. General Manager Jim Campbell and Mayo Smith were concerned by Wert's added weight, which may have contributed to a couple of leg injuries during the season, prompting the acquisition of Mathews. Coming into the season, Wert's weight had increased to about 180 pounds after he quit smoking because of a respiratory infection the season before. But Wert changed his eating habits and had his weight down to the 168 pounds that manager Smith has requested for him before the off-season.

Wert had a new streamlined look as he prepared for 1968. His third-base competition, Mathews, was moved to compete with Norm Cash at first base. As an example of Wert's rediscovered quickness, during a Grapefruit League game against Oakland, he dove to stop a smash off the bat of speedster Bert Campaneris and jumped to his feet to make the throw for the out. "Wert didn't have that kind of quickness last year," said Mayo Smith. "I don't think he could have gotten up to make the throw." Don was excited about the prospects of the new season, saying, "We've got a heck of a chance to win the pennant. We know we need a good start. I can help by doing something with the bat in the early months." Wert added, "A strong first half would help my All-Star chances. I'd like to make the All-Star Game some year. The guys in our league are honest about voting for players who do well early in the year." Up to this point, Wert's All-Star aspirations had been usually dimmed because he played the same position as Brooks Robinson. They were considered to be equals with the glove, but Robinson was seen as being the better batsman.

The Tigers got off to a good start and by May 10 had assumed the lead for keeps. Detroit finished at 103–59, twelve games ahead of Baltimore. But Wert's batting average plunged to a career-low .200. He played in 150 games with 536 at-bats. He scored 44 runs and had 107 hits, 15 doubles, 1 triple, 12 home runs, and 37 RBI. He committed 15 errors while registering 142 putouts and 284 assists. His fielding average was .966. His poor offensive figures may have been a result of his being hit in the head on June 24 by a pitch from Indians sidearmer Hal Kurtz in Cleveland. The pitch shattered his batting helmet. He was carried off the field on a stretcher and spend two nights in the hospital. He was out of the lineup for a week and when he returned, he had added a protective earflap to his batting helmet. "I had no bad headaches," he said, "but I had a numb feeling above my left ear for several days." Over the rest of the season, Wert batted a paltry .179. Despite the injury, he attained one of his career goals by being selected to join teammates Bill Freehan, Denny McLain, and Willie Horton and manager Mayo Smith as members of the American League All-Star team. The game, at the Astrodome in Houston, was the first All-Star Game to be played indoors on artificial turf. As the National League won, 1–0, Wert batted once and doubled off Tom Seaver of the New York Mets for one of only three hits by the AL.

Going into the World Series, the Tigers were the decided underdog against the defending champion St. Louis Cardinals. In Game 1, on October 2 at Busch Stadium in St. Louis, the Cardinals won easily, 4–0, defeating the Tigers' 31 game winner Denny McLain. Bob Gibson struck out 17 Tigers and gave up only five hits. Wert had one of them, a single, going 1-for-2. The next day in St. Louis, Detroit rebounded and walloped the Cardinals, 8–1 behind the six-hit, nine-strikeout performance of Mickey Lolich. Wert went 0-for-2, but contributed an RBI. The series resumed in Detroit and the Cardinals pounded out 13 hits in defeating Detroit, 7–3. Wert went 0-for-4. In what seemed a pivotal Game 4, the Redbirds looked like champions in hammering out 13 hits in a 10–1 triumph. Gibson was once again magnificent, striking out 10 and giving up only five hits. Eddie Mathews assumed Wert's third-base duties in this game and went 1-for-2 against Gibson. Down three games to one, the Tigers came out clawing in Game 5 and eked out a close win, 5–3, a complete-game victory for Lolich. Wert was 0-for-3. The Series shifted back to St. Louis for Game 6 and it proved to be all Tigers as they won going away, 13–1. McLain got the victory. Wert went 0-for-3 but scored a run after getting hit by a pitch. At this point, Wert was a disappointing 1-for-14 going into the deciding game, in which Lolich faced Gibson, both looking for their third win of the Series. The Tigers' Jim Northrup hit a triple in the seventh inning that broke open a scoreless game. Curt Flood, the Cardinals' center fielder, appeared to have a bead on it, but slipped, and the ball fell safely. Wert contributed by driving in pinch-runner Dick Tracewski with a single in the ninth to add an insurance run for the Tigers. With a 4–0 lead, Lolich allowed only a Mike Shannon home run in the ninth inning. Wert played in six games and went 2-for-17 with six walks. Both of his hits were off Gibson. He had two RBI. Although his batting average was only .118, his on-base percentage was .375.

During the off-season, there was concern over Wert's lack of hitting late in the 1968 campaign. Coming up on the age of 31, it wasn't a certainty he would be the regular third baseman in 1969. Wally Moses, the hitting coach, intended to concentrate on Wert in spring training. But after having a good spring training, Wert had problems at the plate once the season started. The Tigers, thinking something might be wrong physically, ordered some medical tests, which found no problems. Wert hit nearly .300 for a midseason stretch, but wound up hitting only .225, with 423 at-bats in 132 games. But he did hit a career-high 14 home runs. His fielding didn't suffer, but the frustration at the plate led Wert to commit himself and his family to staying in Detroit in the off-season instead of going back to New Providence. The Tigers finished the 1969 season in second place in the American League East Division in 1969 with a respectable record of 90–72, but still 19 games behind the Orioles.

Don had a battle on his hands to keep his position in 1970. As the season started, he said confidently, "The job's mine until somebody takes it away," and his competitive fire pleased manager Mayo Smith. Wert's chief competition was from veteran Dalton Jones, acquired from the Red Sox in the off-season, and promising rookie Elliott Maddox, who had been a phenom at the University of Michigan. As the season progressed, Wert's playing time shrank to 117 games, with Maddox playing in 41 games and Jones in 18 at third base. Wert hit .218, with just 79 hits in 363 at-bats. His home run total dropped to six with only 33 RBI. His 14 errors gave him a fielding percentage of .953 at third base, the lowest of his career. The team struggled to a fourth-place finish out of six teams in their division. The Tigers were 79–83, 29 games behind front-running Baltimore. The poor showing cost Mayo Smith his job at the end of the season; he was replaced by Billy Martin. On October 9, 1970, Wert was involved in an eight-player trade between the Tigers and Senators. The Tigers sent Elliott Maddox, Norm McRae, Denny McLain, and Wert to the Senators for Jim Hannan, Joe Coleman, Aurelio Rodriguez, and Ed Brinkman.

The trade spurred Wert on as the 1971 season approached. He said he was "rather excited to play for Mr. [Ted] Williams," the Nats' manager. But things did not go as expected. On March 21, in spring training, Wert was injured in a collision at second base and was hospitalized with a back injury. He began the season on the disabled list. When he returned, he fared poorly. He got into 20 games, only 15 in the field. He had only two hits in 40 at-bats for an .050 average with one double and two RBI. His final appearance with the Senators was on June 11. The Senators released him on June 24. He was 32, and his career in professional baseball was over.

Don returned to his native eastern Pennsylvania. He became involved in farming and business; at one point he was associated full-time with the Jay Advertising Co. of Ronks, Pennsylvania. In 1976, he took a part-time coaching position with the Franklin and Marshall College. His mentoring skills were acknowledged in a recent article in *Franklin and Marshall Magazine*, in which Donnie Marsh, a 1979 graduate, said, "My coaches—Glenn Robinson and Bill Fry in basketball, and Ken Twiford and Don Wert in baseball—helped a guy who had never been away from home to grow up and become a leader in a very tough, very competitive environment." As the 1968 club's 40th anniversary neared, Wert continues to live in eastern Pennsylvania.

References

Publications
National Baseball Hall of Fame Biographies
Sullivan, George, and David Cataneo. *Detroit Tigers: The Complete Record of Detroit Tigers Baseball.* New York: Collier. 1985.
The Sporting News
Christian Science Monitor
Total Baseball

Web Sites
www.answers.com
www.baseball-almanac.com
www.baseball-reference.com
www.wikipedia.org
www.thebaseballcube.com
www.tigerscentral.com

Rich Shook presents:

Tigers In the News

Saturday, September 21
Kaline showed why Mayo Smith wanted to get his bat into the World Series lineup with a game-winning single in the seventh inning of Detroit's 4–3 win at Washington, the Tigers' 11th win in a row. Detroit worked a successful double steal in the first with Mickey Stanley on third and Kaline on first. Singles in the fourth by Cash, Northrup, and Eddie Mathews—plus a throwing error by the right fielder—produced two runs. Consecutive singles by McAuliffe, Stanley, and Kaline produced the win. Joe Sparma (10–10) won in relief of Earl Wilson.

Sunday, September 22
Camilo Pascual ended Detroit's 11-game winning streak with a four-hit shutout in Washington's 6–0 victory. John Hiller, Daryl Patterson, and Don McMahon split the pitching for Detroit.

Monday, Sept 23
Mayo Smith officially announced something he'd clearly been mulling over for days: He would be trying Stanley at shortstop "to get another bat into the lineup" for the World Series, only eight days away. "I'm going to start Stanley at short the rest of the way," Smith said, "and if I think he can handle it, I'll use him there in the World Series. I'd just be changing one position. Northrup can play a good center field, so it wouldn't be weakening two positions." Stanley played short and batted second at Baltimore as the Orioles edged the Tigers, 2–1, and handed McLain only his sixth loss of the season. He pitched seven innings and was due for a five-inning tune-up in his final start of the regular season before opening against Bob Gibson in St. Louis for the start of the Series. Stanley made a pair of errors, the first setting up Baltimore's run in the opening inning. Kaline also made an error in right field.

Tuesday, September 24
Mickey Lolich (17–9) allowed just six hits in six innings of Detroit's 5–3 victory at Baltimore. Bill Freehan highlighted a three-run fourth by hitting a two-run home run, his 25th. Stanley, still batting second, played errorless ball at short.

Wednesday, September 25
The Tigers came up with their 30th win of the season in their last turn at bat when Gates Brown hit a three-run home run in the ninth for a 4–3 victory over the host Orioles. Earl Wilson worked seven five-hit innings but Don McMahon (5–1) received credit for the win. Stanley turned in another errorless game at short but Willie Horton was still ailing and Brown started for him in left. Freehan was hit by a pitch for the 24th time to set a new AL record. Smith had yet to announce whether Wilson or Lolich would pitch the second game of the World Series after McLain pitches the opener.

Thursday, September 26
No game. Smith has three games against visiting Washington to certify Stanley as his shortstop for the World Series. His alternatives would be the .203-hitting Tom Matchick, the .156-hitting Dick Tracewski or the 135-hitting Oyler. Horton was scheduled to return to left field after recovering from a sinus infection.

Friday, September 27
The Tigers dropped a 3–1 decision to the Senators. Mickey Stanley turned in another mistake-free game at shortstop, dimming Matchick's chances of playing there. "I thought I had a hell of a good year, considering the time I lost in the service," the dejected Matchick said. The rookie was the Tigers' primary shortstop the second half of the season although he was on military duty from late July to mid-August. Joe Sparma started but Pat Dobson (5–7) took the loss in relief. Norm Cash hit his 25th home run of the season for Detroit.

Earl Wilson

by Don Hyslop

Season	Age	W	L	Pct	G	GS	CG	SV	IP	H	R	ER	BB	SO	ERA
1968 Tigers	33	13	12	.520	34	33	10	0	224	192	77	71	65	168	2.85
Career Totals		121	109	.526	338	310	69	0	2052	1863	934	842	796	1452	3.69

Ponchatoula, Louisiana, in the 1930s was a small town that had suffered a number of lumber mills closing in the previous decade. By the 1930s, it was known primarily as a strawberry farming region. It was into this area that on October 2, 1934, Earl Lawrence Wilson was born. He later changed his name to Robert Earl Wilson. The family's roots were in this area as both, his father, Earl, and mother, Amanda, were from the region. Amanda's father, in fact, ran a nearby strawberry farm. Earl had been preceded by a sister and eventually would become the middle child upon the birth of another sister. Both his parents were known as hard workers with his father employed as a school custodian and his mother, besides looking after her own household, was employed as a housekeeper.

Wilson grew up loving sports. He went to Hammond Colored High School, where he played varsity basketball. His passion, however, was baseball and he played whenever and wherever he could get the chance. He played at Athletic Park in Ponchatoula for as many community teams as he could. As he grew, his parents, according to son Greg, instilled in him a strong work ethic and desire to always strive to be successful. These characteristics would be very important in Earl's life as it unfolded.

Wilson began playing as an outfielder but soon switched to catching. He was always a strong hitter. In 1953, in what the Baseball Library web site describes as his first real season as a professional, he, because of his strong arm, was changed into a pitcher. He went he went 4–5 with a 3.81 ERA—and more walks (61) than strikeouts (56) for the Brisbee-Douglas Copper Kings of the Arizona-Texas League.

It was during this season that the Boston Red Sox began to notice the young ballplayer. The scouting report sent to the team's head office is indicative of the racial bias that Wilson had to overcome in his early years as a professional ballplayer. It stated, "He is a well mannered colored boy, not too black, pleasant to talk to, well educated, has a very good appearance and conducts himself as a gentleman." That year the Red Sox signed Earl; the first African American to play a game for the Bosox, Elijah "Pumpsie" Green, wasn't signed until 1956. Still, these were the first two African Americans ever signed by Boston. Earl was drafted into the Marines in 1957. Although he continued to play military ball his opportunity to become the first black player to crack the Red Sox lineup was delivered a setback. It looked like Pumpsie Green would get there first

In 1959, Green had hit .400 during spring training with the parent Sox and was named "Camp Rookie of The Year" by the press. Even with those accomplishments, Green had not secured anything. When writers asked owner Tom Yawkey if Green would make the team, he replied, "The Sox will bring up a Negro if he meets our standards." By the time camp had broken, General Manager Bucky Harris seemed to indicate that Green had made the team—but this was not the case. Reports were that manager Pinky Higgins had gone to Yawkey and had Harris overruled. Boston sportswriter Al Hirshberg later claimed that Higgins had made the following statement, "There will be no niggers on this team as long as I have anything to do with it."

The demotion of Green caused a furor among civil rights groups. The NAACP called for an investigation into the affair. The Massachusetts Commission Against Discrimination held hearings into the matter. Neither Yawkey nor Harris attended. They put the team's defense into the hands of a young team lawyer by the name of Dick O'Connell. He argued the Red Sox were employing eight black personnel at the time, one at Fenway Park and eight in the minor leagues. The outcome of the hearing resulted in the Red Sox being absolved of any charges of discrimination for the promise of making every effort to end the apparent segregation that existed on the team.

By that July, Green was hitting .325 at Minneapolis and had just been named an American Association All-Star for the second straight year. On July 21, 1959, Green made his debut for Boston to become the first African American to play for the Red Sox. One week later, Robert Earl Wilson, who had a record of 10–2 at the time, made his first appearance.

During the remainder of that season, Wilson appeared in nine games and compiled a modest 1–1 record with a 6.08 ERA. He recorded his first victory in the majors August 20 in an 11–10 win over the Kansas City A's. Besides picking up his first big-league win, he also showed his bat was a serious weapon as he picked up three RBI in the game.

In the 1960 season, Wilson appeared in 13 games and had a 3–2 record. He lowered his ERA to 4.71 and lowered his walk to strikeout ratio as well. His control at this early stage of his career was always a concern. In spite of what appeared like good progress Wilson would not make a major league start in 1961.

The following season, 1962, saw Wilson come back to stay. It did not take long for him to distinguish himself. On June 26 of that year, he took the mound against the Los Angeles Angels and Bo Belinsky in front of 14,002 fans in Fenway Park. That night he became the first African American to hurl a no-hitter in the American League, pitching the Sox to a 2–0 win. He helped his own cause by hitting a home run, which proved to be the game-winning run. During the contest, Wilson faced 31 Angels hitters. He gave up four base on balls, struck out five, had eight ground-ball outs and 14 fly-ball outs. The Red Sox made several key defensive plays behind Wilson, as happens in most no-hitters. These included a fine catch at the wall by Carl Yastrzemski, a grab of a line drive by shortstop Eddie Bressoud, and a catch of a 400-foot fly ball to center field by Gary Geiger. Following the game, Wilson commented, "Honestly, I didn't think I had as good as stuff as I had in other games I've had this year. I never had any idea anything like this would ever happen to me. The good man was with me tonight." Owner Yawkey gave Wilson a $1,000 bonus for his achievement, declaring, "I am more excited now than I was during Mel Parnell's no-hitter as Wilson is just arriving at what could be a brilliant career."

The victory was Wilson's sixth of the season. He went on to finish the year with a 12–8 won-lost record with a 3.90 ERA. He pitched 191.1 innings. For the first time his strikeouts outnumbered his walks (137–111). It was also in 1962 that Wilson became one of the first professional athletes to have an agent represent him in contract negotiations. It occurred as a result of a minor accident in which Earl was involved. He was referred to a young lawyer by the name of Bob Woolf. The association of Woolf with Wilson marked the start of Woolf's career as a sports agent. It worked out well for both parties as besides being involved in contract discussions for Earl, Woolf also achieved several endorsement deals for the player.

Wilson's next few seasons saw his won-lost record reflect the overall ineptitude of the Red Sox. In 1963, he earned 11 victories and 16 defeats. Still, he lowered his ERA to 3.76. He also threw more than 200 innings for the first time in his career.

The 1964 season saw Wilson compile an 11–12 record with a 4.49 ERA. He once again had more than 200 innings of work. In the 1965 season Earl had 13 wins to lead the Red Sox. He had 14 losses with an ERA of 3.98 and threw 230.2 innings. He gave up 77 walks but struck out 164 opposing hitters. Two of the highlights of that season for Earl occurred in August. On August 16 he hit two home runs but ended up losing the game 5–4 to the Chicago White Sox. On August 25, he struck out 13 Washington Senators in an 8–3 victory.

Early 1966 saw an event occur that had a monumental effect on the rest of Wilson's life. During spring training, while in Lakeland, Florida—the spring home of Wilson's next team, the Detroit Tigers—Wilson and a couple of his teammates, Dennis Bennett and Dave Morehead, decided to go to a local bar named the Cloud 9 for a drink after a day at the park. In Bennett's words he describes what happened that night: "The bartender asked Dave and I what we wanted. He then turned to Earl and said, `We don't serve niggers in here.' So we all got up and left the place. Earl was upset at first as he had never been refused service before."

Author Peter Golenbock, in his book *Red Sox Nation*, wrote that incidents such as this tended to bring negative publicity to the team rather than to the racist attitudes in the South. Wilson understood this was the case and although he revealed the incident to Boston writer Larry Claflin, he asked that the writer keep it to himself and not write about it. Claflin agreed but another writer found out about it and instead of exposing the racism of the incident focused his story on the Red Sox players going out drinking.

Most observers—including Wilson, according to his son—felt this incident was the reason the Red Sox decided to deal him. To Earl the writing was on the wall when on June 13, the Red Sox acquired two black players, John Wyatt and Jose Tartabull. That night, Earl told his roommate

Lenny Green, who was also an African American, "There are too many black players on the team, someone will have to go!" The next morning manager Billy Herman informed Wilson that that he and a black outfielder, Joe Christopher, had been traded to Detroit for veteran outfielder Don Demeter and a player to be named later (a week afterward, Detroit shipped reliever Julio Navarro to the Bosox). Earl at the time had appeared in 15 games with the Sox that season and had a 5–5 record. His ERA was 3.84. Although upset at first, Earl quickly rebounded and went on to post a 13–6 record for the Tigers to finish the year with 18 wins overall and a sparkling Tigers ERA of 2.59. As it turned out, the trade was one-sided in the Tigers' favor with Demeter retiring at the end of the 1967 season.

For Wilson, though, 1967 was without doubt his finest season. He appeared in 39 games and led the Tigers with 22 wins against just 11 defeats. He also racked up 184 strikeouts. Detroit finished the season just one game behind the "Impossible Dream" Red Sox.

The 1968 season saw the Tigers capture the American League pennant, dominating their opponents. They finished 12 games ahead of their nearest rival, the Baltimore Orioles. Besides Wilson, who finished with a 13–12 record and a 2.85 ERA, Detroit also had Denny McLain win 31 games and Mickey Lolich win 17. Wilson tied his career high with seven home runs during the season. In the World Series, the Tigers came from behind to take the fall classic over St. Louis in seven games. Earl pitched the third game of the Series, going 4.1 innings. He gave up three runs, all earned, on four hits and six walks. He had three strikeouts. The Tigers went on to lose the game 7–3. It was Earl's only appearance in the Series.

In 1969, Wilson had his last winning season as a pitcher. He finished with a 12–10 record and a 3.31 ERA. He also pitched more than 200 innings for the last time. The Tigers finished the year in second place, 19 games behind the pennant-winning Orioles.

During his final season in Detroit, Earl was involved in one of the most unusual plays ever to occur in baseball. On April 25, 1970, in a game against the Twins, Wilson swung and missed on a pitch for what appeared to be the third out. The umpire believed the catcher had trapped the ball and did not call Wilson out. Not realizing this, the catcher rolled the ball toward the mound and the Twins began to leave the field. Earl started running around the bases and before the Twins recovered he had rounded third. He tried to get back to third but ended up getting tagged out by the left fielder. It probably was the only strikeout ever to be recorded in the scorebook as 7–6–7. The 1970 season was his final one in the majors.

When he was sold to the San Diego Padres July 15, his record was 4–6 with an ERA of 4.41. The Padres were a terrible club that season and finished the year with 99 losses. Earl's record with the Padres was 1–6 with an ERA of 4.85. He was subsequently released by the Padres on January 13, 1971, at which time he promptly retired from baseball.

In 11 seasons in the big leagues, Wilson had a 121–109 (.526) record. His lifetime ERA was 3.69 and he had 1,452 strikeouts, a rate of better than six for every nine innings pitched. He was a dangerous hitter as well. He had 35 home runs in 740 at bats—a ratio of one homer for every 21 at-bat. (a ratio many regulars would covet). Two of his home runs occurred in the role of a pinch-hitter. He was such a good hitter that Tigers broadcaster Ernie Harwell commented in Wilson's obituary that appeared in the *San Diego Union-Tribune* that he recalled Wilson pinch-hitting on numerous occasions. Former Tigers catcher Bill Freehan commented in the same story that Earl was a better hitter than some in the regular Tiger lineup.

Upon his retirement, Wilson decided to move back to Detroit for several reasons. Detroit was one of the few areas that he had been where blacks actually owned businesses rather than being employees. He also remembered the summers he had spent picking strawberries on his grandfather's farm as a reason he did not return to his Louisiana birthplace. In fact, Earl was just more comfortable in Detroit than anywhere else. His greatest success as a major leaguer happened there and the area had a large number of successful middle-class blacks, many of whom were also entrepreneurs. In a book published by the *Detroit Free Press* titled *The Corner: A Century of Memories at Michigan and Trumbull*, Wilson made the following comment: "Back home in Louisiana, I had never seen black people who owned businesses. When I came to Detroit, I saw this. They had big homes. Just a lot of things I wasn't accustomed to. I just fell in love with the Tigers and knew this was the place I wanted to be."

Moving back to Michigan, Wilson established the Earl Wilson Company, which repaired forklift trucks for the Big Three automakers. He later started Auto Tech Fillings, a company that manufactured a substance that stopped echoes from occurring inside automobiles.

By 1989, Wilson had decided that he once again wanted to be involved in baseball but not in the usual way. He joined the Baseball Assistance Team (BAT) because he had a strong desire to help former major league baseball players and their families who were not as fortunate as he was. After three years in the organization, Earl was elected its vice president, and in 2000 he was elected president, holding the position until 2004. The organization was formed to provide assistance, especially to those who played before salaries or pensions were as generous as they are now. The assistance BAT offers takes many forms including health care, financial grants to those in need, rehabilitative counseling, or whatever is required to attain comfort and dignity for former ballplayers and their families.

According to BAT officials at Major League Baseball headquarters, Wilson was a very active member of the group. Besides holding executive positions, he helped raise financial contributions in a variety of ways, including the Earl Wilson Celebrity Golf Tournament, which ran for five years. Ted Sizemore, the current BAT president in 2007, said, "Earl was one of a kind. As a former ballplayer, he knew how important it was to help one of our own and that's why he became involved with BAT and excelled in his duties as president and CEO."

In 2002, as BAT president, Earl returned to Boston to attend the memorial service for Ted Williams. According to Earl's son Greg, Wilson thought a lot of Teddy Ballgame. One of the few pieces of baseball memorabilia Wilson kept was a Ted Williams autographed baseball.

The world lost Robert Earl Wilson April 23, 2005, to a heart attack at his home in Southfield, Michigan, at age 70. In the words of ESPN announcer and Hall of Famer Joe Morgan, "I appreciated how he cared about former baseball players who were facing tough times. His death was not a loss for just his family but also for all of baseball."

References

Publications

Golenbock, Peter. *Red Sox Nation*. Chicago: Triumph Books. 2004.

Nowlin, Bill. *Mr. Red Sox: The Johnny Pesky Story*. Cambridge, Mass.: Rounder Books. 2004.

Stout, Glen and Richard Johnson. *Red Sox Century*. Boston: Houghton Mifflin. 2004.

Articles

Boston Globe, April 26, 2005.
San Diego Union-Tribune, April 25, 2005.

Web Sites

www.baseballlibrary.com/baseballlibrary/ballplayers/W/Wils
www.baseballreference.com
www.boston.com/sports/baseball/redsox/articles/2005/04/26
www.fergiejenkinsfoundation.org/13
www.insider.espn.go.com/columns
www.1967alpennant.com/1967-tiger-retrospective-earl-wilson/
www.ponchatoula.com
www.wikipedia.org/wiki/Earl_Wilson
www.retrosheet.org
www.signonsandiego.com/uniontrib/20050426/news

Other Sources

Interviews with Greg Lawrence, son of Earl Wilson.
Interviews with the Office of the Baseball Assistance Team, New York.

Rich Shook presents:

Tigers In the News

Saturday, September 28
Denny McLain made his final tune-up for the World Series but failed in his bid for his 32nd victory. He went the first seven innings, allowing no runs on two hits, and Don McMahon (5-2) took the loss in relief. Stanley had Detroit's lone RBI, a single in the seventh that gave Detroit the lead in a game it lost, 2-1. He played mistake-free ball again.

Sunday, September 29
"The shortstop," Mayo Smith told reporters when they entered the clubhouse following Detroit's season-ending 3-2 loss to Washington, "will be Mickey Stanley." The loss left Detroit with a 103-59 record for 1968 and the club exceeded 2 million in attendance for the first time. "Now don't ask me why, that's all," Smith said of his decision. "This is not done for sentiment to get an Al Kaline into the lineup. I want you to understand that. I just want to get an extra bat in the lineup." Stanley hit .259, much better than Mayo's shortstop alternatives, yet he did not make an error all year in center field. Now he would be asked to play an unfamiliar position on the biggest baseball stage of all. "I would no more put any undue pressure on Mickey Stanley if I didn't think he could do the job. He has indicated in the last three days he can do the job. Away from the bag he handles things pretty well, but up in close to it, that's where he has his problems," Smith declared. "I'm really happy he had enough confidence to try me there," Stanley said. "If he wasn't afraid, I shouldn't be." Bill Freehan and Norm Cash hit RBI singles in the first but Detroit didn't score again. Mickey Lolich and Earl Wilson each pitched four innings with Pat Dobson (5-8) taking the loss in the ninth. Smith announced he was pitching Lolich in the second game of the Series. Smith also announced the Tigers were dropping Wyatt from the World Series roster in favor of veteran Mathews, who missed most of the season due to back surgery. Also not eligible for the World Series was veteran relief pitcher Roy Face, who worked just two innings for the Tigers in September.

John Wyatt

by Andrew Blume

Season	Age	W	L	Pct	G	GS	CG	SV	IP	H	R	ER	BB	SO	ERA
1968 Tigers	33	1	0	1.000	22	0	0	2	30.1	26	9	8	11	25	2.37
Career Totals		42	44	.488	435	9	0	103	686.2	600	290	265	346	540	3.47

Reliever John Wyatt may have been considered a journeyman reliever in his day, but his journeys led him to two fortuitous stops. One was in Boston, where he anchored the bullpen of the "Impossible Dream" Red Sox, which came within one game of winning their first World Series in nearly a half-century. The next year, Wyatt found himself in Detroit as a bullpen contributor in the Tigers' drive to the AL pennant. Though Detroit won the World Series that was denied Boston, Wyatt was not on the 25-man roster for the fall classic

Johnathon Thomas Wyatt Jr. was born April 19, 1935, in Chicago. He graduated from Hutchinson High School in Buffalo, New York, in 1953, though it certainly wasn't an easy life. When he was 16, he worked racking balls in a billiards parlor and became a pretty good player (on a four-hour layover in Atlanta on the way to his first spring training, he won $300). Soon after, he took on a much more demanding job, Wyatt told Will McDonough: "I worked in a steel mill from 11 at night until 7 in the morning. I'd go right from work to school. After school I practiced football and wouldn't get home until 6:30. Then I'd sleep four hours and my mother would wake me up to go to work in the steel mill again." He added, "I did most of my sleeping in school."

His professional baseball career began in the Negro Leagues, starting with the Indianapolis Clowns of the Negro American League from 1953 to 1955. The 1954 Clowns, managed by Hall of Famer Oscar Charleston in the final year of his career, won the Negro American League title. In 1954, Wyatt was signed as an amateur free agent by the St. Louis Cardinals, the franchise he would later face in the 1967 World Series. Offered a $1,000 bonus, he leapt to sign. "I never had seen that kind of money in one lump sum and I wasn't going to let it get away," he reminisced. In 1954, he compiled a 12–11 record with a 5.08 ERA in 156 innings for Hannibal of the Class D Mississippi-Ohio Valley League. In 1955, though, he spent the whole year playing again for the Clowns, having been released by the Cardinals.

In April 1956, Wyatt was sent by the Indianapolis Clowns to the Milwaukee Braves, where he appeared in a pair of games for Jacksonville of the Class A South Atlantic (Sally) League. He was returned to Indianapolis in May and then compiled a 4–3 record and 4.14 ERA in 17 games for the unaffiliated El Paso club of the Class B Southwestern League. In July, he was sold by El Paso to the Kansas City Athletics organization and was 2–8, 8.84 for the A's Pocatello club of the Class C Pioneer League. Wyatt served in the military during the 1957 and 1958 seasons. In 1959, he was 1-6, 5.55 in 19 games for Albany in the Single A Eastern League and 4–4, 3.41 in 74 innings for Sioux City of the Class B Three I League over 26 games.

The 1960 season was Wyatt's last full season in the minor leagues. He was 1–2, 5.21 in 38 innings for Dallas-Fort Worth of the Triple A American Association, 4–6, 4.55 in 79 innings for Monterrey of the Mexican League, and 2–2, 3.66 in four games for Sioux City. He described his Mexican League experience in Bill Reynolds' *Lost Summer*: "It was bad down there. Bad baseball. Bad lights. Bad everything. It was as bad as when I was playing in the Negro Leagues, playing as much as three games a day. The ball had raised seams, and one day my finger blistered and began to bleed. When I told the manager I couldn't continue, he took a poke at me. Just as I pulled my fist back to let him have it, nine Mexican guys stood up. 'Cool it, man' they said. I cooled it."

In 1961, Wyatt earned his ticket to the show with Portsmouth of the Sally League. In 52 games, he struck out 91 and gave up only 87 hits in 101 innings, posting a 9–3 record and a 3.13 ERA. On Friday night, September 8, 1961, he made his major league debut for the Kansas City Athletics against the Minnesota Twins at K.C.'s Municipal Stadium. He entered the game in the eighth inning to face Bob Allison and retired him on a foul pop to the catcher. After walking Joe Altobelli, he recorded his first strikeout, fanning Earl Battey. In the ninth, Zoilo Versalles earned the first hit allowed by Wyatt in his major league career. Wyatt wound up finishing the game, and earned what is now called a save, shutting out the Twins over two innings in a 6–4 win. Wyatt appeared in 7.1 innings over five September games for Kansas City. Over the next six seasons, he averaged more than 64 appearances a season. Wyatt established himself as the workhorse of the A's bullpen. In 1962, he made the only nine starts of his major league career, establishing his career high in strikeouts with 106 in 125 innings. In 59 games, Wyatt was 10–7, with a 4.46 ERA and 11 saves. Ten victories were his one-season high, a number he matched in 1967. In 1963, he was 6–4 with a 3.13 ERA and a career-high 21 saves.

In 1964, Wyatt appeared in 81 games, a major league record at the time. Wyatt recorded a 9–8 record with a 3.59 ERA and 20 saves. He gave up only 111 hits in a career-high 128 innings. He pitched three innings or more in relief 10 times during that season. He was named for the only time in his career to the American League All-Star team. In a 7–4 loss to the National League, Wyatt came on in the fourth inning in relief of Dean Chance and had a less than stellar outing: Billy Williams and Ken Boyer homered, accounting for the two runs Wyatt allowed in his single inning.

In 1965, Wyatt was 2–6 with a 3.25 ERA and 18 saves in 88.2 innings over 65 games. In 1966, Wyatt pitched poorly and lost the primary reliever role to Jack Aker (8–4, 1.99 ERA, 32 saves). Wyatt was 0–3 with a 5.32 ERA in 19 games. Meanwhile, in Boston, ace reliever Dick Radatz had been equally disappointing, carrying an 0–2 mark with a 4.74 ERA in 16 games. On June 2, 1966, Radatz was traded by the Red Sox to the Cleveland Indians for Don McMahon and Lee Stange. The Sox followed up on June 13 with the acquisition of Wyatt, Rollie Sheldon, and José Tartabull from the A's for Jim Gosger, Ken Sanders, and Guido Grilli, securing additional help for the bullpen. McMahon and Wyatt split the important relief duties during the balance of the 1966 season with McMahon going 8–7 with a 2.65 ERA and nine saves in 49 games and Wyatt posting numbers of 3–4, 3.14, and eight saves in 42 games.

The 1967 Red Sox were much more potent at the plate than on the mound, though much of this can be explained by the hitter-friendly ballpark they called home. The Sox offense led the league in average (.255), slugging (.395), runs (722), hits (1,394), and home runs (158). The pitching staff finished eighth in the 10-team American League with a 3.36 ERA. The league ERA that year was 3.23, with the White Sox the front-runners, thanks to their impressive staff ERA of 2.45. Crucial to keeping the pitching afloat and the team in pennant contention were the starting of Jim Lonborg and the finishing of John Wyatt. Wyatt, acting as Boston's ace reliever in '67, appeared in 60 games during the pennant drive, finishing 43, saving 20, and finishing fourth on the staff with 10 wins.

It wasn't a smooth start for Wyatt in 1967 as he failed to endear himself to rookie skipper Dick Williams by hitting the hot-swinging Tony Conigliaro on the left arm with a fastball in batting practice during spring training. But as Wyatt heated up, it gave the team the luxury of trading McMahon on June 2 to the White Sox along with minor leaguer Bob Snow in exchange for infielder Jerry Adair, who would become a clutch performer for the '67 AL champs. Wyatt helped stabilize the pitching staff in a year in which Jim Lonborg threw 273.1 innings in 39 starts, winning 22. After Lonborg, there was a huge dropoff in starts, innings pitched, and wins. Lee Stange and Gary Bell were the only other starters with more than 20 starts (each had 24), though Bell had only been acquired on June 4. Stange was second on the staff in innings with 181.2. After Lonborg, only three other Red Sox pitchers recorded 10 or more wins: Bell (12), José Santiago (12), and Wyatt (10). In contrast, the 1967 Cardinals had much more balance and stability in their starting rotation. Five Cards pitchers recorded 23 or more starts. Six pitched 152 or more innings. Five won 10 or more games. Wyatt's worth to the Sox was great in terms of filling a gap in the starting rotation.

The right-handed Wyatt, weighing in at 200 pounds and measuring a half-inch shy of 6 feet, appeared in 60 games in 1967, including 17 in August and 10 in September, compiling a record of 10–7 with a 2.60 ERA (1.45 on the road) in 93.1 innings with 20 saves (10 at home, 10 on the road). He allowed only 71 hits and six home runs, striking out 68 and walking 39. He held opposing hitters to a .217 average (right-handed batters hit only .205). He pitched more than one inning in 33 of his appearances. Four times, he pitched three or more innings in relief, including 5.2 innings against the A's on April 29 and four innings against the Yankees on August 30.

On April 29 at Fenway Park, he threw 5.2 scoreless innings in a 15-inning, 11–10 win over the A's, won on a José Tartabull single that scored Tony Conigliaro and George Scott. Wyatt's outing, according to Ken Coleman in *The Impossible Dream Remembered*, led Kansas City manager Alvin Dark to complain about Wyatt's alleged Vaseline ball. Wyatt's out pitch was alleged to have been a Vaseline-assisted forkball. According to Glenn Stout and Richard A. Johnson in *Red Sox Century*, Wyatt had "think" written on four of the fingers of his glove. On the fifth finger was written "When in doubt—Use Forkball."

Bill Reynolds wrote in *Lost Summer: The '67 Red Sox and the Impossible Dream* that the Vaseline charges originated, according to Wyatt, from ex-White Sox manager Al Lopez. Wyatt is reported to have said: "In a doubleheader they beat me in the first game and I saved the second. That's when Al Lopez claimed I was doctoring the ball. 'How come you didn't say that in the first game?' I asked him. It's only when I win that anyone accuses me of anything illegal. The only time I ever threw a spitter was against Yaz. He hit it off the scoreboard. I never threw another spitter." Later in the season, the Yankees' Joe Pepitone groused, in the words of Reynolds, that "Wyatt has so much Vaseline on him that if he slid into second base he would keep right on going until he hit the outfield fence." Jim Prime and Bill Nowlin lend some credence to the Vaseline allegations in *More Tales from the Red Sox Dugout*: "Caught in a rundown between third and home, pitcher John Wyatt dropped several items from his Sox pitching jacket. The excess baggage included a tube of Vaseline, a pack of cigarettes, and his car keys. We're not sure what Sherlock Holmes would deduce from those clues, but possibly, Wyatt was up to no good."

Wyatt had two appearances in the 1967 World Series against the Cardinals. In the Series opener on October 4 at Fenway Park, Wyatt relieved starter José Santiago, who had held St. Louis to single runs in the third and seventh and supplied the only Red Sox score with a third-inning homer off Bob Gibson. Wyatt set the Cards down in order in the eighth, striking out Julian Javier. In the ninth, he surrendered two walks and committed a balk but completed his second inning of scoreless, hitless relief in the 2–1 Red Sox loss.

Wyatt's second appearance in the Series, in Game 6 on October 11 in Boston, was not as impressive as his first but was far more meaningful in the end result. Starter Gary Waslewski had held the Cards to a pair of third-inning runs in 5.1 innings on the hill. Rico Petrocelli homered in the second off Cardinals starter Dick Hughes. In the fourth, Yastrzemski led off with a homer. After Harrelson and Scott were retired, Smith and Petrocelli sent Hughes to the showers with solo homers for a 4–2 Red Sox lead (the three homers hit by the Red Sox in the inning set a World Series record that still stands). Wyatt entered the game with runners on first and second with one out in the sixth. He got Mike Shannon to pop to the shortstop and Javier to ground out to third to end the Cardinals' threat. However, in the seventh, Wyatt walked Bobby Tolan and surrendered a one-out game-tying homer to Lou Brock. He retired Curt Flood and Roger Maris to avoid any further damage. In the Red Sox' seventh, reliever Jack Lamabe retired Howard on a grounder to third. Jones, batting for Wyatt, singled to right. Foy doubled Jones home, going to third on the throw to the plate. Joe Hoerner succeeded Lamabe on the hill. Mike Andrews singled to left, scoring Foy. Yastrzemski singled Andrews to third. Larry Jaster entered the game in relief and pinch-hitter Adair got Andrews home with a fly to center. Scott singled to left and Smith singled Yastrzemski home to give the Red Sox an 8–4 lead, which would hold up as Gary Bell earned the save with two innings of scoreless relief. Wyatt picked up the win, the fourth African American pitcher in history to record a World Series win.

In the off-season before the 1968 season, Bosox skipper Dick Williams is reported by Peter Golenbock in *Red Sox Nation* to have made critical comments about Wyatt. Wyatt attempted to refute the comments in a letter to the *Boston Record American*. Wyatt got off to a slow start in 1968, losing his ace reliever role to Lee Stange and Sparky Lyle. Wyatt appeared in eight games from April 11 through May 16, giving up earned runs in his first four appearances. In posting a 1–2 record with a 4.22 ERA, he allowed nine hits and five earned runs in 10.2 innings. On May 17, 1968, Wyatt was sold to the Yankees. After the trade, Golenbock wrote, Wyatt said, "I been sold not because of my ability, but because of a personal thing. If that man [Williams] is your enemy, forget it." In seven games for New York, Wyatt was 0–2 with a 2.16 ERA. On June 15, he was again sold, this time to the Tigers. In 22 games for pennant-winning Detroit from June 19 through August 24, Wyatt was 1–0 with a 2.37 ERA and two saves in 30.1 innings. He was left off the Bengals' World Series roster in favor of third baseman (and future Hall of Famer) Eddie Mathews, whose back injuries had sidelined him for much of the season.

On April 3, 1969, Wyatt was released by the Tigers and signed April 7 by the Oakland A's. He was 0–1 with a 5.40 ERA in four games for the A's, allowing five earned runs in 8.1 innings. He pitched his final game in the major leagues on May 1, 1969, in a 3–2 loss to the Angels in Anaheim. He threw a scoreless inning in relief of Jim Hunter, retiring Aurelio Rodriguez on a comebacker to conclude his career. He was released on May 27, 1969.

Wyatt finished his big league career with a 42–44 record, 103 saves, and a 3.47 ERA. During his playing career, he had begun work as a real estate developer in Kansas City, Missouri, in the off-season. Wyatt's mother had owned some property in Buffalo and made a living off the rent, so John resolved to do the same. He saved $7,000 over his first seven years in pro ball and built a 12-unit apartment building on East 29th Street in Kansas City. "No one had ever built a new housing facility in Kansas City for Negroes," he told Will McDonough. "It was a long shot, but I'm a long shot player… you can't win if you never take the chance.… The proudest day of my life came with the construction of that building. In one day, I sold three apartments and got a citation from the president [Lyndon B. Johnson]."

He moved to Omaha, Nebraska, in 1987. On April 6, 1998, a couple of weeks why of his 63rd birthday, Wyatt died after a heart attack at his Omaha home. His survivors included his wife, Barbara, four children, three stepchildren, a brother, a sister, and 11 grandchildren.

References

Publications

Clark, Dick, and Larry Lester. *The Negro Leagues Book*. Cleveland: The Society for American Baseball Research. 1994.

Prime, Jim, and Bill Nowlin. *More Tales from the Red Sox Dugout*. Champaign Ill.: Sports Publishing LLC. 2002.

Articles

McDonough, Will. "Sox' John Wyatt Gambled Savings On Dream And Won." *American League News*, July 1967.

Web Sites

www.NLBPA.com, the Negro Leagues Baseball Players Association site

Notes

An earlier version of this biography appeared in *The 1967 Impossible Dream Red Sox: Pandemonium on the Field*, published by Rounder Books.

The Management

Mayo Smith

by David Raglin

Season	Age	G*	W	L	Pct.
1968 Tigers	53	164	103	59	.636
Career Totals		1279	662	612	.520

Note: The wins and losses do not add to the games managed because of ties.
The Tigers had two ties in 1968 and Smith managed in five tie games in his career.

Mayo Smith was a baseball lifer who served the game in many ways in his 38-year career. Except for being the manager of the 1968 World Series champion Detroit Tigers, he was not well-known by the public. However, within the game, he was a very well-known and well-liked figure who had the nickname "America's Guest" for the amount of time he spent in ballpark press rooms during his time as the New York Yankees' superscout. Jerry Green, in his book *Year of the Tiger*, said he and other writers thought of Smith "as a bland man without imagination—just another conservative baseball manager." However, a detailed look at Smith's life shows that Green and his fellow writers missed the mark. Mayo was an innovator throughout his career. He is best known for his signature move of Mickey Stanley to shortstop for the 1968 World Series, but that isn't the only such example.

Edward Mayo Smith was born in New London, Missouri, on January 17, 1915, to Eva Lake Barkley Smith and George Frederick "Fred" Smith. Smith's middle name, Mayo, came from his grandmother, who had been a patient at the Mayo Clinic in Minnesota and liked the name. From a young age, he was known by that middle name. Mayo's family moved to Lake Worth, Florida, near West Palm Beach, when he was 10, and that area was home to him for the rest of his life. He received the nickname "Catfish" during his high school years, after Georgia Bulldogs end Vernon (Catfish) Smith, an All-American in 1931.

As a youngster, Smith excelled in several sports. At age 16, he was a professional billiards player, playing exhibitions against star pool players Ralph Greenleaf and Willie Hoppe. He played high school football in Lake Worth, too.

However, his favorite sport after baseball was clearly golf. At the time he went into pro baseball, he also had chances to become a pro golfer. There are many ties to Smith and golf in baseball publications of the time. Probably the most amusing story took place in 1943 when a sportswriter, not knowing what he was doing, lost a bet to Smith on the links early in the day and, chagrined, made the mistake of challenging him to a game of pool that evening -- and got whipped there, too. He often played in the National Baseball Players Golf Tournament in the spring, reaching the semifinals in 1959. When he was hired to manage the Tigers in late 1966, he had a 10 handicap and lamented, "I love to play golf and I'm at it all winter. From now on, I won't play as much as I'd like to" because of the new job. In 1956, Smith and fellow Lake Worth major leaguer Herb Score were on the tournament committee for the "Cavalcade of Champions" sponsored by the local Exchange Club. After his retirement from baseball, the Mayo Smith Golf Tournament was established at the Atlantis Country Club in Lake Worth to benefit the Palm Beach Junior (now Community) College.

As a youngster, Smith's main position was third base. Although he was right-handed in golf and pool, he was a lefty hitter at the plate. Lake Worth High School did not have a baseball team at the time, so Mayo played for an Elks team in a county league. At age 18, former Cincinnati Reds and St. Louis Browns manager Dan Howley signed Smith to play outfield for the Toronto Maple Leafs of the International League, the highest level of minor league ball. Mayo immediately made a good impression in the 1933 Toronto training camp, and was described in the *Toronto Star* as a player who "appears to have that little something [who] is destined to go places." In fact, legendary St. Louis Cardinals General Manager Branch Rickey attempted to trade for Smith that spring, but was rebuffed by the Leafs. Smith did not have a lot of power but was very fast; there were many references to his speed as a rookie, and he finished second in a team race to Detroit outfield prospect Hub Walker during a team field day in August. However, minor injuries and illness derailed him, and he did not make his official pro debut until July 24, 1933, subbing for a player with a troublesome molar. Smith made a great catch against the wall and got a hit in his debut. However, a hand injury set him back in August, and Smith, seemingly overmatched as an 18-year-old, only went just 3-for-29 (.103) in his first pro season.

Smith was farmed out by Toronto in 1934 to the Wilmington (North Carolina) Pirates of the Class B Piedmont League. He spent most of the 1935 season in Wilmington too—although another illness caused him to miss time—before returning to the Leafs in September. In 1936, the Wilmington team became the Durham Bulls, and Smith spent all season there. He did not show much power in the Piedmont League, hitting only four home runs in his three seasons, but he did hit .315 in 1935 in Wilmington. A broken collarbone limited him to 66 games in 1936.

In 1937, he stuck with Toronto and played three seasons with the Maple Leafs. Again, he was not a big power hitter, slugging just 66 extra-base hits, including nine home runs, over the 1937–1939 seasons. He was traded in the fall of 1939 to the Buffalo Bisons of the International League for John Tyler. That off-season he married the former Louise Otto on March 10, 1940. Two years later, on July 16, 1942, daughter Judith Ann was born.

Mayo spent five seasons (1940–1944) as the Bisons' center fielder, later described by a Buffalo writer as "the happiest days of [Smith's] career." He was a popular player in Buffalo, a Tigers farm team 1941–1944; Bisons fans gave him a "Mayo Smith Day" in his home town of Lake Worth in the spring of 1942. Later, when he managed in Amsterdam, New York, in 1949 and 1950, it was reported that Buffalo fans were often seen at Amsterdam games. Smith crossed paths with the Tigers in his first spring training as a Bison when he made a classic catch against the Tigers in Lakeland off the bat of Hank Greenberg. The line drive went an estimated 475 feet; those who saw it would compare it favorably to the higher-profile catch by Willie Mays in the 1954 World Series. Smith was not called into service during the war because he was married with a child, and later, because of an illness that delayed his major league debut. One of the many friends Mayo made in Buffalo was a fellow named Bob Smith, who later became better known as "Buffalo Bob" Smith, creator and co-star of the *Howdy Doody* TV show.

Smith's best season was 1944, when he won the International League batting title. Manager Bucky Harris made it his goal to help Smith win the title, hitting Mayo second to allow him to hit the ball through the hole. Whether that, or something else, was the reason, Smith hit .340 with eight home runs, 55 RBIs, and 123 runs scored to win the title. His major competition for the title was his roommate, Shovels Kobesky. The respect Mayo earned was evident when Kobesky was quoted as saying, "I got more of a wallop over Mayo Smith winning that batting championship than if I had won it myself." That fall, Smith realized his dream of making the major leagues when Connie Mack drafted him for the Philadelphia Athletics on November 1, 1944.

However, that winter was one of the hardest times in Mayo's life, as he contracted rheumatic fever in February 1945. The prognosis was that he would miss the entire 1945 season, which left Smith heartbroken. He worked through the spring to get back into shape, but he had a relapse June 6. Doctors recommended that he miss the season—and even thought he might never play again—but on June 24, Mayo Smith made his big-league debut for the Philadelphia Athletics. He pinch-hit for Bobby Estalella in the eighth inning of the first game of a doubleheader, went into center field, and was 0-for-1 at the plate. This was a terrible Athletics team; Smith's first game was the sixth loss of a 14-game losing streak, and gave Philadelphia a 20–35 record.

Smith was pretty much a regular after being called up, playing in 73 of the 98 remaining games of the season, including 68 of the final 82 after being inserted into the lineup. He was a regular in left field from July 13 to August 3 before becoming the regular center fielder. Despite having only five doubles and no triples or homers, he batted third 16 times, hitting sixth and seventh most of the rest of the time. In September, after missing about a week, he was inserted into the leadoff spot, where he played for about a week. Mayo played his last game in the majors on September 27, 1945. Playing right field and batting second, he went 1-for-4 and scored a run. It was also the last game of the season for the Athletics, who finished last with a 52–98 record. After the season, Smith and pitcher Steve Gerkin (0–12 for the 1945 Athletics despite a 3.62 ERA) were traded to the Portland Beavers of the Triple A Pacific Coast

League for pitcher Wandel (Lefty) Mossor, who never pitched in the big leagues.

Smith played for Portland from 1946 to 1948. His best year as a Beaver was 1947, when he hit .311 with 30 doubles. His manager in 1946 was former Tiger Marv Owen, and in 1947 Jim Turner, future pitching coach of the New York Yankees, became manager after the Beavers and Yankees established an informal working agreement. Turner recommended Smith to the Yanks, who hired him to manage their team in the Class C Canadian-American League, the Amsterdam Rugmakers. Smith was player-manager in Amsterdam in 1949 and 1950. The Rugmakers went 67–71 to finish fifth in 1949 but moved up to fourth in 1950, going 72–65. As a player, moving down to Class C, Mayo showed he could hit—with a .297 average, 16 home runs, 116 RBI, and 95 runs scored in only 119 games in 1949, including three homers in a doubleheader.

The Yankees promoted Smith to manage the Norfolk Tides of the Class B Piedmont League, in 1951. The Tides won the pennant both years Smith was at the helm; in 1951, they went 81–58, winning the playoffs; in 1952, they went an astounding 96–36, winning the pennant by 26.5 games, but they lost in the first round of the playoffs. Smith was later named to the initial class of the Tidewater Baseball Hall of Fame in 1962.

Mayo continued to move up the Yankees' chain, managing the Double A Birmingham Barons in 1952 and 1953. He posted winning records for both teams, going 78–76 for a fourth-place finish in 1953 and 81–70 to end up third in 1954. There were rumors that when Casey Stengel retired, Smith could be the man to replace him. Stengel said of Smith: "There's one minor [league] manager who comes to our preliminary camps loaded with curiosity and questions. He watches everything and asks about everything. He never forgets. He is headed, for sure, for a big [league] job." Stengel was right.

The Philadelphia Phillies named Smith their manager on October 14, 1954, replacing Terry Moore. He was hired by Roy Hamey, the Phils' general manager, who had gotten to know Mayo from his years assisting Yankees GM George Weiss. Another factor in Smith's favor was his experience as a manager, which interim manager Moore did not have. One of Smith's first moves as Philly manager was to acquire a pitching machine, which was rather new at the time.

The Phillies struggled often in 1955, falling to a 37–48 record at their worst, before rebounding to finish .500 at 77–77, good for fourth place, 21.5 games behind Brooklyn, still better than the 75–79 mark of 1954. In 1956, Smith ran the Phillies' first instructional camp. Unlike today's fall camps, this one was held in the spring, during the last three weeks of February. Forty-four players were in the camp, including future big leaguers Don Cardwell and Dick Farrell.

The 1956 season was tough for Mayo and the Phillies. They started 5–15, but Smith remained patient with his players. On August 8, they were only one game under .500 before another slump consigned them to a 71–83 finish, in fifth place, 22 games behind the Dodgers.

The Phils had their best season under Smith in 1957. In mid-July, for two days they were just percentage points out of first place in a tight five-team race involving Brooklyn, Milwaukee, St. Louis, and Cincinnati. However, they slumped to 5–15 in their next 20 games and never recovered, ending up at .500 again (77–77).

Philadelphia started slow again in 1958 before inching above .500 at 39–38. They then lost their next seven matches and eight of nine, and Phillies management had seen enough. Mayo was fired as manager and replaced by former Phils Whiz Kids skipper Eddie Sawyer.

Smith was rumored to be in line for the Buffalo managerial job, thanks in part to the goodwill he'd built up there during his playing career, as well as the Reds job as early as August. It turned out that the Reds rumors were true, as Cincinnati hired Smith on September 29 to replace interim manager Jimmy Dykes. It was a controversial move, since Dykes had gone 24–17 after replacing Birdie Tebbetts, who'd gone 52–61. The 43-year-old Smith got the job because the Reds wanted a younger man than the 62-year-old Dykes. His record of a fourth place and two fifth-place finishes did not impress the Cincinnati locals. In Cincinnati, he rented Jim Bunning's house while the Kentucky native was off pitching for the Tigers.

Smith needed to start fast in 1959, and he did; the Reds were in first place at 14–9 on May 9, making the move of Frank Robinson to first base look good. They then lost their next four games, and at the All-Star break, they were 35–45, one step above the basement and 10.5 games back, when Smith received bad news for the second straight July: He'd been fired, replaced by his good friend Fred Hutchinson. Hutch and Mayo knew it was happening; shortly before the firing, Hutchinson called Smith to tell him the Reds had offered him the job, but Hutchinson had turned it down out of respect for his friend. Smith told Hutchinson to take it because if he didn't, somebody else would.

Smith did not stay jobless for long. However, his next job was unique. The Yankees hired him in September 1959 for a "field executive" position to serve as a combination advance man and scout of the other league—an important role with the new interleague trading period—basically what are called these days "superscouts." While a superscout, he shared some of his observations with writers and fans; it was not unusual to see a one-line tidbit in a *Sporting News* column giving Mayo's opinion about a player. Smith wrote an article for *Sport* magazine in the summer of 1962 in which he described his job, and he listed "ten stars of tomorrow," who included Lou Brock, then two years away from his trade to the Cardinals and certainly had not shown much. Smith scouted for the Yankees from 1959 until 1966, when he was hired by the Tigers.

While a superscout, he had been mentioned in conjunction with several other jobs. After the 1960 season, broadcaster Harry Wisner said categorically that Casey Stengel would retire and that Smith would replace him. Lee MacPhail listed Smith as one of many candidates for the Baltimore Orioles job after the 1963 season. Certainly the closest Smith came to another major league managerial job was after the 1965 season when he almost replaced the retiring Al Lopez, Smith's good friend, with the Chicago White Sox. In fact, Jerome Holtzman said in *The Sporting News* that Smith would be named manager, even speculating on his coaching choices. Mayo's chances were scuttled in the interview with Sox owner Arthur Allyn. Chicago had finished second for three straight seasons, but Smith said in his interview that the club was not that good and had done that well only because of Lopez' ability, and supposedly asked for a three-year contract. That statement reportedly angered Allyn so much that he rejected the advice of Lopez and club vice president Ed Short and instead gave the job to Eddie Stanky. The 1966 White Sox finished fourth with an 83–79 record.

The 1966 Tigers suffered through a difficult season in which they lost two managers to illness, Charlie Dressen and Bob Swift both dying before the year was out. The second interim manager, Frank Skaff, was not given consideration to keep the job because Tigers General Manager Jim Campbell wanted someone with major league experience. Smith was not Campbell's first choice. The Tigers tried hard to woo Al Lopez back to the dugout after a year away, but he turned the Tigers down. The next choice was the Yankees' Ralph Houk, to whom the Tigers reportedly offered a $100,000 contract. However, the Yankees had finished last in 1966, and Houk did not want to be seen as deserting a sinking ship. The Tigers also tried to lure Bill Rigney from the California Angels, but after consideration, Rigney decided to stay in California. A long phone conversation between GM Campbell and recently retired Casey Stengel fueled rumors that the former Yankee skipper might be coming to Detroit, but given Stengel's knowledge of Smith, it is likely that he was a main topic of their conversation.

Mayo Smith was named manager of the Detroit Tigers on October 3, 1966. He was basically unknown to Tiger fans, who were asking, "Who's Mayo Smith?" His first move as manager was to ask All-Star shortstop Dick McAuliffe, a fine hitter but not a great fielder, to move to second base, and to make Ray Oyler his shortstop. Mayo didn't waste time getting to know his new players. He touched base with Al Kaline, whom he'd known through golf. A meeting with Bill Freehan at the winter meetings went well, with Freehan praising Smith's knowledge of opposing hitters and his direct style. He called many of his new players during the winter to introduce himself. The word on Smith was that he had been too indecisive with the Phillies and Reds, and he worked hard early in camp to dispel those thoughts.

The 1967 Tigers came out of the gate on fire, winning 17 of their first 24 games to put them a half-game ahead of, ironically, the White Sox, the only other club in the league with a winning record. The Tigers had their biggest lead of the season on June 6, when their 31–18 record led the league by two games. After that they faltered, losing 10 of 12, and it became a five-team race for the pennant. The Angels hung around the race; on August 13, they were actually in fourth place, ahead of the Red Sox, 1.5 games back, but a seven-game losing streak to fellow contenders Minnesota and Boston knocked them out of contention.

Smith worked to keep the team in the race by keeping his cool and not overreacting to events. Mayo rarely had team meetings, and after one meeting, some of the veteran players asked if they could have a players-only meeting, and the manager Mayo said yes. He made it clear that it was his club and he was running it. Mayo spent his time helping to build his players' confidence. "The big thing is to not let the guys get down on themselves," he said. "There's nothing you can do about the mistakes you made or the games you lost. You just have to show up for the next game and do a better job." As the race heated up, Smith seemed to be the calmest man in the dugout. He even quit smoking in the summer of 1967. The Tigers were last in first place on September 18; the Red Sox won the pennant on the last day of the season. The consensus was that the bullpen had failed the Tigers, and Mayo was quoted as saying, "Our bullpen was not consistent enough."

Smith said over the winter that rebuilding the bullpen and finding a consistent right-handed pinch-hitter were the main off-season priorities. He succeeded with the pen; only three of the 13 relievers who pitched on the 1967 Tigers were back in 1968, and the bullpen was a strength of the 1968 club. He was not as successful with the pinch-hitter; Al Kaline, with 16 appearances, was the Tigers' main right-handed pinch-hitter. (In fact, Kaline walked and scored the pennant-winning run as a pinch-hitter.)

There was a feeling that Smith was much more serious in 1968 after the close call in 1967. While several preseason forecasters had the Tigers as the bridesmaids, none of them had them winning it all. *The Sporting News* picked the White Sox; *Sporting News* readers and the baseball writers (as a group) picked the Twins.

Dissatisfied with the left-hand hitting Norm Cash at first base, Smith had considered platooning Eddie Mathews (also left-handed), but on Opening Day, it was Mickey Stanley out there. Other first basemen Mayo tried included Freehan and Kaline. Cash had hit only .214 with three home runs in 145 at-bats against left-handers in 1967. Another player whose playing time was cut back was Joe Sparma, perhaps the Tiger who disliked Smith the most.

In the first game of a June 2 doubleheader, Mayo's 582nd game as a major league manager, he was ejected for the first time. In the ninth inning of a 3–3 game, Tom Tresh of the Yankees was out on a play at the plate (later supported by photographic evidence), but plate umpire Bill Kinnamon called him safe to break the tie, and Smith was ejected in the ensuing argument. Five days later, Smith was ejected again in similar circumstances—another play at the plate to break a tie in the ninth—this time involving Mike Paul of the Indians as the runner, Bill Freehan as the catcher, and Jim Honochick as the home plate umpire. However, the result of this game was different as the Tigers came back in the bottom of the ninth to win 5–4.

The Tigers ran away with the American League in 1968. After an Opening Day loss to the Red Sox, they won nine in a row. They were never more than 2.5 games out of first and went into first place to stay on May 10. At the All-Star break, they were up by 9.5 games with a 55–27 record, causing Las Vegas bookmakers to refuse to accept any more bets on the American League race. The Orioles got to within four games on August 27, but three days later, the Tigers expanded their lead to seven games, and a week after that, to nine full games. The Tigers clinched the pennant September 17, beating the Yankees, 2–1.

The big question going into the World Series concerned Al Kaline and how to get him into the lineup. While Kaline was out with a broken arm, the outfield of Willie Horton, Mickey Stanley, and Jim Northrup had helped lead the Tigers to the Series. Smith considered playing Kaline at third base in place of Don Wert, who hit .200 (when carried out to six decimals,.199626) in 1968, before trying Stanley at shortstop. While it was a surprise to see Stanley at short, the clues had been there. Early in the 1967 season, Dick Young had written in *The Sporting News* that Stanley could be Mayo's savior at short, a thought he most likely got from Smith himself. Smith was also asked about Stanley at short in early 1968, and he did not deny the possibility. In the Series, Stanley started every game at short, but Oyler came into the four Detroit wins as a defensive sub, replacing left fielder Willie Horton (Stanley went to center and Northrup to left).

Mayo made two other notable strategic decisions in the Series. He started Earl Wilson in Game 3 in Detroit, even though the right-hander was more vulnerable to the home run in Tiger Stadium than left-hander Mickey Lolich, to get Wilson's bat in the lineup (Wilson had hit seven home runs in 88 at-bats in 1968). Wilson went 0-for-3 in Game 3, but light-hitting Mickey Lolich hit his only major league home run in Game 2 in St. Louis. Perhaps buoyed by the homer, Smith let Lolich hit for himself in Game 5, down 3–2 in the bottom of the seventh with one out and nobody on. Lolich blooped a single to right to start a game-winning three-run rally.

The Tigers won the Series in seven games after being down three games to one, and Detroit had its first World Series championship in 23 years. Mayo was rewarded with *The Sporting News*' Manager of the Year Award and a new two-year contract, the first multiyear contract of his big-league managerial career.

The 1969 season got off to a poor start. On May 4, the Tigers were already seven games behind the Orioles at 11–13. Baltimore would run away with the first American League East Division pennant race. At the All-Star break, the Tigers were 52–41, 11 games behind the O's, and finished the season 90–72, 19 games behind Baltimore after a season-ending 2–1 loss in 10 innings.

After the season, Smith said the players' boycott of spring training hurt the team. "I know the boycott affected everybody when the players reported late, but we had additional problems on the Detroit club because we had won the pennant and the salary negotiations ... took most of spring training," he asserted. While the Tigers tried to avoid complacency, some observers felt that was a major problem. The main reason according to the players was that nobody was going to beat Baltimore, which went 109–53. Bill Freehan, in his diary of the 1969 season, *Behind the Mask*, often discussed how discouraging it was to be chasing a team that did not seem to lose. For example, the Tigers had a seven-game winning streak in early June but gained only one game on Baltimore, going from 9.5 to 8.5 back.

The biggest controversy of the season was the firing of pitching coach Johnny Sain in August. Sain was highly popular with his pitchers and was known for his belief in positive thinking but also for isolating his pitchers from the rest of the team. George Cantor said in the *Detroit Free Press* that "Sain saw his pitchers as delicate, sensitive performers who must be understood and protected. Mayo saw them as playing cards, the 'hot hand,' tools for a specific function." Sain complained that his advice was not being taken by Smith, who kept control of how pitchers were used. Mayo saw it differently. "I don't know to whom he was making these suggestions. They certainly weren't being made to me. In fact, that was the biggest trouble with him. I could never get a straight yes or no answer from him. We would discuss something and it seemed he would be talking all around it, without coming to a point." By the end, Smith and Sain were barely talking, and when Sain complained to the papers, he was fired.

The 1970 season was a disaster for the Tigers. It started in the spring when Denny McLain was suspended for gambling and Freehan's book was published. While the book in general was complimentary of Mayo, the excerpts in the newspaper were not. The Tigers started out strong at 10–3 after an eight-game winning streak, but in less than a month, they were 17–18, 7.5 back. They were back over .500 at 38–33 by the time McLain returned July 1 from his suspension. They were still well over .500 as late as August 23 (68–57) but they only went 11–26 the rest of the way to finish 79–83. As the Tigers headed for their first losing season since 1963 and their worst record since 1960, Smith came under increasing criticism from fans and the press as his players quit on him. It finally came out after he was fired October 2, 1970. Sharing one last drink with the Detroit media, he uncharacteristically lashed out, saying, "The baseball fans in this town are ignorant. They couldn't tell a baseball player from a Japanese aviator. And that's a quote."

What kind of manager was Mayo Smith? He was a low-key person who believed that if he treated the players like men, they would act like men. When that happened, as in 1967 and 1968, it worked. However, he let players walk over him at times. One of the themes throughout Freehan's book is the players' resentment of the privileges given McLain, allowing him to fly solo to team games and even showing up late to the ballpark even on days he pitched. Smith justified his actions by pointing to McLain's record. More than once, players said they wished Smith would chew them out more. The 1967 players-only meeting was initiated by the recently acquired Eddie Mathews because of his disgust at the contempt his new teammates showed toward their manager.

Mayo also seemed to have great confidence in his ability to judge talent and player capabilities. While the Stanley move received the most attention, he was continually moving players to other positions, from Frank Robinson (first base) with the Reds to McAuliffe (second base) and Freehan and Stanley (first base) with the Tigers. Generally, he did it to improve the offense, but not always; the move of McAuliffe to second was for defensive reasons. Mayo was the right manager for the Tigers when he was hired, when they healing after the deaths of two managers in 1966, but General Manager Campbell did the right thing by replacing Smith with the fiery Billy Martin.

Smith reportedly had several opportunities in the game after being fired by the Tigers, including a managerial offer from the Athletics, but his only job after Detroit was a temporary one, scouting the Orioles for the Athletics in preparation for the 1971 playoffs. He retired to his longtime home of Lake Worth as a millionaire thanks to real estate and other investments. In 1974, he became a grandfather for the first time. On November 22, 1977, while enjoying dinner with his family at a restaurant in Lake Worth, he suffered a stroke and, never regaining consciousness, died two days later in Boynton Beach, Florida.

References

Publications

Green, Jerry. *Year of the Tiger: The Diary of Detroit's World Champions.* New York: Coward-McCann. 1969.

Freehan, Bill. *Behind the Mask: An Inside Baseball Diary.* New York: The World Publishing Company. 1970.

1970 Detroit Tiger Media Guide. Detroit: Detroit Tigers. 1970.

Johnson, Lloyd, and Miles Wolff, eds. *The Encyclopedia of Minor League Baseball*, 2nd ed. Durham, N. C.: Baseball America, Inc. 1997.

The Sporting News' 1969 Baseball Guide. St. Louis: The Sporting News. 1969.

Articles

Detroit Free Press and *Detroit News,* September 24, 1966 to October 4, 1966, August 4, 1969 to August 10, 1969, and September 27, 1970 to October 4, 1970.

Philadelphia Inquirer, June 25, 1945 to October 3, 1945.

Smith, Mayo, as told to Joe Reichler, "Ratings of the Major League Stars." *Sport,* July 1962.

The Sporting News, October 20, 1954; October 27, 1954; January 21, 1967; November 9, 1944; December 12, 1945; March 14, 1946; October 27, 1954; January 18, 1956; February 8, 1956; August 2, 1956; October 8, 1956; August 6, 1958; October 15, 1958; April 1, 1959; September 30, 1959; April 20, 1960; June 8, 1960; July 6, 1960; January 4, 1961; February 8, 1961; June 2, 1962; October 12, 1963; October 23, 1965; November 27, 1965; December 25, 1965; June 23, 1966; October 15, 1966; November 19, 1966; January 7, 1967; January 14, 1967; February 25, 1967; March 4, 1967; March 11, 1967; April 15, 1967; July 29, 1967; August 5, 1967; September 2, 1967; October 14, 1967; March 23, 1968; April 13, 1968; October 26, 1968; December 7, 1968; December 14, 1968; October 4, 1969; May 30, 1970; October 17, 1970; December 19, 1970; January 2, 1971; April 17, 1971; May 15, 1971; October 2, 1971; October 23, 1971; January 8, 1972; February 23, 1972; and December 10, 1977.

Toronto Star, March 23, 1933; March 24, 1933; March 27, 1933; July 25, 1933; July 25, 1933; August 11, 1933; September 11, 1933; September 7, 1935; and December 22, 1939.

Web Sites

Mike McCann's Minor League Baseball Page, *http://www.geocities.com/big_bunko/total.htm*

www.baseballreference.com

www.retrosheet.org

Other Sources

Raglin, David. E-mail exchange with Smith family friend Dave Cantley, who relayed my questions to Louise Smith and Judith Wolfe (Mayo's daughter) and their answers back to me.

Raglin, David. Interview with Bob Buege (writer of Eddie Mathews' autobiography).

Jim Campbell

by Jeanne M. Mallett

By the end of 1987 Jim Campbell had set the major league record for most years as a general manager or president of one club (26), the Detroit Tigers. He continued to add to that record as president and CEO until his abrupt dismissal in August 1992. In all, Jim worked for the Tigers for 43 years, his entire career. He often said his first love was the Tigers, and there is little doubt that the Tigers benefited from that dedication.

James Arthur Campbell was born in the small Lake Erie town of Huron, Ohio, February 5, 1924. He was one of two children of Arthur A. and Vanessa Hart Campbell. His father, a salesman, died while Jim was still in high school, several years after he was severely burned in a freak electrical accident. Jim's mother, in addition to raising him and his sister Betty, was a school teacher and later the first woman postmaster for Huron, a post she held for 25 years. Young Jim excelled in athletics at Huron High School. He played six-man football, basketball, and ran track for the Huron Tigers. The school did not have a baseball team, but Jim played baseball for the Huron G's, a local department store team that played teams from nearby towns. Jim went to Ohio State University in 1942 on a football scholarship. He was part of the "Baby Buckeyes" coached by Paul Brown before he interrupted college following his freshman year to serve in World War II with the Naval Air Corps. Discharged in October 1945, Jim returned to Ohio State in 1946 and graduated in 1949 with a BS degree in commerce (now business administration). This time at OSU Jim's main sport was baseball. He was a star outfielder for the Buckeyes, lettering three straight years, and batting a respectable .271 his senior year. But, as his lifelong friend and classmate, Dick Klein, noted, Jim already knew that what he wanted was a career in the management end of baseball. In December 1949 he got his first break—the only break he would ever need. A local Huron businessman with connections to then-Detroit Tigers General Manager Billy Evans got Jim an interview. Evans hired Campbell as business manager of the Tigers' Class D farm team in Thomasville, Georgia, for the 1950 season.

The challenge presented the new business grad was one for which his schooling could never have prepared him. The first night of the home season the baseball park burned to the ground. "I thought that was it for me," Campbell later told baseball writer Dan Ewald. But Jim's response to the catastrophe showed the Tigers' organization plenty. He borrowed uniforms to keep the team playing and had the field roped off so ticket admissions could be collected. He then had the stadium rebuilt in record time and, along with the rebuilding, added amenities like a popcorn machine and renovated women's restrooms. The Tigers' bosses were impressed enough to promote Jim the next year to business manager of the Tigers' top farm club, the Toledo Mud Hens. Including the 1952 season as business manager at Buffalo, it took only three years for Jim to get his first organization-wide job as business manager for Detroit's minor league system in 1953. In that post, Jim undertook the building of the Tigertown complex at the Tigers' spring training site in Lakeland, Florida. He personally designed the buildings, dormitories, and diamonds. Though built in 1953, Tigertown is still considered one of the finest spring training facilities in major league baseball.

When Campbell began his rise through the Detroit organizational ranks, the team was still owned by the Briggs family. Jim faced a second critical point in his career when the Briggs heirs sold the team to an 11-man syndicate. Jim later told Dan Ewald, "We were just like the fans. We didn't know what to expect. There were so many owners; it looked like most just wanted to be around a major league team. They wanted to make decisions about things they really knew nothing about." Jim did not need to worry. Instead of a setback the arrival of new ownership proved to cement Jim's relationship with the Tigers for the rest of his career. Once the dust settled and John Fetzer emerged as the lead owner of the group and later the primary owner, Campbell's future was assured. He became overall business manager in May 1957 at age 33. A year later Fetzer named him vice-president in charge of farm operations, making Jim one of the youngest men at the time to hold an officer's job at the major league level. After a disastrous experience with veteran baseball man Bill DeWitt running the operation, Fetzer installed himself as president with Rick Ferrell as interim GM. After looking at all his options, Fetzer took a risk, naming Campbell general manager—the office with which his name later became synonymous in Tigers lore. Jim Campbell was 38.

To fully appreciate the boldness of Fetzer's move, it is necessary to know that in 1962, when Jim was named to the post, the general manager was the chief policy maker. General managers, not the owners, ran the whole show, from signing and trading players to deciding ticket prices and choosing ballpark food. It was a time, Dan Ewald wrote, "when any baseball executive under 40 was considered to be just a greenhorn learning the intricacies of the game." Fetzer himself told Ewald that when he started his search for a new permanent general manager he thought Jim was "about ten years away" from being able to step in and run the ballclub. But Fetzer soon recognized that Campbell "demonstrated an ability to take charge. He knew our whole system. He knew the game. And more than anything else, Jim Campbell was probably the most honest man I had ever encountered." Fetzer never regretted his choice. The two worked together to build the Tigers into a winning franchise and keep the team competitive for 21 years, until Fetzer sold the team to Tom Monaghan, who wisely left the team in Jim's capable hands until shortly before he sold the team to Mike Ilitch in 1992. John Fetzer set down three basic principles to guide the team's operations: Stay competitive; build from within; and don't lose money in the process. Jim Campbell implemented those principles. But it was the way he implemented them that made his reputation as one of the great baseball executives of all time. He proved that the traditional small-town values he had brought with him from Huron—honesty, integrity, loyalty and hard work—could produce and maintain a successful major league franchise even in the modern era.

One of Campbell's first and most difficult tasks was not purely in the baseball realm. John Fetzer ordered Jim to make certain that all Tiger players were treated equally regardless of race. Although the Tigers had had black major league players since the late 1950s and had integrated their farm system with future major league prospects without regard to race, black major league players and their families still had to deal with segregation when they went to spring training in Florida. They had the choice of staying with local black families or living at the integrated Tigertown complex. They could not eat at area restaurants. As the civil rights movement grew in intensity in the early 1960s, Fetzer determined that he wanted to be on the right side of history. Yet he knew the situation could be explosive. Jim brought together the mayor of Lakeland, members of the city commission, and the Lakeland Chamber of Commerce. The deal he negotiated required the local Holiday Inn, close to where the major league team trained, to house all major league players on a nonsegregated basis starting with spring training in 1963. The talks also yielded concessions to integrate dining establishments in the area. Typically, Campbell's report to his boss gave the credit to others: "All of these men have recognized this problem, not only with baseball, but in other enterprises. ... They feel the time has come when they want to take a stand."

Fetzer's gamble with Campbell was soon rewarded on the baseball field as well. Jim built the Tigers into consistent winners in only three seasons and world champions in six. The 1968 Tigers were built around homegrown talent. Joining veterans like Al Kaline and Dick McAuliffe were the likes of pitchers Denny McLain, Mickey Lolich, and John Hiller, and in the field, Mickey Stanley, Jim Northrup, Willie Horton, Gates Brown, and Bill Freehan, all Detroit farm products. These Tigers were a far cry from the "Fat Cats" of the 1950s, so named because they were overpaid and underperforming, consistently finishing below .500 and out of contention in the American League. Starting with his years as head of the farm system, Jim Campbell had developed an eye for talent—and just the right kind of talent to make the Tigers winners. *New Yorker* writer Roger Angell paid tribute to both general managers in describing the teams in this last "pre-inflationary, pre-playoff" World Series as "deep, experienced and exciting teams, whose individual attributes were admirably designed for the dimensions of their home parks—the Cardinals, the defending world champions, quick on the bases, brilliant in defense, knowing in the subtleties of the cutoff, sacrifice, and hit-and-run; the Tigers a band of free-swingers who had bashed a hundred and eighty-one homers and could eschew the delicate touch in the knowledge that their runs would come, probably late and in clusters." When the Tigers capped off their comeback from a three-games-to-one deficit to capture the Series with a win over the previously indomitable Bob Gibson, Jim Campbell, as the architect of that team, stood at the pinnacle of his profession. Recognizing his accomplishment, *The Sporting News* named him Major League Baseball Executive of the Year for 1968.

Just as he reached the heights, however, Campbell faced new challenges. Baseball was changing. Continued expansion, playoffs, and free agency altered the staid baseball world. But Campbell, although a baseball traditionalist until his death, managed not only to survive but prosper in the new environment. It was Campbell's style, and Fetzer's, not to snow Tiger fans with a lot of promotions and gimmicks. The Tigers held few promotions. Jim built the best teams he could, believing that what attracted the fans most was a winning team. Hewing to the Fetzer principles, Campbell continued to keep the Tigers competitive most years, building from within and still turning a profit. There were two 100-loss seasons, in 1975 and 1989, but many more years with exciting teams and races. Despite tight budgets, the Tigers under Campbell finished second seven times, won the American League East titles in 1972 and 1987, and won one more World Series in 1984. The 1984 team, like the 1968 team, featured a nucleus of players who had grown up in the Tigers' minor league system, among them Lance Parrish, Kirk Gibson, Alan Trammell, Lou Whitaker, Jack Morris, and Dan Petry. At the postgame celebration following the 1984 World Series victory, Campbell told a Detroit newspaper reporter, "You know, a lot of guys have been in baseball for 34 years like I have and have never won anything. To win a league championship and a World Series is anyone's goal. But it's a long grind. You take a lot of heat. But the reward in the end is worth it all."

While some general managers promoted, marketed, and bought high-priced free agents to attract fans and build champions, Jim Campbell stayed true to his principles. In choosing this path his own personal values helped him. John Fetzer was not the only man who thought Jim Campbell was the most honest man he knew. Although jokingly called "Buddha" because of his premature baldness, round face, and beer belly, Jim was anything but inscrutable. Tigers Hall of Famer Al Kaline said when Jim died, "one thing I'll never forget is how totally honest he was. You didn't need a signed contract, a handshake was just as good." Even the media, who were often critical of his decisions and with whom he had little patience, admired this quality.

Longtime Tigers broadcaster Ernie Harwell praised Jim: "To the media he is one of the most trusted of all sports executives. His honesty and integrity have never been questioned." *Detroit News* sportswriter Joe Falls noted that, if he got information from a source and wanted to check it with Campbell, Jim would always be truthful, either telling him he was right or saying "I wouldn't use that if I were you."

Campbell's honesty also helped him bridge the gap between labor and management and make the transition to the free agent era. Players trusted him. They felt free to come into his office and collar him at the ballpark or on the team bus just to talk baseball with him. They knew his passion for the game was a great as theirs. But they also knew he would be honest and fair with them regarding their contracts. Players from different eras tell the same story. In 1969 Tigers catcher Bill Freehan, a thoughtful university graduate, felt comfortable enough with Jim to informally negotiate with him while a dispute between the owners and the Major League Baseball Players Association was pending. Once the dispute was settled, they were able to compromise on a figure with just over an hour of man-to-man talk at the ballpark. After his 1976 breakout year the free-spirited and talented young pitcher, Mark "The Bird" Fidrych, who had become a media sensation, had offers from many agents to negotiate million-dollar contracts for him. But Jim Campbell chose a typically low-key, direct approach. Treating Fidrych as he had other players in the past, Jim called him and asked when he wanted to talk contract and whether he was going to get an agent. When Fidrych said he wasn't getting an agent, Campbell was concerned enough to ask the young man who was going to help him. When Fidrych answered that his dad would help, Jim promptly offered to fly Mark's father out to Milwaukee, where the Tigers were playing, so they could all negotiate face-to-face. This impressed Fidrych. Even more impressive to him was that the minute he saw the contract he was able to sign it. In his own inimitable style Fidrych related to author Tom Clark: "He had what I wanted. It was weird. It was like we—like he already knew what my mind was talking about before I even got in there." In typical Campbell fashion, after the signing, they all spent the rest of the meeting talking baseball. Even Sparky Anderson claimed he signed his contracts with Jim without reading them. All he would ask was whether what they had talked about was in the contract. When Jim said it was, Sparky signed. "He wasn't going to lie to me," Sparky said. "He wasn't going to cheat. He didn't know how to. When Jim Campbell gave his word, it was like the tablets that Moses brought down from the mountain."

Another quality of Campbell's too infrequently seen in powerful men was his loyalty and ability to let others do their jobs without interference. He demanded loyalty and was a tough boss, setting a high standard of work and commitment. But he was loyal as well, not only to John Fetzer and later Tom Monaghan above him, but to those who worked for him. These qualities made it possible for him to snare Sparky Anderson, already a proven field general, as the manager to guide the Tigers in a run that eventually led to the 1984 world championship. Sparky wrote in his memoir *Bless You Boys*: "Throughout all my days with Cincinnati, everyone told me there was no better general manager in baseball than Jim. He's the one man everyone wants to work for. That's because he lets you do your job. He's a real man's man." Campbell also showed that loyalty under difficult circumstances. Shortly after Jim moved himself up to chairman of the board and CEO, ceding the Tigers' presidency to former University of Michigan football coach Glenn "Bo" Schembechler, Bo fired the popular Ernie Harwell at the end of the 1990 season. Despite media criticism and fan outrage that lasted months, Campbell did not overrule Schembechler. Other teams' executives admired Jim's ability to attract loyal staff. One of them, Roland Hemond, noted that the Tigers under Jim were a very consistent organization: "People were still there decades after you met them. That's a credit to leadership." Jim's staff worked long hours with no overtime. Although they were required to be in early each morning and stay until after each game ended, they respected Jim, and he in turn gave them chances to shine. Jim once told *Detroit Free Press* sportswriter George Puscas: "I was grateful that my bosses gave me opportunities and responsibilities and I like to do that with my people."

Campbell demanded nothing of others that he did not demand of himself. In fact, he demanded the most from himself but claimed never to have regretted it. Although he worked seven days a week throughout the year and took only one vacation that he could remember, he refused to call himself a workaholic. "I enjoy my job too much to be a workaholic," he told Joe Falls in 1985. He did admit to Falls that his love of his work had cost him his marriage. On January 16, 1954, he had married Helene Grace Mulligan, of Lakewood, Ohio, after a brief courtship. In July 1969, only a few months after Jim's triumph with the 1968 Tigers, they divorced. "The Tigers are my whole life. Why kid about it?"
Jim said. "I guess you can say I'm married to the ballclub. My wife always said she was no better than fourth in my life—behind the ball club, Ohio State and my home town of Huron, Ohio. You know something? She was right." Jim never remarried.

The Campbell routine was to arrive at the office each day, in suit and tie, promptly at nine in the morning. His staff was expected to be there at 8:30. Jim felt he owed it to the scouts and other people in the field to be there for their calls. They were working for him, and he was working for them. Only on winter Saturdays and Sundays would he allow himself to come in late, to get things done in the quiet office he could not get done earlier in the week. Jim's dedication to the Tigers led him to reject suggestions that he become president of the American League or even commissioner, posts many more ambitious executives would have coveted.

Jim's loyalty to the Tigers ran deeper than to the organization alone. He told more than one reporter that in the final analysis it was the fans and the importance of baseball to the city of Detroit and the state of Michigan that kept him working. From someone other than Jim Campbell such a statement would have seemed cloying and clichéd. But no one doubted that Jim meant exactly what he said. The motivation to win for the fans helped him make one of his most difficult decisions in 1979. It was one time when he had to choose between two loyalties. Jim had hired career professional Les Moss to manage the Tigers at the beginning of the year. Les had the team playing better than .500 ball and beginning to jell when Jim fired him and replaced him with Sparky Anderson. Jim admitted it was one of the most difficult decisions he ever had to make. He felt, however, that he could not pass up the chance to get Anderson, already a proven winner with the Cincinnati Reds. His intuition proved correct. Sparky arrived promising that within five years he would make the Tigers champions, and he did just that. Although Campbell offered Les Moss another job with the Tigers, Les left the organization—a sad moment for Jim.

The businessman in Campbell recognized that he needed to provide for his own succession. Health problems, including a serious angina attack in 1983, may have hastened his planning. When Tom Monaghan bought the Tigers in 1983, Jim became president and CEO, with Bill Lajoie replacing him as general manager. As early as 1985, Jim told Joe Falls that he didn't want to be one of those persons who stayed on too long. He outlined plans to give

Lajoie more responsibilities and to gradually step aside. In 1990 he named Bo Schembechler president and became chairman of the board and CEO. But, despite his best intentions, he remained effectively in charge. For a man who had spent his life working seven days a week, 365 days a year at a job he loved, the temptation to stay on was too strong.

On August 3, 1992, Tigers owner Tom Monaghan fired both Jim Campbell and his hand-picked president, Bo Schembechler. Monaghan reportedly executed the firings as part of a deal with his fellow pizza magnate, Mike Ilitch, to whom he was selling the club. Ilitch wanted the decks clear for him before he took over to minimize negative publicity for the beginning of his tenure as owner. Once he left the Tigers, Jim Campbell never returned to the ballpark despite numerous invitations and an attempt to have a day in his honor. Reportedly he did not so much regret his own firing but did not like the way his longtime employees were treated by the Ilitch group. Many of them were unceremoniously dumped with little or no warning. Still, he never spoke out against the new owners and continued to follow the Tigers and baseball on television. After leaving the Tigers, Jim divided his time between his home in Dearborn, his retirement condo in Lakeland, Florida, and his home town of Huron, Ohio. He did not take another baseball job.

Jim Campbell died October 31, 1995, little more than three years after his firing. He had had heart problems for years and died a few days after being admitted to the Regional Medical Center in Lakeland. The cause was cardio-pulmonary arrest.

When Campbell died, eulogies came from throughout the baseball world remembering Jim for his honesty, loyalty, and passion for baseball. But Campbell was remembered best and is still remembered by those who knew him the longest: the people of Huron, Ohio. Detroit sportswriters who covered him made little if any mention of his continuing connection to his hometown. They assumed that because of his devotion to his work and his simple lifestyle he had few friends. Yet throughout his life Jim maintained contact with friends he had known since childhood and made new friends in Huron. He visited often, not only to see his mother, who lived into her nineties, but to see old friends. And, anyone who wanted to come up to a ball game in Detroit knew they had only to pick up the phone and call Campbell to find box seats waiting for them. But Jim did more. He had become a wealthy man working for the Tigers. Reportedly, John Fetzer had rewarded his loyalty by giving Campbell a 3 percent stake in the ownership of the Tigers. Jim established a scholarship fund of approximately a million dollars in his mother's name to provide four-year college scholarships based on need and activities for Huron High School graduates. In his will he set aside another $1 million for the fund. Today the fund allows scholarships of $6,000 each year ($24,000 total). In some years as many as twenty four-year scholarships have been awarded to deserving Huron students. It is little wonder that the main street leading to Huron High School has been re-named Jim Campbell Boulevard, in honor of the small-town boy who took the values he learned there and left a legacy that beyond baseball.

The Campbells were of Scottish descent. Nineteenth-century Scottish historian Thomas Carlyle provided the perfect epitaph for Jim Campbell when he said: "Blessed is he who has found his work; let him ask no other blessedness; he has a work, a life-purpose; he has found it and will follow it." Jim Campbell found his work and loved it, and that love benefited many others.

References

Publications

Anderson, Sparky, with Dan Ewald. *Bless You Boys*. Chicago: Contemporary Books. 1984.

Angell, Roger. *The Summer Game*. New York: Popular Library. 1972.

Detroit Tiger Yearbook. Detroit: Detroit Tigers. 1976 and 1984.

Detroit Tiger Scorebook and Official Program. New York City: Professional Sports Publications. 1987.

Ewald, Dan. *John Fetzer. On a Handshake*. Dan Ewald, Champaign, Ill.: Sagamore Publishing. 1977.

Fidrych, Mark, and Tom Clark, *No Big Deal*. Philadelphia and New York: Lippincott. 1977.

Freehan, Bill. *Behind the Mask* Bill Freehan, New York: Popular Library. 1970.

Harwell, Ernie. *Tuned to Baseball*. Ernie Harwell, South Bend, Ind.: Diamond Communications. 1985.

Makio (Ohio State University yearbook). Columbus: The Ohio State University. 1948, 1949, and 1950 editions.

Ohio State University Alumni Magazine. Columbus: The Ohio State University. May 1993.

OSU—The Ohio State University Alumni Magazine. Columbus: The Ohio State University. December 1984.

Articles

Falls, Joe. "The Tigers are his life…" *Detroit News*, February 17, 1985.

Falls, Joe. "Campbell loved game, not agents." *Detroit News*, November 1, 1995.

Green, Jerry. "Longtime Tiger GM dies in Florida at 71." *Detroit News*, November 1, 1995.

Guidi, Gene, Steve Kornacki and John Lowe. "Ex-Tigers boss Campbell dies at 71." *Detroit Free Press*, November 1, 1995.

Puscas, George. "Campbell was a symbol of an era's greatness." *Detroit Free Press*, November 1, 1995.

New York Times, November 2, 1995.

Vincent, Charlie. "Campbell devoted a life to his true love." *Detroit Free Press*, November 1, 1995.

Web Sites

www.BaseballLibrary.com

Other Sources

Mallett, Jeanne M. Interview with Richard L. (Dick) Klein, Huron, Ohio, June 14, 2007.

The City of Huron, Ohio, Chamber of Commerce.

The Ohio State University Alumni Association and The Ohio State University Alumni Records Archive.

Tony Cuccinello

by Barb Mantegani

A diminutive Italian from Astoria, New York, on Long Island, who was introduced to baseball on the local sandlots, Tony Cuccinello was involved in what remains the closest batting race in major league history, when, as a member of the Chicago White Sox, he lost the 1945 American League batting title to George "Snuffy" Stirnweiss of the Yankees by a margin of .000087.

Cuccinello had a fast start in 1945, keeping his average in the .380–.390 range for the first few months. The heat of the Chicago summer eventually wore Tony down, however, and at what was then the advanced age (for a ballplayer) of 37, Cuccinello did not play every day, and in fact had to play more in September to achieve sufficient at-bats to qualify for the batting title. Stirnweiss edged out Cuccinello on the final day of the season, when a White Sox doubleheader was rained out and Stirnweiss went 3-for-4 against the Boston Red Sox. One of those hits, however, was scored an error initially, and then changed to a hit by the official scorer, who just happened to be a writer for the *Bronx Home News*. According to Cuccinello, he was told at the time that the official scorer only changed the call after he was informed that the White Sox had been rained out and Cuccinello's season was over. Ironically, Cuccinello later coached Stirnweiss with the Cleveland Indians, and Snuffy confirmed the shenanigans when he told Cuccinello: "He (the writer) gave it to me."

Anthony Francis ("Tony" or "Cootch") Cuccinello was born November 8, 1907, in Long Island City, New York. Tony played in a semipro league in New York City and eventually signed a contract to play for the Syracuse Stars of the International League in 1926, while still a teenager. After two months Cuccinello was sent to the Class B Lawrence (Massachusetts) Merry Macks, where he spent the rest of 1926 and 1927, when he hit .310. In 1928 he was assigned to the Danville Veterans of the Three I League. After another season hitting .310, Cuccinello caught the attention of Branch Rickey, who saw him play and bought him for the Columbus Senators in the American Association. Cuccinello's performance at Columbus (.358 batting average with 20 home runs and 111 runs batted in, and a league-leading 227 hits and 56 doubles) earned him a quick promotion to the major leagues, when the Reds purchased his contract after the 1929 season. Tony made his debut on Opening Day, April 15, 1930, playing third base in a losing effort against the Pittsburgh Pirates.

Cuccinello had a solid rookie season, batting .312 with 10 home runs and 78 RBIs. In 1931 the Reds shifted Tony to second base and he responded with a .315 average and 93 RBIs, a club record for second basemen until broken by Joe Morgan in 1975. In his best offensive performance that year he got hits in six consecutive at-bats, including two doubles and a triple. He led the league's second basemen in putouts, assists, errors, and double plays.

Despite Cuccinello's performances on the field, he refused to sign the contract the Reds tendered to him and found himself shipped to the Brooklyn Dodgers to begin the 1932 season. Tony played in all 154 games that year, turning in respectable offensive numbers for a second baseman (.281, 12 homers, 32 doubles, and 77 RBIs) but, more importantly, becoming a teammate of future Hall of Fame manager Al Lopez, with whom he would begin a lifelong friendship. That same year Cuccinello married Clara Caroselli (after the season, on October 29), and they produced three children: Anthony Jr. in 1936, Darlene Ann in 1938, and Alan Joseph on their 13th wedding anniversary in 1945. Cuccinello's performance in '32 earned him a spot on the roster of first All-Star Game in 1933 (the so-called "Game of the Century"), where he had the dubious distinction of pinch-hitting for Carl Hubbell in the top of the ninth and striking out to end the game.

In 1935, Cuccinello's younger brother, Al, made his major league debut and played in 54 games with the New York Giants, the only major league experience Al would have. The brothers played against each other several times that year and both homered in the same game on July 5. Tony's homer was a solo shot in the top of the eighth and Al's a two-run blast in the bottom of the ninth inning of a game Brooklyn won 14–4. After four years with the Dodgers, Cuccinello was on the move again when Brooklyn traded him to the Boston Braves. In Boston in 1936, Cuccinello had one of his best offensive seasons, batting .308 and driving in 86 runs. Tony's excellent defensive performances continued in Boston, as well, and he teamed with a player he later described as the finest of the shortstops he played with in his career, Eddie Miller.

In 1939 Cuccinello suffered a knee injury after Dick Bartell of the Chicago Cubs slid into him at second base, and surgery sidelined him for two months. His first game back after the surgery Cuccinello had 10 assists in a 22-inning game while playing third base. The knee never really improved despite the surgery, and Cuccinello was traded to the Giants midway through the 1940 season. At the end of that season Cuccinello retired for the first time, so that he could manage the Jersey City Giants in the International League. Jersey City finished fifth in the eight-team league in 1941, and Cuccinello was prepared to manage again in 1942, but instead was called by his former Brooklyn manager Casey Stengel, then with the Braves, who asked Cuccinello to join his staff as a player-coach. In 1942 Cuccinello threw batting practice, coached third base, and pinch-hit for Stengel, and in mid-season 1943 was released so that he could sign with the Chicago White Sox, a team desperately in need of players to replace those who enlisted in the military. Cuccinello, who suffered from chronic laryngitis, was not drafted into military service, and therefore was able to continue his career.

From mid-1943 through the 1944 season Cuccinello was a reserve infielder who appeared in fewer than 50 games each year, and he later said that but for the war he likely would have retired before the 1945 season. But in 1945 Cuccinello went to a northern spring training in French Lick, Indiana (later made famous by native son Larry Bird), where he had a mineral bath every day, followed by a rubdown and a nap, and entered the season feeling the best he had ever felt. Perhaps it was the mineral baths or the naps, but nevertheless after the Indiana spring training Cuccinello embarked on his near-title-winning year, and retired from playing for good at the end of that campaign.

Cuccinello was out of baseball in 1946, but managed the Tampa Smokers in the Florida International League to 104 wins and a second-place finish in 1947. The following year he reunited with Al Lopez in Indianapolis, where they coached the Indianapolis Indians of the American Association to a 100-win season and a online ranking among the 100 best minor league teams of the 20th century. In 1949 Cuccinello began a three-year stint as a coach with his first major league team, the Reds, and in 1952 he joined Al Lopez's coaching staff on the Cleveland Indians, the first of several such positions he would hold. Coincidentally, 1952 was also the last year of former nemesis Snuffy Stirnweiss's career, also with the Indians.

Cuccinello's first postseason experience came as a coach with the Indians in the 1954 World Series, which the heavily favored Indians lost to the San Francisco Giants. In 1957, Cuccinello followed Lopez to the Chicago White Sox, and in 1959, as third base coach, was involved in a controversial play that some said at the time led to the White Sox' demise at the hands of the Los Angeles Dodgers in the 1959 World Series. In Game 2 of the Series, Sherm Lollar, the White Sox catcher, was on first base in the bottom of the eighth with nobody out, a man on second, and the score 4–2 in favor of the Dodgers. The next batter, Al Smith, doubled to left-center. The runner at second (Earl Torgeson, running for Ted Kluszewski) scored easily. Cuccinello waved Lollar home, where he was thrown out—by a good margin, by all accounts. When the Sox went on to lose the Series four games to two, Cuccinello immediately was awarded goat horns and tagged with the blame for the Series loss.

Lopez defended his friend and fellow coach, telling a *Chicago Daily News* reporter first, that in his opinion the play itself was fine, and more importantly, that the play was not the turning point of the Series, that the Sox' inability to run in the Coliseum was what led to their demise.

Lopez repeated that opinion in an interview with *The Sporting News*, noting that it took a perfect play by the Dodgers' defense to nail Lollar at the plate. One of the Dodgers involved in the play, outfielder Wally Moon, expressed the same opinion during the off-season after the World Series when he said that he also might have sent Lollar if he were in Cuccinello's shoes, because the odds were against the Dodgers making the play.

In any event, Cuccinello survived the controversy and continued coaching in Chicago into Eddie Stanky's managerial tenure, which started in 1966. In 1967 Cuccinello joined the staff of new Tigers manager Mayo Smith, and at the beginning of the season Cuccinello took on Dick McAuliffe as a private project, to help McAuliffe make the switch from shortstop to second base. At the time Cuccinello said McAuliffe had to work on slowing himself down, and in 1968 the work seemed to bear fruit, as McAuliffe's defensive improvement was cited by both opposing manager Alvin Dark of the Cleveland Indians and Tigers coach Hal Naragon as a key factor in the Tigers' success. Cuccinello enjoyed his first and only World Series championship in 1968 when the Tigers defeated the St. Louis Cardinals in seven games.

Cuccinello left the Tigers in 1969 to reunite with Al Lopez, who managed the White Sox for 17 games that season. Cuccinello then retired to Tampa, Florida, where he worked as a Yankees scout in the area until retiring from baseball completely in 1985. Cuccinello passed away of congestive heart failure September 21, 1995, at a hospital in Tampa.

References

Articles

Carmichael, J. "Lollar Play Not Series Key—Lopez." *Baseball Digest*, Vol. 19 p. 71 (February 1960).

Chastain, B., "This Was the Closest Race Ever for a Batting Title." *Baseball Digest*, Vol. 52, p. 63 (December. 1993).

Daniel, Dan. "Over the Fence: Two Big Breaks Influenced Outcome of Series." *The Sporting News*, October 21, 1959, p. 10.

"'Dodgers Reeled Off Perfect Play to Nail Lollar'—Lopez." *The Sporting News*, January 20, 1960, p. 4.

Holmes, T. "Carey Experiments With Dodger Infield." *The Sporting News*, March 31, 1932, p. 1.

"Majors' All-Stars Meet In 'Game of the Century.'" *The Sporting News*, July 6, 1933, p. 1.

Oates, B. "It Took Five Perfect Plays to Get Lollar at Plate!" *Baseball Digest*, vol. 19, p. 69 (February 1960).

Spoelstra, Watson. "Relaxed McAuliffe Gave Tigers Their Flag Spark." *The Sporting News*, October 5, 1968, p. 33.

New York Times, September 23, 1995.

The Sporting News, October 21, 1959, p. 12. The play was also included in a summary of the worst coaching blunders in *The Baseball Hall of Shame*, written by Bruce Nash and Allan Zullo and published in 1985 by Pocket Books, New York.

Westcott, Rich, "Tony Cuccinello-A Great Way to Spend a Lifetime," from *Diamond Greats, Profiles and Interviews with 65 of Baseball's History Makers*, p. 94 (Westport, Conn.: Meckler Books, 1988).

Web Sites

http://web.minorleaguebaseball.com/milb/history/top_about.jsp for top 100 minor league teams (accessed September 16, 2007)

www.baseball-reference.com.

www.retrosheet.org stats

SABR Home Run Log, www.sabr.org

Wally Moses

by Doug Skipper

A highly regarded hitting mentor who spent much of his life in baseball, veteran coach Wally Moses was Mayo Smith's right-hand man for the 1968 world champion Detroit Tigers. Moses, who also served under Smith during his stints in Philadelphia and Cincinnati, spent four seasons in Detroit, tutoring the Tigers' hitters and acting as a buffer between players and their manager. A well-liked and respected Georgian, Moses spent 41 seasons in the majors, 17 as a player, 16 as a coach, three as a scout and five more as a hitting instructor.

As a player, Moses was a speedy line-drive-lashing left-handed outfielder. In 2,012 games, all in the American League, he collected 2,138 hits and batted .291. A 5-foot-10, 160-pound, top-of-the-order slap hitter, Moses laced 435 doubles, 110 triples, and 89 home runs. He drew 821 walks, stole 174 bases, scored 1,124 runs, and was an AL All-Star. A stellar and fearless fly chaser who sometimes struggled with grounders and often dropped to one knee to field them, Moses possessed exceptional range and a strong arm. He collected exactly 4,000 career putouts, and recorded 147 career assists.

Between 1935 and 1951, he turned in some of baseball's least predictable seasons. Moses spent his first seven big-league campaigns with Connie Mack's Philadelphia Athletics, and batted better than .300 in each of those seven seasons—but never did so again during the rest of his 17-year career. In 1937, Moses blasted 25 home runs—but he never hit more than nine in any other year, and smacked just 64 in his other 16 seasons. Mack dealt Moses to the White Sox before the 1942 campaign, and a year later the fleet-footed outfielder stole 56 bases—35 more than his next-best season and nearly a third of his career production. Moses also tied for the league lead with 12 triples in 1943, and two years later, he belted an AL-best 35 doubles and led the league's outfielders in putouts.

The easygoing lefty spent two-and-a-half years with Boston before he went back to Mack to close out his playing days and launch his coaching career in Philadelphia. Between 1952 and 1970, he served five different teams. As a player, he had hit with an open stance and a grip so loose it looked like he might drop the bat. As one of baseball's first—and most respected—full-time hitting coaches, he taught batters to take a short stroke, direct the ball with the bat, and run to first base fast; and was adept at correcting flaws in a hitter's swing. Involved in baseball into his sixties, Moses served as a hitting instructor for several seasons after his coaching career was over, still able to lace lengthy line drives in batting practice, dissect and correct a swing, or spellbind a crowd with tales of hitters and hitting, past and present.

Wallace "Wally" Moses Jr. was born October 8, 1909, in Uvalda, Georgia, the first child of Wallace Moses Sr. and Martha Louise "Mattie Lou" (Smith) Moses. Although baseball references list his birth year as 1910, the U.S. Census of that year, taken on April 10, indicated that Wallace Sr. and Mattie Lou were living with their 6-month-old son, Wallace Jr., and her parents in nearby Tattnall County. Three brothers and a sister followed, the family moved to Vidalia, Georgia, today famous as home of the Vidalia onion, and Wallace Sr. and Mattie Lou separated. After he graduated from high school in Vidalia, Wally left home and journeyed 12 miles west to play baseball at Brewton-Parker College in Mt. Vernon, Georgia, from 1926 to 1928, and then toiled for local teams. It was reported that in 1930 he stole eight bases in a game and hit a pair of bases-loaded triples in the same inning. According to legend, he was "discovered" by Georgia native Ty Cobb, who had been asked to umpire a sandlot game. Moses embarked on his professional career with the Augusta (Georgia) Wolves of the short-lived Palmetto League in 1931. A 1936 *Sporting News* story suggested that New York Giants manager John McGraw saw his name and dispatched a scout to meet Moses in search of a "Hebrew player" who could be a box office star in New York. The speedy youngster of Scots-Irish and English descent pointed out that he wasn't Jewish, the scout replied, "Ah, hell!" and didn't sign him. Moses reportedly had stolen 22 bases and Augusta led the Class D level Palmetto League when it folded in July. The young lefty moved on to the Elmira (New York) Pioneers in the Class B New York-Pennsylvania League.

He returned to the South for the 1932 season. Moses toiled for the Monroe (Louisiana) Drillers of the Class D Cotton States League before that circuit disbanded in July, then the Tyler Sports of the Texas League, who played the second half of the season in Texas after a midyear fire destroyed their ballpark in Shreveport, Louisiana. The Sports moved back to Shreveport and jumped to the Dixie League, but Moses stayed in the Texas League and led the Galveston Buccaneers to a second-place finish in 1933 and the league championship the following year. Near the end of the season, on August 9, 1934, Connie Mack's Philadelphia Athletics purchased Moses and directed him to report the next spring.

Moses joined a franchise in rapid decline. Mack had guided the Athletics to three consecutive AL titles and two world championships between 1929 and 1931 and a second-place finish in 1932. But as the Great Depression deepened and box-office revenues plummeted, Mack, past age 70, sold off his stars, and by spring training 1935, first baseman Jimmie Foxx and outfielder Roger "Doc" Cramer were about the only holdovers. The A's were about to embark on a stretch where they finished last in the AL nine times in 12 years, and never out of the second division in that stretch.

Moses was a bright spot. The Georgian made his major league debut Wednesday, April 17, 1935, in a 4–2 opening day loss to the Senators at Griffith Stadium in Washington. Splitting time with another Southern left-hander, Alabaman Lou Finney, in right field, Moses hit .325 with five home runs, 21 doubles, and 60 runs scored. His season ended August 17 when he crashed into a wall at Chicago's Comiskey Park and fractured his left wrist, but he was still named the AL's top rookie by baseball writers.

The showing was impressive enough that the cash-strapped Mack—who had already pocketed $150,000 in a deal that sent Foxx (and offered Moses) to Boston—shipped Cramer to the Red Sox before the 1936 season in a deal that netted $75,000 and installed Moses in center field. The depleted A's lost 100 games and finished last, but Moses responded by batting a career-best .345, rifled 202 hits, including 35 doubles, 11 triples, and seven homers, stole 12 bases, scored 98 runs, drove in 66, and amassed a career-best 396 putouts.

He was called "Wallace" by the venerable Mack and dubbed "the Georgia Express" by *The Sporting News*. "If a spectacular dive over the turf is necessary to snare a fly ball seemingly out of his reach, Wally dives," the "Baseball Bible" reported. "Moses is a little fellow who hustles every minute." Teammate Bill Werber called him the league's premier leadoff hitter and the fastest man getting from the batter's box to first base. Moses hustled to the altar that winter. He married Billie Mae Haines, a native of Houston, Texas, whom he had met when he played in the Texas League, on December 2, 1936.

Philadelphia managed to climb out of the cellar to seventh-place in 1937. Moses enjoyed the finest season of his career, when he batted .320 and slammed 25 home runs—the only time he hit more than nine. "I reported late to Mexico by 10 days," Moses told baseball biographer Norman Macht. "Connie Mack sent two pitchers to throw for me for extra hitting, Bud Thomas and Al Williams. I was a straightaway or up-the-alleys hitter, always swung from the end of the bat. The pitchers were throwing pretty good, so I had to shorten up on my grip about three inches, and they pitched inside to me and I found when they pitched me high and tight, I could pull the ball, so that year, I hit 25 home runs. I'd always been a lowball hitter, so the AL pitchers kept pitching me high and tight, and now I could pull it." Along the way, he collected 208 hits—the final A's player of the 20th century to reach the 200 mark. He also achieved career highs with 154 games played, 48 doubles, 86 RBI, 357 total bases, and a .550 slugging percentage.

That summer, Moses became one of the first baseball players to grace a Wheaties cereal box and was named to the American League team for baseball's fifth All-Star Game. Moses and ex-teammate Cramer sat on the bench while Dizzy Dean took an Earl Averill line drive off his toe and Lou Gehrig homered to lead the AL to an 8–3 victory at Griffith Stadium in Washington.

Though he hit a respectable .307 and scored 86 runs, the 1938 season was a disappointment. Moses held out for a second straight spring, this time for a month, and settled for a two-year, $12,500-per-season deal instead of a big raise from the taciturn Mack. He joined the team in Atlanta on its way north in early April, but suffered a devastating injury sliding into home in his second game. "A catcher fell on me in Portsmouth, Virginia, and broke my shoulder and I could never swing the same again," Moses told Macht. "It ruined my career." He managed just eight home runs, slugged only .424, and drove in but 49 runs. The Athletics lost 99 games and finished dead last in the American League; then lost 97 more in 1939. Moses represented the Athletics at a game that marked the opening of baseball's Hall of Fame in 1939 and again batted .307, but battled a spring training ankle injury, played in only 115 games, homered just three times, slugged only .423, and drove in but 33 runs.

Looking to cut costs again, Mack moved Moses to Detroit in a trade for Benny McCoy, a reserve infielder, on December 9, 1939. But a month later, on January 14, 1940, baseball Commissioner Kenesaw Mountain Landis declared 91 Tigers and farmhands, including McCoy and pitcher Johnny Sain, free agents because of signing improprieties and a subsequent organizational cover-up. The edict nullified the trade, Moses returned to Philadelphia, and Mack ended up with McCoy anyway when he won a bidding war for the second sacker's services. Moses and McCoy played together for the Athletics, who managed to lose 100 games and finish eighth, while the Tigers went on to win the 1940 AL title. Moses injured his ankle in an exhibition game at Lafayette (Pennsylvania) College, but still batted .309 in 142 games in 1940, hit nine homers, and scored 91 runs, one on a 10th-inning game-winning steal of home in the second game of the August 20 doubleheader with the White Sox. In 1941, Moses injured his shoulder in an automobile accident while traveling from "boiling out" in Hot Springs, Arkansas, to spring training in Anaheim, California. Moses and Athletics outfielder Al Simmons were traveling in Simmons' new car. On February 24, outside of Lubbock, Texas, Moses tried to pass a slow-moving school bus, but the bus turned and Moses drove into the ditch to avoid it. The car rolled once and landed right side up. Simmons, a future Hall of Famer, was unhurt, but Moses missed the first month of the season. He rebounded to hit .301 (the last time he would exceed .300) in 116 games. Philadelphia lost 90 more times.

Two days after the Japanese attack on Pearl Harbor and exactly two years after he traded him the first time, Mack once again dealt Moses. He sent the seven-year veteran to Chicago for outfielder Mike Kreevich and pitcher Jack Hallett. Fiery White Sox manager Jimmy Dykes, who had played third base for Mack, moved the 31-year-old Moses from center to right field and gave him the green light on the base paths. In his first season with the White Sox, Moses hit .270, with 28 doubles and 16 stolen bases. He also smacked seven home runs to lead the White Sox, who bopped a total of 25—11 fewer than Ted Williams slugged for the Red Sox.

A year later, Moses stunned the baseball world when he stole 56 bases—40 more than he had ever stolen before in a full season, and 53 more than two years earlier under Mack. "Connie Mack wouldn't let me run," Moses remembered. "I stole a few bases my first year, but Connie Mack said, 'Wally, I don't want you to run. You got Cramer, Foxx and Johnson behind you. They might hit one and you can walk around.' But when I went to Chicago with Dykes, he told me to run. 'We have to steal runs,' and I had speed. Joe Kuhel was my roommate and he'd steal on guys I'd get thrown out on. I asked him, 'What do you know that I don't know?' He started pointing out things pitchers did." On May 5, in the second game of a doubleheader at Cleveland, Moses swiped home in the top of the 11th inning in a 5–2 White Sox win, his second career steal of home in extra innings, to tie Tony Lazzeri's major league record. He would have had a third that season, but teammate Don Kolloway got hit by the pitch. As a team, the White Sox stole a league-leading 173 bases and were dubbed the "Wild West Boys." Moses earned his own moniker—"Peep Sight"—because of his patience and keen batting eye, and though he finished second in the AL to Washington's George Case, who stole 61 bases, Moses tied the New York Yankees' Johnny Lindell for the league lead with 12 triples. By most other measures, the 1943 season was a disappointment. Moses hit a paltry .245, slugged just .337, and grounded into nine double plays, his worst total since that statistic had been tabulated, starting in 1939.

Like his 25 home runs in 1937, the 56 stolen bases in 1943 turned out to be an aberration. Moses did steal 21 bases—the second-highest total of his career—in 1944, bounced back to hit .280, and clubbed three of Chicago's team total of 23 home runs. He also suffered a pulled groin muscle that would bother him for several seasons. Moses (who had a bad shoulder from the auto accident), Senators pitcher Dutch Leonard, and Yankees pitcher Allie Reynolds were among those called up into military service before the 1945 season, but received deferrals. Moses batted .295 in 1945, sixth in the war-depleted AL, led the league with 35 doubles, and was second with 15 triples and 168 hits. The fleet-footed outfielder also managed 11 steals, the last time he posted double figures, and led the American League in putouts with 329. Because of wartime travel restrictions, major league owners canceled the 1945 All-Star Game, scheduled for Fenway Park. After the season, the

Associated Press asked NL and AL managers to nominate standouts from the two leagues. With 13 of the 16 pilots voting, Moses was named to the AP's AL team.

Moses was back with the White Sox in 1946 when many of the players who had served in the military returned. But after Dykes was fired just 30 games into the season, new manager Ted Lyons moved Taffy Wright to right field and Moses became surplus. The White Sox waived him, and on July 23, league-leading Boston claimed him. "Words couldn't express my happiness," Moses said. "I'm glad to get my nose out of the mud." With Williams in left and Dom DiMaggio in center, the Red Sox needed a regular right fielder, having employed George Metkovich, Tom McBride, Leon Culberson, and Johnny Lazor. Though he hit just .206 with a pair of home runs, Moses led off, which allowed DiMaggio to bat third, was solid defensively, played in 43 of Boston's remaining 63 games, and the Red Sox finished 12 games ahead of second-place Detroit. "Veteran though he is," manager Joe Cronin said, "Wally can still fly as a runner, as he proved. He is still a skillful sun fielder."

Moses saw action only against Redbird right-handers in the Series. His crowning moment came in Game 4, when he became the 23rd player to collect four hits in a World Series game—although the Cards pounded out 20 hits and beat the Red Sox 12–3 at Fenway. In the decisive Game 7, Moses singled to center, his fifth straight hit, to lead off and scored the game's first run on DiMaggio's fly ball. But he was retired his next three times up, and struck out with a pair of runners in scoring position in the top of the eighth. After Enos Slaughter scored the run that gave St. Louis the lead for good in the bottom of the inning, he was on deck when McBride grounded into a force play to end the Series.

Back with Boston in 1947, Moses hit .275, lost playing time to rookie Sam Mele, and the Red Sox slipped to third place. The next year, Mele and Moses shared time with off-season acquisition Stan Spence, a three-time American League All-Star, and all three struggled to hit for new manager Joe McCarthy. Moses batted just .259, with two homers in 78 games. Spence hit 12 home runs but batted just .235, and Mele managed just a meager .233 average. Along the way, McCarthy grew frustrated with his team's injuries and chastised Moses when he found him on the training table with a stiff neck.

On November 15, 1948, the Red Sox issued the veteran outfielder his release. Two weeks later, Moses rejoined his old mentor, Connie Mack, in Philadelphia. After more than a decade at the bottom of the AL standings, the Athletics had posted winning records in 1947 and 1948 for the Tall Tactician. Moses appeared in 110 games and batted .276 as Mack's regular right fielder in 1949. The Athletics finished 81–73, good for fifth in the AL. On July 26, Moses collected his 2,000th career hit, off Joe Ostrowski of the St. Louis Browns. The only other active hitter who had reached the milestone was former White Sox teammate Luke Appling; Joe DiMaggio joined the group the following year.

He was 40 in 1950, and other than the 43-year-old Appling, no AL player was older than Moses. He hit .264 in 88 games, but the Athletics floundered, and the 87-year old Mack released the reins after five decades as Philadelphia manager. "Earle Mack (Connie's son) contacted me and offered me the job of managing the A's when Connie Mack was going to retire," Moses told Macht. "I knew I couldn't do the job. I recommended Dykes." Dykes took over in 1951, and though Appling had retired, Moses was again the league's second-oldest player, behind St. Louis Browns pitcher Satchel Paige, who was thought to be 44. Moses hit just .191, played his final game on September 30, 1951, and was released January 21, 1952. "In 1948," Moses said later, "when Boston released me, Connie Mack asked me to come back and told me I would have a job with the A's as long as he was there." True to his word, Mack made Moses a coach. "He didn't want to be a manager," Moses' daughter remembered. "He didn't have the temperament for it. He regarded being a manager as political. He knew where his strongest area was, and he went for it."

In his final years as a player, Moses did indeed discover his strength. He tutored the A's hitters, including first baseman Ferris Fain, the 1951 AL batting champion and *Sporting News* Player of the Year. With Moses in uniform as a coach in 1952, Fain, a pesky slap hitter, captured another batting title. After a disappointing 1953 season, Eddie Joost replaced Dykes as manager in 1954. It was a disaster. Moses was caught in the middle of hostility between Joost and outfielder Gus Zernial, the Athletics slid to 51-103, Joost was dismissed, and the franchise was sold and moved to Kansas City.

Moses remained in Philadelphia, hopping to the National League to assist new Phillies manager Mayo Smith, another Mack protégé. His pupils included Richie Ashburn, another slap hitter who won NL batting titles in 1955 and 1958, and 1957 NL Rookie of the Year runner-up Ed Bouchee. "I didn't speak much to Mayo Smith," Bouchee said. "But I talked a great deal to his hitting coach, Wally

Moses. Smith was a so-so manager who was much too iffy if I had a problem. Smith would be helpful, but I talked more to Wally Moses than him."

On July 22, 1958, Smith was fired and replaced by Eddie Sawyer. Mayo moved to Cincinnati the next year, brought along Moses, and guided the Reds for 80 games before he was fired again in midseason, replaced by Fred Hutchinson at the All-Star break. Moses stayed on under Hutchinson through the rest of the 1959 campaign and the 1960 season before Smith came calling once more.

This time Mayo was an assistant to new Yankees manager Ralph Houk, and Moses joined a coaching staff that also included Johnny Sain, Frankie Crosetti, and Jim Hegan. Among Moses' pupils that season were Roger Maris, who hit 61 home runs and Mickey Mantle, who slugged 54. The Yankees won the American League pennant handily, and rolled over Hutchinson's Reds in the World Series. In 1962, the Bronx Bombers again won the World Series, a 4-games-to-3 nail-biter over the San Francisco Giants. Moses served as a Yankees scout from 1963 to 1966, was a frequent visitor to Bernard "Toots" Shor's restaurant on West 51st Street, then returned to the dugout in 1966 when Houk was summoned from the front office 20 games into the season to fix the floundering franchise.

When the season ended, Smith took over the Tigers, and Moses joined him. Detroit finished second to Boston in 1967 in a four-team race that wasn't resolved until the season's final day. The next year, the Tigers won the AL title and rallied from a 3-1 deficit to stun the Cardinals in the World Series. "Wally Moses was Mayo's top assistant and knew the game well," star pitcher Denny McLain later related. "Moses coached us on how to signal to each other when Mayo was asleep at the wheel." Smith, with Moses at his side, managed two more seasons before he was ousted in favor of fiery Billy Martin. Moses elected to retire, but the Phillies convinced him to come back as a batting instructor. He hung up his spikes for good after the 1975 campaign, and he and Billie continued to reside in Philadelphia.

Afflicted by chronic lung problems through most of the 1980s, Moses developed cancer, had a lung removed, suffered from emphysema in the other, and relied on bottled oxygen in the final years of his life. His health deteriorated badly, he and Billie moved to Vidalia, and Wally entered a health care center. On October 10, 1990, two days after he celebrated his 80th birthday (it was actually his 81st), he died at the Meadows Regional Medical Center in Vidalia after he suffered a stroke. He was survived by his wife of 53 years. After Wally's death, Billie Mae moved to Savannah, Georgia. She passed away in 2002, and is buried alongside him, near his parents and several family members, at Vidalia's Pine Crest Cemetery. Wally and Billie's daughter, Judith Moses Latham, of Arlington, Virginia, is an international radio broadcaster in the public affairs unit of Voice of America's English-language division. Judith's son, Ernest "Tiger" Hargraves Latham III, was Wally and Billie Mae's only grandchild, and the recipient of Wally's World Series ring.

Before he died, Moses was selected to the Philadelphia Baseball Wall of Fame in 1988. From 1978 to 1993, one former Athletics player was selected each year, and a plaque hung in their honor at Veterans Stadium. After the Vet closed, the 25 plaques were relocated in March 2004 to the Philadelphia Athletics Historical Society in Hatboro, Pennsylvania. In 1989, Moses was inducted into the Georgia Sports Hall of Fame.

References

Publications

Armour, Mark L., and Daniel R. Levitt. *Paths to Glory: How Great Baseball Teams Got That Way*. Dulles, Va.: Potomac Books. 2003.

Gillette, Gary, and Pete Palmer. *The 2005 ESPN Baseball Encyclopedia*. New York: Sterling. 2005.

Golenbock, Peter. *Red Sox Nation: An Unexpurgated History of the Red Sox*. Chicago: Triumph Books. 2005.

Halberstam, David. *The Teammates: A Portrait of a Friendship*. New York: Hyperion. 2003.

Halberstam, David. *Summer of '49*. New York: William Morrow & Company. 1991.

James, Bill. *The New Bill James Historical Abstract*. New York: The Free Press. 2001.

Keri, Jonah, ed. *Baseball Between the Numbers: Why Everything You Know About the Game Is Wrong*. New York: Basic Books. 2006

Kuklick, Bruce. *To Everything a Season: Shibe Park and Urban Philadelphia, 1909–1976*. Princeton, N.J.: Princeton University Press. 1991.

Kuenster, John. *The Best of Baseball Digest: The Greatest Players, the Greatest Games, the Greatest Writers from the Game's Most Exciting Years*. Chicago: Ivan R. Dee. 2006.

Lee, Bill. *The Baseball Necrology: The Post-Baseball Lives and Deaths of Over 7,600 Major League Players and Others*. Jefferson, N.C.: McFarland & Company. 2003.

Lieb, Fred. *Connie Mack*. New York: Van Rees Press. 1945.

Lindberg, Richard C. *Total White Sox: The Definitive Encyclopedia of the World Champion Franchise*. Chicago: Triumph Books. 2006.

McLain, Denny, and Eli Zaret. *I Told You I Wasn't Perfect*. Chicago: Triumph Books. 2007.

Maiorana, Sal. *A Lifetime of Yankee Octobers*. Chelsea, Mich.: Thomson Gale. 2002.

Mead, William B. *Even the Browns: The Zany, True Story of Baseball in the Early Forties*, Chicago: Contemporary Books. 1978.

Morris, Peter. *A Game of Inches: The Stories Behind the Innovations That Shaped Baseball*. Chicago: Ivan R. Dee. 2006.

Neft, David S., Richard Cohen, and Michael Neft. *The Sports Encyclopedia: Baseball 2004*. 24th ed. New York: St. Martin's Griffin. 2004.

Nowlin, Bill. *Mr. Red Sox: The Johnny Pesky Story*. Cambridge, Mass.: Rounder Books. 2004.

Nowlin, Bill, and Dan Desrochers. *The 1967 Impossible Dream Red Sox: Pandemonium on the Field*. Cambridge, Mass.: Rounder Books. 2007.

Peary, Danny. *We Played the Game: Memories of Baseball's Greatest Era*. New York: Black Dog and Leventhal. 1994.

Peterson, Richard. *The St. Louis Baseball Reader*. Columbia, Mo.: University of Missouri Press. 2006.

Porter, David L. *Biographical Dictionary of American Sports: Baseball*, revised and expanded edition, G-P. Westport, Conn.: Greenwood Press. 2000.

Sheed, Wilfred. *My Life as a Fan: A Memoir*. New York: Simon and Schuster. 1993.

Stout, Glenn, and Richard A. Johnson. *Red Sox Century*. Boston: Houghton-Mifflin. 2000.

Sultans of Swat: The Four Great Sluggers of the New York Yankees. New York: New York Times Company. 2006.

Williams, Ted, and John Underwood. *My Turn at Bat*. New York: Pocket Books. 1970.

Articles

Macht, Norman. "Wally Moses: He Was a Premier Leadoff Hitter." *Baseball Digest*, February, 1991, pp. 79–83.

Time, May 28, 1956.

New York Times.

The Sporting News.

Web Sites

www.baseball-almanac.com
www.baseballfever.com
www.baseball-reference.com
www.retrosheet.org
www.baseballlibrary.com
www.minorleaguebaseball.com
www.boston.com
www.thedeadballera.com
www.time.com
www.mlb.com

Other Sources

Skipper, Doug. Interview with Judith Moses Latham, August, 2007.

Special Thanks

Judith Moses Latham
Norman Macht

Hal Naragon

by Tracy J.R. Collins

Hal Naragon gave up two years of his professional baseball career when he was drafted into the Marines in 1951. Like many players of his era, he was proud to serve his country. His story is not unique in that respect. Yet, unlike many players, Hal thought that he was lucky. With his atypical unselfish and positive personality Hal said that his time in the Marines was "a good thing." Still, luck is nothing without talent and hard work. In fact, Naragon's story is one Horatio Alger could have written. Like Alger's characters, Naragon experienced success through hard work, courage, determination, and concern for others. Yet, don't tell him this. He would say it was all luck. But it's a story any American would dream about: A young boy grows up in small-town Ohio, dreams of playing professional baseball, marries his high school sweetheart, and plays in a World Series. It is exactly this quietly effective personality that served him well not only as a player but also later as a respected bullpen coach for the Minnesota Twins and the 1968 world champion Detroit Tigers.

Harold Richard Naragon was born October 1, 1928, the third of four children, to Dwight and Dorothy Naragon in Zanesville, Ohio. When he was in the seventh grade, his parents moved to Barberton, Ohio, outside of Akron, "because there were more jobs there during the war," he said. Hal essentially never left Barberton again. He is exceptionally proud of his hometown. He is quick to recite the city's proud sporting history, which includes figures such as Glenn "Bo" Schembechler, the famous University of Michigan football coach, who began his own sporting career on the Barberton High School baseball team as a teammate of Naragon's, and Bob Addis, the first Barberton High School graduate to sign a contract with a major league baseball team (Boston Braves, 1950). Hal's hometown pride rubbed off on his only child, Pam Naragon Bradley, author of the "Barberton Facts and History" section of the Barberton website [barbertonmagics.com].

While Hal was in high school, the Barberton Magics were not always successful. According to the 1944 Barberton High School yearbook, "The 1944 season was unsuccessful in wins and losses, but a green team gained valuable experience for another season." Naragon, a right-handed-throwing, left-handed-hitting freshman catcher, nonetheless earned his varsity letter. The 1946–1947 school year proved to be a good one for "Haddie" Naragon, as he was referred to in the yearbook. To begin with, Hal spent summer 1946 playing on a Class A baseball team in Akron that fielded former major league players as well as college players. One day a friend on the team told Hal that a group of guys were driving up to Cleveland to try out for "Mr. Veeck," the new owner of the Cleveland Indians. Bill Veeck had decided to conduct open tryouts throughout Ohio to increase interest in the team. Hal played well at the tryouts, earning a contract. But, as he tells the story, "I was not supposed to be there. I wasn't going to graduate until next year and couldn't sign the contract until I graduated. I asked Mr. Veeck if I could let him know my decision tomorrow. My dad was going to kill me if he knew I was in Cleveland trying out for the Indians. So, I came home and explained what happened to my dad, and he drove up to Cleveland with me the next day. Mr. Veeck explained his interest in me to my dad and my dad told him I had not yet graduated from high school, and so Mr. Veeck asked if I would give the Indians the opportunity to sign him the following spring. My dad asked, 'Will a handshake do?' Mr. Veeck said yes. The two men shook hands and that was that."

Back in Barberton, 1947 was declared the year of sports champions. In the winter Hal was on the basketball team and helped the Magics get their first Ohio State Athletic Association trophy for winning the district championships. The Magics lost to Ashtabula in the regional tournament. Then there was the baseball season. The 1947 team, described in *A Bicentennial Remembrance: Barberton Ohio the Magic City*, as "the greatest group of athletes ever to play together on a single team in the City," won all of their games during the regular season with three shutouts and one no-hitter. They were district and regional champions and lost the state championship game in extra innings. "The team's slugger was Hal Naragon, who could be counted on to hit one 'out of the park' every third game. People still speak of those 'Naragon shots.'" Even at the beginning of that "magical" season the *Barberton Herald* published an article, "B.H.S. Baseball Team Captures Three Contests," referring to Naragon as "a fixture behind the plate" and "a good sticker as well as receiver." Naragon posted a .444 batting average in his senior year and batted over .400 for his high school career.

Naragon was ready to begin his career with the Indians. He signed in the spring of 1947 and in July headed off for Pittsfield (Massachusetts) Electrics of the Class C Canadian-American League. It was his first time away from home, but "with a strong arm and good defensive catching skills" Hal was ready to be a professional baseball player, the only career he said he ever wanted. By April 1948 he was the first-string catcher for Harrisburg of the Class B Interstate League where, according to his hometown *Herald*: "Down in Harrisburg Naragon has been credited with having one of the best throwing arms ever seen in those parts working from behind the plate." In midseason he was sent down to Watertown, New York, of the Class C Border League to work on his hitting, but went back up to Harrisburg when it began to improve. That year was important for Naragon in at least two ways. First, Fred Gerkin, manager of the Watertown team, helped him improve his hitting, and second, in what Hal says was the most important and best decision he ever made, on October 10, 1948, he married his high school sweetheart, Joanne Schake, in Barberton.

Naragon ended the 1948 season with a .295 average and was back in Harrisburg for 1949. Muddy Ruel, the Indians' assistant farm director, sang Naragon's praises, saying, "If anyone in this camp has a chance to become a solid major leaguer it's Hal Naragon. He has a very fine chance to become a good catcher. He has the physique and the natural aptitude of a catcher, and he has a sure pair of hands when he comes to catching foul flies," and was "willing to learn." That willingness to learn helped him immensely as he worked his way up to playing for Oklahoma City in the Texas League in 1950 and by 1951 he was in spring training with the Indians. After spring training he was sent to San Diego of the Pacific Coast League, and earned a call-up to the Indians at the end of the season. He singled as a pinch-hitter in his first game, against Detroit, then played in two more games before the season ended—enough to keep his name in the minds of his coaches as the Korean War then intervened.

After the season, Naragon was drafted into the Marines and was stationed at Quantico, Virginia. He was discharged in December 1953. Asked if he felt his career suffered during those years, Hal responded, "I didn't miss a thing. In fact, I got stronger physically during those years. I always thought everything I have done has been a positive experience. Frankly, when all those other guys weren't coming back I thought I was lucky." After his discharge, former Tigers great Hank Greenberg, then the Indians' general manager, sent him to Panama to play winter ball.

Naragon started 1954 season with the Indians and was part of the winningest team in American League history to that point (111 victories). He became friends with all-star outfielder Dale Mitchell, who he says was the person who helped him the most in his baseball career: "He helped me a lot with my hitting." The left-handed-batting Naragon says his best moment as a player occurred during the season. "We were playing the Philadelphia A's and it was the top of the tenth inning and the bases were loaded. I hit a trip a triple off of a left-handed pitcher!" Most remarkably for him, during that season he caught four future Hall of Fame pitchers—Bob Feller, Early Wynn, Hal Newhouser, and Bob Lemon. The Indians would have won the World Series had it started in Cleveland, Naragon maintains. They were instead swept by the New York Giants. Playing backup to Jim Hegan, Naragon finished the season with a .238 batting average perfect 1.000 fielding percentage in 45 games, He returned to Panama to play winter ball after the 1954 season, and in 1955 played 57 games with a batting average of .323. In 1956 and 1957, still in a backup role, he hit .287 and .256, playing in about 50 games each season, and he was sent back to San Diego for 1958, coming back to the Indians for only nine plate appearances.

On May 25, 1959, Naragon was traded by Cleveland with pitcher Hal Woodeshick to the Washington Senators for catcher Ed Fitz Gerald. Of the team's lackluster record in Washington Hal said, with his characteristic tact, "We had some good players there, but maybe we didn't all belong together on the same team." Hal moved in 1961 to Minnesota when Calvin Griffith relocated his franchise from Washington to become the Minnesota Twins. In his first year with the Twins when they returned Washington to play the expansion Senators, he hit the last sacrifice bunt in Griffith Stadium September 21, 1961, in the seventh inning. That first year in Minnesota was one of Naragon's better years hitting (.302 in 57 games as a backup to Earl Battey), but it was no roster guarantee. In 1962, he had only 35 at-bats, and played his last game August 5 of that season. He was released by the Twins on October 19, 1962, having played his entire 10-year career in the American League. (Asked what he thought of not playing in the National League, he chuckled and replied, "I was glad to be playing in any league.")

During an era in baseball history when players spent their off-seasons working, Naragon was no exception, spending his winters working at the rubber factory in Barberton. However, when his playing career was over, Hal was not quite ready to return to the factory. The Twins named Naragon their bullpen coach. As a coach, Naragon found another calling. In 1965, the Twins won the American League pennant in 1965 only to lose the World Series in Game 7 against the Los Angeles Dodgers' unhittable Sandy Koufax. From 1965 to 1969, when he left baseball, Hal was in tandem with pitching coach Johnny Sain, moving with Sain to Detroit after both were released by the Twins after the 1966 season.

According to Naragon, "There were some disagreements—we had a great time at Minnesota—but some people thought that John only got along with the pitchers, which was not true. John, in his career, he always seemed to have a run-in with the managers or different ideas than the managers." What it came down to was that Sain and manager Sam Mele could not work together any longer and, "because Naragon supported Sain strongly," Mele also asked for Naragon's release. *Sports Illustrated* quoted Twins pitcher Jim Kaat, who won 25 games for the Twins in 1965, as calling the firing of Sain and Naragon "the Great Mistake." Kaat added, "This is the worst thing that could happen to our club at this time. Every move John Sain and Hal Naragon made was in the best interest of the Minnesota Twins.... Hal Naragon was the last instrument of communication between Mr. Mele and the players. Now there is complete division."

The combination of Sain and Naragon proved just as effective in Detroit as in Minnesota. When they arrived for the 1967 season the Tigers had just finished in third place, but the 1967 season found them climbing. They finished second, only one game behind the Boston Red Sox. With pitchers like Denny McLain and Mickey Lolich, first baseman Norm Cash and Hall of Fame outfielder Al Kaline, the Tigers would not be denied in 1968. McLain won 31 games that season, and, in the World Series against the St. Louis Cardinals, Mickey Lolich pitched three complete-game victories, allowing only five earned runs in 27 innings. Toward the end of that memorable 1968 season Watson Spoelstra, longtime Detroit sportswriter, wrote, "There's no question that Sain and his close friend and associate, coach Hal Naragon, know about as much as anyone on pitching. They are dedicated baseball men with a low-key selling job." Spoelstra reported that during the 1968 off-season Naragon was given a vote of confidence by the Tigers when they signed him for the 1969 season. Spoelstra quoted Lolich as saying, "Sain and Naragon are my boys. They know how to get a guy straightened out." The Tigers were not as successful in 1969; Naragon finished the season with them and retired from professional baseball. Writers had always said that "Naragon goes where Sain goes," but when Sain landed with the Chicago White Sox in 1971, Naragon decided to try something different. "Could I make a living outside of baseball was always at the back of my mind and when John went to Chicago I decided it was time to answer that question for myself," he says.

Naragon returned to Barberton, to live with his wife and daughter. He did indeed make a living outside of baseball. "I am proud to say that I owned the largest and best sporting goods store in Barberton, Ohio. Of course, it was also the only sporting goods store in Barberton." According to Barberton historian Phyllis Taylor, Naragon bought the local sporting goods store in 1974. He sold the business and retired in 1990. He is active in charitable fundraising events through an association of major league alumni. He also enjoys playing golf with his two grandsons and his wife, a team they affectionately call "the family foursome," and watching the Barberton Magics play baseball on Naragon Field, built in 2000 and named in his honor in April 2006. When asked what he thought his best attributes were as a coach, he laughed and said, "I had trouble with that question. I asked my wife and she said I was a good listener. I guess I was a positive thinker. I learned in pro ball that folks started off negatively because they were so used to hearing criticism, but I thought the power of positive suggestion was much stronger. At a 1965 Twins reunion in 2005 Jerry Kindall said I was very even-tempered and it was always a new day with me. John [Sain] was a very positive person too and we were a good team." Watson Spoelstra, in a June 22, 1968, article for *The Sporting News*, called Naragon "the quiet man who ran the bullpen." Naragon's quiet effectiveness, love of baseball, and good-natured positive attitude is evident not only in reports of interviews with players during his career, but it is also clear in the tone of his voice. "I have met some wonderful people playing baseball," Naragon said. "I don't think anything else I could have done would have put me in contact with as many good people." Such people include Naragon himself, by all accounts a truly good man among baseball's alumni.

References

Publications

A Bicentennial Remembrance: Barberton Ohio, the Magic City. Akron: Beaumarc Publications. 1975.

Taylor, Phyllis. *100 Years of Magic: The Story of Barberton, Ohio, 1891–1991.* Akron: Summit County Historical Press. 1991.

Thielman, Jim. *Cool of the Evening: The 1965 Minnesota Twins.* Minneapolis: Kirkhouse Publishers. 2005.

Articles

"B.H.S. Baseball Team Captures Three Contests." *Barberton Herald*, April 18, 1947.

"Barberton High Wins District Baseball Title." *Barberton Herald*, May 23, 1947.

"Barberton Wins First Tournament Game in Baseball." *Barberton Herald*, May 16, 1947.

"Baseball 1944." *Barberton High School Yearbook.* Barberton, Ohio,.1945.

"Baseball 1947." *Barberton High School Yearbook.* Barberton, Ohio. 1948.

Bradley, Pam Naragon. "Barberton Facts and History." 2004. http://www.barbertonmagics.com/history.htm. Accessed May 31, 2007.

"Hal Naragon." Baseball-Reference. May 30, 2007. http://www.baseball-reference.com/n/naraga01.shtml. Accessed May 31, 2007.

"Harold Naragon Begins New Baseball Season at Harrisburg." *Barberton Herald*, April 29, 1949.

"Hat Naragon Booked as Harrisburg Catcher." *Barberton Herald*, April 30, 1948.

"Johnny Sain, RIP." *The Southpaw*, November 8, 2006. http://108mag.typepad.com/the_southpaw/2006/11/index.html. Accessed May 15, 2007.

"Kaat's Meow." *Sports Illustrated* October 17, 1966, pp. 24–25.

"Magics Play in State Baseball Tournament This Weekend." *Barberton Herald*, May 30, 1947.

"Naragon May Play in Indians Minors Game." *Barberton Herald*, September 23,. 1949.

Nichols, Max. "Dropped by Twins, Sain and Naragon Join Tigers." *The Sporting News*, October 15, 1966.

Spoelstra, Watson. "Price Is Right as No.2 Backstop, Bengals Learn." *The Sporting News*, June 22, 1968.

—-. "Sain's Advice Huge Plus for Tiger Hurlers." *The Sporting News*. September 7, 1968. p. 9.

—-. "Sain, Naragon Give Tigers Early Line on '69." *The Sporting News*. November 2, 1968. p. 29.

Stann, Francis. "How Grant Takes Washington." *Baseball Digest*, September 1960: pp.18–19 and 45–46.

"The Big Defeat." *Barberton High School Yearbook.* Barberton, Ohio, 1947.

Other Sources

All quotations from Hal Naragon comes from several interviews the author had with him in June and July 2007.

Acknowledgements

The author would also like to thank Lynn O'Neil and the Barberton Public Library Local History Room for assistance with finding yearbooks and other early material regarding Hal Naragon.

Johnny Sain

by Jan Finkel

> First we'll use Spahn
> then we'll use Sain
> Then an off day
> followed by rain
> Back will come Spahn
> followed by Sain
> And followed
> we hope
> by two days of rain.
> —Gerald Hern, *Boston Post*, September 1948

> Johnny Sain loves pitchers.
> Maybe he doesn't love baseball so much,
> but he loves pitchers.
> Only he understands them.
> —Mickey Lolich

Nobody would mistake Gerald Hern's most famous work for "Casey at the Bat" or even poetry, but it sums up most of what many people know about Johnny Sain. That's unfortunate because he was much more than someone whose name, fortuitously for Hern, rhymes with rain—trainer of fighter pilots, ace pitcher, one of the great pitching coaches, and holder of one of baseball's little-known but remarkable records.

He was born John Franklin Sain in the tiny town of Havana, Arkansas (population 392 in the 2000 Census), September 25, 1917, to Eva and John Sain. A mechanic and a good semipro ballplayer, the elder Sain would profoundly affect his son's career. Graduating from Havana High School in 1935, Sain was pitching semipro ball in Little Rock in 1936 when St. Louis Browns scout Pat Monahan spotted him and signed him to a contract. The young man spent 1936 and 1937 with Osceola (which in 1937 formalized its loose affiliation with the Browns) of the Class D Northeast Arkansas League.

Osceola left the Northeast Arkansas League after the 1937 season, and Sain moved on to the Newport Cardinals of the same league. Newport became affiliated with Detroit in 1939 and changed its name from Cardinals to Tigers. Two good seasons in Newport in 1938 and 1939 (16–4, 2.72 ERA in 1938 and 18–10, 3.27 ERA and a league-record 27 complete games the next season) weren't enough to get Sain to the majors as he unwittingly approached the turning point in his career.

It started innocuously December 9, 1939, when the Tigers traded second baseman Benny McCoy to the Philadelphia Athletics for outfielder Wally Moses. Citing corruption and cover-ups in the Tiger organization, Commissioner Kenesaw Mountain Landis nullified the trade and on January 14, 1940, granted free agency to 91 Detroit players and farmhands. Sain was among the fortunate new free agents and one of 23 released players who made it to the majors, although it would take two more years in the minors.

After middling seasons with the unaffiliated Class A1 Nashville Vols of the Southern Association in 1940 and 1941, Sain didn't seem to be going anywhere, but the Boston Braves, possibly on the advice of Pat Monahan or Memphis native James Thompson (Doc) Prothro, purchased his contract from Nashville and signed him to a major league contract in March 1942.

Sain made his debut with the Braves April 24, 1942—in relief—giving up a walk and a wild pitch in one and two-thirds innings in a 3–1 loss to the Giants at the Polo Grounds. He picked up his first win April 29 at Wrigley Field in relief of Al Javery. Sain went 4–7 with a 3.90 ERA, mostly in relief for Casey Stengel's last Boston team, buried in seventh place, 44 games behind the Cardinals but 18-and-a-half games ahead of the hopeless Phillies.

Despite the war, Sain completed the season. He reported to Naval Aviation cadet training November 15, and was sent to Amherst College. After completing flight training and several stops at various bases, Sain taught flying at Corpus Christi through the end of the war, receiving his discharge November 25, 1945. The experience proved seminal for the young man, who noted, "I think learning to fly an airplane helped me as much as anything. I was 25 years old. Learning to fly helped me to concentrate and restimulated my ability to learn." Shortly before his discharge, on October 1, Sain married Doris McBride; the couple had four children—John Jr., Sharyl, Rhonda, and Randy—but their marriage ended in divorce.

Military service benefited Sain. He threw whenever he could and pitched on several teams. Service ball was competitive, with many major leaguers involved (Ted Williams, Johnny Pesky, Joe Coleman Sr., and Buddy Gremp were all at Amherst with Sain). Sain was learning his craft well enough to go 12–4 with the North Carolina Pre-Flight team in 1943. He gained self-awareness, recognizing that although he was large for his era at 6-foot-2 and 180 to 200 pounds, he'd never be overpowering. Relying on mechanics, finesse, and guile, he'd make batters hit the ball and let the fielders do their jobs. Moreover, he changed his delivery. Up through 1942, he constantly varied his arm action, even occasionally throwing from a cross-fire motion. Sain saw two problems with his approach. One, he'd wind up hurting his arm. Two, what he'd been doing wasn't effective; 63 walks in 97 innings in 1942 was ample proof. After the war, according to Bill James and Rob Neyer, he kept his windmill windup (one of the last pitchers to do so) and threw almost exclusively overhand, occasionally dropping down to sidearm if he was ahead of the hitter. Finally, there was the curve ball his father had taught him how to throw, in the heat of battle, as Ed Rumill tells it:

"He was hurling in a kid game one day when, with the score tied and two men on base, up to the plate walked the neighborhood slugger. John knew he might have trouble if he threw nothing but fastballs, so he put down his glove and ran across the street to his dad. 'How do you throw a curve, Pop?' the youngster asked. Pop showed him how and he ran back across the street to fan the young slugger."

The knowledge of aerodynamics Sain had absorbed helped him make his best pitch so effective that he earned the nickname "The Man of a Thousand Curves."

Showing no signs of rustiness after four years away from the majors, Sain became a star and staff ace for the Braves in 1946, turning in a 20–14 slate with a career-best 2.21 ERA. From 1946 through 1948 he was a top pitcher in the National League with a 65–41 record and 2.77 ERA. Indeed, he fit in nicely with his American League counterparts Bob Feller (65–41, 2.75) and Hal Newhouser (64–38, 2.59). He was also helping himself with the bat, striking out just once in of 1946 and 1947 combined.

Life was improving for the Braves. Tommy Holmes was a solid contact hitter. Bob Elliott would be acquired from the Pirates over the winter and win the Most Valuable Player Award. And there was a decorated war hero, a southpaw who would be the perfect complement to Johnny Sain—Warren Spahn.

Spahn and Sain became a factor in 1947. Spahn had a great year, going 21–10 with a 2.33 ERA. Sain turned in a 21–12 mark and 3.52 ERA, the relatively high ERA tempered by his own hitting: a .346 average with only one strikeout. Sain became a part of history on opening day, April 15, becoming the first major league pitcher to face Jackie Robinson. Robinson went hitless in three trips to the plate, but the Dodgers won 5–3.

The 1948 season nearly brought baseball nirvana to Boston and New England. The Red Sox finished the season at 96–58, two games ahead of the Yankees but tied with the Indians. The first playoff game in American League history saw Boston go down, 8–3, in Fenway Park as Lou Boudreau put on a one-man show with two homers. The Braves, a perennial poor cousin to the Red Sox, took the National League flag with a 91–62 mark.

It was a magical year. The pennant race gave rise to Gerald Hern's often misquoted lines about "Spahn and Sain." Hern employed some poetic license. He got the Sain part right, but at 15–12 with a 3.71 ERA Spahn had one of the lesser seasons of his career. Arguably, Vern Bickford (11–5, 3.27) and Bill Voiselle (13–13, 3.63) were a touch more effective.

Nevertheless, the Braves got off to a terrible start in 1948, dropping six of their first seven games. They won nine of their next 13 to pull even at 10–10 on May 13. Playing steady, consistent ball from that point on, they took off.

Sain was spectacular. He led the league in wins (24), games started (39), complete games (28), innings pitched (314.2) and batters faced (1,313). Pitching the Braves into first place on June 15, he beat the Cubs, 6–3, in the first game televised in the Boston area. On July 15 he beat the Cubs, 2–1, in Wrigley Field. He often pitched well in defeat, falling 1–0 to Johnny Schmitz in Chicago on August 27, 2–1 to Fritz Ostermueller in Pittsburgh three days later and 3–2 to Sheldon Jones and the Giants in Boston on September 25. The loss to Jones was Sain's last of the season, coming late in an extraordinary streak of personal endurance. From August 30 to September 29, Sain started and completed nine games, winning seven of them. Backed by Sain's efforts, the Braves took 20 of their final 26 games to take the National League pennant by 6-and-one-half games over

St. Louis. *The Sporting News* named Sain National League Pitcher of the Year, even though the hometown Cardinals' Harry Brecheen had been outstanding. In further recognition of his contributions, Sain was runner-up to Stan Musial in voting for the Most Valuable Player Award.

The World Series opened in Boston on October 6, with Sain squaring off against Bob Feller. It was all a Series game should be, with both pitchers at the top of their game. The details are well known: Sain beat Feller, 1–0, the lone run coming after a controversial safe call on a pickoff play. Sain came back to face Steve Gromek in Game 4 in Cleveland and pitch superbly while losing, 2–1. The Indians took the Series in six games. Sain was magnificent in defeat—two complete games, a shutout, a heartbreaking loss, nine strikeouts, no walks, nine hits, and a 1.06 ERA.

Sain's decline was sudden: Between 1949 and 1951 he was a combined 37–44 with a horrendous 4.31 ERA. On August 29, 1951, the Braves sold him to the Yankees for $50,000 and a young pitcher who would pay long-term dividends to the Braves and haunt the Yankees a few years hence—Lew Burdette. For once, the Yankees seemed to get the short end of the deal, as Sain appeared in seven games, starting four and completing one, while posting a 2–1 mark and 4.14 ERA. It was hardly an auspicious start, especially for a team that had come to consider World Series titles its birthright.

One key to the Yankees' phenomenal success from the late 1940s to the mid-1960s was a genius for resurrecting the careers of players thought to be finished. Johnny Mize and Enos Slaughter had several productive years added to their careers. Johnny Sain was a chief beneficiary among the pitching fraternity. The Yankees' approach was simplicity itself. They made him a spot starter and reliever so that slightly fewer than half of his appearances were starts—16 of 35 in 1952 and 19 of 40 in 1953. He completed half of his starts, eight in 1952 and 10 in 1953, and relieved superbly the rest of the time. In 1954, his last full year in pinstripes, all 45 of his appearances were in relief.

Adapting to his new role, Sain began to pay off in 1952 as both starter and reliever. On May 20, he scattered six hits to beat the Chicago White Sox, 3–1. He rescued the Yankees twice at Fenway Park on September 24, coming on in the 10th to preserve a 3–2 win in the opener of the doubleheader, then saving an 8–6 win in the nightcap. Two days later he relieved in the Yankees' 11-inning pennant-clinching 5–2 win in Philadelphia. For the year he was 11–6 with a decent 3.46 ERA and seven saves.

Now a vital part of the Yankees' machine, Sain was outstanding in 1953. Again dividing his duties between starting and relieving, he posted a 14–7 mark with nine saves and a 3.00 ERA, earning a spot on the All-Star team.

By 1954, Sain was a full-time reliever, going 6–6 with a 3.16 ERA and a league-leading 22 saves, becoming the second pitcher (Ellis Kinder achieved it in 1953) to win 20 games in one season and save 20 in another. Wilbur Wood, Dennis Eckersley, John Smoltz, and Derek Lowe were the only other pitchers to have accomplished the feat in the following half-century. The Yankees had their best season under Casey Stengel with a 103–51 record, second to the Indians' record-setting 111–43 mark.

After three appearances, no decisions, and a 6.75 ERA, it was clear early in 1955 that Sain was finished with the Bronx Bombers. On May 11, the Yankees traded Sain and future Hall of Famer Enos Slaughter to the Kansas City Athletics for pitcher Sonny Dixon and cash. Sain appeared in 25 games for Kansas City, winning two and losing five while posting no saves and an ERA of 5.44. He pitched his final game on July 15 and was released eight days later.

Sain had a fine career: 139 wins against 116 losses, a solid 3.49 ERA; a *Sporting News* Pitcher of the Year Award; four 20-win seasons; three trips to the All-Star Game; four World Series; the league lead in wins once; and the league lead in saves once.

An effective contact hitter, Sain helped himself with the bat. He sported a .245 average, led the National League in sacrifice hits in 1948, led his league's pitchers in runs batted in five times, and struck out a mere 20 times in 774 at-bats.

Upon retirement, Sain returned to Arkansas, to Walnut Ridge, raising his children there. He was a prospering Chevrolet dealer in the town from 1952 to 1972, but at heart he was a baseball man. Sain got back into baseball in 1959, signing on as pitching coach for the A's. Working with a veteran staff on a team that could do no better than 66–88, he got adequate seasons out of Ned Garver, Bud Daley, Ray Herbert, and Johnny Kucks.

Catching on with the Yankees when Ralph Houk replaced Casey Stengel, Sain showed what he could do with good material. Persuading Houk to go with a four-man rotation, he transformed Whitey Ford from a perennially very good pitcher into a great one. Ford, who credits Sain with rekindling his career, in 1961 posted a 25–4 mark with a 3.21 ERA, to garner his only Cy Young Award; he had excellent seasons in 1962 and 1963. Ralph Terry found his groove in 1962, leading the league with 23 wins.

Jim Bouton, who called Sain "the greatest pitching coach who ever lived," had a career year in 1963 with a 21–7 slate and 2.53 ERA. Despite three World Series appearances and two world championships in three seasons, Houk fired Sain after the 1963 season. The move mystified many people, but Bouton offered a possible explanation: "What general—Houk started thinking of himself as a general—wants a lieutenant on his staff who's smarter than he is?"

After sitting out for a year, Sain joined the Minnesota Twins in 1965. Helping the Twins to their first pennant, he got Jim "Mudcat" Grant to achieve a 21–7 mark, to lead the league in wins. Under Sain's tutelage lefty Jim Kaat went 25–13 with a 2.75 ERA in 1966 to lead the league in wins and help the Twins to second place.

Sain moved to Detroit in 1967. Working with Mayo Smith's staff, he turned Earl Wilson into a 20-game winner for the only time in his career. In 1968, Sain crafted his masterpiece—Denny McLain, whose 31 wins (six losses and 1.96 ERA) were the most since Lefty Grove's 31 in 1931, a mark not challenged since. McLain took home the Cy Young and Most Valuable Player awards. With lefty Mickey Lolich picking up three wins, the Tigers won the World Series over the Cardinals and Bob Gibson. Sain kept McLain sufficiently focused in 1969 to go 24–9 and share the Cy Young Award with southpaw Mike Cuellar of the Orioles.

World Series victory aside, Sain and Smith (both independently wealthy) were barely speaking. Sain's tenure with the Tigers soured for good in 1969. Sain took time off to handle personal business. In his absence, Smith had the pitchers run, angering Sain. By June 15, Sain favorite Dick Radatz was traded to Montreal for cash. By August 10, Sain was fired.

Sain spent the 1970 season until late September as farm system pitching coach for the California Angels.

Leaving California, Sain was off to the White Sox, where he stayed for six years, largely because Chuck Tanner was manager the whole time and left Sain alone. Sain produced extraordinary results. Wilbur Wood, originally a reliever, became a workhorse starter and won 20 games each year from 1971 to 1974. Wood's ERA in 1971 was a miniscule 1.91, and his work in 1972 earned him *The Sporting News'* Pitcher of the Year Award. Reunited with Sain, Jim Kaat won 21 and 20 in 1974 and 1975. Stan Bahnsen, Rookie of the Year with the Yankees in 1968, reached his career high in wins in 1972 with a 21–16 slate. Making those win totals remarkable was that the White Sox weren't even a .500 club during his tenure, whereas the Yankees, Twins, and Tigers had all been pennant winners.

When Tanner left the Sox to manage the Oakland A's, Sain didn't go with him.

The years on the South Side of Chicago paid an even greater dividend than all those 20-game winners. On July 3, 1972, the divorced Sain was introduced to the widowed Mary Ann Zaremba at a club in the suburbs. Sain was smitten. Mary Ann remembers, "He called me the next day and said, 'You have to marry me.'" That seemed impetuous, so they compromised on a date at Comiskey Park the next day, Independence Day. The date presumably went well: They were married on August 24.

Sain coached Braves pitchers in 1977, but on a miserable team that went 61–101 and saw owner Ted Turner manage (and lose) for a day, he had only one first-rate pitcher, future Hall of Famer Phil Niekro. Sain spent a few years in the Braves' minor league system, then, reunited with Chuck Tanner, went back to the Braves for one final fling from 1985 to 1986, but Rick Mahler was the best he had to work with on two second-division teams.

Most of Sain's coaching career followed a pattern: Almost immediate success, the devotion of his pitchers, inevitable conflict with management, and the search for another job. Houk, Mele, and Smith all won a Manager of the Year award with Sain as their pitching coach, then left town not long after Sain's departure.

Sain's success consisted of several personal qualities. He was credible. Because he'd been successful with superior mechanics, pitchers figured he knew what he was talking about. Sain was loyal, sticking up for his pitchers even if it meant tangling with the manager or the front office. Indeed, he clashed with most of his employers, leading to frequent job searches. Finally, he accepted each pitcher on his unique terms, never trying to make a pitcher a clone of himself.

Nevertheless, some of Sain's teaching methods were strictly his own. He endeared himself to pitchers by not making them run. Some baseball people found this strange, but Sain had two reasons for the tactic. On the practical side he noted, "You don't run the ball up to home plate." On the pedagogical side, Sain said, "I've always felt that a lot of pitching coaches made a living out of running pitchers so they wouldn't have to spend that same time teaching them how to pitch." But he also believed that pitchers had to keep their arms strong, so he had them throw almost every day, even after a long stint on the mound the day or night before. To keep pitchers mentally focused, he had, for example, Wednesday's pitcher chart pitches for Tuesday's game; that way, the pitcher could observe both his teammates and the opposing pitchers and hitters. The benefits seem obvious, and most managers and pitching coaches now have their pitchers chart games, but Sain seems to have been the first to make it a practice.

Finally, Sain brought his own brilliant creation to the table. Roger Kahn describes it concisely in *The Head Game*:

"The Yankees hired Sain in 1961 as pitching coach. He showed up with a briefcase full of inspirational books and tapes and a machine he was patenting as the 'Baseball Pitching Educational Device,' which everyone soon called 'the Baseball Spinner.' Baseballs were mounted on rotating axes—one axis per ball—and you could snap one in a variety of fast-ball spins and the other in rotations for sliders and curves. The baseballs were anchored. Except for rotating, they didn't move. Using John Sain's Baseball Pitching Educational Device, you could practice spinning your delivery at home or in a taxi or in a hotel room without endangering lamps, mirrors, or companions."

What Sain achieved as a pitching coach (16 20-game winners) is impressive, given the diversity of talents he worked with. Whitey Ford and Denny McLain had experienced considerable success. Jim Bouton, Jim Kaat, and Mudcat Grant had yet to reach their potential. Then there was Wilbur Wood, undergoing the transformation from reliever to starter.

Suffering from ill health after a stroke in 2002, Johnny Sain died November 7, 2006, in Resthaven West Nursing Home in Downers Grove, Illinois. Surviving him were his wif,e Mary Ann, his four children, 11 grandchildren, and two great-grandchildren. Returning to Havana, he was buried in Walker Cemetery.

References

Publications

Allen, Thomas E. *If They Hadn't Gone: How World War II Affected Major League Baseball*. Springfield, Mo.: Southwest Missouri State University. 2004.

Gilbert, Bill. *They Also Served: Baseball and the Home Front: 1941–1945*. New York: Crown Publishers. 1992.

James, Bill, and Rob Neyer. *The Neyer/James Guide to Pitchers: An Historical Compendium of Pitching, Pitchers, and Pitches*. New York and London: Simon & Schuster. 2004.

Kahn, Roger. *The Head Game: Baseball Seen from the Pitcher's Mound*. New York: Harcourt. 2000.

Kelley, Brent. *The Case For: Those Overlooked by the Baseball Hall of Fame*. Jefferson, N.C.: McFarland. 1992.

Peary, Danny, ed. *We Played the Game: 65 Players Remember Baseball's Greatest Era, 1947–1964*. New York: Hyperion. 1994.

Shalin, Mike, and Neil Shalin. *Out by a Step: The 100 Best Players NOT in the Baseball Hall of Fame*. South Bend, Ind., and New York: Diamond Communications. 2002.

Thorn, John, and John Holway. *The Pitcher: The Ultimate Compendium of Pitching Lore: Featuring Flakes and Fruitcakes, Wildmen and Control Artists, Strategies, Deliveries, Statistics, and More*. New York and London: Prentice Hall. 1988.

Vincent, David, Lyle Spatz, and David W. Smith. *The Midsummer Classic: The Complete History of Baseball's All-Star Game*. Lincoln, Neb., and London: University of Nebraska Press. 2001.

Wright, Craig R., and Tom House. *The Diamond Appraised*. New York and London: Fireside Books at Simon & Schuster. 1989.

Articles

Rumill, Ed. "Johnny Sain—Hero of the Hub." *Sport Pix* (February 1949), 68–69, 96.

Rumill, Ed. "20 for Sain." *Baseball Magazine* (January 1947), 277–278.

Web sites

www.baseball-almanac.com
www.baseballindex.org
www.baseballlibrary.com
www.baseball-reference.com
www.paperofrecord.com
www.proquest.com
www.retrosheet.org
www.sabr.org

Software

Baseball Oracle (available for purchase from Lucid Software at *www.lucidsoftware.com/baseball/*)

Complete Baseball Encyclopedia by Lee Sinins (available for purchase from *www.baseball-encyclopedia.com*); also known as Sabrmetric Baseball Encyclopedia

National Pastime Almanac 1876–2006 by Ron Gudykunst (RonLG@aol.com) (available for download at *http://hometown.aol.com/ronlg/index.html*)

Professional Baseball Player Database 1922–2004 Version 6.0 (available for purchase from Old-Time Data, Inc. at *www.baseball-almanac.com/minor-league*)

Other Sources

Johnny Sain files at the National Baseball Hall of Fame and Museum Library in Cooperstown, New York.

The Broadcasters

Ernie Harwell

by Matt Bohn

For 55 seasons, baseball fans were able to get a greater enjoyment out of baseball because of the play-by-play descriptions of Ernie Harwell. In his easygoing, laidback Southern drawl, he would exclaim that a home run was "long gone," that a batter on a called third strike "stood there like the house by the side of the road." Ernie might announce that a foul ball in Tiger Stadium might be snatched by a fan from Saginaw or St. Clair Shores. Modest about his own contributions to baseball, Harwell said in a 2005 interview about baseball broadcasting, "The game has got to be paramount. People are going to listen to the game no matter who's announcing it, they want to find out who's winning and what the score is and everything else is pretty much secondary."

Ernie Harwell was born in Washington, Georgia, on January 25, 1918. His father and uncle ran a furniture store that also served as a funeral parlor. As a child, Ernie loved baseball, playing the game as much as possible and listening to it on radio. The local druggist, knowing of young Ernie's enthusiasm for the sport, encouraged him to broadcast an imaginary Atlanta Crackers game for patrons of the drugstore. Harwell's attempts at play-by-play were greeted with gentle gales of laughter by drugstore patrons as young Ernie had a speech impediment that hindered his attempts to pronounce the letter "s." His parents eventually paid for him to take elocution lessons.

In 1934, the 16-year-old Harwell saw his first major league game while visiting a relative in Chicago. That same year, he also gained a job. Dissatisfied with the amount of space devoted to Atlanta baseball in *The Sporting News*, Harwell wrote the paper a letter offering to serve as their Atlanta correspondent. Hoping to seem older than his 16 years, Harwell signed his name "W. Earnest Harwell." Impressed with samples of Harwell's writing, the paper invited him to write regularly.

Through his high school and college years, Harwell also worked part-time for the *Atlanta Constitution* sports department. In 1940, during his senior year at Emory University, he made his radio debut, landing a job as sports director at radio station WSB. Hosting a twice-nightly fifteen-minute sports program, Ernie was able to interview some of the biggest names in sports at the time including Ty Cobb, Ted Williams, Connie Mack, and heavyweight boxer Jack Dempsey.

A year after graduating from Emory University in 1940, Harwell married Lulu Tankersley. Ernie and Lulu's union would be a lasting one. In August 2007, the Harwells celebrated 66 years of married life. They raised four children together.

In 1942, with World War II raging, Harwell enlisted with the Marines. During his time in the service, he was a correspondent for the Marine newspaper *Leatherneck*. He got his first taste of baseball play-by-play in 1943, while still serving in the Marines. Atlanta Crackers owner Earl Mann asked Ernie to do the Crackers broadcasts and he agreed, provided that he could donate his pay to the Red Cross. His stint as a Crackers announcer quickly came to a halt, though. Some civilian listeners felt it was wrong for a serviceman to broadcast baseball games. The Marines told Ernie he could no longer work Crackers games. Mann, however, impressed with Harwell's style, told him that when he was discharged from the service, the Crackers' announcing job was his.

Discharged from the Marines in early 1946, Harwell approached Mann about the Crackers job. At this time, station WATL had obtained the rights to Crackers broadcasts. The station wanted to hire its sports director, Stan Raymond, as the Crackers' voice. Mann, true to his word, insisted that Ernie be the Crackers' radio voice. Pushing for Ernie's hiring, Mann finally won out on the day before the 1946 season opener.

After losing out on an opportunity to broadcast for the New York Giants in 1947 because of a sponsor conflict, Harwell got the chance to broadcast the Brooklyn

Dodgers' games the following year. Regular play-by-play man Red Barber was scheduled to cover the Olympics for CBS that summer. The Dodgers asked Harwell to fill in; then, when Barber was stricken with an ulcer that July, the Dodgers needed another announcer immediately. Crackers' president Mann was willing to let Ernie go to Brooklyn, but for a price. So, in the only deal of its kind, Harwell was traded to the Brooklyn Dodgers in exchange for catcher Cliff Dapper. Harwell became a member of the Dodgers' broadcast crew August 4, 1948. Lead announcer Red Barber, still recovering from the effects of a bleeding ulcer, rejoined the team a month later. Ernie said in a 2005 interview, "He [Red] was still weak and he couldn't do a whole lot, so Connie [Desmond] and I did pretty much the bulk of the work the rest of the season. The first game he came back to was when Rex Barney pitched a no-hitter at the Polo Grounds. And that was the first game I ever worked with Red."

In 1949, Ernie added television to his duties as a Dodgers announcer. Barber, Desmond, and Harwell took turns handling the television portion of the home broadcasts that year—one man on TV, the other two on the radio. Harwell realized right away that television dictated a different approach to play-by-play than radio. "I thought that came pretty much automatic," he said. "I realized that you had to keep your mouth shut a lot more on TV than you did on radio and it wasn't too difficult for me to move back and forth from one medium to another." Only home games were broadcast on television at the time. On road trips, only two of the three broadcasters would make the trip with the team: "We sort of usually had two guys rather than three in the booth at a time. One guy just sort of took off and didn't do that particular game."

Offered a better opportunity with the Giants in 1950, Ernie moved from Ebbets Field to the Polo Grounds, where he was teamed with announcer Russ Hodges. His second year with the Giants turned out to be what he called in his memoir, *Tuned to Baseball*, "the most thrilling season of my broadcasting career." That season, the Giants and Dodgers tied for the pennant, leading to a three-game playoff series before the World Series. The coaxial cable having just been laid, the series was the first sporting event to be broadcast live from coast to coast. On the day of the third and deciding game, Ernie was assigned to cover the game nationally over NBC-TV. In *Tuned to Baseball*, he recalled "I would be on NBC-TV coast-to-coast on the biggest game in baseball history. Hodges, my partner, would have to settle for radio." Ernie felt fortunate—there would be four radio announcers from various outlets that day, but he would be the only television announcer covering the game.

As it turned out, Russ Hodges' description of the famous game-winning Bobby Thomson home run ("The Giants win the pennant!") became one of the most famous play-by-play moments in sports history. Ernie's contribution to the "shot heard 'round the world" was largely forgotten. In those days, few games were recorded for future play. When accepting the Ford Frick Award in 1981 at the Hall of Fame induction ceremony, he said, "Television had no instant replay, no recording in those days. Only Mrs. Harwell knows that I did the telecast of Bobby Thomson's home run."

Dropped by the Giants after the 1953 season, Harwell moved to Baltimore, becoming the first broadcaster for the new American League Orioles. Working in Baltimore, Ernie covered subpar baseball teams (the Orioles, formerly the St. Louis Browns, went 54–100 their first season) but had the opportunity to work with other great baseball voices, including Chuck Thompson and Herb Carneal. In 1957, Orioles (and former Tigers) third baseman George Kell spent some time with Harwell in the broadcast booth while recovering from a beaning. At Harwell's invitation, Kell broadcast some innings of play-by-play. Kell's broadcasting was well received and eventually led to his becoming a full-time baseball announcer with the Detroit Tigers.

Kell later returned the favor. In 1959, while he was doing Tigers radio and TV with Van Patrick, the sponsorship of the Tigers broadcasts changed from the Goebel brewery to Stroh's, the new sponsor decided to replace Patrick with a voice not identified with Goebel. Kell recommended Harwell for the job and told him of the opening. Though he had a strong position in Baltimore, Ernie always liked Detroit and decided to make the move, signing with the Tigers during the 1959 World Series

Kell and Harwell teamed up on Tigers radio and television, splitting play-by-play duties equally from 1960 to 1963. Ernie told *Detroit News* reporter Lynn Henning in 2002, "I'd do the first four-and-a-half innings on TV, and George would do the same thing on radio. Then we'd swap." After Kell left radio in 1963, Harwell was teamed with former Tiger manager Bob Scheffing for a year before being assigned to radio only beginning in 1965.

Ernie, an avid baseball historian, was known for his generosity to his broadcast colleagues. Ray Lane told of an example of Ernie's willingness to help a colleague when he became Harwell's broadcast partner in 1967. Forty years later, Lane remembered how Harwell called him and kindly offered him the use of his vast personal collection of baseball books and records. Lane recalls Harwell saying, "Listen—I have all these things from past history. I have record books…down in my basement. Anything that you ever need concerning baseball—it's yours to use. I'll make the offer one time and any time you want to take a look at any of this stuff, you're welcome to it." Ernie's collection of baseball books and memorabilia was later donated to the Detroit Public Library. Lane, appreciative of Harwell's kindness to a fledgling broadcaster, called him "the true Southern gentleman."

Harwell and Lane first worked together during 1967, a season marked by riots in Detroit and a near-miss of the AL flag for the Tigers. When the Tigers won the American League pennant the following season, Ernie covered the World Series on NBC radio with Pee Wee Reese. He was also asked to select the national anthem singers for the games played at Tiger Stadium. For one of the games, Harwell asked singer Jose Feliciano to sing the anthem. Feliciano's nontraditional rendition was met with angry public reaction and even some calls for Harwell to lose his job. But Ernie stood by his selection of Feliciano and weathered the controversy.

Though Harwell felt fortunate to work alongside a number of good broadcast partners in Detroit, his longest professional association began in 1973 when he was teamed with Paul Carey. Ernie and Paul worked together for 19 seasons. In sharp contrast to later Tiger broadcasters, there was very little on-air banter between the two. Harwell worked the first three and last three innings and rarely commented during Carey's middle three innings of play-by-play. Harwell explained this in an April 5, 1987, *Detroit Free Press* article, saying, "I talk enough during six innings. That's the way I feel about it. With Paul I don't want to interrupt the flow of his game. There are so many times guys come in just to be coming in and we just try to avoid that." Reflecting on their approach in a 2005 interview, Ernie said, "I guess our philosophy was we were there for each other, but we didn't do a lot of chit-chat. If there was a pitching change and Paul was on the air, I'd probably come in and give some other scores or make some comments—or vice versa. I think if anything really significant happened that we felt like needed discussion, we would discuss it. But we didn't talk about stuff after every pitch like some of the guys do now. We concentrated on the game."

Though the two had little on-air conversation, they were known for having a good working relationship. Carey told *Detroit Free Press* sportswriter Joe Lapointe in 1987,

"Basically what it comes down to is we have very different personalities. And I think that's why it works well. I'm a fretter and a worrier. I like the responsibility of the small details. I think Ernie does not. Ernie would like to come in and enjoy the overall atmosphere of the ballpark. Ernie feels that everything is going to come out all right." Carey said in all their years together, they had never had an argument. "I've never had a harsh word between us. I don't think anybody ever has arguments with Ernie Harwell. I have a temper. People might get mad at me. But I don't think anybody could ever get mad at Ernie Harwell."

While still covering the Tigers every day during the regular season, Harwell was no stranger to network baseball audiences at All-Star or postseason time. Ernie broadcast the 1958 and 1961 All-Star games for NBC Radio. He covered many American League Championship Series on CBS Radio from the mid-1970s to the late 1980s as well as providing play-by-play for NBC radio during the 1963 and 1968 World Series.

Harwell was also a football voice as well, working Baltimore Colts games during the 1950s. After his arrival in Detroit, Harwell covered football for one more year (1963) as a voice of the Michigan State Spartans. Asked by Lynn Henning in 2002 if he felt his style was better suited to baseball than football, Harwell said, "I probably fit it [baseball] better than I did with football. There were some people in my early days who thought I was a better football than baseball broadcaster. I think, in football, it moves along, and if you have an authoritative voice, and don't correct yourself and can call the play quickly, and beat the crowd noise, you can be a great football announcer. Nowadays they have a lot more advantages. They can look at videos, at replays. I enjoyed football, but baseball is a better game for radio than any other sport."

On August 2, 1981, Harwell was presented with the Ford Frick Award by the National Baseball Hall of Fame. Ernie was only the fifth broadcaster to receive the honor, and the first living broadcaster—let alone active broadcaster—to be selected. In his acceptance speech, Harwell was modest about his accomplishments, saying "I know that this is an award that is supposed to be for my contribution to baseball. But let me say this: I have given a lot less to baseball than it's given to me. And the greatest gift that I've received from baseball is the way that the people in the game have responded to me with their warmth and their friendship."

After the 1990 season, the 72-year-old Harwell tried to negotiate for three more seasons as a Tigers broadcaster.

However, he was flatly told by Tigers president Bo Schembechler that radio station WJR and the Tigers wanted Harwell to broadcast for just one more year and then announce his retirement. The Tigers and WJR refused to allow Harwell to go on broadcasting beyond 1991.

Announcing his firing at a December 19, 1990, press conference, Harwell said, "I wanted to go on longer, but they decided they didn't want me to go on longer. Bo was very forthright. He told me, 'We don't want you to come back.' I have no bitterness. I was surprised when the one-year deal came up. My health is fine." Harwell was quoted as saying in the *Detroit News*, "I was told they wanted to go in a different direction. I would have preferred to have the decision on my shoulders rather than have somebody tell me."

Schembechler countered that Harwell was asked to retire because the team and the radio station were afraid he would retire suddenly and they would be left scrambling to find a replacement. The December 20, 1990, edition of the *Detroit News* quoted Schembechler as saying "It's our judgment that he's coming down close to the end of his career. We didn't want to have to go out and search." However, Schembechler's explanation rang hollow with fans. Reaction from the public was swift and negative—shock and anger. Former Tigers pitcher Denny McLain called the move "classless and gutless." A volunteer at a Grosse Pointe hospital told *The Sporting News* that when the nuns working there heard of the Harwell firing "they said some words I didn't think they knew." It was a public relations disaster for the team and the radio station.

Harwell, while hurt by the firing, harbored no bitterness about it. A deeply spiritual man, he preferred to forgive and move on. After an emotional farewell to Tigers fans at the end of the 1991 season (as well as to radio partner Paul Carey, who had announced his retirement that year), Harwell found work elsewhere in 1992. Broadcasting 14 games on radio for the California Angels as well as CBS Radio's Game of the Week, he found he missed covering one team day after day. He told *Detroit News* reporter Dave Dye in 1993, "Working for CBS was great. I think it gave me an added dimension. But I don't think there's anything an announcer enjoys more than being with one team. You do a much better job when you're there every day. As a national announcer, you don't have the familiarity or the feeling for a team as a guy that is there all the time."

After Michael Ilitch bought the Tigers in 1992, he asked Harwell to come back for one more season as a radio voice of the team. Working with Rick Rizzs and Bob Rathbun, Ernie provided play-by-play for the third, fourth, and fifth innings of Tigers broadcasts during the 1993 season. Originally planning to retire after that season, Harwell was persuaded to come back the following year on TV. Joining 1968 Tigers alumni Jim Price and Jim Northrup, Harwell became a member of the Tigers' cable broadcasting crew on PASS (Pro Am Sports System, a pay-cable channel) in 1994. That season, he appeared in 25 PASS telecasts providing play-by-play for the first three and last three innings.

Harwell continued covering Tigers games for PASS (and eventually for over-the-air station WKBD) through the 1998 season. He returned to WJR-AM for the final season at Tiger Stadium in 1999 and provided continuity in the narration of Tiger games as the team moved to Comerica Park. In 2002, at age 84, Harwell announced he was retiring. The season became one long goodbye. In each city that the Tigers visited Harwell was honored. In most visiting stadiums, he was asked to throw out the ceremonial first pitch. In Cleveland, the visitors' broadcast booth was renamed in his honor. Comerica Park's press box was renamed the Ernie Harwell Media Center. The respect and appreciation shown to Harwell by the fans and the teams were reminiscent of the outpouring from the fans when it seemed that 1991 would be the final year of his career. The only difference was that this time Ernie was leaving of his own accord.

When the Tigers played their last game, in Toronto, that season, Ernie signed off saying, "I have just finished my baseball broadcasting career. And it's time to say goodbye, but I think goodbyes are sad and I'd much rather say hello. Hello to a new adventure. I'm not leaving, folks. I'll still be with you, living my life in Michigan—my home state—surrounded by family and friends. And rather than goodbye, please allow me to say thank you. Thank you for letting me be part of your family. Thank you for taking me with you to that cottage up north, to the beach, the picnic, your work place and your back yard. Thank you for sneaking your transistor under the pillow as you grew up loving the Tigers. Now I might have been a small part of your life. But you've been a very large part of mine. And it's my privilege and honor to share with you the greatest game of all."

Since his retirement, Harwell has returned to the booth on a few special occasions. During the 2006 AL Division Series between the Tigers and the Yankees, he provided a few innings of play-by-play over the Tigers radio network and ESPN. "I'm going to drop in for a bit," he said. "I'm so honored. Anything they want me to do suits me fine. It's nice to be thought of again." In May 2007, Harwell joined Mario Impemba for a few Tigers games on Fox

Sports Net Detroit. Outside of baseball, he still keeps busy as a spokesman for Blue Cross/Blue Shield of Michigan. Harwell said in 2006, "I'm fine and I'm working hard. I've got a ten-year contract with Blue Cross/Blue Shield with a ten-year option, so I've got to live to be one hundred and six." He laughed, "I'm going to do that or die trying."

References

Publications

Carneal, Herb, and Stew Thornley. *Hi Everybody!* Minneapolis: Nodin Press. 1996.

Harwell, Ernie. *Life After Baseball*. Detroit: Detroit Free Press. 2004.

Harwell, Ernie. *Tuned to Baseball*. South Bend, Ind.: Diamond Communications. 1985.

Keegan, Tom. *Ernie Harwell: My Sixty Years in Baseball*. Chicago: Triumph Books. 2002.

Kell, George, and Dan Ewald. *Hello Everybody, I'm George Kell*. Champaign, Ill.: Sports Publishing. 1998.

Patterson, Ted. *The Golden Voices of Football*. Champaign, Ill.: Sports Publishing. 2004.

Articles

Crowe, Steve. "Harwell succeeds Kell as Tigers' TV Voice." *Detroit Free Press*, March 8, 1997, p. 1A.

Dye, Dave. "Say It Isn't So, Bo: Tigers did Harwell wrong." *The Sporting News*, December 31, 1990, p. 3.

Dye, Dave, and Bill Halls. "Harwell joins Price, Northrup on PASS." *The Detroit News*, April 19, 1994, p. 4C.

Green, Jerry. "Tigers, Ernie Harwell call it quits." *Detroit News*, December 19, 1990, pp. 1A and 4A.

"Harwell back in a familiar chair." *Detroit News*, March 4, 1993, pp. 1C and 6C.

"Harwell to call two games." *Grand Rapids Press*, May 22, 2007, p. D1.

Henning, Lynn. "Ernie Harwell Signs Off, Detroit will miss man, voice. Retiring Tigers announcer regards fans, city fondly." *The Detroit News*, September 26, 2002, p. 1F.

"Insiders Say." *The Sporting News*, December 31, 1990, p. 3.

Lapointe, Joe. "Ernie and Paul: Together 15 years and still in tune." *Detroit Free Press*, April 15, 1987, pp. 9E and 11E.

Parker, Rob. "Harwell leaves booth with class." *The Detroit News*, September 30, 2002, p. 1D.

Reidenbaugh, Lowell. "Reichler, Richman Saluted as Winners of Spink Award." *The Sporting News*, August 15, 1981, p. 30.

Spadafore, Jim. "Harwell makes return in visitors' radio booth." *Detroit News*, May 5, 1992, p. 5C.

Spoelstra, Watson. "Harwell-Kell Combo Will Air Tiger Tilts." *The Sporting News*, October 21, 1959, p. 18.

Spoelstra, Watson. "Kell Will Return to Motor City Mike." *The Sporting News*, February 13, 1965, p. 9.

VanOchten, Brian. "Sound familiar? Ernie's back at mike tonight. Harwell will join ESPN, radio announcing teams for guest appearance." *Grand Rapids Press*, October 6, 2006, p. E2.

Other Sources

Bohn, Matt. Phone interview with Ernie Harwell, June 29, 2005.

Bohn, Matt. Phone interview with Ray Lane, June 28, 2007.

George Kell

by Matt Bohn

In a career that spanned 15 seasons, George Kell batted .306 in 1,795 career games. Narrowly beating out Ted Williams for the batting title in 1949, he hit over .300 in nine seasons. A 10-time All-Star, Kell was finally inducted into the Baseball Hall of Fame in 1983. When his playing career was over, he turned to the microphone and was a Tigers broadcaster for 37 seasons. Kell's Arkansas twang endeared him to Detroit fans with such "Kell-isms" as "It's a bright, sunshiny day," "It's a bunt, and a dandy," and "I don't think you can hit a ball any harder than that."

The son of Clyde and Alma Kell, George Clyde Kell was born August 23, 1922, in Swifton, Arkansas. George's father, a barber, had been a pitcher on the Swifton town team. Clyde, a native of Imboden, Arkansas, was such a great pitcher that the Swifton Town Team offered to buy him a barber shop if he moved to Swifton and pitched for the team all of the time. Clyde accepted the offer.

George, the oldest of three boys (brother Everett "Skeeter" Kell played for the Philadelphia Athletics in 1952), loved baseball from an early age. "I was a [St. Louis] Cardinal fan as a kid," Kell told the Associated Press in 1950. "We used to make the trip up to St. Louis a couple of times a season. I worshipped the old Gas House Gang—Dizzy Dean, Pepper Martin, Joe Medwick, Leo Durocher." In his autobiography *Hello Everybody, I'm George Kell*, he recalled, "There was never a time in my life when I didn't think about playing baseball. I loved the game. I loved every part about it."

Graduating from high school at 16, Kell enrolled at Arkansas State University at Jonesboro in the fall of 1939. Since the university did not have a baseball team, Kell played on the intramural softball team and then for the Swifton town team in the spring of 1940. It was also in the spring of 1940 that Kell got his first chance to play baseball professionally.

The Brooklyn Dodgers had an affiliate in Newport of the Class D Northeast Arkansas League. The Swifton postmaster, Clyde Mitts, often traveled to watch the team play. One day, after the Newport team lost a doubleheader, Mitts told the team's general manager about the baseball playing ability of George Kell. The GM was interested. After discussing it with his father (who would have preferred that young George stay in college), he agreed to join the Newport team the next day. In the 1940 season, Kell played in 48 games and batted a puny .160. During the 1941 season, Kell fared better—this time batting .310 in 118 games. Following the 1941 season, Kell's contract was sold to the Durham Bulls of the Class B Piedmont League.

After a brief stint with Durham, Kell was signed by Lancaster of the Class B Interstate League, then affiliated with the Philadelphia Athletics. Leading all of professional baseball with a .396 average in 1943, Kell attracted the attention of Athletics owner-manager Connie Mack, who offered him the opportunity to play for the A's after Lancaster was finished with the playoffs. Mack wanted Kell to play just one game with Philadelphia. In his debut with the A's on September 28, 1943, Kell hit a triple in his first at bat. "I tried to act very calmly like it was just another time at-bat for me," Kell wrote in his autobiography. "But I was dying to pinch myself to make sure this was all really happening."

Kell then returned to Arkansas to teach at a junior high school. Kell remembered, "Because of the war, they were using anyone who had at least some college experience. I also coached the basketball team and studied as hard as the kids so that I wouldn't get shown up in class."

Playing on a regular basis with the A's in 1944, Kell hit for a .268 average in 139 games. Nearly repeating his numbers in 1945, he batted .272 in 147 games. In early 1946, hitting .299, Kell found himself traded. On May 18, he went to the Detroit Tigers for outfielder Barney McCosky. Kell commented in the May 23, 1946, issue of *The Sporting News*, "It's the biggest break I've ever had in baseball."

Sixty years later, Kell told reporter Bill Dow, "Mr. Mack said, 'George, come up to my suite; I need to talk with you,' and that's when he told me I was traded to the Tigers for Barney McCosky, It was such a shock and felt like a rejection, but Mr. Mack told me, 'George, you're going to be a good ballplayer, and I'm sending you to a team that will pay you the kind of money that I can't.' As it turned out, it was the greatest day in my life."

Kell made his Detroit debut in the first game of a doubleheader against the league-leading Boston Red Sox in a jam-packed Briggs Stadium: "I was scared to death. ... In the first inning, Johnny Pesky slashed one down third base, I made a backhand stab and threw him out, which really calmed me down. I was young, full of enthusiasm and played hard, and the Detroit fans accepted me and were so good. It was the beginning of a great romance."

With the Tigers, Kell had his greatest years—batting better than .300 average every season from 1946 to 1951. In 1946, while batting .327, Kell struck out just 20 times. The next season, Kell made the American League All-Star team for the first time, but as he recalled in his autobiography, "I felt I had to prove myself all over again. I had to prove the previous season was not a one-year fluke." He finished 1947 with a .320 average in 152 games.

"From a personal standpoint, 1948 turned out to be the worst year of my career," Kell wrote. That season he was sidelined with two injuries. The first injury came in the second game of a May 8 doubleheader at Yankee Stadium when Kell's wrist was broken by a pitch from Vic Raschi. The injury prevented him from playing until May 31. At Yankee Stadium again on August 29, Kell's jaw was fractured by a ground ball from Joe DiMaggio. Talking to an Associated Press reporter about the injury two years later, Kell said, "I must have been out on my feet. They tell me afterwards that manager Steve O'Neill tried to take the ball away from me, and I wouldn't let them have it." This injury ended his season, leaving him with a still-impressive .304 average in just 92 games played.

If 1948 was the worst year of Kell's career, 1949 was perhaps the best. That season, he edged out Ted Williams for the batting title on the last day of the season. Fifty years later, Kell recalled the final day for *Detroit Free Press* reporter Gene Guidi: "I went into the game trailing Ted Williams by a couple of points and didn't think I had a chance because I figured Ted was good for a couple of hits that day. Bob Lemon was pitching for Cleveland against us and he was always tough, but I got a double and single my first two at-bats." Later in the game, Bob Feller came out of the bullpen to face Kell. George remembered, "He walked me in the fifth inning and then got me out in the seventh." Late in the game,

it was learned that Williams had been hitless in the Red Sox game against the Yankees. Kell's 2-for-3 game would give him an average of .3429—enough to push him past Williams (.3427) for the batting title. In the ninth inning, manager Red Rolfe wanted to put in a pinch-hitter to bat for the third baseman. Kell insisted on batting. "I remembered Ted Williams not sitting out the last day of the (1941) season after he was already at .400, and I wasn't about to back into a batting title against him." As Kell stood on deck in the ninth inning, batter Eddie Lake grounded into a double play to end the game. "I celebrated by throwing my bats in the air," Kell said. "It was quite a feeling."

In 1950, a season in which the Tigers narrowly missed winning a pennant, Kell hit .340 in 157 games. His average was second only to Boston Red Sox second baseman Billy Goodman's league-leading .354. Kell had a career-high 114 runs and 101 RBI. In addition, he led the league with 218 hits and 56 doubles, and committed only nine errors. In that season, "I was confident about every aspect of my game," he said in his autobiography.

Kell followed that season up with another great year, batting .319 in 1951 and leading the AL with 191 hits and 36 doubles. But on June 3, 1952, Kell's playing career as a Tiger ended when he was traded to the Boston Red Sox. The blockbuster deal included eight other players. Kell, pitcher Dizzy Trout, shortstop Johnny Lipon, and outfielder Hoot Evers were traded for pitcher Bill Wight, first baseman Walt Dropo, third baseman Fred Hatfield, shortstop Johnny Pesky, and outfielder Don Lenhardt. General Manager Charlie Gehringer told Kell that the Tigers hadn't wanted to trade him, but they needed to do something to shake up the team, and the Red Sox wouldn't accept any deal that didn't include Kell. "I sure didn't want to leave Detroit, but the only thing that made it better was going to Boston because that's the other great baseball town in the American League," Kell said later. He finished the 1952 season with a .311 batting average.

In Boston, Kell's closest teammate became his onetime rival for the batting title, Ted Williams. Kell said in 2005, "We were already close when I went to Boston; we were primarily a young ballclub and he was an elder and I was past 30, so we hit it off real good." Continuing his habit of batting over .300, Kell batted .307 in 1953, with 141 hits and 73 RBI, and a career-high 12 home runs that year. His tenure in Boston was brief. On May 23, 1954, he was traded to the Chicago White Sox for Grady Hatton and $100,000.

"It was a totally different feeling in 1954 when the Red Sox traded me to the White Sox," Kell said in his autobiography. "More than anything else, I felt like I was being used." For the first time since 1945, his average dipped below the .300 mark that year. Playing in only 97 games, Kell hit .276 in 1954. In 1955, he bounced back in 1955 and led the Chisox with a .312 average and 81 RBI, but wasn't completely happy: "(T)hat trade took something out of me. I had lost something. That deal got me to thinking about retiring."

At the end of the 1955 season, White Sox manager Paul Richards left to pilot the Baltimore Orioles. Once with the Orioles, Richards wanted Kell to join him there and on May 21, 1956, George, along with pitchers Mike Fornieles and Connie Johnson and outfielder Bob Nieman, was traded to the O's in exchange for pitcher Jim Wilson and outfielder Dave Philley. Though he was flattered that Richards would want him as his third baseman, Kell's thoughts of retirement grew stronger. "After that season … I made up my mind I would play one more year. I really didn't even feel like doing that, but the Orioles had made quite a commitment to get me. I figured I owed it to them," Kell said.

Kell was beaned twice in 1957, his final season. On May 6, at Briggs Stadium, Kell was knocked down when he was hit above the right ear by a Steve Gromek pitch. Though Kell wasnot seriously injured, he was sidelined for 10 days. Then just five weeks later, in a June 9 game at Comiskey Park in Chicago, Kell was beaned again, this time by pitcher Dick Donovan. Though again avoiding serious injury, he once more sat out for 10 days.

During his period of recovery, George sat in the Orioles' radio-TV booth with Ernie Harwell. Kell was no stranger to broadcasting by this time, having worked with Harry Heilmann on a 15-minute radio show in Detroit in the early 1950s. In his memoir *Tuned to Baseball*, Harwell recalls joking with George, "Now you're learning the art of free-loading.… All the hot dogs you can eat and all the pop you can drink." Harwell remembered, "After a couple of games, I asked him to broadcast an inning for us. He did. He liked it and the listening audience liked him."

Kell retired after the 1957 season, saying in January 1958, "It's hard to retire, but it's a lot easier than waiting around until someone tells you you're through." He expressed a desire to spend more time with his 12-year-old son and 9-year-old daughter, saying, "A baseball player just doesn't get to see much of his family. I was away from them entirely for three months a year and at least half the time during the season."

Kell had planned to spend his retirement tending to his 800-acre farm in Swifton. However, CBS Television was interested in hiring a former player to host a 10-minute pre-game interview during the "Game of the Week" telecasts. Paul Richards recommended Kell for the job. Kell told Neal Russo in May 1958, "I jumped at the offer. I didn't want to turn my back on baseball completely.… Besides, I'm away from home only one night a week and I never work more than two days a week."

Kell discovered that as a former player, he had an advantage as a sports interviewer. He told Fred Petrucelli in November 1958, "My connections in baseball proved to be very valuable and that's where I had an edge. After all, I was talking and working with people with whom I had played for many years." Kell was able to set up the interviews himself, citing as an example, "I was able to line up baseball personalities pretty easily myself. I called Ted Williams for a spot on the show and he agreed readily. I don't know how some of the players would have reacted if the advertising boys had signed 'em up."

When Tigers broadcaster Mel Ott was killed in an automobile accident in November 1958, Detroit business manager Harry Sisson offered Kell the job as his replacement. Kell was hesitant to give up so much time away from his family. After talking with Tigers owner John Fetzer, Kell agreed to team up on radio and TV with Van Patrick. Kell reflected in his autobiography, "Before I left that room, I had signed a five-year contract to work all one hundred fifty-four Tigers games as the No. 2 broadcaster. To this day I can only speculate as to why I changed my mind and signed that contract. I'm really not certain." He credited John Fetzer's sincerity and his own love of the Tigers for helping persuade him to take the job.

During the 1959 season, Kell provided play-by-play for the middle three innings of each Tigers game. At the end of the 1959 season, he covered the playoff games between the Los Angeles Dodgers and Milwaukee Braves for ABC Television. Originally, the plan was for Kell to work with Buddy Blattner, but when Dizzy Dean used his connections with the sponsor to block Blattner from doing the broadcast, Kell found himself providing all of the play-by-play and color commentary by himself.

After his broadcast partner, Van Patrick, was fired in 1959, Kell's old friend Ernie Harwell became his new partner. Together, they broadcast Tigers games on radio and television beginning in 1960. Wanting to spend more time with his family, Kell resigned the 1963 season. Tigers owner Fetzer did not want Kell to leave the broadcasts, however. Kell recalls that Fetzer told him, "We are going to work this out some way so that you're still part of the team and everyone is satisfied."

Kell sat out the 1964 season and was rumored to be in line to replace Mel Allen as the voice of the New York Yankees. However, his heart was with the Tigers, and when Fetzer arranged for him to do only 40 to 50 broadcasts a season rather than a full schedule of games, Kell couldn't resist coming back. He rejected an offer from ABC to do the Game of the Week. With the Tigers, he told reporter Jack Craig in 1970, "I just drive to Memphis and take a jet to wherever the Tigers are playing. And if it's a Saturday day game, I get home late the same night."

Though a Tigers fan, Kell resisted being a "homer" on the air. "I'm for the Tigers, but I'm not a cheerleader," he told writer Joe Falls. "When he [Fetzer] hired me, he told me there were some announcers who irritated him by rooting so openly for their team. He told me to report accurately and fairly. Naturally, I'm for the Tigers—you've got to be honest about this thing—but he told me I could show my allegiance by the tone of my voice, rather than going rah-rah-rah."

One of the highlights of his broadcasting career was to be able to provide play-by-play for the 1968 World Series. In *Hello Everybody, I'm George Kell*, he said, "If I have one regret from my playing career, it's the fact that I never had the opportunity to play in a World Series. Every player wants to get that chance at least once in his career. So getting into one as a broadcaster for the Tigers was very special for me." Having previously provided play-by-play for the 1962 World Series over NBC radio, George covered the World Series games from Detroit for NBC television in 1968.

Kell's achievements on the field were recognized when he was elected to the Baseball Hall of Fame in 1983. Though proud of his accomplishments as a player, Kell was overwhelmed by the honor, telling Joe Falls that July, "[W]hen I think of being there with Babe Ruth and all the rest, I'm in awe."

Aside from his baseball broadcasting duties, Kell had other business and political interests to keep him busy. Besides raising Black Angus cattle on his farm in Swifton, he had also invested in an automobile dealership in Newport, Arkansas. He accepted an appointment to a 10-year term on the Arkansas Highway Commission. Proud of his appointment to the office, Kell said "I treated that appointment very seriously. I felt as though I not only was representing the Kell name, but also all the good hard working people of the state of Arkansas."

In 1991, Kell missed 20 Tigers broadcasts to take care of his wife, Charlene, as she battled cancer. George and Charlene Felts had met in the fifth grade and were high school sweethearts. Secretly married May 24, 1941, they spent 50 years together and raised two children (George Jr. and Terrie) before Charlene's death on August 20, 1991. Devastated by his wife's passing, George, a devout Methodist, relied on his deep religious faith to give him strength as he grieved the passing of his wife.

A few years after Charlene died, George met a woman named Carolyn at a local bank for which he was a director. Eventually working up the nerve to ask her to dinner, George said in his autobiography, "I suppose one thing led to another until finally I asked her if she wanted to be tied down to an older man and marry me." George and Carolyn were married May 7, 1994.

After enduring surgeries on his knee and on a broken disk in his back, Kell announced his retirement from broadcasting in January 1997.

Kell's home in Swifton was destroyed by fire in 2001. Miraculously, Kell was rescued from the burning home. Carolyn Kell told *Detroit News* sportswriter Tom Gage, "We don't like to think of what might have happened if a volunteer fireman hadn't been driving by the house at that very time. He went up the stairs and dragged George out. God was on his shoulder that night. That's what I tell George. From playing to broadcasting, all his life, God has been on his shoulder."

Kell, still an avid Tigers fan, returned to Detroit on October 14, 2006, to throw out the first pitch before Game 4 of the American League Championship Series between the Tigers and the Oakland Athletics. Greeted by a standing ovation at Comerica Park, the 84-year-old Kell threw the ball to Tigers coach Andy Van Slyke. Kell commented, "Andy said I threw it better than (Mickey) Lolich." (Lolich had thrown out the first pitch the previous night.) Kell was touched and overwhelmed by the reaction the Detroit fans had to his return to Detroit. "I'm overwhelmed," Kell said. "I didn't expect all of this. The standing ovation sounded like Joe DiMaggio was on the field. It was a little bit more than I expected."

References
Publications
Kell, George, and Dan Ewald. *Hello Everybody, I'm George Kell*. Champaign, Ill.: Sports Publishing. 1998.
Smith, Curt. *Voices of the Game*. New York: Simon & Schuster. 1987.

Articles

Associated Press. "George Kell Never Argues With Umpires, Says Players Get Better Deal If Quiet." *Danville* (Virginia) *Bee*, September 13, 1950, p. 9.

Associated Press. "Kell Quits Baseball Without 'Pink' Slip." *Lawton Constitution* (Oklahoma), January 7, 1958, p. 11.

Basenfelder, Don. "Wheaton and Kell Bloom as Red Roses; A's Believed Holding Inside Track for Slugging Pair; George Tops Hitters." *The Sporting News*, September 9, 1943, p. 7.

"Blattner Charges Dizzy Threw Curve, Quits Duet; Tiff Over Playoff TV Job Led to Blowup." *The Sporting News*, October 28, 1959, p. 23.

"Cadillac Agency, Golf Resort Helped Kell to Make up Mind." *The Sporting News*, August 31, 1963, p. 18.

Chi, Victor. "Charlene Kell, George's wife, dies of cancer." *Detroit Free Press*, August 22, 1991, p. 1F.

Craig, Jack. "Airing Ball Games an Honor." *The Sporting News*, July 25, 1970, p. 54.

Crowe, Steve. "Kell came to Detroit and brought Harwell with him." *Detroit Free Press*, January 29, 1997, p. 3E.

Crowe, Steve. "For openers, Kell pays a visit. Retired announcer admits: 'Yeah, this really does seem strange.'" *Detroit Free Press*, April 8, 1997, p. 6C.

Crowe, Steve, and John Lowe. "As George Kell, who retired Tuesday after 37 seasons as a Tigers broadcaster might say . . . 'It's all over!' Hall of Famer Announces Retirement." *Detroit Free Press*, January 29, 1997, p. 1E.

Dow, Bill. "Kell's Well. Ex-Tiger third sacker returns to Detroit for 'Baseball as America.'" *Detroit Free Press*. March 7, 2006, p. 1D.

Ellis, Jim. "Big Gus Unlimbers Big Guns on Return to Limping Orioles." *The Sporting News*, May 15, 1957, p. 15.

Ellis, Jim. "Birds Take Wing Despite Injuries to Kell, Francona." *The Sporting News*, June 1, 1957, p. 20.

Falls, Joe. "Another Chapter on Baseball Broadcasters." *The Sporting News*, August 28, 1965, p. 14.

Falls, Joe. "Fans favor jocks on TV." *The Sporting News*, May 31, 1980, p. 34.

Falls, Joe. "Kell realizes dream in Hall of Fame." *The Detroit News*, July 31, 1983, p. 1D.

Gage, Tom. "Talking with ... George Kell. *The Detroit News*, April 30, 2001, p. 4F.

Gage, Tom. "Kell misses calling games, remains an avid Tiger fan. He had Hall of Fame playing career, but never lost enthusiasm for broadcasting." *The Detroit News*, June 23, 2003, p. 4F.

"George Kell Now Cattle Raiser." *The Sporting News,* March 16, 1949, p. 25.

Guidi, Gene. "Tigers Corner: Kell traveled tough road to 1949 batting crown." *Detroit Free Press*, September 25, 1999, p. 5B.

Hammer, Dave. "Former Tiger Kell remembers career—Trip to Cooperstown helps 82-year-old forget pain from accident." *Grand Rapids Press*, August 7, 2005.

"Kell stays a fan." *Grand Rapids Press*, October 15, 2006, p. C1.

"NBC and CBS Saturday TV Starts April 5; Brave-Dodger, Yank-Phil Tilts First to Air." *The Sporting News*, April 2, 1958, p. 32.

Petrucelli, Fred. "Kell a Smash Hit First Season on TV and Happy in Role." *The Sporting News*, November 19, 1958, p. 15.

Russo, Neal. "He's 'Old Pro' of Video in Rookie Season; Kell Clouting at .300 Clip as Aircaster. Ex-Hot Sack Star Making Grade on TV." *The Sporting News*, May 28, 1958, pp. 13–14.

Silva, Chris. "Tigers great Kell a hit with first pitch." *Detroit Free Press*, October 15, 2006, p. 2D.

Spoelstra, Warren. "With Tigers All's Well, After Club Acquires Kell." *The Sporting News*, May 23, 1946, p. 6.

"Tiger Kell rescued from his burning home." *Grand Rapids Press*, October 9, 2001.

"Yanks Swamp Tigers After Losing 3–2 Tilt." *Syracuse Herald Journal*, May 9, 1949, p. 59.

Young, Dick. "Kell Reported in Line For Yank Radio Job." *The Sporting News*, October 24, 1964, p. 32.

Web Sites

www.retrosheet.com

Other Sources

McClary, Mike. Interview with George Kell, March 14, 2007. http://www.detroittigerspodcast.com/2007/03/14/the-detroit-tigers-podcast-episode-4-its-a-dandy/Accessed June 23, 2007.

Ray Lane

by Matt Bohn

Born in Detroit in 1930, some of Ray Lane's earliest memories were of listening to Ty Tyson and Harry Heilmann broadcast Detroit Tigers games on radio. Lane found he had an early passion for radio. "My mother always said I had the loudest mouth in the neighborhood," Lane recalled in 2007. "I wasn't sure I wanted to be a sports announcer, but I wanted to be a radio announcer." An outfielder at Mackenzie High School in Detroit, Lane would do the play-by-play from his position during the games.

Enrolling at Michigan State University with a baseball scholarship, Lane majored in radio and television journalism. During the summers, he played baseball in various amateur leagues and after graduation briefly played professionally with the Chicago White Sox organization. Ray said, "I went down faster than the elevator did! I went to spring training with Colorado Springs. By the time they broke camp I was with Waterloo—that was Class B at that time. And then I wound up playing at Topeka—but not very much. They found out that I couldn't hit anymore and that was it."

After a stint in the Army where he played baseball at Fort Sheridan, Lane gave up on dreams of playing baseball and focused on finding work in broadcasting. Answering an ad in *Broadcasting* magazine, Ray first found radio and TV work as an announcer in Cadillac, Michigan. After spending six months in Cadillac, he moved to station KWWL in Waterloo, Iowa, working as a staff announcer. It was at KWWL that he had his first experience as a play-by-play baseball broadcaster, filling in on broadcasts of the Waterloo White Hawks. Leaving Waterloo after a year, Lane worked at WNEM-TV in Saginaw, Michigan, for more than three years before getting a chance to work in his home town of Detroit.

Hired at WJBK-TV, Channel 2, in Detroit, Lane's background in baseball quickly became an asset for him. Within a few months of his arrival at WJBK, the station began looking for someone to host a five-minute evening sports show. Lane recounted, "They had me audition for that and I beat out a few guys and all of a sudden my sports career took off again." Soon, Lane was providing color commentary on Detroit Lions broadcasts. When the Tigers were looking for a new broadcaster after the 1964 season, Tigers owner John Fetzer asked Lane to send him an audition tape. "He called me up and ... asked me if I would go to Puerto Rico where he had a winter team down there and do a couple of days of broadcasting ... on a tape recorder as if I was doing it on radio ... and also do a couple of games as if I was doing it on TV. So I went down there and made about four or five tapes ... brought them back ... he looked at them and that's when he hired me to work with George Kell for two years."

Lane's arrival in the baseball broadcast booth spelled an end to his stint as a Detroit Lions announcer, however. Lane recalled that it was in his second season with the Tigers, "Mr. Fetzer said 'This will be your last year of doing pro football.' And I said 'Well why is that?' And he said 'No Major League announcer is going to work pro football.' He was really against that." It didn't upset Lane. Baseball was his favorite sport and he was thrilled to be covering his hometown team.

After two years on television, Lane moved to the radio booth. "They decided they were going to get rid of the other fellow [Gene Osborn] who was working radio with Ernie Harwell and asked me if I'd be interested in the radio job. That's how I got the radio job." It was a dream come true: "To do all the games—that was outstanding—that's what I've been thinking of probably all of my life!"

Lane's first year on Tigers radio, 1967, was also the year rioting erupted in Detroit. As the riots began, Ray and broadcast partner Harwell sat in the Tiger Stadium radio booth watching thick black smoke rising beyond the left field roof. "When you saw the black smoke it almost looked as if someone was burning a bunch of tires," he recalled. Soon, the announcers received a message from

Tigers general manager Jim Campbell warning them not to mention the smoke over the air. "So we were told not to mention it and we STILL—even while the game was on, had no idea that the riots were going on…and we didn't find out until after we came out of the booth after the ballgame."

For the 1968 fall classic, Lane hosted a World Series pregame show which included analysis on each game by Vic Wertz and Dizzy Dean. "And that was a lot of fun," Lane reminisced, "because you didn't know what Dean was going to say." Although Lane didn't have the opportunity to broadcast the World Series in 1968, he did provide play-by-play with Ernie Harwell on local radio during the 1972 postseason. The 1972 American League playoffs turned out to be his last as a Tigers radio announcer.

Announcer Van Patrick had hosted a late-night sports show on WJBK, but by 1972 had to reduce his schedule due to illness. The station's general manager asked Lane to recommend someone to pick up the slack given Patrick's reduced schedule. Lane said he'd be interested in even giving up his baseball schedule if a good enough offer was made to do the studio work. Lane recalled the station's general manager telling him, "'Tell you what: You do the TV shows…you'll be off the radio broadcasts in '73,' but he said, 'you'll sit out one year and we'll make arrangements that you come back on television with Kell in 1974.' Funny thing happened…I got a call probably just before the end of the year…and it was a fellow by the name of Hal Middlesworth who was the public relations director of the Tigers…and he said 'Ray, I've got some bad news… Channel 2, WJBK, has just lost the rights to do the television games of the Tigers…it's going over to Channel 4.' And so, instead of sitting out one year and getting back on TV, I ended up doing a TV scoreboard.… So that took care of that and there was no way I could get back in."

Lane spent the next few years focused on his studio work at WJBK as well as coverage of other sports. He broadcast Michigan State football and basketball, called the Big Ten Game of the Week over various cable outlets, and spent 16 years covering Red Wings games. "I would do interviews between the first and second periods and then the wrap-up at the end of the game. So I got involved in that but I didn't do any of the play-by-play."

In 1979, Lane returned to baseball broadcasting, this time for the Cincinnati Reds. The Reds were looking for an announcer to broadcast the Reds games of WLWT-TV and Jim Campbell recommended Lane to the Reds. "I still kept my home here. I was going back and forth—they only did about fifty games a year. Only three at home and the rest were on the road." Lane continued his studio work on WJBK while announcing Reds games until new management took over the Detroit station. Previously, the management at WJBK had promoted Lane's status as a Reds announcer. The new management, however, wanted Lane to give up his position with the Reds and focus solely on his work with WJBK. Lane refused. "So after twenty-one years I was through at Channel 2."

In the late 1990s, Lane returned to Tigers play-by-play from time to time. When Tigers announcer Frank Beckmann had a conflict due to a University of Michigan football game, Lane would substitute. By 2001, when Al Kaline left broadcasting to take on other duties with the Tigers, Lane was asked to fill in for him the rest of the season. Following the 2001 season, Lane continued to fill in for Beckmann on Tigers telecasts. "It was a thrill filling in because all of a sudden after Al left, they brought in different guys," Lane said as he recalled his delight at working with such former Tigers as Jack Morris, Lance Parrish, and Dan Petry.

Lane and his wife, the former Carolyn Loose, were high school sweethearts. At the time of her death in 2004, they had been married for 50 years. They had three children.

References

Publications
Eichorn, George B. *Detroit's Sports Broadcasters on the Air.* Charleston, S.C.: Arcadia Publishing. 2003.

Articles
Green, Jerry. "Memory Lane: Detroit Sportscasting Legend Covered It All." *Detroit News.* June 28, 1996.
"Lane Quits as Tiger Voice." *Detroit News,* January 20, 1973, 1D.
Obituary of Carolyn Loose Lane. *Detroit News,* May 21, 2004, 5B.
Spoelstra, Watson. "Kell Will Return to Motor City Mike." *The Sporting News,* February 13, 1965, 9.

Other sources
Bohn, Matt. Phone interview with Ray Lane, June 28, 2007.

Larry Osterman

by Matt Bohn

Larry Osterman's career as a Detroit Tigers broadcaster spanned 20 seasons over four different decades, including two world championships. A modest, hardworking sportscaster, Osterman was known and respected by his colleagues for his professionalism. George Kell, his television broadcasting partner, said of Osterman, "I learned more about broadcasting from Larry Osterman than anyone I ever worked with."

Born in the small town of Malcolm, Nebraska, in 1935, Osterman spent the summer months of his childhood searching the radio dial for baseball games. A St. Louis Cardinals fan, Larry would listen to the St. Louis games over KMOX, and would sometimes pull in the broadcasts of the Triple A Kansas City Blues, as well as the Chicago Cubs and the Chicago White Sox. "On Sunday afternoons I would lie on the living room floor and listen to baseball games that were re-created on KOWH, Omaha," Larry recalled in a 2005 interview conducted by mail. "They had a continuous loop of crowd noise running behind the announcer. About every minute, you would hear a guy groan. A minute later, the same guy would groan. Another minute later... same guy... same groan..."

From an early age, Osterman knew what career he wanted to pursue. "Becoming a play-by-play man was the first and only thing I set for myself as a career goal," Osterman told Jack Moss in the May 12, 1974, issue of the *Kalamazoo Gazette*. The hours young Larry spent listening to sports broadcasts on the radio prepared him for his future path. "Every night I would be turning the radio dial, trying to pick up the broadcast of baseball games," Osterman recalled in 2005. "In the fall and winter, I'd do the same, checking out announcers doing football, basketball and hockey radio play-by-play." Osterman was most impressed by the styles of such broadcasters as Bill King, Chuck Thompson, Ken Coleman, and Ray Scott: "I believe they were instrumental in how I eventually worked a game. I felt they had an approach to the game that would wear well with the radio listeners. I never copied them, but their styles certainly had an influence on my broadcasts."

After graduating from Malcolm High School in the top four of his class in 1953, Osterman enrolled at the University of Nebraska. Leaving college (later earning a degree from Western Michigan University), he took a job as sports director at KCOW in Alliance, Nebraska. It was at KCOW that he broadcast baseball play-by-play for the first time. "We were to do the radio broadcast of a semipro baseball game in Minitara, Nebraska," Osterman told the *Kalamazoo Gazette* in 1974. "There was no press box at the field, so we drove our car up near the diamond and put a batting cage in front of it for protection and I broadcast from the front seat."

In 1959, Osterman went to Kalamazoo to serve as sports director for the John Fetzer–owned radio station, WKZO. By 1961, Osterman was assigned to cover the Detroit Tigers' spring training camp in Lakeland, Florida. "I'll never forget the first time that I covered spring training in Florida in 1961. George and his then-partner, Ernie Harwell, invited me to accompany them to Ybor City for dinner at a Spanish restaurant," Osterman remembered in 2005. "I couldn't wait to get back to Lakeland, to call my wife, and tell her that I had dinner with George Kell and Ernie Harwell!" Osterman's coverage of Tigers spring training camps gave him the opportunity to become acquainted with many of the Detroit players, but his dream of being a play-by-play announcer of a baseball team still eluded him. Whenever a position became available on the Tigers broadcast crew, Osterman made it clear to John Fetzer that he was interested in the job. Finally, in 1967, Osterman got his chance.

At the close of the 1966 season, Tigers radio broadcaster Gene Osborn was fired. When TV announcer Ray Lane moved from television to radio, Osterman was hired as Kell's partner on WJBK-TV's Tigers broadcasts. Beginning in 1967, Osterman would broadcast play-by-play for the middle three innings of each Tigers telecast.

Though he had a great deal of experience broadcasting college sports for WKZO, Osterman quickly discovered that being a major league broadcaster was a different proposition entirely. Stepping onto the field at Yankee Stadium for the first time in 1967, he thought to himself, "This is a hell of a long way from Malcolm, Nebraska!" He credited his broadcast partner with making the transition to the major leagues more smoothly. "I learned more about the game of baseball from George Kell than anyone in my entire life!" Osterman said. "George Kell took the time to introduce me to people in the major leagues. He always introduced me as his 'partner.' He provided guidance on how to become a big-leaguer, how to fend for yourself on the road. He provided a tremendous bridge between my previous career working college games to a much higher profile level of sports broadcasting."

Osterman was able to broadcast many memorable moments in his early seasons as a Tigers telecaster. In 1967, the Tigers barely missed winning the pennant for the first time since 1945. The following year, Osterman had the pleasure of describing the Tigers' championship season. "Individually, the highlight was the game in which McLain won his thirtieth," Osterman told Kalamazoo's *Encore* magazine in 1989. "That was pretty exciting stuff because it was the only time that George missed doing a game in his entire broadcasting career. His daughter was getting married that day, so I did the entire nine innings."

In 1975, the rights of the Tigers telecasts went from WJBK-TV to WWJ-TV. The new rightsholder wanted to use members of its own sports staff on Tigers telecasts as a cross-promotion. As a result, Osterman's role on the telecasts was reduced. Beginning in 1975, he went from broadcasting three innings of play-by-play on each televised game to working only as color commentator on road telecasts.

By 1977, Al Kaline had been added as a color commentator to Tigers telecasts, making the broadcast booth even more crowded. Osterman said in 2005, "I have always been of the opinion (and still am) that three in a booth is one too many. I also was of the opinion that two Hall of Famers were ultimately going to be the main men and I was going to be the odd man out." He found himself without a place in the Tigers broadcast booth the following year.

Leaving his post at WKZO in early 1978, Osterman began hosting sports radio shows over WWJ-AM in Detroit. While Osterman was also providing coverage for University of Michigan football during this time, he quickly realized that he missed doing baseball play-by-play. Hearing about an opening on the Cincinnati Reds' TV crew, Osterman contacted the team about the job, only to be informed that they had just hired his friend, Ray Lane. "That same day I ran into Lane at the Detroit Sports Broadcasters Association luncheon. I told him of my interest in the Reds job and congratulated him on his successful application. He asked me if I had heard about the Minnesota Twins switching rights-holders and that they were looking for an announcer. I called KMSP that afternoon, sent a tape, flew to Minneapolis and joined the Twins broadcast crew within a couple of weeks."

From 1979 to 1983, Osterman paired with Bob Kurtz to cover telecasts of the Twins. On the air, he did all nine innings of play-by-play. During this time, Osterman was versatile in covering other sports as well. He provided coverage for the Detroit Red Wings, the Major Indoor Soccer League, and Michigan and Michigan State football—all on ON-TV, a pay-TV service—as well as the 1980 U.S. Olympic hockey exhibition schedule on ESPN.

Osterman also was active in producing instructional baseball videos. In the early 1980s, he produced a series of instructional baseball tapes marketed to Little League baseball players from the ages of 8 to 18. The series, "The Baseball Masters," included baseball tips from Al Kaline, George Kell and former Twins manager Frank Quilici.

In 1984, Osterman returned to broadcasting Tigers games, this time over a new cable channel, PASS (Pro-Am Sports System.) Larry remembered, "The startup of PASS was unique in that there weren't many sports broadcast companies in the entire country. In fact in our first year we were feeding cable systems throughout the U.S. One of my daughters watched our games regularly on a Florida cable system. We fed a lot of our games to NESN, a new and similar operation serving the New England area out of Boston. The timing could not have been more favorable. A 35–5 start does a lot to increase the interest in a ball club."

Teamed first with Bill Freehan and later with Jim Northrup, Osterman provided play-by-play for 70 to 85 Tigers games on PASS from 1984 to 1992. After being assured in December 1992 by the general manager of PASS that he would return to the booth the following year, Osterman was shocked to learn a month later that he was fired. The firing was explained as a "marketing decision" by PASS. Osterman told Steve Crowe of the *Detroit Free Press* at the time, "I'm shocked and more than a little disappointed about the whole thing for a lot of reasons. There was nothing that led up to it; nobody said they were unhappy with my work."

Osterman continued to work on other PASS programs including the Central Collegiate Hockey Association game of the week. Though Osterman continued to look for work with a major league baseball broadcast crew, he kept busy covering college basketball and the International Hockey League's Kalamazoo Wings.

In 1998, Osterman moved to Florida to become an educational television producer for the Pinellas County School district. Although the job has an educational focus, he finds it sometimes bring him back to his baseball roots. "We're doing some interesting stuff," Osterman reported in the April 9, 2001, edition of the *Kalamazoo Gazette*. "We did some more things with the Tampa Bay Devil Rays major league baseball team, using some of the players and our kids for word-usage educational messages. We spent two days in the Devil Rays' camp shooting and have gotten some great reviews on the final product." Osterman and his wife, Shirley, currently live in Largo, Florida. Married in 1957, they have four children.

References

Publications
Kell, George, and Dan Ewald. *Hello Everybody, I'm George Kell*. Champaign, Ill.: Sports Publishing. 1998.

Articles
"As a voice of the Tigers, Kalamazoo's Larry Osterman is a PASS master." *Encore* magazine (Kalamazoo, Michigan), February 1989.

Crowe, Steve. "PASS fires Osterman, teams Price, Northrup." *Detroit Free Press*. January 21, 1993.

Hawkins, Jim. "Campbell Sees Tiger Crisis as Springboard For Rise." *The Sporting News*, February 1, 1975.

Moss, Jack. "Career gamble pays off for Osterman." *Kalamazoo Gazette*, May 7, 1980.

Moss, Jack. "It's Not Easy For TV 'Pro'; But WKZO's Larry Osterman Takes a Realistic View." *Kalamazoo Gazette*, June 26, 1977.

Moss, Jack. "Larry Osterman going strong these days in Florida." *Kalamazoo Gazette*, April 9, 2001.

Moss, Jack. "Osterman a Television Big Leaguer." *Kalamazoo Gazette*, May 12, 1974.

Moss, Jack. "Osterman Gets Job in Detroit." *Kalamazoo Gazette*, February 16, 1978.

Moss, Jack. "Osterman gives the Wings a class voice." *Kalamazoo Gazette*, October 14, 1993.

"Osborn Out: Osterman New Member of Tiger Air Team." *The Sporting News*, December 31, 1966.

"Osterman on move." *Kalamazoo Gazette*, March 14, 1979.

Wagner, Bob. "From hockey to baseball; Osterman, Neal friendship leads to video productions." *Kalamazoo Gazette*, December 6, 1981.

Other Sources
Bohn, Matt. Interview with Larry Osterman conducted by mail, June 28, 2005.

Sock It To 'Em Tigers

Detroit in 1968

by Rick Vosik

The story of Detroit in 1968 is, at its heart, a story of two things: race and baseball. It's a story of transition—from a mob in full riot one year and a mob in wild celebration the next. It's about the journey from 15,000 empty seats for 1967's pennant-deciding closing game to raucous sellout crowds for the 1968 World Series.

To understand 1968 Detroit, rewind first to July 23, 1967. While many parts of the country enjoyed what came to be called the Summer of Love, Detroit was about to experience something very different.

It's 4 A.M., and undercover police are raiding a "blind pig," an illegal gambling establishment and bar, at 9125 12th Street. Typically, the owners are fined $100; patrons were booked and released. The cops expect to find a dozen or so customers; instead, they find over 80 blacks celebrating the return of two servicemen from Vietnam. As arrests are made and paddy wagons ferry the prisoners to jail, a crowd gathers. The crowd grows to more than 200 angry citizens, tired of what they view as police brutality.

Soon, shoving starts, a rock is thrown, and a full-blown riot erupts. By 8 a.m., the crowd on 12th Street has swelled to 2,000. Fires are started; businesses are looted. Police are outnumbered and cannot stop the growing riot. The riot spreads to cover 25 square miles of the city.

Later that day, a crowd of more than 34,000 gathered at Tiger Stadium, unaware of the bedlam on 12th Street except for the column of smoke rising from the north. The Sunday papers were already on the presses by the time the riot started, and television and radio stations had been asked to downplay the situation.

And so it was that Mickey Lolich took the mound for the Tigers against the Yankees for the first game of a doubleheader. Lolich pitched eight innings and took his 12th loss of the year. He arrived home after the games only to receive a call to report to his National Guard unit for riot duty. Lolich spent the night guarding a public works building on Detroit's west side; later he would be assigned to a police station downtown.

Another Tiger, Willie Horton, took a different kind of role. Horton, still dressed in his Tigers uniform, showed up on 12th Street (he'd grown up not far from the blind pig where the whole thing started) to try and calm the crowds. However, his pleas fell on deaf ears as the riot raged on.

In response to the violence, the Tigers' series with Baltimore, set to begin the following day, was moved to Baltimore and televised. Officials hoped that people would stay home and watch the game, quelling the riot. Instead, the game was halted in a rainstorm in the second inning and called off an hour later.

It took five days to restore order in Detroit. President Lyndon Johnson ordered federal troops to Detroit, and they combined with local law enforcement and National Guardsmen to form a combined force of 17,000. After five days of violence, 43 people were dead, 30 killed by law enforcement personnel. More than 7,200 men and women were arrested on riot-related charges. Rioters looted and burned 2,500 buildings, causing more than $30 million in insured property damage and undoubtedly millions of dollars additional damage to uninsured buildings.

To be sure, black dissatisfaction and resulting riots were not new to Detroit, nor to 1960s America. On June 20, 1943, black and white youths fought on the bridge linking Belle Isle to the city, setting off rioting and violence and resulting in 34 fatalities. In the end President Franklin Roosevelt ordered in federal troops to stop the violence; 350 of them guarded Briggs Stadium during a Tigers game.

In the 1960s, black riots started in Birmingham, Alabama, in 1963; the Watts riots in Los Angeles in 1965 lasted six days. Riots were also reported in Philadelphia, Harlem, Cleveland, Omaha, Milwaukee, Newark and York, Pennsylvania. In addition, riots occurred in more than 100 cities upon the assassination of Dr. Martin Luther King Jr. in Memphis, Tennessee, on April 4, 1968.

In Detroit, the underlying causes of racial tension were many. Blacks had migrated to the city in great numbers in the 1940s and '50s to fill the labor needs of the burgeoning automobile industry. In 1940, the percentage of black residents in Detroit was 9 percent, but this figure grew to 44 percent by 1970. (In 2000, the black population of Detroit was 82 percent of the total population of the city—by far the largest percentage of any major city.) The black population of Detroit more than doubled between 1950 and 1970 (from 300,506 to 660,428), while the number of white residents plunged 46 percent (from 1,545,847 to 838,877). Whites fled the city, often to the suburbs, and blacks took their place.

The rapid change in population brought with it crime, poverty, and crowding. Population density in the 12th Street area in 1960 was almost double the city's average, as housing was subdivided to make room for new residents. Urban renewal exacerbated crowding and caused anger as inner-city neighborhoods, mostly filled with black residents, were razed for freeways. Enrollment in Detroit schools increased by 60,000 in the six years prior to 1967; 57 percent of the students were black. This number of students would have required 1,700 more teachers and 1,000 more classrooms to meet the state average. The dropout rate was 50 percent.

Economically, blacks struggled. In the 1950s, Detroit auto manufacturers increased automation and outsourced parts production. Black workers were hit by this change, exacerbated by institutional discrimination within the auto industry. As a result, the economic gap between black and white widened.

Black militancy was on the rise as well in the 1960s. In 1967, for example, Black Panther H. Rap Brown told a "black power" rally that if Motown didn't come around, "we are going to burn you down".

Police discrimination and brutality played a major role in the events in Detroit in the 1960s. In a survey conducted by the *Detroit Free Press* after the riots in 1967, black respondents cited police brutality as the leading cause of the riots. (Other leading causes included overcrowded living conditions and poor housing.) At the time, blacks made up only 5 percent of the police force, and only one of eight held a rank higher than patrolman. Excessive use of force was alleged in the shooting of a prostitute in the back in 1962, in the beating of another prostitute in 1964, and the beating of a black teenager for "allegedly disturbing the peace."

A commission formed by President Johnson in July 1967, the National Advisory Commission on Civil Disorders, found that the three causes "have merged and reinforced each other in post-World War II years to create the inflammatory mixture which has exploded in the form of our terrible urban disorders of the past several years. Those three causes . . . are racism, powerlessness, and poverty."

This volatile mix existed in Detroit in the 1960s and fueled the riots in 1967. The atmosphere in Detroit continued to be tense throughout the year. In fact, as the hometown favorite Detroit Tigers began their final doubleheader of 1967 in Tiger Stadium on Sunday, October 1, only a half-game back of the Boston Red Sox, there were 15,000 empty seats in the stadium.

In 1968, though, the Tigers were credited with playing an integral role in bringing the city together. After it was over, owner John Fetzer told manager Mayo Smith, "You may not only have won the pennant, you might have saved the city."

That the Tigers would play a role in salving the wounds of racial tension is ironic, since, except for the Boston Red Sox, they were the last major league baseball team to integrate—in 1958, a full 11 years after Jackie Robinson's debut. Former owner Walter Briggs had said that the team would be integrated only over his dead body.

By 1968, however, Briggs was long dead, and black players like Willie Horton, Gates Brown, and Earl Wilson were integral to the success of the Tigers. As a result, both black and white fans had players of their own color to root for, while the players prided themselves on being color-blind. Nevertheless, on the national day of mourning for Martin Luther King Jr., Tigers management scheduled a mandatory practice. By contrast, major league baseball postponed its opening day because of the assassination.

By 1968, Detroit showed the loss of innocence that stemmed from the events of 1967 in the city, as well as the ongoing Vietnam War. Detroit's famed Motown Sound changed, became grittier, as the Supremes sang "Love Child," the Temptations performed the psychedelic-tinged "Cloud 9," and Marvin Gaye reached Number One with "I Heard It Through the Grapevine." The MC5, political revolutionaries and proto-punks, recorded their debut album live at the Grande Ballroom, while Iggy and the Stooges were likewise participating in the birth of punk. Regional favorite Bob Seger released his first album, featuring the antiwar "2 + 2 = ?". In November, the

Beatles launched the musically ambitious "white album." Meanwhile, *2001: A Space Odyssey, Rosemary's Baby,* and *Planet of the Apes* were popular in theaters.

In Vietnam, the Tet offensive began in late January, and the My Lai massacre occurred in mid-March, although the latter was not public knowledge until much later. Eugene McCarthy's strong support as an antiwar candidate led to Johnson's decision not to run for reelection.

Martin Luther King Jr. fell to an assassin's bullet in April; Bobby Kennedy suffered the same fate in June. Tommie Smith and John Carlos raised their black-gloved fists in support of black power at the medal ceremony for the 200-meter dash at the Mexico City Olympics. Saddam Hussein played a key role in a coup d'état that brought the Ba'ath party to power in Iraq. In August, police and anti-war demonstrators clashed at the Democratic National Convention in Chicago, using nightsticks, tear gas, and Mace to beat back the protestors. In October, the first manned Apollo mission was launched; in December, Apollo 8 orbited the moon. In November, Richard M. Nixon defeated Hubert H. Humphrey and third-party candidate George Wallace to win the presidency.

In January, former Tiger Goose Goslin was elected to the Hall of Fame. In early April, another former Tiger, Jim Bunning, became the first pitcher since Cy Young to notch 1,000 strikeouts in both the American and National leagues. In July, the first indoor All-Star Game was played in Houston's Astrodome, and Hank Aaron hit his 500th home run. Tom Phoebus of the Baltimore Orioles threw a no-hitter in April, and in September, Gaylord Perry of the San Francisco Giants and Ray Washburn of the St. Louis Cardinals tossed back-to-back no-hitters in Candlestick Park.

Meanwhile, the Year of the Pitcher was in full force. Carl Yastrzemski won the batting title as the only .300 hitter (.301) in the American League (Pete Rose managed to hit .335 in the NL) while Bob Gibson chalked up a 1.12 ERA, lowest in the majors since Dutch Leonard's 0.96 for the Boston Red Sox in 1914. And Denny McLain of the Tigers won 31 games—the first time a pitcher had won 30 games since Dizzy Dean did so in 1934 for the Cardinals.

Detroit baseball was hot. The Tigers remained in first place from early May until the end of the year, finishing 12 games ahead of the Orioles. The Tigers set an attendance record, topping 2 million fans for the first time in history.

Detroit baseball has been credited with bringing the city together in 1968, both black and white. In *A City on Fire: The Story of the '68 Detroit Tigers*, a TV documentary, Willie Horton said, "What really struck me is how the blacks and the whites were both celebrating. You know, they was just huggin' each other. I mean, like, it was a year before, just about, and they was at each other's throats." Said Ernie Harwell, longtime voice of the Tigers, "I think for that one year, people could tune in on the radio or TV, and have a common interest to root for. They'd want Willie Horton to hit a home run, or Jim Northrup to hit one. Whether he was black or white didn't make any difference, they were Tigers and the people could rally behind that one cause."

In the same documentary, Detroit sportswriter George Cantor said "[F]or those few months that surrounded that pennant race and that World Series, this was a wonderful place to live again."

While Detroit might have been, as Cantor says, a wonderful place to live, in many ways it has never recovered from the 1960s. The economic declines, tied to the difficulties of the automotive industry, continue. In 2005, the unemployment rate in the city of Detroit was 14 percent—the highest among the 50 largest U.S. cities. Detroit has one of the highest poverty rates in the country. Per capita income is but 60 percent of the national average.

Detroit's population decline from 1990 to 2000 was the second largest of all U.S. cities; only Baltimore posted a larger decline. Between 2000 and 2006, only hurricane-ravaged New Orleans had a larger decline in population. Detroit's was the fifth-largest city in the country in 1960. By 2006, the population had dropped by 48 percent, to 871,121 residents, 11th in the country.

White flight, exacerbated by the 1967 riots and court-ordered busing in the 1970s, continues. The proportion of white people in the city of Detroit was nearly 71 percent in 1940, but dropped to just over 12 percent in 2001.

Shells of thousands of abandoned and burned buildings litter the landscape of Detroit, many left over from the riots. As 2008 dawns, the city of Detroit does not have a shopping mall and has only one movie theater.

Recently, however, Detroit has enjoyed a surge of new downtown development. In the 1990s, the Comerica Tower was constructed, along with three casinos. Comerica Park, new home of the Detroit Tigers, replaced Tiger Stadium in 2000, and hosted the All-Star Game in 2005. Ford Field, home of the NFL's Detroit Lions, was opened in 2002, and the Super Bowl was played there in 2006. New office space and hotel redevelopment give additional signs of new hope to downtown.

References

Publications

Cantor, George. *The Tigers of '68: Baseball's Last Real Champions*. Dallas: Taylor Trade Publishing. 1997.

Farley, Reynolds, Sheldon Danziger, and Harry J. Holzer. *Detroit Divided*. New York: Russell Sage Foundation. 2000.

Fine, Sidney. *Violence in the Model City: The Cavanagh Administration, Race Relations, and the Detroit Riot of 1967*. East Lansing: Michigan State University Press. 2007.

Freehan, Bill. *Behind the Mask*. New York: The World Publishing Company. 1970.

Spreen, Johannes F., and Diane Holloway. *Who Killed Detroit?* Lincoln: iUniverse. 2005.

Stanton, Tom, ed. *The Detroit Tigers Reader*. Ann Arbor: The University of Michigan Press. 2005.

Sugrue, Thomas J. *The Origins of the Urban Crisis: Race and Inequality in Postwar Detroit*. Princeton: Princeton University Press. 1996.

Articles

Berliner, Dana. "How Detroit Drives Out Motor City Entrepreneurs." Available from *http://www.ij.org/publications/city_study/CitStud_Detroit.html*. Internet. Accessed July 2, 2007.

Folsom Jr., Burton. "The Costs of Segregation to the Detroit Tigers," in *The Freeman*, December, 2003. Available from *http://www.fee.org/publications/the-freeman/article.asp?aid=5335*. Internet. Accessed June 15, 2007.

Nuechterlein, James. "Remembering the riots. (Detroit race riots of 1967) (Editorial)," in *First Things: A Monthly Journal of Religion and Public Life*. October 1, 1997. Available from *http://www.leaderu.com/ftissues/ft9710/opinion/nuechterlein.html*. Internet. Accessed July 3, 2007.

"Our Nation Is Moving Toward Two Societies, One Black, One White—Separate and Unequal: Excerpts from the Kerner Report." Available from *http://historymatters.gmu.edu/d/6545/*. Internet. Accessed July 8, 2007.

"Report of the National Advisory Commission on Civil Disorders: Summary of Report". Available from *http://www.eisenhowerfoundation.org/docs/kerner.pdf*. Internet. Accessed July 7, 2007.

"Resignation in Detroit" in *Time*, February 9, 1976. Available from *http://www.time.com/time/magazine/article/0,9171,917975,00.html*. Internet. Accessed July 3, 2007.

Schweitzer, Karen. "Catching Up with Willie Horton". Available from *http://www.associatedcontent.com/article/2606/catching_up_with_willie_horton.html*. Internet. Accessed July 6, 2007.

"The American Dream Does not Yet Exist for All Our Citizens: Kerner Commission Members Discuss Civil Unrest." Available from *http://historymatters.gmu.edu/d/6465*. Internet. Accessed July 8, 2007.

"The Detroit Riots of 1967: Events." Available from *http://www.67riots.rutgers.edu/d_index.htm*. Internet. Accessed July 8, 2007.

"Thirty Years Later." Available from *http://www.eisenhowerfoundation.org/frames/millennium/chap1.html*. Internet. Access June 30, 2007.

Trowbridge, Gordon. "The Cost of Segregation: Part 2: Paying for Preferences. Busing battles spurred flight" in *The Detroit News*, January 21, 2002. Available from *http://www.detnews.com/specialreports/2002/segregation2/b02-395697.htm*. Internet. Accessed July 2, 2007.

Vitullo-Martin, Julia. "The Day the Music Died" in *The Wall Street Journal*, July 20, 2007.

Web Sites

www.census.gov

factfinder.census.gov/

Other Sources

A City on Fire: The Story of the '68 Detroit Tigers. Home Box Office, July 22, 2002.

Detroit Managers

by Rich Shook

Jim Campbell always wanted the best to manage his baseball teams. Okay, we can't quite put Les Moss and Joe Schultz in that category, but there were special circumstances for those managers. And try to remember they weren't around very long. Look at the list: Sparky Anderson. Ralph Houk. Billy Martin. Mayo Smith. Charlie Dressen. Sometimes it took Campbell a little more time than he would have liked, but generally speaking he knew who would do the best job of managing the teams he put together, and he nearly always got his man.

Campbell had Bob Scheffing as his manager when the 1960s started. Scheffing took over the 1961 team that made a run at the New York Yankees until mid-September, winning 101 games but still finishing so far back you couldn't see them with binoculars. It was different in 1962, especially when Al Kaline got hurt making a diving catch and was out of action a considerable amount of time. The team began splintering, and Campbell began looking for another manager.

The one he wanted was Charlie Dressen, who had a nice thing going with the Brooklyn Dodgers in the early 1950s but messed it up with his insistence on a multiyear contract. That's how Walter Alston made the Hall of Fame. "I got to know him when he was with the [Milwaukee] Braves," Campbell said of Dressen. "He was one of the finest baseball men I've ever known in my life. And that's taking nothing away from Sparky or Houk. I got to know him because [Braves owner John] McHale and I used to go over to Bradenton in spring training. I knew and liked him. Scheffing was the manager then and we had to make a change. Those guys were eating him up, the players, and he knew it.

"Charlie was advance scouting for Buzzie [Bavasi, GM of the Los Angeles Dodgers] then. I called Buzzy, asked him if I could talk to Charlie. He said, 'I'd never stand in his way. Do you want me to call him?' I said sure, and Buzzy said he [Dressen] was in New York scouting the Tiger club. He called me right back and said he'd just talked to Charlie and asked him his opinion about the Tigers. Charlie said, 'That's the worst looking club I've ever seen in my life.' So Buzzy said, 'Well, Jim Campbell called and would like you to take that club over.' Charlie said, 'You know, that's not such a bad-looking club. They've got some things they can do. Some players…'"

The Detroit farm system was producing players in the early 1960s—the farm system that Campbell was in charge of—but Dressen didn't live to see the end result. He had heart attacks in 1965 and 1966 and didn't survive the second one. "I knew Dressen was going to die," Campbell said. "He didn't look very good. But here's a guy who did a heckuva job with our kids. We had a young club and Charlie loved to play kids. And that team basically all came up through our farm system. We got [Norm] Cash for a player from our farm system [Steve Demeter]. [Denny] McLain from Chicago. And we got Earl Wilson in a trade. But everybody else was a product of our farm system, the front-line players."

The Tigers were a maturing club in 1966, but that was the season of three managers—Dressen, Bob Swift, and Frank Skaff, the first two of whom died before the year was out. Campbell spent the winter searching for candidates, and one of the people he talked to was Ralph Houk, then the manager and GM of the New York Yankees. "The guy I admired and would have liked to have had was Ralph Houk," Campbell said. "But he was tied in with the Yankees then. Solid. So I was talking over my dilemma with him and he said, 'We've got a guy I think would be able to handle that club.' I said, 'Who?' He said, 'Mayo.' I hadn't thought about him at all, but when Ralph recommended him . . . bang, bang, we hired him. So I gave Mayo a call and we made a deal. He wanted to hire his own coaches. Two he wanted for sure were 'Mose' [Wally Moses] and [Tony] Cuccinello. As pitching coach, he liked Sain. He'd known him from New York. I said, 'That's fine with me.' And of course Sain wanted to bring [bullpen catcher Hal] Naragon." Cuccinello had a long history of being with winning teams as a coach under Al Lopez with the Chicago White Sox and Cleveland Indians in the 1950s. Moses and Smith were buddies from long ago while Naragon and Sain, the saying went, were joined at the hip.

Smith won't go down as one of the greatest managers of all time, but he was the perfect manager for the 1968 Detroit Tigers. And unlike some of his contemporaries, he wore a World Series championship ring until the day he died. "We couldn't have gotten a better guy to manage our team," Campbell said in an early-1990s interview. "What Mayo did with that ball club.... His style was to say, 'Here's the bat and balls, go play.' And those guys, they were far enough along in their careers that they could go play."

Things started coming apart in 1969 under the pressure of being manhandled by the Baltimore Orioles, much as Detroit had taken apart the defending league champion Boston Red Sox the year before. Sain liked to have complete control of his pitching staff, and his clashes with Smith were becoming more and more open. Once journalists got hold of the feud, it was all over. Campbell journeyed to Chicago, met with Sain and fired him on the spot. Smith was gone after 1970, when Detroit sagged to fourth in the AL East with a 79–83 record.

Who would make the best successor to Smith? A better version of Smith or an anti-Smith? Much like when selecting other leaders, even presidents and popes, you try to go in a new direction without veering off the path altogether.

Campbell decided the aging Tigers needed someone with a managerial Taser to prod the group back to first place and hired incendiary Billy Martin to manage the team. The fiery Martin got Detroit to 20 games over .500 at 91–71—but it was still 10 games behind Earl Weaver's Orioles. Martin goaded the Tigers to the 1972 AL East title and nearly stopped the Oakland A's from starting their three-year reign as AL champions, losing 3–2 in a best-of-five AL playoff. Martin and Jim Northrup feuded openly in the press in 1973. Writers had a field day going from one to the other to get 'can you top this' stories. Martin was platooning Northrup, who was nearing the end of his career, and the equally stubborn outfielder didn't care one bit for part-time playing. Before the end of that season, however, Martin had to be fired, and Joe Schultz stepped in to finish the season.

Houk had had his fill of George Steinbrenner with the Yankees by that time and quit New York following the 1973 season. Campbell snapped him up, believing he could squeeze one more year from the core group that won the 1968 World Series. It was obvious before June there was no more milk to be gotten from that cow, and Campbell began ripping the club apart. He felt Houk was the guy to nurture young players along, a plan that slowly brought the Tigers close to respectability by 1978. Houk tired of managing and quit after the season—he resurfaced with Boston after discovering he wasn't quite as finished with managing as he thought—and the two felt Les Moss, who had flopped in an earlier managerial trial, was ready to grow with the team. Moss, however, proved to be a size 7 shoe on a size 12 foot.

Moss rated dealing with the media right up there with having a finger cut off or sleeping on nails. Writers would come down to his office after games—and find him reading a book. Getting good insights from Moss was like trying to type a story with no ribbon in the typewriter.

Sparky Anderson had quit (or been fired, your choice) as manager of the Cincinnati Reds after the 1978 and was enjoying his time off. Campbell started hearing stories about other teams sending out feelers to Anderson about managing again. He contacted Anderson, they talked, and the future Hall of Famer was hired. Anderson's Reds and the Tigers had played one another in an annual midseason exhibition game for years, so they were familiar with one another. Campbell showed Anderson his contract and asked him to look it over. Anything he didn't like would come out. Anderson replied in effect, well, if you put it in there, it must be all right. He signed the deal. Moss had been canned with a 27–26 record, and Dick Tracewski managed the club to two wins while Anderson straightened out his affairs and came to Detroit.

The Rise and Fall of the Tigers

by Dan Levitt and Mark Armour

The story of the 1968 Tigers has been the stuff of nostalgia for a few decades, but it is not often that one steps back and tries to put the story in perspective. Setting aside the reality of this fine club's 103 wins and World Series victory, two questions interest us here: How did the team come together, and how did it fall apart? The Tigers had a historically stable roster of players, and the story on both sides of their great season is fairly straightforward, but worth the retelling.

Successful amateur scouting has always been essential to building a contending baseball team. But at no time was it more crucial than in the 20 years before the introduction of the amateur draft in 1965. Prior to World War II, teams usually purchased or drafted players from independent minor league teams, and thus had the opportunity to view them against professional competition, often into the player's early 20s. As major league teams began to employ large farm systems, the onus of finding amateur talent shifted from minor league teams to the majors. By the late 1940s and continuing until the draft, the signing of amateur ballplayers was constrained principally by the financial resources, talent evaluation ability, and hustle of a team's scouts and front office.

The 1968 Detroit Tigers stand as a prime example of how to do this job well, owing its success to an intelligent and active team of scouts and front office personnel in the late 1950s and early 1960s. During a period of about six years the Tigers signed the nucleus of the squad that would carry them to the 1968 title. The organization was much less successful in navigating the early years of the draft, failing to come up with necessary replacements for their aging stars and dropping out of regular pennant contention until a new generation of players began appearing in the late 1970s.

After years of contention in the 1930s and 1940s, the Tigers spent the Eisenhower years mired in mediocrity, rising only as high as 82–72 in 1956. The organization produced a number of excellent players, including Hall of Famers Al Kaline and Jim Bunning, and stars Harvey Kuenn and Frank Lary, but were never able to fill out the roster to compete with the Yankees.

For whatever reason, the Tigers shunned the largest source of newly available talent in baseball history—the black players made eligible with the dissolving of the color barrier in 1947. The Tigers were the 15th team (of 16) to integrate, when Ozzie Virgil played 49 games at third base in 1958. By 1961 the team had three black starting position players (Chico Fernandez, Jake Wood, and Bill Bruton) and turned in their best season in many years. This point can be overstated—the Yankees weren't particularly active in signing black players either and won every year—but, the Tigers clearly missed a valuable opportunity by not moving more quickly to bring black talent into the system.

Ownership and executive-level turnover also combined to counteract the development of any sort of long-term strategy. In January 1952 longtime owner Walter Briggs died, leaving the Tigers to a trusteeship, with his son Spike as team president. In 1956 the trustees put the team up for sale and orchestrated a spirited bidding contest, with the winning bid coming from a complicated group led by radio station operator Fred Knorr. He was helped in his offer by Spike Briggs, an investor in one of Knorr's companies but ineligible to bid for the team himself. The new 11-person syndicate named Knorr president and Briggs general manager.

Over the next few years, due partly to changes in power at the ownership level, the personnel of the team was overseen successively by Briggs, John McHale (1957), Rick Ferrell (1959), Bill DeWitt (1960), Ferrell again (1961), and finally Jim Campbell in September 1962. Complicating the front-office structure, a number of the syndicate's members held executive positions in the Detroit organization. In 1960 John Fetzer, part of the original syndicate and a Kalamazoo (Michigan) radio and

TV operator, acquired a controlling interest in the franchise and before 1961 was over had sole ownership. Fetzer and Campbell were a team for two decades.

During Bill Dewitt's single season at the helm, he made two trades with Cleveland that helped immeasurably. On April 12, 1960, he dealt Steve Demeter to the Indians for Norm Cash, a swap of 25-year-old infielders who had yet to break through. Five days later, on the eve of the season, right fielder Harvey Kuenn, a eight-time All-Star and the reigning batting champion, was swapped for Rocky Colavito, who had led the league with 42 home runs. Kuenn was a fine player, but Colavito was three years younger and had a much better all-around game than the singles-hitting Kuenn. Although the club had an off year in 1960, the next year they took the Yankees down to the last month of the season, thanks largely to Cash and Colavito, who hit 86 home runs and drove in 272 between them.

From 1957 to 1962 the Tigers' scouts and front office had a phenomenal run of signing the amateur free agents who would become the core of the 1968 championship squad. The scouting department benefited from a solid team of midlevel front office personnel, who, despite the rapid turnover in ownership and general managers, remained relatively stable. Campbell joined the Detroit organization in 1949, and scouting director Ed Katalinas had teamed with John McHale in 1953 to sign right field mainstay Al Kaline. Some of the more productive scouts included Bernie DeViveiros, Lou D'Annunzio, Edwin Williams, and Katalinas. Of the top 15 players on the 1968 team (the eight position players with at least 250 at bats, six pitchers with at least 70 innings pitched, and pinch-hitter extraordinaire Gates Brown), 10 were signed during this six-year time frame:

Player	Signed
Dick McAuliffe	1957
Mickey Lolich	1958
Don Wert	1958
Pat Dobson	1959
Jim Northrup	1960
Gates Brown	1960
Bill Freehan	1961
Willie Horton	1961
Mickey Stanley	1961
John Hiller	1962

The Detroit scouts secured two more important players in 1963. The club signed amateur free agent Joe Sparma, who developed into an adequate fourth starter. More important was the selection of Denny McLain off waivers from the Chicago White Sox. Under baseball's latest attempt to keep bonuses down, in certain circumstances bonus players not promoted to a major league roster after a single minor league season could be made available to other clubs through the waiver process. The Tiger scouts smartly recognized McLain's ability and claimed him.

Thus by the end of 1963 the Tigers had already corralled 14 of the key 15 championship players within their organization, and many were already contributing at the major league level. In 1964 first baseman Cash, shortstop McAuliffe, third baseman Wert, right fielder Kaline, left fielder Brown, and catcher Freehan were all regulars for the Tigers; Lolich had joined the rotation, and Sparma and McLain were struggling at its fringes.

The team that Campbell and the Tigers put on the field in 1964 was similar in quality and talent to that trotted out over the previous few years: good enough to finish a few games above .500 and offer hope for the future. Crafty veteran manager Charlie Dressen had taken over the managerial reins in June 1963 after the club jettisoned Bob Scheffing. Of the position players, the team could boast one true star in Al Kaline and a budding one in 22-year-old catcher Bill Freehan. The rest offered a challenge for a general manager. Dick McAuliffe was a great hitter for a shortstop, but his fielding was questionable. The others were all adequate, but were also at least 25 years old and offered little obvious upside. The team finished third in the league in runs scored, and with no clear weak spots in the lineup, it was not particularly evident how to best boost the offense. More obviously, the pitching needed upgrading. The team finished seventh in the league in ERA and only the 23-year-old Mickey Lolich was an obvious top-of-the-rotation starter. Of the others, off-season pickup Dave Wickersham turned in a quality season, but he was already 28 years old and more of a journeyman.

The 1965 season marked a turning point in American League history. The Yankee dynasty that ran from 1949 to 1964—New York won 14 out of 16 possible pennants—came to an end as the Bombers slumped to sixth. Several franchises, most notably Minnesota, Baltimore, Chicago, and Detroit, hoped they were positioned to take advantage of the opening at the top.

In Detroit, Dressen solidified his claim as a capable and willing handler of young players. After his successful introduction of Freehan as regular in 1964, he inserted 22-year-old Willie Horton as his starting left fielder. On the mound he added 21-year-old Denny McLain and 23-year-old Joe Sparma to the rotation. They joined the youthful Lolich and veterans Wickersham and Hank Aguirre to form an improved pitching staff. Despite the youth infusion and an improvement to 89 wins, in 1965 the Tigers finished 13 games behind a powerful Twins team. The next season Dressen inserted 26-year-old left fielder Jim Northrup, another product of the Tiger farm system, into the starting lineup.

Dressen and the Tigers' front office deserve a tremendous amount of credit for recognizing the quality of their youngsters and successfully integrating them onto the roster. The Tigers were consistently close enough in the pennant race that they must have been often tempted to trade prospects for veteran stopgap solutions, but Campbell appreciated that the talent coming through the farm system could succeed at the major league level. Dressen too could have lobbied for journeyman veterans, but he accepted the challenge of assimilating the young players. McAuliffe became a regular by the end of 1961; Wert in 1963; Freehan, Lolich, and Brown in 1964; Horton, McLain, and Sparma in 1965; and Northrup in 1966. The Tigers also introduced two light-hitting, good-fielding farm products into part-time roles: shortstop Ray Oyler and center fielder Mickey Stanley.

Campbell completed few significant trades during his first several years as general manager. In June 1966, however, as the Tigers battled at the edge of the pennant race, Campbell made one of his better moves. He helped unclog a crowded outfield and addressed a starting pitching need by swapping veteran Don Demeter to Boston for hurler Earl Wilson. With Wilson on board, the Tigers went on a six-game winning streak to pull within one-and-a-half games of league-leading Baltimore, but they could inch no closer, and Baltimore pulled away from the field. Managerial tragedies may also have hampered the Tigers pennant hopes. When Dressen experienced a heart attack May 16, Campbell promoted coach Bob Swift. Swift lasted barely two months; he was hospitalized July 14 with a suspected case of food poisoning. Neither survived the year. Dressed died three months after his heart attack, and Swift passed away in October after being diagnosed with a lung tumor. With Swift incapacitated, Campbell promoted another coach, Frank Skaff, to finish out the season.

To skipper the team in 1967 Campbell hired Yankees scout Mayo Smith, which, on its surface, did not seem a particularly inspired choice. Smith had not distinguished himself while managing the Philadelphia Phillies and Cincinnati Reds in the '50s and had last managed in the major leagues in 1959. The Tigers also brought in brilliant pitching coach Johnny Sain, who had just been fired by the Twins. Sain had coached Minnesota's pitchers during their pennant-winning season in 1965 and earned the loyalty of a number of his charges. His outspokenness, extreme self-confidence, and tendency to separate pitchers from position players often quickly wore out his welcome. But before his prickly personality spoiled the relationship with his manager, Sain worked wonders with many pitching staffs.

Heading into the 1967 season Campbell had assembled the team that would capture the 1968 World Series. It was not a great team, but a very good one that could compete for a championship during a period in which the league had no dominant club. Catcher Bill Freehan was the American League's best backstop; Norm Cash was still a capable first baseman, although he had slipped since his best seasons several years earlier. In his most important decision Smith shifted power-hitting infielder Dick McAuliffe to second base to make room for Ray Oyler at short; already 28 years old, Oyler was one of the worst hitters in the major leagues. Don Wert, a fine fielder but weak hitter, continued to hold down third. In the outfield Smith rotated four players: Al Kaline, Willie Horton, Jim Northrup, and Mickey Stanley. Smith and Sain retained the established pitching rotation of McLain, Wilson, Lolich, and Sparma. Dressen had earlier complained about the bullpen, but by this time, Campbell had delivered his new manager a pretty good one; three relievers—Mike Marshall, Pat Dobson, and John Hiller—would go on to pretty good careers.

Detroit remained in the pennant race until the last day of the wide-open 1967 pennant race. Five teams stayed in the race through August, when the Angels effectively dropped back. The remaining four—Boston, Minnesota, Chicago, and Detroit—battled to the final weekend. In mid-August Campbell smartly landed onetime great third baseman Eddie Mathews, still only 35. Mathews capably played in 36 games, subbing for both Wert at third and Cash at first. In one of the great final weekends in pennant history Boston ended up edging Detroit and Minnesota by one game and the White Sox by three. Injuries to Kaline and Horton helped thwart Detroit's pennant hopes. The former missed 26 games midseason with a broken bone in his wrist, and the latter missed 40 due to a bone spur in his heel.

Campbell essentially stood pat over the 1967–1968 off-season, believing that with a healthy Kaline and Horton the team could win the pennant. The biggest hole on the team was shortstop; Oyler, Dick Tracewski, and Tom Matchick were woefully inadequate hitters, and the Tigers likely could have addressed this problem with its surplus in the outfield and on the mound. The Tigers were not big traders in the 1960s, and Campbell essentially forced his manager to deal with the holes in the team.

According to Jerry Green, who wrote a fine book on the 1968 Tigers right after the season, the Tigers tried to acquire Luis Aparicio from the Orioles in a deal that would have sent Denny McLain to Baltimore. Although we cannot know how close such a deal came to being, it is interesting to consider how it would have changed the 1968 pennant race. Aparicio was a better player than Oyler, but moving McLain's season to the Orioles would have tightened things considerably. The problem with such mind games is that this trade would have caused many other transactions to happen or not happen, and the fog begins to overwhelm our ability to see this alternative reality.

Campbell spent much of the 1968 season acquiring veteran relief pitchers—Dick Radatz, John Wyatt, Don McMahon, and Roy Face—without giving up any major league players. Of this group, Radatz did not pitch and Face tossed just two innings, but Wyatt and McMahon were effective in the second half of the season. As it happened, the Tigers had a fine relief pitcher under their control— Mike Marshall—whom they did not use. Marshall had enjoyed an outstanding rookie season in 1967: 1.98 ERA and 10 saves in 37 games. According to Marshall, in spring training the team wanted him to be a specialist who would only face right-handers, and therefore wanted him to stop throwing his sinker (which he used to get lefthanders out). Marshall refused to go along with this, so they sent him to Toledo where he was the International League right-handed pitcher of the year as a starter. The Tigers did not protect him in the expansion draft after the season, the Seattle Pilots picked him, and he later became the best relief pitcher in the majors.

Meanwhile, by mid-September the Tigers had five quality major league outfielders (counting Brown, who hit .370 mainly pinch-hitting) and no shortstop, a situation for which Campbell must take some blame. Smith dealt with this problem by moving Mickey Stanley, an outstanding defensive center fielder, to shortstop with a week to go in the season. That this move worked out is to Smith's credit, but one wonders whether he should have been placed in this situation in the first place.

For that magical season the core of players signed and introduced by the Tigers over the previous decade delivered a world championship. That this success did not continue can be attributed to three factors, one of which was out of the front office's control. The Baltimore Orioles of 1969–1971 were one of history's best teams; it is no shame to lose to such a club. The Tigers finished 19 games out in 1969, and 29 the following year. The two other causes were related: the Tigers got nothing out of the first several amateur drafts and the team did not act to replace their core of players as they aged.

After a decade-long debate the first amateur draft was held June 8, 1965. The Tigers selected and signed three players who would eventually play in the major leagues: Gene Lamont (with the 13th overall pick), Gary Taylor, and Bill Butler. This turned out to be one of their better early drafts. Baseball initially conducted two drafts, the one in June and a second in January. The first player the Tigers signed from any draft who went on to a noteworthy major league career was Lerrin LaGrow, picked in June 1969. The Tigers did not land an impact major leaguer until 1974 when they selected Lance Parrish.

Detroit needed these early drafts to supplement the 1968 core as it inevitably began to fade. In the first five years of the draft, the Boston Red Sox, a club the Tigers battled fairly evenly on the field over these years, drafted and signed Amos Otis, Carlton Fisk, Cecil Cooper, Ben Oglivie, Bill Lee, John Curtis, Rick Miller, and Dwight Evans. Had the Tigers drafted anywhere near this successfully, they would not have had to hit bottom in the mid-1970s. When their roster began sprouting the inevitable holes, the Tigers lacked qualified replacements down on the farm.

In fact, the Tigers of this era had the most stable roster in baseball history. Nine Tigers—Gates Brown, Norm Cash, Bill Freehan, Willie Horton, Al Kaline, Mickey Lolich, Dick McAuliffe, Jim Northrup, and Mickey Stanley—were together for the entire decade of 1964–1973, easily a record. John Hiller just missed this list, joining the club in 1965 and staying on for 15 years. Loyalty of this sort has its merits, but by the early 1970s several of these players were barely contributing, and Campbell failed to replace them. Brown, certainly capable of holding down a regular job somewhere in these years, spent 13 years with the Tigers essentially competing for playing time with the same four outfielders. The Tigers inexplicably chose to hang on to Brown rather than using him as trade bait to acquire an infielder and giving him a chance for a more rewarding career.

The Tigers made one big trade after the 1970 season, and it was a beauty. Denny McLain's career and life had begun its bizarre downward spiral that year; nevertheless, in October Campbell found a willing trade partner, the Washington Senators' Bob Short, and in exchange for McLain, Wert, pitcher Norm McRae, and outfielder Elliot Maddox, he snagged pitchers Joe Coleman and Jim Hannan and infielders Eddie Brinkman and Aurelio Rodriguez. Coleman won 62 games for the Tigers over the next three years, and Brinkman and Rodriguez filled the club's two biggest holes. This deal probably delayed the Tigers' collapse for a few years, and, coupled with the newly achieved stardom of Mickey Lolich and John Hiller, helped win a fluky division title in 1972.

Ultimately, the lack of any incoming talent brought about the club's collapse (72 wins in 1974 followed by 57 in 1975). Loyal to the end, most of the 1968 core played out the string in Detroit as the team fell out of contention. The front office eventually reconstructed a successful amateur scouting organization, and in the mid-1970s began drafting a series of stars that allowed them to build another great club in the 1980s. But that is a story for another book.

References

Publications
Dewey, Donald, and Nicholas Acocella. *Ball Clubs.* New York: Harper Collins. 1996.
Green, Jerry. *Year of the Tiger.* New York: Coward-McCann. 1969.
James, Bill. *The Bill James Baseball Abstract.* New York: Ballantine Books. 1984.
Spatz, Lyle, ed. *The SABR Baseball List and Record Book.* New York: Scribner. 2007.
The Sporting News Official Baseball Guide. St. Louis: The Sporting News Publishing Company. 1955–1969.
Zanger, Jack. *Major League Baseball.* New York: Pocket Books, Inc. 196–1969.

Articles
Sports Illustrated: April 13, 1964; April 19, 1965; April 18, 1966; April 17, 1967.
Falls, Joe. "Turmoil on the Tigers: Does It Still Exist?" *Sport,* June 1967.

Web Sites
www.baseballreference.com
www.retrosheet.org

Other Sources
Baseball America: Executive Database
E-mail exchange with Mike Marshall, August 2007
SABR Scouts Committee Who-Signed-Whom Database

"Go Get 'Em, Tigers"

Written by Artie Fields. Commissioned by the National Bank of Detroit. Introduced during the 1967 season when NBD was a Tigers radio sponsor and played during the Tigers' World Series championship year of 1968.

(woman's voice, spoken)
Go GET 'em, Tigers. Rrowr!

(vocal group)
We're all behind our baseball team
Go get 'em, Tigers!
World Series bound and pickin' up steam
Go get 'em, Tigers!

Bridge:
There'll be joy in Tigertown
We'll sing you songs
When the Bengals bring the pennant home
Where it belongs

We're all behind our baseball team
Go get 'em!

(female solo voice)
Detroit Tigers!

(group)
Go get 'em, Tigers!

(bridge instrumental)

(group)
We're all behind our baseball team
Go get 'em!

(female solo voice)
Detroit Tigers!

(group)
Go get 'em, Tigers!

Interesting Facts ...

- Going into the 1968 season, this was the Tigers' rotation, in order of perceived quality: Earl Wilson, Mickey Lolich, Joe Sparma, and Denny McLain. Incredibly, McLain was considered to be the fourth starter. In fact, he was almost traded to Baltimore before the 1968 season. McLain had gone 17–16 with a 3.76 ERA in 1967, the lowest winning percentage and highest ERA in the rotation. Wilson had gone 22–9, 3.27, in 1967; Lolich, 14–13, 3.04; and Sparma, 16–9, 3.76.

- The Tigers lost on Opening Day to the Red Sox 7–3 before winning their next nine games.

- Detroit went into first place for good on May 10 after beating the Senators 12–1.

- Jim Northrup hit five grand slams in 1968. The first one happened May 17. He then bunched together three in one week—two of them in one game June 24, and another June 29. Northrup hit the fifth in Game 6 of the World Series,

- Four players represented the Tigers in the All-Star Game: Denny McLain, Bill Freehan, Northrup, and Don Wert (who was hitting .220 at the break).

- The Tigers suffered one losing streak of four games, August 23–26, all against New York (plus a tie). All of the losses were by one run and all occurred while Dick McAuliffe was suspended for charging the mound after being thrown at by the White Sox' Tommy John.

- Denny McLain won 13 of his 31 games following a Tigers loss.

- Two of the most historic games in Tigers history came within a week of each other that season. On Saturday, September 14, 1968, in front of an NBC *Game of the Week* national audience, Denny McLain won his 30th game, 5–4. On Tuesday, September 17, 1968, the Tigers won their eighth American League pennant with a 2–1 win over the Yankees. The Tigers won both games in the bottom of the ninth.

- The Tigers had 12 straight complete games from September 6–19. This stretch included McLain's 30th victory and the pennant clincher. The Tigers went 10–2 over this stretch.

- Detroit led the majors in home runs with 185, leading the American League by 53. Who hit the most home runs per at-bat? Pitcher Earl Wilson, with seven home runs in 88 at-bats, hit home runs in 8.0 percent of his at-bats. Willie Horton, with 36 home runs in 512 at-bats, was a distant second at 7.0 percent.

- Detroit tallied 40 wins in after being tied or trailing from the seventh inning on.

- The Tigers played more official games in 1968 than in any other season—164. They had two tie games, which don't count in the standings but do in the statistics. They tied Oakland 2–2 in seven innings on May 24 and the Yankees 3-3 in 19 on August 23.

... About the 1968 Tigers

- St. Louis, the 1964 and 1967 World Series champions, was heavily favored to beat Detroit in the 1968 World Series, with 10–17 odds, but looking at the stats, it hard to see why. Compare these numbers:

Team	Record	GA	RS/G	RA/G
Detroit	103–59	12	4.1	3.0
St. Louis	97–65	9	3.6	2.9

  The Tigers had a better record, won by more games, scored a half-run more per game and allowed about the same number of runs per game (the American League and National League both averaged 3.4 runs per game). The Tigers scored the most runs per game in the American League; the Cards were third in the National League (both teams allowed the fewest runs per game in the league). In addition, the Tigers had an 11-game winning streak in September while the Cards went 11–14 in the last month of the season.

- Mickey Stanley was moved from center field to shortstop in the Series to get Al Kaline's bat in the Series. With four top outfielders (Willie Horton and Jim Northrup, too) and no DH, it was the only way to get them all in the lineup at the same time. Stanley got nine games at shortstop to prepare for his Series role, his first nine games there as a major leaguer. Ray Oyler, the Tigers' regular shortstop, hit .135, low even in the Year of the Pitcher.

- Mayo Smith used the same starting eight in the same lineup order in six of the seven Series games:
  Dick McAuliffe, 2B   Willie Horton, LF
  Mickey Stanley, SS   Jim Northrup, CF
  Al Kaline, RF   Bill Freehan, C
  Norm Cash, 1B   Don Wert, 3B

- In Game 4, Eddie Mathews started at third base and batted seventh, with Freehan hitting eighth and Wert benched.

- In the Tigers' World Series wins in Games 2, 5, 6 and 7, late in the game, Oyler came in at shortstop for defensive purposes, moving Stanley to center field, Northrup to left field, and Horton to the bench.

- Initially, manager Mayo Smith planned on starting right-hander Earl Wilson in Game 2 in St. Louis and southpaw Mickey Lolich in Game 3 in Detroit because of the short right-field fence in Detroit. However, he switched them because he wanted Wilson's home run bat in the lineup in Detroit (by contrast, Lolich hit .114 in 1968 and had never hit a home run in the majors). What happened? Lolich hit the only home run in his big league career in Game 2 in St. Louis and Wilson went 0-for-1 and was hit hard in Game 3 in Detroit. Smith let Lolich hit for himself in a key situation in the seventh inning of Game 5 with one out and none on and the Tigers down 3-2. Lolich blooped a single to right to start a game-winning three-run rally.

1968 Tigers

Denny McLain Game-by-Game in 1968

Date	Opponent	Score	IP	H	R	ER	BB	SO	W/L	Rec.
April 11	Boston	4–3	7	6	3	3	3	6	–	0-0
April 17	Cleveland	4-3(10)	7	6	2	2	2	9	–	0-0
April 21	@Chicago	4–2	9	7	2	2	1	8	W	1-0
April 27	@New York	7–0	9	5	0	0	2	6	W	2-0
May 1	Minnesota	3-2	9	6	2	2	0	9	W	3-0
May 5	California	5-2	9	7	2	2	1	7	W	4-0
May 10	@Washington	12-1	9	7	1	1	0	7	W	5-0
May 15	Baltimore	8-10	2	4	4	4	1	0	L	5-1
May 20	@Minnesota	4-3(10)	10	7	3	3	0	7	W	6-1
May 25	@Oakland	7-1	9	6	1	0	1	8	W	7-1
May 29	@California	3-0	9	4	0	0	1	13	W	8-1
June 2	New York	3-4	8	9	3	3	1	4	-	8-1
June 5	@Boston	5-4	6	5	4	3	0	1	W	9-1
June 9	Cleveland	0-2	8	3	2	2	0	4	L	9-2
June 13	Minnesota	3-1	9	6	1	1	1	6	W	10-2
June 16	@Chicago	6-1	7	3	1	1	2	5	W	11-2
June 20	Boston	5-1	9	3	1	1	2	10	W	12-2
June 24	@Cleveland	14-3	9	9	3	3	0	8	W	13-2
June 29	Chicago	5-2	9	8	2	2	2	5	W	14-2
July 3	California	5-2	9	4	2	1	2	10	W	15-2
July 7	Oakland	5-4	9	5	4	4	1	9	W	16-2
July 12	@Minnesota	5-1	9	3	1	0	4	5	W	17-2
July 16	@Oakland	4-0	9	8	0	0	0	8	W	18-2
July 20	Baltimore	3-5	4.1	6	5	5	3	4	L	18-3
July 23	@Washington	6-4	7	8	4	4	4	7	W	19-3
July 27	@Baltimore	9-0	9	3	0	0	2	7	W	20-3
July 31	Washington	4-0	9	4	0	0	1	9	W	21-3
August 4	@Minnesota	2-1	9	5	1	0	4	4	W	22-3
August 8	Cleveland	13-1	9	6	1	1	3	2	W	23-3
August 12	@Cleveland	6-3	9	5	3	3	1	5	W	24-3
August 15	@Boston	4-0	9	7	0	0	1	9	W	25-3
August 20	Chicago	2-10	5.2	9	9	2	2	3	L	25-4
August 24	@New York	1-2	7	5	2	2	0	6	L	25-5
August 28	California	6-1	9	6	1	1	2	11	W	26-5
September 1	Baltimore	7-3	9	7	3	3	2	9	W	27-5
September 6	Minnesota	8-3	9	9	3	3	1	12	W	28-5
Sept. 10	@California	7-2	9	9	2	2	1	12	W	29-5
Sept. 14	Oakland	5-4	9	6	4	4	1	10	W	30-5
Sept. 19	New York	6-2	9	8	2	2	3	7	W	31-5
Sept. 23	@Baltimore	1-2	7	5	2	1	5	4	L	31-6
Sept. 28	Washington	1-2	7	2	0	0	0	4	-	31-6
Totals		**(1.96 ERA)**	**336**	**241**	**86**	**73**	**63**	**280**		**31-6**

Tiger Stadium

by Jeremy Klumpp

Baseball has been played in Detroit for more than 150 years. During those early days baseball was competing with cricket for fans' affections and playing space, but the times were changing and America was looking for an identity, so cricket "fell into disfavor in a young, virile nation desperately searching for a game it could call its own." As fast as they stopped playing cricket they started playing baseball. The old cricket grounds were used to host baseball tournaments, and after 20 years of playing around the city a professional club started up in 1879 at Recreation Park near what is now the Detroit Medical Center. Recreation Park was the first sports complex in Detroit and it housed along with the baseball diamond, a cricket field, tennis courts, bowling alleys, and a gymnasium.

The Detroit Wolverines played at Recreation Park from 1881 until 1888, winning a National League championship in 1887. The team dissolved after the 1888 season. The city would field teams in the International Association and the Northwestern League in the years immediately following, but it wasn't until 1894 that a new club took for good with the formation of Ban Johnson's Western League, a new minor league, with George Vanderbeck as the new Detroit teams owner. The new Detroit team, named the Creams, played its inaugural season at League Park, located near today's Belle Isle Bridge. Vanderbeck cleaned up the park and added bleachers—increasing League Park's capacity to 3,500—but Vanderbeck was not thrilled with his team's facilities and began looking for land to lease. He found his new park on the Woodbridge farm in an area the city had been using as a haymarket. The new park would sit at the corner of Michigan and Trumbull.

Bennett Park

Tuesday, April 28, 1896, was opening day for Bennett Park. The place that would later be nicknamed "The Corner" was named after fan favorite and former Wolverines catcher Charlie Bennett, who lost both legs in a train accident in 1894. Bennett caught the ceremonial first pitch—something he did every opening day through 1926. The day was rainy and cool with the Detroit team, now named the Tigers, crushing the Columbus team 17–2. Team captain George Stallings hit the first home run with a little help from the Detroit fans; fans were allowed to sit in the outfield and helped Stallings when a Columbus outfielder ran into a fan while running down the ball.

The stadium was constructed out of wood and had a seating capacity of 5,000 with another 1,000 or so sitting in trees or on flimsy bleachers erected on private property. The team's clubhouse was placed in center field and home plate was where right field would be after 1912. It was half the size of Tiger Stadium, and had a 12-foot fence surrounding it. The field could have some tricky bounces due to the cobblestone left behind by the old haymarket, but that would eventually be fixed in 1903. Sunday games were outlawed within Detroit, but that did not stop the team from playing on Sundays. They would simply travel to nearby municipalities that didn't have Sunday blue laws, and would continue playing Sunday games outside of Bennett Park until 1907.

The Tigers survived Ban Johnson's re-formation of the Western League into a new major league called the American League; indeed, Detroit is the only Western League franchise still extant in its original location.. On April 25, 1901, major league baseball returned to Detroit with its largest crowd ever to see a game when 10,023 packed into Bennett Park, witnessing a dramatic ninth inning rally with the Tigers winning 14–13 over Milwaukee. During the early part of the 20th century the Tigers played in three straight World Series, 1907–1909, losing all three. They also added players like "Wahoo" Sam Crawford, Herman "Germany" Schaefer and, in 1905, an 18-year-old kid from Augusta, Georgia, named Tyrus Raymond Cobb.

After changing owners four times in seven years the Tigers wound up with Frank Navin as owner in 1907.

Navin's first order of business was an expansion of Bennett Park. He moved the right-field fence back and added a 2,000-seat bleacher section, connected the grandstand to the first base pavilion, and moved the playing field 40 feet. This increased capacity, plus a good team on the field, helped attendance grow at Bennett Park over the next couple of seasons. Another 3,000 seats were added in 1911, bringing Bennett Park's capacity to 13,000. During the 1909 World Series between Cobb's Tigers and Honus Wagner's Pittsburgh Pirates, Forbes Field in Pittsburgh could handle the 30,000 fans who came to see two of the three fall classic contests in the Steel City. Navin had wanted to build a new stadium almost from his first day as owner and in 1911 he finally purchased the remaining land surrounding Bennett Park he needed and in the winter of 1911 the first home of the Detroit Tigers was torn down.

Navin Field

Navin Field was to have opened on Frank Navin's 41st birthday, Thursday April 18, 1912. The weather did not cooperate and the game had to be postponed due to rain until April 20, the same day as the opening of Fenway Park in Boston. The stadium was twice the size of Bennett Park and was erected out of steel and concrete. The official capacity was listed at 24,382. It was 365 feet down the right field line, 400 feet to center field, and 340 feet down the left field line. A 125-foot flagpole was erected in center field where it stood for 87 years, and was the tallest object ever placed in fair territory of any major league park.

Navin was hoping that the new park with a good team would lead to big attendance numbers. The team's lackluster play led to poor attendance figures during the stadium's first few seasons, but the booming automobile industry helped increase ticket sales, as Detroit became the fourth-largest city in the United States early in the Roaring Twenties. Also helping the box office was having the great Ty Cobb playing and managing the team during these years and the emergence of a rivalry between Cobb and a player whose game could not have been more different, George Herman "Babe" Ruth. During his visits to Detroit, Ruth would crush a ball believed by many to have gone almost 600 feet in the air at Navin Field, and in 1934 clout his 700th career home run.

In the winter of 1922 Navin added a second deck to the original stands from first to third base increasing the capacity to 30,000. He also added a press box, and within a few seasons Navin Field was rivaling Yankee Stadium in attendance each season. In 1924 the Tigers became only the second team after the Yankees to draw more than 1 million fans. Cobb left the Tigers after the 1926 season and the team went into a losing spiral for the next seven seasons that caused a major drop in attendance numbers. The Great Depression that coincided also did not help matters and attendance dropped by almost four million from 1929–1933.

The Tigers added such Hall of Famers as Mickey Cochrane and Goose Goslin to a lineup that already included Hank Greenberg and Charlie Gehringer in the early 1930s and by 1934 they won an American League pennant. Attendance was the best in the majors with fans happy to see a championship club again after 25 years.

The World Series of 1934 contained maybe the nastiest moment of baseball in Detroit. After a Game 6 loss that many blamed on a poor call by the umpires, the St. Louis Cardinals were well ahead of the Tigers in the sixth inning of Game 7 when Joe Medwick slid hard into third, and Tigers third baseman Marv Owen stepped on his foot. According to Owen, Medwick kicked him three times and then scored on the next hit, making the score 9–0. When Medwick went into left field in the bottom of the sixth Tigers fans threw fruit, vegetables, bottles, and insults at him resulting in a 20-minute delay, and an order from commissioner Kenesaw Mountain Landis to have Medwick removed from the game. The Cardinals went on to win the game 11–0 and the Series.

The team bounced back and won the American League again in 1935. Although hoping for a rematch of the 1934 World Series they instead faced off against the Chicago Cubs. In front of 48,420 fans at Navin Field the Tigers won their first World Series with a 4–3 victory in Game 6. The happiness was short-lived, though, when owner Frank Navin died of a heart attack less than six weeks after seeing his beloved Tigers win it all for the first time.

Walter Briggs was Navin's silent partner for years and bought the Tigers for $1 million. He continued Navin's work on Navin Field and in the off-season, tore down the old pavilion along the first-base side, and added a new double-decked grandstand down the first-base line and into right field. Worried about the stands' proximity to Trumbull Avenue, he moved the right field fence 42 feet closer to home plate, and the upper deck hung over the field by another ten feet. The distance down the right field line was just 325 feet and 315 feet in the upper deck. When the Texas Rangers built their new stadium in the early 1990s they included an overhanging right field porch that is reminiscent of Navin Field.

Briggs Stadium

After a disappointing 1937 season Briggs spent $1 million to finish the expansion of Navin Field. The third-base pavilion was demolished and a double-decked grandstand was added along the third-base line and into left field. The city ordered the closing of Cherry Street to accommodate the left-field expansion. The new section connected to the center-field bleachers, thus creating the first stadium in the major leagues to be fully enclosed. The additions upped the capacity from 36,000 to 53,000. Briggs also added the largest press box in the majors, hanging from the grandstand roof to the overhang in right field. A hand-operated scoreboard was installed above the bleachers with smaller electronic boards behind first and third base. The new dimensions of the field were 340 feet down the left-field line, 365 to left center, 440 to dead center, 370 to right center, and 325 down the right field line. The last change to the stadium was the name, with Briggs renaming the stadium after himself with a dedication ceremony on opening day 1938.

The new stadium was a success not only with the local fans—thanks in part to another AL flag in 1940—but with the visiting players as well. Outfielder Doc Cramer called the outfield grass "carpet" because you would slide along the field instead of sticking in the ground. The outfield walls were green, which helped batters see the ball better. Ted Williams, maybe the game's greatest hitter, liked playing at Briggs Stadium and hit 55 of his 521 career home runs in Detroit, the most in any opponent's stadium, surely made easier by the short porch in right field.

Attendance boomed in the postwar era—and a World Series championship in 1945 helped. Between 1945–1950 the Tigers averaged 1.6 million fans a season, the best in the American League. Briggs was turning a profit season after season with all but one of the stadium's top 20 crowds filling the seats between 1940 and 1950. This also had to do with the elimination of standing room tickets and the installation of wider seats during the next decade, but the Tigers were the pride of Detroit and the city was alive when the team was in town.

Also helping with attendance figures were the addition of lights in 1948. Briggs Stadium was the last American League stadium to install lights, but no one knew exactly what time to switch on the lights that June 15 evening. Fans began arriving at 6 p.m. and after more three hours of waiting the lights were finally turned on at 9:30 p.m. to the amazement of all in attendance. The Tigers played 14 games under the lights at Briggs in 1948 with an average of 45,000 fans attending each contest.

The 1950s were a time of change not only for the Tigers, but also for the area surrounding Briggs Stadium. The new freeway system was moving families out of Detroit and into the suburbs. Televisions were popping up in homes all around the metro Detroit area with many fans deciding to stay home and watch the games on WWJ, Channel 4. The streetcars that brought fans to the games were shut down in 1955 with more people driving automobiles to the park. The Tigers never had a parking lot for the public so fans had to rely on local private lots to park and walk to the stadium.

There were some small changes to Briggs Stadium as well. The bullpens were moved from center field and situated in the outfield corners in 1953. Also, the dirt path connecting the pitcher's mound to home plate—called the keyhole—was filled in with grass sometime around 1955. The Tigers would bring back the keyhole for their new stadium, Comerica Park.

In January 1952 Walter Briggs died in Miami, weeks away from his 65th birthday. He made the stadium that bore his name one of the premier ballparks in the major leagues. He led the club and the stadium through the Great Depression, World War II, and a mass migration out of Detroit. He kept ticket prices low and cared about his baseball team, their fans, and his stadium. After his death Tigers manager Red Rolfe called Briggs "the last owner with the viewpoint of the fans."

After Briggs' death the team fell into disarray not only on the field, but in the front office as well. The team hovered right in the middle of the pack in the American League even with such greats as right fielder Al Kaline, shortstop Harvey Kuenn, and pitcher Jim Bunning on the field. The ownership problem was finally decided in 1956 when a group of investors including Fred Knorr and John Fetzer bought the club for $5.5 million. The Briggs era in Detroit was over.

Tiger Stadium and 1968

It cost the Tigers $20,000 to change the name of Briggs Stadium over the winter of 1961. A new sign was erected to replace the old electric one, and the change was complete. John Fetzer bought out his fellow investors and became sole owner of the Tigers in November 1961 and quickly made the Tigers into contenders. Over the years, Detroit added Norm Cash, Denny McLain, and Earl Wilson to a team with good homegrown talent that matured into veteran leadership. The team finished in the top half of the American League in every season between 1961 and 1966, and only had one losing season in 1963.

The 1967 season was a turning point for the Tigers and the city of Detroit. In the predawn hours of July 23, Detroit police raided a printing shop and as police arrested the men inside a crowd grew outside. At first things were calm, but the mood soon turned sour as the crowd began looting and a riot broke out. The Tigers were playing a doubleheader against the Yankees at Tiger Stadium unaware of the trouble that was building outside. The players were ordered to stay home, but hometown hero Willie Horton ventured into the chaos wearing his uniform, hoping to calm the madness but with no success. Pitcher Mickey Lolich missed a start after being assigned to riot duty as a member of the Michigan National Guard. After four days 43 people had died and the city would never be the same.

The team was in the middle of a battle of its own against Minnesota, Boston, and Chicago for the top spot in the American League all season long. With Chicago out and the Red Sox beating the Twins, the Tigers needed to sweep a doubleheader against the California Angels on the last day of the season. The fans who had stayed away after the riots did return for this final series hoping for a Tigers sweep. The team won the first game 6–4 and a win in the second game would set up a playoff game against the Red Sox. With the team down 8–5 in the ninth but two men on base, Dick McAuliffe hit into only his second double play of the season for the final outs of the season.

The team was determined to make 1968 its season and in early May reached the top of the American League to stay. Even with a team in first place many area fans were reluctant at first to head to Detroit and watch them. Even though the Tigers started in 1964 a streak (continued to this day) of one million-plus attendance each season, the home opener had 12,000 empty seats, with early games against Chicago, Cleveland, and Oakland each bringing fewer than 11,000 fans. Also hurting attendance was the fact that both newspapers in Detroit were on strike and could not drum up support for the club. ESPN and the Internet were distant dreams in 1968, so most fans depended on radio, the occasional TV game, the *Detroit American* (the renamed *Polish Daily News* for the duration of the strike) and early editions of the *Toledo Blade* for their Tigers fix.

Still, the fans found their way to Tiger Stadium in 1968. How could they not with a first-place team? Unfortunately, a couple of ugly incidents dimmed the glow of having a first-place team.. In a scene reminiscent to the 1934 World Series the fans littered the field after manager Mayo Smith was thrown out of one early June game after disputing a call. A few weeks later, with the Tigers losing badly to the Boston Red Sox, a fan threw a cherry bomb at Red Sox right fielder Ken Harrelson, who jumped out of the way after the bomb hit him in the back. General Manager Jim Campbell instituted a policy for searching bags and fans were no longer allowed to bring in beer from outside the stadium.

The team finally clinched the American League pennant September 17 in front of 46,512 against the New York Yankees. Baltimore had lost to Boston clinching the pennant for the Tigers with or without a win, but Campbell did not want fans to know before the end of the game and ordered that the score not appear on the scoreboard. The Tigers won the game with a Don Wert single to bring home Al Kaline from third in the bottom of the ninth. Fans began pouring over the fences and onto the field tearing apart the turf, stealing bases and anything else they could. The club had bought fireworks and they were ignited while fans were still destroying the stadium. Only after the fireworks display did security intervene and move fans out of the stadium.

With all the partying that occurred after the Tigers clinched the pennant a casual observer might have thought the Tigers had already won the World Series. That was not the case, of course, and the Tigers went into the 1968 World Series as heavy underdogs to the defending champion St. Louis Cardinals. The teams split the first two games in St. Louis, but the Cards thumped the Tigers in the first two games in Detroit.

Game 5 started with the singing of "The Star Spangled Banner" by Jose Feliciano, who was invited by Tigers broadcaster Ernie Harwell to sing the anthem. Feliciano's rendition was not a straight singing, and the fans were not impressed. Outraged fans called the stadium in protest beyond the switchboard's capacity. The day was rainy and both teams were hoping for a delay or postponement, but none was coming. The Cardinals had a 3–2 lead in the fifth when the speedy Lou Brock hit a one-out double, and Julian Javier followed with a single. Brock took off for home on the hit, and Willie Horton threw the ball on one hop to catcher Bill Freehan, who was blocking the plate. Umpire Doug Harvey called Brock out at the plate, and the momentum was back with the Tigers, who won the game, 5–3, and swept the final three games of the Series to claim the championship.. The photograph of Freehan tagging Brock out is one of the most iconic images in Tiger Stadium history.

The last game played at Tiger Stadium that season became the turning point for the Tigers in the World Series. They went back to St. Louis and trounced the Cardinals 13–1 in Game 6. Game 7 was a showdown Bob Gibson and Mickey Lolich, but Lolich outpitched Gibson and the Tigers won the game 4–1 for their first championship since 1945.

Many consider the 1968 season at Tiger Stadium a time of healing for the city of Detroit. A year after the worst riots in American history the people of Detroit had a common cause to cheer for. The truth is that the damage was done in 1967, and Detroit has never been the same since. People continued to leave for the suburbs and the city fell on hard times. The Tigers continued to play at the corner of Michigan and Trumbull for 31 more seasons. They made it to the postseason in 1972, won another World Series in 1984, and made it back to the playoffs in 1987. The stadium did not host another postseason game after that, and in the summer of 1996 new owner Mike Ilitch announced that the Tigers would be moving to a new stadium along Woodward Avenue.

The stadium that held court for players like Cobb, Greenberg, and Kaline—and later Alan Trammell, Lou Whitaker, and Kirk Gibson—hosted its last game September 27, 1999. The Tigers won 8–2 over the Kansas City Royals and after 103 years major league baseball would not be played again at "The Corner."

References

Publications

Bak, Richard. *A Place For Summer.* Detroit: Wayne State University Press. 1998.

Cantor, George. *The Tigers of '68: Baseball's Last Real Champions.* Dallas: Taylor. 1997.

Stanton, Tom. *The Final Season: Fathers, Sons, and One Last Season in a Classic American Ballpark.* New York: Thomas Dunne. 2001.

Web Sites

www.ballparks.com
www.detroittigers.com
www.wikipedia.com

Other Sources

Michigan and Trumbull: The History of Tiger Stadium. Produced by John Owens. Mort Crim Communications, 1999

The Greatest Inning in Tigers World Series History

It was the third inning of Game 6 of the 1968 Series. The Tigers scored 10 runs in the inning and in the process set or tied a number of records that still stand to this day. Here's what happened, batter by batter:

- Dick McAuliffe was walked on four straight pitches by St. Louis Cardinals starter Ray Washburn.

- Mickey Stanley hit a single to left field, sending McAuliffe to second base.

- Al Kaline hit a line single to center field; McAuliffe scored and Stanley took third base. Cards manager Red Schoendienst brought in Larry Jaster to relieve Washburn.

- Norm Cash hit a first-pitch single to center; Stanley scored and Kaline took third base.

- Jaster walked Willie Horton to load the bases, Cash moving to second.

- Jim Northrup hit a grand slam home run—the 11th in World Series history, and Northrup's fifth of 1968—into the right-field seats in Busch Stadium, driving in four runs. Schoendinst pulled Jaster in favor of Ron Willis.

- Bill Freehan was walked by Willis.

- Willis hit Don Wert with a pitch, moving Freehan to second.

- Denny McLain laid a bunt down the third base line, sacrificing Freehan to third and Wert to second. McLain, the ninth Tigers batter, was the first out of the inning.

- McAuliffe, up for the second time in the inning, was walked intentionally to load the bases.

- Stanley, in his second at-bat of the third, grounded to first baseman Orlando Cepeda, who forced Freehan at home for the second out. Stanley was safe at first; Wert took third base and McAuliffe second.

- Kaline then hit his second single of the inning, driving in Wert and McAuliffe and sending Stanley to third. Schoendinst then brought in Dick Hughes to relieve Willis.

- Cash, next up, hit his second single of the inning as well, scoring Stanley as before and moving Kaline to third base.

- Horton lined a pitch off Hughes' glove, which landed safely for a single, scoring Kaline and moving Cash to second.

- Northrup made the third out of the inning with a fly out to left fielder Lou Brock.

- The totals: 10 runs, seven hits, no errors, two men left on base, and as the game headed into the bottom of the third inning it was Detroit 12, St. Louis 0.

The Switch

by Rich Shook

Mayo Smith knocked on Jim Campbell's office entrance one glorious September morning, walked in and closed the door.

"Whenever he did that, you knew he was going to say something [important] to you," Campbell recalled.

"Are you in a good mood?" the Tigers' manager asked, sneaking out that nervous little chuckle he used whenever he was going to pull a fast one on you or give an unexpected answer.

"Well, I should have been in a good mood. We were about 30 games up at that time," Campbell remembered, snickering himself at the memory of what should have been one of the more startling events in World Series history but one that turned out as strictly ordinary because of the principals involved.

"If you say no, I won't do it," Smith said. "I'm going to play Mickey at shortstop."

"Son of a gun, are you serious?"

"I'm going to start him there. [Jim] Northrup will play center, Willie [Horton] is in left and Al [Kaline] will be in right. Once we get ahead, [Ray] Oyler goes in and Mickey goes back to center."

Campbell thought for a minute.

"Well, I'll tell you, you've got us this far, so if you want to do it, then go ahead and do it. You caught me by surprise."

Smith chortled again.

"I knew I would."

It turned out to be the boldest, brassiest move in World Series history—moving your starting center fielder to shortstop on the eve of the fall classic—yet it's barely a footnote in baseball history because Mickey Stanley's athleticism made the move work so well. We think it no big deal because we know the lore and the individuals involved.

But imagine Kirby Puckett being moved from center field for Minnesota in 1991 to replace Greg Gagne at shortstop or the 1968 Cardinals moving Curt Flood to short because Dal Maxvill was such a woeful hitter. Think John Shelby could have taken over for the weak shortstops the 1988 Los Angeles Dodgers had? Can you picture Joe Torre asking Bernie Williams to take over the position if something had happened to Derek Jeter on the New York Yankees' championship teams? Anybody got an image of Chet Lemon moving to short for the '84 Tigers if Alan Trammell had gotten injured?

Mayo Smith was a hot-hand manager and a skipper who played hunches. If one of his relievers was going well, Smith would ride him until he dropped, then move on to the next one. For in-game strategy, Smith did things based on his knowledge of his own players plus things he had observed in his long career in baseball as a player, manager, coach, and scout.

Smith had been puzzling for a long time over how to work Kaline, the face of the franchise and its best-known player on the national scene, back into the lineup. He had broken his hand in May, and when he came back in July was tried at first base, where Norm Cash's sporadic hitting was cause for concern.

Horton, the club's chief power threat, was not going to be moved out of left field. Stanley was playing well in center, and Northrup was having an excellent season offensively along with being more than capable in right field while Kaline was out. Northrup also showed center field skills if Smith decided Stanley needed a day off.

Concern indeed. How could the Tigers be in the World Series and not feature one of the game's all-time great right fielders in the lineup? Yet how could you sit any of the other three outfielders, each of whom had played a key role in the team's successful season? Platooning was an option, but not entirely satisfactory for any of the principals involved.

The other concern Smith had entering the World Series was his offense. He would be taking a team against the defending World Series champions that featured two automatic outs at the bottom of the order. Ray Oyler, aging Dick Tracewski, and young Tom Matchick shared shortstop that season. Oyler hit a robust .135, Tracewski a hefty .156, and Matchick, not nearly the equal of the other two defensively, was the hitting heavyweight at .203. So if the bottom three hitters in the lineup bat three times each, a surety, Smith was faced with the likelihood that two to three innings of every game was likely to produce a zero on the scoreboard. The rest of the order thus has six or seven innings to put together enough runs to win. Tough.

Over the course of the remarkable season, though, Smith saw something. And what he saw was his center fielder out at shortstop taking ground balls during infield practice.

"Mickey was there every day, or every other day," teammate John Hiller remembered. "He had a lot of nervous energy. He was always out there messing around, taking ground balls, fly balls. I think that might have influenced Mayo. Whether it was for his bat or for who Al Kaline was, he wanted to get him in the World Series."

Other teammates had similar thoughts.

"I think the consensus was, everybody knew what kind of athlete Mickey was," second baseman Dick McAuliffe said. "He could have played third, or first and he would have done the job. You could have put him behind the plate and he'd have done the job. During warmups, infield, he'd never go out in the outfield and take fly balls. He was always in the infield screwing around, taking ground balls. Everybody knew that and nobody said anything. Because they knew Mickey could do the job."

"He thought that Mickey was a good enough athlete that he could do it," Campbell said. "He could play golf, basketball, you name it and Mickey could play it. He wanted to get Kaline in the lineup and this was one way to resolve that situation."

"Mickey was a tremendous athlete," third baseman Don Wert said. "All through the year, he liked to clown around the infield. He'd come in, take ground balls, throw, stuff like that. I don't think there was a man there who thought he couldn't do it. I'm sure there was a lot of pressure on him. But as far as we were concerned, we thought he could do the job. There were a couple of raised eyebrows, that Mayo would even do something like that. But not as far as his ability was concerned."

Smith always denied he made the move for Kaline's sake. "This is not done out of sentiment to get an Al Kaline in the lineup for the World Series," Smith said at the time. "All I'm trying to do is put an extra bat in the lineup. I would not put Mickey under that pressure if I didn't think he could do the job. We haven't seen what he can do on the double plays when he's close to the base. But if I didn't think he could make them I'd be using Matchick at shortstop."

Playing shortstop looks like playing the banjo—real easy until someone hands you the sheet music and banjo and says, "Start playing."

There was just one more thing: What if Stanley refused?

Detroit had a set of games in Baltimore, the next-to-last series of the season, and one that looked like it would be huge after the Orioles went from Hank Bauer to Earl Weaver as manager in the middle of the year. The Tigers clinched the pennant on September 17 and a week later went to Baltimore for crab cakes and Orioles.

Smith called Stanley up to his room on the eve of the series.

"You're playing shortstop in the World Series."

"I was dumbfounded," Stanley remembered. "I had never played the position before. Anywhere."

Smith had been watching Stanley cavort around the position, taking ground balls before games, and decided the move was worth the risk.

"I had a lot of nervous energy before games and used to blow off steam by taking grounders," Stanley said. "Norm [Cash] used to tell me I was pretty good there. I think he put a bug in Mayo's ear."

"I don't think he had any choice," backup outfielder Wayne Comer said of Smith. "He had to get Kaline back in there. He didn't want to hurt anybody else's feelings. If you take Oyler out, it wouldn't come back on you. He's the lesser of the choices. But why wouldn't you make that move earlier, if he's going to make it? I remember we clinched on the 17th [of September]. Why not try that from that day forth?"

That's a question only Smith could answer. It could be he wanted to limit the amount of time Stanley would have to think about it. It could be he wanted just a handful of games so he could reverse course without much harm being done. Kaline assured Smith he would understand if the manager kept him on the bench or used him part-time.

"I know what kind of pressure you're under," he told his manager, "but it was the kids who won the pennant. I wouldn't feel badly if you played them in the Series and not me."

Smith told Kaline in his hometown he would be playing right field "for the first game, at least. We'll see how Mickey does at shortstop."

Through the last six games of the regular season, Stanley did fine. Still, there were doubters—even on the team.

"I thought he was out of his mind," Daryl Patterson said. "I thought he'd gone off the deep end. But Mayo didn't give a hoot about what it did do to somebody else. That didn't bother him. He just did what he felt was right. That was his hunch. He was a hunch guy. But he'd seen a lot more to make that decision … that typified Mayo."

"There were a lot of smirks," Tracewski said. "Everybody just looked at everybody. We felt he was just going to do it for one game, maybe a few innings. You felt Mickey was going to drop a pop fly, kick a ground ball, and he'd be out of the game. But it went from one game to the next and we didn't get hurt by it."

"At first, personally, I thought, 'Aw, he's got to be kidding. There's no way he'd do something like that,'" Jon Warden said. "But realistically, this makes us a stronger team offensively. How else are you going to get [Al] Kaline in the lineup? I think guys in the locker room were laughing. He played there the last few games of the season and it turned out just fine."

"I thought it was odd," Comer said, "to take a center fielder, your best center fielder, and put him at shortstop in a World Series. Bat or no bat, you've gone through the regular season with Oyler at shortstop exclusively, maybe with Matchick for a few games. I think he just ran into a problem where he had to get Kaline back in the lineup, and that's the way he chose to do it. He rolled the dice. And it came up sevens. I felt he [Stanley] could do it. It was just a brave move on Mayo's part, doing that."

"Now you have Horton, Northrup and Kaline in the outfield," Warden said, "which is still pretty good. Northrup could run. But Stanley had such great instincts. Guy starts to swing and Stanley is already on his way to where the ball's going to end up."

Stanley actually played nine games at short in 1968, making two errors. But he looked like a shortstop. It wasn't as if the Tigers took Norm Cash and threw him over there. Stanley was an athlete. He looked like an athlete and played like one. Everybody was watching and all they saw was a young man who looked like a shortstop. He looked smooth and in position making the tag play on a steal. Stanley was involved in two double plays, including one on the last game of the season, and he looked comfortable. That must have been what clinched it for Smith.

"It's true we haven't seen the tough DP," the manager said at the time, "but I've seen enough to indicate he can handle it. Away from the bag he can take care of himself very well. What the hell, he may stand out there [in the Series] and never get any heat."

"The only thing Mayo told me," recounted Stanley's double play partner, McAuliffe, "was 'work with him.' So in the 4–5 days before the World Series, we'd go out and take ground balls, practice turning double plays. I'd try to make him aware of situations. I think he only made one error [actually, two] and it wasn't costly at all. He wasn't as fine a shortstop as Ray Oyler, because Ray Oyler was one helluva shortstop, the best I ever played with as far as fielding and having a touch around the bag. But Mickey could certainly do the job there."

"If I can remember correctly," John Hiller said, "I felt sorry for Ray Oyler. I wanted to win, I needed the money. It wasn't a ring thing, I wasn't caught up in that. I needed the money. As little as it was, I needed the money in those days. But I felt so bad for Ray, and our wives were close. But the way I looked at it, I felt Kaline's bat would be better in the lineup than Oyler's. You knew Stanley wasn't going to be as good as Oyler with the glove. But Mickey was a great athlete. We knew Mickey could do it if anybody could. I don't think I questioned it a whole lot. It was more of an emotional thing."

So when the World Series started, there was Mitchell Jack Stanley, running out to shortstop to do something that two weeks earlier must have seemed as likely as a man walking on the moon.

"You know," Campbell said, "one of the most important things that happened was on the first or second pitch of the World Series, Lou Brock hit a ground ball to short, Mickey threw him out and he was relaxed the rest of the way. There are two kinds of athletes when it comes to situations like that. The kind who would worry about it and those who would accept it and just go out and play. Mickey was in the group that would just accept it."

"That helped me relax so much," Stanley recalled. "My biggest thrill of the year."

Relaxed? Must have been, because the rookie shortstop got two hits off Bob Gibson in that first game.

He made two errors, both inconsequential and both in one-sided Detroit victories.

"It turned out that Ray [Oyler] closed every game we won," Campbell said, "so Ray was satisfied." When Smith put Oyler in to finish at short, Stanley went back to center and Northrup moved to left, with Horton going to the bench.

"It created a lot of tension for me," Stanley said later. "I was scared to death. I didn't enjoy the Series like I should have. I kept worrying about situations, concerned that I'd be in the wrong place or react the wrong way." It turned out, though, that Stanley was in the right place at the right time nearly all the time.

In the sixth inning of the seventh game, Brock led off with a single to left. And even with Lolich pitching, everybody knew Brock would be running. He went on first movement, and Lolich threw to first to Cash, who whipped a relay to second where Stanley awaited to apply a tag that erased Brock from the bases. Curt Flood singled later in the inning—and was promptly picked off by Lolich. A rundown ensued and guess who applied the tag that also dried Flood from the bases? Stanley, of course.

The move became a non-issue because Stanley made no glaring mistakes and Detroit came back from a 3–1 deficit to beat St. Louis. Because of Stanley's skill, one of the greatest gambles in World Series history is largely viewed as a yawn today.

"It was a great, great move for us," McAuliffe said. "We needed the offense against the Cardinals. It didn't really hurt us and we needed the offense."

"Ray was a great defensive player," Fred Lasher said, "but he had no bat. Mickey was a pretty good hitter and a good athlete. It probably hurt Ray a little bit—in fact, I'm sure it did—but it was a good move. Mickey could have played any position. He was just a good athlete. And Mickey being the type of person he is, he'd rise to the challenge, too."

"You talk about a guy put under the gun and came through," Patterson said. "What Mickey Stanley did there is probably as outstanding of a thing as I've seen in sport. You move from one position to another, it's a whole different thing. Second base to shortstop, that's a big deal. But you come from the outfield to the infield, that's a whole different story. Look at films of the seventh game, those were tough plays for [even] Ray Oyler to make."

"He did something that no other manager will ever do," Tracewski said of Smith. "He started an outfielder at shortstop in the World Series. Here was our best player, [Kaline], eligible for the World Series. We had to find a way to play him. It was [a move] from left field. It worked out. It was a good thing he didn't have a lot of plays. It was out of character for him [Mayo]. I think he was very conservative."

"If it had been a bust, Mayo would have been chastised," Warden said. "But it worked, so he didn't get the credit he should have. Because it worked out too good." The next spring Detroit was thinking about making the move permanent. But Stanley came down with a sore arm—many feel it was from making the throw from a different position—and he was shifted back to center field. "It's a different throw, definitely," Wert said. "A lot of your throws are sidearm or underhand, which is different than overhand. I would say it could have hurt his arm. His arm was conditioned to throw from the outfield."

"People don't remember but Tom Matchick was our shortstop that year," Tracewski said about 1968. "He started most of the games. Oyler came in for defense. I played shortstop a lot of the time [especially when Matchick went into the service]. I've always felt Matchick was the guy who was slighted. The thing that hurt was that Tom Matchick never recovered. After that he never played very much. He didn't participate because it hurt. I don't think he even played in that World Series [actually, he was 0-for-3 as a pinch-hitter]—and he was our regular. It certainly hurt his career."

"You're damned if you do and damned if you don't," Smith said back then. "But you have to make a decision. That's what they pay you for."

It was a great, great move. So great, few outside the Tiger community know about it except as a "So what?"

Contributors

Chuck Ailsworth (photo support) has a BS and MS from Michigan State University. He is a SABR member and a lifelong Tigers fan who watched the 1968 World Series with his mom on TV. He saw his first Tigers-Cardinals World Series game in person with his dad and his two kids in 2006.

Mark Armour (Denny McLain, The Rise and Fall of the Tigers) is the chair of SABR's Baseball Biography Project, the author of two baseball books, and a contributor to many baseball publications. He lives, writes, and frets about the Red Sox in Oregon's Willamette Valley with Jane, Maya, Drew, and Cassius.

Parker J. Bena (Daryl Patterson) is active in three SABR chapters. He is a lobbyist by trade and is an active member of St. Joseph's Roman Catholic Church in Jefferson City, Missouri. He lives in Jefferson City with his wife, Karen, their three sons, three cats, and a Chocolate Labrador named Shimmy.

Bill Bishop (Pat Dobson) is a graduate of the University of Michigan public health program and works as a safety and health engineer. His two daughters, who are his pride and joy, were raised to be ardent Tiger fans.

Andrew Blume (John Wyatt) writes from a secret undisclosed location.

A native of Hemlock, Michigan, **Matt Bohn** (Ernie Harwell, George Kell, Ray Lane, Larry Osterman) has been a Detroit Tigers fan since childhood. His interests include writing, genealogy, theatre and the history of baseball broadcasting.

A graduate of Michigan State University, **Brian Borawski** (Les Cain, Wayne Comer) is a CPA and has his own private practice. A lifelong Tigers fan, Brian writes about his favorite team at Tiger Blog (*www.tigerblog.net*) and he also writes a weekly Business of Baseball report at The Hardball Times (*www.hardballtimes.com*).

John Cizik (Dick McAuliffe) grew up a Yankees fan in Wilton, Connecticut, living next door to a Red Sox fan. Something must have rubbed off, because he married Jenny, a Sox fan, in 1990. A lawyer practicing in Waterbury, Connecticut, he has always had an interest in researching and collecting memorabilia of Connecticut-born players.

Tracy J.R. Collins (Hal Naragon) earned her Ph.D. in 19th-century British literature from Purdue. When not working as an academic at Central Michigan University she plays softball, watches baseball, plays tennis, reads about baseball, runs marathons, writes articles on baseball literature, and obsesses about a proper diet for her family.

A retired English professor, **Jan Finkel** (Johnny Sain, proofreader) lives with his wife on Deep Creek Lake in western Maryland. Besides great books and baseball, which he sometimes confuses, he enjoys country music and jazz. His son and daughter and their spouses are wonderful people—and, coincidentally, live in Nashville and New Orleans.

David Fleitz (Eddie Mathews), a SABR member from Bowling Green, Ohio, is a systems analyst by day and a baseball writer at night. He has written five books, including biographies of Shoeless Joe Jackson, Louis Sockalexis, and Cap Anson, and is now working on a volume about the Irish and early baseball.

Dave Gagnon (Gates Brown) splits his time between running a small accounting firm and being a baseball fanatic. While completing 1040 returns, he's got a headset on listening to the Tigers in his office. He had to cut short one client consultation to watch Tigers play the Yankees in the 2006 ALDS.

Gary Gillette (Roy Face, Jim Price) is the co-editor of the *ESPN Baseball Encyclopedia* as well as the executive editor of the *ESPN Pro Football Encyclopedia*. He is also the editor of a new Tigers annual, *Tigers Corner*, first published by Maple Street Press in 2007. Gillette lives in Detroit with his wife, Vicki, and their children, Kamil and Karolina.

Jerry Griffin (Lenny Green), like his biography subject, collects a retirement check from Ford Motor Co.; Griffin worked in labor relations for Ford after playing baseball at Eastern Michigan University and coaching baseball at Highland Park (Michigan) High School. Griffin was also a sandlot contemporary of Green's.

Larry Hilliard and **Rob Hilliard** (John Hiller): Larry, who engineers NASA remote sensors, has homing sensors to Michigan and Trumbull. With co-author Rob he has recently had reunions at the 2006 Super Bowl and World Series, both in Detroit, and via teleconference with John Hiller. All three are men of faith, love da UP, and the Tigers.

With his Garry Maddox model glove, **Dan Holmes** (Willie Horton, Mickey Lolich, Jon Warden) spent his youth playing "500" in the backyard or hitting stones with his bat as he imitated the batting stances of nearly every batter in the American League. Author of *Ty Cobb: A Biography* from Greenwood Press, Dan is a web developer, web consultant, blogger, and freelance journalist who formely worked for the National Baseball Hall of Fame and Museum and MLB Advance Media. He lives in Traverse City, Michigan, with his two daughters.

Don Hyslop (Earl Wilson) lives in Nova Scotia's Annapolis Valley. He is a retired educator who taught at the junior high school level for over 30 years. He conducts interviews for the website *www.redsoxnation.net* and writes about Red Sox minor leaguers on *www.soxprospects.com*. He has also written a biography on former major leaguer Fred Lake.

Maxwell Kates (Norm Cash) is an accountant with a midsize Toronto firm. The director of marketing for SABR's Hanlan's Point Chapter, he has lectured at the SABR Convention in Seattle and the Limmud Conference in Toronto. Previous baseball publications include *The National Pastime, Elysian Fields Quarterly*, and *NINE*.

A fan of the Tigers since 1984 when his dad took him to his first game at Tiger Stadium, **Jeremy Klumpp** (Tiger Stadium) is finishing a degree in broadcasting while writing a baseball blog and having a weekly college radio show. This is his first published work.

Alex Kupfer (Dave Campbell) recently finished his master's in cinema and media studies at UCLA and is currently living in Wisconsin. While interested in too many baseball research topics to list, he is particularly interested in researching ex-players working in film and television.

Mike Lassman (Fred Lasher, Tom Matchick) graduated from Eastern Michigan University and served as a sports information assistant. Mike earned a law degree from the University of Detroit and serves as labor and employment counsel for the Department of Army in Virginia, and is a proud husband and father of two sons.

Len Levin (proofreader), a lifelong Rhode Island resident, admires the Tigers but roots for the Red Sox. He is a newspaper copy editor and an active member of SABR. He has edited or helped edit a number of books on baseball and other topics, including several by his wife, a journalism professor.

An international consultant working almost anywhere they ask, **Peter M. Levine** (Dick Tracewski) is expert in finding ways to track those beloved Detroit Tigers. He especially enjoys Latin America where beisbol is life to some and is convincing his six-year-old son that Detroit rocks/Michigan rolls (a struggle with the maternal side).

Dan Levitt (The Rise and Fall of the Tigers) is the author of *Ed Barrow: The Bulldog Who Built the Yankees' First Dynasty* (University of Nebraska Press, 2008) and co-author of *Paths to Glory: How Great Baseball Teams Got That Way*, which won the Sporting News-SABR Baseball Research Award. He lives in Minneapolis with his wife and two boys.

David MacGregor (Dennis Ribant) is a screenwriter and playwright who teaches in the English department of Wayne State University. In the summer, he and his son tour around major and minor league ballparks and are always pleasantly surprised at the number of free tickets they are handed by generous fellow fans.

SABR member **Bruce MacLeod** (proofreader) is a copy editor and Detroit Red Wings beat writer for the *Macomb Daily* in Mt. Clemens, Michigan.

Jeanne Mallett (Jim Campbell) shares two loves with her subject—the Tigers and the Ohio State Buckeyes. She thinks her cousin, Jim Schmakel, Tigers equipment manager, has the best job in the world. With the best job taken, Jeanne wrote plays, then practiced law, and now writes short stories, including baseball stories.

Barb Mantegani (Tony Cuccinello) is a SABR member by heart and a Mayo Smith Society member by marriage, maintaining dual citizenship in both Red Sox and Tigers Nation. She wrote the Bob Tillman profile for 2006's "Impossible Dream" Red Sox book. A tax attorney in real life, she conducts a series of clinics each year to help impoverished Americans fill out their tax forms. She's also a frequent caller to the "MLB This Morning" program on XM Satellite Radio Channel 175.

Kevin McGraw (fact-checker) has been a Tigers fan since 1959, when his dad took him to his first game at Briggs Stadium. A longtime SABR member, Kevin plans to spend more time on genealogy and baseball research after he retires from his Defense Department analyst job. His favorite team is the '68 Tigers.

John Milner (Bob Christian, Don Wert), a high school counselor in Kerrville, Texas, was no more beyond deadline in submitting his autobiographical sketch than he was in submitting his biographical profiles.

Chip Mundy (proofreader), a member of the Mayo Smith Society, is a copy editor for the *Kalamazoo (Michigan) Gazette*.

Jerry Nechal (Mickey Stanley) is an administrator at Wayne State University, residing in Sylvan Lake, Michigan. He has previously written about "The Worst Team Ever" in *The Baseball Research Journal*. Other interests include architecture, bocce ball, and mountain biking. He still longs for a bleacher seat in old Tiger Stadium.

Richard Newhouse (Ray Oyler), a passionate Tigers' fan since the days of "The Bird," has rejoiced with their success and "died hard" with their futility. He chairs the Western Michigan Wally Pipp chapter of SABR and co-chairs a family of four in Holland, Michigan. This is a first contribution to a national publication.

Bill Nowlin (Lenny Green, adviser) is national vice president of SABR and the author of close to 20 Red Sox-related books. Bill is also co-founder of Rounder Records of Massachusetts. One of his big regrets was finding his flight to Detroit canceled for Boston's final visit to Tiger Stadium.

Mark Pattison (project editor, proofreader) is treasurer of the Mayo Smith Society and editor of its *Tigers Stripes* and *E-Mayo Flash* newsletters. He's media editor for Catholic News Service in Washington, an adjunct labor studies professor at Indiana University-Northwest, a Baltimore-Washington SABR chapter activist, an involved PTA dad, and a middlin' banjo picker.

Don Petersen (Fred Lasher) used to ride the bus to Tiger Stadium and join other families so he could get a 50-cent ticket on Family Day. He later went to Lansing Community College, the University of Chicago, and Harvard Law School. He is now a standup comic and professor at Cooley Law School.

David Raglin (Mayo Smith, project editor), is the vice president of the Bob Davids Chapter of SABR in the Baltimore-Washington region, and has been the Mayo Smith Society's sabermetrician and principal writer for its *Tigers Stripes* and *E-Mayo Flash* newsletters since their respective foundings in 1984 and 2004. His Census Bureau job requires him to count America's 300 million-plus residents using both his fingers and his toes.

Jeff Samoray (Joe Sparma) is a freelance writer based in metro Detroit. He's been a Tigers fan literally his whole life, having been born the day the team clinched the 1968 American League pennant. As Jeff likes to say, "Don Wert delivered—and so did my mother!"

History professor **Jim Sargent** (Jim Northrup) has written articles about baseball and football players for several magazines and for the SABR BioProject and Pro Football Researchers Association web sites. Co-author of *Danny Litwhiler* (2006), Sargent is working on a history of Jean Faut and the South Bend Blue Sox of the AAGPBL.

The highlight of **Dan Scott's** (fact-checker) time as a Tigers fan was getting up at 0300 every morning to watch all of the Tigers' 2006 playoff games while supporting Operation Iraqi Freedom in Camp Fallujah as an active-duty Marine. Dan's appropriately painted basement has been dubbed "Tiger Stadium—Baltimore Annex."

Rich Shook (Jim Rooker, Tigers in the News) covered the 1968 and 1984 Tigers for UPI in Detroit, where he luckily toiled until 1990. He was UPI's baseball analyst-columnist for postseason play 1984–1985 and 1987–1989. He's been varsity baseball coach at Fr. Gabriel Richard High School, Ann

Arbor, Michigan, since 2001. He was an official scorer 1984–2004. Shook still covers the Tigers for The Sports Xchange, and also edits the *Bengal Bytes* newsletter; for details e-mail Shook at shookrl@aol.com.

Doug Skipper (Wally Moses), a longtime SABR member from Apple Valley, Minnesota, is a market research consultant, freelance baseball historian, researcher and writer, and plodding member of his daughter's Dads and Kids dance group. He's contributed several biographies to SABR's *Deadball Stars of the American League* and the Boston chapter's series on Red Sox pennant winners.

Trey Strecker (Bill Freehan) teaches English and sport studies at Ball State University. He edited *Dead Balls and Double Curves: An Anthology of Early Baseball Fiction* (Southern Illinois University Press, 2004) and *The Collected Baseball Stories of Charles Van Loan* (McFarland, 2004), and also edits *NINE: A Journal of Baseball History & Culture*.

John Vorperian (Don McMahon) hosts "Beyond the Game," a sports history series cablecast in Westchester County, New York. He also teaches sports law and sports business topics at Concordia College (New York) and Manhattanville College. An avid Red Sox booster, Vorperian got hooked on baseball in '68. His web site is *johnnyvsports.fws1.com*.

Rick Vosik (The City of Detroit in 1968) lives in Omaha, Nebraska. He became a Tigers fan in 1968 when he attended his first major league baseball game at Tiger Stadium. With the Tigers' World Series championship, he was hooked for life. He is an investment banker, and in his spare time coaches youth baseball.

Nick Waddell (Al Kaline) is a Wayne State University graduate in chemical engineering, but more importantly, he is a lifelong Tigers fan. Currently, he resides in Chicago attending law school, and proudly wears his Old English "D" whenever he can.

SABR

The Society for American Baseball Research (SABR) was established in Cooperstown, New York in August, 1971. Our mission is to foster the study of baseball past and present, and to provide an outlet for educational, historical and research information about the game. There is no test to join SABR (pronounced "saber") and membership is open to anyone with a love of baseball. Some members are academics or the top researchers in their field of expertise who enjoy sharing their findings. Other members take a more relaxed approach to SABR by swapping stories with other knowledgeable members at regional chapter meetings. Some join to receive and read our annual publications, research committee newsletters, and gain access to our many electronic forums. Whatever your interest, SABR provides the network for the baseball lover to connect with individuals of the same interest and expertise. A one-year membership costs $60. To join, send to SABR, 812 Huron Rd E #719, Cleveland, OH 44115. For information, call 800-969-7227 or e-mail *info@sabr.org*.

Mayo Smith Society™

Founded in 1983 in Washington, D.C., the Mayo Smith Society is the fan club for followers of the Detroit Tigers. Named after the manager of the Tigers' 1968 championship team, the Society claims nearly 1,000 members in the United States and throughout the world. Members can take part in an annual gathering in Detroit, yearly spring training trips in Lakeland, Florida, group outings to see the Tigers and their minor league affiliates play (particularly in the Mid-Atlantic), monthly dinners on Capitol Hill in Washington, and voting each off-season for the King Tiger award. The Society also publishes the *Tigers Stripes* newsletter and the *E-Mayo Flash* electronic newsletter, has a full-season four-seat box at Comerica Park for members, and gives to Detroit-area charities. To join, send $20 and name, address, phone and e-mail to Mayo Smith Society, P.O. Box 119, Northville, MI 48167.